Nina - 21
Neva - 33
Dave - 3
Don - 12

Opal - 52
Carrie - 65
Ruby - 23
Bob - 64

Lillie

34 Hazel
24 Annie
28 Freda
37 Julian
43 Avo

Carl
Maurin
Lauin
Laurel

NIV
COUNSELOR'S
NEW TESTAMENT
AND PSALMS

must go to Jerusalem and suffer many things at the hands of the elders, chief priests and teachers of the law, and on the third day be raised to life. ²²Peter took him aside and began to rebuke him. "Never, Lord!" he said. "This shall never happen to you!"

²³Jesus turned and said to Peter, "Get behind me, Satan! You are a stumbling block to me; you do not have in mind the things of God, but the things of men."

²⁴Then Jesus said to his disciples, "If anyone would come after me, he must deny himself and take up his cross and follow me. ²⁵For whoever wants to save his life[a] will lose it, but whoever loses his life for me will find it. ²⁶What good will it be for a man if he gains the whole world, yet forfeits his soul? Or what can a man give in exchange for his soul? ²⁷For the Son of Man is going to come in his Father's glory with his angels, and then he will reward each person according to what he has done. ²⁸I tell you the truth, some who are standing here will not taste death before they see the Son of Man coming in his kingdom."

The Transfiguration

17 After six days Jesus took with him Peter, James and John the brother of James, and led them up a high mountain by themselves. ²There he was transfigured before them. His face shone like the sun, and his clothes became as white as the light. ³Just then there appeared before them Moses and Elijah, talking with Jesus.

⁴Peter said to Jesus, "Lord, it is good for us to be here. If you

a25 The Greek word means either life _or_ soul; _also in verse 26._

wish, I will put up three shelters—one for you, one for Moses and one for Elijah."

⁵While he was still speaking, a bright cloud enveloped them, and a voice from the cloud said, "This is my Son, whom I love; with him I am well pleased. Listen to him!"

⁶When the disciples heard this, they fell facedown to the ground, terrified. ⁷But Jesus came and touched them. "Get up," he said. "Don't be afraid." ⁸When they looked up, they saw no one except Jesus.

⁹As they were coming down the mountain, Jesus instructed them, "Don't tell anyone what you have seen, until the Son of Man has been raised from the dead."

¹⁰The disciples asked him, "Why then do the teachers of the law say that Elijah must come first?"

¹¹Jesus replied, "To be sure, Elijah comes and will restore all things. ¹²But I tell you, Elijah has already come, and they did not recognize him, but have done to him everything they wished. In the same way the Son of Man is going to suffer at their hands." ¹³Then the disciples understood that he was talking to them about John the Baptist.

The Healing of a Boy With a Demon

¹⁴When they came to the crowd, a man approached Jesus and knelt before him. ¹⁵"Lord," he said, "have mercy on my son. He has seizures and is suffering greatly. He often falls into the fire or into the water. ¹⁶I brought him to your disciples, but they could not heal him."

¹⁷"O unbelieving and perverse generation," Jesus replied, "how

Lk 9:23-25

a 2 Some early manuscripts do not have the rest of verse 2 and all of verse 3. a 16 Or Messiah; also in verse 20 b 18 Or hell c 18 Or not d 18 Peter means rock. e 18 Or hell f 19 Or have been g ... prove stronger than it

The Demand for a Sign

16 The Pharisees and Sadducees came to Jesus and tested him by asking him to show them a sign from heaven.

²He replied,ᵃ "When evening comes, you say, 'It will be fair weather, for the sky is red,' ³and in the morning, 'Today it will be stormy, for the sky is red and overcast.' You know how to interpret the appearance of the sky, but you cannot interpret the signs of the times. ⁴A wicked and adulterous generation looks for a miraculous sign, but none will be given it except the sign of Jonah." Jesus then left them and went away.

The Yeast of the Pharisees and Sadducees

⁵When they went across the lake, the disciples forgot to take bread. ⁶"Be careful," Jesus said to them. "Be on your guard against the yeast of the Pharisees and Sadducees."

⁷They discussed this among themselves and said, "It is because we didn't bring any bread."

⁸Aware of their discussion, Jesus asked, "You of little faith, why are you talking among yourselves about having no bread? ⁹Do you still not understand? Don't you remember the five loaves for the five thousand, and how many basketfuls you gathered? ¹⁰Or the seven loaves for the four thousand, and how many basketfuls you gathered? ¹¹How is it you don't understand that I was not talking to you about bread? But be on your guard against the yeast of the Pharisees and Sadducees." ¹²Then they understood that he was not telling them to guard against the yeast used in bread, but against the teaching of the Pharisees and Sadducees.

Peter's Confession of Christ

¹³When Jesus came to the region of Caesarea Philippi, he asked his disciples, "Who do people say the Son of Man is?"

¹⁴They replied, "Some say John the Baptist; others say Elijah; and still others, Jeremiah or one of the prophets."

¹⁵"But what about you?" he asked. "Who do you say I am?"

¹⁶Simon Peter answered, "You are the Christ,ᵃ the Son of the living God."

¹⁷Jesus replied, "Blessed are you, Simon son of Jonah, for this was not revealed to you by man, but by my Father in heaven. ¹⁸And I tell you that you are Peter,ᵈ and on this rock I will build my church, and the gatesᵉ of Hadesᵇ will not overcome itᶠ. ¹⁹I will give you the keys of the kingdom of heaven; whatever you bind on earth willᶜ be bound in heaven, and whatever you loose on earth willᶜ be loosed in heaven." ²⁰Then he warned his disciples not to tell anyone that he was the Christ.

Jesus Predicts His Death

²¹From that time on Jesus began to explain to his disciples that he

8 Mt 18:17
15 1 Ti 1:2
16 Jn 20:31

NIV
COUNSELOR'S

NEW TESTAMENT
AND PSALMS

NEW INTERNATIONAL
VERSION

Notes and Indexes by Ben Chapman

ZONDERVAN BIBLE PUBLISHERS

GRAND RAPIDS, MICHIGAN

You will be pleased to know that a portion of the purchase price of your new NIV Bible has been provided to the International Bible Society to help spread the Gospel of Jesus Christ around the world!

Contents

List of Topics

How to Lead a Person to Faith in Christ

One of the most important types of Christian counseling is guiding another person to faith in Christ. There is no experience more fulfilling and rewarding than this.

If you are working as a counselor in a large evangelistic crusade, you will, of course, be carefully instructed in a particular approach or pattern and you should follow it. For those who have an opportunity to help someone find Christ, the following suggestions are offered:

1. Focus your attention on the person to be helped rather than on a list of verses to cover. Be genuinely concerned and caring; God loves this person and wants to communicate his love through you. This might be a good place to relate briefly the circumstances of your own conversion experience.

2. Show that everyone needs to be saved. No one is righteous; we are all guilty of breaking God's law in some way, and therefore already condemned and sentenced. Use Romans 3:19,20.

3. There is hope in Christ. Salvation does not come by keeping laws or being good, but only through faith in Christ. All have sinned, but anyone who receives Christ can be forgiven and accepted by God as righteous. Use Romans 3:21-25; 5:8; 6:23.

4. God forgives and accepts unconditionally anyone who believes in Christ. Use Romans 8:1,2.

5. Encourage your friend to trust Christ in the heart and confess him as Lord with the mouth. Use Romans 10:9,10. Ask your friend to repeat aloud this prayer (or something similar in his or her own words): I thank you, heavenly Father, for sending your own Son, Jesus Christ, to die on the cross and pay the penalty for sin. I now believe in him and accept him as my Lord. Thank you that I am saved in him.

In Jesus' name, Amen.

Plan of Salvation

These are the scripture references that are marked in the text for this topic. For your convenience they are repeated here, arranged in biblical order.

"To some who were confident of their own righteousness and looked down on everybody else, Jesus told this parable: 'Two men went up to the temple to pray, one a Pharisee and the other a tax collector. The Pharisee stood up and prayed about himself: "God, I thank you that I am not like all other men—robbers, evildoers, adulterers—or even like this tax collector. I fast twice a week and give a tenth of all I get."

" 'But the tax collector stood at a distance. He would not even look up to heaven, but beat his breast and said, "God, have mercy on me, a sinner." '

" 'I tell you that this man, rather than the other, went home justified before God. For everyone who exalts himself will be humbled, and he who humbles himself will be exalted' " (Lk 18:9-14).

"Yet to all who received him, to those who believed in his name, he gave the right to become children of God" (Jn 1:12).

"For God so loved the world that he gave his one and only Son, that whoever believes in him shall not perish but have eternal life. For God did not send his Son into the world to condemn the world, but to save the world through him. Whoever believes in him is not condemned, but whoever does not believe stands condemned already because he has not believed in the name of God's one and only Son" (Jn 3:16-18).

"I tell you the truth, whoever hears my word and believes him who sent me has eternal life and will not be condemned; he has crossed over from death to life" (Jn 5:24).

"But these are written that you may believe that Jesus is the Christ, the Son of God, and that by believing you may have life in his name" (Jn 20:31).

"All the prophets testify about him that everyone who believes in him receives forgiveness of sins through his name" (Ac 10:43).

"For all have sinned and fall short of the glory of God" (Ro 3:23).

"What benefit did you reap at that time from the things you are now ashamed of? Those things result in death! But now that you have been set free from sin and have become slaves to God, the benefit you reap leads to holiness, and the result is eternal life. For the wages of sin is death, but the gift of God is eternal life in Christ Jesus our Lord" (Ro 6:21-23).

"Therefore, there is now no condemnation for those who are in Christ Jesus" (Ro 8:1).

"That if you confess with your mouth, 'Jesus is Lord,' and believe in your heart that God raised him from the dead, you will be saved. For it is with your heart that you believe and are justified, and it is with your mouth that you confess and are saved. . . . for, 'Everyone who calls on the name of the Lord will be saved' " (Ro 10:9,10,13).

"For he says, 'In the time of my favor I heard you, and in the day of salvation I helped you.' I tell you, now is the time of God's favor, now is the day of salvation" (2Co 6:2).

"And without faith it is impossible to please God, because anyone who comes to him must believe that he exists and that he rewards those who earnestly seek him" (Heb 11:6).

"If we confess our sins, he is faithful and just and will forgive us our sins and purify us from all unrighteousness" (1Jn 1:9).

"I write these things to you who believe in the name of the Son of God so that you may know that you have eternal life" (1Jn 5:13).

"Here I am! I stand at the door and knock. If anyone hears my voice and opens the door, I will come in and eat with him, and he with me" (Rev 3:20).

How to Use the NIV Counselor's New Testament

All people have problems. Even born-again, maturing believers in Christ encounter problems daily. Some people have major, seemingly insurmountable problems; others have pesky, everyday struggles that they evaluate negatively. There is stress in life for all of us. Stress can waste precious, emotional energy, it can lead to anxiety, and our mental (and even physical) health can become impaired. From the non-Christian who needs (whether he knows it or not) salvation in Christ to the believer who needs only to be reminded of the worthwhile character of his service to Christ—all of us have needs and problems.

Professional psychologists and counselors have become more and more aware of the usefulness of the Scriptures in counseling. The Word of God was in fact designed so that we might be "thoroughly equipped for every good work" (2 Ti 3:17). The NIV *Counselor's New Testament* (NIVCNT) is an up-to-date resource for using the Word of God to meet our own needs as well as the needs of others. It provides a handy reminder of selected passages that are relevant to specific problems, needs, and topics of everyday Christian living. Much of the New Testament and some of the Old Testament is counseling material by nature. The Bible *is* counseling. It is meant to be used for that purpose.

Every Christian Is a Counselor

We must not suppose that counseling should be left to professionals. Every Christian has the responsibility to counsel others; counseling is part of being a Christian. When Paul wrote to the believers in Thessalonica, for example, he reminded them to "warn [a word that is used as a pattern for some kinds of counseling today] those who are idle, encourage [another word for counseling] the timid, help [another aspect of counseling] the weak, be patient [an important attitude in counseling] with everyone" (1 Th 5:14). Remember that Paul gave those important commands to the people of the church in general, and not to the leaders or pastors, as can be seen from the two preceding verses. There is no question at all about the fact that, according to the New Testament, every believer has the responsibility to counsel. We are in a real sense our "brother's keeper."

Who will "see to it that no one misses the grace of God and that no bitter root grows up to cause trouble . . . (Heb 12:15)" if we do not? Counseling is the general ministry of the church—the "works of service" (Eph 4:12) that all believers perform. "Each one should use whatever gift he has received to serve others, faithfully administering God's grace in its various forms" (1 Pe 4:10).

There is a great need for Christian counselors today in evangelistic campaigns, Christian and public schools, colleges, missionary work, local church and Sunday school ministries, and anywhere that one Christian person has the opportunity to show caring love to another.

Be Ready to Minister to Others

The NIVCNT is a convenient guide to those passages where you have found help for yourself in the past; you can now use both the Word of God and your experiences to help others. God is "the God of all comfort, who comforts us in all our troubles, so that we can comfort those in any trouble with the comfort we ourselves have received from God" (2 Co 1:3, 4). The more mature we become in Christ, the more responsible we are for carrying out this ministry of counseling (Heb 5:12, 13). Christian maturity means not only using the Word of God to cope with our own problems but encouraging and counseling others, too (Gal 6:1, 2).

The Index of Topics

Some of the most helpful passages for the various counseling topics have been highlighted in the text of the NIVCNT. In the margin beside these highlighted passages is a number designating which of the ninety-nine topics is treated in that passage. Beneath the marginal topic number is a scripture reference to the next passage for that topic.

The Index of Topics in the back of the NIVCNT is made up of two kinds of entries:

1. the ninety-nine primary topics, with a list of the highlighted scripture passages and a general summary statement of what the Bible has to say about the topic;

2. various secondary subjects, many of which are negative types of feelings, since these are most often the things people are troubled about. These feelings are frequently listed as adjectives (for example, "abused," "afraid," "alone"). Each secondary subject is cross-referenced to one or more of the ninety-nine primary topics.

Using the index can be as simple as looking up a primary topic and turning to the first reference given. The place in the text is highlighted, and the number in the margin confirms the topic; the next reference for the topic can be seen under the margin topic number and it can be found without referring to the index again.

The NIVCNT is not intended as a study aid. Reference works are available for those who wish to study these topics exhaustively. The people who need your counseling help will benefit most from a few selected thoughts from God's Word. The application of these verses to particular human needs is the work of the Holy Spirit. As a general rule, it would probably be best to find the one or two verses that are most appropriate, pray with your friend, and then leave the rest up to God.

Principles of Biblical Counseling

Counseling is often just listening. It should always begin with listening. In order to use the NIVCNT effectively, you will need to be genuinely interested in the person who has come to you for help. Take the trouble to find out precisely what the person needs by way of help. Don't be too quick to read a verse or offer a solution; your selection may meet a need that is not there or solve a problem the person does not have. Listen! Showing love, caring, and help to another person is not possible without first understanding that person's problem. Understanding is not possible without genuine communication from the person in need, and to hear that communication you have to listen. Don't try to psychoanalyze—just listen. If you are willing to listen for a few minutes and just be a friend, the person's need will become apparent.

Getting the person in need to talk about the problem may come about quite naturally. A person may simply say "I'm afraid," and proceed to tell you exactly what he fears (death, harm, failure, rejection, loss of a loved one, or something else). If there seems to be some reluctance or awkwardness in expressing the problem, try showing your interest in some way with a brief question like, "Could you tell me more about your feelings," or "I really want to help; tell me more about your problem." Above all, be genuinely interested, and listen a lot more than you talk.

Professional counselors differ in their general approach to counseling. Some are directive, some are non-directive, some emphasize psychoanalysis, some emphasize learning new behavior, and some deal mainly with interpersonal relationships. Almost all psychologists and counselors, however, agree that before a person's need can be met he must express the need, understand it himself, and want help. It is important, therefore, to talk about needs.

Biblical counseling, which is the responsibility of every Christian, aims at mutual encouragement in Christ. We must remind each other of the grace of God, in whom all our needs are met. The basis of the Christian world and life view is that God is all we need. Most emotional problems and anxieties among Christian people result from failure to understand and appropriate this truth fully. Once a person understands his needs by expressing them, it is easier for him to see how his needs have really been met in God through faith in Christ.

What are the basic human needs? Human beings are physical and spiritual in nature; we have mental, spiritual, and emotional needs that are just as important as air, water, food, and shelter. Perhaps the most important of these spiritual needs is *meaning*. There must be a reason for our existence, and this reason must be understood. We are thinking, spiritual beings, and unless we can justify our existence to ourselves, we have no will to live. When we feel that some other person loves us, enjoys us, or needs us, we understand the reason for our existence and we feel secure. If we feel that our existence does not matter to anyone else, then we cannot understand the reason for existing and we feel insecure. In such an insecure state, without an understanding of the meaning of life, it is impossible to maintain self-respect; without self-respect we have no incentive to protect ourselves either physically or spiritually and are vulnerable and subject to death from the slightest cause.

The Bible reveals the true meaning of life in Christ. God has a plan and purpose for every individual. The failure to understand meaning and existence occurs in differing degrees, and there are, therefore, varying degrees of insecurity, resulting in various spiritual, emotional, and mental problems. Every person reacts differently to stress-producing factors in his environment in accordance with his degree of understanding of the true meaning of life. Sometimes a person needs only a gentle reminder to put him back in touch with the meaning of life. Another person may need complete instruction in the basic facts of the meaning of life. The Bible reveals all that we need to know about God and about the meaning and significance of our existence. A biblical counselor needs to be well grounded in the Bible himself and then, when he wants to help others, be able to recall passages that have helped him.

Feelings are important, too, because feelings can lead to an understanding of needs. If a person is physically and spiritually comfortable, happy, and at peace with God, himself, and the world, he has no needs. Mental and spiritual happiness exists when a person feels no need. However, a person may look happy, but *feel* unloved or rejected because he has a need that is not being met, or at least that he *feels* is not being met. We, as counselors, can help him understand how his basic needs for ultimate meaning and security are met in God through Christ.

People are often unaware of their feelings until they are directed to think specifically about how they feel. It may be necessary to suggest a few possibilities. Are you angry? Do you feel afraid that you will fail? Were you disappointed? What things make you feel good? People in our society are often unaware of feelings. Before we can help we need to know how a person feels.

There are, of course, also secondary, less basic needs in every person's life, but often these are easier to understand after one feels secure in the basic issues of life. For example, meaning in interpersonal relationships is patterned after the meaning of life in general. We need to be accepted by others who understand God's purpose in our lives—and they need to be accepted by us. Humans are social beings. Awareness of our feelings, as well as an understanding of our needs, helps us to maintain self-respect.

Biblical counseling is not so much psychoanalysis as a caring relationship with another person. It is fellowship; it is discipleship. Biblical counseling is a part of our ministry to each other in the church, but it is not preaching or merely giving out information. It is love in action. It is concerned, but patient and kind. It is not rude, or self-seeking, or touchy, or resentful. "It always protects, always trusts, always hopes, always perseveres" (1 Co 13:7).

Biblical counseling does not eliminate the need for counselors, psychologists, and psychiatrists any more than witnessing for Christ eliminates the need for evangelists. It is important for the church to utilize the research and skill of professionals in mobilizing for its counseling ministry. It is also important to recognize our own limitations and learn of good professionals to whom we can recommend our friends. If there are severe, chronic, or recurring problems of despair, depression, or anxiety, refer your friend to a professional counselor you know.

Suggestions for Counseling

1. Be ready always to share your own experiences in the Christian life and watch for opportunities to help others. Witnessing is really counseling and helping others to find faith in Christ. Discipling is also an important part of our counseling ministry; new believers need a friend to help them get started maturing in Christ. There are people in trouble all around us—even in our own families and among our friends at work. Help them. There are people with marriage and family problems who need help and support. Some are depressed (a common problem); encourage them. Someone near you is worried, or harboring bitter resentment, or has lost a loved one; he or she needs a caring friend.

2. Be willing to listen. Sometimes that's all it takes. People may complain, or be touchy, or cry over the wrong things. If there is an opportunity, encourage others to talk through active listening. Let them express their feelings; you may see basic needs that are unfulfilled and you may be able to help just by listening.

3. Be accepting. There is nothing so bad or evil that God cannot forgive it in Christ; there is no situation where God cannot help. God accepts everyone who comes to him—he holds no prejudice, so why should you? See everyone as a person for whom God has a plan; you have a part in God's plan and so does this other person. Explore the meaning of existence for both of you.

4. Be genuine and open—a true friend. The ancient Greeks used to say, "A friend is another self." If you are a real friend to people in need, they will share feelings that they have never told anyone about before. Some people have discovered feelings they themselves were not aware of until they shared them with a friend. To be a true friend you must be vulnerable; let the other person know you (but be careful not to talk too much). Leave the windows of your soul open, and share briefly feelings you have had that are similar to those being discussed.

5. Be selective in reading scripture passages. Try not to be mechanical—counseling is a relationship and involves more than just analyzing and reading verses. Pray in private for the people you are helping, and meditate on the passages you decide to share

with others (when that is possible). In closing a conversation with someone, summarize and restate the aspects of the problem and the person's feelings, pray with your friend, and try to remember basic human needs and redemptive themes from the Bible.

Highlighting

The verses that appear in the Index of Topics are all highlighted in the text. Verses on the subject of salvation are marked with diagonally striped red highlighting. All other verses are marked in a solid red.

Preface

THE NEW INTERNATIONAL VERSION is a completely new translation of the Holy Bible made by over a hundred scholars working directly from the best available Hebrew, Aramaic and Greek texts. It had its beginning in 1965 when, after several years of exploratory study by committees from the Christian Reformed Church and the National Association of Evangelicals, a group of scholars met at Palos Heights, Illinois, and concurred in the need for a new translation of the Bible in contemporary English. This group, though not made up of official church representatives, was transdenominational. Its conclusion was endorsed by a large number of leaders from many denominations who met in Chicago in 1966.

Responsibility for the new version was delegated by the Palos Heights group to a self-governing body of fifteen, the Committee on Bible Translation, composed for the most part of biblical scholars from colleges, universities and seminaries. In 1967 the New York Bible Society (now the New York International Bible Society) generously undertook the financial sponsorship of the project—a sponsorship that made it possible to enlist the help of many distinguished scholars. The fact that participants from the United States, Great Britain, Canada, Australia and New Zealand worked together gave the project its international scope. That they were from many denominations—including Anglican, Assemblies of God, Baptist, Brethren, Christian Reformed, Church of Christ, Evangelical Free, Lutheran, Mennonite, Methodist, Nazarene, Presbyterian, Wesleyan and other churches—helped to safeguard the translation from sectarian bias.

How it was made helps to give the New International Version its distinctiveness. The translation of each book was assigned to a team of scholars. Next, one of the Intermediate Editorial Committees revised the initial translation, with constant reference to the Hebrew, Aramaic or Greek. Their work then went to one of the General Editorial Committees, which checked it in detail and made another thorough revision. This revision in turn was carefully reviewed by the Committee on Bible Translation, which made further changes and then released the final version for publication. In this way the entire Bible underwent three revisions, during each of which the translation was examined for its faithfulness to the original languages and for its English style.

All this involved many thousands of hours of research and discussion regarding the meaning of the texts and the precise way of putting them into English. It may well be that no other translation has been made by a more thorough process of review and revision from committee to committee than this one.

From the beginning of the project, the Committee on Bible Translation held to certain goals for the New International Version: that it would be an accurate translation and one that would have clarity and literary quality and so prove suitable for public and private reading, teaching, preaching, memorizing and liturgical use. The Committee also sought to preserve some measure of continuity with the long tradition of translating the Scriptures into English.

In working toward these goals, the translators were united in their commitment to the authority and infallibility of the Bible as God's Word in written form. They believe that it contains the divine answer to the deepest needs of humanity, that it sheds unique light on our path in a dark world, and that it sets forth the way to our eternal well-being.

The first concern of the translators has been the accuracy of the translation and its fidelity to the thought of the biblical writers. They have weighed the significance of the lexical and grammatical details of the Hebrew, Aramaic and Greek texts. At the same time, they have striven for more than a word-for-word translation. Because thought patterns and syntax differ from language to language, faithful communication of the meaning of the writers of the Bible demands frequent modifications in sentence structure and constant regard for the contextual meanings of words.

A sensitive feeling for style does not always accompany scholarship. Accordingly the Committee on Bible Translation submitted the developing version to a number of stylistic consultants. Two of them read every book of both Old and New Testaments twice—once before and once after the last major revision—and made invaluable suggestions. Samples of the translation were tested for clarity and ease of reading by various kinds of people—young and old, highly educated and less well educated, ministers and laymen.

Concern for clear and natural English—that the New International Version should be idiomatic but not idiosyncratic, contemporary but not dated—motivated the translators and consultants. At the same time, they tried to reflect the differing styles of the biblical writers. In view of the international use of English, the translators sought to avoid obvious Americanisms on the one hand and obvious Anglicisms on the other. A British edition reflects the comparatively few differences of significant idiom and of spelling.

As for the traditional pronouns "thou," "thee" and "thine" in reference to the Deity, the translators judged that to use these archaisms (along with the old verb forms such as "doest," "wouldest" and "hadst") would violate accuracy in translation. Neither Hebrew, Aramaic nor Greek uses special pronouns for the persons of the Godhead. A present-day translation is not enhanced by forms that in the time of the King James Version were used in everyday speech, whether referring to God or man.

For the Old Testament the standard Hebrew text, the Masoretic Text as published in the latest editions of *Biblia Hebraica*, was used throughout. The Dead Sea Scrolls contain material bearing on an earlier stage of the Hebrew text. They were consulted, as were the Samaritan Pentateuch and the ancient scribal traditions relating to textual changes. Sometimes a variant Hebrew reading in the margin of the Masoretic Text was followed instead of the text itself. Such instances, being variants within the Masoretic tradition, are not specified by footnotes. In rare cases, words in the consonantal text were divided differently from the way they appear in the Masoretic Text. Footnotes indicate this. The translators also consulted the more important early versions—the Septuagint; Aquila, Symmachus and Theodotion; the Vulgate; the Syriac Peshitta; the Targums; and for the Psalms the *Juxta Hebraica* of Jerome. Readings from these versions were occasionally followed where the Masoretic Text seemed doubtful and where accepted principles of textual criticism showed that one or more of these textual witnesses appeared to provide the correct reading. Such instances are footnoted. Sometimes vowel letters and vowel signs did not, in the judgment of the translators, represent the correct vowels for the original consonantal text. Accordingly some words were read with a different set of vowels. These instances are usually not indicated by footnotes.

The Greek text used in translating the New Testament was an eclectic one. No other piece of ancient literature has such an abundance of manuscript witnesses as does the New Testament. Where existing manuscripts differ, the translators made their choice of readings according to accepted principles of New Testament textual criticism. Footnotes call attention to places where there was uncertainty about what the original text was. The best current printed texts of the Greek New Testament were used.

There is a sense in which the work of translation is never wholly finished. This applies to all great literature and uniquely so to the Bible. In 1973 the New Testament in the New International Version was published. Since then, suggestions for corrections and revisions have been received from various sources. The Committee on Bible Translation carefully considered the suggestions and adopted a number of them. These were incorporated in the first printing of the entire Bible in 1978. Additional revisions were made by the Committee on Bible Translation in 1983 and appear in printings after that date.

As in other ancient documents, the precise meaning of the biblical texts is sometimes uncertain. This is more often the case with the Hebrew and Aramaic texts than with the Greek text. Although archaeological and linguistic discoveries in this century aid in understanding difficult passages, some uncertainties remain. The more significant of these have been called to the reader's attention in the footnotes.

In regard to the divine name *YHWH*, commonly referred to as the *Tetragrammaton*, the translators adopted the device used in most English versions of rendering that name as "Lord" in capital letters to distinguish it from *Adonai*, another Hebrew word rendered "Lord," for which small letters are used. Wherever the two names stand together in the Old Testament as a compound name of God, they are rendered "Sovereign LORD."

Because for most readers today the phrases "the LORD of hosts" and "God of hosts" have little meaning, this version renders them "the LORD Almighty" and "God Almighty." These renderings convey the sense of the Hebrew, namely, "he who is sovereign over all the 'hosts' (powers) in heaven and on earth, especially over the 'hosts' (armies) of Israel." For readers unacquainted with Hebrew this does not make clear the distinction between *Sabaoth* ("hosts" or "Almighty") and *Shaddai* (which can also be translated "Almighty"), but the latter occurs infrequently and is always footnoted. When *Adonai* and *YHWH Sabaoth* occur together, they are rendered "the Lord, the LORD Almighty."

As for other proper nouns, the familiar spellings of the King James Version are generally retained. Names traditionally spelled with "ch," except where it is final, are usually spelled in this translation with "k" or "c," since the biblical languages do not have the sound that "ch" frequently indicates in English—for example, in *chant*. For well-known names such as Zechariah, however, the traditional spelling has been retained. Variation in the spelling of names in the original languages has usually not been indicated. Where a person or place has two or more different names in the Hebrew, Aramaic or Greek texts, the more familiar one has generally been used, with footnotes where needed.

To achieve clarity the translators sometimes supplied words not in the original texts but required by the context. If there was uncertainty about such material, it is enclosed in brackets. Also for the sake of clarity or style, nouns, including some proper nouns, are sometimes substituted for pronouns, and vice versa. And though the Hebrew writers often shifted back and forth between first, second and third personal pronouns without change of antecedent, this translation often makes them uniform, in accordance with English style and without the use of footnotes.

Poetical passages are printed as poetry, that is, with indentation of lines and with separate stanzas. These are generally designed to reflect the structure of Hebrew poetry. This poetry is normally characterized by parallelism in balanced lines. Most of the poetry in the Bible is in the Old Testament, and scholars differ regarding the scansion of Hebrew lines. The translators determined the stanza divisions for the most part by analysis of the subject matter. The stanzas therefore serve as poetic paragraphs.

As an aid to the reader, italicized sectional headings are inserted in most of the books. They are not to be regarded as part of the NIV text, are not for oral reading, and are not intended to dictate the interpretation of the sections they head.

The footnotes in this version are of several kinds, most of which need no explanation. Those giving alternative translations begin with "Or" and generally introduce the alternative with the last word preceding it in the text, except when it is a single-word alternative; in poetry quoted in a footnote a slant mark indicates a line division. Footnotes introduced by "Or" do not have uniform significance. In some cases two possible translations were considered to have about equal validity. In other cases, though the translators were convinced that the translation in the text was correct, they judged that another interpretation was possible and of sufficient importance to be represented in a footnote.

In the New Testament, footnotes that refer to uncertainty regarding the original text are introduced by "Some manuscripts" or similiar expressions. In the Old Testament, evidence for the reading chosen is given first and evidence for the alternative is added after a semicolon (for example: Septuagint; Hebrew *father*). In such notes the term "Hebrew" refers to the Masoretic Text.

It should be noted that minerals, flora and fauna, architectural other articles cannot always be identified with precision. Also measures of capacity in the biblical period are particularly uncertain (see the table of weights and measures following the text).

Like all translations of the Bible, made as they are by imperfect man, this one undoubtedly falls short of its goals. Yet we are grateful to God for the extent to which he has enabled us to realize these goals and for the strength he has given us and our colleagues to complete our task. We offer this version of the Bible to him in whose name and for whose glory it has been made. We pray that it will lead many into a better understanding of the Holy Scriptures and a fuller knowledge of Jesus Christ the incarnate Word, of whom the Scriptures so faithfully testify.

The Committee on Bible Translation

June 1978

Names of the translators and editors may be secured
from the International Bible Society,
translation sponsors of the New International Version,
P.O. Box 62970, Colorado Springs, Colorado 80962-2970 U.S.A.

The
New Testament

Matthew

The Genealogy of Jesus

1 A record of the genealogy of
Jesus Christ the son of David,
the son of Abraham:

²Abraham was the father of
Isaac,
Isaac the father of Jacob,
Jacob the father of Judah and
his brothers,
³Judah the father of Perez and
Zerah, whose mother was
Tamar,
Perez the father of Hezron,
Hezron the father of Ram,
⁴Ram the father of Am-
minadab,
Amminadab the father of
Nahshon,
Nahshon the father of Sal-
mon,
⁵Salmon the father of Boaz,
whose mother was Rahab,
Boaz the father of Obed,
whose mother was Ruth,
Obed the father of Jesse,
⁶and Jesse the father of King
David.

David was the father of Solomon, whose mother had
been Uriah's wife,
⁷Solomon the father of Rehoboam,
Rehoboam the father of Abijah,
Abijah the father of Asa,
⁸Asa the father of Jehoshaphat,
Jehoshaphat the father of Jehoram,
Jehoram the father of Uz-
ziah,
⁹Uzziah the father of Jotham,
Jotham the father of Ahaz,
Ahaz the father of Hezekiah,
¹⁰Hezekiah the father of Manasseh,
Manasseh the father of
Amon,
Amon the father of Josiah,
¹¹and Josiah the father of Jeco-
niahᵃ and his brothers at
the time of the exile to Babylon.

¹²After the exile to Babylon:
Jeconiah was the father of
Shealtiel,
Shealtiel the father of Zerub-
babel,
¹³Zerubbabel the father of Abi-
ud,
Abiud the father of Eliakim,
Eliakim the father of Azor,
¹⁴Azor the father of Zadok,
Zadok the father of Akim,
Akim the father of Eliud,
¹⁵Eliud the father of Eleazar,
Eleazar the father of Mat-
than,
Matthan the father of Jacob,
¹⁶and Jacob the father of Jo-
seph, the husband of
Mary, of whom was born
Jesus, who is called Christ.

¹⁷Thus there were fourteen generations in all from Abraham to
David, fourteen from David to
the exile to Babylon, and fourteen from the exile to the Christ.ᵇ

The Birth of Jesus Christ

¹⁸This is how the birth of Jesus
Christ came about: His mother
Mary was pledged to be married
to Joseph, but before they came
together, she was found to be
with child through the Holy

ᵃ11 That is, Jehoiachin; also in verse 12   ᵇ17 Or Messiah. "The Christ" (Greek) and
"the Messiah" (Hebrew) both mean "the Anointed One."

Spirit. [19]Because Joseph her husband was a righteous man and did not want to expose her to public disgrace, he had in mind to divorce her quietly.

[20]But after he had considered this, an angel of the Lord appeared to him in a dream and said, "Joseph son of David, do not be afraid to take Mary home as your wife, because what is conceived in her is from the Holy Spirit. [21]She will give birth to a son, and you are to give him the name Jesus,*a* because he will save his people from their sins."

[22]All this took place to fulfill what the Lord had said through the prophet: [23]"The virgin will be with child and will give birth to a son, and they will call him Immanuel"*b*—which means, "God with us."

[24]When Joseph woke up, he did what the angel of the Lord commanded him and took Mary home as his wife. [25]But he had no union with her until she gave birth to a son. And he gave him the name Jesus.

The Visit of the Magi

2 After Jesus was born in Bethlehem in Judea, during the time of King Herod, Magi*c* from the east came to Jerusalem [2]and asked, "Where is the one who has been born king of the Jews? We saw his star in the east*d* and have come to worship him."

[3]When King Herod heard this he was disturbed, and all Jerusalem with him. [4]When he had called together all the people's chief priests and teachers of the law, he asked them where the Christ*e* was to be born. [5]"In Bethlehem in Judea," they replied,

"for this is what the prophet has written:

[6]" 'But you, Bethlehem, in the
    land of Judah,
  are by no means least
    among the rulers of
    Judah;
for out of you will come a
    ruler
  who will be the shepherd of
    my people Israel.'*f*"

[7]Then Herod called the Magi secretly and found out from them the exact time the star had appeared. [8]He sent them to Bethlehem and said, "Go and make a careful search for the child. As soon as you find him, report to me, so that I too may go and worship him."

[9]After they had heard the king, they went on their way, and the star they had seen in the east*g* went ahead of them until it stopped over the place where the child was. [10]When they saw the star, they were overjoyed. [11]On coming to the house, they saw the child with his mother Mary, and they bowed down and worshiped him. Then they opened their treasures and presented him with gifts of gold and of incense and of myrrh. [12]And having been warned in a dream not to go back to Herod, they returned to their country by another route.

The Escape to Egypt

[13]When they had gone, an angel of the Lord appeared to Joseph in a dream. "Get up," he said, "take the child and his mother and escape to Egypt. Stay there until I tell you, for Herod is

---

*a*21 *Jesus* is the Greek form of *Joshua*, which means *the LORD saves.*   *b*23 Isaiah 7:14
*c*1 Traditionally *Wise Men*   *d*2 Or *star when it rose*   *e*4 Or *Messiah*   *f*6 Micah 5:2
*g*9 Or *seen when it rose*

going to search for the child to kill him."

14So he got up, took the child and his mother during the night and left for Egypt, 15where he stayed until the death of Herod. And so was fulfilled what the Lord had said through the prophet: "Out of Egypt I called my son."[a]

16When Herod realized that he had been outwitted by the Magi, he was furious, and he gave orders to kill all the boys in Bethlehem and its vicinity who were two years old and under, in accordance with the time he had learned from the Magi. 17Then what was said through the prophet Jeremiah was fulfilled:

18"A voice is heard in Ramah,
      weeping and great
          mourning,
   Rachel weeping for her
        children
   and refusing to be
        comforted,
   because they are no more."[b]

The Return to Nazareth

19After Herod died, an angel of the Lord appeared in a dream to Joseph in Egypt 20and said, "Get up, take the child and his mother and go to the land of Israel, for those who were trying to take the child's life are dead."

21So he got up, took the child and his mother and went to the land of Israel. 22But when he heard that Archelaus was reigning in Judea in place of his father Herod, he was afraid to go there. Having been warned in a dream, he withdrew to the district of Galilee, 23and he went and lived in a town called Nazareth. So was fulfilled what was said through the prophets: "He will be called a Nazarene."

John the Baptist Prepares the Way

3 In those days John the Baptist came, preaching in the Desert of Judea 2and saying, "Repent, for the kingdom of heaven is near." 3This is he who was spoken of through the prophet Isaiah:

74
Lk 13:3

"A voice of one calling in the
      desert,
'Prepare the way for the Lord,
     make straight paths for
          him.' "[c]

4John's clothes were made of camel's hair, and he had a leather belt around his waist. His food was locusts and wild honey. 5People went out to him from Jerusalem and all Judea and the whole region of the Jordan. 6Confessing their sins, they were baptized by him in the Jordan River. 7But when he saw many of the Pharisees and Sadducees coming to where he was baptizing, he said to them: "You brood of vipers! Who warned you to flee from the coming wrath? 8Produce fruit in keeping with repentance. 9And do not think you can say to yourselves, 'We have Abraham as our father.' I tell you that out of these stones God can raise up children for Abraham. 10The ax is already at the root of the trees, and every tree that does not produce good fruit will be cut down and thrown into the fire.

7
Ac 26:28

23
Mt 7:24-27

11"I baptize you with[d] water for repentance. But after me will come one who is more powerful than I, whose sandals I am not fit to carry. He will baptize you with the Holy Spirit and with fire. 12His winnowing fork is in his hand, and he will clear his threshing floor, gathering his

---

[a]15 Hosea 11:1   [b]18 Jer. 31:15   [c]3 Isaiah 40:3   [d]11 Or in

wheat into the barn and burning up the chaff with unquenchable fire.''

The Baptism of Jesus

13Then Jesus came from Galilee to the Jordan to be baptized by John. 14But John tried to deter him, saying, "I need to be baptized by you, and do you come to me?''

15Jesus replied, "Let it be so now; it is proper for us to do this to fulfill all righteousness." Then John consented.

16As soon as Jesus was baptized, he went up out of the water. At that moment heaven was opened, and he saw the Spirit of God descending like a dove and lighting on him. 17And a voice from heaven said, "This is my Son, whom I love; with him I am well pleased."

The Temptation of Jesus

4 Then Jesus was led by the Spirit into the desert to be tempted by the devil. 2After fasting forty days and forty nights, he was hungry. 3The tempter came to him and said, "If you are the Son of God, tell these stones to become bread."

4Jesus answered, "It is written: 'Man does not live on bread alone, but on every word that comes from the mouth of God.'*d*"

5Then the devil took him to the holy city and had him stand on the highest point of the temple. 6"If you are the Son of God," he said, "throw yourself down. For it is written:

" 'He will command his angels
    concerning you,
  and they will lift you up in
    their hands,

so that you will not strike
    your foot against a
     stone.'*b*"

7Jesus answered him, "It is also written: 'Do not put the Lord your God to the test.'*c*"

8Again, the devil took him to a very high mountain and showed him all the kingdoms of the world and their splendor. 9"All this I will give you," he said, "if you will bow down and worship me."

10Jesus said to him, "Away from me, Satan! For it is written: 'Worship the Lord your God, and serve him only.'*d*"

11Then the devil left him, and angels came and attended him.

Jesus Begins to Preach

12When Jesus heard that John had been put in prison, he returned to Galilee. 13Leaving Nazareth, he went and lived in Capernaum, which was by the lake in the area of Zebulun and Naphtali— 14to fulfill what was said through the prophet Isaiah:

15"Land of Zebulun and land of
    Naphtali,
the way to the sea, along
    the Jordan,
Galilee of the Gentiles—
16the people living in darkness
  have seen a great light;
on those living in the land of
    the shadow of death
  a light has dawned."*e*

17From that time on Jesus began to preach, "Repent, for the kingdom of heaven is near."

The Calling of the First Disciples

18As Jesus was walking beside the Sea of Galilee, he saw two brothers, Simon called Peter and

---

*a*4 Deut. 8:3   *b*6 Psalm 91:11,12   *c*7 Deut. 6:16   *d*10 Deut. 6:13
*e*16 Isaiah 9:1,2

his brother Andrew. They were casting a net into the lake, for they were fishermen. [19]"Come, follow me," Jesus said, "and I will make you fishers of men." [20]At once they left their nets and followed him.

[21]Going on from there, he saw two other brothers, James son of Zebedee and his brother John. They were in a boat with their father Zebedee, preparing their nets. Jesus called them, [22]and immediately they left the boat and their father and followed him.

Jesus Heals the Sick

[23]Jesus went throughout Galilee, teaching in their synagogues, preaching the good news of the kingdom, and healing every disease and sickness among the people. [24]News about him spread all over Syria, and people brought to him all who were ill with various diseases, those suffering severe pain, the demon-possessed, those having seizures, and the paralyzed, and he healed them. [25]Large crowds from Galilee, the Decapolis,[a] Jerusalem, Judea and the region across the Jordan followed him.

The Beatitudes

5 Now when he saw the crowds, he went up on a mountainside and sat down. His disciples came to him, [2]and he began to teach them, saying:

[3]"Blessed are the poor in spirit,
   for theirs is the kingdom of
   heaven.

53
Jn 11:25,26
[4]Blessed are those who mourn,
   for they will be comforted.
[5]Blessed are the meek,
   for they will inherit the
   earth.

[a]25 That is, the Ten Cities

[6]Blessed are those who hunger
   and thirst for
   righteousness,
   for they will be filled.
[7]Blessed are the merciful,
   for they will be shown
   mercy.
[8]Blessed are the pure in heart,
   for they will see God.
[9]Blessed are the peacemakers,
   for they will be called sons
   of God.
[10]Blessed are those who are
   persecuted because of
   righteousness,
   for theirs is the kingdom of
   heaven.

92
Mt 5:22

[11]"Blessed are you when people insult you, persecute you and falsely say all kinds of evil against you because of me. [12]Rejoice and be glad, because great is your reward in heaven, for in the same way they persecuted the prophets who were before you.

Salt and Light

[13]"You are the salt of the earth. But if the salt loses its saltiness, how can it be made salty again? It is no longer good for anything, except to be thrown out and trampled by men.

[14]"You are the light of the world. A city on a hill cannot be hidden. [15]Neither do people light a lamp and put it under a bowl. Instead they put it on its stand, and it gives light to everyone in the house. [16]In the same way, let your light shine before men, that they may see your good deeds and praise your Father in heaven.

The Fulfillment of the Law

[17]"Do not think that I have come to abolish the Law or the Prophets; I have not come to abolish them but to fulfill them. [18]I tell you the truth, until heaven

and earth disappear, not the smallest letter, not the least stroke of a pen, will by any means disappear from the Law until everything is accomplished. [19]Anyone who breaks one of the least of these commandments and teaches others to do the same will be called least in the kingdom of heaven, but whoever practices and teaches these commands will be called great in the kingdom of heaven. [20]For I tell you that unless your righteousness surpasses that of the Pharisees and the teachers of the law, you will certainly not enter the kingdom of heaven.

Murder

38
Jn 15:23

[21]"You have heard that it was said to the people long ago, 'Do not murder,[a] and anyone who murders will be subject to judgment.' [22]But I tell you that anyone who is angry with his brother[b] will be subject to judgment. Again, anyone who says to his brother, 'Raca,[c]' is answerable to the Sanhedrin. But anyone who says, 'You fool!' will be in danger of the fire of hell.

3
Mk 3:5

92
Ac 14:22

71
1Co 7:11

[23]"Therefore, if you are offering your gift at the altar and there remember that your brother has something against you, [24]leave your gift there in front of the altar. First go and be reconciled to your brother; then come and offer your gift.

[25]"Settle matters quickly with your adversary who is taking you to court. Do it while you are still with him on the way, or he may hand you over to the judge, and the judge may hand you over to the officer, and you may be thrown into prison. [26]I tell you the truth, you will not get out until you have paid the last penny.[d]

Adultery

2
Mt 5:31,32

[27]"You have heard that it was said, 'Do not commit adultery.'[e] [28]But I tell you that anyone who looks at a woman lustfully has already committed adultery with her in his heart. [29]If your right eye causes you to sin, gouge it out and throw it away. It is better for you to lose one part of your body than for your whole body to be thrown into hell. [30]And if your right hand causes you to sin, cut it off and throw it away. It is better for you to lose one part of your body than for your whole body to go into hell.

Divorce

2
Mt 15:19

19
Mt 19:4-6

[31]"It has been said, 'Anyone who divorces his wife must give her a certificate of divorce.'[f] [32]But I tell you that anyone who divorces his wife, except for marital unfaithfulness, causes her to become an adulteress, and anyone who marries the divorced woman commits adultery.

Oaths

[33]"Again, you have heard that it was said to the people long ago, 'Do not break your oath, but keep the oaths you have made to the Lord.' [34]But I tell you, Do not swear at all: either by heaven, for it is God's throne; [35]or by the earth, for it is his footstool; or by Jerusalem, for it is the city of the Great King. [36]And do not swear by your head, for you cannot make even one hair white or black. [37]Simply let your 'Yes' be 'Yes,' and your 'No,' 'No'; anything beyond this comes from the evil one.

An Eye for an Eye

[38]"You have heard that it was

said, 'Eye for eye, and tooth for tooth.'[a] 39But I tell you, Do not resist an evil person. If someone strikes you on the right cheek, turn to him the other also. 40And if someone wants to sue you and take your tunic, let him have your cloak as well. 41If someone forces you to go one mile, go with him two miles. 42Give to the one who asks you, and do not turn away from the one who wants to borrow from you.

Love for Enemies

29
Mt 6:15

43"You have heard that it was said, 'Love your neighbor[b] and hate your enemy.' 44But I tell you: Love your enemies[c] and pray for those who persecute you, 45that you may be sons of your Father in heaven. He causes his sun to rise on the evil and the good, and sends rain on the righteous and the unrighteous. 46If you love those who love you, what reward will you get? Are not even the tax collectors doing that? 47And if you greet only your brothers, what are you doing more than others? Do not even pagans do that? 48Be perfect, therefore, as your heavenly Father is perfect.

Giving to the Needy

6 "Be careful not to do your 'acts of righteousness' before men, to be seen by them. If you do, you will have no reward from your Father in heaven.

76
Ro 12:17

2"So when you give to the needy, do not announce it with trumpets, as the hypocrites do in the synagogues and on the streets, to be honored by men. I tell you the truth, they have received their reward in full. 3But when you give to the needy, do not let your left hand know what your right hand is doing, 4so that your giving may be in secret. Then your Father, who sees what is done in secret, will reward you.

Prayer

5"And when you pray, do not be like the hypocrites, for they love to pray standing in the synagogues and on the street corners to be seen by men. I tell you the truth, they have received their reward in full. 6But when you pray, go into your room, close the door and pray to your Father, who is unseen. Then your Father, who sees what is done in secret, will reward you. 7And when you pray, do not keep on babbling like pagans, for they think that they will be heard because of their many words. 8Do not be like them, for your Father knows what you need before you ask him.

9"This, then, is how you should pray:

69
Mt 7:7,8

" 'Our Father in heaven,
    hallowed be your name,
10your kingdom come,
    your will be done
       on earth as it is in heaven.
11Give us today our daily bread.
12Forgive us our debts,
    as we also have forgiven
       our debtors.
13And lead us not into
       temptation,
    but deliver us from the evil
       one.[d]'

98
Mt 7:21

14For if you forgive men when they sin against you, your heavenly Father will also forgive you. 15But if you do not forgive men

28
Mk 2:10

29
Mk 11:25

---

a38 Exodus 21:24; Lev. 24:20; Deut. 19:21   b43 Lev. 19:18   c44 Some late manuscripts enemies, bless those who curse you, do good to those who hate you   d13 Or from evil; some late manuscripts one, / for yours is the kingdom and the power and the glory forever. Amen.

their sins, your Father will not forgive your sins.

Fasting

16"When you fast, do not look somber as the hypocrites do, for they disfigure their faces to show men they are fasting. I tell you the truth, they have received their reward in full. 17But when you fast, put oil on your head and wash your face, 18so that it will not be obvious to men that you are fasting, but only to your Father, who is unseen; and your Father, who sees what is done in secret, will reward you.

Treasures in Heaven

33
Mt 6:24

37
Lk 12:15

61
Mt 6:24

19"Do not store up for yourselves treasures on earth, where moth and rust destroy, and where thieves break in and steal. 20But store up for yourselves treasures in heaven, where moth and rust do not destroy, and where thieves do not break in and steal. 21For where your treasure is, there your heart will be also.

22"The eye is the lamp of the body. If your eyes are good, your whole body will be full of light. 23But if your eyes are bad, your whole body will be full of darkness. If then the light within you is darkness, how great is that darkness!

33
Mt 23:25

61
Mk 12:41-44

24"No one can serve two masters. Either he will hate the one and love the other, or he will be devoted to the one and despise the other. You cannot serve both God and Money.

Do Not Worry

4
Mt 11:28-30

25"Therefore I tell you, do not worry about your life, what you will eat or drink; or about your body, what you will wear. Is not life more important than food, and the body more important

than clothes? 26Look at the birds of the air; they do not sow or reap or store away in barns, and yet your heavenly Father feeds them. Are you not much more valuable than they? 27Who of you by worrying can add a single hour to his life[a]? 82
Ro 14:16-1

28"And why do you worry about clothes? See how the lilies of the field grow. They do not labor or spin. 29Yet I tell you that not even Solomon in all his splendor was dressed like one of these. 30If that is how God clothes the grass of the field, which is here today and tomorrow is thrown into the fire, will he not much more clothe you, O you of little faith? 31So do not worry, saying, 'What shall we eat?' or 'What shall we drink?' or 'What shall we wear?' 32For the pagans run after all these things, and your heavenly Father knows that you need them. 33But seek first his kingdom and his righteousness, and all these things will be given to you as well. 34Therefore do not worry about tomorrow, for tomorrow will worry about itself. Each day has enough trouble of its own. 77
Mt 9:13

Judging Others

7 "Do not judge, or you too will be judged. 2For in the same way you judge others, you will be judged, and with the measure you use, it will be measured to you. 47
Mt 23:23,2

3"Why do you look at the speck of sawdust in your brother's eye and pay no attention to the plank in your own eye? 4How can you say to your brother, 'Let me take the speck out of your eye,' when all the time there is a plank in your own eye? 5You hypocrite, first take the plank out of your own eye, and then you will see

[a]27 Or single cubit to his height

clearly to remove the speck from your brother's eye.

6"Do not give dogs what is sacred; do not throw your pearls to pigs. If you do, they may trample them under their feet, and then turn and tear you to pieces.

Ask, Seek, Knock

7"Ask and it will be given to you; seek and you will find; knock and the door will be opened to you. 8For everyone who asks receives; he who seeks finds; and to him who knocks, the door will be opened.

9"Which of you, if his son asks for bread, will give him a stone? 10Or if he asks for a fish, will give him a snake? 11If you, then, though you are evil, know how to give good gifts to your children, how much more will your Father in heaven give good gifts to those who ask him! 12So in everything, do to others what you would have them do to you, for this sums up the Law and the Prophets.

The Narrow and Wide Gates

13"Enter through the narrow gate. For wide is the gate and broad is the road the leads to destruction, and many enter through it. 14But small is the gate and narrow the road that leads to life, and only a few find it.

A Tree and Its Fruit

15"Watch out for false prophets. They come to you in sheep's clothing, but inwardly they are ferocious wolves. 16By their fruit you will recognize them. Do people pick grapes from thornbushes, or figs from thistles? 17Likewise every good tree bears good fruit, but a bad tree bears bad fruit. 18A good tree cannot

bear bad fruit, and a bad tree cannot bear good fruit. 19Every tree that does not bear good fruit is cut down and thrown into the fire. 20Thus, by their fruit you will recognize them.

21"Not everyone who says to me, 'Lord, Lord,' will enter the kingdom of heaven, but only he who does the will of my Father who is in heaven. 22Many will say to me on that day, 'Lord, Lord, did we not prophesy in your name, and in your name drive out demons and perform many miracles?' 23Then I will tell them plainly, 'I never knew you. Away from me, you evildoers!'

The Wise and Foolish Builders

24"Therefore everyone who hears these words of mine and puts them into practice is like a wise man who built his house on the rock. 25The rain came down, the streams rose, and the winds blew and beat against that house; yet it did not fall, because it had its foundation on the rock. 26But everyone who hears these words of mine and does not put them into practice is like a foolish man who built his house on sand. 27The rain came down, the streams rose, and the winds blew and beat against that house, and it fell with a great crash."

28When Jesus had finished saying these things, the crowds were amazed at his teaching, 29because he taught as one who had authority, and not as their teachers of the law.

The Man With Leprosy

8 When he came down from the mountainside, large crowds followed him. 2A man with leprosy*a* came and knelt be-

*a2 The Greek word was used for various diseases affecting the skin—not necessarily leprosy.

fore him and said, "Lord, if you are willing, you can make me clean."

³Jesus reached out his hand and touched the man. "I am willing," he said. "Be clean!" Immediately he was cured[a] of his leprosy. ⁴Then Jesus said to him, "See that you don't tell anyone. But go, show yourself to the priest and offer the gift Moses commanded, as a testimony to them."

The Faith of the Centurion

⁵When Jesus had entered Capernaum, a centurion came to him, asking for help. ⁶"Lord," he said, "my servant lies at home paralyzed and in terrible suffering."

⁷Jesus said to him, "I will go and heal him."

⁸The centurion replied, "Lord, I do not deserve to have you come under my roof. But just say the word, and my servant will be healed. ⁹For I myself am a man under authority, with soldiers under me. I tell this one, 'Go,' and he goes; and that one, 'Come,' and he comes. I say to my servant, 'Do this,' and he does it."

24
Mk 11:24

¹⁰When Jesus heard this, he was astonished and said to those following him, "I tell you the truth, I have not found anyone in Israel with such great faith. ¹¹I say to you that many will come from the east and the west, and will take their places at the feast with Abraham, Isaac and Jacob in the kingdom of heaven. ¹²But the subjects of the kingdom will be thrown outside, into the darkness, where there will be weeping and gnashing of teeth."

40
Lk 16:22-26

¹³Then Jesus said to the centurion, "Go! It will be done just as you believed it would." And his servant was healed at that very hour.

Jesus Heals Many

¹⁴When Jesus came into Peter's house, he saw Peter's mother-in-law lying in bed with a fever. ¹⁵He touched her hand and the fever left her, and she got up and began to wait on him.

39
Ac 3:16

¹⁶When evening came, many who were demon-possessed were brought to him, and he drove out the spirits with a word and healed all the sick. ¹⁷This was to fulfill what was spoken through the prophet Isaiah:

"He took up our infirmities
    and carried our diseases."[b]

The Cost of Following Jesus

¹⁸When Jesus saw the crowd around him, he gave orders to cross to the other side of the lake. ¹⁹Then a teacher of the law came to him and said, "Teacher, I will follow you wherever you go."

²⁰Jesus replied, "Foxes have holes and birds of the air have nests, but the Son of Man has no place to lay his head."

²¹Another disciple said to him, "Lord, first let me go and bury my father."

²²But Jesus told him, "Follow me, and let the dead bury their own dead."

Jesus Calms the Storm

²³Then he got into the boat and his disciples followed him. ²⁴Without warning, a furious storm came up on the lake, so that the waves swept over the boat. But Jesus was sleeping. ²⁵The disciples went and woke him, saying, "Lord, save us! We're going to drown!"

²⁶He replied, "You of little faith,

---

[a]3 Greek *made clean*   [b]17 Isaiah 53:4

why are you so afraid?'' Then he got up and rebuked the winds and the waves, and it was completely calm.

27The men were amazed and asked, ''What kind of man is this? Even the winds and the waves obey him!''

The Healing of Two Demon-possessed Men

28When he arrived at the other side in the region of the Gadarenes,[a] two demon-possessed men coming from the tombs met him. They were so violent that no one could pass that way. 29''What do you want with us, Son of God?'' they shouted. ''Have you come here to torture us before the appointed time?''

30Some distance from them a large herd of pigs was feeding. 31The demons begged Jesus, ''If you drive us out, send us into the herd of pigs.''

32He said to them, ''Go!'' So they came out and went into the pigs, and the whole herd rushed down the steep bank into the lake and died in the water. 33Those tending the pigs ran off, went into the town and reported all this, including what had happened to the demon-possessed men. 34Then the whole town went out to meet Jesus. And when they saw him, they pleaded with him to leave their region.

Jesus Heals a Paralytic

9 Jesus stepped into a boat, crossed over and came to his own town. 2Some men brought to him a paralytic, lying on a mat. When Jesus saw their faith, he said to the paralytic, ''Take heart, son; your sins are forgiven.''

3At this, some of the teachers of the law said to themselves, ''This fellow is blaspheming!''

4Knowing their thoughts, Jesus said, ''Why do you entertain evil thoughts in your hearts? 5Which is easier: to say, 'Your sins are forgiven,' or to say, 'Get up and walk'? 6But so that you may know that the Son of Man has authority on earth to forgive sins. . . .'' Then he said to the paralytic, ''Get up, take your mat and go home.'' 7And the man got up and went home. 8When the crowd saw this, they were filled with awe; and they praised God, who had given such authority to men.

The Calling of Matthew

9As Jesus went on from there, he saw a man named Matthew sitting at the tax collector's booth. ''Follow me,'' he told him, and Matthew got up and followed him.

10While Jesus was having dinner at Matthew's house, many tax collectors and ''sinners'' came and ate with him and his disciples. 11When the Pharisees saw this, they asked his disciples, ''Why does your teacher eat with tax collectors and 'sinners'?''

12On hearing this, Jesus said, ''It is not the healthy who need a doctor, but the sick. 13But go and learn what this means: 'I desire mercy, not sacrifice.'[b] For I have not come to call the righteous, but sinners.''

70
1Co 1:26-29

77
Lk 14:14

Jesus Questioned About Fasting

14Then John's disciples came and asked him, ''How is it that we and the Pharisees fast, but your disciples do not fast?''

15Jesus answered, ''How can

the guests of the bridegroom mourn while he is with them? The time will come when the bridegroom will be taken from them; then they will fast.

16"No one sews a patch of unshrunk cloth on an old garment, for the patch will pull away from the garment, making the tear worse. 17Neither do men pour new wine into old wineskins. If they do, the skins will burst, the wine will run out and the wineskins will be ruined. No, they pour new wine into new wineskins, and both are preserved."

A Dead Girl and a Sick Woman

18While he was saying this, a ruler came and knelt before him and said, "My daughter has just died. But come and put your hand on her, and she will live." 19Jesus got up and went with him, and so did his disciples.

20Just then a woman who had been subject to bleeding for twelve years came up behind him and touched the edge of his cloak. 21She said to herself, "If I only touch his cloak, I will be healed."

22Jesus turned and saw her. "Take heart, daughter," he said, "your faith has healed you." And the woman was healed from that moment.

23When Jesus entered the ruler's house and saw the flute players and the noisy crowd, 24he said, "Go away. The girl is not dead but asleep." But they laughed at him. 25After the crowd had been put outside, he went in and took the girl by the hand, and she got up. 26News of this spread through all that region.

Jesus Heals the Blind and Mute

27As Jesus went on from there,

two blind men followed him, calling out, "Have mercy on us, Son of David!"

28When he had gone indoors, the blind men came to him, and he asked them, "Do you believe that I am able to do this?"

"Yes, Lord," they replied.

29Then he touched their eyes and said, "According to your faith will it be done to you"; 30and their sight was restored. Jesus warned them sternly, "See that no one knows about this." 31But they went out and spread the news about him all over that region.

32While they were going out, a man who was demon-possessed and could not talk was brought to Jesus. 33And when the demon was driven out, the man who had been mute spoke. The crowd was amazed and said, "Nothing like this has ever been seen in Israel."

34But the Pharisees said, "It is by the prince of demons that he drives out demons."

The Workers Are Few

35Jesus went through all the towns and villages, teaching in their synagogues, preaching the good news of the kingdom and healing every disease and sickness. 36When he saw the crowds, he had compassion on them, because they were harassed and helpless, like sheep without a shepherd. 37Then he said to his disciples, "The harvest is plentiful but the workers are few. 38Ask the Lord of the harvest, therefore, to send out workers into his harvest field."

Jesus Sends Out the Twelve

10 He called his twelve disciples to him and gave them

authority to drive out evil[a] spirits and to heal every disease and sickness.

[2]These are the names of the twelve apostles: first, Simon (who is called Peter) and his brother Andrew; James son of Zebedee, and his brother John; [3]Philip and Bartholomew; Thomas and Matthew the tax collector; James son of Alphaeus, and Thaddaeus; [4]Simon the Zealot and Judas Iscariot, who betrayed him.

[5]These twelve Jesus sent out with the following instructions: "Do not go among the Gentiles or enter any town of the Samaritans. [6]Go rather to the lost sheep of Israel. [7]As you go, preach this message: 'The kingdom of heaven is near.' [8]Heal the sick, raise the dead, cleanse those who have leprosy,[b] drive out demons. Freely you have received, freely give. [9]Do not take along any gold or silver or copper in your belts; [10]take no bag for the journey, or extra tunic, or sandals or a staff; for the worker is worth his keep.

[11]"Whatever town or village you enter, search for some worthy person there and stay at his house until you leave. [12]As you enter the home, give it your greeting. [13]If the home is deserving, let your peace rest on it; if it is not, let your peace return to you. [14]If anyone will not welcome you or listen to your words, shake the dust off your feet when you leave that home or town. [15]I tell you the truth, it will be more bearable for Sodom and Gomorrah on the day of judgment than for that town. [16]I am sending you out like sheep among wolves. Therefore be as shrewd as snakes and as innocent as doves.

[17]"Be on your guard against men; they will hand you over to the local councils and flog you in their synagogues. [18]On my account you will be brought before governors and kings as witnesses to them and to the Gentiles. [19]But when they arrest you, do not worry about what to say or how to say it. At that time you will be given what to say, [20]for it will not be you speaking, but the Spirit of your Father speaking through you.

[21]"Brother will betray brother to death, and a father his child; children will rebel against their parents and have them put to death. [22]All men will hate you because of me, but he who stands firm to the end will be saved. [23]When you are persecuted in one place, flee to another. I tell you the truth, you will not finish going through the cities of Israel before the Son of Man comes.

[24]"A student is not above his teacher, nor a servant above his master. [25]It is enough for the student to be like his teacher, and the servant like his master. If the head of the house has been called Beelzebub,[c] how much more the members of his household!

[26]"So do not be afraid of them. There is nothing concealed that will not be disclosed, or hidden that will not be made known. [27]What I tell you in the dark, speak in the daylight; what is whispered in your ear, proclaim from the roofs. [28]Do not be afraid of those who kill the body but cannot kill the soul. Rather, be afraid of the One who can destroy both soul and body in hell. [29]Are not two sparrows sold for a penny[d]? Yet not one of them will fall to the ground apart from the

73
Mt 23:37-39

---

[a]1 Greek *unclean*   [b]8 The Greek word was used for various diseases affecting the skin—not necessarily leprosy.   [c]25 Greek *Beezeboul* or *Beelzeboul*   [d]29 Greek *an assarion*

will of your Father. ³⁰And even the very hairs of your head are all numbered. ³¹So don't be afraid; you are worth more than many sparrows.

10
Ac 19:8

³²"Whoever acknowledges me before men, I will also acknowledge him before my Father in heaven. ³³But whoever disowns me before men, I will disown him before my Father in heaven.

³⁴"Do not suppose that I have come to bring peace to the earth. I did not come to bring peace, but a sword. ³⁵For I have come to turn

" 'a man against his father,
a daughter against her
        mother,
a daughter-in-law against her
        mother-in-law—
³⁶   a man's enemies will be the
        members of his own
        household.'ᵃ

³⁷"Anyone who loves his father or mother more than me is not worthy of me; anyone who loves his son or daughter more than me is not worthy of me; ³⁸and anyone who does not take his cross and follow me is not worthy of me. ³⁹Whoever finds his life will lose it, and whoever loses his life for my sake will find it.

⁴⁰"He who receives you receives me, and he who receives me receives the one who sent me. ⁴¹Anyone who receives a prophet because he is a prophet will receive a prophet's reward, and anyone who receives a righteous man because he is a righteous man will receive a righteous man's reward. ⁴²And if anyone gives even a cup of cold water to one of these little ones because he is my disciple, I tell you the truth, he will certainly not lose his reward."

Jesus and John the Baptist

11 After Jesus had finished instructing his twelve disciples, he went on from there to teach and preach in the towns of Galilee.ᵇ

²When John heard in prison what Christ was doing, he sent his disciples ³to ask him, "Are you the one who was to come, or should we expect someone else?"

⁴Jesus replied, "Go back and report to John what you hear and see: ⁵The blind receive sight, the lame walk, those who have leprosyᶜ are cured, the deaf hear, the dead are raised, and the good news is preached to the poor. ⁶Blessed is the man who does not fall away on account of me."

⁷As John's disciples were leaving, Jesus began to speak to the crowd about John: "What did you go out into the desert to see? A reed swayed by the wind? ⁸If not, what did you go out to see? A man dressed in fine clothes? No, those who wear fine clothes are in kings' palaces. ⁹Then what did you go out to see? A prophet? Yes, I tell you, and more than a prophet. ¹⁰This is the one about whom it is written:

" 'I will send my messenger
        ahead of you,
who will prepare your way
        before you.'ᵈ

¹¹I tell you the truth: Among those born of women there has not risen anyone greater than John the Baptist; yet he who is least in the kingdom of heaven is greater than he. ¹²From the days of John the Baptist until now, the kingdom of heaven has been forcefully advancing, and force-

---

ᵃ36 Micah 7:6   ᵇ1 Greek *in their towns*   ᶜ5 The Greek word was used for various diseases affecting the skin—not necessarily leprosy.   ᵈ10 Mal. 3:1

ful men lay hold of it. [13]For all the Prophets and the Law prophesied until John. [14]And if you are willing to accept it, he is the Elijah who was to come. [15]He who has ears, let him hear.

[16]"To what can I compare this generation? They are like children sitting in the marketplaces and calling out to others:

[17]" 'We played the flute for you,
     and you did not dance;
  we sang a dirge,
     and you did not mourn.'

[18]For John came neither eating nor drinking, and they say, 'He has a demon.' [19]The Son of Man came eating and drinking, and they say, 'Here is a glutton and a drunkard, a friend of tax collectors and "sinners." ' But wisdom is proved right by her actions."

Woe on Unrepentant Cities

[20]Then Jesus began to denounce the cities in which most of his miracles had been performed, because they did not repent. [21]"Woe to you, Korazin! Woe to you, Bethsaida! If the miracles that were performed in you had been performed in Tyre and Sidon, they would have repented long ago in sackcloth and ashes. [22]But I tell you, it will be more bearable for Tyre and Sidon on the day of judgment than for you. [23]And you, Capernaum, will you be lifted up to the skies? No, you will go down to the depths.[a] If the miracles that were performed in you had been performed in Sodom, it would have remained to this day. [24]But I tell you that it will be more bearable for Sodom on the day of judgment than for you."

Rest for the Weary

[25]At that time Jesus said, "I praise you, Father, Lord of heaven and earth, because you have hidden these things from the wise and learned, and revealed them to little children. [26]Yes, Father, for this was your good pleasure.

[27]"All things have been committed to me by my Father. No one knows the Son except the Father, and no one knows the Father except the Son and those to whom the Son chooses to reveal him.

[28]"Come to me, all you who are weary and burdened, and I will give you rest. [29]Take my yoke upon you and learn from me, for I am gentle and humble in heart, and you will find rest for your souls. [30]For my yoke is easy and my burden is light."

4
Lk 12:22-26

52
Mt 18:20

65
Mt 14:27

Lord of the Sabbath

12 At that time Jesus went through the grainfields on the Sabbath. His disciples were hungry and began to pick some heads of grain and eat them. [2]When the Pharisees saw this, they said to him, "Look! Your disciples are doing what is unlawful on the Sabbath."

[3]He answered, "Haven't you read what David did when he and his companions were hungry? [4]He entered the house of God, and he and his companions ate the consecrated bread—which was not lawful for them to do, but only for the priests? [5]Or haven't you read in the Law that on the Sabbath the priests in the temple desecrate the day and yet are innocent? [6]I tell you that one[b] greater than the temple is here. [7]If you had known what these words mean, 'I desire mercy, not sacrifice,'[c] you would not have condemned the innocent. [8]For

---

[a]23 Greek *Hades*   [b]6 Or *something*; also in verses 41 and 42   [c]7 Hosea 6:6

the Son of Man is Lord of the Sabbath.''

⁹Going on from that place, he went into their synagogue, ¹⁰and a man with a shriveled hand was there. Looking for a reason to accuse Jesus, they asked him, ''Is it lawful to heal on the Sabbath?''

¹¹He said to them, ''If any of you has a sheep and it falls into a pit on the Sabbath, will you not take hold of it and lift it out? ¹²How much more valuable is a man than a sheep! Therefore it is lawful to do good on the Sabbath.''

¹³Then he said to the man, ''Stretch out your hand.'' So he stretched it out and it was completely restored, just as sound as the other. ¹⁴But the Pharisees went out and plotted how they might kill Jesus.

God's Chosen Servant

¹⁵Aware of this, Jesus withdrew from that place. Many followed him, and he healed all their sick, ¹⁶warning them not to tell who he was. ¹⁷This was to fulfill what was spoken through the prophet Isaiah:

¹⁸''Here is my servant whom I
  have chosen,
  the one I love, in whom I
   delight;
 I will put my Spirit on him,
   and he will proclaim justice
    to the nations.
¹⁹He will not quarrel or cry out;
   no one will hear his voice in
    the streets.
²⁰A bruised reed he will not
    break,
   and a smoldering wick he
    will not snuff out,
 till he leads justice to victory.
²¹ In his name the nations will
   put their hope.''ᵃ

Jesus and Beelzebub

²²Then they brought him a demon-possessed man who was blind and mute, and Jesus healed him, so that he could both talk and see. ²³All the people were astonished and said, ''Could this be the Son of David?''

²⁴But when the Pharisees heard this, they said, ''It is only by Beelzebub,ᵇ the prince of demons, that this fellow drives out demons.''

²⁵Jesus knew their thoughts and said to them, ''Every kingdom divided against itself will be ruined, and every city or household divided against itself will not stand. ²⁶If Satan drives out Satan, he is divided against himself. How then can his kingdom stand? ²⁷And if I drive out demons by Beelzebub, by whom do your people drive them out? So then, they will be your judges. ²⁸But if I drive out demons by the Spirit of God, then the kingdom of God has come upon you.

²⁹''Or again, how can anyone enter a strong man's house and carry off his possessions unless he first ties up the strong man? Then he can rob his house.

³⁰''He who is not with me is against me, and he who does not gather with me scatters. ³¹And so I tell you, every sin and blasphemy will be forgiven men, but the blasphemy against the Spirit will not be forgiven. ³²Anyone who speaks a word against the Son of Man will be forgiven, but anyone who speaks against the Holy Spirit will not be forgiven, either in this age or in the age to come.

³³''Make a tree good and its fruit will be good, or make a tree bad and its fruit will be bad, for a tree

---

ᵃ21 Isaiah 42:1-4   ᵇ24 Greek *Beezeboul* or *Beelzeboul*; also in verse 27

is recognized by its fruit. ³⁴You brood of vipers, how can you who are evil say anything good? For out of the overflow of the heart the mouth speaks. ³⁵The good man brings good things out of the good stored up in him, and the evil man brings evil things out of the evil stored up in him. ³⁶But I tell you that men will have to give account on the day of judgment for every careless word they have spoken. ³⁷For by your words you will be acquitted, and by your words you will be condemned."

The Sign of Jonah

³⁸Then some of the Pharisees and teachers of the law said to him, "Teacher, we want to see a miraculous sign from you."

³⁹He answered, "A wicked and adulterous generation asks for a miraculous sign! But none will be given it except the sign of the prophet Jonah. ⁴⁰For as Jonah was three days and three nights in the belly of a huge fish, so the Son of Man will be three days and three nights in the heart of the earth. ⁴¹The men of Nineveh will stand up at the judgment with this generation and condemn it; for they repented at the preaching of Jonah, and now one*ᵃ* greater than Jonah is here. ⁴²The Queen of the South will rise at the judgment with this generation and condemn it; for she came from the ends of the earth to listen to Solomon's wisdom, and now one greater than Solomon is here.

⁴³"When an evil*ᵇ* spirit comes out of a man, it goes through arid places seeking rest and does not find it. ⁴⁴Then it says, 'I will return to the house I left.' When it arrives, it finds the house unoc-

cupied, swept clean and put in order. ⁴⁵Then it goes and takes with it seven other spirits more wicked than itself, and they go in and live there. And the final condition of that man is worse than the first. That is how it will be with this wicked generation."

Jesus' Mother and Brothers

⁴⁶While Jesus was still talking to the crowd, his mother and brothers stood outside, wanting to speak to him. ⁴⁷Someone told him, "Your mother and brothers are standing outside, wanting to speak to you."*ᶜ*

⁴⁸He replied to him, "Who is my mother, and who are my brothers?" ⁴⁹Pointing to his disciples, he said, "Here are my mother and my brothers. ⁵⁰For whoever does the will of my Father in heaven is my brother and sister and mother."

The Parable of the Sower

13 That same day Jesus went out of the house and sat by the lake. ²Such large crowds gathered around him that he got into a boat and sat in it, while all the people stood on the shore. ³Then he told them many things in parables, saying: "A farmer went out to sow his seed. ⁴As he was scattering the seed, some fell along the path, and the birds came and ate it up. ⁵Some fell on rocky places, where it did not have much soil. It sprang up quickly, because the soil was shallow. ⁶But when the sun came up, the plants were scorched, and they withered because they had no root. ⁷Other seed fell among thorns, which grew up and choked the plants. ⁸Still other seed fell on good soil,

---

ᵃ41 Or something; also in verse 42   ᵇ43 Greek unclean   ᶜ47 Some manuscripts do not have verse 47.

where it produced a crop—a hundred, sixty or thirty times what was sown. [9]He who has ears, let him hear."

[10]The disciples came to him and asked, "Why do you speak to the people in parables?"

[11]He replied, "The knowledge of the secrets of the kingdom of heaven has been given to you, but not to them. [12]Whoever has will be given more, and he will have an abundance. Whoever does not have, even what he has will be taken from him. [13]This is why I speak to them in parables:

"Though seeing, they do not
　　see;
　　though hearing, they do not
　　　　hear or understand.

[14]In them is fulfilled the prophecy of Isaiah:

" 'You will be ever hearing
　　but never understanding;
　you will be ever seeing but
　　never perceiving.
[15]For this people's heart has
　　become calloused;
　they hardly hear with their
　　　ears,
　and they have closed their
　　　eyes.
Otherwise they might see
　　with their eyes,
　hear with their ears,
　understand with their hearts
and turn, and I would heal
　　them.'[a]

[16]But blessed are your eyes because they see, and your ears because they hear. [17]For I tell you the truth, many prophets and righteous men longed to see what you see but did not see it, and to hear what you hear but did not hear it.

[18]"Listen then to what the parable of the sower means: [19]When anyone hears the message about the kingdom and does not understand it, the evil one comes and snatches away what was sown in his heart. This is the seed sown along the path. [20]The one who received the seed that fell on rocky places is the man who hears the word and at once receives it with joy. [21]But since he has no root, he lasts only a short time. When trouble or persecution comes because of the word, he quickly falls away. [22]The one who received the seed that fell among the thorns is the man who hears the word, but the worries of this life and the deceitfulness of wealth choke it, making it unfruitful. [23]But the one who received the seed that fell on good soil is the man who hears the word and understands it. He produces a crop, yielding a hundred, sixty or thirty times what was sown."

The Parable of the Weeds

[24]Jesus told them another parable: "The kingdom of heaven is like a man who sowed good seed in his field. [25]But while everyone was sleeping, his enemy came and sowed weeds among the wheat, and went away. [26]When the wheat sprouted and formed heads, then the weeds also appeared.

[27]"The owner's servants came to him and said, 'Sir, didn't you sow good seed in your field? Where then did the weeds come from?'

[28]" 'An enemy did this,' he replied.

"The servants asked him, 'Do you want us to go and pull them up?'

[29]" 'No,' he answered, 'because while you are pulling the weeds, you may root up the wheat with them. [30]Let both grow together

---

[a]15 Isaiah 6:9,10

until the harvest. At that time I will tell the harvesters: First collect the weeds and tie them in bundles to be burned; then gather the wheat and bring it into my barn.' "

The Parables of the Mustard Seed and the Yeast

31He told them another parable: "The kingdom of heaven is like a mustard seed, which a man took and planted in his field. 32Though it is the smallest of all your seeds, yet when it grows, it is the largest of garden plants and becomes a tree, so that the birds of the air come and perch in its branches."

33He told them still another parable: "The kingdom of heaven is like yeast that a woman took and mixed into a large amount[a] of flour until it worked all through the dough."

34Jesus spoke all these things to the crowd in parables; he did not say anything to them without using a parable. 35So was fulfilled what was spoken through the prophet:

"I will open my mouth in
        parables,
  I will utter things hidden
        since the creation of the
        world."[b]

The Parable of the Weeds Explained

36Then he left the crowd and went into the house. His disciples came to him and said, "Explain to us the parable of the weeds in the field."

37He answered, "The one who sowed the good seed is the Son of Man. 38The field is the world, and the good seed stands for the sons of the kingdom. The weeds are the sons of the evil one, 39and the enemy who sows them is the devil. The harvest is the end of the age, and the harvesters are angels.

40"As the weeds are pulled up and burned in the fire, so it will be at the end of the age. 41The Son of Man will send out his angels, and they will weed out of his kingdom everything that causes sin and all who do evil. 42They will throw them into the fiery furnace, where there will be weeping and gnashing of teeth. 43Then the righteous will shine like the sun in the kingdom of their Father. He who has ears, let him hear.

The Parables of the Hidden Treasure and the Pearl

44"The kingdom of heaven is like treasure hidden in a field. When a man found it, he hid it again, and then in his joy went and sold all he had and bought that field.

45"Again, the kingdom of heaven is like a merchant looking for fine pearls. 46When he found one of great value, he went away and sold everything he had and bought it.

The Parable of the Net

47"Once again, the kingdom of heaven is like a net that was let down into the lake and caught all kinds of fish. 48When it was full, the fishermen pulled it up on the shore. Then they sat down and collected the good fish in baskets, but threw the bad away. 49This is how it will be at the end of the age. The angels will come and separate the wicked from the righteous 50and throw them into the fiery furnace, where there will be weeping and gnashing of teeth.

---

a33 Greek three satas (probably about 1/2 bushel or 22 liters)   b35 Psalm 78:2

51"Have you understood all these things?" Jesus asked.

"Yes," they replied.

52He said to them, "Therefore every teacher of the law who has been instructed about the kingdom of heaven is like the owner of a house who brings out of his storeroom new treasures as well as old."

A Prophet Without Honor

53When Jesus had finished these parables, he moved on from there. 54Coming to his hometown, he began teaching the people in their synagogue, and they were amazed. "Where did this man get this wisdom and these miraculous powers?" they asked. 55"Isn't this the carpenter's son? Isn't his mother's name Mary, and aren't his brothers James, Joseph, Simon and Judas? 56Aren't all his sisters with us? Where then did this man get all these things?" 57And they took offense at him.

But Jesus said to them, "Only in his hometown and in his own house is a prophet without honor."

58And he did not do many miracles there because of their lack of faith.

John the Baptist Beheaded

14 At that time Herod the tetrarch heard the reports about Jesus, 2and he said to his attendants, "This is John the Baptist; he has risen from the dead! That is why miraculous powers are at work in him."

3Now Herod had arrested John and bound him and put him in prison because of Herodias, his brother Philip's wife, 4for John had been saying to him: "It is not lawful for you to have her." 5Herod wanted to kill John, but he was afraid of the people, because they considered him a prophet.

6On Herod's birthday the daughter of Herodias danced for them and pleased Herod so much 7that he promised with an oath to give her whatever she asked. 8Prompted by her mother, she said, "Give me here on a platter the head of John the Baptist." 9The king was distressed, but because of his oaths and his dinner guests, he ordered that her request be granted 10and had John beheaded in the prison. 11His head was brought in on a platter and given to the girl, who carried it to her mother. 12John's disciples came and took his body and buried it. Then they went and told Jesus.

Jesus Feeds the Five Thousand

13When Jesus heard what had happened, he withdrew by boat privately to a solitary place. Hearing of this, the crowds followed him on foot from the towns. 14When Jesus landed and saw a large crowd, he had compassion on them and healed their sick.

15As evening approached, the disciples came to him and said, "This is a remote place, and it's already getting late. Send the crowds away, so they can go to the villages and buy themselves some food."

16Jesus replied, "They do not need to go away. You give them something to eat."

17"We have here only five loaves of bread and two fish," they answered.

18"Bring them here to me," he said. 19And he directed the people to sit down on the grass. Taking the five loaves and the two fish and looking up to heaven, he gave thanks and broke the loaves. Then he gave them to the disciples, and the dis-

ciples gave them to the people.
[20]They all ate and were satisfied,
and the disciples picked up
twelve basketfuls of broken
pieces that were left over. [21]The
number of those who ate was
about five thousand men, besides women and children.

Jesus Walks on the Water

[22]Immediately Jesus made the
disciples get into the boat and go
on ahead of him to the other side,
while he dismissed the crowd.
[23]After he had dismissed them,
he went up on a mountainside by
himself to pray. When evening
came, he was there alone, [24]but
the boat was already a considerable distance[a] from land, buf-
feted by the waves because the
wind was against it.

[25]During the fourth watch of
the night Jesus went out to them,
walking on the lake. [26]When the
disciples saw him walking on the
lake, they were terrified. "It's a
ghost," they said, and cried out
in fear.

65
Ro 5:1,2
[27]But Jesus immediately said to
them: "Take courage! It is I.
Don't be afraid."

[28]"Lord, if it's you," Peter replied, "tell me to come to you on
the water."

[29]"Come," he said.

Then Peter got down out of the
boat, walked on the water and
came toward Jesus. [30]But when
he saw the wind, he was afraid
and, beginning to sink, cried out,
"Lord, save me!"

[31]Immediately Jesus reached
out his hand and caught him.
"You of little faith," he said,
"why did you doubt?"

[32]And when they climbed into
the boat, the wind died down.
[33]Then those who were in the
boat worshiped him, saying,

"Truly you are the Son of God."

[34]When they had crossed over,
they landed at Gennesaret. [35]And
when the men of that place
recognized Jesus, they sent word
to all the surrounding country.
People brought all their sick to
him [36]and begged him to let the
sick just touch the edge of his
cloak, and all who touched him
were healed.

Clean and Unclean

15 Then some Pharisees and
teachers of the law came to
Jesus from Jerusalem and asked,
[2]"Why do your disciples break
the tradition of the elders? They
don't wash their hands before
they eat!"

[3]Jesus replied, "And why do
you break the command of God
for the sake of your tradition?
[4]For God said, 'Honor your father
and mother'[b] and 'Anyone who
curses his father or mother must
be put to death.'[c] [5]But you say
that if a man says to his father or
mother, 'Whatever help you
might otherwise have received
from me is a gift devoted to God,'
[6]he is not to 'honor his father'[d]
with it. Thus you nullify the
word of God for the sake of your
tradition. [7]You hypocrites! Isaiah
was right when he prophesied
about you:

[8]"'These people honor me
      with their lips,
   but their hearts are far from
      me.
[9]They worship me in vain;
   their teachings are but rules
      taught by men.'[e]

[10]Jesus called the crowd to him
and said, "Listen and understand. [11]What goes into a man's
mouth does not make him 'unclean,' but what comes out of his

---

[a]24 Greek *many stadia*   [b]4 Exodus 20:12; Deut. 5:16   [c]4 Exodus 21:17; Lev. 20:9
[d]6 Some manuscripts *father or his mother*   [e]9 Isaiah 29:13

mouth, that is what makes him 'unclean.' "

12Then the disciples came to him and asked, "Do you know that the Pharisees were offended when they heard this?"

13He replied, "Every plant that my heavenly Father has not planted will be pulled up by the roots. 14Leave them; they are blind guides.*a* If a blind man leads a blind man, both will fall into a pit."

15Peter said, "Explain the parable to us."

16"Are you still so dull?" Jesus asked them. 17"Don't you see that whatever enters the mouth goes into the stomach and then out of the body? 18But the things that come out of the mouth come from the heart, and these make a man 'unclean.' 19For out of the heart come evil thoughts, murder, adultery, sexual immorality, theft, false testimony, slander. 20These are what make a man 'unclean'; but eating with unwashed hands does not make him 'unclean.' "

Mt 19:9

The Faith of the Canaanite Woman

21Leaving that place, Jesus withdrew to the region of Tyre and Sidon. 22A Canaanite woman from that vicinity came to him, crying out, "Lord, Son of David, have mercy on me! My daughter is suffering terribly from demon-possession."

23Jesus did not answer a word. So his disciples came to him and urged him, "Send her away, for she keeps crying out after us."

24He answered, "I was sent only to the lost sheep of Israel."

25The woman came and knelt before him. "Lord, help me!" she said.

26He replied, "It is not right to take the children's bread and toss it to their dogs."

27"Yes, Lord," she said, "but even the dogs eat the crumbs that fall from their masters' table."

28Then Jesus answered, "Woman, you have great faith! Your request is granted." And her daughter was healed from that very hour.

Jesus Feeds the Four Thousand

29Jesus left there and went along the Sea of Galilee. Then he went up on a mountainside and sat down. 30Great crowds came to him, bringing the lame, the blind, the crippled, the mute and many others, and laid them at his feet; and he healed them. 31The people were amazed when they saw the mute speaking, the crippled made well, the lame walking and the blind seeing. And they praised the God of Israel.

32Jesus called his disciples to him and said, "I have compassion for these people; they have already been with me three days and have nothing to eat. I do not want to send them away hungry, or they may collapse on the way."

33His disciples answered, "Where could we get enough bread in this remote place to feed such a crowd?"

34"How many loaves do you have?" Jesus asked.

"Seven," they replied, "and a few small fish."

35He told the crowd to sit down on the ground. 36Then he took the seven loaves and the fish, and when he had given thanks, he broke them and gave them to the disciples, and they in turn to the people. 37They all ate and

a14 Some manuscripts guides of the blind

long shall I stay with you? How long shall I put up with you? Bring the boy here to me." [18]Jesus rebuked the demon, and it came out of the boy, and he was healed from that moment.

[19]Then the disciples came to Jesus in private and asked, "Why couldn't we drive it out?"

[20]He replied, "Because you have so little faith. I tell you the truth, if you have faith as small as a mustard seed, you can say to this mountain, 'Move from here to there' and it will move. Nothing will be impossible for you.*"

[22]When they came together in Galilee, he said to them, "The Son of Man is going to be betrayed into the hands of men. [23]They will kill him, and on the third day he will be raised to life." And the disciples were filled with grief.

The Temple Tax

[24]After Jesus and his disciples arrived in Capernaum, the collectors of the two-drachma tax came to Peter and asked, "Doesn't your teacher pay the temple tax*?"

[25]"Yes, he does," he replied.

When Peter came into the house, Jesus was the first to speak. "What do you think, Simon?" he asked. "From whom do the kings of the earth collect duty and taxes—from their own sons or from others?"

[26]"From others," Peter answered.

"Then the sons are exempt," Jesus said to him. [27]"But so that we may not offend them, go to the lake and throw out your line. Take the first fish you catch; open its mouth and you will find a four-drachma coin. Take it and give it to them for my tax and yours."

The Greatest in the Kingdom of Heaven

18 At that time the disciples came to Jesus and asked, "Who is the greatest in the kingdom of heaven?"

[2]He called a little child and had him stand among them. [3]And he said: "I tell you the truth, unless you change and become like little children, you will never enter the kingdom of heaven. [4]Therefore, whoever humbles himself like this child is the greatest in the kingdom of heaven.

[5]"And whoever welcomes a little child like this in my name welcomes me. [6]But if anyone causes one of these little ones who believe in me to sin, it would be better for him to have a large millstone hung around his neck and to be drowned in the depths of the sea.

[7]"Woe to the world because of the things that cause people to sin! Such things must come, but woe to the man through whom they come! [8]If your hand or your foot causes you to sin, cut it off and throw it away. It is better for you to enter life maimed or crippled than to have two hands or two feet and be thrown into eternal fire. [9]And if your eye causes you to sin, gouge it out and throw it away. It is better for you to enter life with one eye than to have two eyes and be thrown into the fire of hell.

The Parable of the Lost Sheep

[10]"See that you do not look down on one of these little ones. For I tell you that their angels in

---

*20 Some manuscripts *you*. [21]*But this kind does not go out except by prayer and fasting.*
*24 Greek *the two drachmas*

heaven always see the face of my Father in heaven.ª

12"What do you think? If a man owns a hundred sheep, and one of them wanders away, will he not leave the ninety-nine on the hills and go to look for the one that wandered off? 13And if he finds it, I tell you the truth, he is happier about that one sheep than about the ninety-nine that did not wander off. 14In the same way your Father in heaven is not willing that any of these little ones should be lost.

A Brother Who Sins Against You

15"If your brother sins against you,ᵇ go and show him his fault, just between the two of you. If he listens to you, you have won your brother over. 16But if he will not listen, take one or two others along, so that 'every matter may be established by the testimony of two or three witnesses.'ᶜ 17If he refuses to listen to them, tell it to the church; and if he refuses to listen even to the church, treat him as you would a pagan or a tax collector.

18"I tell you the truth, whatever you bind on earth will beᵈ bound in heaven, and whatever you loose on earth will beᵈ loosed in heaven.

19"Again, I tell you that if two of you on earth agree about anything you ask for, it will be done for you by my Father in heaven. 20For where two or three come together in my name, there am I with them."

The Parable of the Unmerciful Servant

21Then Peter came to Jesus and asked, "Lord, how many times

shall I forgive my brother when he sins against me? Up to seven times?"

22Jesus answered, "I tell you, not seven times, but seventy-seven times.ᵉ

23"Therefore, the kingdom of heaven is like a king who wanted to settle accounts with his servants. 24As he began the settlement, a man who owed him ten thousand talentsᶠ was brought to him. 25Since he was not able to pay, the master ordered that he and his wife and his children and all that he had be sold to repay the debt.

26"The servant fell on his knees before him. 'Be patient with me,' he begged, 'and I will pay back everything.' 27The servant's master took pity on him, canceled the debt and let him go.

28"But when that servant went out, he found one of his fellow servants who owed him a hundred denarii.ᵍ He grabbed him and began to choke him. 'Pay back what you owe me!' he demanded.

29"His fellow servant fell to his knees and begged him, 'Be patient with me, and I will pay you back.'

30"But he refused. Instead, he went off and had the man thrown into prison until he could pay the debt. 31When the other servants saw what had happened, they were greatly distressed and went and told their master everything that had happened.

32"Then the master called the servant in. 'You wicked servant,' he said, 'I canceled all that debt of yours because you begged me to. 33Shouldn't you have had mercy on your fellow servant just as I had on you?' 34In anger his mas-

---

ᵃ10 Some manuscripts heaven. 11The Son of Man came to save what was lost.   ᵇ15 Some manuscripts do not have against you.   ᶜ16 Deut. 19:15   ᵈ18 Or have been   ᵉ22 Or seventy times seven   ᶠ24 That is, millions of dollars   ᵍ28 That is, a few dollars

---

(margin references)

8
Ac 9:31

69
Lk 18:1

52
Mt 28:20

ter turned him over to the jailers to be tortured, until he should pay back all he owed.

35"This is how my heavenly Father will treat each of you unless you forgive your brother from your heart."

Divorce

19 When Jesus had finished saying these things, he left Galilee and went into the region of Judea to the other side of the Jordan. 2Large crowds followed him, and he healed them there.

3Some Pharisees came to him to test him. They asked, "Is it lawful for a man to divorce his wife for any and every reason?"

19
Mk 10:11,12

4"Haven't you read," he replied, "that at the beginning the Creator 'made them male and female,'a 5and said, 'For this reason a man will leave his father and mother and be united to his wife, and the two will become one flesh'b? 6So they are no longer two, but one. Therefore what God has joined together, let man not separate."

7"Why then," they asked, "did Moses command that a man give his wife a certificate of divorce and send her away?"

8Jesus replied, "Moses permitted you to divorce your wives because your hearts were hard. But it was not this way from the beginning. 9I tell you that anyone who divorces his wife, except for marital unfaithfulness, and marries another woman commits adultery."

2
Jn 8:2-11

10The disciples said to him, "If this is the situation between a husband and wife, it is better not to marry."

11Jesus replied, "Not everyone can accept this word, but only those to whom it has been given.

12For some are eunuchs because they were born that way; others were made that way by men; and others have renounced marriage because of the kingdom of heaven. The one who can accept this should accept it."

The Little Children and Jesus

13Then little children were brought to Jesus for him to place his hands on them and pray for them. But the disciples rebuked those who brought them.

14Jesus said, "Let the little children come to me, and do not hinder them, for the kingdom of heaven belongs to such as these." 15When he had placed his hands on them, he went on from there.

The Rich Young Man

16Now a man came up to Jesus and asked, "Teacher, what good thing must I do to get eternal life?"

17"Why do you ask me about what is good?" Jesus replied. "There is only One who is good. If you want to enter life, obey the commandments."

18"Which ones?" the man inquired.

Jesus replied, " 'Do not murder, do not commit adultery, do not steal, do not give false testimony, 19honor your father and mother,'d and 'love your neighbor as yourself.'e"

20"All these I have kept," the young man said. "What do I still lack?"

21Jesus answered, "If you want to be perfect, go, sell your possessions and give to the poor, and you will have treasure in heaven. Then come, follow me."

22When the young man heard

---

a4 Gen. 1:27   b5 Gen. 2:24   c12 Or have made themselves eunuchs
d19 Exodus 20:12-16; Deut. 5:16-20   e19 Lev. 19:18

this, he went away sad, because he had great wealth.

²³Then Jesus said to his disciples, "I tell you the truth, it is hard for a rich man to enter the kingdom of heaven. ²⁴Again I tell you, it is easier for a camel to go through the eye of a needle than for a rich man to enter the kingdom of God."

²⁵When the disciples heard this, they were greatly astonished and asked, "Who then can be saved?"

²⁶Jesus looked at them and said, "With man this is impossible, but with God all things are possible."

²⁷Peter answered him, "We have left everything to follow you! What then will there be for us?"

²⁸Jesus said to them, "I tell you the truth, at the renewal of all things, when the Son of Man sits on his glorious throne, you who have followed me will also sit on twelve thrones, judging the twelve tribes of Israel. ²⁹And everyone who has left houses or brothers or sisters or father or motherᵃ or children or fields for my sake will receive a hundred times as much and will inherit eternal life. ³⁰But many who are first will be last, and many who are last will be first.

The Parable of the Workers in the Vineyard

20 "For the kingdom of heaven is like a landowner who went out early in the morning to hire men to work in his vineyard. ²He agreed to pay them a denarius for the day and sent them into his vineyard.

³"About the third hour he went out and saw others standing in the marketplace doing nothing. ⁴He told them, 'You also go and work in my vineyard, and I will pay you whatever is right.' ⁵So they went.

"He went out again about the sixth hour and the ninth hour and did the same thing. ⁶About the eleventh hour he went out and found still others standing around. He asked them, 'Why have you been standing here all day long doing nothing?'

⁷"'Because no one has hired us,' they answered.

"He said to them, 'You also go and work in my vineyard.'

⁸"When evening came, the owner of the vineyard said to his foreman, 'Call the workers and pay them their wages, beginning with the last ones hired and going on to the first.'

⁹"The workers who were hired about the eleventh hour came and each received a denarius. ¹⁰So when those came who were hired first, they expected to receive more. But each one of them also received a denarius. ¹¹When they received it, they began to grumble against the landowner. ¹²'These men who were hired last worked only one hour,' they said, 'and you have made them equal to us who have borne the burden of the work and the heat of the day.'

¹³"But he answered one of them, 'Friend, I am not being unfair to you. Didn't you agree to work for a denarius? ¹⁴Take your pay and go. I want to give the man who was hired last the same as I gave you. ¹⁵Don't I have the right to do what I want with my own money? Or are you envious because I am generous?'

¹⁶"So the last will be first, and the first will be last."

ᵃ29 Some manuscripts *mother or wife*

Jesus Again Predicts His Death

17Now as Jesus was going up to Jerusalem, he took the twelve disciples aside and said to them, 18"We are going up to Jerusalem, and the Son of Man will be betrayed to the chief priests and the teachers of the law. They will condemn him to death 19and will turn him over to the Gentiles to be mocked and flogged and crucified. On the third day he will be raised to life!"

A Mother's Request

20Then the mother of Zebedee's sons came to Jesus with her sons and, kneeling down, asked a favor of him.

21"What is it you want?" he asked.

She said, "Grant that one of these two sons of mine may sit at your right and the other at your left in your kingdom."

22"You don't know what you are asking," Jesus said to them. "Can you drink the cup I am going to drink?"

"We can," they answered.

23Jesus said to them, "You will indeed drink from my cup, but to sit at my right or left is not for me to grant. These places belong to those for whom they have been prepared by my Father."

24When the ten heard about this, they were indignant with the two brothers. 25Jesus called them together and said, "You know that the rulers of the Gentiles lord it over them, and their high officials exercise authority over them. 26Not so with you. Instead, whoever wants to become great among you must be your servant, 27and whoever wants to be first must be your slave— 28just as the Son of Man did not come to be served, but to serve, and to give his life as a ransom for many."

Two Blind Men Receive Sight

29As Jesus and his disciples were leaving Jericho, a large crowd followed him. 30Two blind men were sitting by the roadside, and when they heard that Jesus was going by, they shouted, "Lord, Son of David, have mercy on us!"

31The crowd rebuked them and told them to be quiet, but they shouted all the louder, "Lord, Son of David, have mercy on us!"

32Jesus stopped and called them. "What do you want me to do for you?" he asked.

33"Lord," they answered, "we want our sight."

34Jesus had compassion on them and touched their eyes. Immediately they received their sight and followed him.

The Triumphal Entry

21 As they approached Jerusalem and came to Bethphage on the Mount of Olives, Jesus sent two disciples, 2saying to them, "Go to the village ahead of you, and at once you will find a donkey tied there, with her colt by her. Untie them and bring them to me. 3If anyone says anything to you, tell him that the Lord needs them, and he will send them right away."

4This took place to fulfill what was spoken through the prophet:

5"Say to the Daughter of Zion,
   'See, your king comes to
      you,
gentle and riding on a
      donkey,
   on a colt, the foal of a
      donkey.' "[a]

a5 Zech. 9:9

6The disciples went and did as Jesus had instructed them. 7They brought the donkey and the colt, placed their cloaks on them, and Jesus sat on them. 8A very large crowd spread their cloaks on the road, while others cut branches from the trees and spread them on the road. 9The crowds that went ahead of him and those that followed shouted,

"Hosanna*a* to the Son of David!"

"Blessed is he who comes in the name of the Lord!"*b*

"Hosanna*a* in the highest!"

10When Jesus entered Jerusalem, the whole city was stirred and asked, "Who is this?" 11The crowds answered, "This is Jesus, the prophet from Nazareth in Galilee."

Jesus at the Temple

12Jesus entered the temple area and drove out all who were buying and selling there. He overturned the tables of the money changers and the benches of those selling doves. 13"It is written," he said to them, " 'My house will be called a house of prayer,'*c* but you are making it a 'den of robbers.'*d*"

14The blind and the lame came to him at the temple, and he healed them. 15But when the chief priests and the teachers of the law saw the wonderful things he did and the children shouting in the temple area, "Hosanna to the Son of David," they were indignant.

16"Do you hear what these children are saying?" they asked him.

"Yes," replied Jesus, "have you never read,

" 'From the lips of children
    and infants
  you have ordained praise'*e*?"

17And he left them and went out of the city to Bethany, where he spent the night.

The Fig Tree Withers

18Early in the morning, as he was on his way back to the city, he was hungry. 19Seeing a fig tree by the road, he went up to it but found nothing on it except leaves. Then he said to it, "May you never bear fruit again!" Immediately the tree withered.

20When the disciples saw this, they were amazed. "How did the fig tree wither so quickly?" they asked.

21Jesus replied, "I tell you the truth, if you have faith and do not doubt, not only can you do what was done to the fig tree, but also you can say to this mountain, 'Go, throw yourself into the sea,' and it will be done. 22If you believe, you will receive whatever you ask for in prayer.

The Authority of Jesus Questioned

23Jesus entered the temple courts, and, while he was teaching, the chief priests and the elders of the people came to him. "By what authority are you doing these things?" they asked. "And who gave you this authority?"

24Jesus replied, "I will also ask you one question. If you answer me, I will tell you by what authority I am doing these things. 25John's baptism—where did it come from? Was it from heaven, or from men?"

They discussed it among themselves and said, "If we say, 'From heaven,' he will ask, 'Then why

*a9 A Hebrew expression meaning "Save!" which became an exclamation of praise; also in verse 15   *b9 Psalm 118:26   *c13 Isaiah 56:7   *d13 Jer. 7:11   *e16 Psalm 8:2

didn't you believe him?' ²⁶But if we say, 'From men'—we are afraid of the people, for they all hold that John was a prophet."

²⁷So they answered Jesus, "We don't know."

Then he said, "Neither will I tell you by what authority I am doing these things.

The Parable of the Two Sons

²⁸"What do you think? There was a man who had two sons. He went to the first and said, 'Son, go and work today in the vineyard.'

²⁹" 'I will not,' he answered, but later he changed his mind and went.

³⁰"Then the father went to the other son and said the same thing. He answered, 'I will, sir,' but he did not go.

³¹"Which of the two did what his father wanted?"

"The first," they answered.

Jesus said to them, "I tell you the truth, the tax collectors and the prostitutes are entering the kingdom of God ahead of you. ³²For John came to you to show you the way of righteousness, and you did not believe him, but the tax collectors and the prostitutes did. And even after you saw this, you did not repent and believe him.

The Parable of the Tenants

³³"Listen to another parable: There was a landowner who planted a vineyard. He put a wall around it, dug a winepress in it and built a watchtower. Then he rented the vineyard to some farmers and went away on a journey. ³⁴When the harvest time approached, he sent his servants to the tenants to collect his fruit.

³⁵"The tenants seized his servants; they beat one, killed another, and stoned a third. ³⁶Then he sent other servants to them, more than the first time, and the tenants treated them the same way. ³⁷Last of all, he sent his son to them. 'They will respect my son,' he said.

³⁸"But when the tenants saw the son, they said to each other, 'This is the heir. Come, let's kill him and take his inheritance.' ³⁹So they took him and threw him out of the vineyard and killed him.

⁴⁰"Therefore, when the owner of the vineyard comes, what will he do to those tenants?"

⁴¹"He will bring those wretches to a wretched end," they replied, "and he will rent the vineyard to other tenants, who will give him his share of the crop at harvest time."

⁴²Jesus said to them, "Have you never read in the Scriptures:

" 'The stone the builders
      rejected
   has become the capstone*ᵃ*;
   the Lord has done this,
      and it is marvelous in our
      eyes'*ᵇ*?

⁴³"Therefore I tell you that the kingdom of God will be taken away from you and given to a people who will produce its fruit. ⁴⁴He who falls on this stone will be broken to pieces, but he on whom it falls will be crushed."*ᶜ*

⁴⁵When the chief priests and the Pharisees heard Jesus' parables, they knew he was talking about them. ⁴⁶They looked for a way to arrest him, but they were afraid of the crowd because the people held that he was a prophet.

ᵃ42 Or *cornerstone*   *ᵇ42* Psalm 118:22,23   *ᶜ44* Some manuscripts do not have verse 44.

The Parable of the Wedding Banquet

22 Jesus spoke to them again in parables, saying: 2"The kingdom of heaven is like a king who prepared a wedding banquet for his son. 3He sent his servants to those who had been invited to the banquet to tell them to come, but they refused to come.

4"Then he sent some more servants and said, 'Tell those who have been invited that I have prepared my dinner: My oxen and fattened cattle have been butchered, and everything is ready. Come to the wedding banquet.'

5"But they paid no attention and went off—one to his field, another to his business. 6The rest seized his servants, mistreated them and killed them. 7The king was enraged. He sent his army and destroyed those murderers and burned their city.

8"Then he said to his servants, 'The wedding banquet is ready, but those I invited did not deserve to come. 9Go to the street corners and invite to the banquet anyone you find.' 10So the servants went out into the streets and gathered all the people they could find, both good and bad, and the wedding hall was filled with guests.

11"But when the king came in to see the guests, he noticed a man there who was not wearing wedding clothes. 12'Friend,' he asked, 'how did you get in here without wedding clothes?' The man was speechless.

13"Then the king told the attendants, 'Tie him hand and foot, and throw him outside, into the darkness, where there will be weeping and gnashing of teeth.'

14"For many are invited, but few are chosen."

Paying Taxes to Caesar

15Then the Pharisees went out and laid plans to trap him in his words. 16They sent their disciples to him along with the Herodians. "Teacher," they said, "we know you are a man of integrity and that you teach the way of God in accordance with the truth. You aren't swayed by men, because you pay no attention to who they are. 17Tell us then, what is your opinion? Is it right to pay taxes to Caesar or not?"

18But Jesus, knowing their evil intent, said, "You hypocrites, why are you trying to trap me? 19Show me the coin used for paying the tax." They brought him a denarius, 20and he asked them, "Whose portrait is this? And whose inscription?"

21"Caesar's," they replied.

Then he said to them, "Give to Caesar what is Caesar's, and to God what is God's."

22When they heard this, they were amazed. So they left him and went away.

Marriage at the Resurrection

23That same day the Sadducees, who say there is no resurrection, came to him with a question. 24"Teacher," they said, "Moses told us that if a man dies without having children, his brother must marry the widow and have children for him. 25Now there were seven brothers among us. The first one married and died, and since he had no children, he left his wife to his brother. 26The same thing happened to the second and third brother, right on down to the seventh. 27Finally, the woman died. 28Now then, at the resurrection, whose wife will she be of the seven, since all of them were married to her?"

29Jesus replied, "You are in error because you do not know the Scriptures or the power of God. [30]At the resurrection people will neither marry nor be given in marriage; they will be like the angels in heaven. [31]But about the resurrection of the dead—have you not read what God said to you, [32]'I am the God of Abraham, the God of Isaac, and the God of Jacob'[a]? He is not the God of the dead but of the living."

[33]When the crowds heard this, they were astonished at his teaching.

The Greatest Commandment

[34]Hearing that Jesus had silenced the Sadducees, the Pharisees got together. [35]One of them, an expert in the law, tested him with this question: [36]"Teacher, which is the greatest commandment in the Law?"

[37]Jesus replied: " 'Love the Lord your God with all your heart and with all your soul and with all your mind.'[b] [38]This is the first and greatest commandment. [39]And the second is like it: 'Love your neighbor as yourself.'[c] [40]All the Law and the Prophets hang on these two commandments."

Whose Son Is the Christ?

[41]While the Pharisees were gathered together, Jesus asked them, [42]"What do you think about the Christ[d]? Whose son is he?"

"The son of David," they replied.

[43]He said to them, "How is it then that David, speaking by the Spirit, calls him 'Lord'? For he says,

[44] " 'The Lord said to my Lord:
    "Sit at my right hand

until I put your enemies
    under your feet." '[e]

[45]If then David calls him 'Lord,' how can he be his son?" [46]No one could say a word in reply, and from that day on no one dared to ask him any more questions.

Seven Woes

23 Then Jesus said to the crowds and to his disciples: [2]"The teachers of the law and the Pharisees sit in Moses' seat. [3]So you must obey them and do everything they tell you. But do not do what they do, for they do not practice what they preach. [4]They tie up heavy loads and put them on men's shoulders, but they themselves are not willing to lift a finger to move them.

[5]"Everything they do is done for men to see: They make their phylacteries[f] wide and the tassels on their garments long; [6]they love the place of honor at banquets and the most important seats in the synagogues; [7]they love to be greeted in the marketplaces and to have men call them 'Rabbi.'

[8]"But you are not to be called 'Rabbi,' for you have only one Master and you are all brothers. [9]And do not call anyone on earth 'father,' for you have one Father, and he is in heaven. [10]Nor are you to be called 'teacher,' for you have one Teacher, the Christ.[d] [11]The greatest among you will be your servant. [12]For whoever exalts himself will be humbled, and whoever humbles himself will be exalted.

[13]"Woe to you, teachers of the law and Pharisees, you hypocrites! You shut the kingdom of heaven in men's faces. You yourselves do not enter, nor will you

[a]32 Exodus 3:6   [b]37 Deut. 6:5   [c]39 Lev. 19:18   [d]42,10 Or *Messiah*   [e]44 Psalm 110:1   [f]5 That is, boxes containing Scripture verses, worn on forehead and arm

9
Eph 5:8-14

let those enter who are trying to.ᵃ

¹⁵"Woe to you, teachers of the law and Pharisees, you hypocrites! You travel over land and sea to win a single convert, and when he becomes one, you make him twice as much a son of hell as you are.

¹⁶"Woe to you, blind guides! You say, 'If anyone swears by the temple, it means nothing; but if anyone swears by the gold of the temple, he is bound by his oath.' ¹⁷You blind fools! Which is greater: the gold, or the temple that makes the gold sacred? ¹⁸You also say, 'If anyone swears by the altar, it means nothing; but if anyone swears by the gift on it, he is bound by his oath.' ¹⁹You blind men! Which is greater: the gift, or the altar that makes the gift sacred? ²⁰Therefore, he who swears by the altar swears by it and by everything on it. ²¹And he who swears by the temple swears by it and by the one who dwells in it. ²²And he who swears by heaven swears by God's throne and by the one who sits on it.

47
Ro 2:1-4

²³"Woe to you, teachers of the law and Pharisees, you hypocrites! You give a tenth of your spices—mint, dill and cummin. But you have neglected the more important matters of the law—justice, mercy and faithfulness. You should have practiced the latter, without neglecting the former. ²⁴You blind guides! You strain out a gnat but swallow a camel.

33
Mk 7:22

²⁵"Woe to you, teachers of the law and Pharisees, you hypocrites! You clean the outside of the cup and dish, but inside they are full of greed and self-indulgence. ²⁶Blind Pharisee! First clean the inside of the cup and dish, and then the outside also will be clean.

²⁷"Woe to you, teachers of the law and Pharisees, you hypocrites! You are like whitewashed tombs, which look beautiful on the outside but on the inside are full of dead men's bones and everything unclean. ²⁸In the same way, on the outside you appear to people as righteous but on the inside you are full of hypocrisy and wickedness.

²⁹"Woe to you, teachers of the law and Pharisees, you hypocrites! You build tombs for the prophets and decorate the graves of the righteous. ³⁰And you say, 'If we had lived in the days of our forefathers, we would not have taken part with them in shedding the blood of the prophets.' ³¹So you testify against yourselves that you are the descendants of those who murdered the prophets. ³²Fill up, then, the measure of the sin of your forefathers!

³³"You snakes! You brood of vipers! How will you escape being condemned to hell? ³⁴Therefore I am sending you prophets and wise men and teachers. Some of them you will kill and crucify; others you will flog in your synagogues and pursue from town to town. ³⁵And so upon you will come all the righteous blood that has been shed on earth, from the blood of righteous Abel to the blood of Zechariah son of Berekiah, whom you murdered between the temple and the altar. ³⁶I tell you the truth, all this will come upon this generation.

³⁷"O Jerusalem, Jerusalem, you who kill the prophets and stone those sent to you, how often I have longed to gather your children together, as a hen gathers

54
Jn 3:16

73
Jn 5:40

ᵃ13 Some manuscripts to. ¹⁴Woe to you, teachers of the law and Pharisees, you hypocrites! You devour widows' houses and for a show make lengthy prayers. Therefore you will be punished more severely.

her chicks under her wings, but you were not willing. ³⁸Look, your house is left to you desolate. ³⁹For I tell you, you will not see me again until you say, 'Blessed is he who comes in the name of the Lord.'ᵃ⁹

Signs of the End of the Age

24 Jesus left the temple and was walking away when his disciples came up to him to call his attention to its buildings. ²"Do you see all these things?" he asked. "I tell you the truth, not one stone here will be left on another; every one will be thrown down."

³As Jesus was sitting on the Mount of Olives, the disciples came to him privately. "Tell us," they said, "when will this happen, and what will be the sign of your coming and of the end of the age?"

⁴Jesus answered: "Watch out that no one deceives you. ⁵For many will come in my name, claiming, 'I am the Christ,'ᵇ and will deceive many. ⁶You will hear of wars and rumors of wars, but see to it that you are not alarmed. Such things must happen, but the end is still to come. ⁷Nation will rise against nation, and kingdom against kingdom. There will be famines and earthquakes in various places. ⁸All these are the beginning of birth pains.

⁹"Then you will be handed over to be persecuted and put to death, and you will be hated by all nations because of me. ¹⁰At that time many will turn away from the faith and will betray and hate each other, ¹¹and many false prophets will appear and deceive many people. ¹²Because of the increase of wickedness, the love of most will grow cold, ¹³but he who stands firm to the end will be

saved. ¹⁴And this gospel of the kingdom will be preached in the whole world as a testimony to all nations, and then the end will come.

¹⁵"So when you see standing in the holy place 'the abomination that causes desolation,'ᶜ spoken of through the prophet Daniel—let the reader understand—¹⁶then let those who are in Judea flee to the mountains. ¹⁷Let no one on the roof of his house go down to take anything out of the house. ¹⁸Let no one in the field go back to get his cloak. ¹⁹How dreadful it will be in those days for pregnant women and nursing mothers! ²⁰Pray that your flight will not take place in winter or on the Sabbath. ²¹For then there will be great distress, unequaled from the beginning of the world until now—and never to be equaled again. ²²If those days had not been cut short, no one would survive, but for the sake of the elect those days will be shortened. ²³At that time if anyone says to you, 'Look, here is the Christ!' or, 'There he is!' do not believe it. ²⁴For false Christs and false prophets will appear and perform great signs and miracles to deceive even the elect—if that were possible. ²⁵See, I have told you ahead of time.

²⁶"So if anyone tells you, 'There he is, out in the desert,' do not go out; or, 'Here he is, in the inner rooms,' do not believe it. ²⁷For as lightning that comes from the east is visible even in the west, so will be the coming of the Son of Man. ²⁸Wherever there is a carcass, there the vultures will gather.

²⁹"Immediately after the distress of those days

" 'the sun will be darkened,

80
Ac 1:11

ᵃ39 Psalm 118:26   ᵇ5 Or *Messiah*; also in verse 23   ᶜ15 Daniel 9:27; 11:31; 12:11

and the moon will not give
its light;
the stars will fall from the sky,
and the heavenly bodies will
be shaken.'ᵃ

³⁰"At that time the sign of the
Son of Man will appear in the
sky, and all the nations of the
earth will mourn. They will see
the Son of Man coming on the
clouds of the sky, with power
and great glory. ³¹And he will
send his angels with a loud trumpet call, and they will gather his
elect from the four winds, from
one end of the heavens to the
other.

³²"Now learn this lesson from
the fig tree: As soon as its twigs
get tender and its leaves come
out, you know that summer is
near. ³³Even so, when you see all
these things, you know that itᵇ is
near, right at the door. ³⁴I tell you
the truth, this generationᶜ will
certainly not pass away until all
these things have happened.
³⁵Heaven and earth will pass
away, but my words will never
pass away.

The Day and Hour Unknown

³⁶"No one knows about that
day or hour, not even the angels
in heaven, nor the Son,ᵈ but only
the Father. ³⁷As it was in the days
of Noah, so it will be at the coming of the Son of Man. ³⁸For in the
days before the flood, people
were eating and drinking, marrying and giving in marriage, up to
the day Noah entered the ark;
³⁹and they knew nothing about
what would happen until the
flood came and took them all
away. That is how it will be at the
coming of the Son of Man. ⁴⁰Two
men will be in the field; one will
be taken and the other left. ⁴¹Two

women will be grinding with a
hand mill; one will be taken and
the other left.

⁴²"Therefore keep watch, because you do not know on what
day your Lord will come. ⁴³But
understand this: If the owner of
the house had known at what
time of night the thief was coming, he would have kept watch
and would not have let his house
be broken into. ⁴⁴So you also
must be ready, because the Son
of Man will come at an hour
when you do not expect him.

⁴⁵"Who then is the faithful and
wise servant, whom the master
has put in charge of the servants
in his household to give them
their food at the proper time? ⁴⁶It
will be good for that servant
whose master finds him doing so
when he returns. ⁴⁷I tell you the
truth, he will put him in charge of
all his possessions. ⁴⁸But suppose
that servant is wicked and says to
himself, 'My master is staying
away a long time,' ⁴⁹and he then
begins to beat his fellow servants
and to eat and drink with drunkards. ⁵⁰The master of that servant
will come on a day when he does
not expect him and at an hour he
is not aware of. ⁵¹He will cut him
to pieces and assign him a place
with the hypocrites, where there
will be weeping and gnashing of
teeth.

The Parable of the Ten Virgins

25 "At that time the kingdom
of heaven will be like ten
virgins who took their lamps and
went out to meet the bridegroom. ²Five of them were foolish and five were wise. ³The foolish ones took their lamps but did
not take any oil with them. ⁴The

ᵃ29 Isaiah 13:10; 34:4   ᵇ33 Or he   ᶜ34 Or race   ᵈ36 Some manuscripts do not
have nor the Son.

wise, however, took oil in jars along with their lamps. ⁵The bridegroom was a long time in coming, and they all became drowsy and fell asleep.

⁶"At midnight the cry rang out: 'Here's the bridegroom! Come out to meet him!'

⁷"Then all the virgins woke up and trimmed their lamps. ⁸The foolish ones said to the wise, 'Give us some of your oil; our lamps are going out.'

⁹"'No,' they replied, 'there may not be enough for both us and you. Instead, go to those who sell oil and buy some for yourselves.'

¹⁰"But while they were on their way to buy the oil, the bridegroom arrived. The virgins who were ready went in with him to the wedding banquet. And the door was shut.

¹¹"Later the others also came. 'Sir! Sir!' they said. 'Open the door for us!'

¹²"But he replied, 'I tell you the truth, I don't know you.'

¹³"Therefore keep watch, because you do not know the day or the hour.

The Parable of the Talents

¹⁴"Again, it will be like a man going on a journey, who called his servants and entrusted his property to them. ¹⁵To one he gave five talents[a] of money, to another two talents, and to another one talent, each according to his ability. Then he went on his journey. ¹⁶The man who had received the five talents went at once and put his money to work and gained five more. ¹⁷So also, the one with the two talents gained two more. ¹⁸But the man who had received the one talent went off, dug a hole in the ground and hid his master's money.

¹⁹"After a long time the master of those servants returned and settled accounts with them. ²⁰The man who had received the five talents brought the other five. 'Master,' he said, 'you entrusted me with five talents. See, I have gained five more.'

²¹"His master replied, 'Well done, good and faithful servant! You have been faithful with a few things; I will put you in charge of many things. Come and share your master's happiness!'

²²"The man with the two talents also came. 'Master,' he said, 'you entrusted me with two talents; see, I have gained two more.'

²³"His master replied, 'Well done, good and faithful servant! You have been faithful with a few things; I will put you in charge of many things. Come and share your master's happiness!'

²⁴"Then the man who had received the one talent came. 'Master,' he said, 'I knew that you are a hard man, harvesting where you have not sown and gathering where you have not scattered seed. ²⁵So I was afraid and went out and hid your talent in the ground. See, here is what belongs to you.'

²⁶"His master replied, 'You wicked, lazy servant! So you knew that I harvest where I have not sown and gather where I have not scattered seed? ²⁷Well then, you should have put my money on deposit with the bankers, so that when I returned I would have received it back with interest.

²⁸"'Take the talent from him and give it to the one who has the ten talents. ²⁹For everyone who has will be given more, and he

_____
a15 A talent was worth more than a thousand dollars.

will have an abundance. Whoever does not have, even what he has will be taken from him. ³⁰And throw that worthless servant outside, into the darkness, where there will be weeping and gnashing of teeth.'

The Sheep and the Goats

³¹"When the Son of Man comes in his glory, and all the angels with him, he will sit on his throne in heavenly glory. ³²All the nations will be gathered before him, and he will separate the people one from another as a shepherd separates the sheep from the goats. ³³He will put the sheep on his right and the goats on his left.

³⁴"Then the King will say to those on his right, 'Come, you who are blessed by my Father; take your inheritance, the kingdom prepared for you since the creation of the world. ³⁵For I was hungry and you gave me something to eat, I was thirsty and you gave me something to drink, I was a stranger and you invited me in, ³⁶I needed clothes and you clothed me, I was sick and you looked after me, I was in prison and you came to visit me.'

³⁷"Then the righteous will answer him, 'Lord, when did we see you hungry and feed you, or thirsty and give you something to drink? ³⁸When did we see you a stranger and invite you in, or needing clothes and clothe you? ³⁹When did we see you sick or in prison and go to visit you?'

⁴⁰"The King will reply, 'I tell you the truth, whatever you did for one of the least of these brothers of mine, you did for me.'

⁴¹"Then he will say to those on his left, 'Depart from me, you who are cursed, into the eternal fire prepared for the devil and his angels. ⁴²For I was hungry and you gave me nothing to eat, I was

thirsty and you gave me nothing to drink, ⁴³I was a stranger and you did not invite me in, I needed clothes and you did not clothe me, I was sick and in prison and you did not look after me.'

⁴⁴"They also will answer, 'Lord, when did we see you hungry or thirsty or a stranger or needing clothes or sick or in prison, and did not help you?'

⁴⁵"He will reply, 'I tell you the truth, whatever you did not do for one of the least of these, you did not do for me.'

⁴⁶"Then they will go away to eternal punishment, but the righteous to eternal life."

The Plot Against Jesus

26 When Jesus had finished saying all these things, he said to his disciples, ²"As you know, the Passover is two days away—and the Son of Man will be handed over to be crucified."

³Then the chief priests and the elders of the people assembled in the palace of the high priest, whose name was Caiaphas, ⁴and they plotted to arrest Jesus in some sly way and kill him. ⁵"But not during the Feast," they said, "or there may be a riot among the people."

Jesus Anointed at Bethany

⁶While Jesus was in Bethany in the home of a man known as Simon the Leper, ⁷a woman came to him with an alabaster jar of very expensive perfume, which she poured on his head as he was reclining at the table.

⁸When the disciples saw this, they were indignant. "Why this waste?" they asked. ⁹"This perfume could have been sold at a high price and the money given to the poor."

¹⁰Aware of this, Jesus said to

them, "Why are you bothering this woman? She has done a beautiful thing to me. ¹¹The poor you will always have with you, but you will not always have me. ¹²When she poured this perfume on my body, she did it to prepare me for burial. ¹³I tell you the truth, wherever this gospel is preached throughout the world, what she has done will also be told, in memory of her."

Judas Agrees to Betray Jesus

¹⁴Then one of the Twelve—the one called Judas Iscariot—went to the chief priests ¹⁵and asked, "What are you willing to give me if I hand him over to you?" So they counted out for him thirty silver coins. ¹⁶From then on Judas watched for an opportunity to hand him over.

The Lord's Supper

¹⁷On the first day of the Feast of Unleavened Bread, the disciples came to Jesus and asked, "Where do you want us to make preparations for you to eat the Passover?"

¹⁸He replied, "Go into the city to a certain man and tell him, 'The Teacher says: My appointed time is near. I am going to celebrate the Passover with my disciples at your house.'" ¹⁹So the disciples did as Jesus had directed them and prepared the Passover.

²⁰When evening came, Jesus was reclining at the table with the Twelve. ²¹And while they were eating, he said, "I tell you the truth, one of you will betray me."

²²They were very sad and began to say to him one after the other, "Surely not I, Lord?"

²³Jesus replied, "The one who has dipped his hand into the bowl with me will betray me.

²⁴The Son of Man will go just as it is written about him. But woe to that man who betrays the Son of Man! It would be better for him if he had not been born."

²⁵Then Judas, the one who would betray him, said, "Surely not I, Rabbi?"

Jesus answered, "Yes, it is you."ᵃ

²⁶While they were eating, Jesus took bread, gave thanks and broke it, and gave it to his disciples, saying, "Take and eat; this is my body."

²⁷Then he took the cup, gave thanks and offered it to them, saying, "Drink from it, all of you. ²⁸This is my blood of theᵇ covenant, which is poured out for many for the forgiveness of sins. ²⁹I tell you, I will not drink of this fruit of the vine from now on until that day when I drink it anew with you in my Father's kingdom."

³⁰When they had sung a hymn, they went out to the Mount of Olives.

Jesus Predicts Peter's Denial

³¹Then Jesus told them, "This very night you will all fall away on account of me, for it is written:

" 'I will strike the shepherd,
    and the sheep of the flock
        will be scattered.'ᶜ

³²But after I have risen, I will go ahead of you into Galilee."

³³Peter replied, "Even if all fall away on account of you, I never will."

³⁴"I tell you the truth," Jesus answered, "this very night, before the rooster crows, you will disown me three times."

³⁵But Peter declared, "Even if I have to die with you, I will never disown you." And all the other disciples said the same.

ᵃ25 Or "You yourself have said it"   ᵇ28 Some manuscripts the new   ᶜ31 Zech. 13:7

Gethsemane

³⁶Then Jesus went with his disciples to a place called Gethsemane, and he said to them, "Sit here while I go over there and pray." ³⁷He took Peter and the two sons of Zebedee along with him, and he began to be sorrowful and troubled. ³⁸Then he said to them, "My soul is overwhelmed with sorrow to the point of death. Stay here and keep watch with me."

³⁹Going a little farther, he fell with his face to the ground and prayed, "My Father, if it is possible, may this cup be taken from me. Yet not as I will, but as you will."

⁴⁰Then he returned to his disciples and found them sleeping. "Could you men not keep watch with me for one hour?" he asked Peter. ⁴¹"Watch and pray so that you will not fall into temptation. The spirit is willing, but the body is weak."

⁴²He went away a second time and prayed, "My Father, if it is not possible for this cup to be taken away unless I drink it, may your will be done."

⁴³When he came back, he again found them sleeping, because their eyes were heavy. ⁴⁴So he left them and went away once more and prayed the third time, saying the same thing.

⁴⁵Then he returned to the disciples and said to them, "Are you still sleeping and resting? Look, the hour is near, and the Son of Man is betrayed into the hands of sinners. ⁴⁶Rise, let us go! Here comes my betrayer!"

Jesus Arrested

⁴⁷While he was still speaking, Judas, one of the Twelve, arrived. With him was a large crowd armed with swords and clubs, sent from the chief priests and the elders of the people. ⁴⁸Now the betrayer had arranged a signal with them: "The one I kiss is the man; arrest him." ⁴⁹Going at once to Jesus, Judas said, "Greetings, Rabbi!" and kissed him.

⁵⁰Jesus replied, "Friend, do what you came for."ᵃ

Then the men stepped forward, seized Jesus and arrested him. ⁵¹With that, one of Jesus' companions reached for his sword, drew it out and struck the servant of the high priest, cutting off his ear.

⁵²"Put your sword back in its place," Jesus said to him, "for all who draw the sword will die by the sword. ⁵³Do you think I cannot call on my Father, and he will at once put at my disposal more than twelve legions of angels? ⁵⁴But how then would the Scriptures be fulfilled that say it must happen in this way?"

⁵⁵At that time Jesus said to the crowd, "Am I leading a rebellion, that you have come out with swords and clubs to capture me? Every day I sat in the temple courts teaching, and you did not arrest me. ⁵⁶But this has all taken place that the writings of the prophets might be fulfilled." Then all the disciples deserted him and fled.

Before the Sanhedrin

⁵⁷Those who had arrested Jesus took him to Caiaphas, the high priest, where the teachers of the law and the elders had assembled. ⁵⁸But Peter followed him at a distance, right up to the courtyard of the high priest. He entered and sat down with the guards to see the outcome. ⁵⁹The chief priests and the

---

ᵃ50 Or "Friend, why have you come?"

whole Sanhedrin were looking for false evidence against Jesus so that they could put him to death. [60]But they did not find any, though many false witnesses came forward.

Finally two came forward [61]and declared, "This fellow said, 'I am able to destroy the temple of God and rebuild it in three days.'"

[62]Then the high priest stood up and said to Jesus, "Are you not going to answer? What is this testimony that these men are bringing against you?" [63]But Jesus remained silent.

The high priest said to him, "I charge you under oath by the living God: Tell us if you are the Christ,[a] the Son of God."

[64]"Yes, it is as you say," Jesus replied. "But I say to all of you: In the future you will see the Son of Man sitting at the right hand of the Mighty One and coming on the clouds of heaven."

[65]Then the high priest tore his clothes and said, "He has spoken blasphemy! Why do we need any more witnesses? Look, now you have heard the blasphemy. [66]What do you think?"

"He is worthy of death," they answered.

[67]Then they spit in his face and struck him with their fists. Others slapped him [68]and said, "Prophesy to us, Christ. Who hit you?"

Peter Disowns Jesus

[69]Now Peter was sitting out in the courtyard, and a servant girl came to him. "You also were with Jesus of Galilee," she said.

[70]But he denied it before them all. "I don't know what you're talking about," he said.

[71]Then he went out to the gateway, where another girl saw him and said to the people there, "This fellow was with Jesus of Nazareth."

[72]He denied it again, with an oath: "I don't know the man!"

[73]After a little while, those standing there went up to Peter and said, "Surely you are one of them, for your accent gives you away."

[74]Then he began to call down curses on himself and he swore to them, "I don't know the man!"

Immediately a rooster crowed. [75]Then Peter remembered the word Jesus had spoken: "Before the rooster crows, you will disown me three times." And he went outside and wept bitterly.

Judas Hangs Himself

27 Early in the morning, all the chief priests and the elders of the people came to the decision to put Jesus to death. [2]They bound him, led him away and handed him over to Pilate, the governor.

[3]When Judas, who had betrayed him, saw that Jesus was condemned, he was seized with remorse and returned the thirty silver coins to the chief priests and the elders. [4]"I have sinned," he said, "for I have betrayed innocent blood."

"What is that to us?" they replied. "That's your responsibility."

[5]So Judas threw the money into the temple and left. Then he went away and hanged himself.

[6]The chief priests picked up the coins and said, "It is against the law to put this into the treasury, since it is blood money." [7]So they decided to use the money to buy the potter's field as a burial place for foreigners. [8]That is why it has been called the Field of Blood to this day. [9]Then what was spoken by Jeremiah the prophet was ful-

[a] 63 Or *Messiah*; also in verse 68

filled: "They took the thirty silver coins, the price set on him by the people of Israel, [10]and they used them to buy the potter's field, as the Lord commanded me."[a]

Jesus Before Pilate

[11]Meanwhile Jesus stood before the governor, and the governor asked him, "Are you the king of the Jews?"

"Yes, it is as you say," Jesus replied.

[12]When he was accused by the chief priests and the elders, he gave no answer. [13]Then Pilate asked him, "Don't you hear the testimony they are bringing against you?" [14]But Jesus made no reply, not even to a single charge—to the great amazement of the governor.

[15]Now it was the governor's custom at the Feast to release a prisoner chosen by the crowd. [16]At that time they had a notorious prisoner, called Barabbas. [17]So when the crowd had gathered, Pilate asked them, "Which one do you want me to release to you: Barabbas, or Jesus who is called Christ?" [18]For he knew it was out of envy that they had handed Jesus over to him.

[19]While Pilate was sitting on the judge's seat, his wife sent him this message: "Don't have anything to do with that innocent man, for I have suffered a great deal today in a dream because of him."

[20]But the chief priests and the elders persuaded the crowd to ask for Barabbas and to have Jesus executed.

[21]"Which of the two do you want me to release to you?" asked the governor.

"Barabbas," they answered.

[22]"What shall I do, then, with Jesus who is called Christ?" Pilate asked.

They all answered, "Crucify him!"

[23]"Why? What crime has he committed?" asked Pilate.

But they shouted all the louder, "Crucify him!"

[24]When Pilate saw that he was getting nowhere, but that instead an uproar was starting, he took water and washed his hands in front of the crowd. "I am innocent of this man's blood," he said. "It is your responsibility!"

[25]All the people answered, "Let his blood be on us and on our children!"

[26]Then he released Barabbas to them. But he had Jesus flogged, and handed him over to be crucified.

The Soldiers Mock Jesus

[27]Then the governor's soldiers took Jesus into the Praetorium and gathered the whole company of soldiers around him. [28]They stripped him and put a scarlet robe on him, [29]and then twisted together a crown of thorns and set it on his head. They put a staff in his right hand and knelt in front of him and mocked him. "Hail, king of the Jews!" they said. [30]They spit on him, and took the staff and struck him on the head again and again. [31]After they had mocked him, they took off the robe and put his own clothes on him. Then they led him away to crucify him.

The Crucifixion

[32]As they were going out, they met a man from Cyrene, named Simon, and they forced him to carry the cross. [33]They came to a place called Golgotha (which means The Place of the Skull).

[a]10 See Zech. 11:12,13; Jer. 19:1-13; 32:6-9.

[34]There they offered Jesus wine to drink, mixed with gall; but after tasting it, he refused to drink it. [35]When they had crucified him, they divided up his clothes by casting lots.[a] [36]And sitting down, they kept watch over him there. [37]Above his head they placed the written charge against him: THIS IS JESUS, THE KING OF THE JEWS. [38]Two robbers were crucified with him, one on his right and one on his left. [39]Those who passed by hurled insults at him, shaking their heads [40]and saying, "You who are going to destroy the temple and build it in three days, save yourself! Come down from the cross, if you are the Son of God!"

[41]In the same way the chief priests, the teachers of the law and the elders mocked him. [42]"He saved others," they said, "but he can't save himself! He's the King of Israel! Let him come down now from the cross, and we will believe in him. [43]He trusts in God. Let God rescue him now if he wants him, for he said, 'I am the Son of God.'" [44]In the same way the robbers who were crucified with him also heaped insults on him.

The Death of Jesus

[45]From the sixth hour until the ninth hour darkness came over all the land. [46]About the ninth hour Jesus cried out in a loud voice, "Eloi, Eloi,[b] lama sabachthani?"—which means, "My God, my God, why have you forsaken me?"[c]

[47]When some of those standing there heard this, they said, "He's calling Elijah."

[48]Immediately one of them ran and got a sponge. He filled it with wine vinegar, put it on a stick, and offered it to Jesus to drink. [49]The rest said, "Now leave him alone. Let's see if Elijah comes to save him."

[50]And when Jesus had cried out again in a loud voice, he gave up his spirit.

[51]At that moment the curtain of the temple was torn in two from top to bottom. The earth shook and the rocks split. [52]The tombs broke open and the bodies of many holy people who had died were raised to life. [53]They came out of the tombs, and after Jesus' resurrection they went into the holy city and appeared to many people.

[54]When the centurion and those with him who were guarding Jesus saw the earthquake and all that had happened, they were terrified, and exclaimed, "Surely he was the Son[d] of God!"

[55]Many women were there, watching from a distance. They had followed Jesus from Galilee to care for his needs. [56]Among them were Mary Magdalene, Mary the mother of James and Joses, and the mother of Zebedee's sons.

The Burial of Jesus

[57]As evening approached, there came a rich man from Arimathea, named Joseph, who had himself become a disciple of Jesus. [58]Going to Pilate, he asked for Jesus' body, and Pilate ordered that it be given to him. [59]Joseph took the body, wrapped it in a clean linen cloth, [60]and placed it in his own new tomb that he had cut out of the rock. He rolled a big stone in front of the entrance to the tomb and went away. [61]Mary Magda-

[a]35 A few late manuscripts lots that the word spoken by the prophet might be fulfilled: "They divided my garments among themselves and cast lots for my clothing" (Psalm 22:18)   [b]46 Some manuscripts Eli, Eli   [c]46 Psalm 22:1   [d]54 Or a son

lene and the other Mary were sitting there opposite the tomb.

The Guard at the Tomb

62The next day, the one after Preparation Day, the chief priests and the Pharisees went to Pilate. 63"Sir," they said, "we remember that while he was still alive that deceiver said, 'After three days I will rise again.' 64So give the order for the tomb to be made secure until the third day. Otherwise, his disciples may come and steal the body and tell the people that he has been raised from the dead. This last deception will be worse than the first."

65"Take a guard," Pilate answered. "Go, make the tomb as secure as you know how." 66So they went and made the tomb secure by putting a seal on the stone and posting the guard.

The Resurrection

28 After the Sabbath, at dawn on the first day of the week, Mary Magdalene and the other Mary went to look at the tomb.

2There was a violent earthquake, for an angel of the Lord came down from heaven and, going to the tomb, rolled back the stone and sat on it. 3His appearance was like lightning, and his clothes were white as snow. 4The guards were so afraid of him that they shook and became like dead men.

5The angel said to the women, "Do not be afraid, for I know that you are looking for Jesus, who was crucified. 6He is not here; he has risen, just as he said. Come and see the place where he lay. 7Then go quickly and tell his disciples: 'He has risen from the dead and is going ahead of you into Galilee. There you will see him.' Now I have told you."

8So the women hurried away from the tomb, afraid yet filled with joy, and ran to tell his disciples. 9Suddenly Jesus met them. "Greetings," he said. They came to him, clasped his feet and worshiped him. 10Then Jesus said to them, "Do not be afraid. Go and tell my brothers to go to Galilee; there they will see me."

The Guards' Report

11While the women were on their way, some of the guards went into the city and reported to the chief priests everything that had happened. 12When the chief priests had met with the elders and devised a plan, they gave the soldiers a large sum of money, 13telling them, "You are to say, 'His disciples came during the night and stole him away while we were asleep.' 14If this report gets to the governor, we will satisfy him and keep you out of trouble." 15So the soldiers took the money and did as they were instructed. And this story has been widely circulated among the Jews to this very day.

The Great Commission

16Then the eleven disciples went to Galilee, to the mountain where Jesus had told them to go. 17When they saw him, they worshiped him; but some doubted. 18Then Jesus came to them and said, "All authority in heaven and on earth has been given to me. 19Therefore go and make disciples of all nations, baptizing them in*a* the name of the Father and of the Son and of the Holy Spirit, 20and teaching them to

23
Lk 4:18

52
Heb 13:5

---

*a19 Or into; see Acts 8:16; 19:5; Romans 6:3; 1 Cor. 1:13; 10:2 and Gal. 3:27.

obey everything I have commanded you. And surely I am with you always, to the very end of the age."

Mark

John the Baptist Prepares the Way

1 The beginning of the gospel about Jesus Christ, the Son of God.[a]

[2]It is written in Isaiah the prophet:

"I will send my messenger
      ahead of you,
  who will prepare your
      way"[b]—
[3]"a voice of one calling in the desert,
'Prepare the way for the Lord,
  make straight paths for
      him.' "[c]

[4]And so John came, baptizing in the desert region and preaching a baptism of repentance for the forgiveness of sins. [5]The whole Judean countryside and all the people of Jerusalem went out to him. Confessing their sins, they were baptized by him in the Jordan River. [6]John wore clothing made of camel's hair, with a leather belt around his waist, and he ate locusts and wild honey. [7]And this was his message: "After me will come one more powerful than I, the thongs of whose sandals I am not worthy to stoop down and untie. [8]I baptize you with[d] water, but he will baptize you with the Holy Spirit."

The Baptism and Temptation of Jesus

[9]At that time Jesus came from Nazareth in Galilee and was baptized by John in the Jordan. [10]As Jesus was coming up out of the water, he saw heaven being torn open and the Spirit descending on him like a dove. [11]And a voice came from heaven: "You are my Son, whom I love; with you I am well pleased."

[12]At once the Spirit sent him out into the desert, [13]and he was in the desert forty days, being tempted by Satan. He was with the wild animals, and angels attended him.

The Calling of the First Disciples

[14]After John was put in prison, Jesus went into Galilee, proclaiming the good news of God. [15]"The time has come," he said. "The kingdom of God is near. Repent and believe the good news!"

[16]As Jesus walked beside the Sea of Galilee, he saw Simon and his brother Andrew casting a net into the lake, for they were fishermen. [17]"Come, follow me," Jesus said, "and I will make you fishers of men." [18]At once they left their nets and followed him.

[19]When he had gone a little farther, he saw James son of Zebedee and his brother John in a boat, preparing their nets. [20]Without delay he called them, and they left their father Zebedee in the boat with the hired men and followed him.

---

[a]1 Some manuscripts do not have the Son of God.   [b]2 Mal. 3:1   [c]3 Isaiah 40:3
[d]8 Or in

Jesus Drives Out an Evil Spirit

21They went to Capernaum, and when the Sabbath came, Jesus went into the synagogue and began to teach. 22The people were amazed at his teaching, because he taught them as one who had authority, not as the teachers of the law. 23Just then a man in their synagogue who was possessed by an evil*a* spirit cried out, 24"What do you want with us, Jesus of Nazareth? Have you come to destroy us? I know who you are—the Holy One of God!"

25"Be quiet!" said Jesus sternly. "Come out of him!" 26The evil spirit shook the man violently and came out of him with a shriek.

27The people were all so amazed that they asked each other, "What is this? A new teaching—and with authority! He even gives orders to evil spirits and they obey him." 28News about him spread quickly over the whole region of Galilee.

Jesus Heals Many

29As soon as they left the synagogue, they went with James and John to the home of Simon and Andrew. 30Simon's mother-in-law was in bed with a fever, and they told Jesus about her. 31So he went to her, took her hand and helped her up. The fever left her and she began to wait on them.

32That evening after sunset the people brought to Jesus all the sick and demon-possessed. 33The whole town gathered at the door, 34and Jesus healed many who had various diseases. He also drove out many demons, but he would not let the demons speak because they knew who he was.

Jesus Prays in a Solitary Place

35Very early in the morning, while it was still dark, Jesus got up, left the house and went off to a solitary place, where he prayed. 36Simon and his companions went to look for him, 37and when they found him, they exclaimed: "Everyone is looking for you!"

38Jesus replied, "Let us go somewhere else—to the nearby villages—so I can preach there also. That is why I have come." 39So he traveled throughout Galilee, preaching in their synagogues and driving out demons.

A Man With Leprosy

40A man with leprosy*b* came to him and begged him on his knees, "If you are willing, you can make me clean."

41Filled with compassion, Jesus reached out his hand and touched the man. "I am willing," he said. "Be clean!" 42Immediately the leprosy left him and he was cured.

43Jesus sent him away at once with a strong warning: 44"See that you don't tell this to anyone. But go, show yourself to the priest and offer the sacrifices that Moses commanded for your cleansing, as a testimony to them." 45Instead he went out and began to talk freely, spreading the news. As a result, Jesus could no longer enter a town openly but stayed outside in lonely places. Yet the people still came to him from everywhere.

Jesus Heals a Paralytic

2 A few days later, when Jesus again entered Capernaum, the people heard that he had come home. 2So many gathered

---

*a*23 Greek *unclean*; also in verses 26 and 27   *b*40 The Greek word was used for various diseases affecting the skin—not necessarily leprosy.

that there was no room left, not even outside the door, and he preached the word to them. ³Some men came, bringing to him a paralytic, carried by four of them. ⁴Since they could not get him to Jesus because of the crowd, they made an opening in the roof above Jesus and, after digging through it, lowered the mat the paralyzed man was lying on. ⁵When Jesus saw their faith, he said to the paralytic, "Son, your sins are forgiven."

⁶Now some teachers of the law were sitting there, thinking to themselves, ⁷"Why does this fellow talk like that? He's blaspheming! Who can forgive sins but God alone?"

⁸Immediately Jesus knew in his spirit that this was what they were thinking in their hearts, and he said to them, "Why are you thinking these things? ⁹Which is easier: to say to the paralytic, 'Your sins are forgiven,' or to say, 'Get up, take your mat and walk'? ¹⁰But that you may know

Jn 8:2-11

that the Son of Man has authority on earth to forgive sins . . . ." He said to the paralytic, ¹¹"I tell you, get up, take your mat and go home." ¹²He got up, took his mat and walked out in full view of them all. This amazed everyone and they praised God, saying, "We have never seen anything like this!"

The Calling of Levi

¹³Once again Jesus went out beside the lake. A large crowd came to him, and he began to teach them. ¹⁴As he walked along, he saw Levi son of Alphaeus sitting at the tax collector's booth. "Follow me," Jesus told him, and Levi got up and followed him.

¹⁵While Jesus was having dinner at Levi's house, many tax collectors and "sinners" were eating

with him and his disciples, for there were many who followed him. ¹⁶When the teachers of the law who were Pharisees saw him eating with the "sinners" and tax collectors, they asked his disciples: "Why does he eat with tax collectors and 'sinners'?"

¹⁷On hearing this, Jesus said to them, "It is not the healthy who need a doctor, but the sick. I have not come to call the righteous, but sinners."

Jesus Questioned About Fasting

¹⁸Now John's disciples and the Pharisees were fasting. Some people came and asked Jesus, "How is it that John's disciples and the disciples of the Pharisees are fasting, but yours are not?"

¹⁹Jesus answered, "How can the guests of the bridegroom fast while he is with them? They cannot, so long as they have him with them. ²⁰But the time will come when the bridegroom will be taken from them, and on that day they will fast.

²¹"No one sews a patch of unshrunk cloth on an old garment. If he does, the new piece will pull away from the old, making the tear worse. ²²And no one pours new wine into old wineskins. If he does, the wine will burst the skins, and both the wine and the wineskins will be ruined. No, he pours new wine into new wineskins."

Lord of the Sabbath

²³One Sabbath Jesus was going through the grainfields, and as his disciples walked along, they began to pick some heads of grain. ²⁴The Pharisees said to him, "Look, why are they doing what is unlawful on the Sabbath?"

²⁵He answered, "Have you never read what David did when he and his companions were hungry and in need? ²⁶In the days of Abiathar the high priest, he entered the house of God and ate the consecrated bread, which is lawful only for priests to eat. And he also gave some to his companions."

²⁷Then he said to them, "The Sabbath was made for man, not man for the Sabbath. ²⁸So the Son of Man is Lord even of the Sabbath."

3 Another time he went into the synagogue, and a man with a shriveled hand was there. ²Some of them were looking for a reason to accuse Jesus, so they watched him closely to see if he would heal him on the Sabbath. ³Jesus said to the man with the shriveled hand, "Stand up in front of everyone."

⁴Then Jesus asked them, "Which is lawful on the Sabbath: to do good or to do evil, to save life or to kill?" But they remained silent.

3
Lk 15:28

⁵He looked around at them in anger and, deeply distressed at their stubborn hearts, said to the man, "Stretch out your hand." He stretched it out, and his hand was completely restored. ⁶Then the Pharisees went out and began to plot with the Herodians how they might kill Jesus.

Crowds Follow Jesus

⁷Jesus withdrew with his disciples to the lake, and a large crowd from Galilee followed. ⁸When they heard all he was doing, many people came to him from Judea, Jerusalem, Idumea, and the regions across the Jordan and around Tyre and Sidon. ⁹Because of the crowd he told his disciples to have a small boat ready for him, to keep the people from crowding him. ¹⁰For he had healed many, so that those with diseases were pushing forward to touch him. ¹¹Whenever the evil* spirits saw him, they fell down before him and cried out, "You are the Son of God." ¹²But he gave them strict orders not to tell who he was.

The Appointing of the Twelve Apostles

¹³Jesus went up on a mountainside and called to him those he wanted, and they came to him. ¹⁴He appointed twelve—designating them apostlesᵇ—that they might be with him and that he might send them out to preach ¹⁵and to have authority to drive out demons. ¹⁶These are the twelve he appointed: Simon (to whom he gave the name Peter); ¹⁷James son of Zebedee and his brother John (to them he gave the name Boanerges, which means Sons of Thunder); ¹⁸Andrew, Philip, Bartholomew, Matthew, Thomas, James son of Alphaeus, Thaddaeus, Simon the Zealot ¹⁹and Judas Iscariot, who betrayed him.

Jesus and Beelzebub

²⁰Then Jesus entered a house, and again a crowd gathered, so that he and his disciples were not even able to eat. ²¹When his family heard about this, they went to take charge of him, for they said, "He is out of his mind."

²²And the teachers of the law who came down from Jerusalem said, "He is possessed by Beelzebubᶜ! By the prince of demons he is driving out demons."

---

*11 Greek *unclean*; also in verse 30   *14 Some manuscripts do not have *designating them apostles*.   *22 Greek *Beezeboul* or *Beelzeboul*

²³So Jesus called them and spoke to them in parables: "How can Satan drive out Satan? ²⁴If a kingdom is divided against itself, that kingdom cannot stand. ²⁵If a house is divided against itself, that house cannot stand. ²⁶And if Satan opposes himself and is divided, he cannot stand; his end has come. ²⁷In fact, no one can enter a strong man's house and carry off his possessions unless he first ties up the strong man. Then he can rob his house. ²⁸I tell you the truth, all the sins and blasphemies of men will be forgiven them. ²⁹But whoever blasphemes against the Holy Spirit will never be forgiven; he is guilty of an eternal sin."

³⁰He said this because they were saying, "He has an evil spirit."

Jesus' Mother and Brothers

³¹Then Jesus' mother and brothers arrived. Standing outside, they sent someone in to call him. ³²A crowd was sitting around him, and they told him, "Your mother and brothers are outside looking for you."

³³"Who are my mother and my brothers?" he asked.

³⁴Then he looked at those seated in a circle around him and said, "Here are my mother and my brothers! ³⁵Whoever does God's will is my brother and sister and mother."

The Parable of the Sower

4 Again Jesus began to teach by the lake. The crowd that gathered around him was so large that he got into a boat and sat in it out on the lake, while all the people were along the shore at the water's edge. ²He taught them many things by parables, and in his teaching said: ³"Listen! A farmer went out to sow his seed. ⁴As he was scattering the seed, some fell along the path, and the birds came and ate it up. ⁵Some fell on rocky places, where it did not have much soil. It sprang up quickly, because the soil was shallow. ⁶But when the sun came up, the plants were scorched, and they withered because they had no root. ⁷Other seed fell among thorns, which grew up and choked the plants, so that they did not bear grain. ⁸Still other seed fell on good soil. It came up, grew and produced a crop, multiplying thirty, sixty, or even a hundred times."

⁹Then Jesus said, "He who has ears to hear, let him hear."

¹⁰When he was alone, the Twelve and the others around him asked him about the parables. ¹¹He told them, "The secret of the kingdom of God has been given to you. But to those on the outside everything is said in parables ¹²so that,

"'they may be ever seeing but
    never perceiving,
and ever hearing but never
    understanding;
otherwise they might turn and
    be forgiven!' ᵃ"

¹³Then Jesus said to them, "Don't you understand this parable? How then will you understand any parable? ¹⁴The farmer sows the word. ¹⁵Some people are like seed along the path, where the word is sown. As soon as they hear it, Satan comes and takes away the word that was sown in them. ¹⁶Others, like seed sown on rocky places, hear the word and at once receive it with joy. ¹⁷But since they have no root, they last only a short time. When trouble or persecution comes because of the word, they quickly

---

ᵃ12 Isaiah 6:9,10

fall away. [18]Still others, like seed sown among thorns, hear the word; [19]but the worries of this life, the deceitfulness of wealth and the desires for other things come in and choke the word, making it unfruitful. [20]Others, like seed sown on good soil, hear the word, accept it, and produce a crop—thirty, sixty or even a hundred times what was sown."

A Lamp on a Stand

[21]He said to them, "Do you bring in a lamp to put it under a bowl or a bed? Instead, don't you put it on its stand? [22]For whatever is hidden is meant to be disclosed, and whatever is concealed is meant to be brought out into the open. [23]If anyone has ears to hear, let him hear."

[24]"Consider carefully what you hear," he continued. "With the measure you use, it will be measured to you—and even more. [25]Whoever has will be given more; whoever does not have, even what he has will be taken from him."

The Parable of the Growing Seed

[26]He also said, "This is what the kingdom of God is like. A man scatters seed on the ground. [27]Night and day, whether he sleeps or gets up, the seed sprouts and grows, though he does not know how. [28]All by itself the soil produces grain—first the stalk, then the head, then the full kernel in the head. [29]As soon as the grain is ripe, he puts the sickle to it, because the harvest has come."

The Parable of the Mustard Seed

[30]Again he said, "What shall we say the kingdom of God is like, or what parable shall we use to describe it? [31]It is like a mustard seed, which is the smallest seed you plant in the ground. [32]Yet when planted, it grows and becomes the largest of all garden plants, with such big branches that the birds of the air can perch in its shade."

[33]With many similar parables Jesus spoke the word to them, as much as they could understand. [34]He did not say anything to them without using a parable. But when he was alone with his own disciples, he explained everything.

Jesus Calms the Storm

[35]That day when evening came, he said to his disciples, "Let us go over to the other side." [36]Leaving the crowd behind, they took him along, just as he was, in the boat. There were also other boats with him. [37]A furious squall came up, and the waves broke over the boat, so that it was nearly swamped. [38]Jesus was in the stern, sleeping on a cushion. The disciples woke him and said to him, "Teacher, don't you care if we drown?"

[39]He got up, rebuked the wind and said to the waves, "Quiet! Be still!" Then the wind died down and it was completely calm.

[40]He said to his disciples, "Why are you so afraid? Do you still have no faith?" 26
Mk 5:36

[41]They were terrified and asked each other, "Who is this? Even the wind and the waves obey him!"

The Healing of a Demon-possessed Man

5 They went across the lake to the region of the Gerasenes.[a]

---

[a]1 Some manuscripts *Gadarenes*; other manuscripts *Gergesenes*

[2]When Jesus got out of the boat, a man with an evil[c] spirit came from the tombs to meet him. [3]This man lived in the tombs, and no one could bind him any more, not even with a chain. [4]For he had often been chained hand and foot, but he tore the chains apart and broke the irons on his feet. No one was strong enough to subdue him. [5]Night and day among the tombs and in the hills he would cry out and cut himself with stones.

[6]When he saw Jesus from a distance, he ran and fell on his knees in front of him. [7]He shouted at the top of his voice, "What do you want with me, Jesus, Son of the Most High God? Swear to God that you won't torture me!" [8]For Jesus had said to him, "Come out of this man, you evil spirit!"

[9]Then Jesus asked him, "What is your name?"

"My name is Legion," he replied, "for we are many." [10]And he begged Jesus again and again not to send them out of the area.

[11]A large herd of pigs was feeding on the nearby hillside. [12]The demons begged Jesus, "Send us among the pigs; allow us to go into them." [13]He gave them permission, and the evil spirits came out and went into the pigs. The herd, about two thousand in number, rushed down the steep bank into the lake and were drowned.

[14]Those tending the pigs ran off and reported this in the town and countryside, and the people went out to see what had happened. [15]When they came to Jesus, they saw the man who had been possessed by the legion of demons, sitting there, dressed and in his right mind; and they were afraid. [16]Those who had seen it told the people what had happened to the demon-possessed man—and told about the pigs as well. [17]Then the people began to plead with Jesus to leave their region.

[18]As Jesus was getting into the boat, the man who had been demon-possessed begged to go with him. [19]Jesus did not let him, but said, "Go home to your family and tell them how much the Lord has done for you, and how he has had mercy on you." [20]So the man went away and began to tell in the Decapolis[b] how much Jesus had done for him. And all the people were amazed.

A Dead Girl and a Sick Woman

[21]When Jesus had again crossed over by boat to the other side of the lake, a large crowd gathered around him while he was by the lake. [22]Then one of the synagogue rulers, named Jairus, came there. Seeing Jesus, he fell at his feet [23]and pleaded earnestly with him, "My little daughter is dying. Please come and put your hands on her so that she will be healed and live." [24]So Jesus went with him.

A large crowd followed and pressed around him. [25]And a woman was there who had been subject to bleeding for twelve years. [26]She had suffered a great deal under the care of many doctors and had spent all she had, yet instead of getting better she grew worse. [27]When she heard about Jesus, she came up behind him in the crowd and touched his cloak, [28]because she thought, "If I just touch his clothes, I will be healed." [29]Immediately her bleeding stopped and she felt in

---

[a]2 Greek *unclean*; also in verses 8 and 13　　　[b]20 That is, the Ten Cities

her body that she was freed from her suffering.

³⁰At once Jesus realized that power had gone out from him. He turned around in the crowd and asked, "Who touched my clothes?"

³¹"You see the people crowding against you," his disciples answered, "and yet you can ask, 'Who touched me?'"

³²But Jesus kept looking around to see who had done it. ³³Then the woman, knowing what had happened to her, came and fell at his feet and, trembling with fear, told him the whole truth. ³⁴He said to her, "Daughter, your faith has healed you. Go in peace and be freed from your suffering."

³⁵While Jesus was still speaking, some men came from the house of Jairus, the synagogue ruler. "Your daughter is dead," they said. "Why bother the teacher any more?"

³⁶Ignoring what they said, Jesus told the synagogue ruler, "Don't be afraid; just believe."

³⁷He did not let anyone follow him except Peter, James and John the brother of James. ³⁸When they came to the home of the synagogue ruler, Jesus saw a commotion, with people crying and wailing loudly. ³⁹He went in and said to them, "Why all this commotion and wailing? The child is not dead but asleep." ⁴⁰But they laughed at him.

After he put them all out, he took the child's father and mother and the disciples who were with him, and went in where the child was. ⁴¹He took her by the hand and said to her, "*Talitha koum!*" (which means, "Little girl, I say to you, get up!"). ⁴²Immediately the girl stood up and walked around (she was twelve years old). At this

they were completely astonished. ⁴³He gave strict orders not to let anyone know about this, and told them to give her something to eat.

A Prophet Without Honor

6 Jesus left there and went to his hometown, accompanied by his disciples. ²When the Sabbath came, he began to teach in the synagogue, and many who heard him were amazed.

"Where did this man get these things?" they asked. "What's this wisdom that has been given him, that he even does miracles? ³Isn't this the carpenter? Isn't this Mary's son and the brother of James, Joseph,ᵃ Judas and Simon? Aren't his sisters here with us?" And they took offense at him.

⁴Jesus said to them, "Only in his hometown, among his relatives and in his own house is a prophet without honor." ⁵He could not do any miracles there, except lay his hands on a few sick people and heal them. ⁶And he was amazed at their lack of faith.

Jesus Sends Out the Twelve

Then Jesus went around teaching from village to village. ⁷Calling the Twelve to him, he sent them out two by two and gave them authority over evilᵇ spirits.

⁸These were his instructions: "Take nothing for the journey except a staff—no bread, no bag, no money in your belts. ⁹Wear sandals but not an extra tunic. ¹⁰Whenever you enter a house, stay there until you leave that town. ¹¹And if any place will not welcome you or listen to you, shake the dust off your feet when you leave, as a testimony against them."

¹²They went out and preached

26
Lk 12:32

ᵃ3 Greek *Joses*, a variant of *Joseph*   ᵇ7 Greek *unclean*

that people should repent. [13]They drove out many demons and anointed many sick people with oil and healed them.

John the Baptist Beheaded

[14]King Herod heard about this, for Jesus' name had become well known. Some were saying,[a] "John the Baptist has been raised from the dead, and that is why miraculous powers are at work in him."

[15]Others said, "He is Elijah."

And still others claimed, "He is a prophet, like one of the prophets of long ago."

[16]But when Herod heard this, he said, "John, the man I beheaded, has been raised from the dead!"

[17]For Herod himself had given orders to have John arrested, and he had him bound and put in prison. He did this because of Herodias, his brother Philip's wife, whom he had married. [18]For John had been saying to Herod, "It is not lawful for you to have your brother's wife." [19]So Herodias nursed a grudge against John and wanted to kill him. But she was not able to, [20]because Herod feared John and protected him, knowing him to be a righteous and holy man. When Herod heard John, he was greatly puzzled[b]; yet he liked to listen to him.

[21]Finally the opportune time came. On his birthday Herod gave a banquet for his high officials and military commanders and the leading men of Galilee. [22]When the daughter of Herodias came in and danced, she pleased Herod and his dinner guests.

The king said to the girl, "Ask me for anything you want, and I'll give it to you." [23]And he promised her with an oath, "Whatever you ask I will give you, up to half my kingdom."

[24]She went out and said to her mother, "What shall I ask for?"

"The head of John the Baptist," she answered.

[25]At once the girl hurried in to the king with the request: "I want you to give me right now the head of John the Baptist on a platter."

[26]The king was greatly distressed, but because of his oaths and his dinner guests, he did not want to refuse her. [27]So he immediately sent an executioner with orders to bring John's head. The man went, beheaded John in the prison, [28]and brought back his head on a platter. He presented it to the girl, and she gave it to her mother. [29]On hearing of this, John's disciples came and took his body and laid it in a tomb.

Jesus Feeds the Five Thousand

[30]The apostles gathered around Jesus and reported to him all they had done and taught. [31]Then, because so many people were coming and going that they did not even have a chance to eat, he said to them, "Come with me by yourselves to a quiet place and get some rest."

[32]So they went away by themselves in a boat to a solitary place. [33]But many who saw them leaving recognized them and ran on foot from all the towns and got there ahead of them. [34]When Jesus landed and saw a large crowd, he had compassion on them, because they were like sheep without a shepherd. So he began teaching them many things.

[35]By this time it was late in the

---

[a]14 Some early manuscripts *He was saying things*

[b]20 Some early manuscripts *he did many*

day, so his disciples came to him. "This is a remote place," they said, "and it's already very late. ³⁶Send the people away so they can go to the surrounding countryside and villages and buy themselves something to eat."

³⁷But he answered, "You give them something to eat."

They said to him, "That would take eight months of a man's wages*! Are we to go and spend that much on bread and give it to them to eat?"

³⁸"How many loaves do you have?" he asked. "Go and see."

When they found out, they said, "Five—and two fish."

³⁹Then Jesus directed them to have all the people sit down in groups on the green grass. ⁴⁰So they sat down in groups of hundreds and fifties. ⁴¹Taking the five loaves and the two fish and looking up to heaven, he gave thanks and broke the loaves. Then he gave them to his disciples to set before the people. He also divided the two fish among them all. ⁴²They all ate and were satisfied, ⁴³and the disciples picked up twelve basketfuls of broken pieces of bread and fish. ⁴⁴The number of the men who had eaten was five thousand.

Jesus Walks on the Water

⁴⁵Immediately Jesus made his disciples get into the boat and go on ahead of him to Bethsaida, while he dismissed the crowd. ⁴⁶After leaving them, he went up on a mountainside to pray.

⁴⁷When evening came, the boat was in the middle of the lake, and he was alone on land. ⁴⁸He saw the disciples straining at the oars, because the wind was against them. About the fourth watch of the night he went out to them,

walking on the lake. He was about to pass by them, ⁴⁹but when they saw him walking on the lake, they thought he was a ghost. They cried out, ⁵⁰because they all saw him and were terrified.

Immediately he spoke to them and said, "Take courage! It is I. Don't be afraid." ⁵¹Then he climbed into the boat with them, and the wind died down. They were completely amazed, ⁵²for they had not understood about the loaves; their hearts were hardened.

⁵³When they had crossed over, they landed at Gennesaret and anchored there. ⁵⁴As soon as they got out of the boat, people recognized Jesus. ⁵⁵They ran throughout that whole region and carried the sick on mats to wherever they heard he was. ⁵⁶And wherever he went—into villages, towns or countryside—they placed the sick in the marketplaces. They begged him to let them touch even the edge of his cloak, and all who touched him were healed.

Clean and Unclean

7 The Pharisees and some of the teachers of the law who had come from Jerusalem gathered around Jesus and ²saw some of his disciples eating food with hands that were "unclean," that is, unwashed. ³(The Pharisees and all the Jews do not eat unless they give their hands a ceremonial washing, holding to the tradition of the elders. ⁴When they come from the marketplace they do not eat unless they wash. And they observe many other traditions, such as the washing of cups, pitchers and kettles.ᵇ)

⁵So the Pharisees and teachers of the law asked Jesus, "Why

ᵃ37 Greek *take two hundred denarii*   ᵇ4 Some early manuscripts *pitchers, kettles and dining couches*

don't your disciples live according to the tradition of the elders instead of eating their food with 'unclean' hands?"

⁶He replied, "Isaiah was right when he prophesied about you hypocrites; as it is written:

" 'These people honor me
  with their lips,
but their hearts are far from
  me.
⁷They worship me in vain;
  their teachings are but rules
    taught by men.'ᵃ

⁸You have let go of the commands of God and are holding on to the traditions of men."

⁹And he said to them: "You have a fine way of setting aside the commands of God in order to observeᵇ your own traditions! ¹⁰For Moses said, 'Honor your father and your mother,'ᶜ and, 'Anyone who curses his father or mother must be put to death.'ᵈ ¹¹But you say that if a man says to his father or mother: 'Whatever help you might otherwise have received from me is Corban' (that is, a gift devoted to God), ¹²then you no longer let him do anything for his father or mother. ¹³Thus you nullify the word of God by your tradition that you have handed down. And you do many things like that."

¹⁴Again Jesus called the crowd to him and said, "Listen to me, everyone, and understand this. ¹⁵Nothing outside a man can make him 'unclean' by going into him. Rather, it is what comes out of a man that makes him 'unclean.'ᵉ"

¹⁷After he had left the crowd and entered the house, his disciples asked him about this para-

ble. ¹⁸"Are you so dull?" he asked. "Don't you see that nothing that enters a man from the outside can make him 'unclean'? ¹⁹For it doesn't go into his heart but into his stomach, and then out of his body." (In saying this, Jesus declared all foods "clean.")

²⁰He went on: "What comes out of a man is what makes him 'unclean.' ²¹For from within, out of men's hearts, come evil thoughts, sexual immorality, theft, murder, adultery, ²²greed, malice, deceit, lewdness, envy, slander, arrogance and folly. ²³All these evils come from inside and make a man 'unclean.' "

33
1Ti 6:6-10

The Faith of a Syrophoenician Woman

²⁴Jesus left that place and went to the vicinity of Tyre.ᶠ He entered a house and did not want anyone to know it; yet he could not keep his presence secret. ²⁵In fact, as soon as she heard about him, a woman whose little daughter was possessed by an evilᵍ spirit came and fell at his feet. ²⁶The woman was a Greek, born in Syrian Phoenicia. She begged Jesus to drive the demon out of her daughter.

²⁷"First let the children eat all they want," he told her, "for it is not right to take the children's bread and toss it to their dogs."

²⁸"Yes, Lord," she replied, "but even the dogs under the table eat the children's crumbs."

²⁹Then he told her, "For such a reply, you may go; the demon has left your daughter."

³⁰She went home and found her child lying on the bed, and the demon gone.

ᵃ6,7 Isaiah 29:13   ᵇ9 Some manuscripts set up   ᶜ10 Exodus 20:12; Deut. 5:16   ᵈ10 Exodus 21:17; Lev. 20:9   ᵉ15 Some early manuscripts 'unclean.' ¹⁶If anyone has ears to hear, let him hear.   ᶠ24 Many early manuscripts Tyre and Sidon   ᵍ25 Greek unclean

The Healing of a Deaf and Mute Man

31Then Jesus left the vicinity of Tyre and went through Sidon, down to the Sea of Galilee and into the region of the Decapolis.*a* 32There some people brought to him a man who was deaf and could hardly talk, and they begged him to place his hand on the man.

33After he took him aside, away from the crowd, Jesus put his fingers into the man's ears. Then he spit and touched the man's tongue. 34He looked up to heaven and with a deep sigh said to him, *"Ephphatha!"* (which means, "Be opened!"). 35At this, the man's ears were opened, his tongue was loosened and he began to speak plainly.

36Jesus commanded them not to tell anyone. But the more he did so, the more they kept talking about it. 37People were overwhelmed with amazement. "He has done everything well," they said. "He even makes the deaf hear and the mute speak."

Jesus Feeds the Four Thousand

8 During those days another large crowd gathered. Since they had nothing to eat, Jesus called his disciples to him and said, 2"I have compassion for these people; they have already been with me three days and have nothing to eat. 3If I send them home hungry, they will collapse on the way, because some of them have come a long distance."

4His disciples answered, "But where in this remote place can anyone get enough bread to feed them?"

5"How many loaves do you have?" Jesus asked.

"Seven," they replied.

6He told the crowd to sit down on the ground. When he had taken the seven loaves and given thanks, he broke them and gave them to his disciples to set before the people, and they did so. 7They had a few small fish as well; he gave thanks for them also and told the disciples to distribute them. 8The people ate and were satisfied. Afterward the disciples picked up seven basketfuls of broken pieces that were left over. 9About four thousand men were present. And having sent them away, 10he got into the boat with his disciples and went to the region of Dalmanutha.

11The Pharisees came and began to question Jesus. To test him, they asked him for a sign from heaven. 12He sighed deeply and said, "Why does this generation ask for a miraculous sign? I tell you the truth, no sign will be given to it." 13Then he left them, got back into the boat and crossed to the other side.

The Yeast of the Pharisees and Herod

14The disciples had forgotten to bring bread, except for one loaf they had with them in the boat. 15"Be careful," Jesus warned them. "Watch out for the yeast of the Pharisees and that of Herod."

16They discussed this with one another and said, "It is because we have no bread."

17Aware of their discussion, Jesus asked them: "Why are you talking about having no bread? Do you still not see or understand? Are your hearts hardened? 18Do you have eyes but fail

---

a31 That is, the Ten Cities

to see, and ears but fail to hear? And don't you remember? [19]When I broke the five loaves for the five thousand, how many basketfuls of pieces did you pick up?"

"Twelve," they replied.

[20]"And when I broke the seven loaves for the four thousand, how many basketfuls of pieces did you pick up?"

They answered, "Seven."

[21]He said to them, "Do you still not understand?"

The Healing of a Blind Man at Bethsaida

[22]They came to Bethsaida, and some people brought a blind man and begged Jesus to touch him. [23]He took the blind man by the hand and led him outside the village. When he had spit on the man's eyes and put his hands on him, Jesus asked, "Do you see anything?"

[24]He looked up and said, "I see people; they look like trees walking around."

[25]Once more Jesus put his hands on the man's eyes. Then his eyes were opened, his sight was restored, and he saw everything clearly. [26]Jesus sent him home, saying, "Don't go into the village.*a*"

Peter's Confession of Christ

[27]Jesus and his disciples went on to the villages around Caesarea Philippi. On the way he asked them, "Who do people say I am?"

[28]They replied, "Some say John the Baptist; others say Elijah; and still others, one of the prophets."

[29]"But what about you?" he asked. "Who do you say I am?"

Peter answered, "You are the Christ.*b*"

[30]Jesus warned them not to tell anyone about him.

Jesus Predicts His Death

[31]He then began to teach them that the Son of Man must suffer many things and be rejected by the elders, chief priests and teachers of the law, and that he must be killed and after three days rise again. [32]He spoke plainly about this, and Peter took him aside and began to rebuke him.

[33]But when Jesus turned and looked at his disciples, he rebuked Peter. "Get behind me, Satan!" he said. "You do not have in mind the things of God, but the things of men."

[34]Then he called the crowd to him along with his disciples and said: "If anyone would come after me, he must deny himself and take up his cross and follow me. [35]For whoever wants to save his life*c* will lose it, but whoever loses his life for me and for the gospel will save it. [36]What good is it for a man to gain the whole world, yet forfeit his soul? [37]Or what can a man give in exchange for his soul? [38]If anyone is ashamed of me and my words in this adulterous and sinful generation, the Son of Man will be ashamed of him when he comes in his Father's glory with the holy angels."

9 And he said to them, "I tell you the truth, some who are standing here will not taste death before they see the kingdom of God come with power."

The Transfiguration

[2]After six days Jesus took Peter,

---

*a*26 Some manuscripts *Don't go and tell anyone in the village*   *b*29 Or *Messiah.* "The Christ" (Greek) and "the Messiah" (Hebrew) both mean "the Anointed One."
*c*35 The Greek word means either *life* or *soul*; also in verse 36.

James and John with him and led them up a high mountain, where they were all alone. There he was transfigured before them. ³His clothes became dazzling white, whiter than anyone in the world could bleach them. ⁴And there appeared before them Elijah and Moses, who were talking with Jesus.

⁵Peter said to Jesus, "Rabbi, it is good for us to be here. Let us put up three shelters—one for you, one for Moses and one for Elijah." ⁶(He did not know what to say, they were so frightened.)

⁷Then a cloud appeared and enveloped them, and a voice came from the cloud: "This is my Son, whom I love. Listen to him!"

⁸Suddenly, when they looked around, they no longer saw anyone with them except Jesus.

⁹As they were coming down the mountain, Jesus gave them orders not to tell anyone what they had seen until the Son of Man had risen from the dead. ¹⁰They kept the matter to themselves, discussing what "rising from the dead" meant.

¹¹And they asked him, "Why do the teachers of the law say that Elijah must come first?"

¹²Jesus replied, "To be sure, Elijah does come first, and restores all things. Why then is it written that the Son of Man must suffer much and be rejected? ¹³But I tell you, Elijah has come, and they have done to him everything they wished, just as it is written about him."

The Healing of a Boy With an Evil Spirit

¹⁴When they came to the other disciples, they saw a large crowd around them and the teachers of the law arguing with them. ¹⁵As soon as all the people saw Jesus, they were overwhelmed with wonder and ran to greet him.

¹⁶"What are you arguing with them about?" he asked.

¹⁷A man in the crowd answered, "Teacher, I brought you my son, who is possessed by a spirit that has robbed him of speech. ¹⁸Whenever it seizes him, it throws him to the ground. He foams at the mouth, gnashes his teeth and becomes rigid. I asked your disciples to drive out the spirit, but they could not."

¹⁹"O unbelieving generation," Jesus replied, "how long shall I stay with you? How long shall I put up with you? Bring the boy to me."

²⁰So they brought him. When the spirit saw Jesus, it immediately threw the boy into a convulsion. He fell to the ground and rolled around, foaming at the mouth.

²¹Jesus asked the boy's father, "How long has he been like this?"

"From childhood," he answered. ²²"It has often thrown him into fire or water to kill him. But if you can do anything, take pity on us and help us."

²³" 'If you can'?" said Jesus. "Everything is possible for him who believes."

²⁴Immediately the boy's father exclaimed, "I do believe; help me overcome my unbelief!"   Lk 12:46   96

²⁵When Jesus saw that a crowd was running to the scene, he rebuked the evilª spirit. "You deaf and mute spirit," he said, "I command you, come out of him and never enter him again."

²⁶The spirit shrieked, convulsed him violently and came out. The boy looked so much like a corpse that many said, "He's dead."

ª25 Greek *unclean*

²⁷But Jesus took him by the hand and lifted him to his feet, and he stood up.

²⁸After Jesus had gone indoors, his disciples asked him privately, "Why couldn't we drive it out?"

²⁹He replied, "This kind can come out only by prayer.ᵈ"

³⁰They left that place and passed through Galilee. Jesus did not want anyone to know where they were, ³¹because he was teaching his disciples. He said to them, "The Son of Man is going to be betrayed into the hands of men. They will kill him, and after three days he will rise." ³²But they did not understand what he meant and were afraid to ask him about it.

Who Is the Greatest?

³³They came to Capernaum. When he was in the house, he asked them, "What were you arguing about on the road?" ³⁴But they kept quiet because on the way they had argued about who was the greatest.

³⁵Sitting down, Jesus called the Twelve and said, "If anyone wants to be first, he must be the very last, and the servant of all."

³⁶He took a little child and had him stand among them. Taking him in his arms, he said to them, ³⁷"Whoever welcomes one of these little children in my name welcomes me; and whoever welcomes me does not welcome me but the one who sent me."

Whoever Is Not Against Us Is for Us

³⁸"Teacher," said John, "we saw a man driving out demons in your name and we told him to stop, because he was not one of us."

³⁹"Do not stop him," Jesus said. "No one who does a miracle in my name can in the next moment say anything bad about me, ⁴⁰for whoever is not against us is for us. ⁴¹I tell you the truth, anyone who gives you a cup of water in my name because you belong to Christ will certainly not lose his reward.

Causing to Sin

⁴²"And if anyone causes one of these little ones who believe in me to sin, it would be better for him to be thrown into the sea with a large millstone tied around his neck. ⁴³If your hand causes you to sin, cut it off. It is better for you to enter life maimed than with two hands to go into hell, where the fire never goes out.ᵇ ⁴⁵And if your foot causes you to sin, cut it off. It is better for you to enter life crippled than to have two feet and be thrown into hell.ᶜ ⁴⁷And if your eye causes you to sin, pluck it out. It is better for you to enter the kingdom of God with one eye than to have two eyes and be thrown into hell, ⁴⁸where

> "'their worm does not die,
>   and the fire is not
>   quenched.'ᵈ

⁴⁹Everyone will be salted with fire.

⁵⁰"Salt is good, but if it loses its saltiness, how can you make it salty again? Have salt in yourselves, and be at peace with each other."

Divorce

10 Jesus then left that place and went into the region of Judea and across the Jordan. Again crowds of people came to

41
Lk 16:22-26

ᵃ29 Some manuscripts *prayer and fasting* ᵇ43 Some manuscripts *out,* ⁴⁴*where* / *"'their worm does not die, / and the fire is not quenched.'* ᶜ45 Some manuscripts *hell,* ⁴⁶*where* / *"'their worm does not die, / and the fire is not quenched.'* ᵈ48 Isaiah 66:24

him, and as was his custom, he taught them.

²Some Pharisees came and tested him by asking, "Is it lawful for a man to divorce his wife?"

³"What did Moses command you?" he replied.

⁴They said, "Moses permitted a man to write a certificate of divorce and send her away."

⁵"It was because your hearts were hard that Moses wrote you this law," Jesus replied. ⁶"But at the beginning of creation God 'made them male and female.'ᵃ ⁷For this reason a man will leave his father and mother and be united to his wife,ᵇ ⁸and the two will become one flesh.'ᶜ So they are no longer two, but one. ⁹Therefore what God has joined together, let man not separate."

¹⁰When they were in the house again, the disciples asked Jesus about this. ¹¹He answered, "Anyone who divorces his wife and marries another woman commits adultery against her. ¹²And if she divorces her husband and marries another man, she commits adultery."

19
Lk 16:18

The Little Children and Jesus

¹³People were bringing little children to Jesus to have him touch them, but the disciples rebuked them. ¹⁴When Jesus saw this, he was indignant. He said to them, "Let the little children come to me, and do not hinder them, for the kingdom of God belongs to such as these. ¹⁵I tell you the truth, anyone who will not receive the kingdom of God like a little child will never enter it." ¹⁶And he took the children in his arms, put his hands on them and blessed them.

The Rich Young Man

¹⁷As Jesus started on his way, a man ran up to him and fell on his knees before him. "Good teacher," he asked, "what must I do to inherit eternal life?"

¹⁸"Why do you call me good?" Jesus answered. "No one is good—except God alone. ¹⁹You know the commandments: 'Do not murder, do not commit adultery, do not steal, do not give false testimony, do not defraud, honor your father and mother.'ᵈ"

90
Ro 2:21

²⁰"Teacher," he declared, "all these I have kept since I was a boy."

²¹Jesus looked at him and loved him. "One thing you lack," he said. "Go, sell everything you have and give to the poor, and you will have treasure in heaven. Then come, follow me."

²²At this the man's face fell. He went away sad, because he had great wealth.

²³Jesus looked around and said to his disciples, "How hard it is for the rich to enter the kingdom of God!"

²⁴The disciples were amazed at his words. But Jesus said again, "Children, how hard it iseᵉ to enter the kingdom of God! ²⁵It is easier for a camel to go through the eye of a needle than for a rich man to enter the kingdom of God."

²⁶The disciples were even more amazed, and said to each other, "Who then can be saved?"

²⁷Jesus looked at them and said, "With man this is impossible, but not with God; all things are possible with God."

31
Jn 1:18

²⁸Peter said to him, "We have left everything to follow you!"

²⁹"I tell you the truth," Jesus re-

ᵃ6 Gen. 1:27   ᵇ7 Some early manuscripts do not have *and be united to his wife.*   ᶜ8 Gen. 2:24   ᵈ19 Exodus 20:12-16; Deut. 5:16-20   ᵉ24 Some manuscripts *is for those who trust in riches*

plied, "no one who has left home or brothers or sisters or mother or father or children or fields for me and the gospel ³⁰will fail to receive a hundred times as much in this present age (homes, brothers, sisters, mothers, children and fields—and with them, persecutions) and in the age to come, eternal life. ³¹But many who are first will be last, and the last first."

Jesus Again Predicts His Death

³²They were on their way up to Jerusalem, with Jesus leading the way, and the disciples were astonished, while those who followed were afraid. Again he took the Twelve aside and told them what was going to happen to him. ³³"We are going up to Jerusalem," he said, "and the Son of Man will be betrayed to the chief priests and teachers of the law. They will condemn him to death and will hand him over to the Gentiles, ³⁴who will mock him and spit on him, flog him and kill him. Three days later he will rise."

The Request of James and John

³⁵Then James and John, the sons of Zebedee, came to him. "Teacher," they said, "we want you to do for us whatever we ask."

³⁶"What do you want me to do for you?" he asked.

³⁷They replied, "Let one of us sit at your right and the other at your left in your glory."

³⁸"You don't know what you are asking," Jesus said. "Can you drink the cup I drink or be baptized with the baptism I am baptized with?"

³⁹"We can," they answered.

Jesus said to them, "You will drink the cup I drink and be baptized with the baptism I am baptized with, ⁴⁰but to sit at my right or left is not for me to grant. These places belong to those for whom they have been prepared."

⁴¹When the ten heard about this, they became indignant with James and John. ⁴²Jesus called them together and said, "You know that those who are regarded as rulers of the Gentiles lord it over them, and their high officials exercise authority over them. ⁴³Not so with you. Instead, whoever wants to become great among you must be your servant, ⁴⁴and whoever wants to be first must be slave of all. ⁴⁵For even the Son of Man did not come to be served, but to serve, and to give his life as a ransom for many."

Blind Bartimaeus Receives His Sight

⁴⁶Then they came to Jericho. As Jesus and his disciples, together with a large crowd, were leaving the city, a blind man, Bartimaeus (that is, the Son of Timaeus), was sitting by the roadside begging. ⁴⁷When he heard that it was Jesus of Nazareth, he began to shout, "Jesus, Son of David, have mercy on me!"

⁴⁸Many rebuked him and told him to be quiet, but he shouted all the more, "Son of David, have mercy on me!"

⁴⁹Jesus stopped and said, "Call him."

So they called to the blind man, "Cheer up! On your feet! He's calling you." ⁵⁰Throwing his cloak aside, he jumped to his feet and came to Jesus.

⁵¹"What do you want me to do for you?" Jesus asked him.

The blind man said, "Rabbi, I want to see."

⁵²"Go," said Jesus, "your faith has healed you." Immediately he received his sight and followed Jesus along the road.

The Triumphal Entry

11 As they approached Jerusalem and came to Bethphage and Bethany at the Mount of Olives, Jesus sent two of his disciples, ²saying to them, "Go to the village ahead of you, and just as you enter it, you will find a colt tied there, which no one has ever ridden. Untie it and bring it here. ³If anyone asks you, 'Why are you doing this?' tell him, 'The Lord needs it and will send it back here shortly.'"

⁴They went and found a colt outside in the street, tied at a doorway. As they untied it, ⁵some people standing there asked, "What are you doing, untying that colt?" ⁶They answered as Jesus had told them to, and the people let them go. ⁷When they brought the colt to Jesus and threw their cloaks over it, he sat on it. ⁸Many people spread their cloaks on the road, while others spread branches they had cut in the fields. ⁹Those who went ahead and those who followed shouted,

"Hosanna!ᵃ"

"Blessed is he who comes in the name of the Lord!"ᵇ

¹⁰"Blessed is the coming kingdom of our father David!"

"Hosanna in the highest!"

¹¹Jesus entered Jerusalem and went to the temple. He looked around at everything, but since it was already late, he went out to Bethany with the Twelve.

Jesus Clears the Temple

¹²The next day as they were leaving Bethany, Jesus was hungry. ¹³Seeing in the distance a fig tree in leaf, he went to find out if it had any fruit. When he reached it, he found nothing but leaves, because it was not the season for figs. ¹⁴Then he said to the tree, "May no one ever eat fruit from you again." And his disciples heard him say it.

¹⁵On reaching Jerusalem, Jesus entered the temple area and began driving out those who were buying and selling there. He overturned the tables of the money changers and the benches of those selling doves, ¹⁶and would not allow anyone to carry merchandise through the temple courts. ¹⁷And as he taught them, he said, "Is it not written:

"'My house will be called
    a house of prayer for all
        nations'ᶜ?

But you have made it 'a den of robbers.'ᵈ"

¹⁸The chief priests and the teachers of the law heard this and began looking for a way to kill him, for they feared him, because the whole crowd was amazed at his teaching.

¹⁹When evening came, theyᵉ went out of the city.

The Withered Fig Tree

²⁰In the morning, as they went along, they saw the fig tree withered from the roots. ²¹Peter remembered and said to Jesus,

ᵃ9 A Hebrew expression meaning "Save!" which became an exclamation of praise; also in verse 10   ᵇ9 Psalm 118:25,26   ᶜ17 Isaiah 56:7   ᵈ17 Jer. 7:11   ᵉ19 Some early manuscripts *he*

"Rabbi, look! The fig tree you cursed has withered!"

[22]"Have[a] faith in God," Jesus answered. [23]"I tell you the truth, if anyone says to this mountain, 'Go, throw yourself into the sea,' and does not doubt in his heart but believes that what he says will happen, it will be done for him. [24]Therefore I tell you, whatever you ask for in prayer, believe that you have received it, and it will be yours. [25]And when you stand praying, if you hold anything against anyone, forgive him, so that your Father in heaven may forgive you your sins.[b]"

24
Jn 20:31

29
Ro 12:19-21

The Authority of Jesus Questioned

[27]They arrived again in Jerusalem, and while Jesus was walking in the temple courts, the chief priests, the teachers of the law and the elders came to him. [28]"By what authority are you doing these things?" they asked. "And who gave you authority to do this?"

[29]Jesus replied, "I will ask you one question. Answer me, and I will tell you by what authority I am doing these things. [30]John's baptism—was it from heaven, or from men? Tell me!"

[31]They discussed it among themselves and said, "If we say, 'From heaven,' he will ask, 'Then why didn't you believe him?' [32]But if we say, 'From men'. . . ." (They feared the people, for everyone held that John really was a prophet.)

[33]So they answered Jesus, "We don't know."

Jesus said, "Neither will I tell you by what authority I am doing these things."

The Parable of the Tenants

12 He then began to speak to them in parables: "A man planted a vineyard. He put a wall around it, dug a pit for the winepress and built a watchtower. Then he rented the vineyard to some farmers and went away on a journey. [2]At harvest time he sent a servant to the tenants to collect from them some of the fruit of the vineyard. [3]But they seized him, beat him and sent him away empty-handed. [4]Then he sent another servant to them; they struck this man on the head and treated him shamefully. [5]He sent still another, and that one they killed. He sent many others; some of them they beat, others they killed.

[6]"He had one left to send, a son, whom he loved. He sent him last of all, saying, 'They will respect my son.'

[7]"But the tenants said to one another, 'This is the heir. Come, let's kill him, and the inheritance will be ours.' [8]So they took him and killed him, and threw him out of the vineyard.

[9]"What then will the owner of the vineyard do? He will come and kill those tenants and give the vineyard to others. [10]Haven't you read this scripture:

" 'The stone the builders rejected
has become the capstone[c];
[11]the Lord has done this,
and it is marvelous in our eyes'[d]?"

[12]Then they looked for a way to arrest him because they knew he had spoken the parable against them. But they were afraid of the crowd; so they left him and went away.

[a]22 Some early manuscripts *If you have not forgive, neither will your Father who is in heaven forgive your sins.*   [b]25 Some manuscripts *sins.* [26]*But if you do not forgive, neither will your Father who is in heaven forgive your sins.*   [c]10 Or *cornerstone*   [d]11 Psalm 118:22,23

Paying Taxes to Caesar

13Later they sent some of the Pharisees and Herodians to Jesus to catch him in his words. 14They came to him and said, "Teacher, we know you are a man of integrity. You aren't swayed by men, because you pay no attention to who they are; but you teach the way of God in accordance with the truth. Is it right to pay taxes to Caesar or not? 15Should we pay or shouldn't we?"

But Jesus knew their hypocrisy. "Why are you trying to trap me?" he asked. "Bring me a denarius and let me look at it." 16They brought the coin, and he asked them, "Whose portrait is this? And whose inscription?"

"Caesar's," they replied.

17Then Jesus said to them, "Give to Caesar what is Caesar's and to God what is God's."

And they were amazed at him.

Marriage at the Resurrection

18Then the Sadducees, who say there is no resurrection, came to him with a question. 19"Teacher," they said, "Moses wrote for us that if a man's brother dies and leaves a wife but no children, the man must marry the widow and have children for his brother. 20Now there were seven brothers. The first one married and died without leaving any children. 21The second one married the widow, but he also died, leaving no child. It was the same with the third. 22In fact, none of the seven left any children. Last of all, the woman died too. 23At the resurrection*a* whose wife will she be, since the seven were married to her?"

24Jesus replied, "Are you not in error because you do not know the Scriptures or the power of God? 25When the dead rise, they will neither marry nor be given in marriage; they will be like the angels in heaven. 26Now about the dead rising—have you not read in the book of Moses, in the account of the bush, how God said to him, 'I am the God of Abraham, the God of Isaac, and the God of Jacob'*b*? 27He is not the God of the dead, but of the living. You are badly mistaken!"

The Greatest Commandment

28One of the teachers of the law came and heard them debating. Noticing that Jesus had given them a good answer, he asked him, "Of all the commandments, which is the most important?"

29"The most important one," answered Jesus, "is this: 'Hear, O Israel, the Lord our God, the Lord is one.*c* 30Love the Lord your God with all your heart and with all your soul and with all your mind and with all your strength.'*d* 31The second is this: 'Love your neighbor as yourself.'*e* There is no commandment greater than these."

32"Well said, teacher," the man replied. "You are right in saying that God is one and there is no other but him. 33To love him with all your heart, with all your understanding and with all your strength, and to love your neighbor as yourself is more important than all burnt offerings and sacrifices."

34When Jesus saw that he had answered wisely, he said to him, "You are not far from the kingdom of God." And from then on no one dared ask him any more questions.

a23 Some manuscripts *resurrection, when men rise from the dead,*   *b26* Exodus 3:6
c29 Or *the Lord our God is one Lord*   *d30* Deut. 6:4,5   *e31* Lev. 19:18

Whose Son Is the Christ?

[35]While Jesus was teaching in the temple courts, he asked, "How is it that the teachers of the law say that the Christ[a] is the son of David? [36]David himself, speaking by the Holy Spirit, declared:

" 'The Lord said to my Lord:
  "Sit at my right hand
until I put your enemies
  under your feet." '[b]

[37]David himself calls him 'Lord.' How then can he be his son?"

The large crowd listened to him with delight.

[38]As he taught, Jesus said, "Watch out for the teachers of the law. They like to walk around in flowing robes and be greeted in the marketplaces, [39]and have the most important seats in the synagogues and the places of honor at banquets. [40]They devour widows' houses and for a show make lengthy prayers. Such men will be punished most severely."

The Widow's Offering

61
Lk 3:14

[41]Jesus sat down opposite the place where the offerings were put and watched the crowd putting their money into the temple treasury. Many rich people threw in large amounts. [42]But a poor widow came and put in two very small copper coins,[c] worth only a fraction of a penny.[d]

[43]Calling his disciples to him, Jesus said, "I tell you the truth, this poor widow has put more into the treasury than all the others. [44]They all gave out of their wealth; but she, out of her poverty, put in everything—all she had to live on."

Signs of the End of the Age

13 As he was leaving the temple, one of his disciples said to him, "Look, Teacher! What massive stones! What magnificent buildings!"

[2]"Do you see all these great buildings?" replied Jesus. "Not one stone here will be left on another; every one will be thrown down."

[3]As Jesus was sitting on the Mount of Olives opposite the temple, Peter, James, John and Andrew asked him privately, [4]"Tell us, when will these things happen? And what will be the sign that they are all about to be fulfilled?"

[5]Jesus said to them: "Watch out that no one deceives you. [6]Many will come in my name, claiming, 'I am he,' and will deceive many. [7]When you hear of wars and rumors of wars, do not be alarmed. Such things must happen, but the end is still to come. [8]Nation will rise against nation, and kingdom against kingdom. There will be earthquakes in various places, and famines. These are the beginning of birth pains.

[9]"You must be on your guard. You will be handed over to the local councils and flogged in the synagogues. On account of me you will stand before governors and kings as witnesses to them. [10]And the gospel must first be preached to all nations. [11]Whenever you are arrested and brought to trial, do not worry beforehand about what to say. Just say whatever is given you at the time, for it is not you speaking, but the Holy Spirit.

[12]"Brother will betray brother to death, and a father his child. Children will rebel against their parents and have them put to death. [13]All men will hate you because of me, but he who stands firm to the end will be saved. [14]"When you see 'the abomina-

[35] Or *Messiah*   [36] Psalm 110:1   [42] Greek *two lepta*   [42] Greek *kodranta*

tion that causes desolation'[a] standing where it[b] does not belong—let the reader understand—then let those who are in Judea flee to the mountains. [15]Let no one on the roof of his house go down or enter the house to take anything out. [16]Let no one in the field go back to get his cloak. [17]How dreadful it will be in those days for pregnant women and nursing mothers! [18]Pray that this will not take place in winter, [19]because those will be days of distress unequaled from the beginning, when God created the world, until now—and never to be equaled again. [20]If the Lord had not cut short those days, no one would survive. But for the sake of the elect, whom he has chosen, he has shortened them. [21]At that time if anyone says to you, 'Look, here is the Christ[c]!' or, 'Look, there he is!' do not believe it. [22]For false Christs and false prophets will appear and perform signs and miracles to deceive the elect—if that were possible. [23]So be on your guard; I have told you everything ahead of time.

[24]"But in those days, following that distress,

" 'the sun will be darkened,
and the moon will not give
its light;
[25]the stars will fall from the sky,
and the heavenly bodies will
be shaken.'[d]

[26]"At that time men will see the Son of Man coming in clouds with great power and glory. [27]And he will send his angels and gather his elect from the four winds, from the ends of the earth to the ends of the heavens.

[28]"Now learn this lesson from the fig tree: As soon as its twigs

get tender and its leaves come out, you know that summer is near. [29]Even so, when you see these things happening, you know that it is near, right at the door. [30]I tell you the truth, this generation[e] will certainly not pass away until all these things have happened. [31]Heaven and earth will pass away, but my words will never pass away.

The Day and Hour Unknown

[32]"No one knows about that day or hour, not even the angels in heaven, nor the Son, but only the Father. [33]Be on guard! Be alert![f] You do not know when that time will come. [34]It's like a man going away: He leaves his house and puts his servants in charge, each with his assigned task, and tells the one at the door to keep watch.

[35]"Therefore keep watch because you do not know when the owner of the house will come back—whether in the evening, or at midnight, or when the rooster crows, or at dawn. [36]If he comes suddenly, do not let him find you sleeping. [37]What I say to you, I say to everyone: 'Watch!' "

Jesus Anointed at Bethany

14 Now the Passover and the Feast of Unleavened Bread were only two days away, and the chief priests and the teachers of the law were looking for some sly way to arrest Jesus and kill him. [2]"But not during the Feast," they said, "or the people may riot."

[3]While he was in Bethany, reclining at the table in the home of a man known as Simon the Leper, a woman came with an alabaster jar of very expensive per-

Ro 8:28-30 (margin at verse 22)

---

[a]14 Daniel 9:27; 11:31; 12:11   [b]14 Or he; also in verse 29   [c]21 Or Messiah
[d]25 Isaiah 13:10; 34:4   [e]30 Or race   [f]33 Some manuscripts alert and pray

fume, made of pure nard. She broke the jar and poured the perfume on his head.

4Some of those present were saying indignantly to one another, "Why this waste of perfume? 5It could have been sold for more than a year's wages[a] and the money given to the poor." And they rebuked her harshly.

6"Leave her alone," said Jesus. "Why are you bothering her? She has done a beautiful thing to me. 7The poor you will always have with you, and you can help them any time you want. But you will not always have me. 8She did what she could. She poured perfume on my body beforehand to prepare for my burial. 9I tell you the truth, wherever the gospel is preached throughout the world, what she has done will also be told, in memory of her."

10Then Judas Iscariot, one of the Twelve, went to the chief priests to betray Jesus to them. 11They were delighted to hear this and promised to give him money. So he watched for an opportunity to hand him over.

The Lord's Supper

12On the first day of the Feast of Unleavened Bread, when it was customary to sacrifice the Passover lamb, Jesus' disciples asked him, "Where do you want us to go and make preparations for you to eat the Passover?"

13So he sent two of his disciples, telling them, "Go into the city, and a man carrying a jar of water will meet him. Follow him. 14Say to the owner of the house he enters, 'The Teacher asks: Where is my guest room, where I may eat the Passover with my disciples?' 15He will show you a large upper room, furnished and ready. Make preparations for us there."

16The disciples left, went into the city and found things just as Jesus had told them. So they prepared the Passover.

17When evening came, Jesus arrived with the Twelve. 18While they were reclining at the table eating, he said, "I tell you the truth, one of you will betray me—one who is eating with me."

19They were saddened, and one by one they said to him, "Surely not I?"

20"It is one of the Twelve," he replied, "one who dips bread into the bowl with me. 21The Son of Man will go just as it is written about him. But woe to that man who betrays the Son of Man! It would be better for him if he had not been born."

22While they were eating, Jesus took bread, gave thanks and broke it, and gave it to his disciples, saying, "Take it; this is my body."

23Then he took the cup, gave thanks and offered it to them, and they all drank from it.

24"This is my blood of the[b] covenant, which is poured out for many," he said to them. 25"I tell you the truth, I will not drink again of the fruit of the vine until that day when I drink it anew in the kingdom of God."

26When they had sung a hymn, they went out to the Mount of Olives.

Jesus Predicts Peter's Denial

27"You will all fall away," Jesus told them, "for it is written:

" 'I will strike the shepherd,
    and the sheep will be
    scattered.'[c]

28But after I have risen, I will go ahead of you into Galilee."

29Peter declared, "Even if all fall away, I will not."

---

[a]5 Greek *than three hundred denarii*   [b]24 Some manuscripts *the new*   [c]27 Zech. 13:7

[30]"I tell you the truth," Jesus answered, "today—yes, tonight —before the rooster crows twice[a] you yourself will disown me three times."

[31]But Peter insisted emphatically, "Even if I have to die with you, I will never disown you." And all the others said the same.

Gethsemane

[32]They went to a place called Gethsemane, and Jesus said to his disciples, "Sit here while I pray." [33]He took Peter, James and John along with him, and he began to be deeply distressed and troubled. [34]"My soul is overwhelmed with sorrow to the point of death," he said to them. "Stay here and keep watch."

[35]Going a little farther, he fell to the ground and prayed that if possible the hour might pass from him. [36]"Abba,[b] Father," he said, "everything is possible for you. Take this cup from me. Yet not what I will, but what you will."

[37]Then he returned to his disciples and found them sleeping. "Simon," he said to Peter, "are you asleep? Could you not keep watch for one hour? [38]Watch and pray so that you will not fall into temptation. The spirit is willing, but the body is weak."

[39]Once more he went away and prayed the same thing. [40]When he came back, he again found them sleeping, because their eyes were heavy. They did not know what to say to him.

[41]Returning the third time, he said to them, "Are you still sleeping and resting? Enough! The hour has come. Look, the Son of Man is betrayed into the hands of sinners. [42]Rise! Let us go! Here comes my betrayer!"

Jesus Arrested

[43]Just as he was speaking, Judas, one of the Twelve, appeared. With him was a crowd armed with swords and clubs, sent from the chief priests, the teachers of the law, and the elders.

[44]Now the betrayer had arranged a signal with them: "The one I kiss is the man; arrest him and lead him away under guard." [45]Going at once to Jesus, Judas said, "Rabbi!" and kissed him. [46]The men seized Jesus and arrested him. [47]Then one of those standing near drew his sword and struck the servant of the high priest, cutting off his ear.

[48]"Am I leading a rebellion," said Jesus, "that you have come out with swords and clubs to capture me? [49]Every day I was with you, teaching in the temple courts, and you did not arrest me. But the Scriptures must be fulfilled." [50]Then everyone deserted him and fled.

[51]A young man, wearing nothing but a linen garment, was following Jesus. When they seized him, [52]he fled naked, leaving his garment behind.

Before the Sanhedrin

[53]They took Jesus to the high priest, and all the chief priests, elders and teachers of the law came together. [54]Peter followed him at a distance, right into the courtyard of the high priest. There he sat with the guards and warmed himself at the fire.

[55]The chief priests and the whole Sanhedrin were looking for evidence against Jesus so that they could put him to death, but they did not find any. [56]Many testified falsely against him, but

---

[a]30 Some early manuscripts do not have twice.   [b]36 Aramaic for Father

their statements did not agree.
⁵⁷Then some stood up and gave this false testimony against him: ⁵⁸"We heard him say, 'I will destroy this man-made temple and in three days will build another, not made by man.'" ⁵⁹Yet even then their testimony did not agree.

⁶⁰Then the high priest stood up before them and asked Jesus, "Are you not going to answer? What is this testimony that these men are bringing against you?" ⁶¹But Jesus remained silent and gave no answer.

Again the high priest asked him, "Are you the Christ,ᵃ the Son of the Blessed One?"

⁶²"I am," said Jesus. "And you will see the Son of Man sitting at the right hand of the Mighty One and coming on the clouds of heaven."

⁶³The high priest tore his clothes. "Why do we need any more witnesses?" he asked. ⁶⁴"You have heard the blasphemy. What do you think?"

They all condemned him as worthy of death. ⁶⁵Then some began to spit at him; they blindfolded him, struck him with their fists, and said, "Prophesy!" And the guards took him and beat him.

Peter Disowns Jesus

⁶⁶While Peter was below in the courtyard, one of the servant girls of the high priest came by. ⁶⁷When she saw Peter warming himself, she looked closely at him.

"You also were with that Nazarene, Jesus," she said.

⁶⁸But he denied it. "I don't know or understand what you're talking about," he said, and went out into the entryway.ᵇ

⁶⁹When the servant girl saw him there, she said again to those standing around, "This fellow is one of them." ⁷⁰Again he denied it.

After a little while, those standing near said to Peter, "Surely you are one of them, for you are a Galilean."

⁷¹He began to call down curses on himself, and he swore to them, "I don't know this man you're talking about."

⁷²Immediately the rooster crowed the second time.ᶜ Then Peter remembered the word Jesus had spoken to him: "Before the rooster crows twiceᵈ you will disown me three times." And he broke down and wept.

Jesus Before Pilate

15 Very early in the morning, the chief priests, with the elders, the teachers of the law and the whole Sanhedrin, reached a decision. They bound Jesus, led him away and handed him over to Pilate.

²"Are you the king of the Jews?" asked Pilate.

"Yes, it is as you say," Jesus replied.

³The chief priests accused him of many things. ⁴So again Pilate asked him, "Aren't you going to answer? See how many things they are accusing you of."

⁵But Jesus still made no reply, and Pilate was amazed.

⁶Now it was the custom at the Feast to release a prisoner whom the people requested. ⁷A man called Barabbas was in prison with the insurrectionists who had committed murder in the uprising. ⁸The crowd came up

---

ᵃ*61* Or *Messiah*   ᵇ*68* Some early manuscripts *entryway and the rooster crowed*
ᶜ*72* Some early manuscripts do not have *the second time.*   ᵈ*72* Some early manuscripts do not have *twice.*

and asked Pilate to do for them what he usually did.

9"Do you want me to release to you the king of the Jews?" asked Pilate, 10knowing it was out of envy that the chief priests had handed Jesus over to him. 11But the chief priests stirred up the crowd to have Pilate release Barabbas instead.

12"What shall I do, then, with the one you call the king of the Jews?" Pilate asked them.

13"Crucify him!" they shouted.

14"Why? What crime has he committed?" asked Pilate.

But they shouted all the louder, "Crucify him!"

15Wanting to satisfy the crowd, Pilate released Barabbas to them. He had Jesus flogged, and handed him over to be crucified.

The Soldiers Mock Jesus

16The soldiers led Jesus away into the palace (that is, the Praetorium) and called together the whole company of soldiers. 17They put a purple robe on him, then twisted together a crown of thorns and set it on him. 18And they began to call out to him, "Hail, king of the Jews!" 19Again and again they struck him on the head with a staff and spit on him. Falling on their knees, they paid homage to him. 20And when they had mocked him, they took off the purple robe and put his own clothes on him. Then they led him out to crucify him.

The Crucifixion

21A certain man from Cyrene, Simon, the father of Alexander and Rufus, was passing by on his way in from the country, and they forced him to carry the cross. 22They brought Jesus to the place called Golgotha (which

means The Place of the Skull). 23Then they offered him wine mixed with myrrh, but he did not take it. 24And they crucified him. Dividing up his clothes, they cast lots to see what each would get.

25It was the third hour when they crucified him. 26The written notice of the charge against him read: THE KING OF THE JEWS. 27They crucified two robbers with him, one on his right and one on his left.*a* 29Those who passed by hurled insults at him, shaking their heads and saying, "So! You who are going to destroy the temple and build it in three days, 30come down from the cross and save yourself!"

31In the same way the chief priests and the teachers of the law mocked him among themselves. "He saved others," they said, "but he can't save himself! 32Let this Christ,*b* this King of Israel, come down now from the cross, that we may see and believe." Those crucified with him also heaped insults on him.

The Death of Jesus

33At the sixth hour darkness came over the whole land until the ninth hour. 34And at the ninth hour Jesus cried out in a loud voice, "Eloi, Eloi, lama sabachthani?"—which means, "My God, my God, why have you forsaken me?"*c*

35When some of those standing near heard this, they said, "Listen, he's calling Elijah."

36One man ran, filled a sponge with wine vinegar, put it on a stick, and offered it to Jesus to drink. "Now leave him alone. Let's see if Elijah comes to take him down," he said.

37With a loud cry, Jesus breathed his last.

---

a27 Some manuscripts left, 28and the scripture was fulfilled which says, "He was counted with the lawless ones" (Isaiah 53:12)   b32 Or Messiah   c34 Psalm 22:1

³⁸The curtain of the temple was torn in two from top to bottom. ³⁹And when the centurion, who stood there in front of Jesus, heard his cry and*^a* saw how he died, he said, "Surely this man was the Son*^b* of God!"

⁴⁰Some women were watching from a distance. Among them were Mary Magdalene, Mary the mother of James the younger and of Joses, and Salome. ⁴¹In Galilee these women had followed him and cared for his needs. Many other women who had come up with him to Jerusalem were also there.

The Burial of Jesus

⁴²It was Preparation Day (that is, the day before the Sabbath). So as evening approached, ⁴³Joseph of Arimathea, a prominent member of the Council, who was himself waiting for the kingdom of God, went boldly to Pilate and asked for Jesus' body. ⁴⁴Pilate was surprised to hear that he was already dead. Summoning the centurion, he asked him if Jesus had already died. ⁴⁵When he learned from the centurion that it was so, he gave the body to Joseph. ⁴⁶So Joseph bought some linen cloth, took down the body, wrapped it in the linen, and placed it in a tomb cut out of rock. Then he rolled a stone against the entrance of the tomb. ⁴⁷Mary Magdalene and Mary the mother of Joses saw where he was laid.

The Resurrection

16 When the Sabbath was over, Mary Magdalene, Mary the mother of James, and Salome bought spices so that they might go to anoint Jesus' body. ²Very early on the first day of the week, just after sunrise,

they were on their way to the tomb ³and they asked each other, "Who will roll the stone away from the entrance of the tomb?"

⁴But when they looked up, they saw that the stone, which was very large, had been rolled away. ⁵As they entered the tomb, they saw a young man dressed in a white robe sitting on the right side, and they were alarmed. ⁶"Don't be alarmed," he said. "You are looking for Jesus the Nazarene, who was crucified. He has risen! He is not here. See the place where they laid him. ⁷But go, tell his disciples and Peter, 'He is going ahead of you into Galilee. There you will see him, just as he told you.'"

⁸Trembling and bewildered, the women went out and fled from the tomb. They said nothing to anyone, because they were afraid.

75
Lk 24:36-46

———————————

[The most reliable early manuscripts and other ancient witnesses do not have Mark 16:9-20.]

⁹When Jesus rose early on the first day of the week, he appeared first to Mary Magdalene, out of whom he had driven seven demons. ¹⁰She went and told those who had been with him and who were mourning and weeping. ¹¹When they heard that Jesus was alive and that she had seen him, they did not believe it.

¹²Afterward Jesus appeared in a different form to two of them while they were walking in the country. ¹³These returned and reported it to the rest; but they did not believe them either.

¹⁴Later Jesus appeared to the Eleven as they were eating; he rebuked them for their lack of

---

^a39 Some manuscripts do not have *heard his cry and.*   *^b39* Or *a son*

faith and their stubborn refusal to believe those who had seen him after he had risen.

15He said to them, "Go into all the world and preach the good news to all creation. 16Whoever believes and is baptized will be saved, but whoever does not believe will be condemned. 17And these signs will accompany those who believe: In my name they will drive out demons; they will speak in new tongues; 18they will pick up snakes with their hands; and when they drink deadly poison, it will not hurt them at all; they will place their hands on sick people, and they will get well."

19After the Lord Jesus had spoken to them, he was taken up into heaven and he sat at the right hand of God. 20Then the disciples went out and preached everywhere, and the Lord worked with them and confirmed his word by the signs that accompanied it.

Luke

Introduction

1 Many have undertaken to draw up an account of the things that have been fulfilleda among us, 2just as they were handed down to us by those who from the first were eyewitnesses and servants of the word. 3Therefore, since I myself have carefully investigated everything from the beginning, it seemed good also to me to write an orderly account for you, most excellent Theophilus, 4so that you may know the certainty of the things you have been taught.

The Birth of John the Baptist Foretold

5In the time of Herod king of Judea there was a priest named Zechariah, who belonged to the priestly division of Abijah; his wife Elizabeth was also a descendant of Aaron. 6Both of them were upright in the sight of God, observing all the Lord's commandments and regulations blamelessly. 7But they had no children, because Elizabeth was barren; and they were both well along in years.

8Once when Zechariah's division was on duty and he was serving as priest before God, 9he was chosen by lot, according to the custom of the priesthood, to go into the temple of the Lord and burn incense. 10And when the time for the burning of incense came, all the assembled worshipers were praying outside.

11Then an angel of the Lord appeared to him, standing at the right side of the altar of incense. 12When Zechariah saw him, he was startled and was gripped with fear. 13But the angel said to him: "Do not be afraid, Zechariah; your prayer has been heard. Your wife Elizabeth will bear you a son, and you are to give him the name John. 14He will be a joy and delight to you, and many will rejoice because of his birth, 15for he will be great in the sight of the Lord. He is never to take wine or other fermented drink, and he will be filled with the Holy Spirit

a1 Or been surely believed

even from birth.[a] 16Many of the people of Israel will he bring back to the Lord their God. 17And he will go on before the Lord, in the spirit and power of Elijah, to turn the hearts of the fathers to their children and the disobedient to the wisdom of the righteous—to make ready a people prepared for the Lord."

18Zechariah asked the angel, "How can I be sure of this? I am an old man and my wife is well along in years."

19The angel answered, "I am Gabriel. I stand in the presence of God, and I have been sent to speak to you and to tell you this good news. 20And now you will be silent and not able to speak until the day this happens, because you did not believe my words, which will come true at their proper time."

21Meanwhile, the people were waiting for Zechariah and wondering why he stayed so long in the temple. 22When he came out, he could not speak to them. They realized he had seen a vision in the temple, for he kept making signs to them but remained unable to speak.

23When his time of service was completed, he returned home. 24After this his wife Elizabeth became pregnant and for five months remained in seclusion. 25"The Lord has done this for me," she said. "In these days he has shown his favor and taken away my disgrace among the people."

The Birth of Jesus Foretold

26In the sixth month, God sent the angel Gabriel to Nazareth, a town in Galilee, 27to a virgin pledged to be married to a man named Joseph, a descendant of David. The virgin's name was Mary. 28The angel went to her and said, "Greetings, you who are highly favored! The Lord is with you."

29Mary was greatly troubled at his words and wondered what kind of greeting this might be. 30But the angel said to her, "Do not be afraid, Mary, you have found favor with God. 31You will be with child and give birth to a son, and you are to give him the name Jesus. 32He will be great and will be called the Son of the Most High. The Lord God will give him the throne of his father David, 33and he will reign over the house of Jacob forever; his kingdom will never end."

34"How will this be," Mary asked the angel, "since I am a virgin?"

35The angel answered, "The Holy Spirit will come upon you, and the power of the Most High will overshadow you. So the holy one to be born will be called[b] the Son of God. 36Even Elizabeth your relative is going to have a child in her old age, and she who was said to be barren is in her sixth month. 37For nothing is impossible with God."

38"I am the Lord's servant," Mary answered. "May it be to me as you have said." Then the angel left her.

Mary Visits Elizabeth

39At that time Mary got ready and hurried to a town in the hill country of Judea, 40where she entered Zechariah's home and greeted Elizabeth. 41When Elizabeth heard Mary's greeting, the baby leaped in her womb, and Elizabeth was filled with the Holy Spirit. 42In a loud voice she exclaimed: "Blessed are you among women, and blessed is the child you will bear! 43But why

---

[a]15 Or *from his mother's womb*   [b]35 Or *So the child to be born will be called holy,*

am I so favored, that the mother of my Lord should come to me? ⁴⁴As soon as the sound of your greeting reached my ears, the baby in my womb leaped for joy. ⁴⁵Blessed is she who has believed that what the Lord has said to her will be accomplished!''

Mary's Song

⁴⁶And Mary said:

"My soul glorifies the Lord
⁴⁷ and my spirit rejoices in
          God my Savior,
⁴⁸for he has been mindful
     of the humble state of his
          servant.
From now on all generations
     will call me blessed,
⁴⁹ for the Mighty One has
          done great things for
          me—
     holy is his name.
⁵⁰His mercy extends to those
          who fear him,
     from generation to
          generation.
⁵¹He has performed mighty
          deeds with his arm;
     he has scattered those who
          are proud in their inmost
          thoughts.
⁵²He has brought down rulers
          from their thrones
     but has lifted up the
          humble.
⁵³He has filled the hungry with
          good things
     but has sent the rich away
          empty.
⁵⁴He has helped his servant
          Israel,
     remembering to be merciful
⁵⁵to Abraham and his
          descendants forever,
     even as he said to our
          fathers.''

⁵⁶Mary stayed with Elizabeth for about three months and then returned home.

The Birth of John the Baptist

⁵⁷When it was time for Elizabeth to have her baby, she gave birth to a son. ⁵⁸Her neighbors and relatives heard that the Lord had shown her great mercy, and they shared her joy.

⁵⁹On the eighth day they came to circumcise the child, and they were going to name him after his father Zechariah, ⁶⁰but his mother spoke up and said, ''No! He is to be called John.''

⁶¹They said to her, ''There is no one among your relatives who has that name.''

⁶²Then they made signs to his father, to find out what he would like to name the child. ⁶³He asked for a writing tablet, and to everyone's astonishment he wrote, ''His name is John.'' ⁶⁴Immediately his mouth was opened and his tongue was loosed, and he began to speak, praising God. ⁶⁵The neighbors were all filled with awe, and throughout the hill country of Judea people were talking about all these things. ⁶⁶Everyone who heard this wondered about it, asking, ''What then is this child going to be?'' For the Lord's hand was with him.

Zechariah's Song

⁶⁷His father Zechariah was filled with the Holy Spirit and prophesied:

⁶⁸''Praise be to the Lord, the
          God of Israel,
     because he has come and
          has redeemed his
          people.
⁶⁹He has raised up a horn^d of
          salvation for us
     in the house of his servant
          David
⁷⁰(as he said through his holy
          prophets of long ago),

^d69 Horn here symbolizes strength.

71salvation from our enemies
　　and from the hand of all
　　who hate us—
72to show mercy to our fathers
　　and to remember his holy
　　covenant,
73　the oath he swore to our
　　father Abraham:
74to rescue us from the hand of
　　our enemies,
　　and to enable us to serve
　　him without fear
75　in holiness and
　　righteousness before him
　　all our days.

76And you, my child, will be
　　called a prophet of the
　　Most High;
　　for you will go on before
　　the Lord to prepare the
　　way for him,
77to give his people the
　　knowledge of
　　salvation
　　through the forgiveness of
　　their sins,
78because of the tender mercy
　　of our God,
　　by which the rising sun will
　　come to us from heaven
79to shine on those living in
　　darkness
　　and in the shadow of death,
　　to guide our feet into the path
　　of peace.''

80And the child grew and
became strong in spirit; and he
lived in the desert until he appeared publicly to Israel.

The Birth of Jesus

2 In those days Caesar Augus-
tus issued a decree that a census should be taken of the entire
Roman world. 2(This was the first
census that took place while
Quirinius was governor of Syria.)

3And everyone went to his own
town to register.

4So Joseph also went up from
the town of Nazareth in Galilee to
Judea, to Bethlehem the town of
David, because he belonged to
the house and line of David. 5He
went there to register with Mary,
who was pledged to be married
to him and was expecting a child.
6While they were there, the time
came for the baby to be born,
7and she gave birth to her firstborn, a son. She wrapped him in
cloths and placed him in a manger, because there was no room
for them in the inn.

The Shepherds and the Angels

8And there were shepherds living out in the fields nearby, keeping watch over their flocks at
night. 9An angel of the Lord appeared to them, and the glory of
the Lord shone around them,
and they were terrified. 10But the
angel said to them, ''Do not be
afraid. I bring you good news of
great joy that will be for all the
people. 11Today in the town of
David a Savior has been born
to you; he is Christ*a* the Lord.
12This will be a sign to you: You
will find a baby wrapped in
cloths and lying in a manger.''

13Suddenly a great company of
the heavenly host appeared with
the angel, praising God and saying,

14''Glory to God in the highest,
　　and on earth peace to men
　　on whom his favor
　　rests.''

15When the angels had left
them and gone into heaven, the
shepherds said to one another,
''Let's go to Bethlehem and see
this thing that has happened,

---

a11 Or Messiah. ''The Christ'' (Greek) and ''the Messiah'' (Hebrew) both mean ''the
Anointed One''; also in verse 26.

which the Lord has told us about."

16So they hurried off and found Mary and Joseph, and the baby, who was lying in the manger. 17When they had seen him, they spread the word concerning what had been told them about this child, 18and all who heard it were amazed at what the shepherds said to them. 19But Mary treasured up all these things and pondered them in her heart. 20The shepherds returned, glorifying and praising God for all the things they had heard and seen, which were just as they had been told.

Jesus Presented in the Temple

21On the eighth day, when it was time to circumcise him, he was named Jesus, the name the angel had given him before he had been conceived.

22When the time of their purification according to the Law of Moses had been completed, Joseph and Mary took him to Jerusalem to present him to the Lord 23(as it is written in the Law of the Lord, "Every firstborn male is to be consecrated to the Lord"a), 24and to offer a sacrifice in keeping with what is said in the Law of the Lord: "a pair of doves or two young pigeons."b

25Now there was a man in Jerusalem called Simeon, who was righteous and devout. He was waiting for the consolation of Israel, and the Holy Spirit was upon him. 26It had been revealed to him by the Holy Spirit that he would not die before he had seen the Lord's Christ. 27Moved by the Spirit, he went into the temple courts. When the parents brought in the child Jesus to do for him what the custom of the

Law required, 28Simeon took him in his arms and praised God, saying:

29"Sovereign Lord, as you have promised,
  you now dismissc your servant in peace.
30For my eyes have seen your salvation,
31 which you have prepared in the sight of all people,
32a light for revelation to the Gentiles
  and for glory to your people Israel."

33The child's father and mother marveled at what was said about him. 34Then Simeon blessed them and said to Mary, his mother: "This child is destined to cause the falling and rising of many in Israel, and to be a sign that will be spoken against, 35so that the thoughts of many hearts will be revealed. And a sword will pierce your own soul too."

36There was also a prophetess, Anna, the daughter of Phanuel, of the tribe of Asher. She was very old; she had lived with her husband seven years after her marriage, 37and then was a widow until she was eighty-four.d She never left the temple but worshiped night and day, fasting and praying. 38Coming up to them at that very moment, she gave thanks to God and spoke about the child to all who were looking forward to the redemption of Jerusalem.

39When Joseph and Mary had done everything required by the Law of the Lord, they returned to Galilee to their own town of Nazareth. 40And the child grew and became strong; he was filled with wisdom, and the grace of God was upon him.

a23 Exodus 13:2,12   b24 Lev. 12:8   c29 Or promised, / now dismiss   d37 Or widow for eighty-four years

The Boy Jesus at the Temple

41Every year his parents went to Jerusalem for the Feast of the Passover. 42When he was twelve years old, they went up to the Feast, according to the custom. 43After the Feast was over, while his parents were returning home, the boy Jesus stayed behind in Jerusalem, but they were unaware of it. 44Thinking he was in their company, they traveled on for a day. Then they began looking for him among their relatives and friends. 45When they did not find him, they went back to Jerusalem to look for him. 46After three days they found him in the temple courts, sitting among the teachers, listening to them and asking them questions. 47Everyone who heard him was amazed at his understanding and his answers. 48When his parents saw him, they were astonished. His mother said to him, "Son, why have you treated us like this? Your father and I have been anxiously searching for you."

49"Why were you searching for me?" he asked. "Didn't you know I had to be in my Father's house?" 50But they did not understand what he was saying to them.

51Then he went down to Nazareth with them and was obedient to them. But his mother treasured all these things in her heart. 52And Jesus grew in wisdom and stature, and in favor with God and men.

John the Baptist Prepares the Way

3 In the fifteenth year of the reign of Tiberius Caesar—when Pontius Pilate was governor of Judea, Herod tetrarch of Galilee, his brother Philip tetrarch of Iturea and Traconitis, and Lysanias tetrarch of Abilene— 2during the high priesthood of Annas and Caiaphas, the word of God came to John son of Zechariah in the desert. 3He went into all the country around the Jordan, preaching a baptism of repentance for the forgiveness of sins. 4As is written in the book of the words of Isaiah the prophet:

"A voice of one calling in the
    desert,
'Prepare the way for the Lord,
    make straight paths for him.
5Every valley shall be filled in,
    every mountain and hill
        made low.
The crooked roads shall
        become straight,
    the rough ways smooth.
6And all mankind will see
        God's salvation.' "a

7John said to the crowds coming out to be baptized by him, "You brood of vipers! Who warned you to flee from the coming wrath? 8Produce fruit in keeping with repentance. And do not begin to say to yourselves, 'We have Abraham as our father.' For I tell you that out of these stones God can raise up children for Abraham. 9The ax is already at the root of the trees, and every tree that does not produce good fruit will be cut down and thrown into the fire."

10"What should we do then?" the crowd asked.

11John answered, "The man with two tunics should share with him who has none, and the one who has food should do the same."

12Tax collectors also came to be baptized. "Teacher," they asked, "what should we do?"

13"Don't collect any more than

a6 Isaiah 40:3-5

you are required to,'' he told
them.

61
Ac 8:20

¹⁴Then some soldiers asked
him, ''And what should we do?''

He replied, ''Don't extort
money and don't accuse people
falsely—be content with your
pay.''

¹⁵The people were waiting ex-
pectantly and were all wondering in their hearts if John might
possibly be the Christ.ᵃ ¹⁶John answered them all, ''I baptize you
withᵇ water. But one more powerful than I will come, the thongs
of whose sandals I am not worthy
to untie. He will baptize you with
the Holy Spirit and with fire.
¹⁷His winnowing fork is in his
hand to clear his threshing floor
and to gather the wheat into his
barn, but he will burn up the
chaff with unquenchable fire.''
¹⁸And with many other words
John exhorted the people and
preached the good news to them.

¹⁹But when John rebuked Herod the tetrarch because of Herodias, his brother's wife, and all
the other evil things he had done,
²⁰Herod added this to them all:
He locked John up in prison.

The Baptism and Genealogy
of Jesus

²¹When all the people were being baptized, Jesus was baptized
too. And as he was praying,
heaven was opened ²²and the
Holy Spirit descended on him in
bodily form like a dove. And a
voice came from heaven: ''You
are my Son, whom I love; with
you I am well pleased.''

²³Now Jesus himself was about
thirty years old when he began
his ministry. He was the son, so
it was thought, of Joseph,

the son of Heli, ²⁴the son of
Matthat,

the son of Levi, the son of
Melki,

the son of Jannai, the son of
Joseph,

²⁵the son of Mattathias, the son
of Amos,

the son of Nahum, the son of
Esli,

the son of Naggai, ²⁶the son
of Maath,

the son of Mattathias, the son
of Semein,

the son of Josech, the son of
Joda,

²⁷the son of Joanan, the son of
Rhesa,

the son of Zerubbabel, the
son of Shealtiel,

the son of Neri, ²⁸the son of
Melki,

the son of Addi, the son of
Cosam,

the son of Elmadam, the son
of Er,

²⁹the son of Joshua, the son of
Eliezer,

the son of Jorim, the son of
Matthat,

the son of Levi, ³⁰the son of
Simeon,

the son of Judah, the son of
Joseph,

the son of Jonam, the son of
Eliakim,

³¹the son of Melea, the son of
Menna,

the son of Mattatha, the son
of Nathan,

the son of David, ³²the son of
Jesse,

the son of Obed, the son of
Boaz,

the son of Salmon,ᶜ the son of
Nahshon,

³³the son of Amminadab, the
son of Ram,ᵈ

ᵃ15 Or Messiah   ᵇ16 Or in   ᶜ32 Some early manuscripts Sala   ᵈ33 Some
manuscripts Amminadab, the son of Admin, the son of Arni; other manuscripts vary
widely.

the son of Hezron, the son of
    Perez,
the son of Judah, ³⁴the son of
    Jacob,
the son of Isaac, the son of
    Abraham,
the son of Terah, the son of
    Nahor,
³⁵the son of Serug, the son of
    Reu,
the son of Peleg, the son of
    Eber,
the son of Shelah, ³⁶the son of
    Cainan,
the son of Arphaxad, the son
    of Shem,
the son of Noah, the son of
    Lamech,
³⁷the son of Methuselah, the
    son of Enoch,
the son of Jared, the son of
    Mahalalel,
the son of Kenan, ³⁸the son of
    Enosh,
the son of Seth, the son of
    Adam,
the son of God.

The Temptation of Jesus

4 Jesus, full of the Holy Spirit,
    returned from the Jordan and
was led by the Spirit in the
desert, ²where for forty days he
was tempted by the devil. He ate
nothing during those days, and
at the end of them he was hungry.

³The devil said to him, "If you
are the Son of God, tell this stone
to become bread."

⁴Jesus answered, "It is written:
'Man does not live on bread
alone.'ᵃ"

⁵The devil led him up to a high
place and showed him in an in-
stant all the kingdoms of the
world. ⁶And he said to him, "I
will give you all their authority
and splendor, for it has been giv-
en to me, and I can give it to anyone I want to. ⁷So if you worship
me, it will all be yours."

⁸Jesus answered, "It is written:
'Worship the Lord your God and
serve him only.'ᵇ"

⁹The devil led him to Jerusalem
and had him stand on the highest
point of the temple. "If you are
the Son of God," he said, "throw
yourself down from here. ¹⁰For it
is written:

   "'He will command his angels
        concerning you
      to guard you carefully;
   ¹¹they will lift you up in their
        hands,
      so that you will not strike
        your foot against a
        stone.'ᶜ"

¹²Jesus answered, "It says: 'Do
not put the Lord your God to the
test.'ᵈ"

¹³When the devil had finished
all this tempting, he left him until
an opportune time.

Jesus Rejected at Nazareth

¹⁴Jesus returned to Galilee in
the power of the Spirit, and news
about him spread through the
whole countryside. ¹⁵He taught
in their synagogues, and everyone praised him.

¹⁶He went to Nazareth, where
he had been brought up, and on
the Sabbath day he went into the
synagogue, as was his custom.
And he stood up to read. ¹⁷The
scroll of the prophet Isaiah was
handed to him. Unrolling it, he
found the place where it is written:

¹⁸"The Spirit of the Lord is on
        me,
    because he has anointed me
        to preach good news to the
        poor.

23
Lk 19:10

ᵃ4 Deut. 8:3   ᵇ8 Deut. 6:13   ᶜ11 Psalm 91:11,12   ᵈ12 Deut. 6:16

He has sent me to proclaim
    freedom for the
    prisoners
  and recovery of sight for the
    blind,
to release the oppressed,
19 to proclaim the year of the
    Lord's favor."[a]

20Then he rolled up the scroll, gave it back to the attendant and sat down. The eyes of everyone in the synagogue were fastened on him, 21and he began by saying to them, "Today this scripture is fulfilled in your hearing."

22All spoke well of him and were amazed at the gracious words that came from his lips. "Isn't this Joseph's son?" they asked.

23Jesus said to them, "Surely you will quote this proverb to me: 'Physician, heal yourself! Do here in your hometown what we have heard that you did in Capernaum.'"

24"I tell you the truth," he continued, "no prophet is accepted in his hometown. 25I assure you that there were many widows in Israel in Elijah's time, when the sky was shut for three and a half years and there was a severe famine throughout the land. 26Yet Elijah was not sent to any of them, but to a widow in Zarephath in the region of Sidon. 27And there were many in Israel with leprosy[b] in the time of Elisha the prophet, yet not one of them was cleansed—only Naaman the Syrian."

28All the people in the synagogue were furious when they heard this. 29They got up, drove him out of the town, and took him to the brow of the hill on which the town was built, in order to throw him down the cliff.

30But he walked right through the crowd and went on his way.

Jesus Drives Out an Evil Spirit

31Then he went down to Capernaum, a town in Galilee, and on the Sabbath began to teach the people. 32They were amazed at his teaching, because his message had authority.

33In the synagogue there was a man possessed by a demon, an evil[c] spirit. He cried out at the top of his voice, 34"Ha! What do you want with us, Jesus of Nazareth? Have you come to destroy us? I know who you are—the Holy One of God!"

35"Be quiet!" Jesus said sternly. "Come out of him!" Then the demon threw the man down before them all and came out without injuring him.

36All the people were amazed and said to each other, "What is this teaching? With authority and power he gives orders to evil spirits and they come out!" 37And the news about him spread throughout the surrounding area.

Jesus Heals Many

38Jesus left the synagogue and went to the home of Simon. Now Simon's mother-in-law was suffering from a high fever, and they asked Jesus to help her. 39So he bent over her and rebuked the fever, and it left her. She got up at once and began to wait on them.

40When the sun was setting, the people brought to Jesus all who had various kinds of sickness, and laying his hands on each one, he healed them. 41More-

---

[a]19 Isaiah 61:1,2 [b]27 The Greek word was used for various diseases affecting the skin—not necessarily leprosy. [c]33 Greek *unclean*; also in verse 36

over, demons came out of many people, shouting, "You are the Son of God!" But he rebuked them and would not allow them to speak, because they knew he was the Christ.*

42At daybreak Jesus went out to a solitary place. The people were looking for him and when they came to where he was, they tried to keep him from leaving them. 43But he said, "I must preach the good news of the kingdom of God to the other towns also, because that is why I was sent." 44And he kept on preaching in the synagogues of Judea.b

The Calling of the First Disciples

5 One day as Jesus was standing by the Lake of Gennesaret,c with the people crowding around him and listening to the word of God, 2he saw at the water's edge two boats, left there by the fishermen, who were washing their nets. 3He got into one of the boats, the one belonging to Simon, and asked him to put out a little from shore. Then he sat down and taught the people from the boat.

4When he had finished speaking, he said to Simon, "Put out into deep water, and let downd the nets for a catch."

5Simon answered, "Master, we've worked hard all night and haven't caught anything. But because you say so, I will let down the nets."

6When they had done so, they caught such a large number of fish that their nets began to break. 7So they signaled their partners in the other boat to come and help them, and they came

and filled both boats so full that they began to sink.

8When Simon Peter saw this, he fell at Jesus' knees and said, "Go away from me, Lord; I am a sinful man!" 9For he and all his companions were astonished at the catch of fish they had taken, 10and so were James and John, the sons of Zebedee, Simon's partners.

Then Jesus said to Simon, "Don't be afraid; from now on you will catch men." 11So they pulled their boats up on shore, left everything and followed him.

The Man With Leprosy

12While Jesus was in one of the towns, a man came along who was covered with leprosy.e When he saw Jesus, he fell with his face to the ground and begged him, "Lord, if you are willing, you can make me clean."

13Jesus reached out his hand and touched the man. "I am willing," he said. "Be clean!" And immediately the leprosy left him.

14Then Jesus ordered him, "Don't tell anyone, but go, show yourself to the priest and offer the sacrifices that Moses commanded for your cleansing, as a testimony to them."

15Yet the news about him spread all the more, so that crowds of people came to hear him and to be healed of their sicknesses. 16But Jesus often withdrew to lonely places and prayed.

Jesus Heals a Paralytic

17One day as he was teaching, Pharisees and teachers of the law, who had come from every

---

a41 Or Messiah   b44 Or the land of the Jews; some manuscripts Galilee   c1 That is, Sea of Galilee   d4 The Greek verb is plural.   e12 The Greek word was used for various diseases affecting the skin—not necessarily leprosy.

village of Galilee and from Judea and Jerusalem, were sitting there. And the power of the Lord was present for him to heal the sick. [18]Some men came carrying a paralytic on a mat and tried to take him into the house to lay him before Jesus. [19]When they could not find a way to do this because of the crowd, they went up on the roof and lowered him on his mat through the tiles into the middle of the crowd, right in front of Jesus.

[20]When Jesus saw their faith, he said, "Friend, your sins are forgiven."

[21]The Pharisees and the teachers of the law began thinking to themselves, "Who is this fellow who speaks blasphemy? Who can forgive sins but God alone?"

[22]Jesus knew what they were thinking and asked, "Why are you thinking these things in your hearts? [23]Which is easier: to say, 'Your sins are forgiven,' or to say, 'Get up and walk'? [24]But that you may know that the Son of Man has authority on earth to forgive sins. . . ." He said to the paralyzed man, "I tell you, get up, take your mat and go home." [25]Immediately he stood up in front of them, took what he had been lying on and went home praising God. [26]Everyone was amazed and gave praise to God. They were filled with awe and said, "We have seen remarkable things today."

The Calling of Levi

[27]After this, Jesus went out and saw a tax collector by the name of Levi sitting at his tax booth. "Follow me," Jesus said to him, [28]and Levi got up, left everything and followed him.

[29]Then Levi held a great banquet for Jesus at his house, and a large crowd of tax collectors and others were eating with them. [30]But the Pharisees and the teachers of the law who belonged to their sect complained to his disciples, "Why do you eat and drink with tax collectors and 'sinners'?"

[31]Jesus answered them, "It is not the healthy who need a doctor, but the sick. [32]I have not come to call the righteous, but sinners to repentance."

Jesus Questioned About Fasting

[33]They said to him, "John's disciples often fast and pray, and so do the disciples of the Pharisees, but yours go on eating and drinking."

[34]Jesus answered, "Can you make the guests of the bridegroom fast while he is with them? [35]But the time will come when the bridegroom will be taken from them; in those days they will fast."

[36]He told them this parable: "No one tears a patch from a new garment and sews it on an old one. If he does, he will have torn the new garment, and the patch from the new will not match the old. [37]And no one pours new wine into old wineskins. If he does, the new wine will burst the skins, the wine will run out and the wineskins will be ruined. [38]No, new wine must be poured into new wineskins. [39]And no one after drinking old wine wants the new, for he says, 'The old is better.'"

Lord of the Sabbath

6 One Sabbath Jesus was going through the grainfields, and his disciples began to pick some heads of grain, rub them in their hands and eat the kernels. [2]Some of the Pharisees asked, "Why are you doing what is unlawful on the Sabbath?"

[3]Jesus answered them, "Have you never read what David did when he and his companions were hungry? [4]He entered the house of God, and taking the consecrated bread, he ate what is lawful only for priests to eat. And he also gave some to his companions." [5]Then Jesus said to them, "The Son of Man is Lord of the Sabbath."

[6]On another Sabbath he went into the synagogue and was teaching, and a man was there whose right hand was shriveled. [7]The Pharisees and the teachers of the law were looking for a reason to accuse Jesus, so they watched him closely to see if he would heal on the Sabbath. [8]But Jesus knew what they were thinking and said to the man with the shriveled hand, "Get up and stand in front of everyone." So he got up and stood there.

[9]Then Jesus said to them, "I ask you, which is lawful on the Sabbath: to do good or to do evil, to save life or to destroy it?"

[10]He looked around at them all, and then said to the man, "Stretch out your hand." He did so, and his hand was completely restored. [11]But they were furious and began to discuss with one another what they might do to Jesus.

The Twelve Apostles

[12]One of those days Jesus went out to a mountainside to pray, and spent the night praying to God. [13]When morning came, he called his disciples to him and chose twelve of them, whom he also designated apostles: [14]Simon (whom he named Peter), his brother Andrew, James, John, Philip, Bartholomew, [15]Matthew, Thomas, James son of Alphaeus, Simon who was called the Zealot, [16]Judas son of James, and Judas Iscariot, who became a traitor.

Blessings and Woes

[17]He went down with them and stood on a level place. A large crowd of his disciples was there and a great number of people from all over Judea, from Jerusalem, and from the coast of Tyre and Sidon, [18]who had come to hear him and to be healed of their diseases. Those troubled by evil[a] spirits were cured, [19]and the people all tried to touch him, because power was coming from him and healing them all.

[20]Looking at his disciples, he said:

"Blessed are you who are
        poor,
    for yours is the kingdom of
        God.
[21]Blessed are you who hunger
        now,
    for you will be satisfied.
Blessed are you who weep
        now,
    for you will laugh.
[22]Blessed are you when men
        hate you,
    when they exclude you and
        insult you
    and reject your name as
        evil,
        because of the Son of
            Man.

[23]"Rejoice in that day and leap for joy, because great is your reward in heaven. For that is how their fathers treated the prophets.

[24]"But woe to you who are rich,
    for you have already
        received your comfort.
[25]Woe to you who are well fed
        now,

---

[a]18 Greek *unclean*

for you will go hungry.
Woe to you who laugh now,
   for you will mourn and
   weep.
26Woe to you when all men
   speak well of you,
   for that is how their fathers
      treated the false
      prophets.

Love for Enemies

55
Jn 13:35 27"But I tell you who hear me: Love your enemies, do good to those who hate you, 28bless those who curse you, pray for those who mistreat you. 29If someone strikes you on one cheek, turn to him the other also. If someone takes your cloak, do not stop him from taking your tunic. 30Give to everyone who asks you, and if anyone takes what belongs to you, do not demand it back. 31Do to others as you would have them do to you.

32"If you love those who love you, what credit is that to you? Even 'sinners' love those who love them. 33And if you do good to those who are good to you, what credit is that to you? Even 'sinners' do that. 34And if you lend to those from whom you expect repayment, what credit is that to you? Even 'sinners' lend to 'sinners,' expecting to be repaid in full. 35But love your enemies, do good to them, and lend to them without expecting to get anything back. Then your reward will be great, and you will be sons of the Most High, because he is kind to the ungrateful and wicked. 36Be merciful, just as your Father is merciful.

Judging Others

37"Do not judge, and you will not be judged. Do not condemn, and you will not be condemned. Forgive, and you will be forgiven. 38Give, and it will be given

to you. A good measure, pressed down, shaken together and running over, will be poured into your lap. For with the measure you use, it will be measured to you."

39He also told them this parable: "Can a blind man lead a blind man? Will they not both fall into a pit? 40A student is not above his teacher, but everyone who is fully trained will be like his teacher.

41"Why do you look at the speck of sawdust in your brother's eye and pay no attention to the plank in your own eye? 42How can you say to your brother, 'Brother, let me take the speck out of your eye,' when you yourself fail to see the plank in your own eye? You hypocrite, first take the plank out of your eye, and then you will see clearly to remove the speck from your brother's eye.

A Tree and Its Fruit

43"No good tree bears bad fruit, nor does a bad tree bear good fruit. 44Each tree is recognized by its own fruit. People do not pick figs from thornbushes, or grapes from briers. 45The good man brings good things out of the good stored up in his heart, and the evil man brings evil things out of the evil stored up in his heart. For out of the overflow of his heart his mouth speaks.

The Wise and Foolish Builders

46"Why do you call me, 'Lord, Lord,' and do not do what I say? 47I will show you what he is like who comes to me and hears my words and puts them into practice. 48He is like a man building a house, who dug down deep and laid the foundation on rock. When a flood came, the torrent struck that house but could not shake it, because it was well built. 49But the one who hears my words and does not put them into practice is like a man who built a house on the ground without a foundation. The moment the torrent struck that house, it collapsed and its destruction was complete."

The Faith of the Centurion

7 When Jesus had finished saying all this in the hearing of the people, he entered Capernaum. 2There a centurion's servant, whom his master valued highly, was sick and about to die. 3The centurion heard of Jesus and sent some elders of the Jews to him, asking him to come and heal his servant. 4When they came to Jesus, they pleaded earnestly with him, "This man deserves to have you do this, 5because he loves our nation and has built our synagogue." 6So Jesus went with them.

He was not far from the house when the centurion sent friends to say to him: "Lord, don't trouble yourself, for I do not deserve to have you come under my roof. 7That is why I did not even consider myself worthy to come to you. But say the word, and my servant will be healed. 8For I myself am a man under authority, with soldiers under me. I tell this one, 'Go,' and he goes; and that one, 'Come,' and he comes. I say to my servant, 'Do this,' and he does it."

9When Jesus heard this, he was amazed at him, and turning to the crowd following him, he said, "I tell you, I have not found such great faith even in Israel." 10Then the men who had been sent returned to the house and found the servant well.

Jesus Raises a Widow's Son

11Soon afterward, Jesus went to a town called Nain, and his disciples and a large crowd went along with him. 12As he approached the town gate, a dead person was being carried out— the only son of his mother, and she was a widow. And a large crowd from the town was with her. 13When the Lord saw her, his heart went out to her and he said, "Don't cry."

14Then he went up and touched the coffin, and those carrying it stood still. He said, "Young man, I say to you, get up!" 15The dead man sat up and began to talk, and Jesus gave him back to his mother.

16They were all filled with awe and praised God. "A great prophet has appeared among us," they said. "God has come to help his people." 17This news about Jesus spread throughout Judea[a] and the surrounding country.

Jesus and John the Baptist

18John's disciples told him about all these things. Calling two of them, 19he sent them to the Lord to ask, "Are you the one who was to come, or should we expect someone else?"

20When the men came to Jesus, they said, "John the Baptist sent us to you to ask, 'Are you the one who was to come, or should we expect someone else?'"

21At that very time Jesus cured many who had diseases, sicknesses and evil spirits, and gave sight to many who were blind. 22So he replied to the messengers, "Go back and report to John what you have seen and heard: The blind receive sight, the lame

a17 Or the land of the Jews

walk, those who have leprosy[a] are cured, the deaf hear, the dead are raised, and the good news is preached to the poor. 23Blessed is the man who does not fall away on account of me.''

24After John's messengers left, Jesus began to speak to the crowd about John: ''What did you go out into the desert to see? A reed swayed by the wind? 25If not, what did you go out to see? A man dressed in fine clothes? No, those who wear expensive clothes and indulge in luxury are in palaces. 26But what did you go out to see? A prophet? Yes, I tell you, and more than a prophet. 27This is the one about whom it is written:

'' 'I will send my messenger
    ahead of you,
who will prepare your way
    before you.'[b]

28I tell you, among those born of women there is no one greater than John; yet the one who is least in the kingdom of God is greater than he.''

29(All the people, even the tax collectors, when they heard Jesus' words, acknowledged that God's way was right, because they had been baptized by John. 30But the Pharisees and experts in the law rejected God's purpose for themselves, because they had not been baptized by John.)

31''To what, then, can I compare the people of this generation? What are they like? 32They are like children sitting in the marketplace and calling out to each other:

'' 'We played the flute for you,
    and you did not dance;

we sang a dirge,
    and you did not cry.'

33For John the Baptist came neither eating bread nor drinking wine, and you say, 'He has a demon.' 34The Son of Man came eating and drinking, and you say, 'Here is a glutton and a drunkard, a friend of tax collectors and ''sinners.' ' 35But wisdom is proved right by all her children.''

Jesus Anointed by a Sinful Woman

36Now one of the Pharisees invited Jesus to have dinner with him, so he went to the Pharisee's house and reclined at the table. 37When a woman who had lived a sinful life in that town learned that Jesus was eating at the Pharisee's house, she brought an alabaster jar of perfume, 38and as she stood behind him at his feet weeping, she began to wet his feet with her tears. Then she wiped them with her hair, kissed them and poured perfume on them.

39When the Pharisee who had invited Jesus saw this, he said to himself, ''If this man were a prophet, he would know who is touching him and what kind of woman she is—that she is a sinner.''

40Jesus answered him, ''Simon, I have something to tell you.''

''Tell me, teacher,'' he said.

41''Two men owed money to a certain moneylender. One owed him five hundred denarii,[c] and the other fifty. 42Neither of them had the money to pay him back, so he canceled the debts of both. Now which of them will love him more?''

43Simon replied, ''I suppose the

---

[a]22 The Greek word was used for various diseases affecting the skin—not necessarily leprosy.   [b]27 Mal. 3:1   [c]41 A denarius was a coin worth about a day's wages.

one who had the bigger debt canceled."

"You have judged correctly," Jesus said.

44Then he turned toward the woman and said to Simon, "Do you see this woman? I came into your house. You did not give me any water for my feet, but she wet my feet with her tears and wiped them with her hair. 45You did not give me a kiss, but this woman, from the time I entered, has not stopped kissing my feet. 46You did not put oil on my head, but she has poured perfume on my feet. 47Therefore, I tell you, her many sins have been forgiven—for she loved much. But he who has been forgiven little loves little."

48Then Jesus said to her, "Your sins are forgiven."

49The other guests began to say among themselves, "Who is this who even forgives sins?"

50Jesus said to the woman, "Your faith has saved you; go in peace."

The Parable of the Sower

8 After this, Jesus traveled about from one town and village to another, proclaiming the good news of the kingdom of God. The Twelve were with him, 2and also some women who had been cured of evil spirits and diseases: Mary (called Magdalene) from whom seven demons had come out; 3Joanna the wife of Cuza, the manager of Herod's household; Susanna; and many others. These women were helping to support them out of their own means.

4While a large crowd was gathering and people were coming to Jesus from town after town, he told this parable: 5"A farmer went out to sow his seed. As he was scattering the seed, some fell along the path; it was trampled on, and the birds of the air ate it up. 6Some fell on rock, and when it came up, the plants withered because they had no moisture. 7Other seed fell among thorns, which grew up with it and choked the plants. 8Still other seed fell on good soil. It came up and yielded a crop, a hundred times more than was sown."

When he said this, he called out, "He who has ears to hear, let him hear."

9His disciples asked him what this parable meant. 10He said, "The knowledge of the secrets of the kingdom of God has been given to you, but to others I speak in parables, so that,

" 'though seeing, they may
     not see;
   though hearing, they may
     not understand.'[a]

11"This is the meaning of the parable: The seed is the word of God. 12Those along the path are the ones who hear, and then the devil comes and takes away the word from their hearts, so that they may not believe and be saved. 13Those on the rock are the ones who receive the word with joy when they hear it, but they have no root. They believe for a while, but in the time of testing they fall away. 14The seed that fell among thorns stands for those who hear, but as they go on their way they are choked by life's worries, riches and pleasures, and they do not mature. 15But the seed on good soil stands for those with a noble and good heart, who hear the word, retain it, and by persevering produce a crop.

A Lamp on a Stand

16"No one lights a lamp and

[a]10 Isaiah 6:9

hides it in a jar or puts it under a bed. Instead, he puts it on a stand, so that those who come in can see the light. ¹⁷For there is nothing hidden that will not be disclosed, and nothing concealed that will not be known or brought out into the open. ¹⁸Therefore consider carefully how you listen. Whoever has will be given more; whoever does not have, even what he thinks he has will be taken from him.''

Jesus' Mother and Brothers

¹⁹Now Jesus' mother and brothers came to see him, but they were not able to get near him because of the crowd. ²⁰Someone told him, ''Your mother and brothers are standing outside, wanting to see you.''

²¹He replied, ''My mother and brothers are those who hear God's word and put it into practice.''

Jesus Calms the Storm

²²One day Jesus said to his disciples, ''Let's go over to the other side of the lake.'' So they got into a boat and set out. ²³As they sailed, he fell asleep. A squall came down on the lake, so that the boat was being swamped, and they were in great danger.

²⁴The disciples went and woke him, saying, ''Master, Master, we're going to drown!''

He got up and rebuked the wind and the raging waters; the storm subsided, and all was calm. ²⁵''Where is your faith?'' he asked his disciples.

In fear and amazement they asked one another, ''Who is this? He commands even the winds and the water, and they obey him.''

The Healing of a Demon-possessed Man

²⁶They sailed to the region of the Gerasenes,ᵃ which is across the lake from Galilee. ²⁷When Jesus stepped ashore, he was met by a demon-possessed man from the town. For a long time this man had not worn clothes or lived in a house, but had lived in the tombs. ²⁸When he saw Jesus, he cried out and fell at his feet, shouting at the top of his voice, ''What do you want with me, Jesus, Son of the Most High God? I beg you, don't torture me!'' ²⁹For Jesus had commanded the evilᵇ spirit to come out of the man. Many times it had seized him, and though he was chained hand and foot and kept under guard, he had broken his chains and had been driven by the demon into solitary places.

³⁰Jesus asked him, ''What is your name?''

''Legion,'' he replied, because many demons had gone into him. ³¹And they begged him repeatedly not to order them to go into the Abyss.

³²A large herd of pigs was feeding there on the hillside. The demons begged Jesus to let them go into them, and he gave them permission. ³³When the demons came out of the man, they went into the pigs, and the herd rushed down the steep bank into the lake and was drowned.

³⁴When those tending the pigs saw what had happened, they ran off and reported this in the town and countryside, ³⁵and the people went out to see what had happened. When they came to Jesus, they found the man from whom the demons had gone out,

---

ᵃ26 Some manuscripts *Gadarenes*; other manuscripts *Gergesenes*; also in verse 37
ᵇ29 Greek *unclean*

sitting at Jesus' feet, dressed and in his right mind; and they were afraid. 36Those who had seen it told the people how the demon-possessed man had been cured. 37Then all the people of the region of the Gerasenes asked Jesus to leave them, because they were overcome with fear. So he got into the boat and left.

38The man from whom the demons had gone out begged to go with him, but Jesus sent him away, saying, 39"Return home and tell how much God has done for you." So the man went away and told all over town how much Jesus had done for him.

A Dead Girl and a Sick Woman

40Now when Jesus returned, a crowd welcomed him, for they were all expecting him. 41Then a man named Jairus, a ruler of the synagogue, came and fell at Jesus' feet, pleading with him to come to his house 42because his only daughter, a girl of about twelve, was dying.

As Jesus was on his way, the crowds almost crushed him. 43And a woman was there who had been subject to bleeding for twelve years,*a* but no one could heal her. 44She came up behind him and touched the edge of his cloak, and immediately her bleeding stopped.

45"Who touched me?" Jesus asked.

When they all denied it, Peter said, "Master, the people are crowding and pressing against you."

46But Jesus said, "Someone touched me; I know that power has gone out from me."

47Then the woman, seeing that she could not go unnoticed, came

trembling and fell at his feet. In the presence of all the people, she told why she had touched him and how she had been instantly healed. 48Then he said to her, "Daughter, your faith has healed you. Go in peace."

49While Jesus was still speaking, someone came from the house of Jairus, the synagogue ruler. "Your daughter is dead," he said. "Don't bother the teacher any more."

50Hearing this, Jesus said to Jairus, "Don't be afraid; just believe, and she will be healed."

51When he arrived at the house of Jairus, he did not let anyone go in with him except Peter, John and James, and the child's father and mother. 52Meanwhile, all the people were wailing and mourning for her. "Stop wailing," Jesus said. "She is not dead but asleep."

53They laughed at him, knowing that she was dead. 54But he took her by the hand and said, "My child, get up!" 55Her spirit returned, and at once she stood up. Then Jesus told them to give her something to eat. 56Her parents were astonished, but he ordered them not to tell anyone what had happened.

Jesus Sends Out the Twelve

9 When Jesus had called the Twelve together, he gave them power and authority to drive out all demons and to cure diseases, 2and he sent them out to preach the kingdom of God and to heal the sick. 3He told them: "Take nothing for the journey—no staff, no bag, no bread, no money, no extra tunic. 4Whatever house you enter, stay there until you leave that town. 5If people do not welcome you,

---

a43 Many manuscripts years, and she had spent all she had on doctors

shake the dust off your feet when you leave their town, as a testimony against them." ⁶So they set out and went from village to village, preaching the gospel and healing people everywhere.

32
Ac 2:22-24

⁷Now Herod the tetrarch heard about all that was going on. And he was perplexed, because some were saying that John had been raised from the dead, ⁸others that Elijah had appeared, and still others that one of the prophets of long ago had come back to life. ⁹But Herod said, "I beheaded John. Who, then, is this I hear such things about?" And he tried to see him.

Jesus Feeds the Five Thousand

¹⁰When the apostles returned, they reported to Jesus what they had done. Then he took them with him and they withdrew by themselves to a town called Bethsaida, ¹¹but the crowds learned about it and followed him. He welcomed them and spoke to them about the kingdom of God, and healed those who needed healing.

¹²Late in the afternoon the Twelve came to him and said, "Send the crowd away so they can go to the surrounding villages and countryside and find food and lodging, because we are in a remote place here."

¹³He replied, "You give them something to eat."

They answered, "We have only five loaves of bread and two fish—unless we go and buy food for all this crowd." ¹⁴(About five thousand men were there.)

But he said to his disciples, "Have them sit down in groups of about fifty each." ¹⁵The disciples did so, and everybody sat down. ¹⁶Taking the five loaves

and the two fish and looking up to heaven, he gave thanks and broke them. Then he gave them to the disciples to set before the people. ¹⁷They all ate and were satisfied, and the disciples picked up twelve basketfuls of broken pieces that were left over.

Peter's Confession of Christ

¹⁸Once when Jesus was praying in private and his disciples were with him, he asked them, "Who do the crowds say I am?"

¹⁹They replied, "Some say John the Baptist; others say Elijah; and still others, that one of the prophets of long ago has come back to life."

²⁰"But what about you?" he asked. "Who do you say I am?"

Peter answered, "The Christ^a of God."

²¹Jesus strictly warned them not to tell this to anyone. ²²And he said, "The Son of Man must suffer many things and be rejected by the elders, chief priests and teachers of the law, and he must be killed and on the third day be raised to life."

²³Then he said to them all: "If anyone would come after me, he must deny himself and take up his cross daily and follow me. ²⁴For whoever wants to save his life will lose it, but whoever loses his life for me will save it. ²⁵What good is it for a man to gain the whole world, and yet lose or forfeit his very self? ²⁶If anyone is ashamed of me and my words, the Son of Man will be ashamed of him when he comes in his glory and in the glory of the Father and of the holy angels. ²⁷I tell you the truth, some who are standing here will not taste death before they see the kingdom of God."

84
1Co 10:24

^a20 Or *Messiah*

The Transfiguration

28About eight days after Jesus said this, he took Peter, John and James with him and went up onto a mountain to pray. 29As he was praying, the appearance of his face changed, and his clothes became as bright as a flash of lightning. 30Two men, Moses and Elijah, 31appeared in glorious splendor, talking with Jesus. They spoke about his departure, which he was about to bring to fulfillment at Jerusalem. 32Peter and his companions were very sleepy, but when they became fully awake, they saw his glory and the two men standing with him. 33As the men were leaving Jesus, Peter said to him, "Master, it is good for us to be here. Let us put up three shelters—one for you, one for Moses and one for Elijah." (He did not know what he was saying.)

34While he was speaking, a cloud appeared and enveloped them, and they were afraid as they entered the cloud. 35A voice came from the cloud, saying, "This is my Son, whom I have chosen; listen to him." 36When the voice had spoken, they found that Jesus was alone. The disciples kept this to themselves, and told no one at that time what they had seen.

The Healing of a Boy With an Evil Spirit

37The next day, when they came down from the mountain, a large crowd met him. 38A man in the crowd called out, "Teacher, I beg you to look at my son, for he is my only child. 39A spirit seizes him and he suddenly screams; it throws him into convulsions so that he foams at the mouth. It scarcely ever leaves him and is destroying him. 40I begged your disciples to drive it out, but they could not."

41"O unbelieving and perverse generation," Jesus replied, "how long shall I stay with you and put up with you? Bring your son here."

42Even while the boy was coming, the demon threw him to the ground in a convulsion. But Jesus rebuked the evil[a] spirit, healed the boy and gave him back to his father. 43And they were all amazed at the greatness of God.

While everyone was marveling at all that Jesus did, he said to his disciples, 44"Listen carefully to what I am about to tell you: The Son of Man is going to be betrayed into the hands of men." 45But they did not understand what this meant. It was hidden from them, so that they did not grasp it, and they were afraid to ask him about it.

Who Will Be the Greatest?

46An argument started among the disciples as to which of them would be the greatest. 47Jesus, knowing their thoughts, took a little child and had him stand beside him. 48Then he said to them, "Whoever welcomes this little child in my name welcomes me; and whoever welcomes me welcomes the one who sent me. For he who is least among you all— he is the greatest."

49"Master," said John, "we saw a man driving out demons in your name and we tried to stop him, because he is not one of us."

50"Do not stop him," Jesus said, "for whoever is not against you is for you."

Samaritan Opposition

51As the time approached for

---

a42 Greek unclean

him to be taken up to heaven, Jesus resolutely set out for Jerusalem. [52]And he sent messengers on ahead, who went into a Samaritan village to get things ready for him; [53]but the people there did not welcome him, because he was heading for Jerusalem. [54]When the disciples James and John saw this, they asked, "Lord, do you want us to call fire down from heaven to destroy them[a]?" [55]But Jesus turned and rebuked them, [56]and[b] they went to another village.

The Cost of Following Jesus

[57]As they were walking along the road, a man said to him, "I will follow you wherever you go."

[58]Jesus replied, "Foxes have holes and birds of the air have nests, but the Son of Man has no place to lay his head."

[59]He said to another man, "Follow me."

But the man replied, "Lord, first let me go and bury my father."

[60]Jesus said to him, "Let the dead bury their own dead, but you go and proclaim the kingdom of God."

[61]Still another said, "I will follow you, Lord; but first let me go back and say good-by to my family."

[62]Jesus replied, "No one who puts his hand to the plow and looks back is fit for service in the kingdom of God."

Jesus Sends Out the Seventy-two

10 After this the Lord appointed seventy-two[c] others and sent them two by two ahead of him to every town and place where he was about to go. [2]He told them, "The harvest is plentiful, but the workers are few. Ask the Lord of the harvest, therefore, to send out workers into his harvest field. [3]Go! I am sending you out like lambs among wolves. [4]Do not take a purse or bag or sandals; and do not greet anyone on the road.

[5]"When you enter a house, first say, 'Peace to this house.' [6]If a man of peace is there, your peace will rest on him; if not, it will return to you. [7]Stay in that house, eating and drinking whatever they give you, for the worker deserves his wages. Do not move around from house to house.

[8]"When you enter a town and are welcomed, eat what is set before you. [9]Heal the sick who are there and tell them, 'The kingdom of God is near you.' [10]But when you enter a town and are not welcomed, go into its streets and say, [11]'Even the dust of your town that sticks to our feet we wipe off against you. Yet be sure of this: The kingdom of God is near.' [12]I tell you, it will be more bearable on that day for Sodom than for that town.

[13]"Woe to you, Korazin! Woe to you, Bethsaida! For if the miracles that were performed in you had been performed in Tyre and Sidon, they would have repented long ago, sitting in sackcloth and ashes. [14]But it will be more bearable for Tyre and Sidon at the judgment than for you. [15]And you, Capernaum, will you be lifted up to the skies? No, you will go down to the depths.[d]

---

[a]54 Some manuscripts them, even as Elijah did [b]55,56 Some manuscripts them. And he said, "You do not know what kind of spirit you are of, for the Son of Man did not come to destroy men's lives, but to save them." [56]And verse 17 [c]15 Greek Hades [c]1 Some manuscripts seventy; also in

¹⁶"He who listens to you listens to me; he who rejects you rejects me; but he who rejects me rejects him who sent me."

¹⁷The seventy-two returned with joy and said, "Lord, even the demons submit to us in your name."

¹⁸He replied, "I saw Satan fall like lightning from heaven. ¹⁹I have given you authority to trample on snakes and scorpions and to overcome all the power of the enemy; nothing will harm you. ²⁰However, do not rejoice that the spirits submit to you, but rejoice that your names are written in heaven."

²¹At that time Jesus, full of joy through the Holy Spirit, said, "I praise you, Father, Lord of heaven and earth, because you have hidden these things from the wise and learned, and revealed them to little children. Yes, Father, for this was your good pleasure.

²²"All things have been committed to me by my Father. No one knows who the Son is except the Father, and no one knows who the Father is except the Son and those to whom the Son chooses to reveal him."

²³Then he turned to his disciples and said privately, "Blessed are the eyes that see what you see. ²⁴For I tell you that many prophets and kings wanted to see what you see but did not see it, and to hear what you hear but did not hear it."

The Parable of the Good Samaritan

²⁵On one occasion an expert in the law stood up to test Jesus. "Teacher," he asked, "what must I do to inherit eternal life?"

²⁶"What is written in the Law?" he replied. "How do you read it?"

²⁷He answered: " 'Love the Lord your God with all your heart and with all your soul and with all your strength and with all your mind'ᵈ; and, 'Love your neighbor as yourself.'ᵉ"

60
1Co 3:5-9

²⁸"You have answered correctly," Jesus replied. "Do this and you will live."

²⁹But he wanted to justify himself, so he asked Jesus, "And who is my neighbor?"

³⁰In reply Jesus said: "A man was going down from Jerusalem to Jericho, when he fell into the hands of robbers. They stripped him of his clothes, beat him and went away, leaving him half dead. ³¹A priest happened to be going down the same road, and when he saw the man, he passed by on the other side. ³²So too, a Levite, when he came to the place and saw him, passed by on the other side. ³³But a Samaritan, as he traveled, came where the man was; and when he saw him, he took pity on him. ³⁴He went to him and bandaged his wounds, pouring on oil and wine. Then he put the man on his own donkey, took him to an inn and took care of him. ³⁵The next day he took out two silver coinsˡ and gave them to the innkeeper. 'Look after him,' he said, 'and when I return, I will reimburse you for any extra expense you may have.'

³⁶"Which of these three do you think was a neighbor to the man who fell into the hands of robbers?"

³⁷The expert in the law replied, "The one who had mercy on him."

Jesus told him, "Go and do likewise."

ᵈ27 Deut. 6:5   ᵉ27 Lev. 19:18   ˡ35 Greek two denarii

At the Home of Martha and Mary

³⁸As Jesus and his disciples were on their way, he came to a village where a woman named Martha opened her home to him. ³⁹She had a sister called Mary, who sat at the Lord's feet listening to what he said. ⁴⁰But Martha was distracted by all the preparations that had to be made. She came to him and asked, "Lord, don't you care that my sister has left me to do the work by myself? Tell her to help me!"

⁴¹"Martha, Martha," the Lord answered, "you are worried and upset about many things, ⁴²but only one thing is needed.ᵃ Mary has chosen what is better, and it will not be taken away from her."

Jesus' Teaching on Prayer

11 One day Jesus was praying in a certain place. When he finished, one of his disciples said to him, "Lord, teach us to pray, just as John taught his disciples."

²He said to them, "When you pray, say:

" 'Father,ᵇ
hallowed be your name,
your kingdom come.ᶜ
³Give us each day our daily
bread.
⁴Forgive us our sins,
for we also forgive everyone
who sins against us.ᵈ
And lead us not into
temptation.ᵉ' "

⁵Then he said to them, "Suppose one of you has a friend, and he goes to him at midnight and says, 'Friend, lend me three loaves of bread, ⁶because a friend of mine on a journey has come to me, and I have nothing to set before him.'

⁷"Then the one inside answers, 'Don't bother me. The door is already locked, and my children are with me in bed. I can't get up and give you anything.' ⁸I tell you, though he will not get up and give him the bread because he is his friend, yet because of the man's boldnessᶠ he will get up and give him as much as he needs.

⁹"So I say to you: Ask and it will be given to you; seek and you will find; knock and the door will be opened to you. ¹⁰For everyone who asks receives; he who seeks finds; and to him who knocks, the door will be opened.

¹¹"Which of you fathers, if your son asks forᵍ a fish, will give him a snake instead? ¹²Or if he asks for an egg, will give him a scorpion? ¹³If you then, though you are evil, know how to give good gifts to your children, how much more will your Father in heaven give the Holy Spirit to those who ask him!"

Jesus and Beelzebub

¹⁴Jesus was driving out a demon that was mute. When the demon left, the man who had been mute spoke, and the crowd was amazed. ¹⁵But some of them said, "By Beelzebub,ʰ the prince of demons, he is driving out demons." ¹⁶Others tested him by asking for a sign from heaven.

¹⁷Jesus knew their thoughts and said to them: "Any kingdom divided against itself will be

ᵃ42 Some manuscripts but few things are needed—or only one   ᵇ2 Some manuscripts Our Father in heaven   ᶜ2 Some manuscripts come. May your will be done on earth as it is in heaven.   ᵈ4 Greek everyone who is indebted to us   ᵉ4 Some manuscripts temptation but deliver us from the evil one   ᶠ8 Or persistence   ᵍ11 Some manuscripts for bread, will give him a stone; or if he asks for   ʰ15 Greek Beezeboul or Beelzeboul; also in verses 18 and 19

ruined, and a house divided against itself will fall. [18]If Satan is divided against himself, how can his kingdom stand? I say this because you claim that I drive out demons by Beelzebub. [19]Now if I drive out demons by Beelzebub, by whom do your followers drive them out? So then, they will be your judges. [20]But if I drive out demons by the finger of God, then the kingdom of God has come to you.

[21]"When a strong man, fully armed, guards his own house, his possessions are safe. [22]But when someone stronger attacks and overpowers him, he takes away the armor in which the man trusted and divides up the spoils.

[23]"He who is not with me is against me, and he who does not gather with me, scatters.

[24]"When an evil[a] spirit comes out of a man, it goes through arid places seeking rest and does not find it. Then it says, 'I will return to the house I left.' [25]When it arrives, it finds the house swept clean and put in order. [26]Then it goes and takes seven other spirits more wicked than itself, and they go in and live there. And the final condition of that man is worse than the first."

[27]As Jesus was saying these things, a woman in the crowd called out, "Blessed is the mother who gave you birth and nursed you."

[28]He replied, "Blessed rather are those who hear the word of God and obey it."

The Sign of Jonah

[29]As the crowds increased, Jesus said, "This is a wicked generation. It asks for a miraculous sign, but none will be given it except the sign of Jonah. [30]For as Jonah was a sign to the Nine-

vites, so also will the Son of Man be to this generation. [31]The Queen of the South will rise at the judgment with the men of this generation and condemn them; for she came from the ends of the earth to listen to Solomon's wisdom, and now one[b] greater than Solomon is here. [32]The men of Nineveh will stand up at the judgment with this generation and condemn it; for they repented at the preaching of Jonah, and now one greater than Jonah is here.

The Lamp of the Body

[33]"No one lights a lamp and puts it in a place where it will be hidden, or under a bowl. Instead he puts it on its stand, so that those who come in may see the light. [34]Your eye is the lamp of your body. When your eyes are good, your whole body also is full of light. But when they are bad, your body also is full of darkness. [35]See to it, then, that the light within you is not darkness. [36]Therefore, if your whole body is full of light, and no part of it dark, it will be completely lighted, as when the light of a lamp shines on you."

Six Woes

[37]When Jesus had finished speaking, a Pharisee invited him to eat with him; so he went in and reclined at the table. [38]But the Pharisee, noticing that Jesus did not first wash before the meal, was surprised.

[39]Then the Lord said to him, "Now then, you Pharisees clean the outside of the cup and dish, but inside you are full of greed and wickedness. [40]You foolish people! Did not the one who made the outside make the inside also? [41]But give what is inside the

[a]24 Greek unclean   [b]31 Or something; also in verse 32

dish,ᵃ to the poor, and everything will be clean for you.

⁴²"Woe to you Pharisees, because you give God a tenth of your mint, rue and all other kinds of garden herbs, but you neglect justice and the love of God. You should have practiced the latter without leaving the former undone.

⁴³"Woe to you Pharisees, because you love the most important seats in the synagogues and greetings in the marketplaces.

⁴⁴"Woe to you, because you are like unmarked graves, which men walk over without knowing it."

⁴⁵One of the experts in the law answered him, "Teacher, when you say these things, you insult us also."

⁴⁶Jesus replied, "And you experts in the law, woe to you, because you load people down with burdens they can hardly carry, and you yourselves will not lift one finger to help them.

⁴⁷"Woe to you, because you build tombs for the prophets, and it was your forefathers who killed them. ⁴⁸So you testify that you approve of what your forefathers did; they killed the prophets, and you build their tombs. ⁴⁹Because of this, God in his wisdom said, 'I will send them prophets and apostles, some of whom they will kill and others they will persecute.' ⁵⁰Therefore this generation will be held responsible for the blood of all the prophets that has been shed since the beginning of the world, ⁵¹from the blood of Abel to the blood of Zechariah, who was killed between the altar and the sanctuary. Yes, I tell you, this generation will be held responsible for it all.

⁵²"Woe to you experts in the law, because you have taken away the key to knowledge. You yourselves have not entered, and you have hindered those who were entering."

⁵³When Jesus left there, the Pharisees and the teachers of the law began to oppose him fiercely and to besiege him with questions, ⁵⁴waiting to catch him in something he might say.

Warnings and Encouragements

12 Meanwhile, when a crowd of many thousands had gathered, so that they were trampling on one another, Jesus began to speak first to his disciples, saying: "Be on your guard against the yeast of the Pharisees, which is hypocrisy. ²There is nothing concealed that will not be disclosed, or hidden that will not be made known. ³What you have said in the dark will be heard in the daylight, and what you have whispered in the ear in the inner rooms will be proclaimed from the roofs.

⁴"I tell you, my friends, do not be afraid of those who kill the body and after that can do no more. ⁵But I will show you whom you should fear: Fear him who, after the killing of the body, has power to throw you into hell. Yes, I tell you, fear him. ⁶Are not five sparrows sold for two penniesᵇ? Yet not one of them is forgotten by God. ⁷Indeed, the very hairs of your head are all numbered. Don't be afraid; you are worth more than many sparrows.

⁸"I tell you, whoever acknowledges me before men, the Son of Man will also acknowledge him before the angels of God. ⁹But he

---

ᵃ41 Or *what you have*   ᵇ6 Greek *two assaria*

who disowns me before men will be disowned before the angels of God. [10]And everyone who speaks a word against the Son of Man will be forgiven, but anyone who blasphemes against the Holy Spirit will not be forgiven.

[11]"When you are brought before synagogues, rulers and authorities, do not worry about how you will defend yourselves or what you will say, [12]for the Holy Spirit will teach you at that time what you should say."

The Parable of the Rich Fool

[13]Someone in the crowd said to him, "Teacher, tell my brother to divide the inheritance with me."

[14]Jesus replied, "Man, who appointed me a judge or an arbiter between you?" [15]Then he said to them, "Watch out! Be on your guard against all kinds of greed; a man's life does not consist in the abundance of his possessions."

[16]And he told them this parable: "The ground of a certain rich man produced a good crop. [17]He thought to himself, 'What shall I do? I have no place to store my crops.'

[18]"Then he said, 'This is what I'll do. I will tear down my barns and build bigger ones, and there I will store all my grain and my goods. [19]And I'll say to myself, "You have plenty of good things laid up for many years. Take life easy; eat, drink and be merry." '

[20]"But God said to him, 'You fool! This very night your life will be demanded from you. Then who will get what you have prepared for yourself?'

[21]"This is how it will be with anyone who stores up things for himself but is not rich toward God."

Do Not Worry

[22]Then Jesus said to his disciples: "Therefore I tell you, do not worry about your life, what you will eat; or about your body, what you will wear. [23]Life is more than food, and the body more than clothes. [24]Consider the ravens: They do not sow or reap, they have no storeroom or barn; yet God feeds them. And how much more valuable you are than birds! [25]Who of you by worrying can add a single hour to his life[a]? [26]Since you cannot do this very little thing, why do you worry about the rest?

[27]"Consider how the lilies grow. They do not labor or spin. Yet I tell you, not even Solomon in all his splendor was dressed like one of these. [28]If that is how God clothes the grass of the field, which is here today, and tomorrow is thrown into the fire, how much more will he clothe you, O you of little faith! [29]And do not set your heart on what you will eat or drink; do not worry about it. [30]For the pagan world runs after all such things, and your Father knows that you need them. [31]But seek his kingdom, and these things will be given to you as well.

[32]"Do not be afraid, little flock, for your Father has been pleased to give you the kingdom. [33]Sell your possessions and give to the poor. Provide purses for yourselves that will not wear out, a treasure in heaven that will not be exhausted, where no thief comes near and no moth destroys. [34]For where your treasure is, there your heart will be also.

25 Or single cubit to his height

---

37 Ac 20:35

4 Php 4:6,7

26 Php 4:13

Watchfulness

³⁵"Be dressed ready for service and keep your lamps burning, ³⁶like men waiting for their master to return from a wedding banquet, so that when he comes and knocks they can immediately open the door for him. ³⁷It will be good for those servants whose master finds them watching when he comes. I tell you the truth, he will dress himself to serve, will have them recline at the table and will come and wait on them. ³⁸It will be good for those servants whose master finds them ready, even if he comes in the second or third watch of the night. ³⁹But understand this: If the owner of the house had known at what hour the thief was coming, he would not have let his house be broken into. ⁴⁰You also must be ready, because the Son of Man will come at an hour when you do not expect him."

⁴¹Peter asked, "Lord, are you telling this parable to us, or to everyone?"

⁴²The Lord answered, "Who then is the faithful and wise manager, whom the master puts in charge of his servants to give them their food allowance at the proper time? ⁴³It will be good for that servant whom the master finds doing so when he returns. ⁴⁴I tell you the truth, he will put him in charge of all his possessions. ⁴⁵But suppose the servant says to himself, 'My master is taking a long time in coming,' and he then begins to beat the menservants and maidservants and to eat and drink and get ⁹⁶ drunk. ⁴⁶The master of that servant will come on a day when he does not expect him and at an hour he is not aware of. He will

cut him to pieces and assign him a place with the unbelievers.

⁴⁷"That servant who knows his master's will and does not get ready or does not do what his master wants will be beaten with many blows. ⁴⁸But the one who does not know and does things deserving punishment will be beaten with few blows. From everyone who has been given much, much will be demanded; and from the one who has been entrusted with much, much more will be asked.

Not Peace but Division

⁴⁹"I have come to bring fire on the earth, and how I wish it were already kindled! ⁵⁰But I have a baptism to undergo, and how distressed I am until it is completed! ⁵¹Do you think I came to bring peace on earth? No, I tell you, but division. ⁵²From now on there will be five in one family divided against each other, three against two and two against three. ⁵³They will be divided, father against son and son against father, mother against daughter and daughter against mother, mother-in-law against daughter-in-law and daughter-in-law against mother-in-law."

Interpreting the Times

⁵⁴He said to the crowd: "When you see a cloud rising in the west, immediately you say, 'It's going to rain,' and it does. ⁵⁵And when the south wind blows, you say, 'It's going to be hot,' and it is. ⁵⁶Hypocrites! You know how to interpret the appearance of the earth and the sky. How is it that you don't know how to interpret this present time?

⁵⁷"Why don't you judge for yourselves what is right? ⁵⁸As

you are going with your adversary to the magistrate, try hard to be reconciled to him on the way, or he may drag you off to the judge, and the judge turn you over to the officer, and the officer throw you into prison. ⁵⁹I tell you, you will not get out until you have paid the last penny.ᵃ'

Repent or Perish

13 Now there were some present at that time who told Jesus about the Galileans whose blood Pilate had mixed with their sacrifices. ²Jesus answered, "Do you think that these Galileans were worse sinners than all the other Galileans because they suffered this way? ³I tell you, no! But unless you repent, you too will all perish. ⁴Or those eighteen who died when the tower in Siloam fell on them—do you think they were more guilty than all the others living in Jerusalem? ⁵I tell you, no! But unless you repent, you too will all perish."

⁶Then he told this parable: "A man had a fig tree, planted in his vineyard, and he went to look for fruit on it, but did not find any. ⁷So he said to the man who took care of the vineyard, 'For three years now I've been coming to look for fruit on this fig tree and haven't found any. Cut it down! Why should it use up the soil?'

⁸"'Sir,' the man replied, 'leave it alone for one more year, and I'll dig around it and fertilize it. ⁹If it bears fruit next year, fine! If not, then cut it down.'"

A Crippled Woman Healed on the Sabbath

¹⁰On a Sabbath Jesus was teaching in one of the synagogues, ¹¹and a woman was there who had been crippled by a spirit for eighteen years. She was bent over and could not straighten up at all. ¹²When Jesus saw her, he called her forward and said to her, "Woman, you are set free from your infirmity." ¹³Then he put his hands on her, and immediately she straightened up and praised God.

¹⁴Indignant because Jesus had healed on the Sabbath, the synagogue ruler said to the people, "There are six days for work. So come and be healed on those days, not on the Sabbath."

¹⁵The Lord answered him, "You hypocrites! Doesn't each of you on the Sabbath untie his ox or donkey from the stall and lead it out to give it water? ¹⁶Then should not this woman, a daughter of Abraham, whom Satan has kept bound for eighteen long years, be set free on the Sabbath day from what bound her?"

¹⁷When he said this, all his opponents were humiliated, but the people were delighted with all the wonderful things he was doing.

The Parables of the Mustard Seed and the Yeast

¹⁸Then Jesus asked, "What is the kingdom of God like? What shall I compare it to? ¹⁹It is like a mustard seed, which a man took and planted in his garden. It grew and became a tree, and the birds of the air perched in its branches."

²⁰Again he asked, "What shall I compare the kingdom of God to? ²¹It is like yeast that a woman took and mixed into a large amountᵇ of flour until it worked all through the dough."

ᵃ59 Greek *lepton*   ᵇ21 Greek *three satas* (probably about 1/2 bushel or 22 liters)

The Narrow Door

22Then Jesus went through the towns and villages, teaching as he made his way to Jerusalem. 23Someone asked him, "Lord, are only a few people going to be saved?"

He said to them, 24"Make every effort to enter through the narrow door, because many, I tell you, will try to enter and will not be able to. 25Once the owner of the house gets up and closes the door, you will stand outside knocking and pleading, 'Sir, open the door for us.'

"But he will answer, 'I don't know you or where you come from.'

26"Then you will say, 'We ate and drank with you, and you taught in our streets.'

27"But he will reply, 'I don't know you or where you come from. Away from me, all you evildoers!'

28"There will be weeping there, and gnashing of teeth, when you see Abraham, Isaac and Jacob and all the prophets in the kingdom of God, but you yourselves thrown out. 29People will come from east and west and north and south, and will take their places at the feast in the kingdom of God. 30Indeed there are those who are last who will be first, and first who will be last."

Jesus' Sorrow for Jerusalem

31At that time some Pharisees came to Jesus and said to him, "Leave this place and go somewhere else. Herod wants to kill you."

32He replied, "Go tell that fox, 'I will drive out demons and heal people today and tomorrow, and on the third day I will reach my goal.' 33In any case, I must keep going today and tomorrow and the next day—for surely no prophet can die outside Jerusalem!

34"O Jerusalem, Jerusalem, you who kill the prophets and stone those sent to you, how often I have longed to gather your children together, as a hen gathers her chicks under her wings, but you were not willing! 35Look, your house is left to you desolate. I tell you, you will not see me again until you say, 'Blessed is he who comes in the name of the Lord.'ᵈ"

Jesus at a Pharisee's House

14 One Sabbath, when Jesus went to eat in the house of a prominent Pharisee, he was being carefully watched. 2There in front of him was a man suffering from dropsy. 3Jesus asked the Pharisees and experts in the law, "Is it lawful to heal on the Sabbath or not?" 4But they remained silent. So taking hold of the man, he healed him and sent him away.

5Then he asked them, "If one of you has a sonᵇ or an ox that falls into a well on the Sabbath day, will you not immediately pull him out?" 6And they had nothing to say.

7When he noticed how the guests picked the places of honor at the table, he told them this parable: 8"When someone invites you to a wedding feast, do not take the place of honor, for a person more distinguished than you may have been invited. 9If so, the host who invited both of you will come and say to you, 'Give this man your seat.' Then, humiliated, you will have to take the least important place. 10But when you are invited, take the lowest

ᵈ35 Psalm 118:26   ᵇ5 Some manuscripts donkey

place, so that when your host comes, he will say to you, 'Friend, move up to a better place.' Then you will be honored in the presence of all your fellow guests. ¹¹For everyone who exalts himself will be humbled, and he who humbles himself will be exalted."

¹²Then Jesus said to his host, "When you give a luncheon or dinner, do not invite your friends, your brothers or relatives, or your rich neighbors; if you do, they may invite you back and so you will be repaid. ¹³But when you give a banquet, invite the poor, the crippled, the lame, **77** ¹⁴and you will be **Ac 3:14** blessed. Although they cannot repay you, you will be repaid at the resurrection of the righteous."

The Parable of the Great Banquet

¹⁵When one of those at the table with him heard this, he said to Jesus, "Blessed is the man who will eat at the feast in the kingdom of God."

¹⁶Jesus replied: "A certain man was preparing a great banquet and invited many guests. ¹⁷At the time of the banquet he sent his servant to tell those who had been invited, 'Come, for everything is now ready.'

¹⁸"But they all alike began to make excuses. The first said, 'I have just bought a field, and I must go and see it. Please excuse me.'

¹⁹"Another said, 'I have just bought five yoke of oxen, and I'm on my way to try them out. Please excuse me.'

²⁰"Still another said, 'I just got married, so I can't come.'

²¹"The servant came back and reported this to his master. Then the owner of the house became angry and ordered his servant, 'Go out quickly into the streets and alleys of the town and bring in the poor, the crippled, the blind and the lame.'

²²"'Sir,' the servant said, 'what you ordered has been done, but there is still room.'

²³"Then the master told his servant, 'Go out to the roads and country lanes and make them come in, so that my house will be full. ²⁴I tell you, not one of those men who were invited will get a taste of my banquet.'"

The Cost of Being a Disciple

²⁵Large crowds were traveling with Jesus, and turning to them he said: ²⁶"If anyone comes to me and does not hate his father and mother, his wife and children, his brothers and sisters—yes, even his own life—he cannot be my disciple. ²⁷And anyone who does not carry his cross and follow me cannot be my disciple.

²⁸"Suppose one of you wants to build a tower. Will he not first sit down and estimate the cost to see if he has enough money to complete it? ²⁹For if he lays the foundation and is not able to finish it, everyone who sees it will ridicule him, ³⁰saying, 'This fellow began to build and was not able to finish.'

³¹"Or suppose a king is about to go to war against another king. Will he not first sit down and consider whether he is able with ten thousand men to oppose the one coming against him with twenty thousand? ³²If he is not able, he will send a delegation while the other is still a long way off and will ask for terms of peace. ³³In the same way, any of you who does not give up everything he has cannot be my disciple.

³⁴"Salt is good, but if it loses its

saltiness, how can it be made salty again? 35It is fit neither for the soil nor for the manure pile; it is thrown out.

"He who has ears to hear, let him hear."

The Parable of the Lost Sheep

15 Now the tax collectors and "sinners" were all gathering around to hear him. 2But the Pharisees and the teachers of the law muttered, "This man welcomes sinners and eats with them."

3Then Jesus told them this parable: 4"Suppose one of you has a hundred sheep and loses one of them. Does he not leave the ninety-nine in the open country and go after the lost sheep until he finds it? 5And when he finds it, he joyfully puts it on his shoulders 6and goes home. Then he calls his friends and neighbors together and says, 'Rejoice with me; I have found my lost sheep.' 7I tell you that in the same way there will be more rejoicing in heaven over one sinner who repents than over ninety-nine righteous persons who do not need to repent.

The Parable of the Lost Coin

8"Or suppose a woman has ten silver coins*a* and loses one. Does she not light a lamp, sweep the house and search carefully until she finds it? 9And when she finds it, she calls her friends and neighbors together and says, 'Rejoice with me; I have found my lost coin.' 10In the same way, I tell you, there is rejoicing in the presence of the angels of God over one sinner who repents."

The Parable of the Lost Son

11Jesus continued: "There was a man who had two sons. 12The younger one said to his father, 'Father, give me my share of the estate.' So he divided his property between them.

13"Not long after that, the younger son got together all he had, set off for a distant country and there squandered his wealth in wild living. 14After he had spent everything, there was a severe famine in that whole country, and he began to be in need. 15So he went and hired himself out to a citizen of that country, who sent him to his fields to feed pigs. 16He longed to fill his stomach with the pods that the pigs were eating, but no one gave him anything.

17"When he came to his senses, he said, 'How many of my father's hired men have food to spare, and here I am starving to death! 18I will set out and go back to my father and say to him: Father, I have sinned against heaven and against you. 19I am no longer worthy to be called your son; make me like one of your hired men.' 20So he got up and went to his father.

"But while he was still a long way off, his father saw him and was filled with compassion for him; he ran to his son, threw his arms around him and kissed him.

21"The son said to him, 'Father, I have sinned against heaven and against you. I am no longer worthy to be called your son.'*b*

22"But the father said to his servants, 'Quick! Bring the best robe and put it on him. Put a ring on his finger and sandals on his feet. 23Bring the fattened calf and kill it. Let's have a feast and celebrate. 24For this son of mine was dead and is alive again; he was

---

*a*8 Greek *ten drachmas*, each worth about a day's wages   *b*21 Some early manuscripts *son. Make me like one of your hired men.*

lost and is found.' So they began to celebrate.

25"Meanwhile, the older son was in the field. When he came near the house, he heard music and dancing. 26So he called one of the servants and asked him what was going on. 27'Your brother has come,' he replied, 'and your father has killed the fattened calf because he has him back safe and sound.'

28"The older brother became angry and refused to go in. So his father went out and pleaded with him. 29But he answered his father, 'Look! All these years I've been slaving for you and never disobeyed your orders. Yet you never gave me even a young goat so I could celebrate with my friends. 30But when this son of yours who has squandered your property with prostitutes comes home, you kill the fattened calf for him!'

31"'My son,' the father said, 'you are always with me, and everything I have is yours. 32But we had to celebrate and be glad, because this brother of yours was dead and is alive again; he was lost and is found.'"

The Parable of the Shrewd Manager

16 Jesus told his disciples: "There was a rich man whose manager was accused of wasting his possessions. 2So he called him in and asked him, 'What is this I hear about you? Give an account of your management, because you cannot be manager any longer.'

3"The manager said to himself, 'What shall I do now? My master is taking away my job. I'm not strong enough to dig, and I'm ashamed to beg— 4I know what

I'll do so that, when I lose my job here, people will welcome me into their houses.'

5"So he called in each one of his master's debtors. He asked the first, 'How much do you owe my master?'

6"'Eight hundred gallons[a] of olive oil,' he replied.

"The manager told him, 'Take your bill, sit down quickly, and make it four hundred.'

7"Then he asked the second, 'And how much do you owe?'

"'A thousand bushels[b] of wheat,' he replied.

"He told him, 'Take your bill and make it eight hundred.'

8"The master commended the dishonest manager because he had acted shrewdly. For the people of this world are more shrewd in dealing with their own kind than are the people of the light. 9I tell you, use worldly wealth to gain friends for yourselves, so that when it is gone, you will be welcomed into eternal dwellings.

10"Whoever can be trusted with very little can also be trusted with much, and whoever is dishonest with very little will also be dishonest with much. 11So if you have not been trustworthy in handling worldly wealth, who will trust you with true riches? 12And if you have not been trustworthy with someone else's property, who will give you property of your own?

13"No servant can serve two masters. Either he will hate the one and love the other, or he will be devoted to the one and despise the other. You cannot serve both God and Money."

14The Pharisees, who loved money, heard all this and were sneering at Jesus. 15He said to

---

*a 6 Greek one hundred batous (probably about 3 kiloliters)   *b 7 Greek one hundred korous (probably about 35 kiloliters) them, "You are the ones who justify yourselves in the eyes of men, but God knows your hearts. What is highly valued among men is detestable in God's sight.

Additional Teachings

16"The Law and the Prophets were proclaimed until John. Since that time, the good news of the kingdom of God is being preached, and everyone is forcing his way into it. 17It is easier for heaven and earth to disappear than for the least stroke of a pen to drop out of the Law.

19
1Co 7:10,11

18"Anyone who divorces his wife and marries another woman commits adultery, and the man who marries a divorced woman commits adultery.

The Rich Man and Lazarus

19"There was a rich man who was dressed in purple and fine linen and lived in luxury every day. 20At his gate was laid a beggar named Lazarus, covered with sores 21and longing to eat what fell from the rich man's table. Even the dogs came and licked his sores.

40
Ro 2:5-11

22"The time came when the beggar died and the angels carried him to Abraham's side. The rich man also died and was buried. 23In hell,ᵃ where he was in torment, he looked up and saw Abraham far away, with Lazarus by his side. 24So he called to him, 'Father Abraham, have pity on me and send Lazarus to dip the tip of his finger in water and cool my tongue, because I am in agony in this fire.'

41
Ro 2:5-11

25"But Abraham replied, 'Son, remember that in your lifetime you received your good things, while Lazarus received bad things, but now he is comforted

here and you are in agony. 26And besides all this, between us and you a great chasm has been fixed, so that those who want to go from here to you cannot, nor can anyone cross over from there to us.'

27"He answered, 'Then I beg you, father, send Lazarus to my father's house, 28for I have five brothers. Let him warn them, so that they will not also come to this place of torment.'

29"Abraham replied, 'They have Moses and the Prophets; let them listen to them.'

30"'No, father Abraham,' he said, 'but if someone from the dead goes to them, they will repent.'

31"He said to him, 'If they do not listen to Moses and the Prophets, they will not be convinced even if someone rises from the dead.'"

Sin, Faith, Duty

17 Jesus said to his disciples: "Things that cause people to sin are bound to come, but woe to that person through whom they come. 2It would be better for him to be thrown into the sea with a millstone tied around his neck than for him to cause one of these little ones to sin. 3So watch yourselves.

"If your brother sins, rebuke him, and if he repents, forgive him. 4If he sins against you seven times in a day, and seven times comes back to you and says, 'I repent,' forgive him."

86
Ro 10:11

5The apostles said to the Lord, "Increase our faith!"

6He replied, "If you have faith as small as a mustard seed, you can say to this mulberry tree, 'Be uprooted and planted in the sea,' and it will obey you.

7"Suppose one of you had a ser-

ᵃ23 Greek *Hades*

vant plowing or looking after the sheep. Would he say to the servant when he comes in from the field, 'Come along now and sit down to eat'? 8Would he not rather say, 'Prepare my supper, get yourself ready and wait on me while I eat and drink; after that you may eat and drink'? 9Would he thank the servant because he did what he was told to do? 10So you also, when you have done everything you were told to do, should say, 'We are unworthy servants; we have only done our duty.'"

Ten Healed of Leprosy

11Now on his way to Jerusalem, Jesus traveled along the border between Samaria and Galilee. 12As he was going into a village, ten men who had leprosy[a] met him. They stood at a distance 13and called out in a loud voice, "Jesus, Master, have pity on us!"

14When he saw them, he said, "Go, show yourselves to the priests." And as they went, they were cleansed.

15One of them, when he saw he was healed, came back, praising God in a loud voice. 16He threw himself at Jesus' feet and thanked him—and he was a Samaritan.

17Jesus asked, "Were not all ten cleansed? Where are the other nine? 18Was no one found to return and give praise to God except this foreigner?" 19Then he said to him, "Rise and go; your faith has made you well."

The Coming of the Kingdom of God

20Once, having been asked by the Pharisees when the kingdom of God would come, Jesus replied, "The kingdom of God does not come with your careful observation, 21nor will people say, 'Here it is,' or 'There it is,' because the kingdom of God is within[b] you."

22Then he said to his disciples, "The time is coming when you will long to see one of the days of the Son of Man, but you will not see it. 23Men will tell you, 'There he is!' or 'Here he is!' Do not go running off after them. 24For the Son of Man in his day[c] will be like the lightning, which flashes and lights up the sky from one end to the other. 25But first he must suffer many things and be rejected by this generation.

26"Just as it was in the days of Noah, so also will it be in the days of the Son of Man. 27People were eating, drinking, marrying and being given in marriage up to the day Noah entered the ark. Then the flood came and destroyed them all.

28"It was the same in the days of Lot. People were eating and drinking, buying and selling, planting and building. 29But the day Lot left Sodom, fire and sulfur rained down from heaven and destroyed them all.

30"It will be just like this on the day the Son of Man is revealed. 31On that day no one who is on the roof of his house, with his goods inside, should go down to get them. Likewise, no one in the field should go back for anything. 32Remember Lot's wife! 33Whoever tries to keep his life will lose it, and whoever loses his life will preserve it. 34I tell you, on that night two people will be in one bed; one will be taken and the other left. 35Two women will be grinding grain together; one

---

*a12 The Greek word was used for various diseases affecting the skin—not necessarily leprosy. *b21 Or among *c24 Some manuscripts do not have in his day.*

will be taken and the other left.[a]

37"Where, Lord?" they asked.

He replied, "Where there is a dead body, there the vultures will gather."

The Parable of the Persistent Widow

16
Jn 16:33
69
Jn 14:13,14

18 Then Jesus told his disciples a parable to show them that they should always pray and not give up. [2]He said: "In a certain town there was a judge who neither feared God nor cared about men. [3]And there was a widow in that town who kept coming to him with the plea, 'Grant me justice against my adversary.'

[4]"For some time he refused. But finally he said to himself, 'Even though I don't fear God or care about men, [5]yet because this widow keeps bothering me, I will see that she gets justice, so that she won't eventually wear me out with her coming!'"

[6]And the Lord said, "Listen to what the unjust judge says. [7]And will not God bring about justice for his chosen ones, who cry out to him day and night? Will he keep putting them off? [8]I tell you, he will see that they get justice, and quickly. However, when the Son of Man comes, will he find faith on the earth?"

The Parable of the Pharisee and the Tax Collector

44
Eph 5:21
48
Jn 5:30
66
Ro 3:23
78
Jn 1:12

[9]To some who were confident of their own righteousness and looked down on everybody else, Jesus told this parable: [10]"Two men went up to the temple to pray, one a Pharisee and the other a tax collector. [11]The Pharisee stood up and prayed about[b] himself: 'God, I thank you that I am not like other men—robbers, evildoers, adulterers—or even like this tax collector. [12]I fast twice a week and give a tenth of all I get.'

[13]"But the tax collector stood at a distance. He would not even look up to heaven, but beat his breast and said, 'God, have mercy on me, a sinner.'

[14]"I tell you that this man, rather than the other, went home justified before God. For everyone who exalts himself will be humbled, and he who humbles himself will be exalted."

The Little Children and Jesus

[15]People were also bringing babies to Jesus to have him touch them. When the disciples saw this, they rebuked them. [16]But Jesus called the children to him and said, "Let the little children come to me, and do not hinder them, for the kingdom of God belongs to such as these. [17]I tell you the truth, anyone who will not receive the kingdom of God like a little child will never enter it."

The Rich Ruler

[18]A certain ruler asked him, "Good teacher, what must I do to inherit eternal life?"

[19]"Why do you call me good?" Jesus answered. "No one is good—except God alone. [20]You know the commandments: 'Do not commit adultery, do not murder, do not steal, do not give false testimony, honor your father and mother.'[c]"

[21]"All these I have kept since I was a boy," he said.

[22]When Jesus heard this, he said to him, "You still lack one thing. Sell everything you have and give to the poor, and you will

---

[a]35 Some manuscripts left. [36]Two men will be in the field; one will be taken and the other left.   [b]11 Or to   [c]20 Exodus 20:12-16; Deut. 5:16-20

have treasure in heaven. Then come, follow me.''

23When he heard this, he became very sad, because he was a man of great wealth. 24Jesus looked at him and said, ''How hard it is for the rich to enter the kingdom of God! 25Indeed, it is easier for a camel to go through the eye of a needle than for a rich man to enter the kingdom of God.''

26Those who heard this asked, ''Who then can be saved?''

27Jesus replied, ''What is impossible with men is possible with God.''

28Peter said to him, ''We have left all we had to follow you!''

29''I tell you the truth,'' Jesus said to them, ''no one who has left home or wife or brothers or parents or children for the sake of the kingdom of God 30will fail to receive many times as much in this age and, in the age to come, eternal life.''

Jesus Again Predicts His Death

31Jesus took the Twelve aside and told them, ''We are going up to Jerusalem, and everything that is written by the prophets about the Son of Man will be fulfilled. 32He will be handed over to the Gentiles. They will mock him, insult him, spit on him, flog him and kill him. 33On the third day he will rise again.''

34The disciples did not understand any of this. Its meaning was hidden from them, and they did not know what he was talking about.

A Blind Beggar Receives His Sight

35As Jesus approached Jericho, a blind man was sitting by the roadside begging. 36When he heard the crowd going by, he asked what was happening. 37They told him, ''Jesus of Nazareth is passing by.''

38He called out, ''Jesus, Son of David, have mercy on me!''

39Those who led the way rebuked him and told him to be quiet, but he shouted all the more, ''Son of David, have mercy on me!''

40Jesus stopped and ordered the man to be brought to him. When he came near, Jesus asked him, 41''What do you want me to do for you?''

''Lord, I want to see,'' he replied.

42Jesus said to him, ''Receive your sight; your faith has healed you.'' 43Immediately he received his sight and followed Jesus, praising God. When all the people saw it, they also praised God.

Zacchaeus the Tax Collector

19 Jesus entered Jericho and was passing through. 2A man was there by the name of Zacchaeus; he was a chief tax collector and was wealthy. 3He wanted to see who Jesus was, but being a short man he could not, because of the crowd. 4So he ran ahead and climbed a sycamore-fig tree to see him, since Jesus was coming that way.

5When Jesus reached the spot, he looked up and said to him, ''Zacchaeus, come down immediately. I must stay at your house today.'' 6So he came down at once and welcomed him gladly.

7All the people saw this and began to mutter, ''He has gone to be the guest of a 'sinner.' ''

8But Zacchaeus stood up and said to the Lord, ''Look, Lord! Here and now I give half of my possessions to the poor, and if I have cheated anybody out of anything, I will pay back four times the amount.''

⁹Jesus said to him, "Today salvation has come to this house, because this man, too, is a son of Abraham. ¹⁰For the Son of Man came to seek and to save what was lost.''

23
Jn 6:29

The Parable of the Ten Minas

¹¹While they were listening to this, he went on to tell them a parable, because he was near Jerusalem and the people thought that the kingdom of God was going to appear at once. ¹²He said: "A man of noble birth went to a distant country to have himself appointed king and then to return. ¹³So he called ten of his servants and gave them ten minas.ᵃ 'Put this money to work,' he said, 'until I come back.'

¹⁴"But his subjects hated him and sent a delegation after him to say, 'We don't want this man to be our king.'

¹⁵"He was made king, however, and returned home. Then he sent for the servants to whom he had given the money, in order to find out what they had gained with it.

¹⁶"The first one came and said, 'Sir, your mina has earned ten more.'

¹⁷" 'Well done, my good servant!' his master replied. 'Because you have been trustworthy in a very small matter, take charge of ten cities.'

¹⁸"The second came and said, 'Sir, your mina has earned five more.'

¹⁹"His master answered, 'You take charge of five cities.'

²⁰"Then another servant came and said, 'Sir, here is your mina; I have kept it laid away in a piece of cloth. ²¹I was afraid of you, because you are a hard man. You

take out what you did not put in and reap what you did not sow.'

²²"His master replied, 'I will judge you by your own words, you wicked servant! You knew, did you, that I am a hard man, taking out what I did not put in, and reaping what I did not sow? ²³Why then didn't you put my money on deposit, so that when I came back, I could have collected it with interest?'

²⁴"Then he said to those standing by, 'Take his mina away from him and give it to the one who has ten minas.'

²⁵" 'Sir,' they said, 'he already has ten!'

²⁶"He replied, 'I tell you that to everyone who has, more will be given, but as for the one who has nothing, even what he has will be taken away. ²⁷But those enemies of mine who did not want me to be king over them—bring them here and kill them in front of me.' "

The Triumphal Entry

²⁸After Jesus had said this, he went on ahead, going up to Jerusalem. ²⁹As he approached Bethphage and Bethany at the hill called the Mount of Olives, he sent two of his disciples, saying to them, ³⁰"Go to the village ahead of you, and as you enter it, you will find a colt tied there, which no one has ever ridden. Untie it and bring it here. ³¹If anyone asks you, 'Why are you untying it?' tell him, 'The Lord needs it.' "

³²Those who were sent ahead went and found it just as he had told them. ³³As they were untying the colt, its owners asked them, "Why are you untying the colt?"

³⁴They replied, "The Lord needs it."

ᵃ13 A mina was about three months' wages.

³⁵They brought it to Jesus, threw their cloaks on the colt and put Jesus on it. ³⁶As he went along, people spread their cloaks on the road.

³⁷When he came near the place where the road goes down the Mount of Olives, the whole crowd of disciples began joyfully to praise God in loud voices for all the miracles they had seen:

³⁸"Blessed is the king who
      comes in the name of the
      Lord!"ᵃ

"Peace in heaven and glory in
      the highest!"

³⁹Some of the Pharisees in the crowd said to Jesus, "Teacher, rebuke your disciples!"

⁴⁰"I tell you," he replied, "if they keep quiet, the stones will cry out."

⁴¹As he approached Jerusalem and saw the city, he wept over it ⁴²and said, "If you, even you, had only known on this day what would bring you peace—but now it is hidden from your eyes. ⁴³The days will come upon you when your enemies will build an embankment against you and encircle you and hem you in on every side. ⁴⁴They will dash you to the ground, you and the children within your walls. They will not leave one stone on another, because you did not recognize the time of God's coming to you."

Jesus at the Temple

⁴⁵Then he entered the temple area and began driving out those who were selling. ⁴⁶"It is written," he said to them, "'My house will be a house of prayer'ᵇ; but you have made it 'a den of robbers.'ᶜ"

⁴⁷Every day he was teaching at the temple. But the chief priests,

the teachers of the law and the leaders among the people were trying to kill him. ⁴⁸Yet they could not find any way to do it, because all the people hung on his words.

The Authority of Jesus Questioned

20 One day as he was teaching the people in the temple courts and preaching the gospel, the chief priests and the teachers of the law, together with the elders, came up to him. ²"Tell us by what authority you are doing these things," they said. "Who gave you this authority?"

³He replied, "I will also ask you a question. Tell me, ⁴John's baptism—was it from heaven, or from men?"

⁵They discussed it among themselves and said, "If we say, 'From heaven,' he will ask, 'Why didn't you believe him?' ⁶But if we say, 'From men,' all the people will stone us, because they are persuaded that John was a prophet."

⁷So they answered, "We don't know where it was from."

⁸Jesus said, "Neither will I tell you by what authority I am doing these things."

The Parable of the Tenants

⁹He went on to tell the people this parable: "A man planted a vineyard, rented it to some farmers and went away for a long time. ¹⁰At harvest time he sent a servant to the tenants so they would give him some of the fruit of the vineyard. But the tenants beat him and sent him away empty-handed. ¹¹He sent another servant, but that one also they beat and treated shamefully and sent away empty-handed. ¹²He sent still a third, and they

---

ᵃ38 Psalm 118:26   ᵇ46 Isaiah 56:7   ᶜ46 Jer. 7:11

wounded him and threw him out.

¹³"Then the owner of the vineyard said, 'What shall I do? I will send my son, whom I love; perhaps they will respect him.'

¹⁴"But when the tenants saw him, they talked the matter over. 'This is the heir,' they said. 'Let's kill him, and the inheritance will be ours.' ¹⁵So they threw him out of the vineyard and killed him.

"What then will the owner of the vineyard do to them? ¹⁶He will come and kill those tenants and give the vineyard to others."

When the people heard this, they said, "May this never be!"

¹⁷Jesus looked directly at them and asked, "Then what is the meaning of that which is written:

"'The stone the builders
        rejected
has become the capstone[a][b]?

¹⁸Everyone who falls on that stone will be broken to pieces, but he on whom it falls will be crushed."

¹⁹The teachers of the law and the chief priests looked for a way to arrest him immediately, because they knew he had spoken this parable against them. But they were afraid of the people.

Paying Taxes to Caesar

²⁰Keeping a close watch on him, they sent spies, who pretended to be honest. They hoped to catch Jesus in something he said so that they might hand him over to the power and authority of the governor. ²¹So the spies questioned him: "Teacher, we know that you speak and teach what is right, and that you do not show partiality but teach the way of God in accordance with the truth. ²²Is it right for us to pay taxes to Caesar or not?"

²³He saw through their duplicity and said to them, ²⁴"Show me a denarius. Whose portrait and inscription are on it?"

²⁵"Caesar's," they replied.

He said to them, "Then give to Caesar what is Caesar's, and to God what is God's."

²⁶They were unable to trap him in what he had said there in public. And astonished by his answer, they became silent.

The Resurrection and Marriage

²⁷Some of the Sadducees, who say there is no resurrection, came to Jesus with a question. ²⁸"Teacher," they said, "Moses wrote for us that if a man's brother dies and leaves a wife but no children, the man must marry the widow and have children for his brother. ²⁹Now there were seven brothers. The first one married a woman and died childless. ³⁰The second ³¹and then the third married her, and in the same way the seven died, leaving no children. ³²Finally, the woman died too. ³³Now then, at the resurrection whose wife will she be, since the seven were married to her?"

³⁴Jesus replied, "The people of this age marry and are given in marriage. ³⁵But those who are considered worthy of taking part in that age and in the resurrection from the dead will neither marry nor be given in marriage, ³⁶and they can no longer die; for they are like the angels. They are God's children, since they are children of the resurrection. ³⁷But in the account of the bush, even Moses showed that the dead rise, for he calls the Lord 'the God of Abraham, and the God of Isaac, and the God of Jacob.'[c] ³⁸He is not

---

[a]17 Or cornerstone   [b]17 Psalm 118:22   [c]37 Exodus 3:6

the God of the dead, but of the living, for to him all are alive."

³⁹Some of the teachers of the law responded, "Well said, teacher!" ⁴⁰And no one dared to ask him any more questions.

Whose Son Is the Christ?

⁴¹Then Jesus said to them, "How is it that they say the Christ*a* is the Son of David? ⁴²David himself declares in the Book of Psalms:

" 'The Lord said to my Lord:
    "Sit at my right hand
⁴³until I make your enemies
    a footstool for your feet." '*b*

⁴⁴David calls him 'Lord.' How then can he be his son?"

⁴⁵While all the people were listening, Jesus said to his disciples, ⁴⁶"Beware of the teachers of the law. They like to walk around in flowing robes and love to be greeted in the marketplaces and have the most important seats in the synagogues and the places of honor at banquets. ⁴⁷They devour widows' houses and for a show make lengthy prayers. Such men will be punished most severely."

The Widow's Offering

21 As he looked up, Jesus saw the rich putting their gifts into the temple treasury. ²He also saw a poor widow put in two very small copper coins.*c* ³"I tell you the truth," he said, "this poor widow has put in more than all the others. ⁴All these people gave their gifts out of their wealth; but she out of her poverty put in all she had to live on."

Signs of the End of the Age

⁵Some of his disciples were remarking about how the temple was adorned with beautiful stones and with gifts dedicated to God. But Jesus said, ⁶"As for what you see here, the time will come when not one stone will be left on another; every one of them will be thrown down."

⁷"Teacher," they asked, "when will these things happen? And what will be the sign that they are about to take place?"

⁸He replied: "Watch out that you are not deceived. For many will come in my name, claiming, 'I am he,' and, 'The time is near.' Do not follow them. ⁹When you hear of wars and revolutions, do not be frightened. These things must happen first, but the end will not come right away."

¹⁰Then he said to them: "Nation will rise against nation, and kingdom against kingdom. ¹¹There will be great earthquakes, famines and pestilences in various places, and fearful events and great signs from heaven.

¹²"But before all this, they will lay hands on you and persecute you. They will deliver you to synagogues and prisons, and you will be brought before kings and governors, and all on account of my name. ¹³This will result in your being witnesses to them. ¹⁴But make up your mind not to worry beforehand how you will defend yourselves. ¹⁵For I will give you words and wisdom that none of your adversaries will be able to resist or contradict. ¹⁶You will be betrayed even by parents, brothers, relatives and friends, and they will put some of you to death. ¹⁷All men will hate you because of me. ¹⁸But not a hair of your head will perish. ¹⁹By standing firm you will gain life.

²⁰"When you see Jerusalem being surrounded by armies, you will know that its desolation is

^a41 Or *Messiah*   ^b43 Psalm 110:1   ^c2 Greek *two lepta*

near. 21Then let those who are in
Judea flee to the mountains, let
those in the city get out, and let
those in the country not enter the
city. 22For this is the time of punishment in fulfillment of all that
has been written. 23How dreadful
it will be in those days for pregnant women and nursing
mothers! There will be great distress in the land and wrath
against this people. 24They will
fall by the sword and will be tak-
en as prisoners to all the nations.
Jerusalem will be trampled on by
the Gentiles until the times of the
Gentiles are fulfilled.

25"There will be signs in the
sun, moon and stars. On the
earth, nations will be in anguish
and perplexity at the roaring and
tossing of the sea. 26Men will faint
from terror, apprehensive of
what is coming on the world, for
the heavenly bodies will be shak-
en. 27At that time they will see the
Son of Man coming in a cloud
with power and great glory.
28When these things begin to take
place, stand up and lift up your
heads, because your redemption
is drawing near."

29He told them this parable:
"Look at the fig tree and all the
trees. 30When they sprout leaves,
you can see for yourselves and
know that summer is near.
31Even so, when you see these
things happening, you know
that the kingdom of God is near.

32"I tell you the truth, this generation*a* will certainly not pass
away until all these things have
happened. 33Heaven and earth
will pass away, but my words
will never pass away.

34"Be careful, or your hearts
will be weighed down with dissipation, drunkenness and the
anxieties of life, and that day will
close on you unexpectedly like a

trap. 35For it will come upon all
those who live on the face of the
whole earth. 36Be always on the
watch, and pray that you may be
able to escape all that is about to
happen, and that you may be
able to stand before the Son of
Man."

37Each day Jesus was teaching
at the temple, and each evening
he went out to spend the night
on the hill called the Mount of
Olives, 38and all the people came
early in the morning to hear him
at the temple.

Judas Agrees to Betray Jesus

22 Now the Feast of Unleavened Bread, called the
Passover, was approaching, 2and
the chief priests and the teachers
of the law were looking for some
way to get rid of Jesus, for they
were afraid of the people. 3Then
Satan entered Judas, called Iscariot, one of the Twelve. 4And
Judas went to the chief priests
and the officers of the temple
guard and discussed with them
how he might betray Jesus. 5They
were delighted and agreed to
give him money. 6He consented,
and watched for an opportunity
to hand Jesus over to them when
no crowd was present.

The Last Supper

7Then came the day of Unleavened Bread on which the Passover lamb had to be sacrificed.
8Jesus sent Peter and John, saying, "Go and make preparations
for us to eat the Passover."

9"Where do you want us to prepare for it?" they asked.

10He replied, "As you enter the
city, a man carrying a jar of water
will meet you. Follow him to the
house that he enters, 11and say to
the owner of the house, 'The
Teacher asks: Where is the guest

<hr>

a32 Or race

room, where I may eat the Passover with my disciples?' ¹²He will show you a large upper room, all furnished. Make preparations there."

¹³They left and found things just as Jesus had told them. So they prepared the Passover.

¹⁴When the hour came, Jesus and his apostles reclined at the table. ¹⁵And he said to them, "I have eagerly desired to eat this Passover with you before I suffer. ¹⁶For I tell you, I will not eat it again until it finds fulfillment in the kingdom of God."

¹⁷After taking the cup, he gave thanks and said, "Take this and divide it among you. ¹⁸For I tell you I will not drink again of the fruit of the vine until the kingdom of God comes."

¹⁹And he took bread, gave thanks and broke it, and gave it to them, saying, "This is my body given for you; do this in remembrance of me."

²⁰In the same way, after the supper he took the cup, saying, "This cup is the new covenant in my blood, which is poured out for you. ²¹But the hand of him who is going to betray me is with mine on the table. ²²The Son of Man will go as it has been decreed, but woe to that man who betrays him." ²³They began to question among themselves which of them it might be who would do this.

²⁴Also a dispute arose among them as to which of them was considered to be greatest. ²⁵Jesus said to them, "The kings of the Gentiles lord it over them; and those who exercise authority over them call themselves Benefactors. ²⁶But you are not to be like that. Instead, the greatest among you should be like the youngest, and the one who rules

like the one who serves. ²⁷For who is greater, the one who is at the table or the one who serves? Is it not the one who is at the table? But I am among you as one who serves. ²⁸You are those who have stood by me in my trials. ²⁹And I confer on you a kingdom, just as my Father conferred one on me, ³⁰so that you may eat and drink at my table in my kingdom and sit on thrones, judging the twelve tribes of Israel.

³¹"Simon, Simon, Satan has asked to sift you*ᵃ* as wheat. ³²But I have prayed for you, Simon, that your faith may not fail. And when you have turned back, strengthen your brothers."

³³But he replied, "Lord, I am ready to go with you to prison and to death."

³⁴Jesus answered, "I tell you, Peter, before the rooster crows today, you will deny three times that you know me."

³⁵Then Jesus asked them, "When I sent you without purse, bag or sandals, did you lack anything?"

"Nothing," they answered.

³⁶He said to them, "But now if you have a purse, take it, and also a bag; and if you don't have a sword, sell your cloak and buy one. ³⁷It is written: 'And he was numbered with the transgressors'ᵇ; and I tell you that this must be fulfilled in me. Yes, what is written about me is reaching its fulfillment."

³⁸The disciples said, "See, Lord, here are two swords."

"That is enough," he replied.

Jesus Prays on the Mount of Olives

³⁹Jesus went out as usual to the Mount of Olives, and his disciples followed him. ⁴⁰On reaching

ᵃ31 The Greek is plural.   ᵇ37 Isaiah 53:12

the place, he said to them, "Pray that you will not fall into temptation." [41]He withdrew about a stone's throw beyond them, knelt down and prayed, [42]"Father, if you are willing, take this cup from me; yet not my will, but yours be done." [43]An angel from heaven appeared to him and strengthened him. [44]And being in anguish, he prayed more earnestly, and his sweat was like drops of blood falling to the ground.[a]

[45]When he rose from prayer and went back to the disciples, he found them asleep, exhausted from sorrow. [46]"Why are you sleeping?" he asked them. "Get up and pray so that you will not fall into temptation."

Jesus Arrested

[47]While he was still speaking a crowd came up, and the man who was called Judas, one of the Twelve, was leading them. He approached Jesus to kiss him, [48]but Jesus asked him, "Judas, are you betraying the Son of Man with a kiss?"

[49]When Jesus' followers saw what was going to happen, they said, "Lord, should we strike with our swords?" [50]And one of them struck the servant of the high priest, cutting off his right ear.

[51]But Jesus answered, "No more of this!" And he touched the man's ear and healed him.

[52]Then Jesus said to the chief priests, the officers of the temple guard, and the elders, who had come for him, "Am I leading a rebellion, that you have come with swords and clubs? [53]Every day I was with you in the temple courts, and you did not lay a hand on me. But this is your hour—when darkness reigns."

Peter Disowns Jesus

[54]Then seizing him, they led him away and took him into the house of the high priest. Peter followed at a distance. [55]But when they had kindled a fire in the middle of the courtyard and had sat down together, Peter sat down with them. [56]A servant girl saw him seated there in the firelight. She looked closely at him and said, "This man was with him."

[57]But he denied it. "Woman, I don't know him," he said.

[58]A little later someone else saw him and said, "You also are one of them."

"Man, I am not!" Peter replied.

[59]About an hour later another asserted, "Certainly this fellow was with him, for he is a Galilean."

[60]Peter replied, "Man, I don't know what you're talking about!" Just as he was speaking, the rooster crowed. [61]The Lord turned and looked straight at Peter. Then Peter remembered the word the Lord had spoken to him: "Before the rooster crows today, you will disown me three times." [62]And he went outside and wept bitterly.

The Guards Mock Jesus

[63]The men who were guarding Jesus began mocking and beating him. [64]They blindfolded him and demanded, "Prophesy! Who hit you?" [65]And they said many other insulting things to him.

Jesus Before Pilate and Herod

[66]At daybreak the council of the elders of the people, both the chief priests and teachers of the law, met together, and Jesus was led before them. [67]"If you are the Christ,[b]" they said, "tell us."

---

[a]44 Some early manuscripts do not have verses 43 and 44.   [b]67 Or *Messiah*

Jesus answered, "If I tell you, you will not believe me, 68and if I asked you, you would not answer. 69But from now on, the Son of Man will be seated at the right hand of the mighty God."

70They all asked, "Are you then the Son of God?"

He replied, "You are right in saying I am."

71Then they said, "Why do we need any more testimony? We have heard it from his own lips."

23 Then the whole assembly rose and led him off to Pilate. 2And they began to accuse him, saying, "We have found this man subverting our nation. He opposes payment of taxes to Caesar and claims to be Christ,*a a king."

3So Pilate asked Jesus, "Are you the king of the Jews?"

"Yes, it is as you say," Jesus replied.

4Then Pilate announced to the chief priests and the crowd, "I find no basis for a charge against this man."

5But they insisted, "He stirs up the people all over Judeab by his teaching. He started in Galilee and has come all the way here."

6On hearing this, Pilate asked if the man was a Galilean. 7When he learned that Jesus was under Herod's jurisdiction, he sent him to Herod, who was also in Jerusalem at that time.

8When Herod saw Jesus, he was greatly pleased, because for a long time he had been wanting to see him. From what he had heard about him, he hoped to see him perform some miracle. 9He plied him with many questions, but Jesus gave him no answer. 10The chief priests and the teachers of the law were standing there, vehemently accusing him.

11Then Herod and his soldiers ridiculed and mocked him. Dressing him in an elegant robe, they sent him back to Pilate. 12That day Herod and Pilate became friends—before this they had been enemies.

13Pilate called together the chief priests, the rulers and the people, 14and said to them, "You brought me this man as one who was inciting the people to rebellion. I have examined him in your presence and have found no basis for your charges against him. 15Neither has Herod, for he sent him back to us; as you can see, he has done nothing to deserve death. 16Therefore, I will punish him and then release him.c"

18With one voice they cried out, "Away with this man! Release Barabbas to us!" 19(Barabbas had been thrown into prison for an insurrection in the city, and for murder.)

20Wanting to release Jesus, Pilate appealed to them again. 21But they kept shouting, "Crucify him! Crucify him!"

22For the third time he spoke to them: "Why? What crime has this man committed? I have found in him no grounds for the death penalty. Therefore I will have him punished and then release him."

23But with loud shouts they insistently demanded that he be crucified, and their shouts prevailed. 24So Pilate decided to grant their demand. 25He released the man who had been thrown into prison for insurrection and murder, the one they asked for, and surrendered Jesus to their will.

The Crucifixion

26As they led him away, they

a2 Or Messiah; also in verses 35 and 39   b5 Or over the land of the Jews   c16 Some manuscripts him." 17Now he was obliged to release one man to them at the Feast.

seized Simon from Cyrene, who was on his way in from the country, and put the cross on him and made him carry it behind Jesus. 27A large number of people followed him, including women who mourned and wailed for him. 28Jesus turned and said to them, "Daughters of Jerusalem, do not weep for me; weep for yourselves and for your children. 29For the time will come when you will say, 'Blessed are the barren women, the wombs that never bore and the breasts that never nursed!' 30Then

" 'they will say to the
    mountains, "Fall on us!"
and to the hills, "Cover
    us!" ' a

31For if men do these things when the tree is green, what will happen when it is dry?"

32Two other men, both criminals, were also led out with him to be executed. 33When they came to the place called the Skull, there they crucified him, along with the criminals—one on his right, the other on his left. 34Jesus said, "Father, forgive them, for they do not know what they are doing." b And they divided up his clothes by casting lots.

35The people stood watching, and the rulers even sneered at him. They said, "He saved others; let him save himself if he is the Christ of God, the Chosen One."

36The soldiers also came up and mocked him. They offered him wine vinegar 37and said, "If you are the king of the Jews, save yourself."

38There was a written notice above him, which read: THIS IS THE KING OF THE JEWS.

39One of the criminals who hung there hurled insults at him: "Aren't you the Christ? Save yourself and us!"

40But the other criminal rebuked him. "Don't you fear God," he said, "since you are under the same sentence? 41We are punished justly, for we are getting what our deeds deserve. But this man has done nothing wrong."

42Then he said, "Jesus, remember me when you come into your kingdom." c

43Jesus answered him, "I tell you the truth, today you will be with me in paradise."

Jesus' Death

44It was now about the sixth hour, and darkness came over the whole land until the ninth hour, 45for the sun stopped shining. And the curtain of the temple was torn in two. 46Jesus called out with a loud voice, "Father, into your hands I commit my spirit." When he had said this, he breathed his last.

47The centurion, seeing what had happened, praised God and said, "Surely this was a righteous man." 48When all the people who had gathered to witness this sight saw what took place, they beat their breasts and went away. 49But all those who knew him, including the women who had followed him from Galilee, stood at a distance, watching these things.

Jesus' Burial

50Now there was a man named Joseph, a member of the Council, a good and upright man, 51who had not consented to their decision and action. He came from the Judean town of Arimathea and he was waiting for the king-

a30 Hosea 10:8   b34 Some early manuscripts do not have this sentence.
c42 Some manuscripts come with your kingly power

dom of God. ⁵²Going to Pilate, he asked for Jesus' body. ⁵³Then he took it down, wrapped it in linen cloth and placed it in a tomb cut in the rock, one in which no one had yet been laid. ⁵⁴It was Preparation Day, and the Sabbath was about to begin.

⁵⁵The women who had come with Jesus from Galilee followed Joseph and saw the tomb and how his body was laid in it. ⁵⁶Then they went home and prepared spices and perfumes. But they rested on the Sabbath in obedience to the commandment.

The Resurrection

24 On the first day of the week, very early in the morning, the women took the spices they had prepared and went to the tomb. ²They found the stone rolled away from the tomb, ³but when they entered, they did not find the body of the Lord Jesus. ⁴While they were wondering about this, suddenly two men in clothes that gleamed like lightning stood beside them. ⁵In their fright the women bowed down with their faces to the ground, but the men said to them, "Why do you look for the living among the dead? ⁶He is not here; he has risen! Remember how he told you, while he was still with you in Galilee: ⁷'The Son of Man must be delivered into the hands of sinful men, be crucified and on the third day be raised again.'" ⁸Then they remembered his words.

⁹When they came back from the tomb, they told all these things to the Eleven and to all the others. ¹⁰It was Mary Magdalene, Joanna, Mary the mother of James, and the others with them who told this to the apostles. ¹¹But they did not believe the women,

because their words seemed to them like nonsense. ¹²Peter, however, got up and ran to the tomb. Bending over, he saw the strips of linen lying by themselves, and he went away, wondering to himself what had happened.

On the Road to Emmaus

¹³Now that same day two of them were going to a village called Emmaus, about seven miles*ᵃ* from Jerusalem. ¹⁴They were talking with each other about everything that had happened. ¹⁵As they talked and discussed these things with each other, Jesus himself came up and walked along with them; ¹⁶but they were kept from recognizing him.

¹⁷He asked them, "What are you discussing together as you walk along?"

They stood still, their faces downcast. ¹⁸One of them, named Cleopas, asked him, "Are you only a visitor to Jerusalem and do not know the things that have happened there in these days?"

¹⁹"What things?" he asked.

"About Jesus of Nazareth," they replied. "He was a prophet, powerful in word and deed before God and all the people. ²⁰The chief priests and our rulers handed him over to be sentenced to death, and they crucified him; ²¹but we had hoped that he was the one who was going to redeem Israel. And what is more, it is the third day since all this took place. ²²In addition, some of our women amazed us. They went to the tomb early this morning ²³but didn't find his body. They came and told us that they had seen a vision of angels, who said he was alive. ²⁴Then some of our companions went to the tomb and

---

ᵃ13 Greek sixty stadia (about 11 kilometers)

found it just as the women had said, but him they did not see."

25He said to them, "How foolish you are, and how slow of heart to believe all that the prophets have spoken! 26Did not the Christ*a* have to suffer these things and then enter his glory?" 27And beginning with Moses and all the Prophets, he explained to them what was said in all the Scriptures concerning himself.

28As they approached the village to which they were going, Jesus acted as if he were going farther. 29But they urged him strongly, "Stay with us, for it is nearly evening; the day is almost over." So he went in to stay with them.

30When he was at the table with them, he took bread, gave thanks, broke it and began to give it to them. 31Then their eyes were opened and they recognized him, and he disappeared from their sight. 32They asked each other, "Were not our hearts burning within us while he talked with us on the road and opened the Scriptures to us?"

33They got up and returned at once to Jerusalem. There they found the Eleven and those with them, assembled together 34and saying, "It is true! The Lord has risen and has appeared to Simon." 35Then the two told what had happened on the way, and how Jesus was recognized by them when he broke the bread.

Jesus Appears to the Disciples

75
Jn 11:25,26
36While they were still talking about this, Jesus himself stood among them and said to them, "Peace be with you."

37They were startled and frightened, thinking they saw a ghost.

38He said to them, "Why are you troubled, and why do doubts rise in your minds? 39Look at my hands and my feet. It is I myself! Touch me and see; a ghost does not have flesh and bones, as you see I have."

40When he had said this, he showed them his hands and feet. 41And while they still did not believe it because of joy and amazement, he asked them, "Do you have anything here to eat?" 42They gave him a piece of broiled fish, 43and he took it and ate it in their presence.

44He said to them, "This is what I told you while I was still with you: Everything must be fulfilled that is written about me in the Law of Moses, the Prophets and the Psalms."

45Then he opened their minds so they could understand the Scriptures. 46He told them, "This is what is written: The Christ will suffer and rise from the dead on the third day, 47and repentance and forgiveness of sins will be preached in his name to all nations, beginning at Jerusalem. 48You are witnesses of these things. 49I am going to send you what my Father has promised; but stay in the city until you have been clothed with power from on high."

45
1Th 2:13

The Ascension

50When he had led them out to the vicinity of Bethany, he lifted up his hands and blessed them. 51While he was blessing them, he left them and was taken up into heaven. 52Then they worshiped him and returned to Jerusalem with great joy. 53And they stayed continually at the temple, praising God.

a26 Or Messiah; also in verse 46

John

The Word Became Flesh

15
Jn 1:14

1 In the beginning was the Word, and the Word was with God, and the Word was God. ²He was with God in the beginning.

³Through him all things were made; without him nothing was made that has been made. ⁴In him was life, and that life was the light of men. ⁵The light shines in the darkness, but the darkness has not understood[a] it.

⁶There came a man who was sent from God; his name was John. ⁷He came as a witness to testify concerning that light, so that through him all men might believe. ⁸He himself was not the light; he came only as a witness to the light. ⁹The true light that gives light to every man was coming into the world.[b]

¹⁰He was in the world, and though the world was made through him, the world did not recognize him. ¹¹He came to that which was his own, but his own did not receive him. ¹²Yet to all who received him, to those who believed in his name, he gave the right to become children of God— ¹³children born not of natural descent,[c] nor of human decision or a husband's will, but born of God.

62
Jn 3:3-7

78
Jn 3:16-18

¹⁴The Word became flesh and made his dwelling among us. We have seen his glory, the glory of the One and Only,[d] who came from the Father, full of grace and truth.

15
Jn 10:30

¹⁵John testifies concerning him. He cries out, saying, "This was he of whom I said, 'He who comes after me has surpassed me because he was before me.'" ¹⁶From the fullness of his grace we have all received one blessing after another. ¹⁷For the law was given through Moses; grace and truth came through Jesus Christ. ¹⁸No one has ever seen God, but God the One and Only,[d,e] who is at the Father's side, has made him known.

50
Ro 3:19,20

31
Ac 17:29

John the Baptist Denies Being the Christ

¹⁹Now this was John's testimony when the Jews of Jerusalem sent priests and Levites to ask him who he was. ²⁰He did not fail to confess, but confessed freely, "I am not the Christ."

²¹They asked him, "Then who are you? Are you Elijah?"

He said, "I am not."

"Are you the Prophet?"

He answered, "No."

²²Finally they said, "Who are you? Give us an answer to take back to those who sent us. What do you say about yourself?"

²³John replied in the words of Isaiah the prophet, "I am the voice of one calling in the desert, 'Make straight the way for the Lord.'"[g]

²⁴Now some Pharisees who had been sent ²⁵questioned him, "Why then do you baptize if you are not the Christ, nor Elijah, nor the Prophet?"

---

[a]5 Or darkness, and the darkness has not overcome   [b]9 Or This was the true light that gives light to every man who comes into the world   [c]13 Greek of bloods   [d]14,18 Or the Only Begotten   [e]18 Some manuscripts but the only (or only begotten) Son   [f]20 Or Messiah. "The Christ" (Greek) and "the Messiah" (Hebrew) both mean "the Anointed One"; also in verse 25.   [g]23 Isaiah 40:3

26"I baptize with^a water," John replied, "but among you stands one you do not know. 27He is the one who comes after me, the thongs of whose sandals I am not worthy to untie."

28This all happened at Bethany on the other side of the Jordan, where John was baptizing.

Jesus the Lamb of God

29The next day John saw Jesus coming toward him and said, "Look, the Lamb of God, who takes away the sin of the world! 30This is the one I meant when I said, 'A man who comes after me has surpassed me because he was before me.' 31I myself did not know him, but the reason I came baptizing with water was that he might be revealed to Israel."

32Then John gave this testimony: "I saw the Spirit come down from heaven as a dove and remain on him. 33I would not have known him, except that the one who sent me to baptize with water told me, 'The man on whom you see the Spirit come down and remain is he who will baptize with the Holy Spirit.' 34I have seen and I testify that this is the Son of God."

Jesus' First Disciples

35The next day John was there again with two of his disciples. 36When he saw Jesus passing by, he said, "Look, the Lamb of God!"

37When the two disciples heard him say this, they followed Jesus. 38Turning around, Jesus saw them following and asked, "What do you want?"

They said, "Rabbi" (which means Teacher), "where are you staying?"

39"Come," he replied, "and you will see."

So they went and saw where he was staying, and spent that day with him. It was about the tenth hour.

40Andrew, Simon Peter's brother, was one of the two who heard what John had said and who had followed Jesus. 41The first thing Andrew did was to find his brother Simon and tell him, "We have found the Messiah" (that is, the Christ). 42And he brought him to Jesus.

Jesus looked at him and said, "You are Simon son of John. You will be called Cephas" (which, when translated, is Peter^b).

Jesus Calls Philip and Nathanael

43The next day Jesus decided to leave for Galilee. Finding Philip, he said to him, "Follow me."

44Philip, like Andrew and Peter, was from the town of Bethsaida. 45Philip found Nathanael and told him, "We have found the one Moses wrote about in the Law, and about whom the prophets also wrote—Jesus of Nazareth, the son of Joseph."

46"Nazareth! Can anything good come from there?" Nathanael asked.

"Come and see," said Philip.

47When Jesus saw Nathanael approaching, he said of him, "Here is a true Israelite, in whom there is nothing false."

48"How do you know me?" Nathanael asked.

Jesus answered, "I saw you while you were still under the fig tree before Philip called you."

49Then Nathanael declared, "Rabbi, you are the Son of God; you are the King of Israel."

^a26 Or in; also in verses 31 and 33   ^b42 Both Cephas (Aramaic) and Peter (Greek) mean rock.

⁵⁰Jesus said, "You believe[a] because I told you I saw you under the fig tree. You shall see greater things than that." ⁵¹He then added, "I tell you[b] the truth, you[b] shall see heaven open, and the angels of God ascending and descending on the Son of Man."

Jesus Changes Water to Wine

2 On the third day a wedding took place at Cana in Galilee. Jesus' mother was there, ²and Jesus and his disciples had also been invited to the wedding. ³When the wine was gone, Jesus' mother said to him, "They have no more wine."

⁴"Dear woman, why do you involve me?" Jesus replied. "My time has not yet come."

⁵His mother said to the servants, "Do whatever he tells you."

⁶Nearby stood six stone water jars, the kind used by the Jews for ceremonial washing, each holding from twenty to thirty gallons.[c]

⁷Jesus said to the servants, "Fill the jars with water"; so they filled them to the brim.

⁸Then he told them, "Now draw some out and take it to the master of the banquet."

They did so, ⁹and the master of the banquet tasted the water that had been turned into wine. He did not realize where it had come from, though the servants who had drawn the water knew. Then he called the bridegroom aside ¹⁰and said, "Everyone brings out the choice wine first and then the cheaper wine after the guests have had too much to drink; but you have saved the best till now."

¹¹This, the first of his miraculous signs, Jesus performed at Cana of Galilee. He thus revealed his glory, and his disciples put their faith in him.

Jesus Clears the Temple

¹²After this he went down to Capernaum with his mother and brothers and his disciples. There they stayed for a few days.

¹³When it was almost time for the Jewish Passover, Jesus went up to Jerusalem. ¹⁴In the temple courts he found men selling cattle, sheep and doves, and others sitting at tables exchanging money. ¹⁵So he made a whip out of cords, and drove all from the temple area, both sheep and cattle; he scattered the coins of the money changers and overturned their tables. ¹⁶To those who sold doves he said, "Get these out of here! How dare you turn my Father's house into a market!"

¹⁷His disciples remembered that it is written: "Zeal for your house will consume me."[d]

¹⁸Then the Jews demanded of him, "What miraculous sign can you show us to prove your authority to do all this?"

¹⁹Jesus answered them, "Destroy this temple, and I will raise it again in three days."

²⁰The Jews replied, "It has taken forty-six years to build this temple, and you are going to raise it in three days?" ²¹But the temple he had spoken of was his body. ²²After he was raised from the dead, his disciples recalled what he had said. Then they believed the Scripture and the words that Jesus had spoken.

²³Now while he was in Jerusalem at the Passover Feast, many people saw the miraculous signs

---

ᵃ50 Or Do you believe . . . ?   ᵇ51 The Greek is plural.   ᶜ6 Greek two to three metretes (probably about 75 to 115 liters)   ᵈ17 Psalm 69:9

he was doing and believed in his name.[a] [24]But Jesus would not entrust himself to them, for he knew all men. [25]He did not need man's testimony about man, for he knew what was in a man.

Jesus Teaches Nicodemus

3 Now there was a man of the Pharisees named Nicodemus, a member of the Jewish ruling council. [2]He came to Jesus at night and said, "Rabbi, we know you are a teacher who has come from God. For no one could perform the miraculous signs you are doing if God were not with him."

[3]In reply Jesus declared, "I tell you the truth, no one can see the kingdom of God unless he is born again.[b]"

[4]"How can a man be born when he is old?" Nicodemus asked. "Surely he cannot enter a second time into his mother's womb to be born!"

[5]Jesus answered, "I tell you the truth, no one can enter the kingdom of God unless he is born of water and the Spirit. [6]Flesh gives birth to flesh, but the Spirit[c] gives birth to spirit. [7]You should not be surprised at my saying, 'You[d] must be born again.' [8]The wind blows wherever it pleases. You hear its sound, but you cannot tell where it comes from or where it is going. So it is with everyone born of the Spirit."

[9]"How can this be?" Nicodemus asked.

[10]"You are Israel's teacher," said Jesus, "and do you not understand these things? [11]I tell you the truth, we speak of what we know, and we testify to what we have seen, but still you people do not accept our testimony. [12]I have spoken to you of earthly things and you do not believe; how then will you believe if I speak of heavenly things? [13]No one has ever gone into heaven except the one who came from heaven—the Son of Man.[e] [14]Just as Moses lifted up the snake in the desert, so the Son of Man must be lifted up, [15]that everyone who believes in him may have eternal life.[f]

[16]"For God so loved the world that he gave his one and only Son,[g] that whoever believes in him shall not perish but have eternal life. [17]For God did not send his Son into the world to condemn the world, but to save the world through him. [18]Whoever believes in him is not condemned, but whoever does not believe stands condemned already because he has not believed in the name of God's one and only Son.[h] [19]This is the verdict: Light has come into the world, but men loved darkness instead of light because their deeds were evil. [20]Everyone who does evil hates the light, and will not come into the light for fear that his deeds will be exposed. [21]But whoever lives by the truth comes into the light, so that it may be seen plainly that what he has done has been done through God."[i]

John the Baptist's Testimony About Jesus

[22]After this, Jesus and his disciples went out into the Judean countryside, where he spent some time with them, and baptized. [23]Now John also was bap-

Margin references:
62 Ro 5:16,17
1   Jn 5:41-44
54 Jn 15:13
78 Jn 5:24
96 Jn 8:24

---

[a]23 Or and believed in him   [b]3 Or born from above; also in verse 7   [c]6 Or but spirit   [d]7 The Greek is plural.   [e]13 Some manuscripts Man, who is in heaven   [f]15 Or believes may have eternal life in him   [g]16 Or his only begotten Son   [h]18 Or God's only begotten Son   [i]21 Some interpreters end the quotation after verse 15.

tizing at Aenon near Salim, because there was plenty of water, and people were constantly coming to be baptized. ²⁴(This was before John was put in prison.) ²⁵An argument developed between some of John's disciples and a certain Jew*ᵃ* over the matter of ceremonial washing. ²⁶They came to John and said to him, "Rabbi, that man who was with you on the other side of the Jordan—the one you testified about—well, he is baptizing, and everyone is going to him."

²⁷To this John replied, "A man can receive only what is given him from heaven. ²⁸You yourselves can testify that I said, 'I am not the Christ*ᵇ* but am sent ahead of him.' ²⁹The bride belongs to the bridegroom. The friend who attends the bridegroom waits and listens for him, and is full of joy when he hears the bridegroom's voice. That joy is mine, and it is now complete. ³⁰He must become greater; I must become less.

³¹"The one who comes from above is above all; the one who is from the earth belongs to the earth, and speaks as one from the earth. The one who comes from heaven is above all. ³²He testifies to what he has seen and heard, but no one accepts his testimony. ³³The man who has accepted it has certified that God is truthful. ³⁴For the one whom God has sent speaks the words of God, for God*ᶜ* gives the Spirit without limit. ³⁵The Father loves the Son and has placed everything in his hands. ³⁶Whoever believes in the Son has eternal life, but whoever rejects the Son will not see life, for God's wrath remains on him."*ᵈ*

Jesus Talks With a Samaritan Woman

4 The Pharisees heard that Jesus was gaining and baptizing more disciples than John, ²although in fact it was not Jesus who baptized, but his disciples. ³When the Lord learned of this, he left Judea and went back once more to Galilee. ⁴Now he had to go through Samaria. ⁵So he came to a town in Samaria called Sychar, near the plot of ground Jacob had given to his son Joseph. ⁶Jacob's well was there, and Jesus, tired as he was from the journey, sat down by the well. It was about the sixth hour.

⁷When a Samaritan woman came to draw water, Jesus said to her, "Will you give me a drink?" ⁸(His disciples had gone into the town to buy food.)

⁹The Samaritan woman said to him, "You are a Jew and I am a Samaritan woman. How can you ask me for a drink?" (For Jews do not associate with Samaritans.*ᵉ*)

¹⁰Jesus answered her, "If you knew the gift of God and who it is that asks you for a drink, you would have asked him and he would have given you living water."

¹¹"Sir," the woman said, "you have nothing to draw with and the well is deep. Where can you get this living water? ¹²Are you greater than our father Jacob, who gave us the well and drank from it himself, as did also his sons and his flocks and herds?"

¹³Jesus answered, "Everyone who drinks this water will be thirsty again, ¹⁴but whoever drinks the water I give him will

51
Ro 8:9-11

ᵃ25 Some manuscripts *and certain Jews*   *ᵇ28* Or *Messiah*   *ᶜ34* Greek *he*   *ᵈ36* Some interpreters end the quotation after verse 30.   *ᵉ9* Or *do not use dishes Samaritans have used*

never thirst. Indeed, the water I give him will become in him a spring of water welling up to eternal life."

¹⁵The woman said to him, "Sir, give me this water so that I won't get thirsty and have to keep coming here to draw water."

¹⁶He told her, "Go, call your husband and come back."

¹⁷"I have no husband," she replied.

Jesus said to her, "You are right when you say you have no husband. ¹⁸The fact is, you have had five husbands, and the man you now have is not your husband. What you have just said is quite true."

¹⁹"Sir," the woman said, "I can see that you are a prophet. ²⁰Our fathers worshiped on this mountain, but you Jews claim that the place where we must worship is in Jerusalem."

²¹Jesus declared, "Believe me, woman, a time is coming when you will worship the Father neither on this mountain nor in Jerusalem. ²²You Samaritans worship what you do not know; we worship what we do know, for salvation is from the Jews.

99
Eph 3:20,21

²³Yet a time is coming and has now come when the true worshipers will worship the Father in spirit and truth, for they are the kind of worshipers the Father seeks. ²⁴God is spirit, and his worshipers must worship in spirit and in truth."

²⁵The woman said, "I know that Messiah" (called Christ) "is coming. When he comes, he will explain everything to us."

²⁶Then Jesus declared, "I who speak to you am he."

The Disciples Rejoin Jesus

²⁷Just then his disciples re-

ᵃ29 Or *Messiah*

turned and were surprised to find him talking with a woman. But no one asked, "What do you want?" or "Why are you talking with her?"

²⁸Then, leaving her water jar, the woman went back to the town and said to the people, ²⁹"Come, see a man who told me everything I ever did. Could this be the Christ*ᵃ*?" ³⁰They came out of the town and made their way toward him.

³¹Meanwhile his disciples urged him, "Rabbi, eat something."

³²But he said to them, "I have food to eat that you know nothing about."

³³Then his disciples said to each other, "Could someone have brought him food?"

³⁴"My food," said Jesus, "is to do the will of him who sent me and to finish his work. ³⁵Do you not say, 'Four months more and then the harvest'? I tell you, open your eyes and look at the fields! They are ripe for harvest. ³⁶Even now the reaper draws his wages, even now he harvests the crop for eternal life, so that the sower and the reaper may be glad together. ³⁷Thus the saying 'One sows and another reaps' is true. ³⁸I sent you to reap what you have not worked for. Others have done the hard work, and you have reaped the benefits of their labor."

98
Jn 7:17

Many Samaritans Believe

³⁹Many of the Samaritans from that town believed in him because of the woman's testimony, "He told me everything I ever did." ⁴⁰So when the Samaritans came to him, they urged him to stay with them, and he stayed two days. ⁴¹And because of his

words many more became believers.

42They said to the woman, "We no longer believe just because of what you said; now we have heard for ourselves, and we know that this man really is the Savior of the world."

Jesus Heals the Official's Son

43After the two days he left for Galilee. 44(Now Jesus himself had pointed out that a prophet has no honor in his own country.) 45When he arrived in Galilee, the Galileans welcomed him. They had seen all that he had done in Jerusalem at the Passover Feast, for they also had been there.

46Once more he visited Cana in Galilee, where he had turned the water into wine. And there was a certain royal official whose son lay sick at Capernaum. 47When this man heard that Jesus had arrived in Galilee from Judea, he went to him and begged him to come and heal his son, who was close to death.

48"Unless you people see miraculous signs and wonders," Jesus told him, "you will never believe."

49The royal official said, "Sir, come down before my child dies."

50Jesus replied, "You may go. Your son will live."

The man took Jesus at his word and departed. 51While he was still on the way, his servants met him with the news that his boy was living. 52When he inquired as to the time when his son got better, they said to him, "The fever left him yesterday at the seventh hour."

53Then the father realized that this was the exact time at which Jesus had said to him, "Your son will live." So he and all his household believed.

54This was the second miraculous sign that Jesus performed, having come from Judea to Galilee.

The Healing at the Pool

5 Some time later, Jesus went up to Jerusalem for a feast of the Jews. 2Now there is in Jerusalem near the Sheep Gate a pool, which in Aramaic is called Bethesda[a] and which is surrounded by five covered colonnades. 3Here a great number of disabled people used to lie—the blind, the lame, the paralyzed.[b] 5One who was there had been an invalid for thirty-eight years. 6When Jesus saw him lying there and learned that he had been in this condition for a long time, he asked him, "Do you want to get well?"

7"Sir," the invalid replied, "I have no one to help me into the pool when the water is stirred. While I am trying to get in, someone else goes down ahead of me."

8Then Jesus said to him, "Get up! Pick up your mat and walk." 9At once the man was cured; he picked up his mat and walked.

The day on which this took place was a Sabbath, 10and so the Jews said to the man who had been healed, "It is the Sabbath; the law forbids you to carry your mat."

11But he replied, "The man who made me well said to me, 'Pick up your mat and walk.'"

12So they asked him, "Who is this fellow who told you to pick it up and walk?"

---

a2 Some manuscripts Bethzatha; other manuscripts Bethsaida   b3 Some less important manuscripts paralyzed—and they waited for the moving of the waters. 4From time to time an angel of the Lord would come down and stir up the waters. The first one into the pool after each such disturbance would be cured of whatever disease he had.

[13]The man who was healed had no idea who it was, for Jesus had slipped away into the crowd that was there.

[14]Later Jesus found him at the temple and said to him, "See, you are well again. Stop sinning or something worse may happen to you." [15]The man went away and told the Jews that it was Jesus who had made him well.

Life Through the Son

[16]So, because Jesus was doing these things on the Sabbath, the Jews persecuted him. [17]Jesus said to them, "My Father is always at his work to this very day, and I, too, am working." [18]For this reason the Jews tried all the harder to kill him; not only was he breaking the Sabbath, but he was even calling God his own Father, making himself equal with God.

[19]Jesus gave them this answer: "I tell you the truth, the Son can do nothing by himself; he can do only what he sees his Father doing, because whatever the Father does the Son also does. [20]For the Father loves the Son and shows him all he does. Yes, to your amazement he will show him even greater things than these. [21]For just as the Father raises the dead and gives them life, even so the Son gives life to whom he is pleased to give it. [22]Moreover, the Father judges no one, but has entrusted all judgment to the Son, [23]that all may honor the Son just as they honor the Father. He who does not honor the Son does not honor the Father, who sent him.

[24]"I tell you the truth, whoever hears my word and believes him who sent me has eternal life and will not be condemned; he has crossed over from death to life. [25]I tell you the truth, a time is com-

ing and has now come when the dead will hear the voice of the Son of God and those who hear will live. [26]For as the Father has life in himself, so he has granted the Son to have life in himself. [27]And he has given him authority to judge because he is the Son of Man.

[28]"Do not be amazed at this, for a time is coming when all who are in their graves will hear his voice [29]and come out—those who have done good will rise to live, and those who have done evil will rise to be condemned. [30]By myself I can do nothing; I judge only as I hear, and my judgment is just, for I seek not to please myself but him who sent me.

Testimonies About Jesus

[31]"If I testify about myself, my testimony is not valid. [32]There is another who testifies in my favor, and I know that his testimony about me is valid.

[33]"You have sent to John and he has testified to the truth. [34]Not that I accept human testimony; but I mention it that you may be saved. [35]John was a lamp that burned and gave light, and you chose for a time to enjoy his light.

[36]"I have testimony weightier than that of John. For the very work that the Father has given me to finish, and which I am doing, testifies that the Father has sent me. [37]And the Father who sent me has himself testified concerning me. You have never heard his voice nor seen his form, [38]nor does his word dwell in you, for you do not believe the one he sent. [39]You diligently study[a] the Scriptures because you think that by them you possess eternal life. These are the Scriptures that testify about me, [40]yet you refuse to come to me to have life.

78
Jn 20:31

81
Jn 10:28

48
Ro 3:26

73
Ro 10:21

_____

[a]39 Or Study diligently (the imperative)

1
Jn 6:37
⁴¹"I do not accept praise from men, ⁴²but I know you. I know that you do not have the love of God in your hearts. ⁴³I have come in my Father's name, and you do not accept me; but if someone else comes in his own name, you will accept him. ⁴⁴How can you believe if you accept praise from one another, yet make no effort to obtain the praise that comes from the only God[a]?

⁴⁵"But do not think I will accuse you before the Father. Your accuser is Moses, on whom your hopes are set. ⁴⁶If you believed Moses, you would believe me, for he wrote about me. ⁴⁷But since you do not believe what he wrote, how are you going to believe what I say?"

Jesus Feeds the Five Thousand

6 Some time after this, Jesus crossed to the far shore of the Sea of Galilee (that is, the Sea of Tiberias), ²and a great crowd of people followed him because they saw the miraculous signs he had performed on the sick. ³Then Jesus went up on a mountainside and sat down with his disciples. ⁴The Jewish Passover Feast was near.

⁵When Jesus looked up and saw a great crowd coming toward him, he said to Philip, "Where shall we buy bread for these people to eat?" ⁶He asked this only to test him, for he already had in mind what he was going to do.

⁷Philip answered him, "Eight months' wages[b] would not buy enough bread for each one to have a bite!"

⁸Another of his disciples, Andrew, Simon Peter's brother, spoke up, ⁹"Here is a boy with five small barley loaves and two small fish, but how far will they go among so many?"

¹⁰Jesus said, "Have the people sit down." There was plenty of grass in that place, and the men sat down, about five thousand of them. ¹¹Jesus then took the loaves, gave thanks, and distributed to those who were seated as much as they wanted. He did the same with the fish.

¹²When they had all had enough to eat, he said to his disciples, "Gather the pieces that are left over. Let nothing be wasted." ¹³So they gathered them and filled twelve baskets with the pieces of the five barley loaves left over by those who had eaten.

¹⁴After the people saw the miraculous sign that Jesus did, they began to say, "Surely this is the Prophet who is to come into the world." ¹⁵Jesus, knowing that they intended to come and make him king by force, withdrew again to a mountain by himself.

Jesus Walks on the Water

¹⁶When evening came, his disciples went down to the lake, ¹⁷where they got into a boat and set off across the lake for Capernaum. By now it was dark, and Jesus had not yet joined them. ¹⁸A strong wind was blowing and the waters grew rough. ¹⁹When they had rowed three or three and a half miles,[c] they saw Jesus approaching the boat, walking on the water; and they were terrified. ²⁰But he said to them, "It is I; don't be afraid." ²¹Then they were willing to take him into the boat, and immediately the boat reached the shore where they were heading.

²²The next day the crowd that had stayed on the opposite shore of the lake realized that only one

---

[a]44 Some early manuscripts the Only One   [b]7 Greek two hundred denarii   [c]19 Greek
rowed twenty-five or thirty stadia (about 5 or 6 kilometers)

boat had been there, and that Jesus had not entered it with his disciples, but that they had gone away alone. ²³Then some boats from Tiberias landed near the place where the people had eaten the bread after the Lord had given thanks. ²⁴Once the crowd realized that neither Jesus nor his disciples were there, they got into the boats and went to Capernaum in search of Jesus.

Jesus the Bread of Life

²⁵When they found him on the other side of the lake, they asked him, "Rabbi, when did you get here?"

²⁶Jesus answered, "I tell you the truth, you are looking for me, not because you saw miraculous signs but because you ate the loaves and had your fill. ²⁷Do not work for food that spoils, but for food that endures to eternal life, which the Son of Man will give you. On him God the Father has placed his seal of approval."

²⁸Then they asked him, "What must we do to do the works God requires?"

²⁹Jesus answered, "The work of God is this: to believe in the one he has sent."

³⁰So they asked him, "What miraculous sign then will you give that we may see it and believe you? What will you do? ³¹Our forefathers ate the manna in the desert; as it is written: 'He gave them bread from heaven to eat.'ᵃ

³²Jesus said to them, "I tell you the truth, it is not Moses who has given you the bread from heaven, but it is my Father who gives you the true bread from heaven. ³³For the bread of God is he who comes down from heaven and gives life to the world."

³⁴"Sir," they said, "from now on give us this bread."

³⁵Then Jesus declared, "I am the bread of life. He who comes to me will never go hungry, and he who believes in me will never be thirsty. ³⁶But as I told you, you have seen me and still you do not believe. ³⁷All that the Father gives me will come to me, and whoever comes to me I will never drive away. ³⁸For I have come down from heaven not to do my will but to do the will of him who sent me. ³⁹And this is the will of him who sent me, that I shall lose none of all that he has given me, but raise them up at the last day. ⁴⁰For my Father's will is that everyone who looks to the Son and believes in him shall have eternal life, and I will raise him up at the last day."

⁴¹At this the Jews began to grumble about him because he said, "I am the bread that came down from heaven." ⁴²They said, "Is this not Jesus, the son of Joseph, whose father and mother we know? How can he now say, 'I came down from heaven'?"

⁴³"Stop grumbling among yourselves," Jesus answered. ⁴⁴"No one can come to me unless the Father who sent me draws him, and I will raise him up at the last day. ⁴⁵It is written in the Prophets: 'They will all be taught by God.'ᵇ Everyone who listens to the Father and learns from him comes to me. ⁴⁶No one has seen the Father except the one who is from God; only he has seen the Father. ⁴⁷I tell you the truth, he who believes has everlasting life. ⁴⁸I am the bread of life. ⁴⁹Your forefathers ate the manna in the desert, yet they died. ⁵⁰But here is the bread that comes down from heaven, which a man may eat and not die. ⁵¹I am the living

23
Ac 1:8

1
Jn 14:23

ᵃ31 Exodus 16:4; Neh. 9:15; Psalm 78:24,25   ᵇ45 Isaiah 54:13

bread that came down from heaven. If anyone eats of this bread, he will live forever. This bread is my flesh, which I will give for the life of the world."

⁵²Then the Jews began to argue sharply among themselves, "How can this man give us his flesh to eat?"

⁵³Jesus said to them, "I tell you the truth, unless you eat the flesh of the Son of Man and drink his blood, you have no life in you. ⁵⁴Whoever eats my flesh and drinks my blood has eternal life, and I will raise him up at the last day. ⁵⁵For my flesh is real food and my blood is real drink. ⁵⁶Whoever eats my flesh and drinks my blood remains in me, and I in him. ⁵⁷Just as the living Father sent me and I live because of the Father, so the one who feeds on me will live because of me. ⁵⁸This is the bread that came down from heaven. Your forefathers ate manna and died, but he who feeds on this bread will live forever." ⁵⁹He said this while teaching in the synagogue in Capernaum.

Many Disciples Desert Jesus

⁶⁰On hearing it, many of his disciples said, "This is a hard teaching. Who can accept it?"

⁶¹Aware that his disciples were grumbling about this, Jesus said to them, "Does this offend you? ⁶²What if you see the Son of Man ascend to where he was before! ⁶³The Spirit gives life; the flesh counts for nothing. The words I have spoken to you are spirit*ᵃ* and they are life. ⁶⁴Yet there are some of you who do not believe." For Jesus had known from the beginning which of them did not believe and who would betray him. ⁶⁵He went on to say, "This is why I told you that no one can

come to me unless the Father has enabled him."

⁶⁶From this time many of his disciples turned back and no longer followed him.

⁶⁷"You do not want to leave too, do you?" Jesus asked the Twelve.

⁶⁸Simon Peter answered him, "Lord, to whom shall we go? You have the words of eternal life. ⁶⁹We believe and know that you are the Holy One of God."

⁷⁰Then Jesus replied, "Have I not chosen you, the Twelve? Yet one of you is a devil!" ⁷¹(He meant Judas, the son of Simon Iscariot, who, though one of the Twelve, was later to betray him.)

Jesus Goes to the Feast of Tabernacles

7 After this, Jesus went around in Galilee, purposely staying away from Judea because the Jews there were waiting to take his life. ²But when the Jewish Feast of Tabernacles was near, ³Jesus' brothers said to him, "You ought to leave here and go to Judea, so that your disciples may see the miracles you do. ⁴No one who wants to become a public figure acts in secret. Since you are doing these things, show yourself to the world." ⁵For even his own brothers did not believe in him.

⁶Therefore Jesus told them, "The right time for me has not yet come; for you any time is right. ⁷The world cannot hate you, but it hates me because I testify that what it does is evil. ⁸You go to the Feast. I am not yet*ᵇ* going up to this Feast, because for me the right time has not yet come." ⁹Having said this, he stayed in Galilee.

¹⁰However, after his brothers had left for the Feast, he went

---

ᵃ63 Or Spirit   ᵇ8 Some early manuscripts do not have yet.

also, not publicly, but in secret.
[11]Now at the Feast the Jews were watching for him and asking, "Where is that man?"

[12]Among the crowds there was widespread whispering about him. Some said, "He is a good man."

Others replied, "No, he deceives the people." [13]But no one would say anything publicly about him for fear of the Jews.

Jesus Teaches at the Feast

[14]Not until halfway through the Feast did Jesus go up to the temple courts and begin to teach. [15]The Jews were amazed and asked, "How did this man get such learning without having studied?"

[16]Jesus answered, "My teaching is not my own. It comes from him who sent me. [17]If anyone chooses to do God's will, he will find out whether my teaching comes from God or whether I speak on my own. [18]He who speaks on his own does so to gain honor for himself, but he who works for the honor of the one who sent him is a man of truth; there is nothing false about him. [19]Has not Moses given you the law? Yet not one of you keeps the law. Why are you trying to kill me?"

[20]"You are demon-possessed," the crowd answered. "Who is trying to kill you?"

[21]Jesus said to them, "I did one miracle, and you are all astonished. [22]Yet, because Moses gave you circumcision (though actually it did not come from Moses, but from the patriarchs), you circumcise a child on the Sabbath. [23]Now if a child can be circumcised on the Sabbath so that the law of Moses may not be broken, why are you angry with me for

healing the whole man on the Sabbath? [24]Stop judging by mere appearances, and make a right judgment."

Is Jesus the Christ?

[25]At that point some of the people of Jerusalem began to ask, "Isn't this the man they are trying to kill? [26]Here he is, speaking publicly, and they are not saying a word to him. Have the authorities really concluded that he is the Christ?[a] [27]But we know where this man is from; when the Christ comes, no one will know where he is from."

[28]Then Jesus, still teaching in the temple courts, cried out, "Yes, you know me, and you know where I am from. I am not here on my own, but he who sent me is true. You do not know him, [29]but I know him because I am from him and he sent me."

[30]At this they tried to seize him, but no one laid a hand on him, because his time had not yet come. [31]Still, many in the crowd put their faith in him. They said, "When the Christ comes, will he do more miraculous signs than this man?"

[32]The Pharisees heard the crowd whispering such things about him. Then the chief priests and the Pharisees sent temple guards to arrest him.

[33]Jesus said, "I am with you for only a short time, and then I go to the one who sent me. [34]You will look for me, but you will not find me; and where I am, you cannot come."

[35]The Jews said to one another, "Where does this man intend to go that we cannot find him? Will he go where our people live scattered among the Greeks, and teach the Greeks? [36]What did he mean when he said, 'You will

98
Ac 20:27

a 26 Or Messiah; also in verses 27, 31, 41 and 42

look for me, but you will not find me,' and 'Where I am, you cannot come'?''

[37]On the last and greatest day of the Feast, Jesus stood and said in a loud voice, "If anyone is thirsty, let him come to me and drink. [38]Whoever believes in me, as[a] the Scripture has said, streams of living water will flow from within him." [39]By this he meant the Spirit, whom those who believed in him were later to receive. Up to that time the Spirit had not been given, since Jesus had not yet been glorified.

[40]On hearing his words, some of the people said, "Surely this man is the Prophet."

[41]Others said, "He is the Christ."

Still others asked, "How can the Christ come from Galilee? [42]Does not the Scripture say that the Christ will come from David's family[h] and from Bethlehem, the town where David lived?" [43]Thus the people were divided because of Jesus. [44]Some wanted to seize him, but no one laid a hand on him.

Unbelief of the Jewish Leaders

[45]Finally the temple guards went back to the chief priests and Pharisees, who asked them, "Why didn't you bring him in?"

[46]"No one ever spoke the way this man does," the guards declared.

[47]"You mean he has deceived you also?" the Pharisees retorted. [48]"Has any of the rulers or of the Pharisees believed in him? [49]No! But this mob that knows nothing of the law—there is a curse on them."

[50]Nicodemus, who had gone to Jesus earlier and who was one

of their own number, asked, [51]"Does our law condemn anyone without first hearing him to find out what he is doing?"

[52]They replied, "Are you from Galilee, too? Look into it, and you will find that a prophet[c] does not come out of Galilee."

[The earliest and most reliable manuscripts and other ancient witnesses do not have John 7:53-8:11.]

[53]Then each went to his own home.

8 But Jesus went to the Mount of Olives. [2]At dawn he appeared again in the temple courts, where all the people gathered around him, and he sat down to teach them. [3]The teachers of the law and the Pharisees brought in a woman caught in adultery. They made her stand before the group [4]and said to Jesus, "Teacher, this woman was caught in the act of adultery. [5]In the Law Moses commanded us to stone such women. Now what do you say?" [6]They were using this question as a trap, in order to have a basis for accusing him.

But Jesus bent down and started to write on the ground with his finger. [7]When they kept on questioning him, he straightened up and said to them, "If any one of you is without sin, let him be the first to throw a stone at her." [8]Again he stooped down and wrote on the ground.

[9]At this, those who heard began to go away one at a time, the older ones first, until only Jesus was left, with the woman still standing there. [10]Jesus straightened up and asked her,

2
1Co 6:9-11

28
Eph 1:17

---

[a]37,38 Or / If anyone is thirsty, let him come to me. / And let him drink, [38]who believes in me. / As   [h]42 Greek seed   [c]52 Two early manuscripts the Prophet

"Woman, where are they? Has no one condemned you?"

¹¹"No one, sir," she said.

"Then neither do I condemn you," Jesus declared. "Go now and leave your life of sin."

The Validity of Jesus' Testimony

¹²When Jesus spoke again to the people, he said, "I am the light of the world. Whoever follows me will never walk in darkness, but will have the light of life."

¹³The Pharisees challenged him, "Here you are, appearing as your own witness; your testimony is not valid."

¹⁴Jesus answered, "Even if I testify on my own behalf, my testimony is valid, for I know where I came from and where I am going. But you have no idea where I come from or where I am going. ¹⁵You judge by human standards; I pass judgment on no one. ¹⁶But if I do judge, my decisions are right, because I am not alone. I stand with the Father, who sent me. ¹⁷In your own Law it is written that the testimony of two men is valid. ¹⁸I am one who testifies for myself; my other witness is the Father, who sent me."

¹⁹Then they asked him, "Where is your father?"

"You do not know me or my Father," Jesus replied. "If you knew me, you would know my Father also." ²⁰He spoke these words while teaching in the temple area near the place where the offerings were put. Yet no one seized him, because his time had not yet come.

²¹Once more Jesus said to them, "I am going away, and you will look for me, and you will die in your sin. Where I go, you cannot come."

²²This made the Jews ask, "Will he kill himself? Is that why he says, 'Where I go, you cannot come'?"

²³But he continued, "You are from below; I am from above. You are of this world; I am not of this world. ²⁴I told you that you would die in your sins; if you do not believe that I am the one I claim to be,ᵃ you will indeed die in your sins."

²⁵"Who are you?" they asked.

"Just what I have been claiming all along," Jesus replied. ²⁶"I have much to say in judgment of you. But he who sent me is reliable, and what I have heard from him I tell the world."

²⁷They did not understand that he was telling them about his Father. ²⁸So Jesus said, "When you have lifted up the Son of Man, then you will know that I am the one I claim to be, and that I do nothing on my own but speak just what the Father has taught me. ²⁹The one who sent me is with me; he has not left me alone, for I always do what pleases him." ³⁰Even as he spoke, many put their faith in him.

The Children of Abraham

³¹To the Jews who had believed him, Jesus said, "If you hold to my teaching, you are really my disciples. ³²Then you will know the truth, and the truth will set you free."

³³They answered him, "We are Abraham's descendantsᵇ and have never been slaves of anyone. How can you say that we shall be set free?"

³⁴Jesus replied, "I tell you the truth, everyone who sins is a slave to sin. ³⁵Now a slave has no

96
2Th 2:11,

30
Ro 8:21

88
Ro 3:10

ᵃ24 Or I am he; also in verse 28   ᵇ33 Greek seed; also in verse 37

permanent place in the family, but a son belongs to it forever. [36]So if the Son sets you free, you will be free indeed. [37]I know you are Abraham's descendants. Yet you are ready to kill me, because you have no room for my word. [38]I am telling you what I have seen in the Father's presence, and you do what you have heard from your father.[a]

[39]"Abraham is our father," they answered.

"If you were Abraham's children," said Jesus, "then you would[b] do the things Abraham did. [40]As it is, you are determined to kill me, a man who has told you the truth that I heard from God. Abraham did not do such things. [41]You are doing the things your own father does."

"We are not illegitimate children," they protested. "The only Father we have is God himself."

The Children of the Devil

[42]Jesus said to them, "If God were your Father, you would love me, for I came from God and now am here. I have not come on my own; but he sent me. [43]Why is my language not clear to you? Because you are unable to hear what I say. [44]You belong to your father, the devil, and you want to carry out your father's desire. He was a murderer from the beginning, not holding to the truth, for there is no truth in him. When he lies, he speaks his native language, for he is a liar and the father of lies. [45]Yet because I tell the truth, you do not believe me! [46]Can any of you prove me guilty of sin? If I am telling the truth, why don't you believe me? [47]He who belongs to God hears what

56
Eph 4:15

God says. The reason you do not hear is that you do not belong to God."

The Claims of Jesus About Himself

[48]The Jews answered him, "Aren't we right in saying that you are a Samaritan and demon-possessed?"

[49]"I am not possessed by a demon," said Jesus, "but I honor my Father and you dishonor me. [50]I am not seeking glory for myself; but there is one who seeks it, and he is the judge. [51]I tell you the truth, if anyone keeps my word, he will never see death."

[52]At this the Jews exclaimed, "Now we know that you are demon-possessed! Abraham died and so did the prophets, yet you say that if anyone keeps your word, he will never taste death. [53]Are you greater than our father Abraham? He died, and so did the prophets. Who do you think you are?"

[54]Jesus replied, "If I glorify myself, my glory means nothing. My Father, whom you claim as your God, is the one who glorifies me. [55]Though you do not know him, I know him. If I said I did not, I would be a liar like you, but I do know him and keep his word. [56]Your father Abraham rejoiced at the thought of seeing my day; he saw it and was glad."

[57]"You are not yet fifty years old," the Jews said to him, "and you have seen Abraham!"

[58]"I tell you the truth," Jesus answered, "before Abraham was born, I am!" [59]At this, they picked up stones to stone him, but Jesus hid himself, slipping away from the temple grounds.

---

[a]38 Or presence. Therefore do what you have heard from the Father.   [b]39 Some early manuscripts "If you are Abraham's children," said Jesus, "then

Jesus Heals a Man Born Blind

9 As he went along, he saw a man blind from birth. [2]His disciples asked him, "Rabbi, who sinned, this man or his parents, that he was born blind?"

[3]"Neither this man nor his parents sinned," said Jesus, "but this happened so that the work of God might be displayed in his life. [4]As long as it is day, we must do the work of him who sent me. Night is coming, when no one can work. [5]While I am in the world, I am the light of the world."

[6]Having said this, he spit on the ground, made some mud with the saliva, and put it on the man's eyes. [7]"Go," he told him, "wash in the Pool of Siloam" (this word means Sent). So the man went and washed, and came home seeing.

[8]His neighbors and those who had formerly seen him begging asked, "Isn't this the same man who used to sit and beg?" [9]Some claimed that he was.

Others said, "No, he only looks like him."

But he himself insisted, "I am the man."

[10]"How then were your eyes opened?" they demanded.

[11]He replied, "The man they call Jesus made some mud and put it on my eyes. He told me to go to Siloam and wash. So I went and washed, and then I could see."

[12]"Where is this man?" they asked him.

"I don't know," he said.

The Pharisees Investigate the Healing

[13]They brought to the Pharisees the man who had been blind. [14]Now the day on which Jesus had made the mud and opened the man's eyes was a Sabbath. [15]Therefore the Pharisees also asked him how he had received his sight. "He put mud on my eyes," the man replied, "and I washed, and now I see."

[16]Some of the Pharisees said, "This man is not from God, for he does not keep the Sabbath."

But others asked, "How can a sinner do such miraculous signs?" So they were divided.

[17]Finally they turned again to the blind man, "What have you to say about him? It was your eyes he opened."

The man replied, "He is a prophet."

[18]The Jews still did not believe that he had been blind and had received his sight until they sent for the man's parents. [19]"Is this your son?" they asked. "Is this the one you say was born blind? How is it that now he can see?"

[20]"We know he is our son," the parents answered, "and we know he was born blind. [21]But how he can see now, or who opened his eyes, we don't know. Ask him. He is of age; he will speak for himself." [22]His parents said this because they were afraid of the Jews, for already the Jews had decided that anyone who acknowledged that Jesus was the Christ[a] would be put out of the synagogue. [23]That was why his parents said, "He is of age; ask him."

[24]A second time they summoned the man who had been blind. "Give glory to God,[b]" they said. "We know this man is a sinner."

[25]He replied, "Whether he is a sinner or not, I don't know. One thing I do know. I was blind but now I see!"

[a]22 Or Messiah   [b]24 A solemn charge to tell the truth (see Joshua 7:19)

²⁶Then they asked him, "What did he do to you? How did he open your eyes?"

²⁷He answered, "I have told you already and you did not listen. Why do you want to hear it again? Do you want to become his disciples, too?"

²⁸Then they hurled insults at him and said, "You are this fellow's disciple! We are disciples of Moses! ²⁹We know that God spoke to Moses, but as for this fellow, we don't even know where he comes from."

³⁰The man answered, "Now that is remarkable! You don't know where he comes from, yet he opened my eyes. ³¹We know that God does not listen to sinners. He listens to the godly man who does his will. ³²Nobody has ever heard of opening the eyes of a man born blind. ³³If this man were not from God, he could do nothing."

³⁴To this they replied, "You were steeped in sin at birth; how dare you lecture us!" And they threw him out.

Spiritual Blindness

³⁵Jesus heard that they had thrown him out, and when he found him, he said, "Do you believe in the Son of Man?"

³⁶"Who is he, sir?" the man asked. "Tell me so that I may believe in him."

³⁷Jesus said, "You have now seen him; in fact, he is the one speaking with you."

³⁸Then the man said, "Lord, I believe," and he worshiped him.

³⁹Jesus said, "For judgment I have come into this world, so that the blind will see and those who see will become blind."

⁴⁰Some Pharisees who were with him heard him say this and asked, "What? Are we blind too?"

⁴¹Jesus said, "If you were blind, you would not be guilty of sin; but now that you claim you can see, your guilt remains.

The Shepherd and His Flock

10 "I tell you the truth, the man who does not enter the sheep pen by the gate, but climbs in by some other way, is a thief and a robber. ²The man who enters by the gate is the shepherd of his sheep. ³The watchman opens the gate for him, and the sheep listen to his voice. He calls his own sheep by name and leads them out. ⁴When he has brought out all his own, he goes on ahead of them, and his sheep follow him because they know his voice. ⁵But they will never follow a stranger; in fact, they will run away from him because they do not recognize a stranger's voice." ⁶Jesus used this figure of speech, but they did not understand what he was telling them.

⁷Therefore Jesus said again, "I tell you the truth, I am the gate for the sheep. ⁸All who ever came before me were thieves and robbers, but the sheep did not listen to them. ⁹I am the gate; whoever enters through me will be saved.ᵃ He will come in and go out, and find pasture. ¹⁰The thief comes only to steal and kill and destroy; I have come that they may have life, and have it to the full.

¹¹"I am the good shepherd. The good shepherd lays down his life for the sheep. ¹²The hired hand is not the shepherd who owns the sheep. So when he sees the wolf coming, he abandons the sheep and runs away. Then the wolf attacks the flock and scatters it.

ᵃ9 Or *kept safe*

¹³The man runs away because he is a hired hand and cares nothing for the sheep.

¹⁴"I am the good shepherd; I know my sheep and my sheep know me— ¹⁵just as the Father knows me and I know the Father—and I lay down my life for the sheep. ¹⁶I have other sheep that are not of this sheep pen. I must bring them also. They too will listen to my voice, and there shall be one flock and one shepherd. ¹⁷The reason my Father loves me is that I lay down my life—only to take it up again. ¹⁸No one takes it from me, but I lay it down of my own accord. I have authority to lay it down and authority to take it up again. This command I received from my Father."

¹⁹At these words the Jews were again divided. ²⁰Many of them said, "He is demon-possessed and raving mad. Why listen to him?"

²¹But others said, "These are not the sayings of a man possessed by a demon. Can a demon open the eyes of the blind?"

The Unbelief of the Jews

²²Then came the Feast of Dedication*a* at Jerusalem. It was winter, ²³and Jesus was in the temple area walking in Solomon's Colonnade. ²⁴The Jews gathered around him, saying, "How long will you keep us in suspense? If you are the Christ,*b* tell us plainly."

²⁵Jesus answered, "I did tell you, but you do not believe. The miracles I do in my Father's name speak for me, ²⁶but you do not believe because you are not my sheep. ²⁷My sheep listen to my voice; I know them, and they fol-low me. ²⁸I give them eternal life, and they shall never perish; no one can snatch them out of my hand. ²⁹My Father, who has given them to me, is greater than all*c*; no one can snatch them out of my Father's hand. ³⁰I and the Father are one."

³¹Again the Jews picked up stones to stone him, ³²but Jesus said to them, "I have shown you many great miracles from the Father. For which of these do you stone me?"

³³"We are not stoning you for any of these," replied the Jews, "but for blasphemy, because you, a mere man, claim to be God."

³⁴Jesus answered them, "Is it not written in your Law, 'I have said you are gods'*d*? ³⁵If he called them 'gods,' to whom the word of God came—and the Scripture cannot be broken— ³⁶what about the one whom the Father set apart as his very own and sent into the world? Why then do you accuse me of blasphemy because I said, 'I am God's Son'? ³⁷Do not believe me unless I do what my Father does. ³⁸But if I do it, even though you do not believe me, believe the miracles, that you may know and understand that the Father is in me, and I in the Father." ³⁹Again they tried to seize him, but he escaped their grasp.

⁴⁰Then Jesus went back across the Jordan to the place where John had been baptizing in the early days. Here he stayed ⁴¹and many people came to him. They said, "Though John never performed a miraculous sign, all that John said about this man was true." ⁴²And in that place many believed in Jesus.

81 Jn 14:18

15 Jn 10:33

15 Jn 20:28

---

*a*22 That is, Hanukkah   *b*24 Or Messiah   *c*29 Many early manuscripts *What my Father has given me is greater than all*   *d*34 Psalm 82:6

The Death of Lazarus

11 Now a man named Lazarus was sick. He was from Bethany, the village of Mary and her sister Martha. ²This Mary, whose brother Lazarus now lay sick, was the same one who poured perfume on the Lord and wiped his feet with her hair. ³So the sisters sent word to Jesus, "Lord, the one you love is sick."

⁴When he heard this, Jesus said, "This sickness will not end in death. No, it is for God's glory so that God's Son may be glorified through it." ⁵Jesus loved Martha and her sister and Lazarus. ⁶Yet when he heard that Lazarus was sick, he stayed where he was two more days.

⁷Then he said to his disciples, "Let us go back to Judea."

⁸"But Rabbi," they said, "a short while ago the Jews tried to stone you, and yet you are going back there?"

⁹Jesus answered, "Are there not twelve hours of daylight? A man who walks by day will not stumble, for he sees by this world's light. ¹⁰It is when he walks by night that he stumbles, for he has no light."

¹¹After he had said this, he went on to tell them, "Our friend Lazarus has fallen asleep; but I am going there to wake him up."

¹²His disciples replied, "Lord, if he sleeps, he will get better." ¹³Jesus had been speaking of his death, but his disciples thought he meant natural sleep.

¹⁴So then he told them plainly, "Lazarus is dead, ¹⁵and for your sake I am glad I was not there, so that you may believe. But let us go to him."

¹⁶Then Thomas (called Didymus) said to the rest of the disciples, "Let us also go, that we may die with him."

Jesus Comforts the Sisters

¹⁷On his arrival, Jesus found that Lazarus had already been in the tomb for four days. ¹⁸Bethany was less than two miles[a] from Jerusalem, ¹⁹and many Jews had come to Martha and Mary to comfort them in the loss of their brother. ²⁰When Martha heard that Jesus was coming, she went out to meet him, but Mary stayed at home.

²¹"Lord," Martha said to Jesus, "if you had been here, my brother would not have died. ²²But I know that even now God will give you whatever you ask."

²³Jesus said to her, "Your brother will rise again."

²⁴Martha answered, "I know he will rise again in the resurrection at the last day."

²⁵Jesus said to her, "I am the resurrection and the life. He who believes in me will live, even though he dies; ²⁶and whoever lives and believes in me will never die. Do you believe this?"

²⁷"Yes, Lord," she told him, "I believe that you are the Christ,[b] the Son of God, who was to come into the world."

²⁸And after she had said this, she went back and called her sister Mary aside. "The Teacher is here," she said, "and is asking for you." ²⁹When Mary heard this, she got up quickly and went to him. ³⁰Now Jesus had not yet entered the village, but was still at the place where Martha had met him. ³¹When the Jews who had been with Mary in the house, comforting her, noticed how quickly she got up and went out, they followed her, supposing she

53
Jn 14:1-6

75
1Co 15:20-23

---

[a]18 Greek *fifteen stadia* (about 3 kilometers)   [b]27 Or *Messiah*

was going to the tomb to mourn there.

32When Mary reached the place where Jesus was and saw him, she fell at his feet and said, "Lord, if you had been here, my brother would not have died."

33When Jesus saw her weeping, and the Jews who had come along with her also weeping, he was deeply moved in spirit and troubled. 34"Where have you laid him?" he asked.

"Come and see, Lord," they replied.

35Jesus wept.

36Then the Jews said, "See how he loved him!"

37But some of them said, "Could not he who opened the eyes of the blind man have kept this man from dying?"

Jesus Raises Lazarus From the Dead

38Jesus, once more deeply moved, came to the tomb. It was a cave with a stone laid across the entrance. 39"Take away the stone," he said.

"But, Lord," said Martha, the sister of the dead man, "by this time there is a bad odor, for he has been there four days."

40Then Jesus said, "Did I not tell you that if you believed, you would see the glory of God?"

41So they took away the stone. Then Jesus looked up and said, "Father, I thank you that you have heard me. 42I knew that you always hear me, but I said this for the benefit of the people standing here, that they may believe that you sent me."

43When he had said this, Jesus called in a loud voice, "Lazarus, come out!" 44The dead man came out, his hands and feet wrapped

with strips of linen, and a cloth around his face.

Jesus said to them, "Take off the grave clothes and let him go."

The Plot to Kill Jesus

45Therefore many of the Jews who had come to visit Mary, and had seen what Jesus did, put their faith in him. 46But some of them went to the Pharisees and told them what Jesus had done. 47Then the chief priests and the Pharisees called a meeting of the Sanhedrin.

"What are we accomplishing?" they asked. "Here is this man performing many miraculous signs. 48If we let him go on like this, everyone will believe in him, and then the Romans will come and take away both our place*ᵃ* and our nation."

49Then one of them, named Caiaphas, who was high priest that year, spoke up, "You know nothing at all! 50You do not realize that it is better for you that one man die for the people than that the whole nation perish."

51He did not say this on his own, but as high priest that year he prophesied that Jesus would die for the Jewish nation, 52and not only for that nation but also for the scattered children of God, to bring them together and make them one. 53So from that day on they plotted to take his life.

54Therefore Jesus no longer moved about publicly among the Jews. Instead he withdrew to a region near the desert, to a village called Ephraim, where he stayed with his disciples.

55When it was almost time for the Jewish Passover, many went up from the country to Jerusalem for their ceremonial cleansing be-

ᵃ48 Or temple

fore the Passover. [56]They kept looking for Jesus, and as they stood in the temple area they asked one another, "What do you think? Isn't he coming to the Feast at all?" [57]But the chief priests and Pharisees had given orders that if anyone found out where Jesus was, he should report it so that they might arrest him.

Jesus Anointed at Bethany

12 Six days before the Passover, Jesus arrived at Bethany, where Lazarus lived, whom Jesus had raised from the dead. [2]Here a dinner was given in Jesus' honor. Martha served, while Lazarus was among those reclining at the table with him. [3]Then Mary took about a pint[a] of pure nard, an expensive perfume; she poured it on Jesus' feet and wiped his feet with her hair. And the house was filled with the fragrance of the perfume.

[4]But one of his disciples, Judas Iscariot, who was later to betray him, objected, [5]"Why wasn't this perfume sold and the money given to the poor? It was worth a year's wages.[b] " [6]He did not say this because he cared about the poor but because he was a thief; as keeper of the money bag, he used to help himself to what was put into it.

[7]"Leave her alone," Jesus replied. "It was intended that she should save this perfume for the day of my burial. [8]You will always have the poor among you, but you will not always have me."

[9]Meanwhile a large crowd of Jews found out that Jesus was there and came, not only because of him but also to see Lazarus,

whom he had raised from the dead. [10]So the chief priests made plans to kill Lazarus as well, [11]for on account of him many of the Jews were going over to Jesus and putting their faith in him.

The Triumphal Entry

[12]The next day the great crowd that had come for the Feast heard that Jesus was on his way to Jerusalem. [13]They took palm branches and went out to meet him, shouting,

"Hosanna![c]"

"Blessed is he who comes in
      the name of the Lord!"[d]

"Blessed is the King of Israel!"

[14]Jesus found a young donkey and sat upon it, as it is written,

[15]"Do not be afraid,
      O Daughter of Zion;
see, your king is coming,
      seated on a donkey's colt."[e]

[16]At first his disciples did not understand all this. Only after Jesus was glorified did they realize that these things had been written about him and that they had done these things to him. [17]Now the crowd that was with him when he called Lazarus from the tomb and raised him from the dead continued to spread the word. [18]Many people, because they had heard that he had given this miraculous sign, went out to meet him. [19]So the Pharisees said to one another, "See, this is getting us nowhere. Look how the whole world has gone after him!"

Jesus Predicts His Death

[20]Now there were some Greeks among those who went up to worship at the Feast. [21]They came

---

*3 Greek *a litra* (probably about 0.5 liter)   *5 Greek *three hundred denarii* which became an exclamation of praise
*13 A Hebrew expression meaning "Save!"
*13 Psalm 118:25, 26   *15 Zech. 9:9

to Philip, who was from Bethsaida in Galilee, with a request. "Sir," they said, "we would like to see Jesus." ²²Philip went to tell Andrew; Andrew and Philip in turn told Jesus.

²³Jesus replied, "The hour has come for the Son of Man to be glorified. ²⁴I tell you the truth, unless a kernel of wheat falls to the ground and dies, it remains only a single seed. But if it dies, it produces many seeds. ²⁵The man who loves his life will lose it, while the man who hates his life in this world will keep it for eternal life. ²⁶Whoever serves me must follow me; and where I am, my servant also will be. My Father will honor the one who serves me.

²⁷"Now my heart is troubled, and what shall I say? 'Father, save me from this hour'? No, it was for this very reason I came to this hour. ²⁸Father, glorify your name!"

Then a voice came from heaven, "I have glorified it, and will glorify it again." ²⁹The crowd that was there and heard it said it had thundered; others said an angel had spoken to him.

³⁰Jesus said, "This voice was for your benefit, not mine. ³¹Now is the time for judgment on this world; now the prince of this world will be driven out. ³²But I, when I am lifted up from the earth, will draw all men to myself." ³³He said this to show the kind of death he was going to die.

³⁴The crowd spoke up, "We have heard from the Law that the Christ*a* will remain forever, so how can you say, 'The Son of Man must be lifted up'? Who is this 'Son of Man'?"

³⁵Then Jesus told them, "You are going to have the light just a little while longer. Walk while you have the light, before darkness overtakes you. The man who walks in the dark does not know where he is going. ³⁶Put your trust in the light while you have it, so that you may become sons of light." When he had finished speaking, Jesus left and hid himself from them.

The Jews Continue in Their Unbelief

³⁷Even after Jesus had done all these miraculous signs in their presence, they still would not believe in him. ³⁸This was to fulfill the word of Isaiah the prophet:

"Lord, who has believed our
        message
    and to whom has the arm of
        the Lord been
        revealed?"*b*

³⁹For this reason they could not believe, because, as Isaiah says elsewhere:

⁴⁰"He has blinded their eyes
        and deadened their hearts,
    so they can neither see with
        their eyes,
    nor understand with their
        hearts,
    nor turn—and I would heal
        them."*c*

⁴¹Isaiah said this because he saw Jesus' glory and spoke about him.

⁴²Yet at the same time many even among the leaders believed in him. But because of the Pharisees they would not confess their faith for fear they would be put out of the synagogue; ⁴³for they loved praise from men more than praise from God.

⁴⁴Then Jesus cried out, "When a man believes in me, he does not believe in me only, but in the one

---

*a*34 Or *Messiah*   *b*38 Isaiah 53:1   *c*40 Isaiah 6:10

who sent me. [45]When he looks at me, he sees the one who sent me. [46]I have come into the world as a light, so that no one who believes in me should stay in darkness.

[47]"As for the person who hears my words but does not keep them, I do not judge him. For I did not come to judge the world, but to save it. [48]There is a judge for the one who rejects me and does not accept my words; that very word which I spoke will condemn him at the last day. [49]For I did not speak of my own accord, but the Father who sent me commanded me what to say and how to say it. [50]I know that his command leads to eternal life. So whatever I say is just what the Father has told me to say."

Jesus Washes His Disciples' Feet

13 It was just before the Passover Feast. Jesus knew that the time had come for him to leave this world and go to the Father. Having loved his own who were in the world, he now showed them the full extent of his love.[a]

[2]The evening meal was being served, and the devil had already prompted Judas Iscariot, son of Simon, to betray Jesus. [3]Jesus knew that the Father had put all things under his power, and that he had come from God and was returning to God; [4]so he got up from the meal, took off his outer clothing, and wrapped a towel around his waist. [5]After that, he poured water into a basin and began to wash his disciples' feet, drying them with the towel that was wrapped around him.

[6]He came to Simon Peter, who said to him, "Lord, are you going to wash my feet?"

[7]Jesus replied, "You do not realize now what I am doing, but later you will understand."

[8]"No," said Peter, "you shall never wash my feet."

Jesus answered, "Unless I wash you, you have no part with me."

[9]"Then, Lord," Simon Peter replied, "not just my feet but my hands and my head as well!"

[10]Jesus answered, "A person who has had a bath needs only to wash his feet; his whole body is clean. And you are clean, though not every one of you." [11]For he knew who was going to betray him, and that was why he said not every one was clean.

[12]When he had finished washing their feet, he put on his clothes and returned to his place. "Do you understand what I have done for you?" he asked them. [13]"You call me 'Teacher' and 'Lord,' and rightly so, for that is what I am. [14]Now that I, your Lord and Teacher, have washed your feet, you also should wash one another's feet. [15]I have set you an example that you should do as I have done for you. [16]I tell you the truth, no servant is greater than his master, nor is a messenger greater than the one who sent him. [17]Now that you know these things, you will be blessed if you do them.

Jesus Predicts His Betrayal

[18]"I am not referring to all of you; I know those I have chosen. But this is to fulfill the scripture: 'He who shares my bread has lifted up his heel against me.'[b]

[19]"I am telling you now before it happens, so that when it does happen you will believe that I am He. [20]I tell you the truth, whoever accepts anyone I send accepts

---

[a]1 Or *he loved them to the last*   [b]18 Psalm 41:9

me; and whoever accepts me accepts the one who sent me."

²¹After he had said this, Jesus was troubled in spirit and testified, "I tell you the truth, one of you is going to betray me."

²²His disciples stared at one another, at a loss to know which of them he meant. ²³One of them, the disciple whom Jesus loved, was reclining next to him. ²⁴Simon Peter motioned to this disciple and said, "Ask him which one he means."

²⁵Leaning back against Jesus, he asked him, "Lord, who is it?"

²⁶Jesus answered, "It is the one to whom I will give this piece of bread when I have dipped it in the dish." Then, dipping the piece of bread, he gave it to Judas Iscariot, son of Simon. ²⁷As soon as Judas took the bread, Satan entered into him.

"What you are about to do, do quickly," Jesus told him, ²⁸but no one at the meal understood why Jesus said this to him. ²⁹Since Judas had charge of the money, some thought Jesus was telling him to buy what was needed for the Feast, or to give something to the poor. ³⁰As soon as Judas had taken the bread, he went out. And it was night.

Jesus Predicts Peter's Denial

³¹When he was gone, Jesus said, "Now is the Son of Man glorified and God is glorified in him. ³²If God is glorified in him,ª God will glorify the Son in himself, and will glorify him at once.

³³"My children, I will be with you only a little longer. You will look for me, and just as I told the Jews, so I tell you now: Where I am going, you cannot come.

³⁴"A new command I give you: Love one another. As I have

loved you, so you must love one another. ³⁵By this all men will know that you are my disciples, if you love one another."

³⁶Simon Peter asked him, "Lord, where are you going?"

Jesus replied, "Where I am going, you cannot follow now, but you will follow later."

³⁷Peter asked, "Lord, why can't I follow you now? I will lay down my life for you."

³⁸Then Jesus answered, "Will you really lay down your life for me? I tell you the truth, before the rooster crows, you will disown me three times!

Jesus Comforts His Disciples

14 "Do not let your hearts be troubled. Trust in God*b*; trust also in me. ²In my Father's house are many rooms; if it were not so, I would have told you. I am going there to prepare a place for you. ³And if I go and prepare a place for you, I will come back and take you to be with me that you also may be where I am. ⁴You know the way to the place where I am going."

Jesus the Way to the Father

⁵Thomas said to him, "Lord, we don't know where you are going, so how can we know the way?"

⁶Jesus answered, "I am the way and the truth and the life. No one comes to the Father except through me. ⁷If you really knew me, you would know* my Father as well. From now on, you do know him and have seen him."

⁸Philip said, "Lord, show us the Father and that will be enough for us."

⁹Jesus answered: "Don't you know me, Philip, even after I have been among you such a long time? Anyone who has seen

55
1Co 13

53
Jn 16:22

27
Ac 2:42

---

*ª32 Many early manuscripts do not have If God is glorified in him.   *b*1 Or You trust in God   *c*7 Some early manuscripts If you really have known me, you will know

me has seen the Father. How can you say, 'Show us the Father'? [10]Don't you believe that I am in the Father, and that the Father is in me? The words I say to you are not just my own. Rather, it is the Father, living in me, who is doing his work. [11]Believe me when I say that I am in the Father and the Father is in me; or at least believe on the evidence of the miracles themselves. [12]I tell you the truth, anyone who has faith in me will do what I have been doing. He will do even greater things than these, because I am going to the Father. [13]And I will do whatever you ask in my name, so that the Son may bring glory to the Father. [14]You may ask me for anything in my name, and I will do it.

69
1Th 5:17

Jesus Promises the Holy Spirit

63
Jn 14:23

[15]"If you love me, you will obey what I command. [16]And I will ask the Father, and he will give you another Counselor to be with you forever— [17]the Spirit of truth. The world cannot accept him, because it neither sees him nor knows him. But you know him, for he lives with you and will be[d] in you. [18]I will not leave you as orphans; I will come to you. [19]Before long, the world will not see me anymore, but you will see me. Because I live, you also will live. [20]On that day you will realize that I am in my Father, and you are in me, and I am in you. [21]Whoever has my commands and obeys them, he is the one who loves me. He who loves me will be loved by my Father, and I too will love him and show myself to him."

81
Ro 8:28

[22]Then Judas (not Judas Iscariot) said, "But, Lord, why do you intend to show yourself to us and not to the world?"

[23]Jesus replied, "If anyone loves me, he will obey my teaching. My Father will love him, and we will come to him and make our home with him. [24]He who does not love me will not obey my teaching. These words you hear are not my own; they belong to the Father who sent me.

1
Ac 10:34,35

63
Ac 3:22,23

[25]"All this I have spoken while still with you. [26]But the Counselor, the Holy Spirit, whom the Father will send in my name, will teach you all things and will remind you of everything I have said to you. [27]Peace I leave with you; my peace I give you. I do not give to you as the world gives. Do not let your hearts be troubled and do not be afraid.

[28]"You heard me say, 'I am going away and I am coming back to you.' If you loved me, you would be glad that I am going to the Father, for the Father is greater than I. [29]I have told you now before it happens, so that when it does happen you will believe. [30]I will not speak with you much longer, for the prince of this world is coming. He has no hold on me, [31]but the world must learn that I love the Father and that I do exactly what my Father has commanded me.

"Come now; let us leave.

The Vine and the Branches

15 "I am the true vine, and my Father is the gardener. [2]He cuts off every branch in me that bears no fruit, while every branch that does bear fruit he prunes[b] so that it will be even more fruitful. [3]You are already clean because of the word I have spoken to you. [4]Remain in me, and I will remain in you. No branch can bear fruit by itself; it must remain in the vine. Neither

---

[a]17 Some early manuscripts *and is*   [b]2 The Greek for *prunes* also means *cleans*.

can you bear fruit unless you remain in me.

5"I am the vine; you are the branches. If a man remains in me and I in him, he will bear much fruit; apart from me you can do nothing. 6If anyone does not remain in me, he is like a branch that is thrown away and withers; such branches are picked up, thrown into the fire and burned. 7If you remain in me and my words remain in you, ask whatever you wish, and it will be given you. 8This is to my Father's glory, that you bear much fruit, showing yourselves to be my disciples.

9"As the Father has loved me, so have I loved you. Now remain in my love. 10If you obey my commands, you will remain in my love, just as I have obeyed my Father's commands and remain in his love. 11I have told you this so that my joy may be in you and that your joy may be complete. 12My command is this: Love each other as I have loved you. 13Greater love has no one than this, that he lay down his life for his friends. 14You are my friends if you do what I command. 15I no longer call you servants, because a servant does not know his master's business. Instead, I have called you friends, for everything that I learned from my Father I have made known to you. 16You did not choose me, but I chose you and appointed you to go and bear fruit—fruit that will last. Then the Father will give you whatever you ask in my name. 17This is my command: Love each other.

The World Hates the Disciples

18"If the world hates you, keep in mind that it hated me first. 19If you belonged to the world, it would love you as its own. As it is, you do not belong to the world, but I have chosen you out of the world. That is why the world hates you. 20Remember the words I spoke to you: 'No servant is greater than his master.'[a] If they persecuted me, they will persecute you also. If they obeyed my teaching, they will obey yours also. 21They will treat you this way because of my name, for they do not know the One who sent me. 22If I had not come and spoken to them, they would not be guilty of sin. Now, however, they have no excuse for their sin. 23He who hates me hates my Father as well. 24If I had not done among them what no one else did, they would not be guilty of sin. But now they have seen these miracles, and yet they have hated both me and my Father. 25But this is to fulfill what is written in their Law: 'They hated me without reason.'[b]

26"When the Counselor comes, whom I will send to you from the Father, the Spirit of truth who goes out from the Father, he will testify about me. 27And you also must testify, for you have been with me from the beginning.

16 "All this I have told you so that you will not go astray. 2They will put you out of the synagogue; in fact, a time is coming when anyone who kills you will think he is offering a service to God. 3They will do such things because they have not known the Father or me. 4I have told you this, so that when the time comes you will remember that I warned you. I did not tell you this at first because I was with you.

The Work of the Holy Spirit

5"Now I am going to him who sent me, yet none of you asks

54
Ro 5:8

91
Ac 5:41

36
Ro 2:5-11

38
Ro 8:7

a20 John 13:16   b25 Psalms 35:19; 69:4

me, 'Where are you going?' ⁶Because I have said these things, you are filled with grief. ⁷But I tell you the truth: It is for your good that I am going away. Unless I go away, the Counselor will not come to you; but if I go, I will send him to you. ⁸When he comes, he will convict the world of guiltᵃ in regard to sin and righteousness and judgment: ⁹in regard to sin, because men do not believe in me; ¹⁰in regard to righteousness, because I am going to the Father, where you can see me no longer; ¹¹and in regard to judgment, because the prince of this world now stands condemned.

¹²"I have much more to say to you, more than you can now bear. ¹³But when he, the Spirit of truth, comes, he will guide you into all truth. He will not speak on his own; he will speak only what he hears, and he will tell you what is yet to come. ¹⁴He will bring glory to me by taking from what is mine and making it known to you. ¹⁵All that belongs to the Father is mine. That is why I said the Spirit will take from what is mine and make it known to you.

¹⁶"In a little while you will see me no more, and then after a little while you will see me."

The Disciples' Grief Will Turn to Joy

¹⁷Some of his disciples said to one another, "What does he mean by saying, 'In a little while you will see me no more, and then after a little while you will see me,' and 'Because I am going to the Father'?" ¹⁸They kept asking, "What does he mean by 'a little while'? We don't understand what he is saying."

¹⁹Jesus saw that they wanted to ask him about this, so he said to them, "Are you asking one another what I meant when I said, 'In a little while you will see me no more, and then after a little while you will see me'? ²⁰I tell you the truth, you will weep and mourn while the world rejoices. You will grieve, but your grief will turn to joy. ²¹A woman giving birth to a child has pain because her time has come; but when her baby is born she forgets the anguish because of her joy that a child is born into the world. ²²So with you: Now is your time of grief, but I will see you again and you will rejoice, and no one will take away your joy. ²³In that day you will no longer ask me anything. I tell you the truth, my Father will give you whatever you ask in my name. ²⁴Until now you have not asked for anything in my name. Ask and you will receive, and your joy will be complete.

²⁵"Though I have been speaking figuratively, a time is coming when I will no longer use this kind of language but will tell you plainly about my Father. ²⁶In that day you will ask in my name. I am not saying that I will ask the Father on your behalf. ²⁷No, the Father himself loves you because you have loved me and have believed that I came from God. ²⁸I came from the Father and entered the world; now I am leaving the world and going back to the Father."

²⁹Then Jesus' disciples said, "Now you are speaking clearly and without figures of speech. ³⁰Now we can see that you know all things and that you do not even need to have anyone ask you questions. This makes us be-

Margin references:
14 — 1Th 1:5
35 — Jn 16:13
35 — 2Co 1:3,4
53 — Ro 14:8

ᵃ8 Or will expose the guilt of the world

lieve that you came from God."
31"You believe at last!"[a] Jesus answered. 32"But a time is coming, and has come, when you will be scattered, each to his own home. You will leave me all alone. Yet I am not alone, for my Father is with me.

33"I have told you these things, so that in me you may have peace. In this world you will have trouble. But take heart! I have overcome the world."

16
2Co 4:1,2

Jesus Prays for Himself

17 After Jesus said this, he looked toward heaven and prayed:

"Father, the time has come. Glorify your Son, that your Son may glorify you. 2For you granted him authority over all people that he might give eternal life to all those you have given him. 3Now this is eternal life: that they may know you, the only true God, and Jesus Christ, whom you have sent. 4I have brought you glory on earth by completing the work you gave me to do. 5And now, Father, glorify me in your presence with the glory I had with you before the world began.

Jesus Prays for His Disciples

6"I have revealed you[b] to those whom you gave me out of the world. They were yours; you gave them to me and they have obeyed your word. 7Now they know that everything you have given me comes from you. 8For I gave them the words you gave me and they accepted them. They knew with certainty that I came from you,

and they believed that you sent me. 9I pray for them. I am not praying for the world, but for those you have given me, for they are yours. 10All I have is yours, and all you have is mine. And glory has come to me through them. 11I will remain in the world no longer, but they are still in the world, and I am coming to you. Holy Father, protect them by the power of your name—the name you gave me—so that they may be one as we are one. 12While I was with them, I protected them and kept them safe by that name you gave me. None has been lost except the one doomed to destruction so that Scripture would be fulfilled.

13"I am coming to you now, but I say these things while I am still in the world, so that they may have the full measure of my joy within them. 14I have given them your word and the world has hated them, for they are not of the world any more than I am of the world. 15My prayer is not that you take them out of the world but that you protect them from the evil one. 16They are not of the world, even as I am not of it. 17Sanctify[c] them by the truth; your word is truth. 18As you sent me into the world, I have sent them into the world. 19For them I sanctify myself, that they too may be truly sanctified.

79
Ac 26:17,18

Jesus Prays for All Believers

20"My prayer is not for them alone. I pray also for those who will believe in me

---

a31 Or "Do you now believe?"   b6 Greek your name; also in verse 26   c17 Greek hagiazo (set apart for sacred use or make holy); also in verse 19

through their message, 21that all of them may be one, Father, just as you are in me and I am in you. May they also be in us so that the world may believe that you have sent me. 22I have given them the glory that you gave me, that they may be one as we are

97
Ro 15:5,6

one: 23I in them and you in me. May they be brought to complete unity to let the world know that you sent me and have loved them even as you have loved me.

24"Father, I want those you have given me to be with me where I am, and to see my glory, the glory you have given me because you loved me before the creation of the world.

25"Righteous Father, though the world does not know you, I know you, and they know that you have sent me. 26I have made you known to them, and will continue to make you known in order that the love you have for me may be in them and that I myself may be in them."

Jesus Arrested

18 When he had finished praying, Jesus left with his disciples and crossed the Kidron Valley. On the other side there was an olive grove, and he and his disciples went into it.

2Now Judas, who betrayed him, knew the place, because Jesus had often met there with his disciples. 3So Judas came to the grove, guiding a detachment of soldiers and some officials from the chief priests and Pharisees. They were carrying torches, lanterns and weapons.

4Jesus, knowing all that was going to happen to him, went out

and asked them, "Who is it you want?"

5"Jesus of Nazareth," they replied.

"I am he," Jesus said. (And Judas the traitor was standing there with them.) 6When Jesus said, "I am he," they drew back and fell to the ground.

7Again he asked them, "Who is it you want?"

And they said, "Jesus of Nazareth."

8"I told you that I am he," Jesus answered. "If you are looking for me, then let these men go." 9This happened so that the words he had spoken would be fulfilled: "I have not lost one of those you gave me."*a*

10Then Simon Peter, who had a sword, drew it and struck the high priest's servant, cutting off his right ear. (The servant's name was Malchus.)

11Jesus commanded Peter, "Put your sword away! Shall I not drink the cup the Father has given me?"

Jesus Taken to Annas

12Then the detachment of soldiers with its commander and the Jewish officials arrested Jesus. They bound him 13and brought him first to Annas, who was the father-in-law of Caiaphas, the high priest that year. 14Caiaphas was the one who had advised the Jews that it would be good if one man died for the people.

Peter's First Denial

15Simon Peter and another disciple were following Jesus. Because this disciple was known to the high priest, he went with Jesus into the high priest's courtyard, 16but Peter had to wait outside at the door. The other disciple, who was known to the high

*a 9 John 6:39

priest, came back, spoke to the girl on duty there and brought Peter in.

[17]"You are not one of his disciples, are you?" the girl at the door asked Peter.

He replied, "I am not."

[18]It was cold, and the servants and officials stood around a fire they had made to keep warm. Peter also was standing with them, warming himself.

The High Priest Questions Jesus

[19]Meanwhile, the high priest questioned Jesus about his disciples and his teaching.

[20]"I have spoken openly to the world," Jesus replied. "I always taught in synagogues or at the temple, where all the Jews come together. I said nothing in secret. [21]Why question me? Ask those who heard me. Surely they know what I said."

[22]When Jesus said this, one of the officials nearby struck him in the face. "Is this the way you answer the high priest?" he demanded.

[23]"If I said something wrong," Jesus replied, "testify as to what is wrong. But if I spoke the truth, why did you strike me?" [24]Then Annas sent him, still bound, to Caiaphas the high priest.[a]

Peter's Second and Third Denials

[25]As Simon Peter stood warming himself, he was asked, "You are not one of his disciples, are you?"

He denied it, saying, "I am not."

[26]One of the high priest's servants, a relative of the man whose ear Peter had cut off, challenged him, "Didn't I see you

with him in the olive grove?" [27]Again Peter denied it, and at that moment a rooster began to crow.

Jesus Before Pilate

[28]Then the Jews led Jesus from Caiaphas to the palace of the Roman governor. By now it was early morning, and to avoid ceremonial uncleanness the Jews did not enter the palace; they wanted to be able to eat the Passover. [29]So Pilate came out to them and asked, "What charges are you bringing against this man?"

[30]"If he were not a criminal," they replied, "we would not have handed him over to you."

[31]Pilate said, "Take him yourselves and judge him by your own law."

"But we have no right to execute anyone," the Jews objected. [32]This happened so that the words Jesus had spoken indicating the kind of death he was going to die would be fulfilled.

[33]Pilate then went back inside the palace, summoned Jesus and asked him, "Are you the king of the Jews?"

[34]"Is that your own idea," Jesus asked, "or did others talk to you about me?"

[35]"Am I a Jew?" Pilate replied. "It was your people and your chief priests who handed you over to me. What is it you have done?"

[36]Jesus said, "My kingdom is not of this world. If it were, my servants would fight to prevent my arrest by the Jews. But now my kingdom is from another place."

[37]"You are a king, then!" said Pilate.

Jesus answered, "You are right in saying I am a king. In fact, for

---

[a]24 Or *(Now Annas had sent him, still bound, to Caiaphas the high priest.)*

this reason I was born, and for this I came into the world, to testify to the truth. Everyone on the side of truth listens to me."

38"What is truth?" Pilate asked. With this he went out again to the Jews and said, "I find no basis for a charge against him. 39But it is your custom for me to release to you one prisoner at the time of the Passover. Do you want me to release 'the king of the Jews'?"

40They shouted back, "No, not him! Give us Barabbas!" Now Barabbas had taken part in a rebellion.

Jesus Sentenced to be Crucified

19 Then Pilate took Jesus and had him flogged. 2The soldiers twisted together a crown of thorns and put it on his head. They clothed him in a purple robe 3and went up to him again and again, saying, "Hail, king of the Jews!" And they struck him in the face.

4Once more Pilate came out and said to the Jews, "Look, I am bringing him out to you to let you know that I find no basis for a charge against him." 5When Jesus came out wearing the crown of thorns and the purple robe, Pilate said to them, "Here is the man!"

6As soon as the chief priests and their officials saw him, they shouted, "Crucify! Crucify!"

But Pilate answered, "You take him and crucify him. As for me, I find no basis for a charge against him."

7The Jews insisted, "We have a law, and according to that law he must die, because he claimed to be the Son of God."

8When Pilate heard this, he was even more afraid, 9and he went back inside the palace. "Where do you come from?" he asked Jesus, but Jesus gave him no an-

swer. 10"Do you refuse to speak to me?" Pilate said. "Don't you realize I have power either to free you or to crucify you?"

11Jesus answered, "You would have no power over me if it were not given to you from above. Therefore the one who handed me over to you is guilty of a greater sin."

12From then on, Pilate tried to set Jesus free, but the Jews kept shouting, "If you let this man go, you are no friend of Caesar. Anyone who claims to be a king opposes Caesar."

13When Pilate heard this, he brought Jesus out and sat down on the judge's seat at a place known as the Stone Pavement (which in Aramaic is Gabbatha). 14It was the day of Preparation of Passover Week, about the sixth hour.

"Here is your king," Pilate said to the Jews.

15But they shouted, "Take him away! Take him away! Crucify him!"

"Shall I crucify your king?" Pilate asked.

"We have no king but Caesar," the chief priests answered.

16Finally Pilate handed him over to them to be crucified.

The Crucifixion

So the soldiers took charge of Jesus. 17Carrying his own cross, he went out to the place of the Skull (which in Aramaic is called Golgotha). 18Here they crucified him, and with him two others—one on each side and Jesus in the middle.

19Pilate had a notice prepared and fastened to the cross. It read: JESUS OF NAZARETH, THE KING OF THE JEWS. 20Many of the Jews read this sign, for the place where Jesus was crucified was near the city, and the sign was written in

Aramaic, Latin and Greek. [21]The chief priests of the Jews protested to Pilate, "Do not write 'The King of the Jews,' but that this man claimed to be king of the Jews."

[22]Pilate answered, "What I have written, I have written."

[23]When the soldiers crucified Jesus, they took his clothes, dividing them into four shares, one for each of them, with the undergarment remaining. This garment was seamless, woven in one piece from top to bottom.

[24]"Let's not tear it," they said to one another. "Let's decide by lot who will get it."

This happened that the scripture might be fulfilled which said,

"They divided my garments
    among them
and cast lots for my
    clothing."[a]

So this is what the soldiers did.

[25]Near the cross of Jesus stood his mother, his mother's sister, Mary the wife of Clopas, and Mary Magdalene. [26]When Jesus saw his mother there, and the disciple whom he loved standing nearby, he said to his mother, "Dear woman, here is your son," [27]and to the disciple, "Here is your mother." From that time on, this disciple took her into his home.

The Death of Jesus

[28]Later, knowing that all was now completed, and so that the Scripture would be fulfilled, Jesus said, "I am thirsty." [29]A jar of wine vinegar was there, so they soaked a sponge in it, put the sponge on a stalk of the hyssop plant, and lifted it to Jesus' lips. [30]When he had received the drink, Jesus said, "It is finished."

With that, he bowed his head and gave up his spirit.

[31]Now it was the day of Preparation, and the next day was to be a special Sabbath. Because the Jews did not want the bodies left on the crosses during the Sabbath, they asked Pilate to have the legs broken and the bodies taken down. [32]The soldiers therefore came and broke the legs of the first man who had been crucified with Jesus, and then those of the other. [33]But when they came to Jesus and found that he was already dead, they did not break his legs. [34]Instead, one of the soldiers pierced Jesus' side with a spear, bringing a sudden flow of blood and water. [35]The man who saw it has given testimony, and his testimony is true. He knows that he tells the truth, and he testifies so that you also may believe. [36]These things happened so that the scripture would be fulfilled: "Not one of his bones will be broken,"[b] [37]and, as another scripture says, "They will look on the one they have pierced."[c]

The Burial of Jesus

[38]Later, Joseph of Arimathea asked Pilate for the body of Jesus. Now Joseph was a disciple of Jesus, but secretly because he feared the Jews. With Pilate's permission, he came and took the body away. [39]He was accompanied by Nicodemus, the man who earlier had visited Jesus at night. Nicodemus brought a mixture of myrrh and aloes, about seventy-five pounds.[d] [40]Taking Jesus' body, the two of them wrapped it, with the spices, in strips of linen. This was in accordance with Jewish burial customs. [41]At the place where Jesus was crucified, there was a gar-

[a]24 Psalm 22:18   [b]36 Exodus 12:46; Num. 9:12; Psalm 34:20   [c]37 Zech. 12:10
[d]39 Greek a hundred litrai (about 34 kilograms)

den, and in the garden a new tomb, in which no one had ever been laid. 42Because it was the Jewish day of Preparation and since the tomb was nearby, they laid Jesus there.

The Empty Tomb

20 Early on the first day of the week, while it was still dark, Mary Magdalene went to the tomb and saw that the stone had been removed from the entrance. 2So she came running to Simon Peter and the other disciple, the one Jesus loved, and said, "They have taken the Lord out of the tomb, and we don't know where they have put him!"

3So Peter and the other disciple started for the tomb. 4Both were running, but the other disciple outran Peter and reached the tomb first. 5He bent over and looked in at the strips of linen lying there but did not go in. 6Then Simon Peter, who was behind him, arrived and went into the tomb. He saw the strips of linen lying there, 7as well as the burial cloth that had been around Jesus' head. The cloth was folded up by itself, separate from the linen. 8Finally the other disciple, who had reached the tomb first, also went inside. He saw and believed. 9(They still did not understand from Scripture that Jesus had to rise from the dead.)

Jesus Appears to Mary Magdalene

10Then the disciples went back to their homes, 11but Mary stood outside the tomb crying. As she wept, she bent over to look into the tomb 12and saw two angels in white, seated where Jesus' body had been, one at the head and the other at the foot.

13They asked her, "Woman, why are you crying?"

"They have taken my Lord away," she said, "and I don't know where they have put him." 14At this, she turned around and saw Jesus standing there, but she did not realize that it was Jesus.

15"Woman," he said, "why are you crying? Who is it you are looking for?"

Thinking he was the gardener, she said, "Sir, if you have carried him away, tell me where you have put him, and I will get him."

16Jesus said to her, "Mary."

She turned toward him and cried out in Aramaic, "Rabboni!" (which means Teacher).

17Jesus said, "Do not hold on to me, for I have not yet returned to the Father. Go instead to my brothers and tell them, 'I am returning to my Father and your Father, to my God and your God.'"

18Mary Magdalene went to the disciples with the news: "I have seen the Lord!" And she told them that he had said these things to her.

Jesus Appears to His Disciples

19On the evening of that first day of the week, when the disciples were together, with the doors locked for fear of the Jews, Jesus came and stood among them and said, "Peace be with you!" 20After he said this, he showed them his hands and side. The disciples were overjoyed when they saw the Lord.

21Again Jesus said, "Peace be with you! As the Father has sent me, I am sending you." 22And with that he breathed on them and said, "Receive the Holy Spirit. 23If you forgive anyone his sins, they are forgiven; if you do not forgive them, they are not forgiven."

Jesus Appears to Thomas

24Now Thomas (called Didymus), one of the Twelve, was not with the disciples when Jesus came. 25So the other disciples told him, "We have seen the Lord!"

But he said to them, "Unless I see the nail marks in his hands and put my finger where the nails were, and put my hand into his side, I will not believe it."

26A week later his disciples were in the house again, and Thomas was with them. Though the doors were locked, Jesus came and stood among them and said, "Peace be with you!" 27Then he said to Thomas, "Put your finger here; see my hands. Reach out your hand and put it into my side. Stop doubting and believe."

28Thomas said to him, "My Lord and my God!"

15
Php 2:6

29Then Jesus told him, "Because you have seen me, you have believed; blessed are those who have not seen and yet have believed."

30Jesus did many other miraculous signs in the presence of his disciples, which are not recorded in this book. 31But these are written that you may[a] believe that Jesus is the Christ, the Son of God, and that by believing you may have life in his name.

6
Ac 4:12

24
Ac 16:31

78
Ac 10:43

Jesus and the Miraculous Catch of Fish

21 Afterward Jesus appeared again to his disciples, by the Sea of Tiberias.[b] It happened this way: 2Simon Peter, Thomas (called Didymus), Nathanael from Cana in Galilee, the sons of Zebedee, and two other disciples were together. 3"I'm going out to fish," Simon Peter told them,

and they said, "We'll go with you." So they went out and got into the boat, but that night they caught nothing.

4Early in the morning, Jesus stood on the shore, but the disciples did not realize that it was Jesus.

5He called out to them, "Friends, haven't you any fish?"

"No," they answered.

6He said, "Throw your net on the right side of the boat and you will find some." When they did, they were unable to haul the net in because of the large number of fish.

7Then the disciple whom Jesus loved said to Peter, "It is the Lord!" As soon as Simon Peter heard him say, "It is the Lord," he wrapped his outer garment around him (for he had taken it off) and jumped into the water. 8The other disciples followed in the boat, towing the net full of fish, for they were not far from shore, about a hundred yards.[c] 9When they landed, they saw a fire of burning coals there with fish on it, and some bread.

10Jesus said to them, "Bring some of the fish you have just caught."

11Simon Peter climbed aboard and dragged the net ashore. It was full of large fish, 153, but even with so many the net was not torn. 12Jesus said to them, "Come and have breakfast." None of the disciples dared ask him, "Who are you?" They knew it was the Lord. 13Jesus came, took the bread and gave it to them, and did the same with the fish. 14This was now the third time Jesus appeared to his disciples after he was raised from the dead.

---

[a]31 Some manuscripts may continue to two hundred cubits (about 90 meters)   [b]1 That is, Sea of Galilee   [c]8 Greek about

Jesus Reinstates Peter

15
Gal 6:1

¹⁵When they had finished eating, Jesus said to Simon Peter, "Simon son of John, do you truly love me more than these?"

"Yes, Lord," he said, "you know that I love you."

Jesus said, "Feed my lambs."

¹⁶Again Jesus said, "Simon son of John, do you truly love me?"

He answered, "Yes, Lord, you know that I love you."

Jesus said, "Take care of my sheep."

¹⁷The third time he said to him, "Simon son of John, do you love me?"

Peter was hurt because Jesus asked him the third time, "Do you love me?" He said, "Lord, you know all things; you know that I love you."

Jesus said, "Feed my sheep. ¹⁸I tell you the truth, when you were younger you dressed yourself and went where you wanted; but when you are old you will stretch out your hands, and someone else will dress you and lead you where you do not want to go." ¹⁹Jesus said this to indicate the kind of death by which Peter would glorify God. Then he said to him, "Follow me!"

²⁰Peter turned and saw that the disciple whom Jesus loved was following them. (This was the one who had leaned back against Jesus at the supper and had said, "Lord, who is going to betray you?") ²¹When Peter saw him, he asked, "Lord, what about him?"

²²Jesus answered, "If I want him to remain alive until I return, what is that to you? You must follow me." ²³Because of this, the rumor spread among the brothers that this disciple would not die. But Jesus did not say that he would not die; he only said, "If I want him to remain alive until I return, what is that to you?"

²⁴This is the disciple who testifies to these things and who wrote them down. We know that his testimony is true.

²⁵Jesus did many other things as well. If every one of them were written down, I suppose that even the whole world would not have room for the books that would be written.

Acts

Jesus Taken Up Into Heaven

1 In my former book, Theophilus, I wrote about all that Jesus began to do and to teach ²until the day he was taken up to heaven, after giving instructions through the Holy Spirit to the apostles he had chosen. ³After his suffering, he showed himself to these men and gave many convincing proofs that he was alive. He appeared to them over a period of forty days and spoke about the kingdom of God. ⁴On one occasion, while he was eating with them, he gave them this command: "Do not leave Jerusalem, but wait for the gift my Father promised, which you have heard me speak about. ⁵For John baptized with*ᵃ* water, but in a few days you will be baptized with the Holy Spirit."

⁶So when they met together, they asked him, "Lord, are you at this time going to restore the kingdom to Israel?"

ᵃ5 Or in

7He said to them: "It is not for you to know the times or dates the Father has set by his own authority. 8But you will receive power when the Holy Spirit comes on you; and you will be my witnesses in Jerusalem, and in all Judea and Samaria, and to the ends of the earth."

9After he said this, he was taken up before their very eyes, and a cloud hid him from their sight.

10They were looking intently up into the sky as he was going, when suddenly two men dressed in white stood beside them. 11"Men of Galilee," they said, "why do you stand here looking into the sky? This same Jesus, who has been taken from you into heaven, will come back in the same way you have seen him go into heaven."

Matthias Chosen to Replace Judas

12Then they returned to Jerusalem from the hill called the Mount of Olives, a Sabbath day's walk*a* from the city. 13When they arrived, they went upstairs to the room where they were staying. Those present were Peter, John, James and Andrew; Philip and Thomas, Bartholomew and Matthew; James son of Alphaeus and Simon the Zealot, and Judas son of James. 14They all joined together constantly in prayer, along with the women and Mary the mother of Jesus, and with his brothers.

15In those days Peter stood up among the believers*b* (a group numbering about a hundred and twenty) 16and said, "Brothers, the Scripture had to be fulfilled which the Holy Spirit spoke long ago through the mouth of David

concerning Judas, who served as guide for those who arrested Jesus— 17he was one of our number and shared in this ministry."

18(With the reward he got for his wickedness, Judas bought a field; there he fell headlong, his body burst open and all his intestines spilled out. 19Everyone in Jerusalem heard about this, so they called that field in their language Akeldama, that is, Field of Blood.)

20"For," said Peter, "it is written in the book of Psalms,

" 'May his place be deserted;
    let there be no one to dwell
    in it,'*c*

and,

" 'May another take his place
    of leadership.'*d*

21Therefore it is necessary to choose one of the men who have been with us the whole time the Lord Jesus went in and out among us, 22beginning from John's baptism to the time when Jesus was taken up from us. For one of these must become a witness with us of his resurrection."

23So they proposed two men: Joseph called Barsabbas (also known as Justus) and Matthias. 24Then they prayed, "Lord, you know everyone's heart. Show us which of these two you have chosen 25to take over this apostolic ministry, which Judas left to go where he belongs." 26Then they cast lots, and the lot fell to Matthias; so he was added to the eleven apostles.

The Holy Spirit Comes at Pentecost

2 When the day of Pentecost came, they were all together

*a12 That is, about 3/4 mile (about 1,100 meters)   *b15 Greek brothers
*c20 Psalm 69:25   *d20 Psalm 109:8

23
Ac 5:42

80
1Th 4:13-18

in one place. ²Suddenly a sound like the blowing of a violent wind came from heaven and filled the whole house where they were sitting. ³They saw what seemed to be tongues of fire that separated and came to rest on each of ⁹⁵ them. ⁴All of them were filled ^{Ac 10:46} with the Holy Spirit and began to speak in other tongues*a* as the Spirit enabled them.

⁵Now there were staying in Jerusalem God-fearing Jews from every nation under heaven. ⁶When they heard this sound, a crowd came together in bewilderment, because each one heard them speaking in his own language. ⁷Utterly amazed, they asked: "Are not all these men who are speaking Galileans? ⁸Then how is it that each of us hears them in his own native language? ⁹Parthians, Medes and Elamites; residents of Mesopotamia, Judea and Cappadocia, Pontus and Asia, ¹⁰Phrygia and Pamphylia, Egypt and the parts of Libya near Cyrene; visitors from Rome ¹¹(both Jews and converts to Judaism); Cretans and Arabs—we hear them declaring the wonders of God in our own tongues!" ¹²Amazed and perplexed, they asked one another, "What does this mean?"

¹³Some, however, made fun of them and said, "They have had too much wine.*b*"

Peter Addresses the Crowd

¹⁴Then Peter stood up with the Eleven, raised his voice and addressed the crowd: "Fellow Jews and all of you who live in Jerusalem, let me explain this to you; listen carefully to what I say. ¹⁵These men are not drunk, as you suppose. It's only nine in the

morning! ¹⁶No, this is what was spoken by the prophet Joel:

¹⁷" 'In the last days, God says,
I will pour out my Spirit on all people.
Your sons and daughters will prophesy,
your young men will see visions,
your old men will dream dreams.
¹⁸Even on my servants, both men and women,
I will pour out my Spirit in those days,
and they will prophesy.
¹⁹I will show wonders in the heaven above
and signs on the earth below,
blood and fire and billows of smoke.
²⁰The sun will be turned to darkness
and the moon to blood
before the coming of the great and glorious day of the Lord.
²¹And everyone who calls on the name of the Lord will be saved.'*c*

²²"Men of Israel, listen to this: ³² Jesus of Nazareth was a man ac- ^{Ac 8:40} credited by God to you by miracles, wonders and signs, which God did among you through him, as you yourselves know. ²³This man was handed over to you by God's set purpose and foreknowledge; and you, with the help of wicked men,*d* put him to death by nailing him to the cross. ²⁴But God raised him from the dead, freeing him from the agony of death, because it was impossible for death to keep its hold on him. ²⁵David said about him:

---

*a*4 Or *languages*; also in verse 11   *b*13 Or *sweet wine*   *c*21 Joel 2:28-32   *d*23 Or *of those not having the law* (that is, Gentiles)

'' 'I saw the Lord always
    before me.
Because he is at my right
    hand,
I will not be shaken.
[26]Therefore my heart is glad
    and my tongue rejoices;
my body also will live in
    hope,
[27]because you will not abandon
    me to the grave,
nor will you let your Holy
    One see decay.
[28]You have made known to me
    the paths of life;
you will fill me with joy in
    your presence.'[a]

[29]"Brothers, I can tell you confidently that the patriarch David died and was buried, and his tomb is here to this day. [30]But he was a prophet and knew that God had promised him on oath that he would place one of his descendants on his throne. [31]Seeing what was ahead, he spoke of the resurrection of the Christ,[b] that he was not abandoned to the grave, nor did his body see decay. [32]God has raised this Jesus to life, and we are all witnesses of the fact. [33]Exalted to the right hand of God, he has received from the Father the promised Holy Spirit and has poured out what you now see and hear. [34]For David did not ascend to heaven, and yet he said,

'' 'The Lord said to my Lord:
    "Sit at my right hand
[35]until I make your enemies
    a footstool for your feet." '[c]

[36]"Therefore let all Israel be assured of this: God has made this Jesus, whom you crucified, both Lord and Christ."

[37]When the people heard this, they were cut to the heart and said to Peter and the other apostles, "Brothers, what shall we do?"

[38]Peter replied, "Repent and be baptized, every one of you, in the name of Jesus Christ for the forgiveness of your sins. And you will receive the gift of the Holy Spirit. [39]The promise is for you and your children and for all who are far off—for all whom the Lord our God will call."

[40]With many other words he warned them; and he pleaded with them, "Save yourselves from this corrupt generation." [41]Those who accepted his message were baptized, and about three thousand were added to their number that day.

The Fellowship of the Believers

[42]They devoted themselves to the apostles' teaching and to the fellowship, to the breaking of bread and to prayer. [43]Everyone was filled with awe, and many wonders and miraculous signs were done by the apostles. [44]All the believers were together and had everything in common. [45]Selling their possessions and goods, they gave to anyone as he had need. [46]Every day they continued to meet together in the temple courts. They broke bread in their homes and ate together with glad and sincere hearts, [47]praising God and enjoying the favor of all the people. And the Lord added to their number daily those who were being saved.

Peter Heals the Crippled Beggar

3 One day Peter and John were going up to the temple at the

74
Ac 17:30

27
Ac 4:32

---

[a]28 Psalm 16:8-11   [b]31 Or Messiah. "The Christ" (Greek) and "the Messiah" (Hebrew) both mean "the Anointed One"; also in verse 36.   [c]35 Psalm 110:1

time of prayer—at three in the afternoon. ²Now a man crippled from birth was being carried to the temple gate called Beautiful, where he was put every day to beg from those going into the temple courts. ³When he saw Peter and John about to enter, he asked them for money. ⁴Peter looked straight at him, as did John. Then Peter said, "Look at us!" ⁵So the man gave them his attention, expecting to get something from them.

⁶Then Peter said, "Silver or gold I do not have, but what I have I give you. In the name of Jesus Christ of Nazareth, walk." ⁷Taking him by the right hand, he helped him up, and instantly the man's feet and ankles became strong. ⁸He jumped to his feet and began to walk. Then he went with them into the temple courts, walking and jumping, and praising God. ⁹When all the people saw him walking and praising God, ¹⁰they recognized him as the same man who used to sit begging at the temple gate called Beautiful, and they were filled with wonder and amazement at what had happened to him.

Peter Speaks to the Onlookers

¹¹While the beggar held on to Peter and John, all the people were astonished and came running to them in the place called Solomon's Colonnade. ¹²When Peter saw this, he said to them: "Men of Israel, why does this surprise you? Why do you stare at us as if by our own power or godliness we had made this man walk? ¹³The God of Abraham, Isaac and Jacob, the God of our fathers, has glorified his servant Jesus. You handed him over to be killed, and you disowned him before Pilate, though he had de-

cided to let him go. ¹⁴You disowned the Holy and Righteous One and asked that a murderer be released to you. ¹⁵You killed the author of life, but God raised him from the dead. We are witnesses of this. ¹⁶By faith in the name of Jesus, this man whom you see and know was made strong. It is Jesus' name and the faith that comes through him that has given this complete healing to him, as you can all see.

¹⁷"Now, brothers, I know that you acted in ignorance, as did your leaders. ¹⁸But this is how God fulfilled what he had foretold through all the prophets, saying that his Christ[a] would suffer. ¹⁹Repent, then, and turn to God, so that your sins may be wiped out, that times of refreshing may come from the Lord, ²⁰and that he may send the Christ, who has been appointed for you—even Jesus. ²¹He must remain in heaven until the time comes for God to restore everything, as he promised long ago through his holy prophets. ²²For Moses said, 'The Lord your God will raise up for you a prophet like me from among your own people; you must listen to everything he tells you. ²³Anyone who does not listen to him will be completely cut off from among his people.'[b]

²⁴"Indeed, all the prophets from Samuel on, as many as have spoken, have foretold these days. ²⁵And you are heirs of the prophets and of the covenant God made with your fathers. He said to Abraham, 'Through your offspring all peoples on earth will be blessed.'[c] ²⁶When God raised up his servant, he sent him first to you to bless you by turning each of you from your wicked ways."

77
Ro 3:21-26

39
Ac 10:38

63
Ac 5:29

---

[a]18 Or *Messiah*; also in verse 20   [b]23 Deut. 18:15,18,19   [c]25 Gen. 22:18; 26:4

Peter and John Before the Sanhedrin

4 The priests and the captain of the temple guard and the Sadducees came up to Peter and John while they were speaking to the people. ²They were greatly disturbed because the apostles were teaching the people and proclaiming in Jesus the resurrection of the dead. ³They seized Peter and John, and because it was evening, they put them in jail until the next day. ⁴But many who heard the message believed, and the number of men grew to about five thousand.

⁵The next day the rulers, elders and teachers of the law met in Jerusalem. ⁶Annas the high priest was there, and so were Caiaphas, John, Alexander and the other men of the high priest's family. ⁷They had Peter and John brought before them and began to question them: "By what power or what name did you do this?"

⁸Then Peter, filled with the Holy Spirit, said to them: "Rulers and elders of the people! ⁹If we are being called to account today for an act of kindness shown to a cripple and are asked how he was healed, ¹⁰then know this, you and all the people of Israel: It is by the name of Jesus Christ of Nazareth, whom you crucified but whom God raised from the dead, that this man stands before you healed. ¹¹He is

" 'the stone you builders rejected,
which has become the capstone,'*ᵇ*

Heb 1:1,2 ¹²Salvation is found in no one else, for there is no other name under heaven given to men by which we must be saved."

¹³When they saw the courage of Peter and John and realized that they were unschooled, ordinary men, they were astonished and they took note that these men had been with Jesus. ¹⁴But since they could see the man who had been healed standing there with them, there was nothing they could say. ¹⁵So they ordered them to withdraw from the Sanhedrin and then conferred together. ¹⁶"What are we going to do with these men?" they asked. "Everybody living in Jerusalem knows they have done an outstanding miracle, and we cannot deny it. ¹⁷But to stop this thing from spreading any further among the people, we must warn these men to speak no longer to anyone in this name."

¹⁸Then they called them in again and commanded them not to speak or teach at all in the name of Jesus. ¹⁹But Peter and John replied, "Judge for yourselves whether it is right in God's sight to obey you rather than God. ²⁰For we cannot help speaking about what we have seen and heard."

²¹After further threats they let them go. They could not decide how to punish them, because all the people were praising God for what had happened. ²²For the man who was miraculously healed was over forty years old.

The Believers' Prayer

²³On their release, Peter and John went back to their own people and reported all that the chief priests and elders had said to them. ²⁴When they heard this, they raised their voices together in prayer to God. "Sovereign Lord," they said, "you made the heaven and the earth and the sea,

---

*11 Or *cornerstone*   ᵇ11 Psalm 118:22

and everything in them. 25You spoke by the Holy Spirit through the mouth of your servant, our father David:

" 'Why do the nations rage
    and the peoples plot in
        vain?
26The kings of the earth take
        their stand
    and the rulers gather
        together
  against the Lord
    and against his Anointed
        One.*'b

27Indeed Herod and Pontius Pilate met together with the Gentiles and the peoplec of Israel in this city to conspire against your holy servant Jesus, whom you anointed. 28They did what your power and will had decided beforehand should happen. 29Now, Lord, consider their threats and enable your servants to speak your word with great boldness. 30Stretch out your hand to heal and perform miraculous signs and wonders through the name of your holy servant Jesus."

31After they prayed, the place where they were meeting was shaken. And they were all filled with the Holy Spirit and spoke the word of God boldly.

The Believers Share Their Possessions

27
Ro 12:9-13
32All the believers were one in heart and mind. No one claimed that any of his possessions was his own, but they shared everything they had. 33With great power the apostles continued to testify to the resurrection of the Lord Jesus, and much grace was upon them all. 34There were no needy persons among them. For from time to time those who owned lands or houses sold them, brought the money from the sales 35and put it at the apostles' feet, and it was distributed to anyone as he had need.

36Joseph, a Levite from Cyprus, whom the apostles called Barnabas (which means Son of Encouragement), 37sold a field he owned and brought the money and put it at the apostles' feet.

Ananias and Sapphira

5 Now a man named Ananias, together with his wife Sapphira, also sold a piece of property. 2With his wife's full knowledge he kept back part of the money for himself, but brought the rest and put it at the apostles' feet.

3Then Peter said, "Ananias, how is it that Satan has so filled your heart that you have lied to the Holy Spirit and have kept for yourself some of the money you received for the land? 4Didn't it belong to you before it was sold? And after it was sold, wasn't the money at your disposal? What made you think of doing such a thing? You have not lied to men but to God."

5When Ananias heard this, he fell down and died. And great fear seized all who heard what had happened. 6Then the young men came forward, wrapped up his body, and carried him out and buried him.

7About three hours later his wife came in, not knowing what had happened. 8Peter asked her, "Tell me, is this the price you and Ananias got for the land?"

"Yes," she said, "that is the price."

9Peter said to her, "How could you agree to test the Spirit of the Lord? Look! The feet of the men

---

a26 That is, Christ or Messiah   b26 Psalm 2:1,2   c27 The Greek is plural.

who buried your husband are at the door, and they will carry you out also."

[10]At that moment she fell down at his feet and died. Then the young men came in and, finding her dead, carried her out and buried her beside her husband. [11]Great fear seized the whole church and all who heard about these events.

The Apostles Heal Many

[12]The apostles performed many miraculous signs and wonders among the people. And all the believers used to meet together in Solomon's Colonnade. [13]No one else dared join them, even though they were highly regarded by the people. [14]Nevertheless, more and more men and women believed in the Lord and were added to their number. [15]As a result, people brought the sick into the streets and laid them on beds and mats so that at least Peter's shadow might fall on some of them as he passed by. [16]Crowds gathered also from the towns around Jerusalem, bringing their sick and those tormented by evil[a] spirits, and all of them were healed.

The Apostles Persecuted

[17]Then the high priest and all his associates, who were members of the party of the Sadducees, were filled with jealousy. [18]They arrested the apostles and put them in the public jail. [19]But during the night an angel of the Lord opened the doors of the jail and brought them out. [20]"Go, stand in the temple courts," he said, "and tell the people the full message of this new life."

[21]At daybreak they entered the temple courts, as they had been told, and began to teach the people.

When the high priest and his associates arrived, they called together the Sanhedrin—the full assembly of the elders of Israel—and sent to the jail for the apostles. [22]But on arriving at the jail, the officers did not find them there. So they went back and reported, [23]"We found the jail securely locked, with the guards standing at the doors; but when we opened them, we found no one inside." [24]On hearing this report, the captain of the temple guard and the chief priests were puzzled, wondering what would come of this.

[25]Then someone came and said, "Look! The men you put in jail are standing in the temple courts teaching the people." [26]At that, the captain went with his officers and brought the apostles. They did not use force, because they feared that the people would stone them.

[27]Having brought the apostles, they made them appear before the Sanhedrin to be questioned by the high priest. [28]"We gave you strict orders not to teach in this name," he said. "Yet you have filled Jerusalem with your teaching and are determined to make us guilty of this man's blood."

[29]Peter and the other apostles replied: "We must obey God rather than men! [30]The God of our fathers raised Jesus from the dead—whom you had killed by hanging him on a tree. [31]God exalted him to his own right hand as Prince and Savior that he might give repentance and forgiveness of sins to Israel. [32]We are witnesses of these things, and so is the Holy Spirit, whom God has

63
Ac 5:32

63
Heb 13:17

[a]16 Greek *unclean*

given to those who obey him."

33When they heard this, they were furious and wanted to put them to death. 34But a Pharisee named Gamaliel, a teacher of the law, who was honored by all the people, stood up in the Sanhedrin and ordered that the men be put outside for a little while. 35Then he addressed them: "Men of Israel, consider carefully what you intend to do to these men. 36Some time ago Theudas appeared, claiming to be somebody, and about four hundred men rallied to him. He was killed, all his followers were dispersed, and it all came to nothing. 37After him, Judas the Galilean appeared in the days of the census and led a band of people in revolt. He too was killed, and all his followers were scattered. 38Therefore, in the present case I advise you: Leave these men alone! Let them go! For if their purpose or activity is of human origin, it will fail. 39But if it is from God, you will not be able to stop these men; you will only find yourselves fighting against God."

40His speech persuaded them. They called the apostles in and had them flogged. Then they ordered them not to speak in the name of Jesus, and let them go.

91
Ac 9:16

41The apostles left the Sanhedrin, rejoicing because they had been counted worthy of suffering

23
Ro 1:16

disgrace for the Name. 42Day after day, in the temple courts and from house to house, they never stopped teaching and proclaiming the good news that Jesus is the Christ.a

The Choosing of the Seven

6 In those days when the number of disciples was increasing, the Grecian Jews among

them complained against the Hebraic Jews because their widows were being overlooked in the daily distribution of food. 2So the Twelve gathered all the disciples together and said, "It would not be right for us to neglect the ministry of the word of God in order to wait on tables. 3Brothers, choose seven men from among you who are known to be full of the Spirit and wisdom. We will turn this responsibility over to them 4and will give our attention to prayer and the ministry of the word."

5This proposal pleased the whole group. They chose Stephen, a man full of faith and of the Holy Spirit; also Philip, Procorus, Nicanor, Timon, Parmenas, and Nicolas from Antioch, a convert to Judaism. 6They presented these men to the apostles, who prayed and laid their hands on them.

7So the word of God spread. The number of disciples in Jerusalem increased rapidly, and a large number of priests became obedient to the faith.

Stephen Seized

8Now Stephen, a man full of God's grace and power, did great wonders and miraculous signs among the people. 9Opposition arose, however, from members of the Synagogue of the Freedmen (as it was called)—Jews of Cyrene and Alexandria as well as the provinces of Cilicia and Asia. These men began to argue with Stephen, 10but they could not stand up against his wisdom or the Spirit by whom he spoke. 11Then they secretly persuaded some men to say, "We have heard Stephen speak words of blasphemy against Moses and against God."

a42 Or Messiah

¹²So they stirred up the people and the elders and the teachers of the law. They seized Stephen and brought him before the Sanhedrin. ¹³They produced false witnesses, who testified, "This fellow never stops speaking against this holy place and against the law. ¹⁴For we have heard him say that this Jesus of Nazareth will destroy this place and change the customs Moses handed down to us."

¹⁵All who were sitting in the Sanhedrin looked intently at Stephen, and they saw that his face was like the face of an angel.

Stephen's Speech to the Sanhedrin

7 Then the high priest asked him, "Are these charges true?"

²To this he replied: "Brothers and fathers, listen to me! The God of glory appeared to our father Abraham while he was still in Mesopotamia, before he lived in Haran. ³'Leave your country and your people,' God said, 'and go to the land I will show you.'ᵃ

⁴"So he left the land of the Chaldeans and settled in Haran. After the death of his father, God sent him to this land where you are now living. ⁵He gave him no inheritance here, not even a foot of ground. But God promised him that he and his descendants after him would possess the land, even though at that time Abraham had no child. ⁶God spoke to him in this way: 'Your descendants will be strangers in a country not their own, and they will be enslaved and mistreated four hundred years. ⁷But I will punish the nation they serve as slaves,' God said, 'and afterward they will come out of that country and worship me in this place.'ᵇ ⁸Then he gave Abraham the covenant of circumcision. And Abraham became the father of Isaac and circumcised him eight days after his birth. Later Isaac became the father of Jacob, and Jacob became the father of the twelve patriarchs.

⁹"Because the patriarchs were jealous of Joseph, they sold him as a slave into Egypt. But God was with him ¹⁰and rescued him from all his troubles. He gave Joseph wisdom and enabled him to gain the goodwill of Pharaoh king of Egypt; so he made him ruler over Egypt and all his palace.

¹¹"Then a famine struck all Egypt and Canaan, bringing great suffering, and our fathers could not find food. ¹²When Jacob heard that there was grain in Egypt, he sent our fathers on their first visit. ¹³On their second visit, Joseph told his brothers who he was, and Pharaoh learned about Joseph's family. ¹⁴After this, Joseph sent for his father Jacob and his whole family, seventy-five in all. ¹⁵Then Jacob went down to Egypt, where he and our fathers died. ¹⁶Their bodies were brought back to Shechem and placed in the tomb that Abraham had bought from the sons of Hamor at Shechem for a certain sum of money.

¹⁷"As the time drew near for God to fulfill his promise to Abraham, the number of our people in Egypt greatly increased. ¹⁸Then another king, who knew nothing about Joseph, became ruler of Egypt. ¹⁹He dealt treacherously with our people and oppressed our forefathers by forcing them to throw out their newborn babies so that they would die.

ᵃ3 Gen. 12:1   ᵇ7 Gen. 15:13,14

²⁰"At that time Moses was born, and he was no ordinary child.ᵃ For three months he was cared for in his father's house. ²¹When he was placed outside, Pharaoh's daughter took him and brought him up as her own son. ²²Moses was educated in all the wisdom of the Egyptians and was powerful in speech and action.

²³"When Moses was forty years old, he decided to visit his fellow Israelites. ²⁴He saw one of them being mistreated by an Egyptian, so he went to his defense and avenged him by killing the Egyptian. ²⁵Moses thought that his own people would realize that God was using him to rescue them, but they did not. ²⁶The next day Moses came upon two Israelites who were fighting. He tried to reconcile them by saying, 'Men, you are brothers; why do you want to hurt each other?'

²⁷"But the man who was mistreating the other pushed Moses aside and said, 'Who made you ruler and judge over us? ²⁸Do you want to kill me as you killed the Egyptian yesterday?'ᵇ ²⁹When Moses heard this, he fled to Midian, where he settled as a foreigner and had two sons.

³⁰"After forty years had passed, an angel appeared to Moses in the flames of a burning bush in the desert near Mount Sinai. ³¹When he saw this, he was amazed at the sight. As he went over to look more closely, he heard the Lord's voice: ³²'I am the God of your fathers, the God of Abraham, Isaac and Jacob.'ᶜ Moses trembled with fear and did not dare to look.

³³"Then the Lord said to him, 'Take off your sandals; the place where you are standing is holy ground. ³⁴I have indeed seen the oppression of my people in Egypt. I have heard their groaning and have come down to set them free. Now come, I will send you back to Egypt.'ᵈ

³⁵"This is the same Moses whom they had rejected with the words, 'Who made you ruler and judge?' He was sent to be their ruler and deliverer by God himself, through the angel who appeared to him in the bush. ³⁶He led them out of Egypt and did wonders and miraculous signs in Egypt, at the Red Seaᵉ and for forty years in the desert.

³⁷"This is that Moses who told the Israelites, 'God will send you a prophet like me from your own people.'ᶠ ³⁸He was in the assembly in the desert, with the angel who spoke to him on Mount Sinai, and with our fathers; and he received living words to pass on to us.

³⁹"But our fathers refused to obey him. Instead, they rejected him and in their hearts turned back to Egypt. ⁴⁰They told Aaron, 'Make us gods who will go before us. As for this fellow Moses who led us out of Egypt—we don't know what has happened to him!'ᵍ ⁴¹That was the time they made an idol in the form of a calf. They brought sacrifices to it and held a celebration in honor of what their hands had made. ⁴²But God turned away and gave them over to the worship of the heavenly bodies. This agrees with what is written in the book of the prophets:

" 'Did you bring me sacrifices
        and offerings
   forty years in the desert,
        O house of Israel?

ᵃ20 Or *was fair in the sight of God*   ᵇ28 Exodus 2:14   ᶜ32 Exodus 3:6
ᵈ34 Exodus 3:5,7,8,10   ᵉ36 That is, Sea of Reeds   ᶠ37 Deut. 18:15   ᵍ40 Exodus 32:1

⁴³You have lifted up the shrine
    of Molech
  and the star of your god
    Rephan,
  the idols you made to
    worship.
Therefore I will send you into
  exile'[a] beyond Babylon.

⁴⁴"Our forefathers had the tabernacle of the Testimony with them in the desert. It had been made as God directed Moses, according to the pattern he had seen. ⁴⁵Having received the tabernacle, our fathers under Joshua brought it with them when they took the land from the nations God drove out before them. It remained in the land until the time of David, ⁴⁶who enjoyed God's favor and asked that he might provide a dwelling place for the God of Jacob.[b] ⁴⁷But it was Solomon who built the house for him.

⁴⁸"However, the Most High does not live in houses made by men. As the prophet says:

⁴⁹" 'Heaven is my throne,
    and the earth is my
      footstool.
  What kind of house will you
    build for me?
          says the Lord.
  Or where will my resting
    place be?
⁵⁰Has not my hand made all
    these things?'[c]

⁵¹"You stiff-necked people, with uncircumcised hearts and ears! You are just like your fathers: You always resist the Holy Spirit! ⁵²Was there ever a prophet your fathers did not persecute? They even killed those who predicted the coming of the Righteous One. And now you have betrayed and murdered him— ⁵³you who have received the law

that was put into effect through angels but have not obeyed it."

The Stoning of Stephen

⁵⁴When they heard this, they were furious and gnashed their teeth at him. ⁵⁵But Stephen, full of the Holy Spirit, looked up to heaven and saw the glory of God, and Jesus standing at the right hand of God. ⁵⁶"Look," he said, "I see heaven open and the Son of Man standing at the right hand of God."

⁵⁷At this they covered their ears and, yelling at the top of their voices, they all rushed at him, ⁵⁸dragged him out of the city and began to stone him. Meanwhile, the witnesses laid their clothes at the feet of a young man named Saul.

⁵⁹While they were stoning him, Stephen prayed, "Lord Jesus, receive my spirit." ⁶⁰Then he fell on his knees and cried out, "Lord, do not hold this sin against them." When he had said this, he fell asleep.

8 And Saul was there, giving approval to his death.

The Church Persecuted and Scattered

On that day a great persecution broke out against the church at Jerusalem, and all except the apostles were scattered throughout Judea and Samaria. ²Godly men buried Stephen and mourned deeply for him. ³But Saul began to destroy the church. Going from house to house, he dragged off men and women and put them in prison.

Philip in Samaria

⁴Those who had been scattered preached the word wherever they went. ⁵Philip went down to a city in Samaria and proclaimed

---

[a]43 Amos 5:25-27   [b]46 Some early manuscripts *the house of Jacob*   [c]50 Isaiah 66:1,2

the Christ[a] there. [6]When the crowds heard Philip and saw the miraculous signs he did, they all paid close attention to what he said. [7]With shrieks, evil[b] spirits came out of many, and many paralytics and cripples were healed. [8]So there was great joy in that city.

Simon the Sorcerer

[9]Now for some time a man named Simon had practiced sorcery in the city and amazed all the people of Samaria. He boasted that he was someone great, [10]and all the people, both high and low, gave him their attention and exclaimed, "This man is the divine power known as the Great Power." [11]They followed him because he had amazed them for a long time with his magic. [12]But when they believed Philip as he preached the good news of the kingdom of God and the name of Jesus Christ, they were baptized, both men and women. [13]Simon himself believed and was baptized. And he followed Philip everywhere, astonished by the great signs and miracles he saw.

[14]When the apostles in Jerusalem heard that Samaria had accepted the word of God, they sent Peter and John to them. [15]When they arrived, they prayed for them that they might receive the Holy Spirit, [16]because the Holy Spirit had not yet come upon any of them; they had simply been baptized into[c] the name of the Lord Jesus. [17]Then Peter and John placed their hands on them, and they received the Holy Spirit.

[18]When Simon saw that the Spirit was given at the laying on of the apostles' hands, he offered them money [19]and said, "Give me also this ability so that everyone on whom I lay my hands may receive the Holy Spirit."

[20]Peter answered: "May your money perish with you, because you thought you could buy the gift of God with money! [21]You have no part or share in this ministry, because your heart is not right before God. [22]Repent of this wickedness and pray to the Lord. Perhaps he will forgive you for having such a thought in your heart. [23]For I see that you are full of bitterness and captive to sin."

[24]Then Simon answered, "Pray to the Lord for me so that nothing you have said may happen to me."

[25]When they had testified and proclaimed the word of the Lord, Peter and John returned to Jerusalem, preaching the gospel in many Samaritan villages.

Philip and the Ethiopian

[26]Now an angel of the Lord said to Philip, "Go south to the road—the desert road—that goes down from Jerusalem to Gaza." [27]So he started out, and on his way he met an Ethiopian[d] eunuch, an important official in charge of all the treasury of Candace, queen of the Ethiopians. This man had gone to Jerusalem to worship, [28]and on his way home was sitting in his chariot reading the book of Isaiah the prophet. [29]The Spirit told Philip, "Go to that chariot and stay near it."

[30]Then Philip ran up to the chariot and heard the man reading Isaiah the prophet. "Do you understand what you are reading?" Philip asked.

[31]"How can I," he said, "unless someone explains it to me?" So he invited Philip to come up and sit with him.

---

[a]5 Or Messiah   [b]7 Greek unclean   [c]16 Or in   [d]27 That is, from the upper Nile region

32The eunuch was reading this passage of Scripture:

"He was led like a sheep to
    the slaughter,
and as a lamb before the
    shearer is silent,
so he did not open his
    mouth.
33In his humiliation he was
    deprived of justice.
Who can speak of his
    descendants?
For his life was taken from
    the earth."[a]

34The eunuch asked Philip, "Tell me, please, who is the prophet talking about, himself or someone else?" 35Then Philip began with that very passage of Scripture and told him the good news about Jesus.

36As they traveled along the road, they came to some water and the eunuch said, "Look, here is water. Why shouldn't I be baptized?"[b] 38And he gave orders to stop the chariot. Then both Philip and the eunuch went down into the water and Philip baptized him. 39When they came up out of the water, the Spirit of the Lord suddenly took Philip away, and the eunuch did not see him again, but went on his way rejoicing. 40Philip, however, appeared at Azotus and traveled about, preaching the gospel in all the towns until he reached Caesarea.

Saul's Conversion

9 Meanwhile, Saul was still breathing out murderous threats against the Lord's disciples. He went to the high priest 2and asked him for letters to the synagogues in Damascus, so that if he found any there who belonged to the Way, whether men

32
Ac 10:34-43

or women, he might take them as prisoners to Jerusalem. 3As he neared Damascus on his journey, suddenly a light from heaven flashed around him. 4He fell to the ground and heard a voice say to him, "Saul, Saul, why do you persecute me?"

5"Who are you, Lord?" Saul asked.

"I am Jesus, whom you are persecuting," he replied. 6"Now get up and go into the city, and you will be told what you must do."

7The men traveling with Saul stood there speechless; they heard the sound but did not see anyone. 8Saul got up from the ground, but when he opened his eyes he could see nothing. So they led him by the hand into Damascus. 9For three days he was blind, and did not eat or drink anything.

10In Damascus there was a disciple named Ananias. The Lord called to him in a vision, "Ananias!"

"Yes, Lord," he answered.

11The Lord told him, "Go to the house of Judas on Straight Street and ask for a man from Tarsus named Saul, for he is praying. 12In a vision he has seen a man named Ananias come and place his hands on him to restore his sight."

13"Lord," Ananias answered, "I have heard many reports about this man and all the harm he has done to your saints in Jerusalem. 14And he has come here with authority from the chief priests to arrest all who call on your name."

15But the Lord said to Ananias, "Go! This man is my chosen instrument to carry my name be-

---

a33 Isaiah 53:7,8   b36 Some late manuscripts *baptized?"* 37*Philip said, "If you believe with all your heart, you may." The eunuch answered, "I believe that Jesus Christ is the Son of God."*

fore the Gentiles and their kings and before the people of Israel. [16]I will show him how much he must suffer for my name."

91
Ro 5:3,4

[17]Then Ananias went to the house and entered it. Placing his hands on Saul, he said, "Brother Saul, the Lord—Jesus, who appeared to you on the road as you were coming here—has sent me so that you may see again and be filled with the Holy Spirit." [18]Immediately, something like scales fell from Saul's eyes, and he could see again. He got up and was baptized, [19]and after taking some food, he regained his strength.

Saul in Damascus and Jerusalem

Saul spent several days with the disciples in Damascus. [20]At once he began to preach in the synagogues that Jesus is the Son of God. [21]All those who heard him were astonished and asked, "Isn't he the man who raised havoc in Jerusalem among those who call on this name? And hasn't he come here to take them as prisoners to the chief priests?" [22]Yet Saul grew more and more powerful and baffled the Jews living in Damascus by proving that Jesus is the Christ.[a]

[23]After many days had gone by, the Jews conspired to kill him, [24]but Saul learned of their plan. Day and night they kept close watch on the city gates in order to kill him. [25]But his followers took him by night and lowered him in a basket through an opening in the wall.

[26]When he came to Jerusalem, he tried to join the disciples, but they were all afraid of him, not believing that he really was a disciple. [27]But Barnabas took him and brought him to the apostles. He told them how Saul on his journey had seen the Lord and that the Lord had spoken to him, and how in Damascus he had preached fearlessly in the name of Jesus. [28]So Saul stayed with them and moved about freely in Jerusalem, speaking boldly in the name of the Lord. [29]He talked and debated with the Grecian Jews, but they tried to kill him. [30]When the brothers learned of this, they took him down to Caesarea and sent him off to Tarsus.

[31]Then the church throughout Judea, Galilee and Samaria enjoyed a time of peace. It was strengthened; and encouraged by the Holy Spirit, it grew in numbers, living in the fear of the Lord.

8
Ac 20:17

Aeneas and Dorcas

[32]As Peter traveled about the country, he went to visit the saints in Lydda. [33]There he found a man named Aeneas, a paralytic who had been bedridden for eight years. [34]"Aeneas," Peter said to him, "Jesus Christ heals you. Get up and take care of your mat." Immediately Aeneas got up. [35]All those who lived in Lydda and Sharon saw him and turned to the Lord.

[36]In Joppa there was a disciple named Tabitha (which, when translated, is Dorcas[b]), who was always doing good and helping the poor. [37]About that time she became sick and died, and her body was washed and placed in an upstairs room. [38]Lydda was near Joppa; so when the disciples heard that Peter was in Lydda, they sent two men to him and urged him, "Please come at once!"

---

[a]22 Or *Messiah*   [b]36 Both *Tabitha* (Aramaic) and *Dorcas* (Greek) mean *gazelle*.

³⁹Peter went with them, and when he arrived he was taken upstairs to the room. All the widows stood around him, crying and showing him the robes and other clothing that Dorcas had made while she was still with them.

⁴⁰Peter sent them all out of the room; then he got down on his knees and prayed. Turning toward the dead woman, he said, "Tabitha, get up." She opened her eyes, and seeing Peter she sat up. ⁴¹He took her by the hand and helped her to her feet. Then he called the believers and the widows and presented her to them alive. ⁴²This became known all over Joppa, and many people believed in the Lord. ⁴³Peter stayed in Joppa for some time with a tanner named Simon.

Cornelius Calls for Peter

10 At Caesarea there was a man named Cornelius, a centurion in what was known as the Italian Regiment. ²He and all his family were devout and God-fearing; he gave generously to those in need and prayed to God regularly. ³One day at about three in the afternoon he had a vision. He distinctly saw an angel of God, who came to him and said, "Cornelius!"

⁴Cornelius stared at him in fear. "What is it, Lord?" he asked.

The angel answered, "Your prayers and gifts to the poor have come up as a memorial offering before God. ⁵Now send men to Joppa to bring back a man named Simon who is called Peter. ⁶He is staying with Simon the tanner, whose house is by the sea."

⁷When the angel who spoke to him had gone, Cornelius called two of his servants and a devout soldier who was one of his atten-

dants. ⁸He told them everything that had happened and sent them to Joppa.

Peter's Vision

⁹About noon the following day as they were on their journey and approaching the city, Peter went up on the roof to pray. ¹⁰He became hungry and wanted something to eat, and while the meal was being prepared, he fell into a trance. ¹¹He saw heaven opened and something like a large sheet being let down to earth by its four corners. ¹²It contained all kinds of four-footed animals, as well as reptiles of the earth and birds of the air. ¹³Then a voice told him, "Get up, Peter. Kill and eat."

¹⁴"Surely not, Lord!" Peter replied. "I have never eaten anything impure or unclean."

¹⁵The voice spoke to him a second time, "Do not call anything impure that God has made clean."

¹⁶This happened three times, and immediately the sheet was taken back to heaven.

¹⁷While Peter was wondering about the meaning of the vision, the men sent by Cornelius found out where Simon's house was and stopped at the gate. ¹⁸They called out, asking if Simon who was known as Peter was staying there.

¹⁹While Peter was still thinking about the vision, the Spirit said to him, "Simon, three* men are looking for you. ²⁰So get up and go downstairs. Do not hesitate to go with them, for I have sent them."

²¹Peter went down and said to the men, "I'm the one you're looking for. Why have you come?"

²²The men replied, "We have

*19 One early manuscript *two*; other manuscripts do not have the number.

come from Cornelius the centurion. He is a righteous and God-fearing man, who is respected by all the Jewish people. A holy angel told him to have you come to his house so that he could hear what you have to say." [23]Then Peter invited the men into the house to be his guests.

Peter at Cornelius' House

The next day Peter started out with them, and some of the brothers from Joppa went along. [24]The following day he arrived in Caesarea. Cornelius was expecting them and had called together his relatives and close friends. [25]As Peter entered the house, Cornelius met him and fell at his feet in reverence. [26]But Peter made him get up. "Stand up," he said, "I am only a man myself."

[27]Talking with him, Peter went inside and found a large gathering of people. [28]He said to them: "You are well aware that it is against our law for a Jew to associate with a Gentile or visit him. But God has shown me that I should not call any man impure or unclean. [29]So when I was sent for, I came without raising any objection. May I ask why you sent for me?"

[30]Cornelius answered: "Four days ago I was in my house praying at this hour, at three in the afternoon. Suddenly a man in shining clothes stood before me [31]and said, 'Cornelius, God has heard your prayer and remembered your gifts to the poor. [32]Send to Joppa for Simon who is called Peter. He is a guest in the home of Simon the tanner, who lives by the sea.' [33]So I sent for you immediately, and it was good of you to come. Now we are all here in the presence of God to listen to everything the Lord has commanded you to tell us."

[34]Then Peter began to speak: "I now realize how true it is that God does not show favoritism [35]but accepts men from every nation who fear him and do what is right. [36]You know the message God sent to the people of Israel, telling the good news of peace through Jesus Christ, who is Lord of all. [37]You know what has happened throughout Judea, beginning in Galilee after the baptism that John preached— [38]how God anointed Jesus of Nazareth with the Holy Spirit and power, and how he went around doing good and healing all who were under the power of the devil, because God was with him.

[39]"We are witnesses of everything he did in the country of the Jews and in Jerusalem. They killed him by hanging him on a tree, [40]but God raised him from the dead on the third day and caused him to be seen. [41]He was not seen by all the people, but by witnesses whom God had already chosen—by us who ate and drank with him after he rose from the dead. [42]He commanded us to preach to the people and to testify that he is the one whom God appointed as judge of the living and the dead. [43]All the prophets testify about him that everyone who believes in him receives forgiveness of sins through his name."

[44]While Peter was still speaking these words, the Holy Spirit came on all who heard the message. [45]The circumcised believers who had come with Peter were astonished that the gift of the Holy Spirit had been poured out even on the Gentiles. [46]For they

1
Ro 15:7
32
Ro 1:16

39
1Co 12:9

78
Ro 3:23

95
Ac 19:6

heard them speaking in tongues[a] and praising God.

Then Peter said, [47]"Can anyone keep these people from being baptized with water? They have received the Holy Spirit just as we have." [48]So he ordered that they be baptized in the name of Jesus Christ. Then they asked Peter to stay with them for a few days.

Peter Explains His Actions

11 The apostles and the brothers throughout Judea heard that the Gentiles also had received the word of God. [2]So when Peter went up to Jerusalem, the circumcised believers criticized him [3]and said, "You went into the house of uncircumcised men and ate with them."

[4]Peter began and explained everything to them precisely as it had happened: [5]"I was in the city of Joppa praying, and in a trance I saw a vision. I saw something like a large sheet being let down from heaven by its four corners, and it came down to where I was. [6]I looked into it and saw four-footed animals of the earth, wild beasts, reptiles, and birds of the air. [7]Then I heard a voice telling me, 'Get up, Peter. Kill and eat.'

[8]"I replied, 'Surely not, Lord! Nothing impure or unclean has ever entered my mouth.'

[9]"The voice spoke from heaven a second time, 'Do not call anything impure that God has made clean.' [10]This happened three times, and then it was all pulled up to heaven again.

[11]"Right then three men who had been sent to me from Caesarea stopped at the house where I was staying. [12]The Spirit told me to have no hesitation about going with them. These six brothers also went with me, and we en-

tered the man's house. [13]He told us how he had seen an angel appear in his house and say, 'Send to Joppa for Simon who is called Peter. [14]He will bring you a message through which you and all your household will be saved.'

[15]"As I began to speak, the Holy Spirit came on them as he had come on us at the beginning. [16]Then I remembered what the Lord had said: 'John baptized with[b] water, but you will be baptized with the Holy Spirit.' [17]So if God gave them the same gift as he gave us, who believed in the Lord Jesus Christ, who was I to think that I could oppose God?"

[18]When they heard this, they had no further objections and praised God, saying, "So then, God has granted even the Gentiles repentance unto life."

The Church in Antioch

[19]Now those who had been scattered by the persecution in connection with Stephen traveled as far as Phoenicia, Cyprus and Antioch, telling the message only to Jews. [20]Some of them, however, men from Cyprus and Cyrene, went to Antioch and began to speak to Greeks also, telling them the good news about the Lord Jesus. [21]The Lord's hand was with them, and a great number of people believed and turned to the Lord.

[22]News of this reached the ears of the church at Jerusalem, and they sent Barnabas to Antioch. [23]When he arrived and saw the evidence of the grace of God, he was glad and encouraged them all to remain true to the Lord with all their hearts. [24]He was a good man, full of the Holy Spirit and faith, and a great number of people were brought to the Lord. [25]Then Barnabas went to Tarsus

[a]46 Or other languages [b]16 Or in

to look for Saul, 26and when he found him, he brought him to Antioch. So for a whole year Barnabas and Saul met with the church and taught great numbers of people. The disciples were called Christians first at Antioch.

27During this time some prophets came down from Jerusalem to Antioch. 28One of them, named Agabus, stood up and through the Spirit predicted that a severe famine would spread over the entire Roman world. (This happened during the reign of Claudius.) 29The disciples, each according to his ability, decided to provide help for the brothers living in Judea. 30This they did, sending their gift to the elders by Barnabas and Saul.

Peter's Miraculous Escape From Prison

12 It was about this time that King Herod arrested some who belonged to the church, intending to persecute them. 2He had James, the brother of John, put to death with the sword. 3When he saw that this pleased the Jews, he proceeded to seize Peter also. This happened during the Feast of Unleavened Bread. 4After arresting him, he put him in prison, handing him over to be guarded by four squads of four soldiers each. Herod intended to bring him out for public trial after the Passover.

5So Peter was kept in prison, but the church was earnestly praying to God for him.

6The night before Herod was to bring him to trial, Peter was sleeping between two soldiers, bound with two chains, and sentries stood guard at the entrance. 7Suddenly an angel of the Lord appeared and a light shone in the cell. He struck Peter on the side and woke him up. "Quick, get up!" he said, and the chains fell off Peter's wrists.

8Then the angel said to him, "Put on your clothes and sandals." And Peter did so. "Wrap your cloak around you and follow me," the angel told him. 9Peter followed him out of the prison, but he had no idea that what the angel was doing was really happening; he thought he was seeing a vision. 10They passed the first and second guards and came to the iron gate leading to the city. It opened for them by itself, and they went through it. When they had walked the length of one street, suddenly the angel left him.

11Then Peter came to himself and said, "Now I know without a doubt that the Lord sent his angel and rescued me from Herod's clutches and from everything the Jewish people were anticipating."

12When this had dawned on him, he went to the house of Mary the mother of John, also called Mark, where many people had gathered and were praying. 13Peter knocked at the outer entrance, and a servant girl named Rhoda came to answer the door. 14When she recognized Peter's voice, she was so overjoyed she ran back without opening it and exclaimed, "Peter is at the door!"

15"You're out of your mind," they told her. When she kept insisting that it was so, they said, "It must be his angel."

16But Peter kept on knocking, and when they opened the door and saw him, they were astonished. 17Peter motioned with his hand for them to be quiet and described how the Lord had brought him out of prison. "Tell James and the brothers about this," he said, and then he left for another place.

¹⁸In the morning, there was no small commotion among the soldiers as to what had become of Peter. ¹⁹After Herod had a thorough search made for him and did not find him, he cross-examined the guards and ordered that they be executed.

Herod's Death

Then Herod went from Judea to Caesarea and stayed there a while. ²⁰He had been quarreling with the people of Tyre and Sidon; they now joined together and sought an audience with him. Having secured the support of Blastus, a trusted personal servant of the king, they asked for peace, because they depended on the king's country for their food supply.

²¹On the appointed day Herod, wearing his royal robes, sat on his throne and delivered a public address to the people. ²²They shouted, "This is the voice of a god, not of a man." ²³Immediately, because Herod did not give praise to God, an angel of the Lord struck him down, and he was eaten by worms and died.

²⁴But the word of God continued to increase and spread.

²⁵When Barnabas and Saul had finished their mission, they returned from*a* Jerusalem, taking with them John, also called Mark.

Barnabas and Saul Sent Off

13 In the church at Antioch there were prophets and teachers: Barnabas, Simeon called Niger, Lucius of Cyrene, Manaen (who had been brought up with Herod the tetrarch) and Saul. ²While they were worshiping the Lord and fasting, the Holy Spirit said, "Set apart for me Barnabas and Saul for the

work to which I have called them." ³So after they had fasted and prayed, they placed their hands on them and sent them off.

On Cyprus

⁴The two of them, sent on their way by the Holy Spirit, went down to Seleucia and sailed from there to Cyprus. ⁵When they arrived at Salamis, they proclaimed the word of God in the Jewish synagogues. John was with them as their helper.

⁶They traveled through the whole island until they came to Paphos. There they met a Jewish sorcerer and false prophet named Bar-Jesus, ⁷who was an attendant of the proconsul, Sergius Paulus. The proconsul, an intelligent man, sent for Barnabas and Saul because he wanted to hear the word of God. ⁸But Elymas the sorcerer (for that is what his name means) opposed them and tried to turn the proconsul from the faith. ⁹Then Saul, who was also called Paul, filled with the Holy Spirit, looked straight at Elymas and said, ¹⁰"You are a child of the devil and an enemy of everything that is right! You are full of all kinds of deceit and trickery. Will you never stop perverting the right ways of the Lord? ¹¹Now the hand of the Lord is against you. You are going to be blind, and for a time you will be unable to see the light of the sun."

Immediately mist and darkness came over him, and he groped about, seeking someone to lead him by the hand. ¹²When the proconsul saw what had happened, he believed, for he was amazed at the teaching about the Lord.

*²⁵ Some manuscripts *to*

In Pisidian Antioch

[13]From Paphos, Paul and his companions sailed to Perga in Pamphylia, where John left them to return to Jerusalem. [14]From Perga they went on to Pisidian Antioch. On the Sabbath they entered the synagogue and sat down. [15]After the reading from the Law and the Prophets, the synagogue rulers sent word to them, saying, "Brothers, if you have a message of encouragement for the people, please speak."

[16]Standing up, Paul motioned with his hand and said: "Men of Israel and you Gentiles who worship God, listen to me! [17]The God of the people of Israel chose our fathers; he made the people prosper during their stay in Egypt, with mighty power he led them out of that country, [18]he endured their conduct[a] for about forty years in the desert, [19]he overthrew seven nations in Canaan and gave their land to his people as their inheritance. [20]All this took about 450 years.

"After this, God gave them judges until the time of Samuel the prophet. [21]Then the people asked for a king, and he gave them Saul son of Kish, of the tribe of Benjamin, who ruled forty years. [22]After removing Saul, he made David their king. He testified concerning him: 'I have found David son of Jesse a man after my own heart; he will do everything I want him to do.'

[23]"From this man's descendants God has brought to Israel the Savior Jesus, as he promised. [24]Before the coming of Jesus, John preached repentance and baptism to all the people of Israel. [25]As John was completing his work, he said: 'Who do you think I am? I am not that one. No, but he is coming after me, whose sandals I am not worthy to untie.'

[26]"Brothers, children of Abraham, and you God-fearing Gentiles, it is to us that this message of salvation has been sent. [27]The people of Jerusalem and their rulers did not recognize Jesus, yet in condemning him they fulfilled the words of the prophets that are read every Sabbath. [28]Though they found no proper ground for a death sentence, they asked Pilate to have him executed. [29]When they had carried out all that was written about him, they took him down from the tree and laid him in a tomb. [30]But God raised him from the dead, [31]and for many days he was seen by those who had traveled with him from Galilee to Jerusalem. They are now his witnesses to our people.

[32]"We tell you the good news: What God promised our fathers [33]he has fulfilled for us, their children, by raising up Jesus. As it is written in the second Psalm:

" 'You are my Son;
    today I have become your
        Father.'[b][c]

[34]The fact that God raised him from the dead, never to decay, is stated in these words:

" 'I will give you the holy and
    sure blessings promised
        to David.'[d]

[35]So it is stated elsewhere:

" 'You will not let your Holy
    One see decay.'[e]

[36]"For when David had served God's purpose in his own generation, he fell asleep; he was

---

[a]18 Some manuscripts *and cared for them*   [b]33 Or *have begotten you*   [c]33 Psalm 2:7
[d]34 Isaiah 55:3   [e]35 Psalm 16:10

buried with his fathers and his body decayed. ³⁷But the one whom God raised from the dead did not see decay.

³⁸Therefore, my brothers, I want you to know that through Jesus the forgiveness of sins is proclaimed to you. ³⁹Through him everyone who believes is justified from everything you could not be justified from by the law of Moses. ⁴⁰Take care that what the prophets have said does not happen to you:

⁴¹" 'Look, you scoffers,
    wonder and perish,
  for I am going to do
      something in your days
    that you would never
      believe,
  even if someone told you.'ᵈ"

⁴²As Paul and Barnabas were leaving the synagogue, the people invited them to speak further about these things on the next Sabbath. ⁴³When the congregation was dismissed, many of the Jews and devout converts to Judaism followed Paul and Barnabas, who talked with them and urged them to continue in the grace of God.

⁴⁴On the next Sabbath almost the whole city gathered to hear the word of the Lord. ⁴⁵When the Jews saw the crowds, they were filled with jealousy and talked abusively against what Paul was saying.

⁴⁶Then Paul and Barnabas answered them boldly: "We had to speak the word of God to you first. Since you reject it and do not consider yourselves worthy of eternal life, we now turn to the Gentiles. ⁴⁷For this is what the Lord has commanded us:

" 'I have made youᵇ a light for
    the Gentiles,

that youᵇ may bring
    salvation to the ends of
    the earth.'ᶜ"

⁴⁸When the Gentiles heard this, they were glad and honored the word of the Lord; and all who were appointed for eternal life believed.

⁴⁹The word of the Lord spread through the whole region. ⁵⁰But the Jews incited the God-fearing women of high standing and the leading men of the city. They stirred up persecution against Paul and Barnabas, and expelled them from their region. ⁵¹So they shook the dust from their feet in protest against them and went to Iconium. ⁵²And the disciples were filled with joy and with the Holy Spirit.

In Iconium

14 At Iconium Paul and Barnabas went as usual into the Jewish synagogue. There they spoke so effectively that a great number of Jews and Gentiles believed. ²But the Jews who refused to believe stirred up the Gentiles and poisoned their minds against the brothers. ³So Paul and Barnabas spent considerable time there, speaking boldly for the Lord, who confirmed the message of his grace by enabling them to do miraculous signs and wonders. ⁴The people of the city were divided; some sided with the Jews, others with the apostles. ⁵There was a plot afoot among the Gentiles and Jews, together with their leaders, to mistreat them and stone them. ⁶But they found out about it and fled to the Lycaonian cities of Lystra and Derbe and to the surrounding country, ⁷where they continued to preach the good news.

ᵃ41 Hab. 1:5   ᵇ47 The Greek is singular.   ᶜ47 Isaiah 49:6

In Lystra and Derbe

⁸In Lystra there sat a man crippled in his feet, who was lame from birth and had never walked. ⁹He listened to Paul as he was speaking. Paul looked directly at him, saw that he had faith to be healed ¹⁰and called out, "Stand up on your feet!" At that, the man jumped up and began to walk.

¹¹When the crowd saw what Paul had done, they shouted in the Lycaonian language, "The gods have come down to us in human form!" ¹²Barnabas they called Zeus, and Paul they called Hermes because he was the chief speaker. ¹³The priest of Zeus, whose temple was just outside the city, brought bulls and wreaths to the city gates because he and the crowd wanted to offer sacrifices to them.

¹⁴But when the apostles Barnabas and Paul heard of this, they tore their clothes and rushed out into the crowd, shouting: ¹⁵"Men, why are you doing this? We too are only men, human like you. We are bringing you good news, telling you to turn from these worthless things to the living God, who made heaven and earth and sea and everything in them. ¹⁶In the past, he let all nations go their own way. ¹⁷Yet he has not left himself without testimony: He has shown kindness by giving you rain from heaven and crops in their seasons; he provides you with plenty of food and fills your hearts with joy." ¹⁸Even with these words, they had difficulty keeping the crowd from sacrificing to them.

¹⁹Then some Jews came from Antioch and Iconium and won the crowd over. They stoned Paul and dragged him outside the city, thinking he was dead. ²⁰But after the disciples had gathered around him, he got up and went back into the city. The next day he and Barnabas left for Derbe.

The Return to Antioch in Syria

²¹They preached the good news in that city and won a large number of disciples. Then they returned to Lystra, Iconium and Antioch, ²²strengthening the disciples and encouraging them to remain true to the faith. "We must go through many hardships to enter the kingdom of God," they said. ²³Paul and Barnabas appointed eldersª for them in each church and, with prayer and fasting, committed them to the Lord, in whom they had put their trust. ²⁴After going through Pisidia, they came into Pamphylia, ²⁵and when they had preached the word in Perga, they went down to Attalia.

²⁶From Attalia they sailed back to Antioch, where they had been committed to the grace of God for the work they had now completed. ²⁷On arriving there, they gathered the church together and reported all that God had done through them and how he had opened the door of faith to the Gentiles. ²⁸And they stayed there a long time with the disciples.

The Council at Jerusalem

15 Some men came down from Judea to Antioch and were teaching the brothers: "Unless you are circumcised, according to the custom taught by Moses, you cannot be saved." ²This brought Paul and Barnabas into sharp dispute and debate

92
2Th 3:3

ª23 Or *Barnabas ordained elders*; or *Barnabas had elders elected*

with them. So Paul and Barnabas were appointed, along with some other believers, to go up to Jerusalem to see the apostles and elders about this question. ³The church sent them on their way, and as they traveled through Phoenicia and Samaria, they told how the Gentiles had been converted. This news made all the brothers very glad. ⁴When they came to Jerusalem, they were welcomed by the church and the apostles and elders, to whom they reported everything God had done through them.

⁵Then some of the believers who belonged to the party of the Pharisees stood up and said, "The Gentiles must be circumcised and required to obey the law of Moses."

⁶The apostles and elders met to consider this question. ⁷After much discussion, Peter got up and addressed them: "Brothers, you know that some time ago God made a choice among you that the Gentiles might hear from my lips the message of the gospel and believe. ⁸God, who knows the heart, showed that he accepted them by giving the Holy Spirit to them, just as he did to us. ⁹He made no distinction between us and them, for he purified their hearts by faith. ¹⁰Now then, why do you try to test God by putting on the necks of the disciples a yoke that neither we nor our fathers have been able to bear? ¹¹No! We believe it is through the grace of our Lord Jesus that we are saved, just as they are."

¹²The whole assembly became silent as they listened to Barnabas and Paul telling about the miraculous signs and wonders God had done among the Gen-

tiles through them. ¹³When they finished, James spoke up: "Brothers, listen to me. ¹⁴Simon[a] has described to us how God at first showed his concern by taking from the Gentiles a people for himself. ¹⁵The words of the prophets are in agreement with this, as it is written:

¹⁶" 'After this I will return
    and rebuild David's fallen
        tent.
Its ruins I will rebuild,
    and I will restore it,
¹⁷that the remnant of men may
        seek the Lord,
    and all the Gentiles who
        bear my name,
says the Lord, who does these
        things'[b]
¹⁸   that have been known for
        ages.[c]

¹⁹"It is my judgment, therefore, that we should not make it difficult for the Gentiles who are turning to God. ²⁰Instead we should write to them, telling them to abstain from food polluted by idols, from sexual immorality, from the meat of strangled animals and from blood. ²¹For Moses has been preached in every city from the earliest times and is read in the synagogues on every Sabbath."

The Council's Letter to Gentile Believers

²²Then the apostles and elders, with the whole church, decided to choose some of their own men and send them to Antioch with Paul and Barnabas. They chose Judas (called Barsabbas) and Silas, two men who were leaders among the brothers. ²³With them they sent the following letter:

---

[a]14 Greek *Simeon*, a variant of *Simon*; that is, Peter   [b]17 Amos 9:11,12
[c]17,18 Some manuscripts *things'—* / ¹⁸*known to the Lord for ages is his work*

The apostles and elders, your brothers,

To the Gentile believers in Antioch, Syria and Cilicia:

Greetings.

24We have heard that some went out from us without our authorization and disturbed you, troubling your minds by what they said. 25So we all agreed to choose some men and send them to you with our dear friends Barnabas and Paul— 26men who have risked their lives for the name of our Lord Jesus Christ. 27Therefore we are sending Judas and Silas to confirm by word of mouth what we are writing. 28It seemed good to the Holy Spirit and to us not to burden you with anything beyond the following requirements: 29You are to abstain from food sacrificed to idols, from blood, from the meat of strangled animals and from sexual immorality. You will do well to avoid these things.

Farewell.

30The men were sent off and went down to Antioch, where they gathered the church together and delivered the letter. 31The people read it and were glad for its encouraging message. 32Judas and Silas, who themselves were prophets, said much to encourage and strengthen the brothers. 33After spending some time there, they were sent off by the brothers with the blessing of peace to return to those who had sent them.a 35But Paul and Barnabas remained in Antioch, where they and many others taught and preached the word of the Lord.

Disagreement Between Paul and Barnabas

36Some time later Paul said to Barnabas, "Let us go back and visit the brothers in all the towns where we preached the word of the Lord and see how they are doing." 37Barnabas wanted to take John, also called Mark, with them, 38but Paul did not think it wise to take him, because he had deserted them in Pamphylia and had not continued with them in the work. 39They had such a sharp disagreement that they parted company. Barnabas took Mark and sailed for Cyprus, 40but Paul chose Silas and left, commended by the brothers to the grace of the Lord. 41He went through Syria and Cilicia, strengthening the churches.

Timothy Joins Paul and Silas

16 He came to Derbe and then to Lystra, where a disciple named Timothy lived, whose mother was a Jewess and a believer, but whose father was a Greek. 2The brothers at Lystra and Iconium spoke well of him. 3Paul wanted to take him along on the journey, so he circumcised him because of the Jews who lived in that area, for they all knew that his father was a Greek. 4As they traveled from town to town, they delivered the decisions reached by the apostles and elders in Jerusalem for the people to obey. 5So the churches were strengthened in the faith and grew daily in numbers.

Paul's Vision of the Man of Macedonia

6Paul and his companions traveled throughout the region of Phrygia and Galatia, having been kept by the Holy Spirit from

---

a33 Some manuscripts them, 34but Silas decided to remain there preaching the word in the province of Asia. 7When they came to the border of Mysia, they tried to enter Bithynia, but the Spirit of Jesus would not allow them to. 8So they passed by Mysia and went down to Troas. 9During the night Paul had a vision of a man of Macedonia standing and begging him, "Come over to Macedonia and help us." 10After Paul had seen the vision, we got ready at once to leave for Macedonia, concluding that God had called us to preach the gospel to them.

Lydia's Conversion in Philippi

11From Troas we put out to sea and sailed straight for Samothrace, and the next day on to Neapolis. 12From there we traveled to Philippi, a Roman colony and the leading city of that district of Macedonia. And we stayed there several days.

13On the Sabbath we went outside the city gate to the river, where we expected to find a place of prayer. We sat down and began to speak to the women who had gathered there. 14One of those listening was a woman named Lydia, a dealer in purple cloth from the city of Thyatira, who was a worshiper of God. The Lord opened her heart to respond to Paul's message. 15When she and the members of her household were baptized, she invited us to her home. "If you consider me a believer in the Lord," she said, "come and stay at my house." And she persuaded us.

Paul and Silas in Prison

16Once when we were going to the place of prayer, we were met by a slave girl who had a spirit by which she predicted the future. She earned a great deal of money for her owners by fortune-telling.

17This girl followed Paul and the rest of us, shouting, "These men are servants of the Most High God, who are telling you the way to be saved." 18She kept this up for many days. Finally Paul became so troubled that he turned around and said to the spirit, "In the name of Jesus Christ I command you to come out of her!" At that moment the spirit left her.

19When the owners of the slave girl realized that their hope of making money was gone, they seized Paul and Silas and dragged them into the marketplace to face the authorities. 20They brought them before the magistrates and said, "These men are Jews, and are throwing our city into an uproar 21by advocating customs unlawful for us Romans to accept or practice."

22The crowd joined in the attack against Paul and Silas, and the magistrates ordered them to be stripped and beaten. 23After they had been severely flogged, they were thrown into prison, and the jailer was commanded to guard them carefully. 24Upon receiving such orders, he put them in the inner cell and fastened their feet in the stocks.

25About midnight Paul and Silas were praying and singing hymns to God, and the other prisoners were listening to them. 26Suddenly there was such a violent earthquake that the foundations of the prison were shaken. At once all the prison doors flew open, and everybody's chains came loose. 27The jailer woke up, and when he saw the prison doors open, he drew his sword and was about to kill himself because he thought the prisoners had escaped. 28But Paul shouted, "Don't harm yourself! We are all here!"

²⁹The jailer called for lights, rushed in and fell trembling before Paul and Silas. ³⁰He then brought them out and asked, "Sirs, what must I do to be saved?"

³¹They replied, "Believe in the Lord Jesus, and you will be saved—you and your household." ³²Then they spoke the word of the Lord to him and to all the others in his house. ³³At that hour of the night the jailer took them and washed their wounds; then immediately he and all his family were baptized. ³⁴The jailer brought them into his house and set a meal before them; he was filled with joy because he had come to believe in God—he and his whole family.

³⁵When it was daylight, the magistrates sent their officers to the jailer with the order: "Release those men." ³⁶The jailer told Paul, "The magistrates have ordered that you and Silas be released. Now you can leave. Go in peace."

³⁷But Paul said to the officers: "They beat us publicly without a trial, even though we are Roman citizens, and threw us into prison. And now do they want to get rid of us quietly? No! Let them come themselves and escort us out."

³⁸The officers reported this to the magistrates, and when they heard that Paul and Silas were Roman citizens, they were alarmed. ³⁹They came to appease them and escorted them from the prison, requesting them to leave the city. ⁴⁰After Paul and Silas came out of the prison, they went to Lydia's house, where they met with the brothers and encouraged them. Then they left.

In Thessalonica

17 When they had passed through Amphipolis and Apollonia, they came to Thessalonica, where there was a Jewish synagogue. ²As his custom was, Paul went into the synagogue, and on three Sabbath days he reasoned with them from the Scriptures, ³explaining and proving that the Christᵃ had to suffer and rise from the dead. "This Jesus I am proclaiming to you is the Christ,ᵃ" he said. ⁴Some of the Jews were persuaded and joined Paul and Silas, as did a large number of God-fearing Greeks and not a few prominent women.

⁵But the Jews were jealous; so they rounded up some bad characters from the marketplace, formed a mob and started a riot in the city. They rushed to Jason's house in search of Paul and Silas in order to bring them out to the crowd.ᵇ ⁶But when they did not find them, they dragged Jason and some other brothers before the city officials, shouting: "These men who have caused trouble all over the world have now come here, ⁷and Jason has welcomed them into his house. They are all defying Caesar's decrees, saying that there is another king, one called Jesus." ⁸When they heard this, the crowd and the city officials were thrown into turmoil. ⁹Then they made Jason and the others post bond and let them go.

In Berea

¹⁰As soon as it was night, the brothers sent Paul and Silas away to Berea. On arriving there, they went to the Jewish synagogue.

¹¹Now the Bereans were of more noble character than the Thessalonians, for they received the message with great eagerness and examined the Scriptures every day to see if what Paul said was true. ¹²Many of the Jews believed, as did also a number of prominent Greek women and many Greek men.

¹³When the Jews in Thessalonica learned that Paul was preaching the word of God at Berea, they went there too, agitating the crowds and stirring them up. ¹⁴The brothers immediately sent Paul to the coast, but Silas and Timothy stayed at Berea. ¹⁵The men who escorted Paul brought him to Athens and then left with instructions for Silas and Timothy to join him as soon as possible.

In Athens

¹⁶While Paul was waiting for them in Athens, he was greatly distressed to see that the city was full of idols. ¹⁷So he reasoned in the synagogue with the Jews and the God-fearing Greeks, as well as in the marketplace day by day with those who happened to be there. ¹⁸A group of Epicurean and Stoic philosophers began to dispute with him. Some of them asked, "What is this babbler trying to say?" Others remarked, "He seems to be advocating foreign gods." They said this because Paul was preaching the good news about Jesus and the resurrection. ¹⁹Then they took him and brought him to a meeting of the Areopagus, where they said to him, "May we know what this new teaching is that you are presenting? ²⁰You are bringing some strange ideas to our ears, and we want to know what they mean." ²¹(All the Athenians and the foreigners who lived there spent their time doing nothing but talking about and listening to the latest ideas.)

²²Paul then stood up in the meeting of the Areopagus and said: "Men of Athens! I see that in every way you are very religious. ²³For as I walked around and looked carefully at your objects of worship, I even found an altar with this inscription: TO AN UNKNOWN GOD. Now what you worship as something unknown I am going to proclaim to you.

²⁴"The God who made the world and everything in it is the Lord of heaven and earth and does not live in temples built by hands. ²⁵And he is not served by human hands, as if he needed anything, because he himself gives all men life and breath and everything else. ²⁶From one man he made every nation of men, that they should inhabit the whole earth; and he determined the times set for them and the exact places where they should live. ²⁷God did this so that men would seek him and perhaps reach out for him and find him, though he is not far from each one of us. ²⁸'For in him we live and move and have our being.' As some of your own poets have said, 'We are his offspring.'

²⁹"Therefore since we are God's offspring, we should not think that the divine being is like gold or silver or stone—an image made by man's design and skill. ³⁰In the past God overlooked such ignorance, but now he commands all people everywhere to repent. ³¹For he has set a day when he will judge the world with justice by the man he has appointed. He has given proof of this to all men by raising him from the dead."

³²When they heard about the

31
Ro 8:32

74
Ac 20:21

resurrection of the dead, some of them sneered, but others said, "We want to hear you again on this subject." ³³At that, Paul left the Council. ³⁴A few men became followers of Paul and believed. Among them was Dionysius, a member of the Areopagus, also a woman named Damaris, and a number of others.

In Corinth

18 After this, Paul left Athens and went to Corinth. ²There he met a Jew named Aquila, a native of Pontus, who had recently come from Italy with his wife Priscilla, because Claudius had ordered all the Jews to leave Rome. Paul went to see them, ³and because he was a tentmaker as they were, he stayed and worked with them. ⁴Every Sabbath he reasoned in the synagogue, trying to persuade Jews and Greeks.

⁵When Silas and Timothy came from Macedonia, Paul devoted himself exclusively to preaching, testifying to the Jews that Jesus was the Christ.ᵃ ⁶But when the Jews opposed Paul and became abusive, he shook out his clothes in protest and said to them, "Your blood be on your own heads! I am clear of my responsibility. From now on I will go to the Gentiles."

⁷Then Paul left the synagogue and went next door to the house of Titius Justus, a worshiper of God. ⁸Crispus, the synagogue ruler, and his entire household believed in the Lord; and many of the Corinthians who heard him believed and were baptized.

⁹One night the Lord spoke to Paul in a vision: "Do not be afraid; keep on speaking, do not be silent. ¹⁰For I am with you, and no one is going to attack and

harm you, because I have many people in this city." ¹¹So Paul stayed for a year and a half, teaching them the word of God.

¹²While Gallio was proconsul of Achaia, the Jews made a united attack on Paul and brought him into court. ¹³"This man," they charged, "is persuading the people to worship God in ways contrary to the law."

¹⁴Just as Paul was about to speak, Gallio said to the Jews, "If you Jews were making a complaint about some misdemeanor or serious crime, it would be reasonable for me to listen to you. ¹⁵But since it involves questions about words and names and your own law—settle the matter yourselves. I will not be a judge of such things." ¹⁶So he had them ejected from the court. ¹⁷Then they all turned on Sosthenes the synagogue ruler and beat him in front of the court. But Gallio showed no concern whatever.

Priscilla, Aquila and Apollos

¹⁸Paul stayed on in Corinth for some time. Then he left the brothers and sailed for Syria, accompanied by Priscilla and Aquila. Before he sailed, he had his hair cut off at Cenchrea because of a vow he had taken. ¹⁹They arrived at Ephesus, where Paul left Priscilla and Aquila. He himself went into the synagogue and reasoned with the Jews. ²⁰When they asked him to spend more time with them, he declined. ²¹But as he left, he promised, "I will come back if it is God's will." Then he set sail from Ephesus. ²²When he landed at Caesarea, he went up and greeted the church and then went down to Antioch.

²³After spending some time in Antioch, Paul set out from there and traveled from place to place

---

ᵃ5 Or *Messiah;* also in verse 28

throughout the region of Galatia and Phrygia, strengthening all the disciples.

²⁴Meanwhile a Jew named Apollos, a native of Alexandria, came to Ephesus. He was a learned man, with a thorough knowledge of the Scriptures. ²⁵He had been instructed in the way of the Lord, and he spoke with great fervor*ᵃ* and taught about Jesus accurately, though he knew only the baptism of John. ²⁶He began to speak boldly in the synagogue. When Priscilla and Aquila heard him, they invited him to their home and explained to him the way of God more adequately.

²⁷When Apollos wanted to go to Achaia, the brothers encouraged him and wrote to the disciples there to welcome him. On arriving, he was a great help to those who by grace had believed. ²⁸For he vigorously refuted the Jews in public debate, proving from the Scriptures that Jesus was the Christ.

Paul in Ephesus

19 While Apollos was at Corinth, Paul took the road through the interior and arrived at Ephesus. There he found some disciples ²and asked them, "Did you receive the Holy Spirit when*ᵇ* you believed?"

They answered, "No, we have not even heard that there is a Holy Spirit."

³So Paul asked, "Then what baptism did you receive?"

"John's baptism," they replied.

⁴Paul said, "John's baptism was a baptism of repentance. He told the people to believe in the one coming after him, that is, in Jesus." ⁵On hearing this, they were baptized into*ᶜ* the name of

the Lord Jesus. ⁶When Paul placed his hands on them, the Holy Spirit came on them, and they spoke in tongues*ᵈ* and prophesied. ⁷There were about twelve men in all.

⁸Paul entered the synagogue and spoke boldly there for three months, arguing persuasively about the kingdom of God. ⁹But some of them became obstinate; they refused to believe and publicly maligned the Way. So Paul left them. He took the disciples with him and had discussions daily in the lecture hall of Tyrannus. ¹⁰This went on for two years, so that all the Jews and Greeks who lived in the province of Asia heard the word of the Lord.

¹¹God did extraordinary miracles through Paul, ¹²so that even handkerchiefs and aprons that had touched him were taken to the sick, and their illnesses were cured and the evil spirits left them.

¹³Some Jews who went around driving out evil spirits tried to invoke the name of the Lord Jesus over those who were demon-possessed. They would say, "In the name of Jesus, whom Paul preaches, I command you to come out." ¹⁴Seven sons of Sceva, a Jewish chief priest, were doing this. ¹⁵One day, the evil spirit answered them, "Jesus I know, and I know about Paul, but who are you?" ¹⁶Then the man who had the evil spirit jumped on them and overpowered them all. He gave them such a beating that they ran out of the house naked and bleeding.

¹⁷When this became known to the Jews and Greeks living in Ephesus, they were all seized with fear, and the name of the Lord Jesus was held in high honor. ¹⁸Many of those who believed

95
1Co 12:10

10
Php 2:11

now came and openly confessed their evil deeds. ¹⁹A number who had practiced sorcery brought their scrolls together and burned them publicly. When they calculated the value of the scrolls, the total came to fifty thousand drachmas.ᵃ ²⁰In this way the word of the Lord spread widely and grew in power.

²¹After all this had happened, Paul decided to go to Jerusalem, passing through Macedonia and Achaia. "After I have been there," he said, "I must visit Rome also." ²²He sent two of his helpers, Timothy and Erastus, to Macedonia, while he stayed in the province of Asia a little longer.

The Riot in Ephesus

²³About that time there arose a great disturbance about the Way. ²⁴A silversmith named Demetrius, who made silver shrines of Artemis, brought in no little business for the craftsmen. ²⁵He called them together, along with the workmen in related trades, and said: "Men, you know we receive a good income from this business. ²⁶And you see and hear how this fellow Paul has convinced and led astray large numbers of people here in Ephesus and in practically the whole province of Asia. He says that man-made gods are no gods at all. ²⁷There is danger not only that our trade will lose its good name, but also that the temple of the great goddess Artemis will be discredited, and the goddess herself, who is worshiped throughout the province of Asia and the world, will be robbed of her divine majesty."

²⁸When they heard this, they were furious and began shouting: "Great is Artemis of the

Ephesians!" ²⁹Soon the whole city was in an uproar. The people seized Gaius Aristarchus, Paul's traveling companions from Macedonia, and rushed as one man into the theater. ³⁰Paul wanted to appear before the crowd, but the disciples would not let him. ³¹Even some of the officials of the province, friends of Paul, sent him a message begging him not to venture into the theater.

³²The assembly was in confusion: Some were shouting one thing, another. Most of the people did not even know why they were there. ³³The Jews pushed Alexander to the front, and some of the crowd shouted instructions to him. He motioned for silence in order to make a defense before the people. ³⁴But when they realized he was a Jew, they all shouted in unison for about two hours: "Great is Artemis of the Ephesians!"

³⁵The city clerk quieted the crowd and said: "Men of Ephesus, doesn't all the world know that the city of Ephesus is the guardian of the temple of the great Artemis and of her image, which fell from heaven? ³⁶Therefore, since these facts are undeniable, you ought to be quiet and not do anything rash. ³⁷You have brought these men here, though they have neither robbed temples nor blasphemed our goddess. ³⁸If, then, Demetrius and his fellow craftsmen have a grievance against anybody, the courts are open and there are proconsuls. They can press charges. ³⁹If there is anything further you want to bring up, it must be settled in a legal assembly. ⁴⁰As it is, we are in danger of being charged with rioting because of today's events. In that case we

---

ᵃ19 A drachma was a silver coin worth about a day's wages.

would not be able to account for this commotion, since there is no reason for it." [41]After he had said this, he dismissed the assembly.

Through Macedonia and Greece

20 When the uproar had ended, Paul sent for the disciples and, after encouraging them, said good-by and set out for Macedonia. [2]He traveled through that area, speaking many words of encouragement to the people, and finally arrived in Greece, [3]where he stayed three months. Because the Jews made a plot against him just as he was about to sail for Syria, he decided to go back through Macedonia. [4]He was accompanied by Sopater son of Pyrrhus from Berea, Aristarchus and Secundus from Thessalonica, Gaius from Derbe, Timothy also, and Tychicus and Trophimus from the province of Asia. [5]These men went on ahead and waited for us at Troas. [6]But we sailed from Philippi after the Feast of Unleavened Bread, and five days later joined the others at Troas, where we stayed seven days.

Eutychus Raised From the Dead at Troas

[7]On the first day of the week we came together to break bread. Paul spoke to the people and, because he intended to leave the next day, kept on talking until midnight. [8]There were many lamps in the upstairs room where we were meeting. [9]Seated in a window was a young man named Eutychus, who was sinking into a deep sleep as Paul talked on and on. When he was sound asleep, he fell to the ground from the third story and was picked up dead. [10]Paul went down, threw himself on the

young man and put his arms around him. "Don't be alarmed," he said. "He's alive!" [11]Then he went upstairs again and broke bread and ate. After talking until daylight, he left. [12]The people took the young man home alive and were greatly comforted.

Paul's Farewell to the Ephesian Elders

[13]We went on ahead to the ship and sailed for Assos, where we were going to take Paul aboard. He had made this arrangement because he was going there on foot. [14]When he met us at Assos, we took him aboard and went on to Mitylene. [15]The next day we set sail from there and arrived off Kios. The day after that we crossed over to Samos, and on the following day arrived at Miletus. [16]Paul had decided to sail past Ephesus to avoid spending time in the province of Asia, for he was in a hurry to reach Jerusalem, if possible, by the day of Pentecost.

[17]From Miletus, Paul sent to **8** Ephesus for the elders of the Ac 20:28 church. [18]When they arrived, he said to them: "You know how I lived the whole time I was with you, from the first day I came into the province of Asia. [19]I served the Lord with great humility and with tears, although I was severely tested by the plots of the Jews. [20]You know that I have not hesitated to preach anything that would be helpful to you but have taught you publicly and from house to house. [21]I have declared to both **74** Jews and Greeks that they must Ro 2:1-4 turn to God in repentance and have faith in our Lord Jesus. [22]"And now, compelled by the Spirit, I am going to Jerusalem, not knowing what will happen to

me there. 23I only know that in every city the Holy Spirit warns me that prison and hardships are facing me. 24However, I consider my life worth nothing to me, if only I may finish the race and complete the task the Lord Jesus has given me—the task of testifying to the gospel of God's grace.

25"Now I know that none of you among whom I have gone about preaching the kingdom will ever see me again. 26Therefore, I declare to you today that I am innocent of the blood of all men. 27For I have not hesitated to proclaim to you the whole will of God. 28Keep watch over yourselves and all the flock of which the Holy Spirit has made you overseers.ᵃ Be shepherds of the church of God,ᵇ which he bought with his own blood. 29I know that after I leave, savage wolves will come in among you and will not spare the flock. 30Even from your own number men will arise and distort the truth in order to draw away disciples after them. 31So be on your guard! Remember that for three years I never stopped warning each of you night and day with tears.

32"Now I commit you to God and to the word of his grace, which can build you up and give you an inheritance among all those who are sanctified. 33I have not coveted anyone's silver or gold or clothing. 34You yourselves know that these hands of mine have supplied my own needs and the needs of my companions. 35In everything I did, I showed you that by this kind of hard work we must help the weak, remembering the words the Lord Jesus himself said: 'It is more blessed to give than to receive.'"

36When he had said this, he knelt down with all of them and prayed. 37They all wept as they embraced him and kissed him. 38What grieved them most was his statement that they would never see his face again. Then they accompanied him to the ship.

On to Jerusalem

21 After we had torn ourselves away from them, we put out to sea and sailed straight to Cos. The next day we went to Rhodes and from there to Patara. 2We found a ship crossing over to Phoenicia, went on board and set sail. 3After sighting Cyprus and passing to the south of it, we sailed on to Syria. We landed at Tyre, where our ship was to unload its cargo. 4Finding the disciples there, we stayed with them seven days. Through the Spirit they urged Paul not to go on to Jerusalem. 5But when our time was up, we left and continued on our way. All the disciples and their wives and children accompanied us out of the city, and there on the beach we knelt to pray. 6After saying good-by to each other, we went aboard the ship, and they returned home.

7We continued our voyage from Tyre and landed at Ptolemais, where we greeted the brothers and stayed with them for a day. 8Leaving the next day, we reached Caesarea and stayed at the house of Philip the evangelist, one of the Seven. 9He had four unmarried daughters who prophesied.

10After we had been there a number of days, a prophet named Agabus came down from Judea. 11Coming over to us, he took Paul's belt, tied his own hands and feet with it and said, "The Holy Spirit says, 'In this

98
Eph 5:17

8
Ro 16:5

37
1Ti 6:17

ᵃ28 Traditionally *bishops*   ᵇ28 Many manuscripts *of the Lord*

way the Jews of Jerusalem will bind the owner of this belt and will hand him over to the Gentiles.' "

¹²When we heard this, we and the people there pleaded with Paul not to go up to Jerusalem. ¹³Then Paul answered, "Why are you weeping and breaking my heart? I am ready not only to be bound, but also to die in Jerusalem for the name of the Lord Jesus." ¹⁴When he would not be dissuaded, we gave up and said, "The Lord's will be done."

¹⁵After this, we got ready and went up to Jerusalem. ¹⁶Some of the disciples from Caesarea accompanied us and brought us to the home of Mnason, where we were to stay. He was a man from Cyprus and one of the early disciples.

Paul's Arrival at Jerusalem

¹⁷When we arrived at Jerusalem, the brothers received us warmly. ¹⁸The next day Paul and the rest of us went to see James, and all the elders were present. ¹⁹Paul greeted them and reported in detail what God had done among the Gentiles through his ministry.

²⁰When they heard this, they praised God. Then they said to Paul: "You see, brother, how many thousands of Jews have believed, and all of them are zealous for the law. ²¹They have been informed that you teach all the Jews who live among the Gentiles to turn away from Moses, telling them not to circumcise their children or live according to our customs. ²²What shall we do? They will certainly hear that you have come, ²³so do what we tell you. There are four men with us who have made a vow. ²⁴Take these men, join in their purification rites and pay their expenses,

so that they can have their heads shaved. Then everybody will know there is no truth in these reports about you, but that you yourself are living in obedience to the law. ²⁵As for the Gentile believers, we have written to them our decision that they should abstain from food sacrificed to idols, from blood, from the meat of strangled animals and from sexual immorality."

²⁶The next day Paul took the men and purified himself along with them. Then he went to the temple to give notice of the date when the days of purification would end and the offering would be made for each of them.

Paul Arrested

²⁷When the seven days were nearly over, some Jews from the province of Asia saw Paul at the temple. They stirred up the whole crowd and seized him, ²⁸shouting, "Men of Israel, help us! This is the man who teaches all men everywhere against our people and our law and this place. And besides, he has brought Greeks into the temple area and defiled this holy place." ²⁹(They had previously seen Trophimus the Ephesian in the city with Paul and assumed that Paul had brought him into the temple area.)

³⁰The whole city was aroused, and the people came running from all directions. Seizing Paul, they dragged him from the temple, and immediately the gates were shut. ³¹While they were trying to kill him, news reached the commander of the Roman troops that the whole city of Jerusalem was in an uproar. ³²He at once took some officers and soldiers and ran down to the crowd. When the rioters saw the com-

mander and his soldiers, they stopped beating Paul.

[33]The commander came up and arrested him and ordered him to be bound with two chains. Then he asked who he was and what he had done. [34]Some in the crowd shouted one thing and some another, and since the commander could not get at the truth because of the uproar, he ordered that Paul be taken into the barracks. [35]When Paul reached the steps, the violence of the mob was so great he had to be carried by the soldiers. [36]The crowd that followed kept shouting, "Away with him!"

Paul Speaks to the Crowd

[37]As the soldiers were about to take Paul into the barracks, he asked the commander, "May I say something to you?"

"Do you speak Greek?" he replied. [38]"Aren't you the Egyptian who started a revolt and led four thousand terrorists out into the desert some time ago?"

[39]Paul answered, "I am a Jew, from Tarsus in Cilicia, a citizen of no ordinary city. Please let me speak to the people."

[40]Having received the commander's permission, Paul stood on the steps and motioned to the crowd. When they were all silent, he said to them in Aramaic[a]:

22 [1]"Brothers and fathers, listen now to my defense."

[2]When they heard him speak to them in Aramaic, they became very quiet.

Then Paul said: [3]"I am a Jew, born in Tarsus of Cilicia, but brought up in this city. Under Gamaliel I was thoroughly trained in the law of our fathers and was just as zealous for God as any of you are today. [4]I persecuted the followers of this Way to their death, arresting both men and women and throwing them into prison, [5]as also the high priest and all the Council can testify. I even obtained letters from them to their brothers in Damascus, and went there to bring these people as prisoners to Jerusalem to be punished.

[6]"About noon as I came near Damascus, suddenly a bright light from heaven flashed around me. [7]I fell to the ground and heard a voice say to me, 'Saul! Saul! Why do you persecute me?'

[8]"'Who are you, Lord?' I asked.

"'I am Jesus of Nazareth, whom you are persecuting,' he replied. [9]My companions saw the light, but they did not understand the voice of him who was speaking to me.

[10]"'What shall I do, Lord?' I asked.

"'Get up,' the Lord said, 'and go into Damascus. There you will be told all that you have been assigned to do.' [11]My companions led me by the hand into Damascus, because the brilliance of the light had blinded me.

[12]"A man named Ananias came to see me. He was a devout observer of the law and highly respected by all the Jews living there. [13]He stood beside me and said, 'Brother Saul, receive your sight!' And at that very moment I was able to see him.

[14]"Then he said: 'The God of our fathers has chosen you to know his will and to see the Righteous One and to hear words from his mouth. [15]You will be his witness to all men of what you have seen and heard. [16]And now what are you waiting for? Get up, be baptized and wash your sins away, calling on his name.'

[a]40 Or possibly *Hebrew*; also in 22:2

[17]"When I returned to Jerusalem and was praying at the temple, I fell into a trance [18]and saw the Lord speaking. 'Quick!' he said to me. 'Leave Jerusalem immediately, because they will not accept your testimony about me.'

[19]"'Lord,' I replied, 'these men know that I went from one synagogue to another to imprison and beat those who believe in you. [20]And when the blood of your martyr[a] Stephen was shed, I stood there giving my approval and guarding the clothes of those who were killing him.'

[21]"Then the Lord said to me, 'Go; I will send you far away to the Gentiles.'"

Paul the Roman Citizen

[22]The crowd listened to Paul until he said this. Then they raised their voices and shouted, "Rid the earth of him! He's not fit to live!"

[23]As they were shouting and throwing off their cloaks and flinging dust into the air, [24]the commander ordered Paul to be taken into the barracks. He directed that he be flogged and questioned in order to find out why the people were shouting at him like this. [25]As they stretched him out to flog him, Paul said to the centurion standing there, "Is it legal for you to flog a Roman citizen who hasn't even been found guilty?"

[26]When the centurion heard this, he went to the commander and reported it. "What are you going to do?" he asked. "This man is a Roman citizen."

[27]The commander went to Paul and asked, "Tell me, are you a Roman citizen?"

"Yes, I am," he answered.

[28]Then the commander said, "I had to pay a big price for my citizenship."

"But I was born a citizen," Paul replied.

[29]Those who were about to question him withdrew immediately. The commander himself was alarmed when he realized that he had put Paul, a Roman citizen, in chains.

Before the Sanhedrin

[30]The next day, since the commander wanted to find out exactly why Paul was being accused by the Jews, he released him and ordered the chief priests and all the Sanhedrin to assemble. Then he brought Paul and had him stand before them.

23 Paul looked straight at the Sanhedrin and said, "My brothers, I have fulfilled my duty to God in all good conscience to this day." [2]At this the high priest Ananias ordered those standing near Paul to strike him on the mouth. [3]Then Paul said to him, "God will strike you, you white-washed wall! You sit there to judge me according to the law, yet you yourself violate the law by commanding that I be struck!"

[4]Those who were standing near Paul said, "You dare to insult God's high priest?"

[5]Paul replied, "Brothers, I did not realize that he was the high priest; for it is written: 'Do not speak evil about the ruler of your people.'[b]"

[6]Then Paul, knowing that some of them were Sadducees and the others Pharisees, called out in the Sanhedrin, "My brothers, I am a Pharisee, the son of a Pharisee. I stand on trial because of my hope in the resurrection of the dead." [7]When he said this, a dispute broke out between the Pharisees and the Sadducees, and the as-

---

a20 Or witness   *b5 Exodus 22:28*

sembly was divided. 8(The Sadducees say that there is no resurrection, and that there are neither angels nor spirits, but the Pharisees acknowledge them all.)

9There was a great uproar, and some of the teachers of the law who were Pharisees stood up and argued vigorously. "We find nothing wrong with this man," they said. "What if a spirit or an angel has spoken to him?" 10The dispute became so violent that the commander was afraid Paul would be torn to pieces by them. He ordered the troops to go down and take him away from them by force and bring him into the barracks.

11The following night the Lord stood near Paul and said, "Take courage! As you have testified about me in Jerusalem, so you must also testify in Rome."

The Plot to Kill Paul

12The next morning the Jews formed a conspiracy and bound themselves with an oath not to eat or drink until they had killed Paul. 13More than forty men were involved in this plot. 14They went to the chief priests and elders and said, "We have taken a solemn oath not to eat anything until we have killed Paul. 15Now then, you and the Sanhedrin petition the commander to bring him before you on the pretext of wanting more accurate information about his case. We are ready to kill him before he gets here."

16But when the son of Paul's sister heard of this plot, he went into the barracks and told Paul.

17Then Paul called one of the centurions and said, "Take this young man to the commander; he has something to tell him." 18So he took him to the commander.

The centurion said, "Paul, the prisoner, sent for me and asked me to bring this young man to you because he has something to tell you."

19The commander took the young man by the hand, drew him aside and asked, "What is it you want to tell me?"

20He said: "The Jews have agreed to ask you to bring Paul before the Sanhedrin tomorrow on the pretext of wanting more accurate information about him. 21Don't give in to them, because more than forty of them are waiting in ambush for him. They have taken an oath not to eat or drink until they have killed him. They are ready now, waiting for your consent to their request."

22The commander dismissed the young man and cautioned him, "Don't tell anyone that you have reported this to me."

Paul Transferred to Caesarea

23Then he called two of his centurions and ordered them, "Get ready a detachment of two hundred soldiers, seventy horsemen and two hundred spearmen a to go to Caesarea at nine tonight. 24Provide mounts for Paul so that he may be taken safely to Governor Felix."

25He wrote a letter as follows:

26Claudius Lysias,

To His Excellency, Governor Felix:

Greetings.

27This man was seized by the Jews and they were about to kill him, but I came with my troops and rescued him, for I had learned that he is a Roman citizen. 28I wanted to know why they were accus-

---

a23 The meaning of the Greek for this word is uncertain.

ing him, so I brought him to their Sanhedrin. ²⁹I found that the accusation had to do with questions about their law, but there was no charge against him that deserved death or imprisonment. ³⁰When I was informed of a plot to be carried out against the man, I sent him to you at once. I also ordered his accusers to present to you their case against him.

³¹So the soldiers, carrying out their orders, took Paul with them during the night and brought him as far as Antipatris. ³²The next day they let the cavalry go on with him, while they returned to the barracks. ³³When the cavalry arrived in Caesarea, they delivered the letter to the governor and handed Paul over to him. ³⁴The governor read the letter and asked what province he was from. Learning that he was from Cilicia, ³⁵he said, "I will hear your case when your accusers get here." Then he ordered that Paul be kept under guard in Herod's palace.

The Trial Before Felix

24 Five days later the high priest Ananias went down to Caesarea with some of the elders and a lawyer named Tertullus, and they brought their charges against Paul before the governor. ²When Paul was called in, Tertullus presented his case before Felix: "We have enjoyed a long period of peace under you, and your foresight has brought about reforms in this nation. ³Everywhere and in every way, most excellent Felix, we acknowledge this with profound grati-

tude. ⁴But in order not to weary you further, I would request that you be kind enough to hear us briefly.

⁵"We have found this man to be a troublemaker, stirring up riots among the Jews all over the world. He is a ringleader of the Nazarene sect ⁶and even tried to desecrate the temple; so we seized him. ⁸By ᵃ examining him yourself you will be able to learn the truth about all these charges we are bringing against him."

⁹The Jews joined in the accusation, asserting that these things were true.

¹⁰When the governor motioned for him to speak, Paul replied: "I know that for a number of years you have been a judge over this nation; so I gladly make my defense. ¹¹You can easily verify that no more than twelve days ago I went up to Jerusalem to worship. ¹²My accusers did not find me arguing with anyone at the temple, or stirring up a crowd in the synagogues or anywhere else in the city. ¹³And they cannot prove to you the charges they are now making against me. ¹⁴However, I admit that I worship the God of our fathers as a follower of the Way, which they call a sect. I believe everything that agrees with the Law and that is written in the Prophets, ¹⁵and I have the same hope in God as these men, that there will be a resurrection of both the righteous and the wicked. ¹⁶So I strive always to keep my conscience clear before God and man.

¹⁷"After an absence of several years, I came to Jerusalem to bring my people gifts for the poor and to present offerings. ¹⁸I was ceremonially clean when they

---

ᵃ6-8 Some manuscripts *him and wanted to judge him according to our law. ⁷But the commander, Lysias, came and with the use of much force snatched him from our hands* ⁸*and ordered his accusers to come before you.* By

found me in the temple courts doing this. There was no crowd with me, nor was I involved in any disturbance. [19]But there are some Jews from the province of Asia, who ought to be here before you and bring charges if they have anything against me. [20]Or these who are here should state what crime they found in me when I stood before the Sanhedrin— [21]unless it was this one thing I shouted as I stood in their presence: 'It is concerning the resurrection of the dead that I am on trial before you today.' "

[22]Then Felix, who was well acquainted with the Way, adjourned the proceedings. "When Lysias the commander comes," he said, "I will decide your case." [23]He ordered the centurion to keep Paul under guard but to give him some freedom and permit his friends to take care of his needs.

[24]Several days later Felix came with his wife Drusilla, who was a Jewess. He sent for Paul and listened to him as he spoke about faith in Christ Jesus. [25]As Paul discoursed on righteousness, self-control and the judgment to come, Felix was afraid and said, "That's enough for now! You may leave. When I find it convenient, I will send for you." [26]At the same time he was hoping that Paul would offer him a bribe, so he sent for him frequently and talked with him.

[27]When two years had passed, Felix was succeeded by Porcius Festus, but because Felix wanted to grant a favor to the Jews, he left Paul in prison.

The Trial Before Festus

25 Three days after arriving in the province, Festus went up from Caesarea to Jerusalem, [2]where the chief priests and Jewish leaders appeared before him and presented the charges against Paul. [3]They urgently requested Festus, as a favor to them, to have Paul transferred to Jerusalem, for they were preparing an ambush to kill him along the way. [4]Festus answered, "Paul is being held at Caesarea, and I myself am going there soon. [5]Let some of your leaders come with me and press charges against the man there, if he has done anything wrong."

[6]After spending eight or ten days with them, he went down to Caesarea, and the next day he convened the court and ordered that Paul be brought before him. [7]When Paul appeared, the Jews who had come down from Jerusalem stood around him, bringing many serious charges against him, which they could not prove.

[8]Then Paul made his defense: "I have done nothing wrong against the law of the Jews or against the temple or against Caesar."

[9]Festus, wishing to do the Jews a favor, said to Paul, "Are you willing to go up to Jerusalem and stand trial before me there on these charges?"

[10]Paul answered: "I am now standing before Caesar's court, where I ought to be tried. I have not done any wrong to the Jews, as you yourself know very well. [11]If, however, I am guilty of doing anything deserving death, I do not refuse to die. But if the charges brought against me by these Jews are not true, no one has the right to hand me over to them. I appeal to Caesar!"

[12]After Festus had conferred with his council, he declared: "You have appealed to Caesar. To Caesar you will go!"

Festus Consults King Agrippa

13A few days later King Agrippa and Bernice arrived at Caesarea to pay their respects to Festus. 14Since they were spending many days there, Festus discussed Paul's case with the king. He said: "There is a man here whom Felix left as a prisoner. 15When I went to Jerusalem, the chief priests and elders of the Jews brought charges against him and asked that he be condemned.

16"I told them that it is not the Roman custom to hand over any man before he has faced his accusers and has had an opportunity to defend himself against their charges. 17When they came here with me, I did not delay the case, but convened the court the next day and ordered the man to be brought in. 18When his accusers got up to speak, they did not charge him with any of the crimes I had expected. 19Instead, they had some points of dispute with him about their own religion and about a dead man named Jesus who Paul claimed was alive. 20I was at a loss how to investigate such matters; so I asked if he would be willing to go to Jerusalem and stand trial there on these charges. 21When Paul made his appeal to be held over for the Emperor's decision, I ordered him held until I could send him to Caesar."

22Then Agrippa said to Festus, "I would like to hear this man myself."

He replied, "Tomorrow you will hear him."

Paul Before Agrippa

23The next day Agrippa and Bernice came with great pomp and entered the audience room with the high ranking officers and the leading men of the city. At the command of Festus, Paul was brought in. 24Festus said: "King Agrippa, and all who are present with us, you see this man! The whole Jewish community has petitioned me about him in Jerusalem and here in Caesarea, shouting that he ought not to live any longer. 25I found he had done nothing deserving of death, but because he made his appeal to the Emperor I decided to send him to Rome. 26But I have nothing definite to write to His Majesty about him. Therefore I have brought him before all of you, and especially before you, King Agrippa, so that as a result of this investigation I may have something to write. 27For I think it is unreasonable to send on a prisoner without specifying the charges against him."

26 Then Agrippa said to Paul, "You have permission to speak for yourself."

So Paul motioned with his hand and began his defense: 2"King Agrippa, I consider myself fortunate to stand before you today as I make my defense against all the accusations of the Jews, 3and especially so because you are well acquainted with all the Jewish customs and controversies. Therefore, I beg you to listen to me patiently.

4"The Jews all know the way I have lived ever since I was a child, from the beginning of my life in my own country, and also in Jerusalem. 5They have known me for a long time and can testify, if they are willing, that according to the strictest sect of our religion, I lived as a Pharisee. 6And now it is because of my hope in what God has promised our fathers that I am on trial today. 7This is the promise our twelve tribes are hoping to see fulfilled as they earnestly serve God day and night. O king, it is because of this hope that the Jews are accusing me. 8Why should any of you consider it incredible that God raises the dead?

9"I too was convinced that I ought to do all that was possible to oppose the name of Jesus of Nazareth. 10And that is just what I did in Jerusalem. On the authority of the chief priests I put many of the saints in prison, and when they were put to death, I cast my vote against them. 11Many a time I went from one synagogue to another to have them punished, and I tried to force them to blaspheme. In my obsession against them, I even went to foreign cities to persecute them.

12"On one of these journeys I was going to Damascus with the authority and commission of the chief priests. 13About noon, O king, as I was on the road, I saw a light from heaven, brighter than the sun, blazing around me and my companions. 14We all fell to the ground, and I heard a voice saying to me in Aramaic,[a] 'Saul, Saul, why do you persecute me? It is hard for you to kick against the goads.'

15"Then I asked, 'Who are you, Lord?'

" 'I am Jesus, whom you are persecuting,' the Lord replied. 16'Now get up and stand on your feet. I have appeared to you to appoint you as a servant and as a witness of what you have seen of me and what I will show you. 17I will rescue you from your own people and from the Gentiles. I am sending you to them 18to open their eyes and turn them from darkness to light, and from the power of Satan to God, so that they may receive forgiveness of sins and a place among those who are sanctified by faith in me.'

19"So then, King Agrippa, I was not disobedient to the vision from heaven. 20First to those in Damascus, then to those in Jerusalem and in all Judea, and to the Gentiles also, I preached that they should repent and turn to God and prove their repentance by their deeds. 21That is why the Jews seized me in the temple courts and tried to kill me. 22But I have had God's help to this very day, and so I stand here and testify to small and great alike. I am saying nothing beyond what the prophets and Moses said would happen— 23that the Christ[b] would suffer and, as the first to rise from the dead, would proclaim light to his own people and to the Gentiles."

24At this point Festus interrupted Paul's defense. "You are out of your mind, Paul!" he shouted. "Your great learning is driving you insane."

25"I am not insane, most excellent Festus," Paul replied. "What I am saying is true and reasonable. 26The king is familiar with these things, and I can speak freely to him. I am convinced that none of this has escaped his notice, because it was not done in a corner. 27King Agrippa, do you believe the prophets? I know you do."

28Then Agrippa said to Paul, "Do you think that in such a short time you can persuade me to be a Christian?"

29Paul replied, "Short time or long—I pray God that not only you but all who are listening to me today may become what I am, except for these chains."

30The king rose, and with him the governor and Bernice and those sitting with them. 31They

7
Ro 14:17,18

79
o 12:1,2

left the room, and while talking with one another, they said, "This man is not doing anything that deserves death or imprisonment."

³²Agrippa said to Festus, "This man could have been set free if he had not appealed to Caesar."

Paul Sails for Rome

27 When it was decided that we would sail for Italy, Paul and some other prisoners were handed over to a centurion named Julius, who belonged to the Imperial Regiment. ²We boarded a ship from Adramyttium about to sail for ports along the coast of the province of Asia, and we put out to sea. Aristarchus, a Macedonian from Thessalonica, was with us.

³The next day we landed at Sidon; and Julius, in kindness to Paul, allowed him to go to his friends so they might provide for his needs. ⁴From there we put out to sea again and passed to the lee of Cyprus because the winds were against us. ⁵When we had sailed across the open sea off the coast of Cilicia and Pamphylia, we landed at Myra in Lycia. ⁶There the centurion found an Alexandrian ship sailing for Italy and put us on board. ⁷We made slow headway for many days and had difficulty arriving off Cnidus. When the wind did not allow us to hold our course, we sailed to the lee of Crete, opposite Salmone. ⁸We moved along the coast with difficulty and came to a place called Fair Havens, near the town of Lasea.

⁹Much time had been lost, and sailing had already become dangerous because by now it was after the Fast.ᵃ So Paul warned them, ¹⁰"Men, I can see that our voyage is going to be disastrous

and bring great loss to ship and cargo, and to our own lives also." ¹¹But the centurion, instead of listening to what Paul said, followed the advice of the pilot and of the owner of the ship. ¹²Since the harbor was unsuitable to winter in, the majority decided that we should sail on, hoping to reach Phoenix and winter there. This was a harbor in Crete, facing both southwest and northwest.

The Storm

¹³When a gentle south wind began to blow, they thought they had obtained what they wanted; so they weighed anchor and sailed along the shore of Crete. ¹⁴Before very long, a wind of hurricane force, called the "northeaster," swept down from the island. ¹⁵The ship was caught by the storm and could not head into the wind; so we gave way to it and were driven along. ¹⁶As we passed to the lee of a small island called Cauda, we were hardly able to make the lifeboat secure. ¹⁷When the men had hoisted it aboard, they passed ropes under the ship itself to hold it together. Fearing that they would run aground on the sandbars of Syrtis, they lowered the sea anchor and let the ship be driven along. ¹⁸We took such a violent battering from the storm that the next day they began to throw the cargo overboard. ¹⁹On the third day, they threw the ship's tackle overboard with their own hands. ²⁰When neither sun nor stars appeared for many days and the storm continued raging, we finally gave up all hope of being saved.

²¹After the men had gone a long time without food, Paul stood up before them and said: "Men, you should have taken my advice not

ᵃ9 That is, the Day of Atonement (Yom Kippur)

to sail from Crete; then you would have spared yourselves this damage and loss. ²²But now I urge you to keep up your courage, because not one of you will be lost; only the ship will be destroyed. ²³Last night an angel of the God whose I am and whom I serve stood beside me ²⁴and said, 'Do not be afraid, Paul. You must stand trial before Caesar; and God has graciously given you the lives of all who sail with you.' ²⁵So keep up your courage, men, for I have faith in God that it will happen just as he told me. ²⁶Nevertheless, we must run aground on some island."

The Shipwreck

²⁷On the fourteenth night we were still being driven across the Adriatic[a] Sea, when about midnight the sailors sensed they were approaching land. ²⁸They took soundings and found that the water was a hundred and twenty feet[b] deep. A short time later they took soundings again and found it was ninety feet[c] deep. ²⁹Fearing that we would be dashed against the rocks, they dropped four anchors from the stern and prayed for daylight. ³⁰In an attempt to escape from the ship, the sailors let the lifeboat down into the sea, pretending they were going to lower some anchors from the bow. ³¹Then Paul said to the centurion and the soldiers, "Unless these men stay with the ship, you cannot be saved." ³²So the soldiers cut the ropes that held the lifeboat and let it fall away.

³³Just before dawn Paul urged them all to eat. "For the last fourteen days," he said, "you have been in constant suspense and

have gone without food—you haven't eaten anything. ³⁴Now I urge you to take some food. You need it to survive. Not one of you will lose a single hair from his head." ³⁵After he said this, he took some bread and gave thanks to God in front of them all. Then he broke it and began to eat. ³⁶They were all encouraged and ate some food themselves. ³⁷Altogether there were 276 of us on board. ³⁸When they had eaten as much as they wanted, they lightened the ship by throwing the grain into the sea.

³⁹When daylight came, they did not recognize the land, but they saw a bay with a sandy beach, where they decided to run the ship aground if they could. ⁴⁰Cutting loose the anchors, they left them in the sea and at the same time untied the ropes that held the rudders. Then they hoisted the foresail to the wind and made for the beach. ⁴¹But the ship struck a sandbar and ran aground. The bow stuck fast and would not move, and the stern was broken to pieces by the pounding of the surf.

⁴²The soldiers planned to kill the prisoners to prevent any of them from swimming away and escaping. ⁴³But the centurion wanted to spare Paul's life and kept them from carrying out their plan. He ordered those who could swim to jump overboard first and get to land. ⁴⁴The rest were to get there on planks or on pieces of the ship. In this way everyone reached land in safety.

Ashore on Malta

28 Once safely on shore, we found out that the island was called Malta. ²The islanders

94
1Co 15:10

---

[a]27 In ancient times the name referred to an area extending well south of Italy.   [b]28 Greek *twenty orguias* (about 37 meters)   [c]28 Greek *fifteen orguias* (about 27 meters)

showed us unusual kindness. They built a fire and welcomed us all because it was raining and cold. ³Paul gathered a pile of brushwood and, as he put it on the fire, a viper, driven out by the heat, fastened itself on his hand. ⁴When the islanders saw the snake hanging from his hand, they said to each other, "This man must be a murderer; for though he escaped from the sea, Justice has not allowed him to live." ⁵But Paul shook the snake off into the fire and suffered no ill effects. ⁶The people expected him to swell up or suddenly fall dead, but after waiting a long time and seeing nothing unusual happen to him, they changed their minds and said he was a god.

⁷There was an estate nearby that belonged to Publius, the chief official of the island. He welcomed us to his home and for three days entertained us hospitably. ⁸His father was sick in bed, suffering from fever and dysentery. Paul went in to see him and, after prayer, placed his hands on him and healed him. ⁹When this had happened, the rest of the sick on the island came and were cured. ¹⁰They honored us in many ways and when we were ready to sail, they furnished us with the supplies we needed.

Arrival at Rome

¹¹After three months we put out to sea in a ship that had wintered in the island. It was an Alexandrian ship with the figurehead of the twin gods Castor and Pollux. ¹²We put in at Syracuse and stayed there three days. ¹³From there we set sail and arrived at Rhegium. The next day the south wind came up, and on the following day we reached Puteoli. ¹⁴There we found some brothers who invited us to spend a week

with them. And so we came to Rome. ¹⁵The brothers there had heard that we were coming, and they traveled as far as the Forum of Appius and the Three Taverns to meet us. At the sight of these men Paul thanked God and was encouraged. ¹⁶When we got to Rome, Paul was allowed to live by himself, with a soldier to guard him.

Paul Preaches at Rome Under Guard

¹⁷Three days later he called together the leaders of the Jews. When they had assembled, Paul said to them: "My brothers, although I have done nothing against our people or against the customs of our ancestors, I was arrested in Jerusalem and handed over to the Romans. ¹⁸They examined me and wanted to release me, because I was not guilty of any crime deserving death. ¹⁹But when the Jews objected, I was compelled to appeal to Caesar—not that I had any charge to bring against my own people. ²⁰For this reason I have asked to see you and talk with you. It is because of the hope of Israel that I am bound with this chain."

²¹They replied, "We have not received any letters from Judea concerning you, and none of the brothers who have come from there has reported or said anything bad about you. ²²But we want to hear what your views are, for we know that people everywhere are talking against this sect."

²³They arranged to meet Paul on a certain day, and came in even larger numbers to the place where he was staying. From morning till evening he explained and declared to them the kingdom of God and tried to con-

vince them about Jesus from the Law of Moses and from the Prophets. ²⁴Some were convinced by what he said, but others would not believe. ²⁵They disagreed among themselves and began to leave after Paul had made this final statement: "The Holy Spirit spoke the truth to your forefathers when he said through Isaiah the prophet:

²⁶" 'Go to this people and say,
    "You will be ever hearing but
        never understanding;
    you will be ever seeing but
        never perceiving."
²⁷For this people's heart has
        become calloused;
    they hardly hear with their
        ears,

and they have closed their
        eyes.
Otherwise they might see
        with their eyes,
    hear with their ears,
    understand with their
        hearts
and turn, and I would heal
    them.'ᵃ

²⁸"Therefore I want you to know that God's salvation has been sent to the Gentiles, and they will listen!"ᵇ

³⁰For two whole years Paul stayed there in his own rented house and welcomed all who came to see him. ³¹Boldly and without hindrance he preached the kingdom of God and taught about the Lord Jesus Christ.

Romans

1 Paul, a servant of Christ Jesus, called to be an apostle and set apart for the gospel of God— ²the gospel he promised beforehand through his prophets in the Holy Scriptures ³regarding his Son, who as to his human nature was a descendant of David, ⁴and who through the Spiritᶜ of holiness was declared with power to be the Son of Godᵈ by his resurrection from the dead: Jesus Christ our Lord. ⁵Through him and for his name's sake, we received grace and apostleship to call people from among all the Gentiles to the obedience that comes from faith. ⁶And you also are among those who are called to belong to Jesus Christ.

⁷To all in Rome who are loved by God and called to be saints:

Grace and peace to you from God our Father and from the Lord Jesus Christ.

Paul's Longing to Visit Rome

⁸First, I thank my God through Jesus Christ for all of you, because your faith is being reported all over the world. ⁹God, whom I serve with my whole heart in preaching the gospel of his Son, is my witness how constantly I remember you ¹⁰in my prayers at all times; and I pray that now at last by God's will the way may be opened for me to come to you.

¹¹I long to see you so that I may impart to you some spiritual gift to make you strong— ¹²that is, that you and I may be mutually encouraged by each other's faith. ¹³I do not want you to be un-

---

ᵃ27 Isaiah 6:9,10   ᵇ28 Some manuscripts listen!" ²⁹After he said this, the Jews left, arguing vigorously among themselves.   ᶜ4 Or who as to his spirit   ᵈ4 Or was appointed to be the Son of God with power

aware, brothers, that I planned many times to come to you (but have been prevented from doing so until now) in order that I might have a harvest among you, just as I have had among the other Gentiles.

¹⁴I am obligated both to Greeks and non-Greeks, both to the wise and the foolish. ¹⁵That is why I am so eager to preach the gospel also to you who are at Rome.

23
1Co 1:18

32
Ro 2:12-16

¹⁶I am not ashamed of the gospel, because it is the power of God for the salvation of everyone who believes: first for the Jew, then for the Gentile. ¹⁷For in the gospel a righteousness from God is revealed, a righteousness that is by faith from first to last,ᵃ just as it is written: "The righteous will live by faith."ᵇ

God's Wrath Against Mankind

¹⁸The wrath of God is being revealed from heaven against all the godlessness and wickedness of men who suppress the truth by their wickedness, ¹⁹since what may be known about God is plain to them, because God has made it plain to them. ²⁰For since the creation of the world God's invisible qualities—his eternal power and divine nature—have been clearly seen, being understood from what has been made, so that men are without excuse.

²¹For although they knew God, they neither glorified him as God nor gave thanks to him, but their thinking became futile and their foolish hearts were darkened. ²²Although they claimed to be wise, they became fools ²³and exchanged the glory of the immortal God for images made to look like mortal man and birds and animals and reptiles.

²⁴Therefore God gave them over in the sinful desires of their hearts to sexual impurity for the degrading of their bodies with one another. ²⁵They exchanged the truth of God for a lie, and worshiped and served created things rather than the Creator— who is forever praised. Amen. ²⁶Because of this, God gave them over to shameful lusts. Even their women exchanged natural relations for unnatural ones. ²⁷In the same way the men also abandoned natural relations with women and were inflamed with lust for one another. Men committed indecent acts with other men, and received in themselves the due penalty for their perversion.

²⁸Furthermore, since they did not think it worthwhile to retain the knowledge of God, he gave them over to a depraved mind, to do what ought not to be done. ²⁹They have become filled with every kind of wickedness, evil, greed and depravity. They are full of envy, murder, strife, deceit and malice. They are gossips, ³⁰slanderers, God-haters, insolent, arrogant and boastful; they invent ways of doing evil; they disobey their parents; ³¹they are senseless, faithless, heartless, ruthless. ³²Although they know God's righteous decree that those who do such things deserve death, they not only continue to do these very things but also approve of those who practice them.

God's Righteous Judgment

2 You, therefore, have no excuse, you who pass judgment on someone else, for at whatever point you judge the other, you are condemning your-

47
Jas 2:1-

74
2Co 7:9

ᵃ17 Or *is from faith to faith* ᵇ17 Hab. 2:4

self, because you who pass judgment do the same things. ²Now we know that God's judgment against those who do such things is based on truth. ³So when you, a mere man, pass judgment on them and yet do the same things, do you think you will escape God's judgment? ⁴Or do you show contempt for the riches of his kindness, tolerance and patience, not realizing that God's kindness leads you toward repentance?

⁵But because of your stubbornness and your unrepentant heart, you are storing up wrath against yourself for the day of God's wrath, when his righteous judgment will be revealed. ⁶God "will give to each person according to what he has done."*a* ⁷To those who by persistence in doing good seek glory, honor and immortality, he will give eternal life. ⁸But for those who are self-seeking and who reject the truth and follow evil, there will be wrath and anger. ⁹There will be trouble and distress for every human being who does evil: first for the Jew, then for the Gentile; ¹⁰but glory, honor and peace for everyone who does good: first for the Jew, then for the Gentile. ¹¹For God does not show favoritism.

¹²All who sin apart from the law will also perish apart from the law, and all who sin under the law will be judged by the law. ¹³For it is not those who hear the law who are righteous in God's sight, but it is those who obey the law who will be declared righteous. ¹⁴(Indeed, when Gentiles, who do not have the law, do by nature things required by the law, they are a law for themselves, even though they do not have the law, ¹⁵since they show

that the requirements of the law are written on their hearts, their consciences also bearing witness, and their thoughts now accusing, now even defending them.) ¹⁶This will take place on the day when God will judge men's secrets through Jesus Christ, as my gospel declares.

The Jews and the Law

¹⁷Now you, if you call yourself a Jew; if you rely on the law and brag about your relationship to God; ¹⁸if you know his will and approve of what is superior because you are instructed by the law; ¹⁹if you are convinced that you are a guide for the blind, a light for those who are in the dark, ²⁰an instructor of the foolish, a teacher of infants, because you have in the law the embodiment of knowledge and truth—²¹you, then, who teach others, do you not teach yourself? You who preach against stealing, do you steal? ²²You who say that people should not commit adultery, do you commit adultery? You who abhor idols, do you rob temples? ²³You who brag about the law, do you dishonor God by breaking the law? ²⁴As it is written: "God's name is blasphemed among the Gentiles because of you."*b*

²⁵Circumcision has value if you observe the law, but if you break the law, you have become as though you had not been circumcised. ²⁶If those who are not circumcised keep the law's requirements, will they not be regarded as though they were circumcised? ²⁷The one who is not circumcised physically and yet obeys the law will condemn you who, even though you have the*c* written code and circumcision, are a lawbreaker.

²⁸A man is not a Jew if he is only

---

*a*6 Psalm 62:12; Prov. 24:12   *b*24 Isaiah 52:5; Ezek. 36:22   *c*27 Or *who, by means of a*

36
⊙ 3:19,20

40
Co 2:9,10

41
10:26-31

90
Ro 13:9

32

12
⊙ 8:10-12

one outwardly, nor is circumcision merely outward and physical. [29]No, a man is a Jew if he is one inwardly; and circumcision is circumcision of the heart, by the Spirit, not by the written code. Such a man's praise is not from men, but from God.

God's Faithfulness

3 What advantage, then, is there in being a Jew, or what value is there in circumcision? [2]Much in every way! First of all, they have been entrusted with the very words of God.

[3]What if some did not have faith? Will their lack of faith nullify God's faithfulness? [4]Not at all! Let God be true, and every man a liar. As it is written:

> "So that you may be proved right when you speak and prevail when you judge."[a]

[5]But if our unrighteousness brings out God's righteousness more clearly, what shall we say? That God is unjust in bringing his wrath on us? (I am using a human argument.) [6]Certainly not! If that were so, how could God judge the world? [7]Someone might argue, "If my falsehood enhances God's truthfulness and so increases his glory, why am I still condemned as a sinner?" [8]Why not say—as we are being slanderously reported as saying and as some claim that we say—"Let us do evil that good may result"? Their condemnation is deserved.

No One Is Righteous

[9]What shall we conclude then? Are we any better[b]? Not at all! We have already made the charge that Jews and Gentiles alike are all under sin. [10]As it is written:

> "There is no one righteous, not even one;
> [11] there is no one who understands, no one who seeks God.
> [12]All have turned away, they have together become worthless;
> there is no one who does good, not even one."[c]
> [13]"Their throats are open graves; their tongues practice deceit."[d]
> "The poison of vipers is on their lips."[e]
> [14] "Their mouths are full of cursing and bitterness."[f]
> [15]"Their feet are swift to shed blood;
> [16] ruin and misery mark their ways,
> [17]and the way of peace they do not know."[g]
> [18] "There is no fear of God before their eyes."[h]

[19]Now we know that whatever the law says, it says to those who are under the law, so that every mouth may be silenced and the whole world held accountable to God. [20]Therefore no one will be declared righteous in his sight by observing the law; rather, through the law we become conscious of sin.

Righteousness Through Faith

[21]But now a righteousness from God, apart from law, has been made known, to which the Law and the Prophets testify. [22]This righteousness from God comes through faith in Jesus Christ to all who believe. There is no difference, [23]for all have sinned and fall short of the glory of God, [24]and

Cross references (right margin): 88 Gal 5:15 · 36 Ro 8:1 · 50 Ro 4:13 · 77 Ro 4:15 · 72 Gal 3:13 · 66 Ro 4:2-5

[a]4 Psalm 51:4   [b]9 Or *worse*   [c]12 Psalms 14:1-3; 53:1-3; Eccles. 7:20   [d]13 Psalm 5:9   [e]13 Psalm 140:3   [f]14 Psalm 10:7   [g]17 Isaiah 59:7,8   [h]18 Psalm 36:1

78 are justified freely by his grace
Ro 6:21-23 through the redemption that
came by Christ Jesus. ²⁵God
presented him as a sacrifice of
atonement,^a through faith in his
blood. He did this to demon-
strate his justice, because in his
forbearance he had left the sins
committed beforehand unpun-
48 ished— ²⁶he did it to demon-
Ro 5:1 strate his justice at the present
time, so as to be just and the one
who justifies those who have
faith in Jesus.

²⁷Where, then, is boasting? It is
excluded. On what principle? On
that of observing the law? No,
but on that of faith. ²⁸For we
maintain that a man is justified
by faith apart from observing the
law. ²⁹Is God the God of Jews
only? Is he not the God of Gentiles too? Yes, of Gentiles too,
³⁰since there is only one God,
who will justify the circumcised
by faith and the uncircumcised
through that same faith. ³¹Do we,
then, nullify the law by this faith?
Not at all! Rather, we uphold the
law.

Abraham Justified by Faith

4 What then shall we say that
Abraham, our forefather, dis-
66 covered in this matter? ²If, in fact,
1Co 8:12 Abraham was justified by works,
he had something to boast
about—but not before God.
20 ³What does the Scripture say?
Ro 4:18-21 "Abraham believed God, and it
was credited to him as righteousness."^b

⁴Now when a man works, his
wages are not credited to him as
a gift, but as an obligation. ⁵How-
ever, to the man who does not
work but trusts God who justifies
the wicked, his faith is credited as
righteousness. ⁶David says the
same thing when he speaks of

the blessedness of the man to
whom God credits righteousness
apart from works:

⁷"Blessed are they
     whose transgressions are
        forgiven,
     whose sins are covered.
⁸Blessed is the man
     whose sin the Lord will
        never count against
        him."^c

⁹Is this blessedness only for the
circumcised, or also for the uncircumcised? We have been saying
that Abraham's faith was credit-
ed to him as righteousness. ¹⁰Un-
der what circumstances was it
credited? Was it after he was circumcised, or before? It was not
after, but before! ¹¹And he received the sign of circumcision, a
seal of the righteousness that he
had by faith while he was still
uncircumcised. So then, he is the
father of all who believe but have
not been circumcised, in order
that righteousness might be credited to them. ¹²And he is also the
father of the circumcised who not
only are circumcised but who
also walk in the footsteps of the
faith that our father Abraham
had before he was circumcised.

¹³It was not through law that   50
Abraham and his offspring re-   Gal 3:10,11
ceived the promise that he would
be heir of the world, but through   77
the righteousness that comes by   1Co 1:30
faith. ¹⁴For if those who live by
law are heirs, faith has no value
and the promise is worthless,
¹⁵because law brings wrath. And
where there is no law there is no
transgression.

¹⁶Therefore, the promise comes
by faith, so that it may be by
grace and may be guaranteed to
all Abraham's offspring—not
only to those who are of the law

^a25 Or as the one who would turn aside his wrath, taking away sin   ^b3 Gen. 15:6; also in
verse 22   ^c8 Psalm 32:1,2

but also to those who are of the faith of Abraham. He is the father of us all. [17]As it is written: "I have made you a father of many nations."[a] He is our father in the sight of God, in whom he believed—the God who gives life to the dead and calls things that are not as though they were.

43
Ro 5:5

[18]Against all hope, Abraham in hope believed and so became the father of many nations, just as it had been said to him, "So shall your offspring be."[b] [19]Without weakening in his faith, he faced the fact that his body was as good as dead—since he was about a hundred years old—and that Sarah's womb was also dead. [20]Yet he did not waver through unbelief regarding the promise of God, but was strengthened in his faith and gave glory to God, [21]being fully persuaded that God had power to do what he had promised. [22]This is why "it was credited to him as righteousness." [23]The words "it was credited to him" were written not for him alone, [24]but also for us, to whom God will credit righteousness—for us who believe in him who raised Jesus our Lord from the dead. [25]He was delivered over to death for our sins and was raised to life for our justification.

20
Ro 8:16

Peace and Joy

5 Therefore, since we have been justified through faith, we[c] have peace with God through our Lord Jesus Christ, [2]through whom we have gained access by faith into this grace in which we now stand. And we[c] rejoice in the hope of the glory of God. [3]Not only so, but we[c] also rejoice in our sufferings, because we know that suffering produces perseverance; [4]perseverance, character; and character, hope.

48
Ro 5:11

65
Php 4:8,9

91
Ro 8:16-18

[5]And hope does not disappoint us, because God has poured out his love into our hearts by the Holy Spirit, whom he has given us.

43
Php 4:19

[6]You see, at just the right time, when we were still powerless, Christ died for the ungodly. [7]Very rarely will anyone die for a righteous man, though for a good man someone might possibly dare to die. [8]But God demonstrates his own love for us in this: While we were still sinners, Christ died for us.

54
Ro 8:35-39

[9]Since we have now been justified by his blood, how much more shall we be saved from God's wrath through him! [10]For if, when we were God's enemies, we were reconciled to him through the death of his Son, how much more, having been reconciled, shall we be saved through his life! [11]Not only is this so, but we also rejoice in God through our Lord Jesus Christ, through whom we have now received reconciliation.

48
Ps 37:27,28

Death Through Adam, Life Through Christ

[12]Therefore, just as sin entered the world through one man, and death through sin, and in this way death came to all men, because all sinned— [13]for before the law was given, sin was in the world. But sin is not taken into account when there is no law. [14]Nevertheless, death reigned from the time of Adam to the time of Moses, even over those who did not sin by breaking a command, as did Adam, who was a pattern of the one to come.

[15]But the gift is not like the trespass. For if the many died by the trespass of the one man, how much more did God's grace and

[a]17 Gen. 17:5   [b]18 Gen. 15:5   [c]1,2,3 Or let us

the gift that came by the grace of the one man, Jesus Christ, overflow to the many! [16]Again, the gift of God is not like the result of the one man's sin: The judgment followed one sin and brought condemnation, but the gift followed many trespasses and brought justification. [17]For if, by the trespass of the one man, death reigned through that one man, how much more will those who receive God's abundant provision of grace and of the gift of righteousness reign in life through the one man, Jesus Christ.

[18]Consequently, just as the result of one trespass was condemnation for all men, so also the result of one act of righteousness was justification that brings life for all men. [19]For just as through the disobedience of the one man the many were made sinners, so also through the obedience of the one man the many will be made righteous.

[20]The law was added so that the trespass might increase. But where sin increased, grace increased all the more, [21]so that, just as sin reigned in death, so also grace might reign through righteousness to bring eternal life through Jesus Christ our Lord.

Dead to Sin, Alive in Christ

6 What shall we say, then? Shall we go on sinning so that grace may increase? [2]By no means! We died to sin; how can we live in it any longer? [3]Or don't you know that all of us who were baptized into Christ Jesus were baptized into his death? [4]We were therefore buried with him through baptism into death in order that, just as Christ was raised from the dead through the glory

of the Father, we too may live a new life.

[5]If we have been united with him like this in his death, we will certainly also be united with him in his resurrection. [6]For we know that our old self was crucified with him so that the body of sin might be done away with,[a] that we should no longer be slaves to sin— [7]because anyone who has died has been freed from sin.

[8]Now if we died with Christ, we believe that we will also live with him. [9]For we know that since Christ was raised from the dead, he cannot die again; death no longer has mastery over him. [10]The death he died, he died to sin once for all; but the life he lives, he lives to God.

[11]In the same way, count yourselves dead to sin but alive to God in Christ Jesus. [12]Therefore do not let sin reign in your mortal body so that you obey its evil desires. [13]Do not offer the parts of your body to sin, as instruments of wickedness, but rather offer yourselves to God, as those who have been brought from death to life; and offer the parts of your body to him as instruments of righteousness. [14]For sin shall not be your master, because you are not under law, but under grace.

Slaves to Righteousness

[15]What then? Shall we sin because we are not under law but under grace? By no means! [16]Don't you know that when you offer yourselves to someone to obey him as slaves, you are slaves to the one whom you obey—whether you are slaves to sin, which leads to death, or to obedience, which leads to righteousness? [17]But thanks be to God that, though you used to be

62
Tit 3:5

42
1Co 6:9-11

[a]6 Or be rendered powerless

slaves to sin, you wholeheartedly obeyed the form of teaching to which you were entrusted. ¹⁸You have been set free from sin and have become slaves to righteousness.

¹⁹I put this in human terms because you are weak in your natural selves. Just as you used to offer the parts of your body in slavery to impurity and to ever-increasing wickedness, so now offer them in slavery to righteousness leading to holiness. ²⁰When you were slaves to sin, you were free from the control of righteousness. ²¹What benefit did you reap at that time from the things you are now ashamed of? Those things result in death! ²²But now that you have been set free from sin and have become slaves to God, the benefit you reap leads to holiness, and the result is eternal life. ²³For the wages of sin is death, but the gift of God is eternal life in ᵃ Christ Jesus our Lord.

An Illustration From Marriage

7 Do you not know, brothers— for I am speaking to men who know the law—that the law has authority over a man only as long as he lives? ²For example, by law a married woman is bound to her husband as long as he is alive, but if her husband dies, she is released from the law of marriage. ³So then, if she marries another man while her husband is still alive, she is called an adulteress. But if her husband dies, she is released from that law and is not an adulteress, even though she marries another man.

⁴So, my brothers, you also died to the law through the body of Christ, that you might belong to

another, to him who was raised from the dead, in order that we might bear fruit to God. ⁵For when we were controlled by the sinful nature, ᵇ the sinful passions aroused by the law were at work in our bodies, so that we bore fruit for death. ⁶But now, by dying to what once bound us, we have been released from the law so that we serve in the new way of the Spirit, and not in the old way of the written code.

Struggling With Sin

⁷What shall we say, then? Is the law sin? Certainly not! Indeed I would not have known what sin was except through the law. For I would not have known what coveting really was if the law had not said, "Do not covet." ᶜ ⁸But sin, seizing the opportunity afforded by the commandment, produced in me every kind of covetous desire. For apart from law, sin is dead. ⁹Once I was alive apart from law; but when the commandment came, sin sprang to life and I died. ¹⁰I found that the very commandment that was intended to bring life actually brought death. ¹¹For sin, seizing the opportunity afforded by the commandment, deceived me, and through the commandment put me to death. ¹²So then, the law is holy, and the commandment is holy, righteous and good.

¹³Did that which is good, then, become death to me? By no means! But in order that sin might be recognized as sin, it produced death in me through what was good, so that through the commandment sin might become utterly sinful.

¹⁴We know that the law is spiritual; but I am unspiritual, sold as

---

ᵃ23 Or *through*   ᵇ5 Or *the flesh*; also in verse 25   ᶜ7 Exodus 20:17; Deut. 5:21

a slave to sin. [15]I do not understand what I do. For what I want to do I do not do, but what I hate I do. [16]And if I do what I do not want to do, I agree that the law is good. [17]As it is, it is no longer I myself who do it, but it is sin living in me. [18]I know that nothing good lives in me, that is, in my sinful nature.[a] For I have the desire to do what is good, but I cannot carry it out. [19]For what I do is not the good I want to do; no, the evil I do not want to do—this I keep on doing. [20]Now if I do what I do not want to do, it is no longer I who do it, but it is sin living in me that does it.

[21]So I find this law at work: When I want to do good, evil is right there with me. [22]For in my inner being I delight in God's law; [23]but I see another law at work in the members of my body, waging war against the law of my mind and making me a prisoner of the law of sin at work within my members. [24]What a wretched man I am! Who will rescue me from this body of death? [25]Thanks be to God—through Jesus Christ our Lord!

So then, I myself in my mind am a slave to God's law, but in the sinful nature a slave to the law of sin.

Life Through the Spirit

36
b 10:26,27

78
Ro 10:9,10

8 Therefore, there is now no condemnation for those who are in Christ Jesus,[b] [2]because through Christ Jesus the law of the Spirit of life set me free from the law of sin and death. [3]For what the law was powerless to do in that it was weakened by the sinful nature,[c] God did by send-ing his own Son in the likeness of sinful man to be a sin offering.[d] And so he condemned sin in sinful man,[e] [4]in order that the righteous requirements of the law might be fully met in us, who do not live according to the sinful nature but according to the Spirit.

59
Ro 12:1,2

[5]Those who live according to the sinful nature have their minds set on what that nature desires; but those who live in accordance with the Spirit have their minds set on what the Spirit desires. [6]The mind of sinful man[f] is death, but the mind controlled by the Spirit is life and peace; [7]the sinful mind[g] is hostile to God. It does not submit to God's law, nor can it do so. [8]Those controlled by the sinful nature cannot please God.

3
Eph 4:26

38
Ro 12:18,19

51
Col 3:1-4

[9]You, however, are controlled not by the sinful nature but by the Spirit, if the Spirit of God lives in you. And if anyone does not have the Spirit of Christ, he does not belong to Christ. [10]But if Christ is in you, your body is dead because of sin, yet your spirit is alive because of righteousness. [11]And if the Spirit of him who raised Jesus from the dead is living in you, he who raised Christ from the dead will also give life to your mortal bodies through his Spirit, who lives in you.

[12]Therefore, brothers, we have an obligation—but it is not to the sinful nature, to live according to it. [13]For if you live according to the sinful nature, you will die; but if by the Spirit you put to death the misdeeds of the body, you will live, [14]because those who are led by the Spirit of God

---

*a18 Or my flesh   *b1 Some later manuscripts Jesus, who do not live according to the
sinful nature but according to the Spirit,   *c3 Or the flesh; also in verses 4, 5, 8, 9, 12
and 13   *d3 Or man, for sin   *e3 Or in the flesh   *f6 Or mind set on the flesh
*g7 Or the mind set on the flesh

are sons of God. ¹⁵For you did not receive a spirit that makes you a slave again to fear, but you received the Spirit of sonship.ᵃ And by him we cry, "Abba,ᵇ Father."

20
2Ti 1:7

¹⁶The Spirit himself testifies with our spirit that we are God's children. ¹⁷Now if we are children, then we are heirs—heirs of God and co-heirs with Christ, if indeed we share in his sufferings in order that we may also share in his glory.

91
2Co 12:9,10

Future Glory

¹⁸I consider that our present sufferings are not worth comparing with the glory that will be revealed in us. ¹⁹The creation waits in eager expectation for the sons of God to be revealed. ²⁰For the creation was subjected to frustration, not by its own choice, but by the will of the one who subjected it, in hope ²¹thatᶜ the creation itself will be liberated from its bondage to decay and brought into the glorious freedom of the children of God.

30
1Co 8:9

²²We know that the whole creation has been groaning as in the pains of childbirth right up to the present time. ²³Not only so, but we ourselves, who have the firstfruits of the Spirit, groan inwardly as we wait eagerly for our adoption as sons, the redemption of our bodies. ²⁴For in this hope we were saved. But hope that is seen is no hope at all. Who hopes for what he already has? ²⁵But if we hope for what we do not yet have, we wait for it patiently.

²⁶In the same way, the Spirit helps us in our weakness. We do not know what we ought to pray for, but the Spirit himself inter-

cedes for us with groans that words cannot express. ²⁷And he who searches our hearts knows the mind of the Spirit, because the Spirit intercedes for the saints in accordance with God's will.

More Than Conquerors

²⁸And we know that in all things God works for the good of those who love him,ᵈ whoᵉ have been called according to his purpose. ²⁹For those God foreknew he also predestined to be conformed to the likeness of his Son, that he might be the firstborn among many brothers. ³⁰And those he predestined, he also called; those he called, he also justified; those he justified, he also glorified.

22
Ro 9:11

81
Ro 8:37-3

87
1Co 12:4

³¹What, then, shall we say in response to this? If God is for us, who can be against us? ³²He who did not spare his own Son, but gave him up for us all—how will he not also, along with him, graciously give us all things? ³³Who will bring any charge against those whom God has chosen? It is God who justifies. ³⁴Who is he that condemns? Christ Jesus, who died—more than that, who was raised to life—is at the right hand of God and is also interceding for us. ³⁵Who shall separate us from the love of Christ? Shall trouble or hardship or persecution or famine or nakedness or danger or sword? ³⁶As it is written:

68
Heb 13:1

31
1Ti 6:15,

54
Ro 10:21

"For your sake we face death
all day long;
we are considered as sheep
to be slaughtered."ᶠ

³⁷No, in all these things we are more than conquerors through

81
2Co 9:8

ᵃ15 Or adoption   ᵇ15 Aramaic for Father   ᶜ20,21 Or subjected it in hope. ²¹For
ᵈ28 Some manuscripts And we know that all things work together for good to those who love God   ᵉ28 Or works together with those who love him to bring about what is good—with those who   ᶠ36 Psalm 44:22

him who loved us. ³⁸For I am convinced that neither death nor life, neither angels nor demons,ᵃ neither the present nor the future, nor any powers, ³⁹neither height nor depth, nor anything else in all creation, will be able to separate us from the love of God that is in Christ Jesus our Lord.

God's Sovereign Choice

9 I speak the truth in Christ—I am not lying, my conscience confirms it in the Holy Spirit— ²I have great sorrow and unceasing anguish in my heart. ³For I could wish that I myself were cursed and cut off from Christ for the sake of my brothers, those of my own race, ⁴the people of Israel. Theirs is the adoption as sons; theirs the divine glory, the covenants, the receiving of the law, the temple worship and the promises. ⁵Theirs are the patriarchs, and from them is traced the human ancestry of Christ, who is God over all, forever praised!ᵇ Amen.

⁶It is not as though God's word had failed. For not all who are descended from Israel are Israel. ⁷Nor because they are his descendants are they all Abraham's children. On the contrary, "It is through Isaac that your offspring will be reckoned."ᶜ ⁸In other words, it is not the natural children who are God's children, but it is the children of the promise who are regarded as Abraham's offspring. ⁹For this was how the promise was stated: "At the appointed time I will return, and Sarah will have a son."ᵈ

¹⁰Not only that, but Rebekah's children had one and the same father, our father Isaac. ¹¹Yet, be-

fore the twins were born or had done anything good or bad—in order that God's purpose in election might stand: ¹²not by works but by him who calls—she was told, "The older will serve the younger."ᵉ ¹³Just as it is written: "Jacob I loved, but Esau I hated."ᶠ

¹⁴What then shall we say? Is God unjust? Not at all! ¹⁵For he says to Moses,

"I will have mercy on whom I
    have mercy,
and I will have compassion
    on whom I have
    compassion."ᵍ

¹⁶It does not, therefore, depend on man's desire or effort, but on God's mercy. ¹⁷For the Scripture says to Pharaoh: "I raised you up for this very purpose, that I might display my power in you and that my name might be proclaimed in all the earth."ʰ ¹⁸Therefore God has mercy on whom he wants to have mercy, and he hardens whom he wants to harden.

¹⁹One of you will say to me: "Then why does God still blame us? For who resists his will?" ²⁰But who are you, O man, to talk back to God? "Shall what is formed say to him who formed it, 'Why did you make me like this?'"ⁱ ²¹Does not the potter have the right to make out of the same lump of clay some pottery for noble purposes and some for common use?

²²What if God, choosing to show his wrath and make his power known, bore with great patience the objects of his wrath—prepared for destruction? ²³What if he did this to make

22 Ro 11:7

ᵃ38 Or *nor heavenly rulers*   ᵇ5 Or *Christ, who is over all. God be forever praised!* Or *Christ. God who is over all be forever praised!*   ᶜ7 Gen. 21:12   ᵈ9 Gen. 18:10,14   ᵉ12 Gen. 25:23   ᶠ13 Mal. 1:2,3   ᵍ15 Exodus 33:19   ʰ17 Exodus 9:16   ⁱ20 Isaiah 29:16; 45:9

the riches of his glory known to the objects of his mercy, whom he prepared in advance for glory— ²⁴even us, whom he also called, not only from the Jews but also from the Gentiles? ²⁵As he says in Hosea:

"I will call them 'my people'
  who are not my people;
and I will call her 'my loved
    one' who is not my
    loved one,"[a]

²⁶and,

"It will happen that in the
    very place where it was
    said to them,
  'You are not my people,'
they will be called 'sons of the
    living God.' "[b]

²⁷Isaiah cries out concerning Israel:

"Though the number of the
    Israelites be like the sand
    by the sea,
  only the remnant will be
    saved.
²⁸For the Lord will carry out
    his sentence on earth with
    speed and finality."[c]

²⁹It is just as Isaiah said previously:

"Unless the Lord Almighty
    had left us descendants,
we would have become like
    Sodom,
  we would have been like
    Gomorrah."[d]

Israel's Unbelief

³⁰What then shall we say? That the Gentiles, who did not pursue righteousness, have obtained it, a righteousness that is by faith; ³¹but Israel, who pursued a law of

righteousness, has not attained it. ³²Why not? Because they pursued it not by faith but as if it were by works. They stumbled over the "stumbling stone." ³³As it is written:

"See, I lay in Zion a stone
    that causes men to
    stumble
  and a rock that makes them
    fall,
and the one who trusts in him
    will never be put to
    shame."[e]

10 Brothers, my heart's desire and prayer to God for the Israelites is that they may be saved. ²For I can testify about them that they are zealous for God, but their zeal is not based on knowledge. ³Since they did not know the righteousness that comes from God and sought to establish their own, they did not submit to God's righteousness. ⁴Christ is the end of the law so that there may be righteousness for everyone who believes.

⁵Moses describes in this way the righteousness that is by the law: "The man who does these things will live by them."[f] ⁶But the righteousness that is by faith says: "Do not say in your heart, 'Who will ascend into heaven?'[g] (that is, to bring Christ down) ⁷or 'Who will descend into the deep?'[h] (that is, to bring Christ up from the dead). ⁸But what does it say? "The word is near you; it is in your mouth and in your heart,"[i] that is, the word of faith we are proclaiming: ⁹That if you confess with your mouth, "Jesus is Lord," and believe in your heart that God raised him from the dead, you will be saved.

78
Ro 10:13

---

^a25 Hosea 2:23   ^b26 Hosea 1:10   ^c28 Isaiah 10:22,23   ^d29 Isaiah 1:9
^e33 Isaiah 8:14; 28:16   ^f5 Lev. 18:5   ^g6 Deut. 30:12   ^h7 Deut. 30:13
ⁱ8 Deut. 30:14

[10]For it is with your heart that you believe and are justified, and it is with your mouth that you confess and are saved. [11]As the Scripture says, "Anyone who trusts in him will never be put to shame."[d]

[12]For there is no difference between Jew and Gentile—the same Lord is Lord of all and richly blesses all who call on him, [13]for, "Everyone who calls on the name of the Lord will be saved."[b]

[14]How, then, can they call on the one they have not believed in? And how can they believe in the one of whom they have not heard? And how can they hear without someone preaching to them? [15]And how can they preach unless they are sent? As it is written, "How beautiful are the feet of those who bring good news!"[c]

[16]But not all the Israelites accepted the good news. For Isaiah says, "Lord, who has believed our message?"[d] [17]Consequently, faith comes from hearing the message, and the message is heard through the word of Christ. [18]But I ask: Did they not hear? Of course they did:

"Their voice has gone out into
    all the earth,
  their words to the ends of
    the world."[e]

[19]Again I ask: Did Israel not understand? First, Moses says,

"I will make you envious by
    those who are not a
    nation;
  I will make you angry by a
    nation that has no
    understanding."[f]

86
1Co 4:14

78
2Co 6:2

24
Gal 3:26

[20]And Isaiah boldly says,

"I was found by those who
    did not seek me;
  I revealed myself to those
    who did not ask for
    me."[g]

[21]But concerning Israel he says,

"All day long I have held out
    my hands
  to a disobedient and
    obstinate people."[h]

85
1Co 3:16,17

18
Eph 2:1,2
54
1Jn 4:13-16
73
1Co 4:11-13

The Remnant of Israel

11 I ask then: Did God reject his people? By no means! I am an Israelite myself, a descendant of Abraham, from the tribe of Benjamin. [2]God did not reject his people, whom he foreknew. Don't you know what the Scripture says in the passage about Elijah—how he appealed to God against Israel: [3]"Lord, they have killed your prophets and torn down your altars; I am the only one left, and they are trying to kill me"[i]? [4]And what was God's answer to him? "I have reserved for myself seven thousand who have not bowed the knee to Baal."[j] [5]So too, at the present time there is a remnant chosen by grace. [6]And if by grace, then it is no longer by works; if it were, grace would no longer be grace.[k]

[7]What then? What Israel sought so earnestly it did not obtain, but the elect did. The others were hardened, [8]as it is written:

"God gave them a spirit of
    stupor,
  eyes so that they could not
    see

22
2Ti 2:10

---

[d]11 Isaiah 28:16   *[b]13* Joel 2:32   *[c]15* Isaiah 52:7   *[d]16* Isaiah 53:1   *[e]18* Psalm 19:4
[f]19 Deut. 32:21   *[g]20* Isaiah 65:1   *[h]21* Isaiah 65:2   *[i]3* 1 Kings 19:10,14
[j]4 1 Kings 19:18   *[k]6* Some manuscripts *by grace. But if by works, then it is no longer grace; if it were, work would no longer be work.*

and ears so that they could
not hear,
to this very day."[a]

9And David says:

"May their table become a
snare and a trap,
a stumbling block and a
retribution for them.
10May their eyes be darkened so
they cannot see,
and their backs be bent
forever."[b]

Ingrafted Branches

11Again I ask: Did they stumble
so as to fall beyond recovery? Not
at all! Rather, because of their
transgression, salvation has
come to the Gentiles to make Israel
envious. 12But if their transgression
means riches for the
world, and their loss means
riches for the Gentiles, how
much greater riches will their
fullness bring!

13I am talking to you Gentiles.
Inasmuch as I am the apostle to
the Gentiles, I make much of my
ministry 14in the hope that I may
somehow arouse my own people
to envy and save some of them.
15For if their rejection is the reconciliation
of the world, what will
their acceptance be but life from
the dead? 16If the part of the
dough offered as firstfruits is
holy, then the whole batch is
holy; if the root is holy, so are the
branches.

17If some of the branches have
been broken off, and you,
though a wild olive shoot, have
been grafted in among the others
and now share in the nourishing
sap from the olive root, 18do not
boast over those branches. If you
do, consider this: You do not
support the root, but the root
supports you. 19You will say

then, "Branches were broken off
so that I could be grafted in."
20Granted. But they were broken
off because of unbelief, and you
stand by faith. Do not be arrogant,
but be afraid. 21For if God
did not spare the natural
branches, he will not spare you
either.

22Consider therefore the kindness
and sternness of God: sternness
to those who fell, but kindness
to you, provided that you
continue in his kindness. Otherwise,
you also will be cut off.
23And if they do not persist in unbelief,
they will be grafted in, for
God is able to graft them in again.
24After all, if you were cut out of
an olive tree that is wild by nature,
and contrary to nature were
grafted into a cultivated olive
tree, how much more readily will
these, the natural branches, be
grafted into their own olive tree!

All Israel Will Be Saved

25I do not want you to be ignorant
of this mystery, brothers, so
that you may not be conceited:
Israel has experienced a hardening
in part until the full number
of the Gentiles has come in.
26And so all Israel will be saved,
as it is written:

"The deliverer will come from
Zion;
he will turn godlessness
away from Jacob.
27And this is[c] my covenant with
them
when I take away their
sins."[d]

28As far as the gospel is concerned,
they are enemies on your
account; but as far as election is
concerned, they are loved on account
of the patriarchs, 29for
God's gifts and his call are irrevo-

[a]8 Deut. 29:4; Isaiah 29:10   [b]10 Psalm 69:22,23   [c]27 Or *will be*
[d]27 Isaiah 59:20,21; 27:9; Jer. 31:33,34

cable. [30]Just as you who were at one time disobedient to God have now received mercy as a result of their disobedience, [31]so they too have now become disobedient in order that they too may now[a] receive mercy as a result of God's mercy to you. [32]For God has bound all men over to disobedience so that he may have mercy on them all.

Doxology

[33]Oh, the depth of the riches of
     the wisdom and[b]
     knowledge of God!
  How unsearchable his
     judgments,
  and his paths beyond
     tracing out!
[34]"Who has known the mind of
     the Lord?
  Or who has been his
     counselor?"[c]
[35]"Who has ever given to God,
     that God should repay
     him?"[d]
[36]For from him and through
     him and to him are all
     things.
  To him be the glory forever!
     Amen.

Living Sacrifices

59
2Co 4:4

79
2Co 13:9

12 Therefore, I urge you, brothers, in view of God's mercy, to offer your bodies as living sacrifices, holy and pleasing to God—this is your spiritual[e] act of worship. [2]Do not conform any longer to the pattern of this world, but be transformed by the renewing of your mind. Then you will be able to test and approve what God's will is—his good, pleasing and perfect will.

[3]For by the grace given me I say to every one of you: Do not think of yourself more highly than you

ought, but rather think of yourself with sober judgment, in accordance with the measure of faith God has given you. [4]Just as each of us has one body with many members, and these members do not all have the same function, [5]so in Christ we who are many form one body, and each member belongs to all the others. [6]We have different gifts, according to the grace given us. If a man's gift is prophesying, let him use it in proportion to his[f] faith. [7]If it is serving, let him serve; if it is teaching, let him teach; [8]if it is encouraging, let him encourage; if it is contributing to the needs of others, let him give generously; if it is leadership, let him govern diligently; if it is showing mercy, let him do it cheerfully.

Love

27
Phm 4-7

[9]Love must be sincere. Hate what is evil; cling to what is good. [10]Be devoted to one another in brotherly love. Honor one another above yourselves. [11]Never be lacking in zeal, but keep your spiritual fervor, serving the Lord. [12]Be joyful in hope, patient in affliction, faithful in prayer. [13]Share with God's people who are in need. Practice hospitality.

64
Ro 15:4

[14]Bless those who persecute you; bless and do not curse. [15]Rejoice with those who rejoice; mourn with those who mourn. [16]Live in harmony with one another. Do not be proud, but be willing to associate with people of low position.[g] Do not be conceited.

1Co 3:11-15

[17]Do not repay anyone evil for evil. Be careful to do what is right in the eyes of everybody. [18]If it is

76

38
1Th 2:14-16

---

[a]31 Some manuscripts do not have *now.*   [b]33 Or *riches and the wisdom and the*
[c]34 Isaiah 40:13   [d]35 Job 41:11   [e]1 Or *reasonable*   [f]6 Or *in agreement with the*
[g]16 Or *willing to do menial work*

possible, as far as it depends on you, live at peace with everyone.
29 **19**Do not take revenge, my
Eph 4:32 friends, but leave room for God's wrath, for it is written: "It is mine to avenge; I will repay,"[a] says the Lord. **20**On the contrary:

"If your enemy is hungry,
    feed him;
 if he is thirsty, give him
    something to drink.
 In doing this, you will heap
    burning coals on his
    head."[b]

21Do not be overcome by evil, but overcome evil with good.

Submission to the Authorities

13 Everyone must submit himself to the governing authorities, for there is no authority except that which God has established. The authorities that exist have been established by God. **2**Consequently, he who rebels against the authority is rebelling against what God has instituted, and those who do so will bring judgment on themselves. **3**For rulers hold no terror for those who do right, but for those who do wrong. Do you want to be free from fear of the one in authority? Then do what is right and he will commend you. **4**For he is God's servant to do you good. But if you do wrong, be afraid, for he does not bear the sword for nothing. He is God's servant, an agent of wrath to bring punishment on the wrongdoer. **5**Therefore, it is necessary to submit to the authorities, not only because of possible punishment but also because of conscience.

6This is also why you pay taxes, for the authorities are God's servants, who give their full time to

governing. **7**Give everyone what you owe him: If you owe taxes, pay taxes; if revenue, then revenue; if respect, then respect; if honor, then honor.

Love, for the Day Is Near

8Let no debt remain outstanding, except the continuing debt to love one another, for he who loves his fellowman has fulfilled the law. **9**The commandments, **90** "Do not commit adultery," "Do **Eph 4:28** not murder," "Do not steal," "Do not covet,"[c] and whatever other commandment there may be, are summed up in this one rule: "Love your neighbor as yourself."[d] **10**Love does no harm to its neighbor. Therefore love is the fulfillment of the law.

11And do this, understanding the present time. The hour has come for you to wake up from your slumber, because our salvation is nearer now than when we first believed. **12**The night is nearly over; the day is almost here. So let us put aside the deeds of darkness and put on the armor of light. **13**Let us behave **46** decently, as in the daytime, not **1Co 3:3** in orgies and drunkenness, not in sexual immorality and debauchery, not in dissension and jealousy. **14**Rather, clothe yourselves with the Lord Jesus Christ, and do not think about how to gratify the desires of the sinful nature.[e]

The Weak and the Strong

14 Accept him whose faith is weak, without passing judgment on disputable matters. **2**One man's faith allows him to eat everything, but another man, whose faith is weak, eats only vegetables. **3**The man who eats everything must not look down

a19 Deut. 32:35 *b20* Prov. 25:21,22 *c9* Exodus 20:13-15,17; Deut. 5:17-19,21 *d9* Lev. 19:18 *e14* Or *the flesh*

on him who does not, and the man who does not eat everything must not condemn the man who does, for God has accepted him. [4]Who are you to judge someone else's servant? To his own master he stands or falls. And he will stand, for the Lord is able to make him stand.

[5]One man considers one day more sacred than another; another man considers every day alike. Each one should be fully convinced in his own mind. [6]He who regards one day as special, does so to the Lord. He who eats meat, eats to the Lord, for he gives thanks to God; and he who abstains, does so to the Lord and gives thanks to God. [7]For none of us lives to himself alone and none of us dies to himself alone. [8]If we live, we live to the Lord; and if we die, we die to the Lord. So, whether we live or die, we belong to the Lord.

[9]For this very reason, Christ died and returned to life so that he might be the Lord of both the dead and the living. [10]You, then, why do you judge your brother? Or why do you look down on your brother? For we will all stand before God's judgment seat. [11]It is written:

" 'As surely as I live,' says the Lord,
'every knee will bow before me;
every tongue will confess to God.' " [a]

[12]So then, each of us will give an account of himself to God.

[13]Therefore let us stop passing judgment on one another. Instead, make up your mind not to put any stumbling block or obstacle in your brother's way. [14]As one who is in the Lord Jesus, I am fully convinced that no food[b] is

unclean in itself. But if anyone regards something as unclean, then for him it is unclean. [15]If your brother is distressed because of what you eat, you are no longer acting in love. Do not by your eating destroy your brother for whom Christ died. [16]Do not allow what you consider good to be spoken of as evil. [17]For the kingdom of God is not a matter of eating and drinking, but of righteousness, peace and joy in the Holy Spirit, [18]because anyone who serves Christ in this way is pleasing to God and approved by men.

[19]Let us therefore make every effort to do what leads to peace and to mutual edification. [20]Do not destroy the work of God for the sake of food. All food is clean, but it is wrong for a man to eat anything that causes someone else to stumble. [21]It is better not to eat meat or drink wine or to do anything else that will cause your brother to fall.

[22]So whatever you believe about these things keep between yourself and God. Blessed is the man who does not condemn himself by what he approves. [23]But the man who has doubts is condemned if he eats, because his eating is not from faith; and everything that does not come from faith is sin.

15

We who are strong ought to bear with the failings of the weak and not to please ourselves. [2]Each of us should please his neighbor for his good, to build him up. [3]For even Christ did not please himself but, as it is written: "The insults of those who insult you have fallen on me." [c] [4]For everything that was written in the past was written to teach us, so that through endurance and the encouragement of

53
Co 15:54-58

93
1Co 10:13

82
Ro 14:22

7
Eph 4:1-6

21
1Co 6:9-11

82
1Co 4:3

64
1Co 13:4

[a]11 Isaiah 45:23   [b]14 Or *that nothing*   [c]3 Psalm 69:9

the Scriptures we might have hope.

97
1Co 1:10

⁵May the God who gives endurance and encouragement give you a spirit of unity among yourselves as you follow Christ Jesus, ⁶so that with one heart and mouth you may glorify the God and Father of our Lord Jesus Christ.

1
Eph 2:19-22

⁷Accept one another, then, just as Christ accepted you, in order to bring praise to God. ⁸For I tell you that Christ has become a servant of the Jews*a* on behalf of God's truth, to confirm the promises made to the patriarchs ⁹so that the Gentiles may glorify God for his mercy, as it is written:

"Therefore I will praise you
        among the Gentiles;
    I will sing hymns to your
        name."*b*

¹⁰Again, it says,

"Rejoice, O Gentiles, with his
    people."*c*

¹¹And again,

"Praise the Lord, all you
        Gentiles,
    and sing praises to him, all
        you peoples."*d*

¹²And again, Isaiah says,

"The Root of Jesse will spring
        up,
    one who will arise to rule
        over the nations;
    the Gentiles will hope in
        him."*e*

¹³May the God of hope fill you with all joy and peace as you trust in him, so that you may overflow with hope by the power of the Holy Spirit.

Paul the Minister to the Gentiles

¹⁴I myself am convinced, my brothers, that you yourselves are full of goodness, complete in knowledge and competent to instruct one another. ¹⁵I have written you quite boldly on some points, as if to remind you of them again, because of the grace God gave me ¹⁶to be a minister of Christ Jesus to the Gentiles with the priestly duty of proclaiming the gospel of God, so that the Gentiles might become an offering acceptable to God, sanctified by the Holy Spirit.

¹⁷Therefore I glory in Christ Jesus in my service to God. ¹⁸I will not venture to speak of anything except what Christ has accomplished through me in leading the Gentiles to obey God by what I have said and done— ¹⁹by the power of signs and miracles, through the power of the Spirit. So from Jerusalem all the way around to Illyricum, I have fully proclaimed the gospel of Christ. ²⁰It has always been my ambition to preach the gospel where Christ was not known, so that I would not be building on someone else's foundation. ²¹Rather, as it is written:

"Those who were not told
        about him will see,
    and those who have not
        heard will understand."*f*

²²This is why I have often been hindered from coming to you.

Paul's Plan to Visit Rome

²³But now that there is no more place for me to work in these re-

---

*a8 Greek *circumcision*   *b9 2 Samuel 22:50; Psalm 18:49   *c10 Deut. 32:43
*d11 Psalm 117:1   *e12 Isaiah 11:10   *f21 Isaiah 52:15

gions, and since I have been longing for many years to see you, [21] I plan to do so when I go to Spain. I hope to visit you while passing through and to have you assist me on my journey there, after I have enjoyed your company for a while. [25] Now, however, I am on my way to Jerusalem in the service of the saints there. [26] For Macedonia and Achaia were pleased to make a contribution for the poor among the saints in Jerusalem. [27] They were pleased to do it, and indeed they owe it to them. For if the Gentiles have shared in the Jews' spiritual blessings, they owe it to the Jews to share with them their material blessings. [28] So after I have completed this task and have made sure that they have received this fruit, I will go to Spain and visit you on the way. [29] I know that when I come to you, I will come in the full measure of the blessing of Christ.

[30] I urge you, brothers, by our Lord Jesus Christ and by the love of the Spirit, to join me in my struggle by praying to God for me. [31] Pray that I may be rescued from the unbelievers in Judea and that my service in Jerusalem may be acceptable to the saints there, [32] so that by God's will I may come to you with joy and together with you be refreshed. [33] The God of peace be with you all. Amen.

Personal Greetings

16 I commend to you our sister Phoebe, a servant[a] of the church in Cenchrea. [2] I ask you to receive her in the Lord in a way worthy of the saints and to give her any help she may need from you, for she has been a great help to many people, including me.

[3] Greet Priscilla[b] and Aquila, my fellow workers in Christ Jesus. [4] They risked their lives for me. Not only I but all the churches of the Gentiles are grateful to them. [5] Greet also the church that meets at their house.

Greet my dear friend Epenetus, who was the first convert to Christ in the province of Asia.

[6] Greet Mary, who worked very hard for you.

[7] Greet Andronicus and Junias, my relatives who have been in prison with me. They are outstanding among the apostles, and they were in Christ before I was.

[8] Greet Ampliatus, whom I love in the Lord.

[9] Greet Urbanus, our fellow worker in Christ, and my dear friend Stachys.

[10] Greet Apelles, tested and approved in Christ.

Greet those who belong to the household of Aristobulus.

[11] Greet Herodion, my relative.

Greet those in the household of Narcissus who are in the Lord.

[12] Greet Tryphena and Tryphosa, those women who work hard in the Lord.

Greet my dear friend Persis, another woman who has worked very hard in the Lord.

[13] Greet Rufus, chosen in the Lord, and his mother, who has been a mother to me, too.

[14] Greet Asyncritus, Phlegon, Hermes, Patrobas, Hermas and the brothers with them.

[15] Greet Philologus, Julia, Nereus and his sister, and Olympas and all the saints with them.

8 1Co 11:22

---

a1 Or *deaconess*   b3 Greek *Prisca*, a variant of *Priscilla*

¹⁶Greet one another with a holy kiss.

All the churches of Christ send greetings.

¹⁷I urge you, brothers, to watch out for those who cause divisions and put obstacles in your way that are contrary to the teaching you have learned. Keep away from them. ¹⁸For such people are not serving our Lord Christ, but their own appetites. By smooth talk and flattery they deceive the minds of naive people. ¹⁹Everyone has heard about your obedience, so I am full of joy over you; but I want you to be wise about what is good, and innocent about what is evil.

²⁰The God of peace will soon crush Satan under your feet.

The grace of our Lord Jesus be with you.

²¹Timothy, my fellow worker, sends his greetings to you, as do Lucius, Jason and Sosipater, my relatives.

²²I, Tertius, who wrote down this letter, greet you in the Lord.

²³Gaius, whose hospitality I and the whole church here enjoy, sends you his greetings.

Erastus, who is the city's director of public works, and our brother Quartus send you their greetings.ᵃ

²⁵Now to him who is able to establish you by my gospel and the proclamation of Jesus Christ, according to the revelation of the mystery hidden for long ages past, ²⁶but now revealed and made known through the prophetic writings by the command of the eternal God, so that all nations might believe and obey him— ²⁷to the only wise God be glory forever through Jesus Christ! Amen.

1 Corinthians

1 Paul, called to be an apostle of Christ Jesus by the will of God, and our brother Sosthenes,

²To the church of God in Corinth, to those sanctified in Christ Jesus and called to be holy, together with all those everywhere who call on the name of our Lord Jesus Christ—their Lord and ours:

³Grace and peace to you from God our Father and the Lord Jesus Christ.

Thanksgiving

⁴I always thank God for you because of his grace given you in Christ Jesus. ⁵For in him you have been enriched in every way—in all your speaking and in all your knowledge— ⁶because our testimony about Christ was confirmed in you. ⁷Therefore you do not lack any spiritual gift as you eagerly wait for our Lord Jesus Christ to be revealed. ⁸He will keep you strong to the end, so that you will be blameless on the day of our Lord Jesus Christ. ⁹God, who has called you into fellowship with his Son Jesus Christ our Lord, is faithful.

Divisions in the Church

¹⁰I appeal to you, brothers, in the name of our Lord Jesus Christ, that all of you agree with

97
Eph 4:1-6

ᵃ23 Some manuscripts *their greetings.* ²⁴*May the grace of our Lord Jesus Christ be with all of you. Amen.*

one another so that there may be no divisions among you and that you may be perfectly united in mind and thought. ¹¹My brothers, some from Chloe's household have informed me that there are quarrels among you. ¹²What I mean is this: One of you says, "I follow Paul"; another, "I follow Apollos"; another, "I follow Cephas*"; still another, "I follow Christ."

¹³Is Christ divided? Was Paul crucified for you? Were you baptized into* the name of Paul? ¹⁴I am thankful that I did not baptize any of you except Crispus and Gaius, ¹⁵so no one can say that you were baptized into my name. ¹⁶(Yes, I also baptized the household of Stephanas; beyond that, I don't remember if I baptized anyone else.) ¹⁷For Christ did not send me to baptize, but to preach the gospel—not with words of human wisdom, lest the cross of Christ be emptied of its power.

Christ the Wisdom and Power of God

23
2Co 5:17-21

¹⁸For the message of the cross is foolishness to those who are perishing, but to us who are being saved it is the power of God. ¹⁹For it is written:

"I will destroy the wisdom of the wise;
the intelligence of the intelligent I will frustrate."*

²⁰Where is the wise man? Where is the scholar? Where is the philosopher of this age? Has not God made foolish the wisdom of the world? ²¹For since in the wisdom of God the world through its wisdom did not know him, God was pleased through the foolishness of what was

preached to save those who believe. ²²Jews demand miraculous signs and Greeks look for wisdom, ²³but we preach Christ crucified: a stumbling block to Jews and foolishness to Gentiles, ²⁴but to those whom God has called, both Jews and Greeks, Christ the power of God and the wisdom of God. ²⁵For the foolishness of God is wiser than man's wisdom, and the weakness of God is stronger than man's strength.

²⁶Brothers, think of what you were when you were called. Not many of you were wise by human standards; not many were influential; not many were of noble birth. ²⁷But God chose the foolish things of the world to shame the wise; God chose the weak things of the world to shame the strong. ²⁸He chose the lowly things of this world and despised things—and the things that are not—to nullify the things that are, ²⁹so that no one may boast before him. ³⁰It is because of him that you are in Christ Jesus, who has become for us wisdom from God—that is, our righteousness, holiness and redemption. ³¹Therefore, as it is written: "Let him who boasts boast in the Lord."*

70
Gal 6:3

77
Ps 119:7

2 When I came to you, brothers, I did not come with eloquence or superior wisdom as I proclaimed to you the testimony about God.* ²For I resolved to know nothing while I was with you except Jesus Christ and him crucified. ³I came to you in weakness and fear, and with much trembling. ⁴My message and my preaching were not with wise and persuasive words, but with a demonstration of the Spirit's power, ⁵so that your faith might

---

*12 That is, Peter   *13 Or in; also in verse 15   *19 Isaiah 29:14   *31 Jer. 9:24
*1 Some manuscripts as I proclaimed to you God's mystery

not rest on men's wisdom, but on God's power.

Wisdom From the Spirit

[6]We do, however, speak a message of wisdom among the mature, but not the wisdom of this age or of the rulers of this age, who are coming to nothing. [7]No, we speak of God's secret wisdom, a wisdom that has been hidden and that God destined for our glory before time began. [8]None of the rulers of this age understood it, for if they had, they would not have crucified the Lord of glory. [9]However, as it is written:

> "No eye has seen,
>   no ear has heard,
> no mind has conceived
>   what God has prepared for
>   those who love him"[a]—

[10]but God has revealed it to us by his Spirit.

The Spirit searches all things, even the deep things of God. [11]For who among men knows the thoughts of a man except the man's spirit within him? In the same way no one knows the thoughts of God except the Spirit of God. [12]We have not received the spirit of the world but the Spirit who is from God, that we may understand what God has freely given us. [13]This is what we speak, not in words taught us by human wisdom but in words taught by the Spirit, expressing spiritual truths in spiritual words.[b] [14]The man without the Spirit does not accept the things that come from the Spirit of God, for they are foolishness to him, and he cannot understand them, because they are spiritually discerned. [15]The spiritual man makes judgments about all

things, but he himself is not subject to any man's judgment:

[16]"For who has known the
    mind of the Lord
    that he may instruct him?"[c]

But we have the mind of Christ.

On Divisions in the Church

3 Brothers, I could not address you as spiritual but as worldly—mere infants in Christ. [2]I gave you milk, not solid food, for you were not yet ready for it. Indeed, you are still not ready. [3]You are still worldly. For since there is jealousy and quarreling among you, are you not worldly? Are you not acting like mere men? [4]For when one says, "I follow Paul," and another, "I follow Apollos," are you not mere men?

[5]What, after all, is Apollos? And what is Paul? Only servants, through whom you came to believe—as the Lord has assigned to each his task. [6]I planted the seed, Apollos watered it, but God made it grow. [7]So neither he who plants nor he who waters is anything, but only God, who makes things grow. [8]The man who plants and the man who waters have one purpose, and each will be rewarded according to his own labor. [9]For we are God's fellow workers; you are God's field, God's building.

[10]By the grace God has given me, I laid a foundation as an expert builder, and someone else is building on it. But each one should be careful how he builds. [11]For no one can lay any foundation other than the one already laid, which is Jesus Christ. [12]If any man builds on this foundation using gold, silver, costly stones, wood, hay or straw, [13]his work will be shown for what it is,

Marginal references
40 Rev 21:1-4

34 Eph 4:16

46 2Co 11:2

60 1Co 4:1-5

76 Col 3:23,24

---

[a]9 Isaiah 64:4   [b]13 Or Spirit, interpreting spiritual truths to spiritual men
[c]16 Isaiah 40:13

because the Day will bring it to light. It will be revealed with fire, and the fire will test the quality of each man's work. [14]If what he has built survives, he will receive his reward. [15]If it is burned up, he will suffer loss; he himself will be saved, but only as one escaping through the flames.

[85]
o 6:14-18

[16]Don't you know that you yourselves are God's temple and that God's Spirit lives in you? [17]If anyone destroys God's temple, God will destroy him; for God's temple is sacred, and you are that temple.

[18]Do not deceive yourselves. If any one of you thinks he is wise by the standards of this age, he should become a "fool" so that he may become wise. [19]For the wisdom of this world is foolishness in God's sight. As it is written: "He catches the wise in their craftiness"[a]; [20]and again, "The Lord knows that the thoughts of the wise are futile."[b 21]So then, no more boasting about men! All things are yours, [22]whether Paul or Apollos or Cephas[c] or the world or life or death or the present or the future—all are yours, [23]and you are of Christ, and Christ is of God.

Apostles of Christ

[60]
o 12:4-11

4 So then, men ought to regard us as servants of Christ and as those entrusted with the secret things of God. [2]Now it is required that those who have been given a trust must prove faithful. [3]I care very little if I am judged by you or by any human court; indeed, I do not even judge myself. [4]My conscience is clear, but that does not make me innocent. It is the Lord who judges me. [5]Therefore judge nothing before the appointed time; wait till the Lord comes. He will bring to light what is hidden

[82]
Gal 6:4,5

in darkness and will expose the motives of men's hearts. At that time each will receive his praise from God.

[6]Now, brothers, I have applied these things to myself and Apollos for your benefit, so that you may learn from us the meaning of the saying, "Do not go beyond what is written." Then you will not take pride in one man over against another. [7]For who makes you different from anyone else? What do you have that you did not receive? And if you did receive it, why do you boast as though you did not?

[8]Already you have all you want! Already you have become rich! You have become kings—and that without us! How I wish that you really had become kings so that we might be kings with you! [9]For it seems to me that God has put us apostles on display at the end of the procession, like men condemned to die in the arena. We have been made a spectacle to the whole universe, to angels as well as to men. [10]We are fools for Christ, but you are so wise in Christ! We are weak, but you are strong! You are honored, we are dishonored! [11]To this very hour we go hungry and thirsty, we are in rags, we are brutally treated, we are homeless. [12]We work hard with our own hands. When we are cursed, we bless; when we are persecuted, we endure it; [13]when we are slandered, we answer kindly. Up to this moment we have become the scum of the earth, the refuse of the world.

[73]
2Ti 2:12

[14]I am not writing this to shame you, but to warn you, as my dear children. [15]Even though you have ten thousand guardians in Christ, you do not have many fathers, for in Christ Jesus I became your father through th...

[86]
1Co 6:5

19 Job 5:13   *20* Psalm 94:11   *22* That is, Peter

[16]Therefore I urge you to imitate me. [17]For this reason I am sending to you Timothy, my son whom I love, who is faithful in the Lord. He will remind you of my way of life in Christ Jesus, which agrees with what I teach everywhere in every church.

[18]Some of you have become arrogant, as if I were not coming to you. [19]But I will come to you very soon, if the Lord is willing, and then I will find out not only how these arrogant people are talking, but what power they have. [20]For the kingdom of God is not a matter of talk but of power. [21]What do you prefer? Shall I come to you with a whip, or in love and with a gentle spirit?

Expel the Immoral Brother!

5 It is actually reported that there is sexual immorality among you, and of a kind that does not occur even among pagans: A man has his father's wife. [2]And you are proud! Shouldn't you rather have been filled with grief and have put out of your fellowship the man who did this? [3]Even though I am not physically present, I am with you in spirit. And I have already passed judgment on the one who did this, just as if I were present. [4]When you are assembled in the name of our Lord Jesus and I am with you in spirit, and the power of our Lord Jesus is present, [5]hand this man over to Satan, so that the sinful nature[a] may be destroyed and his spirit saved on the day of the Lord.

[6]Your boasting is not good. Don't you know that a little yeast works through the whole batch of dough? [7]Get rid of the old

[a][5] Or that you may be new
[b][4] Or matter

really are. For Christ, our Passover lamb, has been sacrificed. [8]Therefore let us keep the Festival, not with the old yeast, the yeast of malice and wickedness, but with bread without yeast, the bread of sincerity and truth.

[9]I have written you in my letter not to associate with sexually immoral people— [10]not at all meaning the people of this world who are immoral, or the greedy and swindlers, or idolaters. In that case you would have to leave this world. [11]But now I am writing you that you must not associate with anyone who calls himself a brother but is sexually immoral or greedy, an idolater or a slanderer, a drunkard or a swindler. With such a man do not even eat.

[12]What business is it of mine to judge those outside the church? Are you not to judge those inside? [13]God will judge those outside. "Expel the wicked man from among you."[b]

Lawsuits Among Believers

6 If any of you has a dispute with another, dare he take it before the ungodly for judgment instead of before the saints? [2]Do you not know that the saints will judge the world? And if you are to judge the world, are you not competent to judge trivial cases? [3]Do you not know that we will judge angels? How much more the things of this life! [4]Therefore, if you have disputes about such matters, appoint as judges even men of little account in the church![c] [5]I say this to shame you. Is it possible that there is nobody among you wise enough to judge a dispute between believers? [6]But instead, one brother goes to law against another—and this in front of unbelievers!

86
2Co 11:2

[a][13] *... the flesh*   [b][13] Deut. 17:7; 19:19; 21:21,22; 22:21,24; 24:7
[c][4] *... judges men of little account in the church?*

7The very fact that you have lawsuits among you means you have been completely defeated already. Why not rather be wronged? Why not rather be cheated? 8Instead, you yourselves cheat and do wrong, and you do this to your brothers.

2
Heb 13:4

21
o 10:31,32

42
Col 3:5

9Do you not know that the wicked will not inherit the kingdom of God? Do not be deceived: Neither the sexually immoral nor idolaters nor adulterers nor male prostitutes nor homosexual offenders 10nor thieves nor the greedy nor drunkards nor slanderers nor swindlers will inherit the kingdom of God. 11And that is what some of you were. But you were washed, you were sanctified, you were justified in the name of the Lord Jesus Christ and by the Spirit of our God.

Sexual Immorality

12"Everything is permissible for me"—but not everything is beneficial. "Everything is permissible for me"—but I will not be mastered by anything. 13"Food for the stomach and the stomach for food"—but God will destroy them both. The body is not meant for sexual immorality, but for the Lord, and the Lord for the body. 14By his power God raised the Lord from the dead, and he will raise us also. 15Do you not know that your bodies are members of Christ himself? Shall I then take the members of Christ and unite them with a prostitute? Never! 16Do you not know that he who unites himself with a prostitute is one with her in body? For it is said, "The two will become one flesh."[a] 17But he who unites himself with the Lord is one with him in spirit.

18Flee from sexual immorality. All other sins a man commits are outside his body, but he who sins sexually sins against his own body. 19Do you not know that your body is a temple of the Holy Spirit, who is in you, whom you have received from God? You are not your own; 20you were bought at a price. Therefore honor God with your body.

Marriage

7 Now for the matters you wrote about: It is good for a man not to marry.[b] 2But since there is so much immorality, each man should have his own wife, and each woman her own husband. 3The husband should fulfill his marital duty to his wife, and likewise the wife to her husband. 4The wife's body does not belong to her alone but also to her husband. In the same way, the husband's body does not belong to him alone but also to his wife. 5Do not deprive each other except by mutual consent and for a time, so that you may devote yourselves to prayer. Then come together again so that Satan will not tempt you because of your lack of self-control. 6I say this as a concession, not as a command. 7I wish that all men were as I am. But each man has his own gift from God; one has this gift, another has that.

57
Eph 4:2

8Now to the unmarried and the widows I say: It is good for them to stay unmarried, as I am. 9But if they cannot control themselves, they should marry, for it is better to marry than to burn with passion.

19
1Co 7:27

10To the married I give this command (not I, but the Lord): A wife must not separate from her husband. 11But if she does, she must remain unmarried or else be reconciled to her husband.

71
2Co 5:17-21

a16 Gen. 2:24   b1 Or "It is good for a man not to have sexual relations with a woman."

And a husband must not divorce his wife.

¹²To the rest I say this (I, not the Lord): If any brother has a wife who is not a believer and she is willing to live with him, he must not divorce her. ¹³And if a woman has a husband who is not a believer and he is willing to live with her, she must not divorce him. ¹⁴For the unbelieving husband has been sanctified through his wife, and the unbelieving wife has been sanctified through her believing husband. Otherwise your children would be unclean, but as it is, they are holy. ¹⁵But if the unbeliever leaves, let him do so. A believing man or woman is not bound in such circumstances; God has called us to live in peace. ¹⁶How do you know, wife, whether you will save your husband? Or, how do you know, husband, whether you will save your wife?

¹⁷Nevertheless, each one should retain the place in life that the Lord assigned to him and to which God has called him. This is the rule I lay down in all the churches. ¹⁸Was a man already circumcised when he was called? He should not become uncircumcised. Was a man uncircumcised when he was called? He should not be circumcised. ¹⁹Circumcision is nothing and uncircumcision is nothing. Keeping God's commands is what counts. ²⁰Each one should remain in the situation which he was in when God called him. ²¹Were you a slave when you were called? Don't let it trouble you—although if you can gain your freedom, do so. ²²For he who was a slave when he was called by the Lord is the Lord's freedman; similarly, he who was a free man when he was called is Christ's slave. ²³You were bought at a price; do not become slaves of men. ²⁴Brothers, each man, as responsible to God, should remain in the situation God called him to.

²⁵Now about virgins: I have no command from the Lord, but I give a judgment as one who by the Lord's mercy is trustworthy. ²⁶Because of the present crisis, I think that it is good for you to remain as you are. ²⁷Are you married? Do not seek a divorce. Are you unmarried? Do not look for a wife. ²⁸But if you do marry, you have not sinned; and if a virgin marries, she has not sinned. But those who marry will face many troubles in this life, and I want to spare you this.

²⁹What I mean, brothers, is that the time is short. From now on those who have wives should live as if they had none; ³⁰those who mourn, as if they did not; those who are happy, as if they were not; those who buy something, as if it were not theirs to keep; ³¹those who use the things of the world, as if not engrossed in them. For this world in its present form is passing away.

³²I would like you to be free from concern. An unmarried man is concerned about the Lord's affairs—how he can please the Lord. ³³But a married man is concerned about the affairs of this world—how he can please his wife— ³⁴and his interests are divided. An unmarried woman or virgin is concerned about the Lord's affairs: Her aim is to be devoted to the Lord in both body and spirit. But a married woman is concerned about the affairs of this world—how she can please her husband. ³⁵I am saying this for your own good, not to restrict you, but that you may live in a right way in undivided devotion to the Lord.

³⁶If anyone thinks he is acting

19
Php 2:3

improperly toward the virgin he is engaged to, and if she is getting along in years and he feels he ought to marry, he should do as he wants. He is not sinning. They should get married. [37]But the man who has settled the matter in his own mind, who is under no compulsion but has control over his own will, and who has made up his mind not to marry the virgin—this man also does the right thing. [38]So then, he who marries the virgin does right, but he who does not marry her does even better. [a]

[39]A woman is bound to her husband as long as he lives. But if her husband dies, she is free to marry anyone she wishes, but he must belong to the Lord. [40]In my judgment, she is happier if she stays as she is—and I think that I too have the Spirit of God.

Food Sacrificed to Idols

8 Now about food sacrificed to idols: We know that we all possess knowledge. [b] Knowledge puffs up, but love builds up. [2]The man who thinks he knows something does not yet know as he ought to know. [3]But the man who loves God is known by God.

[4]So then, about eating food sacrificed to idols: We know that an idol is nothing at all in the world and that there is no God but one. [5]For even if there are so-called gods, whether in heaven or on earth (as indeed there are many "gods" and many "lords"), [6]yet for us there is but one God, the Father, from whom all things came and for whom we live; and

there is but one Lord, Jesus Christ, through whom all things came and through whom we live.

[7]But not everyone knows this. Some people are still so accustomed to idols that when they eat such food they think of it as having been sacrificed to an idol, and since their conscience is weak, it is defiled. [8]But food does not bring us near to God; we are no worse if we do not eat, and no better if we do.

[9]Be careful, however, that the exercise of your freedom does not become a stumbling block to the weak. [10]For if anyone with a weak conscience sees you who have this knowledge eating in an idol's temple, won't he be emboldened to eat what has been sacrificed to idols? [11]So this weak brother, for whom Christ died, is destroyed by your knowledge. [12]When you sin against your brothers in this way and wound their weak conscience, you sin against Christ. [13]Therefore, if what I eat causes my brother to fall into sin, I will never eat meat again, so that I will not cause him to fall.

30 1Co 10:29

12 1Ti 1:5

66 1Co 13:10

The Rights of an Apostle

9 Am I not free? Am I not an apostle? Have I not seen Jesus our Lord? Are you not the result of my work in the Lord? [2]Even though I may not be an apostle to others, surely I am to you! For you are the seal of my apostleship in the Lord.

[3]This is my defense to those who sit in judgment on me.

---

[a]36-38 Or [36]If anyone thinks he is not treating his daughter properly, and if she is getting along in years, and he feels she ought to marry, he should do as he wants. He is not sinning. He should let her get married. [37]But the man who has settled the matter in his own mind, who is under no compulsion but has control over his own will, and who has made up his mind to keep the virgin unmarried—this man also does the right thing. [38]So then, he who gives his virgin in marriage does right, but he who does not give her in marriage does even better.   [b]1 Or "We all possess knowledge," as you say

⁴Don't we have the right to food and drink? ⁵Don't we have the right to take a believing wife along with us, as do the other apostles and the Lord's brothers and Cephas*? ⁶Or is it only I and Barnabas who must work for a living?

⁷Who serves as a soldier at his own expense? Who plants a vineyard and does not eat of its grapes? Who tends a flock and does not drink of the milk? ⁸Do I say this merely from a human point of view? Doesn't the Law say the same thing? ⁹For it is written in the Law of Moses: "Do not muzzle an ox while it is treading out the grain."ᵇ Is it about oxen that God is concerned? ¹⁰Surely he says this for us, doesn't he? Yes, this was written for us, because when the plowman plows and the thresher threshes, they ought to do so in the hope of sharing in the harvest. ¹¹If we have sown spiritual seed among you, is it too much if we reap a material harvest from you? ¹²If others have this right of support from you, shouldn't we have it all the more?

But we did not use this right. On the contrary, we put up with anything rather than hinder the gospel of Christ. ¹³Don't you know that those who work in the temple get their food from the temple, and those who serve at the altar share in what is offered on the altar? ¹⁴In the same way, the Lord has commanded that those who preach the gospel should receive their living from the gospel.

¹⁵But I have not used any of these rights. And I am not writing this in the hope that you will do such things for me. I would rather die than have anyone deprive me of this boast. ¹⁶Yet when I preach the gospel, I cannot boast, for I am compelled to preach. Woe to me if I do not preach the gospel! ¹⁷If I preach voluntarily, I have a reward; but if not voluntarily, I am simply discharging the trust committed to me. ¹⁸What then is my reward? Just this: that in preaching the gospel I may offer it free of charge, and so not make use of my rights in preaching it.

¹⁹Though I am free and belong to no man, I make myself a slave to everyone, to win as many as possible. ²⁰To the Jews I became like a Jew, to win the Jews. To those under the law I became like one under the law (though I myself am not under the law), so as to win those under the law. ²¹To those not having the law I became like one not having the law (though I am not free from God's law but am under Christ's law), so as to win those not having the law. ²²To the weak I became weak, to win the weak. I have become all things to all men so that by all possible means I might save some. ²³I do all this for the sake of the gospel, that I may share in its blessings.

²⁴Do you not know that in a race all the runners run, but only one gets the prize? Run in such a way as to get the prize. ²⁵Everyone who competes in the games goes into strict training. They do it to get a crown that will not last; but we do it to get a crown that will last forever. ²⁶Therefore I do not run like a man running aimlessly; I do not fight like a man beating the air. ²⁷No, I beat my body and make it my slave so that after I have preached to others, I myself will not be disqualified for the prize.

ᵃ5 That is, Peter ᵇ9 Deut. 25:4

Warnings From Israel's History

10 For I do not want you to be ignorant of the fact, brothers, that our forefathers were all under the cloud and that they all passed through the sea. ²They were all baptized into Moses in the cloud and in the sea. ³They all ate the same spiritual food ⁴and drank the same spiritual drink; for they drank from the spiritual rock that accompanied them, and that rock was Christ. ⁵Nevertheless, God was not pleased with most of them; their bodies were scattered over the desert.

⁶Now these things occurred as examples*ᵃ* to keep us from setting our hearts on evil things as they did. ⁷Do not be idolaters, as some of them were; as it is written: "The people sat down to eat and drink and got up to indulge in pagan revelry."*ᵇ* ⁸We should not commit sexual immorality, as some of them did—and in one day twenty-three thousand of them died. ⁹We should not test the Lord, as some of them did—and were killed by snakes. ¹⁰And do not grumble, as some of them did—and were killed by the destroying angel.

¹¹These things happened to them as examples and were written down as warnings for us, on whom the fulfillment of the ages has come. ¹²So, if you think you are standing firm, be careful that you don't fall! ¹³No temptation has seized you except what is common to man. And God is faithful; he will not let you be tempted beyond what you can bear. But when you are tempted, he will also provide a way out so that you can stand up under it.

Idol Feasts and the Lord's Supper

¹⁴Therefore, my dear friends, flee from idolatry. ¹⁵I speak to sensible people; judge for yourselves what I say. ¹⁶Is not the cup of thanksgiving for which we give thanks a participation in the blood of Christ? And is not the bread that we break a participation in the body of Christ? ¹⁷Because there is one loaf, we, who are many, are one body, for we all partake of the one loaf.

¹⁸Consider the people of Israel: Do not those who eat the sacrifices participate in the altar? ¹⁹Do I mean then that a sacrifice offered to an idol is anything, or that an idol is anything? ²⁰No, but the sacrifices of pagans are offered to demons, not to God, and I do not want you to be participants with demons. ²¹You cannot drink the cup of the Lord and the cup of demons too; you cannot have a part in both the Lord's table and the table of demons. ²²Are we trying to arouse the Lord's jealousy? Are we stronger than he?

The Believer's Freedom

²³"Everything is permissible" —but not everything is beneficial. "Everything is permissible"—but not everything is constructive. ²⁴Nobody should seek his own good, but the good of others.

²⁵Eat anything sold in the meat market without raising questions of conscience, ²⁶for, "The earth is the Lord's, and everything in it."*ᶜ*

²⁷If some unbeliever invites you to a meal and you want to go, eat whatever is put before you with-

93
Th 3:3,4

84
2Co 5:14,15

ᵃ6 Or *types*; also in verse 11   *ᵇ7* Exodus 32:6   *ᶜ26* Psalm 24:1

out raising questions of conscience. 28But if anyone says to you, "This has been offered in sacrifice," then do not eat it, both for the sake of the man who told you and for conscience' sake^a—

30
2Co 3:17

29the other man's conscience, I mean, not yours. For why should my freedom be judged by another's conscience? 30If I take part in the meal with thankfulness, why am I denounced because of something I thank God for?

21
Eph 5:18

31So whether you eat or drink or whatever you do, do it all for the glory of God. 32Do not cause anyone to stumble, whether Jews, Greeks or the church of God— 33even as I try to please everybody in every way. For I am not seeking my own good but the good of many, so that they may

11 be saved. 1Follow my example, as I follow the example of Christ.

Propriety in Worship

2I praise you for remembering me in everything and for holding to the teachings,^b just as I passed them on to you.

3Now I want you to realize that the head of every man is Christ, and the head of the woman is man, and the head of Christ is God. 4Every man who prays or prophesies with his head covered dishonors his head. 5And every woman who prays or prophesies with her head uncovered dishonors her head—it is just as though her head were shaved. 6If a woman does not cover her head, she should have her hair cut off; and if it is a disgrace for a woman to have her

hair cut or shaved off, she should cover her head. 7A man ought not to cover his head,^c since he is the image and glory of God; but the woman is the glory of man. 8For man did not come from woman, but woman from man; 9neither was man created for woman, but woman for man. 10For this reason, and because of the angels, the woman ought to have a sign of authority on her head.

11In the Lord, however, woman is not independent of man, nor is man independent of woman. 12For as woman came from man, so also man is born of woman. But everything comes from God. 13Judge for yourselves: Is it proper for a woman to pray to God with her head uncovered? 14Does not the very nature of things teach you that if a man has long hair, it is a disgrace to him, 15but that if a woman has long hair, it is her glory? For long hair is given to her as a covering. 16If anyone wants to be contentious about this, we have no other practice—nor do the churches of God.

The Lord's Supper

17In the following directives I have no praise for you, for your meetings do more harm than good. 18In the first place, I hear that when you come together as a church, there are divisions among you, and to some extent I believe it. 19No doubt there have to be differences among you to show which of you have God's approval. 20When you come together, it is not the Lord's Supper

^a28 Some manuscripts conscience' sake, for "the earth is the Lord's and everything in it" ^b2 Or traditions   4-7 Or 4Every man who prays or prophesies with long hair dishonors his head. 5And every woman who prays or prophesies with no covering of hair, on her head dishonors her head—she is just like one of the "shorn women." 6If a woman has no covering, let her be for now with short hair, but since it is a disgrace for a woman to have her hair shorn or shaved, she should grow it again. 7A man ought not to have long hair

you eat, ²¹for as you eat, each of you goes ahead without waiting for anybody else. One remains hungry, another gets drunk. ²²Don't you have homes to eat and drink in? Or do you despise the church of God and humiliate those who have nothing? What shall I say to you? Shall I praise you for this? Certainly not!

²³For I received from the Lord what I also passed on to you: The Lord Jesus, on the night he was betrayed, took bread, ²⁴and when he had given thanks, he broke it and said, "This is my body, which is for you; do this in remembrance of me." ²⁵In the same way, after supper he took the cup, saying, "This cup is the new covenant in my blood; do this, whenever you drink it, in remembrance of me." ²⁶For whenever you eat this bread and drink this cup, you proclaim the Lord's death until he comes.

²⁷Therefore, whoever eats the bread or drinks the cup of the Lord in an unworthy manner will be guilty of sinning against the body and blood of the Lord. ²⁸A man ought to examine himself before he eats of the bread and drinks of the cup. ²⁹For anyone who eats and drinks without recognizing the body of the Lord eats and drinks judgment on himself. ³⁰That is why many among you are weak and sick, and a number of you have fallen asleep. ³¹But if we judged ourselves, we would not come under judgment. ³²When we are judged by the Lord, we are being disciplined so that we will not be condemned with the world.

³³So then, my brothers, when you come together to eat, wait for each other. ³⁴If anyone is hungry, he should eat at home, so that

when you meet together it may not result in judgment.

And when I come I will give further directions.

Spiritual Gifts

12 Now about spiritual gifts, brothers, I do not want you to be ignorant. ²You know that when you were pagans, somehow or other you were influenced and led astray to mute idols. ³Therefore I tell you that no one who is speaking by the Spirit of God says, "Jesus be cursed," and no one can say, "Jesus is Lord," except by the Holy Spirit.

⁴There are different kinds of gifts, but the same Spirit. ⁵There are different kinds of service, but the same Lord. ⁶There are different kinds of working, but the same God works all of them in all men.

⁷Now to each one the manifestation of the Spirit is given for the common good. ⁸To one there is given through the Spirit the message of wisdom, to another the message of knowledge by means of the same Spirit, ⁹to another faith by the same Spirit, to another gifts of healing by that one Spirit, ¹⁰to another miraculous powers, to another prophecy, to another distinguishing between spirits, to another speaking in different kinds of tongues,ᵃ and to still another the interpretation of tongues.ᵃ ¹¹All these are the work of one and the same Spirit, and he gives them to each one, just as he determines.

One Body, Many Parts

¹²The body is a unit, though it is made up of many parts; and though all its parts are many, they form one body. So it is with Christ. ¹³For we were all baptized

---

Margin references:

8 Mth 2:19-22

17 Eph 6:1-4

60 2Co 5:17-21

87 2Co 5:5

39 Heb 2:4

95 1Co 12:28

ᵃ10 Or languages; also in verse 28

by^a one Spirit into one body—whether Jews or Greeks, slave or free—and we were all given the one Spirit to drink.

¹⁴Now the body is not made up of one part but of many. ¹⁵If the foot should say, "Because I am not a hand, I do not belong to the body," it would not for that reason cease to be part of the body. ¹⁶And if the ear should say, "Because I am not an eye, I do not belong to the body," it would not for that reason cease to be part of the body. ¹⁷If the whole body were an eye, where would the sense of hearing be? If the whole body were an ear, where would the sense of smell be? ¹⁸But in fact God has arranged the parts in the body, every one of them, just as he wanted them to be. ¹⁹If they were all one part, where would the body be? ²⁰As it is, there are many parts, but one body.

²¹The eye cannot say to the hand, "I don't need you!" And the head cannot say to the feet, "I don't need you!" ²²On the contrary, those parts of the body that seem to be weaker are indispensable, ²³and the parts that we think are less honorable we treat with special honor. And the parts that are unpresentable are treated with special modesty, ²⁴while our presentable parts need no special treatment. But God has combined the members of the body and has given greater honor to the parts that lacked it, ²⁵so that there should be no division in the body, but that its parts should have equal concern for each other. ²⁶If one part suffers, every part suffers with it; if one part is honored, every part rejoices with it.

²⁷Now you are the body of Christ, and each one of you is a part of it. ²⁸And in the church God has appointed first of all apostles, second prophets, third teachers, then workers of miracles, also those having gifts of healing, those able to help others, those with gifts of administration, and those speaking in different kinds of tongues. ²⁹Are all apostles? Are all prophets? Are all teachers? Do all work miracles? ³⁰Do all have gifts of healing? Do all speak in tongues^b? Do all interpret? ³¹But eagerly desire^c the greater gifts.

Love

And now I will show you the most excellent way.

13 If I speak in the tongues^d of men and of angels, but have not love, I am only a resounding gong or a clanging cymbal. ²If I have the gift of prophecy and can fathom all mysteries and all knowledge, and if I have a faith that can move mountains, but have not love, I am nothing. ³If I give all I possess to the poor and surrender my body to the flames,^e but have not love, I gain nothing.

⁴Love is patient, love is kind. It does not envy, it does not boast, it is not proud. ⁵It is not rude, it is not self-seeking, it is not easily angered, it keeps no record of wrongs. ⁶Love does not delight in evil but rejoices with the truth. ⁷It always protects, always trusts, always hopes, always perseveres.

⁸Love never fails. But where there are prophecies, they will cease; where there are tongues, they will be stilled; where there is knowledge, it will pass away. ⁹For we know in part and we prophesy in part, ¹⁰but when perfection comes, the imperfect

Cross references (right margin):

95 1Co 12:36
95 1Co 13:1
55 Gal 6:2
95 1Co 14:15
64 1Th 5:14
67 2Co 12:12
66 Php 3:12

---

^a13 Or *with; or in*   ^b30 Or *other languages*   ^c31 Or *But you are eagerly desiring*
^d1 Or *languages*   ^e3 Some early manuscripts *body that I may boast*

disappears. [11]When I was a child, I talked like a child, I thought like a child, I reasoned like a child. When I became a man, I put childish ways behind me. [12]Now we see but a poor reflection as in a mirror; then we shall see face to face. Now I know in part; then I shall know fully, even as I am fully known.

[13]And now these three remain: faith, hope and love. But the greatest of these is love.

Gifts of Prophecy and Tongues

95
1Co 14:22

14 Follow the way of love and eagerly desire spiritual gifts, especially the gift of prophecy. [2]For anyone who speaks in a tongue[a] does not speak to men but to God. Indeed, no one understands him; he utters mysteries with his spirit.[b] [3]But everyone who prophesies speaks to men for their strengthening, encouragement and comfort. [4]He who speaks in a tongue edifies himself, but he who prophesies edifies the church. [5]I would like every one of you to speak in tongues,[c] but I would rather have you prophesy. He who prophesies is greater than one who speaks in tongues,[c] unless he interprets, so that the church may be edified.

[6]Now, brothers, if I come to you and speak in tongues, what good will I be to you, unless I bring you some revelation or knowledge or prophecy or word of instruction? [7]Even in the case of lifeless things that make sounds, such as the flute or harp, how will anyone know what tune is being played unless there is a distinction in the notes? [8]Again, if the trumpet does not sound a clear call, who will get ready for battle? [9]So it is

with you. Unless you speak intelligible words with your tongue, how will anyone know what you are saying? You will just be speaking into the air. [10]Undoubtedly there are all sorts of languages in the world, yet none of them is without meaning. [11]If then I do not grasp the meaning of what someone is saying, I am a foreigner to the speaker, and he is a foreigner to me. [12]So it is with you. Since you are eager to have spiritual gifts, try to excel in gifts that build up the church.

[13]For this reason anyone who speaks in a tongue should pray that he may interpret what he says. [14]For if I pray in a tongue, my spirit prays, but my mind is unfruitful. [15]So what shall I do? I will pray with my spirit, but I will also pray with my mind; I will sing with my spirit, but I will also sing with my mind. [16]If you are praising God with your spirit, how can one who finds himself among those who do not understand[d] say "Amen" to your thanksgiving, since he does not know what you are saying? [17]You may be giving thanks well enough, but the other man is not edified.

[18]I thank God that I speak in tongues more than all of you. [19]But in the church I would rather speak five intelligible words to instruct others than ten thousand words in a tongue.

[20]Brothers, stop thinking like children. In regard to evil be infants, but in your thinking be adults. [21]In the Law it is written:

"Through men of strange
        tongues
    and through the lips of
        foreigners
I will speak to this people,

---

[a]2 Or *another language;* also in verses 4, 13, 14, 19, 26 and 27   [b]2 Or *by the Spirit*
[c]5 Or *other languages;* also in verses 6, 18, 22, 23 and 39   [d]16 Or *among the inquirers*

but even then they will not
   listen to me,"[a]
says the Lord.

95
1Co 14:39,40

[22]Tongues, then, are a sign, not for believers but for unbelievers; prophecy, however, is for believers, not for unbelievers. [23]So if the whole church comes together and everyone speaks in tongues, and some who do not understand[b] or some unbelievers come in, will they not say that you are out of your mind? [24]But if an unbeliever or someone who does not understand[c] comes in while everybody is prophesying, he will be convinced by all that he is a sinner and will be judged by all, [25]and the secrets of his heart will be laid bare. So he will fall down and worship God, exclaiming, "God is really among you!"

Orderly Worship

[26]What then shall we say, brothers? When you come together, everyone has a hymn, or a word of instruction, a revelation, a tongue or an interpretation. All of these must be done for the strengthening of the church. [27]If anyone speaks in a tongue, two—or at the most three—should speak, one at a time, and someone must interpret. [28]If there is no interpreter, the speaker should keep quiet in the church and speak to himself and God.

[29]Two or three prophets should speak, and the others should weigh carefully what is said. [30]And if a revelation comes to someone who is sitting down, the first speaker should stop. [31]For you can all prophesy in turn so that everyone may be instructed and encouraged. [32]The spirits of prophets are subject to the control of prophets. [33]For God is not a God of disorder but of peace.

As in all the congregations of the saints, [34]women should remain silent in the churches. They are not allowed to speak, but must be in submission, as the Law says. [35]If they want to inquire about something, they should ask their own husbands at home; for it is disgraceful for a woman to speak in the church.

[36]Did the word of God originate with you? Or are you the only people it has reached? [37]If anybody thinks he is a prophet or spiritually gifted, let him acknowledge that what I am writing to you is the Lord's command. [38]If he ignores this, he himself will be ignored.[d]

[39]Therefore, my brothers, be eager to prophesy, and do not forbid speaking in tongues. [40]But everything should be done in a fitting and orderly way.

95
Heb 2:4

The Resurrection of Christ

15 Now, brothers, I want to remind you of the gospel I preached to you, which you received and on which you have taken your stand. [2]By this gospel you are saved, if you hold firmly to the word I preached to you. Otherwise, you have believed in vain.

[3]For what I received I passed on to you as of first importance[e]: that Christ died for our sins according to the Scriptures, [4]that he was buried, that he was raised on the third day according to the Scriptures, [5]and that he appeared to Peter,[f] and then to the Twelve. [6]After that, he appeared to more

---

[a]21 Isaiah 28:11,12   [b]23 Or some inquirers   [c]24 Or or some inquirer   [d]38 Some
manuscripts If he is ignorant of this, let him be ignorant   [e]3 Or you at the first
[f]5 Greek Cephas

than five hundred of the brothers at the same time, most of whom are still living, though some have fallen asleep. [7]Then he appeared to James, then to all the apostles, [8]and last of all he appeared to me also, as to one abnormally born.

[9]For I am the least of the apostles and do not even deserve to be called an apostle, because I persecuted the church of God. [10]But by the grace of God I am what I am, and his grace to me was not without effect. No, I worked harder than all of them—yet not I, but the grace of God that was with me. [11]Whether, then, it was I or they, this is what we preach, and this is what you believed.

94
2Co 2:14

The Resurrection of the Dead

[12]But if it is preached that Christ has been raised from the dead, how can some of you say that there is no resurrection of the dead? [13]If there is no resurrection of the dead, then not even Christ has been raised. [14]And if Christ has not been raised, our preaching is useless and so is your faith. [15]More than that, we are then found to be false witnesses about God, for we have testified about God that he raised Christ from the dead. But he did not raise him if in fact the dead are not raised. [16]For if the dead are not raised, then Christ has not been raised either. [17]And if Christ has not been raised, your faith is futile; you are still in your sins. [18]Then those also who have fallen asleep in Christ are lost. [19]If only for this life we have hope in Christ, we are to be pitied more than all men.

[20]But Christ has indeed been raised from the dead, the first-fruits of those who have fallen

75
15:42-44

asleep. [21]For since death came through a man, the resurrection of the dead comes also through a man. [22]For as in Adam all die, so in Christ all will be made alive. [23]But each in his own turn: Christ, the firstfruits; then, when he comes, those who belong to him. [24]Then the end will come, when he hands over the kingdom to God the Father after he has destroyed all dominion, authority and power. [25]For he must reign until he has put all his enemies under his feet. [26]The last enemy to be destroyed is death. [27]For he "has put everything under his feet."[a] Now when it says that "everything" has been put under him, it is clear that this does not include God himself, who put everything under Christ. [28]When he has done this, then the Son himself will be made subject to him who put everything under him, so that God may be all in all.

[29]Now if there is no resurrection, what will those do who are baptized for the dead? If the dead are not raised at all, why are people baptized for them? [30]And as for us, why do we endanger ourselves every hour? [31]I die every day—I mean that, brothers—just as surely as I glory over you in Christ Jesus our Lord. [32]If I fought wild beasts in Ephesus for merely human reasons, what have I gained? If the dead are not raised,

"Let us eat and drink,
  for tomorrow we die."[b]

[33]Do not be misled: "Bad company corrupts good character." [34]Come back to your senses as you ought, and stop sinning; for there are some who are ignorant of God—I say this to your shame.

[a]27 Psalm 8:6   [b]32 Isaiah 22:13

The Resurrection Body

[35]But someone may ask, "How are the dead raised? With what kind of body will they come?" [36]How foolish! What you sow does not come to life unless it dies. [37]When you sow, you do not plant the body that will be, but just a seed, perhaps of wheat or of something else. [38]But God gives it a body as he has determined, and to each kind of seed he gives its own body. [39]All flesh is not the same: Men have one kind of flesh, animals have another, birds another and fish another. [40]There are also heavenly bodies and there are earthly bodies; but the splendor of the heavenly bodies is one kind, and the splendor of the earthly bodies is another. [41]The sun has one kind of splendor, the moon another and the stars another; and star differs from star in splendor.

[42]So will it be with the resurrection of the dead. The body that is sown is perishable, it is raised imperishable; [43]it is sown in dishonor, it is raised in glory; it is sown in weakness, it is raised in power; [44]it is sown a natural body, it is raised a spiritual body.

If there is a natural body, there is also a spiritual body. [45]So it is written: "The first man Adam became a living being"[a]; the last Adam, a life-giving spirit. [46]The spiritual did not come first, but the natural, and after that the spiritual. [47]The first man was of the dust of the earth, the second man from heaven. [48]As was the earthly man, so are those who are of the earth; and as is the man from heaven, so also are those who are of heaven. [49]And just as we have borne the likeness of the earthly man, so shall we[b] bear the likeness of the man from heaven.

[50]I declare to you, brothers, that flesh and blood cannot inherit the kingdom of God, nor does the perishable inherit the imperishable. [51]Listen, I tell you a mystery: We will not all sleep, but we will all be changed— [52]in a flash, in the twinkling of an eye, at the last trumpet. For the trumpet will sound, the dead will be raised imperishable, and we will be changed. [53]For the perishable must clothe itself with the imperishable, and the mortal with immortality. [54]When the perishable has been clothed with the imperishable, and the mortal with immortality, then the saying that is written will come true: "Death has been swallowed up in victory."[c]

[55]"Where, O death, is your victory?
    Where, O death, is your sting?"[d]

[56]The sting of death is sin, and the power of sin is the law. [57]But thanks be to God! He gives us the victory through our Lord Jesus Christ.

[58]Therefore, my dear brothers, stand firm. Let nothing move you. Always give yourselves fully to the work of the Lord, because you know that your labor in the Lord is not in vain.

The Collection for God's People

16 Now about the collection for God's people: Do what I told the Galatian churches to do. [2]On the first day of every week, each one of you should set aside a sum of money in keeping with his income, saving it up, so that when I come no collections

---

[a]45 Gen. 2:7   [b]49 Some early manuscripts *so let us*   [c]54 Isaiah 25:8
[d]55 Hosea 13:14

margin references:
75 1Co 15:50-52
75 Php 3:20
53 2Co 4:8,9

will have to be made. ³Then, when I arrive, I will give letters of introduction to the men you approve and send them with your gift to Jerusalem. ⁴If it seems advisable for me to go also, they will accompany me.

Personal Requests

⁵After I go through Macedonia, I will come to you—for I will be going through Macedonia. ⁶Perhaps I will stay with you awhile, or even spend the winter, so that you can help me on my journey, wherever I go. ⁷I do not want to see you now and make only a passing visit; I hope to spend some time with you, if the Lord permits. ⁸But I will stay on at Ephesus until Pentecost, ⁹because a great door for effective work has opened to me, and there are many who oppose me.

¹⁰If Timothy comes, see to it that he has nothing to fear while he is with you, for he is carrying on the work of the Lord, just as I am. ¹¹No one, then, should refuse to accept him. Send him on his way in peace so that he may return to me. I am expecting him along with the brothers.

¹²Now about our brother Apollos: I strongly urged him to go to you with the brothers. He was quite unwilling to go now, but he will go when he has the opportunity.

¹³Be on your guard; stand firm in the faith; be men of courage; be strong. ¹⁴Do everything in love.

¹⁵You know that the household of Stephanas were the first converts in Achaia, and they have devoted themselves to the service of the saints. I urge you, brothers, ¹⁶to submit to such as these and to everyone who joins in the work, and labors at it. ¹⁷I was glad when Stephanas, Fortunatus and Achaicus arrived, because they have supplied what was lacking from you. ¹⁸For they refreshed my spirit and yours also. Such men deserve recognition.

Final Greetings

¹⁹The churches in the province of Asia send you greetings. Aquila and Priscilla[a] greet you warmly in the Lord, and so does the church that meets at their house. ²⁰All the brothers here send you greetings. Greet one another with a holy kiss.

²¹I, Paul, write this greeting in my own hand.

²²If anyone does not love the Lord—a curse be on him. Come, O Lord[b]!

²³The grace of the Lord Jesus be with you.

²⁴My love to all of you in Christ Jesus. Amen.[c]

2 Corinthians

1 Paul, an apostle of Christ Jesus by the will of God, and Timothy our brother,

To the church of God in Corinth, together with all the saints throughout Achaia:

²Grace and peace to you from God our Father and the Lord Jesus Christ.

The God of All Comfort

³Praise be to the God and Fa-

*19 Greek *Prisca,* a variant of *Priscilla* *22 In Aramaic the expression *Come, O Lord* is *Marana tha.* *24 Some manuscripts do not have *Amen.*

35
Gal 6:2

ther of our Lord Jesus Christ, the Father of compassion and the God of all comfort, [4]who comforts us in all our troubles, so that we can comfort those in any trouble with the comfort we ourselves have received from God. [5]For just as the sufferings of Christ flow over into our lives, so also through Christ our comfort overflows. [6]If we are distressed, it is for your comfort and salvation; if we are comforted, it is for your comfort, which produces in you patient endurance of the same sufferings we suffer. [7]And our hope for you is firm, because we know that just as you share in our sufferings, so also you share in our comfort.

[8]We do not want you to be uninformed, brothers, about the hardships we suffered in the province of Asia. We were under great pressure, far beyond our ability to endure, so that we despaired even of life. [9]Indeed, in our hearts we felt the sentence of death. But this happened that we might not rely on ourselves but on God, who raises the dead. [10]He has delivered us from such a deadly peril, and he will deliver us. On him we have set our hope that he will continue to deliver us, [11]as you help us by your prayers. Then many will give thanks on our[a] behalf for the gracious favor granted us in answer to the prayers of many.

Paul's Change of Plans

[12]Now this is our boast: Our conscience testifies that we have conducted ourselves in the world, and especially in our relations with you, in the holiness and sincerity that are from God. We have done so not according to worldly wisdom but according to God's grace. [13]For we do not write you anything you cannot read or understand. And I hope that, [14]as you have understood us in part, you will come to understand fully that you can boast of us just as we will boast of you in the day of the Lord Jesus.

[15]Because I was confident of this, I planned to visit you first so that you might benefit twice. [16]I planned to visit you on my way to Macedonia and to come back to you from Macedonia, and then to have you send me on my way to Judea. [17]When I planned this, did I do it lightly? Or do I make my plans in a worldly manner so that in the same breath I say, "Yes, yes" and "No, no"?

[18]But as surely as God is faithful, our message to you is not "Yes" and "No." [19]For the Son of God, Jesus Christ, who was preached among you by me and Silas[b] and Timothy, was not "Yes" and "No," but in him it has always been "Yes." [20]For no matter how many promises God has made, they are "Yes" in Christ. And so through him the "Amen" is spoken by us to the glory of God. [21]Now it is God who makes both us and you stand firm in Christ. He anointed us, [22]set his seal of ownership on us, and put his Spirit in our hearts as a deposit, guaranteeing what is to come.

[23]I call God as my witness that it was in order to spare you that I did not return to Corinth. [24]Not that we lord it over your faith, but we work with you for your joy, because it is by faith you stand firm. [1]So I made up my mind that I would not make another painful visit to you. [2]For if I grieve you, who is left to make me glad but you whom I have

2

---

[a]11 Many manuscripts *your*   [b]19 Greek *Silvanus*, a variant of *Silas*

grieved? [3]I wrote as I did so that when I came I should not be distressed by those who ought to make me rejoice. I had confidence in all of you, that you would all share my joy. [4]For I wrote you out of great distress and anguish of heart and with many tears, not to grieve you but to let you know the depth of my love for you.

Forgiveness for the Sinner

[5]If anyone has caused grief, he has not so much grieved me as he has grieved all of you, to some extent—not to put it too severely. [6]The punishment inflicted on him by the majority is sufficient for him. [7]Now instead, you ought to forgive and comfort him, so that he will not be overwhelmed by excessive sorrow. [8]I urge you, therefore, to reaffirm your love for him. [9]The reason I wrote you was to see if you would stand the test and be obedient in everything. [10]If you forgive anyone, I also forgive him. And what I have forgiven—if there was anything to forgive—I have forgiven in the sight of Christ for your sake, [11]in order that Satan might not outwit us. For we are not unaware of his schemes.

Ministers of the New Covenant

[12]Now when I went to Troas to preach the gospel of Christ and found that the Lord had opened a door for me, [13]I still had no peace of mind, because I did not find my brother Titus there. So I said good-by to them and went on to Macedonia.

[14]But thanks be to God, who always leads us in triumphal procession in Christ and through us spreads everywhere the fragrance of the knowledge of him. [15]For we are to God the aroma of Christ among those who are being saved and those who are perishing. [16]To the one we are the smell of death; to the other, the fragrance of life. And who is equal to such a task? [17]Unlike so many, we do not peddle the word of God for profit. On the contrary, in Christ we speak before God with sincerity, like men sent from God.

3 Are we beginning to commend ourselves again? Or do we need, like some people, letters of recommendation to you or from you? [2]You yourselves are our letter, written on our hearts, known and read by everybody. [3]You show that you are a letter from Christ, the result of our ministry, written not with ink but with the Spirit of the living God, not on tablets of stone but on tablets of human hearts.

[4]Such confidence as this is ours through Christ before God. [5]Not that we are competent in ourselves to claim anything for ourselves, but our competence comes from God. [6]He has made us competent as ministers of a new covenant—not of the letter but of the Spirit; for the letter kills, but the Spirit gives life.

The Glory of the New Covenant

[7]Now if the ministry that brought death, which was engraved in letters on stone, came with glory, so that the Israelites could not look steadily at the face of Moses because of its glory, fading though it was, [8]will not the ministry of the Spirit be even more glorious? [9]If the ministry that condemns men is glorious, how much more glorious is the ministry that brings righteous-

ness! [10]For what was glorious has no glory now in comparison with the surpassing glory. [11]And if what was fading away came with glory, how much greater is the glory of that which lasts!

[12]Therefore, since we have such a hope, we are very bold. [13]We are not like Moses, who would put a veil over his face to keep the Israelites from gazing at it while the radiance was fading away. [14]But their minds were made dull, for to this day the same veil remains when the old covenant is read. It has not been removed, because only in Christ is it taken away. [15]Even to this day when Moses is read, a veil covers their hearts. [16]But whenever anyone turns to the Lord, the veil is taken away. [17]Now the Lord is the Spirit, and where the Spirit of the Lord is, there is freedom. [18]And we, who with unveiled faces all reflect[a] the Lord's glory, are being transformed into his likeness with ever-increasing glory, which comes from the Lord, who is the Spirit.

30
Gal 5:1

Treasures in Jars of Clay

16
2Co 4:16,17

4 Therefore, since through God's mercy we have this ministry, we do not lose heart. [2]Rather, we have renounced secret and shameful ways; we do not use deception, nor do we distort the word of God. On the contrary, by setting forth the truth plainly we commend ourselves to every man's conscience in the sight of God. [3]And even if our gospel is veiled, it is veiled to those who are perishing. [4]The god of this age has blinded the minds of unbelievers, so that they cannot see the light of the gospel of the glory of Christ, who is the image of God. [5]For we do

59
2Co 5:16,17

not preach ourselves, but Jesus Christ as Lord, and ourselves as your servants for Jesus' sake. [6]For God, who said, "Let light shine out of darkness,"[b] made his light shine in our hearts to give us the light of the knowledge of the glory of God in the face of Christ.

[7]But we have this treasure in jars of clay to show that this all-surpassing power is from God and not from us. [8]We are hard pressed on every side, but not crushed; perplexed, but not in despair; [9]persecuted, but not abandoned; struck down, but not destroyed. [10]We always carry around in our body the death of Jesus, so that the life of Jesus may also be revealed in our body. [11]For we who are alive are always being given over to death for Jesus' sake, so that his life may be revealed in our mortal body. [12]So then, death is at work in us, but life is at work in you.

53
2Co 5:1

[13]It is written: "I believed; therefore I have spoken."[c] With that same spirit of faith we also believe and therefore speak, [14]because we know that the one who raised the Lord Jesus from the dead will also raise us with Jesus and present us with you in his presence. [15]All this is for your benefit, so that the grace that is reaching more and more people may cause thanksgiving to overflow to the glory of God.

[16]Therefore we do not lose heart. Though outwardly we are wasting away, yet inwardly we are being renewed day by day. [17]For our light and momentary troubles are achieving for us an eternal glory that far outweighs them all. [18]So we fix our eyes not on what is seen, but on what is unseen. For what is seen is temporary, but what is unseen is eternal.

16
Gal 6:9,10

[a]18 Or *contemplate*   [b]6 Gen. 1:3   [c]13 Psalm 116:10

Our Heavenly Dwelling

53
1p 1:21-23

5 Now we know that if the earthly tent we live in is destroyed, we have a building from God, an eternal house in heaven, not built by human hands. ²Meanwhile we groan, longing to be clothed with our heavenly dwelling, ³because when we are clothed, we will not be found naked. ⁴For while we are in this tent, we groan and are burdened, because we do not wish to be unclothed but to be clothed with our heavenly dwelling, so that what is mortal may be swallowed up by life. ⁵Now it is God who has made us for this very purpose and has given us the Spirit as a deposit, guaranteeing what is to come.

87
Gal 2:20

⁶Therefore we are always confident and know that as long as we are at home in the body we are away from the Lord. ⁷We live by faith, not by sight. ⁸We are confident, I say, and would prefer to be away from the body and at home with the Lord. ⁹So we make it our goal to please him, whether we are at home in the body or away from it. ¹⁰For we must all appear before the judgment seat of Christ, that each one may receive what is due him for the things done while in the body, whether good or bad.

The Ministry of Reconciliation

¹¹Since, then, we know what it is to fear the Lord, we try to persuade men. What we are is plain to God, and I hope it is also plain to your conscience. ¹²We are not trying to commend ourselves to you again, but are giving you an opportunity to take pride in us, so that you can answer those who take pride in what is seen rather than in what is in the heart. ¹³If we are out of our mind, it is for the sake of God; if we are in our right mind, it is for you. ¹⁴For Christ's love compels us, because we are convinced that one died for all, and therefore all died. ¹⁵And he died for all, that those who live should no longer live for themselves but for him who died for them and was raised again.

84
Php 2:3

¹⁶So from now on we regard no one from a worldly point of view. Though we once regarded Christ in this way, we do so no longer. ¹⁷Therefore, if anyone is in Christ, he is a new creation; the old has gone, the new has come! ¹⁸All this is from God, who reconciled us to himself through Christ and gave us the ministry of reconciliation: ¹⁹that God was reconciling the world to himself in Christ, not counting men's sins against them. And he has committed to us the message of reconciliation. ²⁰We are therefore Christ's ambassadors, as though God were making his appeal through us. We implore you on Christ's behalf: Be reconciled to God. ²¹God made him who had no sin to be sinᵃ for us, so that in him we might become the righteousness of God.

59
Eph 4:23

23
Ps 126:6

60
1Ti 3:1-13

71
Eph 2:16

6 As God's fellow workers we urge you not to receive God's grace in vain. ²For he says,

78
Heb 11:6

"In the time of my favor I
    heard you,
and in the day of salvation I
    helped you."ᵇ

I tell you, now is the time of God's favor, now is the day of salvation.

Paul's Hardships

³We put no stumbling block in anyone's path, so that our minis-

---

ᵃ21 Or be a sin offering   ᵇ2 Isaiah 49:8

try will not be discredited. [4]Rather, as servants of God we commend ourselves in every way: in great endurance; in troubles, hardships and distresses; [5]in beatings, imprisonments and riots; in hard work, sleepless nights and hunger; [6]in purity, understanding, patience and kindness; in the Holy Spirit and in sincere love; [7]in truthful speech and in the power of God; with weapons of righteousness in the right hand and in the left; [8]through glory and dishonor, bad report and good report; genuine, yet regarded as impostors; [9]known, yet regarded as unknown; dying, and yet we live on; beaten, and yet not killed; [10]sorrowful, yet always rejoicing; poor, yet making many rich; having nothing, and yet possessing everything.

[11]We have spoken freely to you, Corinthians, and opened wide our hearts to you. [12]We are not withholding our affection from you, but you are withholding yours from us. [13]As a fair exchange—I speak as to my children—open wide your hearts also.

Do Not Be Yoked With Unbelievers

85
Eph 5:6,7

[14]Do not be yoked together with unbelievers. For what do righteousness and wickedness have in common? Or what fellowship can light have with darkness? [15]What harmony is there between Christ and Belial[a]? What does a believer have in common with an unbeliever? [16]What agreement is there between the temple of God and idols? For we are the temple of the living God. As God has said: "I will live with them and walk among them, and I will be their God, and they will be my people."[b]

[17]"Therefore come out from them
and be separate,
says the Lord.
Touch no unclean thing,
and I will receive you."[c]
[18]"I will be a Father to you,
and you will be my sons
and daughters,
says the Lord
Almighty."[d]

7 Since we have these promises, dear friends, let us purify ourselves from everything that contaminates body and spirit, perfecting holiness out of reverence for God.

Paul's Joy

[2]Make room for us in your hearts. We have wronged no one, we have corrupted no one, we have exploited no one. [3]I do not say this to condemn you; I have said before that you have such a place in our hearts that we would live or die with you. [4]I have great confidence in you; I take great pride in you. I am greatly encouraged; in all our troubles my joy knows no bounds.

[5]For when we came into Macedonia, this body of ours had no rest, but we were harassed at every turn—conflicts on the outside, fears within. [6]But God, who comforts the downcast, comforted us by the coming of Titus, [7]and not only by his coming but also by the comfort you had given him. He told us about your longing for me, your deep sorrow, your ardent concern for me, so that my joy was greater than ever.

[8]Even if I caused you sorrow by

---

[a]15 Greek *Beliar*, a variant of *Belial*   [b]16 Lev. 26:12; Jer. 32:38; Ezek. 37:27
[c]17 Isaiah 52:11; Ezek. 20:34,41   [d]18 2 Samuel 7:14; 7:8

my letter, I do not regret it. Though I did regret it—I see that my letter hurt you, but only for a little while— ⁹yet now I am happy, not because you were made sorry, but because your sorrow led you to repentance. For you became sorrowful as God intended and so were not harmed in any way by us. ¹⁰Godly sorrow brings repentance that leads to salvation and leaves no regret, but worldly sorrow brings death. ¹¹See what this godly sorrow has produced in you: what earnestness, what eagerness to clear yourselves, what indignation, what alarm, what longing, what concern, what readiness to see justice done. At every point you have proved yourselves to be innocent in this matter. ¹²So even though I wrote to you, it was not on account of the one who did the wrong or of the injured party, but rather that before God you could see for yourselves how devoted to us you are. ¹³By all this we are encouraged.

In addition to our own encouragement, we were especially delighted to see how happy Titus was, because his spirit has been refreshed by all of you. ¹⁴I had boasted to him about you, and you have not embarrassed me. But just as everything we said to you was true, so our boasting about you to Titus has proved to be true as well. ¹⁵And his affection for you is all the greater when he remembers that you were all obedient, receiving him with fear and trembling. ¹⁶I am glad I can have complete confidence in you.

Generosity Encouraged

8 And now, brothers, we want you to know about the grace that God has given the Mac-

edonian churches. ²Out of the most severe trial, their overflowing joy and their extreme poverty welled up in rich generosity. ³For I testify that they gave as much as they were able, and even beyond their ability. Entirely on their own, ⁴they urgently pleaded with us for the privilege of sharing in this service to the saints. ⁵And they did not do as we expected, but they gave themselves first to the Lord and then to us in keeping with God's will. ⁶So we urged Titus, since he had earlier made a beginning, to bring also to completion this act of grace on your part. ⁷But just as you excel in everything—in faith, in speech, in knowledge, in complete earnestness and in your love for us^a—see that you also excel in this grace of giving.

⁸I am not commanding you, but I want to test the sincerity of your love by comparing it with the earnestness of others. ⁹For you know the grace of our Lord Jesus Christ, that though he was rich, yet for your sakes he became poor, so that you through his poverty might become rich.

¹⁰And here is my advice about what is best for you in this matter: Last year you were the first not only to give but also to have the desire to do so. ¹¹Now finish the work, so that your eager willingness to do it may be matched by your completion of it, according to your means. ¹²For if the willingness is there, the gift is acceptable according to what one has, not according to what he does not have.

¹³Our desire is not that others might be relieved while you are hard pressed, but that there might be equality. ¹⁴At the present time your plenty will supply what they need, so that in

^a7 Some manuscripts *in our love for you*

74
2Ti 2:25

turn their plenty will supply what you need. Then there will be equality, [15]as it is written: "He who gathered much did not have too much, and he who gathered little did not have too little."[a]

Titus Sent to Corinth

[16]I thank God, who put into the heart of Titus the same concern I have for you. [17]For Titus not only welcomed our appeal, but he is coming to you with much enthusiasm and on his own initiative. [18]And we are sending along with him the brother who is praised by all the churches for his service to the gospel. [19]What is more, he was chosen by the churches to accompany us as we carry the offering, which we administer in order to honor the Lord himself and to show our eagerness to help. [20]We want to avoid any criticism of the way we administer this liberal gift. [21]For we are taking pains to do what is right, not only in the eyes of the Lord but also in the eyes of men.

[22]In addition, we are sending with them our brother who has often proved to us in many ways that he is zealous, and now even more so because of his great confidence in you. [23]As for Titus, he is my partner and fellow worker among you; as for our brothers, they are representatives of the churches and an honor to Christ. [24]Therefore show these men the proof of your love and the reason for our pride in you, so that the churches can see it.

9 There is no need for me to write to you about this service to the saints. [2]For I know your eagerness to help, and I have been boasting about it to the Macedonians, telling them that since last year you in Achaia were ready to give; and your en-

thusiasm has stirred most of them to action. [3]But I am sending the brothers in order that our boasting about you in this matter should not prove hollow, but that you may be ready, as I said you would be. [4]For if any Macedonians come with me and find you unprepared, we—not to say anything about you—would be ashamed of having been so confident. [5]So I thought it necessary to urge the brothers to visit you in advance and finish the arrangements for the generous gift you had promised. Then it will be ready as a generous gift, not as one grudgingly given.

Sowing Generously

[6]Remember this: Whoever sows sparingly will also reap sparingly, and whoever sows generously will also reap generously. [7]Each man should give what he has decided in his heart to give, not reluctantly or under compulsion, for God loves a cheerful giver. [8]And God is able to make all grace abound to you, so that in all things at all times, having all that you need, you will abound in every good work. [9]As it is written:

> "He has scattered abroad his
>   gifts to the poor;
> his righteousness endures
>   forever."[b]

[10]Now he who supplies seed to the sower and bread for food will also supply and increase your store of seed and will enlarge the harvest of your righteousness. [11]You will be made rich in every way so that you can be generous on every occasion, and through us your generosity will result in thanksgiving to God.

[12]This service that you perform is not only supplying the needs

61
2Co 9:1

81
Php 1:6

61
1Ti 3:3

---

[a]15 Exodus 16:18 [b]9 Psalm 112:9

of God's people but is also overflowing in many expressions of thanks to God. [13]Because of the service by which you have proved yourselves, men will praise God for the obedience that accompanies your confession of the gospel of Christ, and for your generosity in sharing with them and with everyone else. [14]And in their prayers for you their hearts will go out to you, because of the surpassing grace God has given you. [15]Thanks be to God for his indescribable gift!

Paul's Defense of His Ministry

10 By the meekness and gentleness of Christ, I appeal to you—I, Paul, who am "timid" when face to face with you, but "bold" when away! [2]I beg you that when I come I may not have to be as bold as I expect to be toward some people who think that we live by the standards of this world. [3]For though we live in the world, we do not wage war as the world does. [4]The weapons we fight with are not the weapons of the world. On the contrary, they have divine power to demolish strongholds. [5]We demolish arguments and every pretension that sets itself up against the knowledge of God, and we take captive every thought to make it obedient to Christ. [6]And we will be ready to punish every act of disobedience, once your obedience is complete.

[7]You are looking only on the surface of things.[a] If anyone is confident that he belongs to Christ, he should consider again that we belong to Christ just as

much as he. [8]For even if I boast somewhat freely about the authority the Lord gave us for building you up rather than pulling you down, I will not be ashamed of it. [9]I do not want to seem to be trying to frighten you with my letters. [10]For some say, "His letters are weighty and forceful, but in person he is unimpressive and his speaking amounts to nothing." [11]Such people should realize that what we are in our letters when we are absent, we will be in our actions when we are present.

[12]We do not dare to classify or compare ourselves with some who commend themselves. When they measure themselves by themselves and compare themselves with themselves, they are not wise. [13]We, however, will not boast beyond proper limits, but will confine our boasting to the field God has assigned to us, a field that reaches even to you. [14]We are not going too far in our boasting, as would be the case if we had not come to you, for we did get as far as you with the gospel of Christ. [15]Neither do we go beyond our limits by boasting of work done by others.[b] Our hope is that, as your faith continues to grow, our area of activity among you will greatly expand, [16]so that we can preach the gospel in the regions beyond you. For we do not want to boast about work already done in another man's territory. [17]But, "Let him who boasts boast in the Lord."[c] [18]For it is not the one who commends himself who is approved, but the one whom the Lord commends.

*a*7 Or *Look at the obvious facts*   *b*13-15 Or [13]*We, however, will not boast about things that cannot be measured, but we will boast according to the standard of measurement that the God of measure has assigned us—a measurement that relates even to you.* [14] . . . . [15]*Neither do we boast about things that cannot be measured in regard to the work done by others.*
*c*17 Jer. 9:24

Paul and the False Apostles

11 I hope you will put up with a little of my foolishness; but you are already doing that. ²I am jealous for you with a godly jealousy. I promised you to one husband, to Christ, so that I might present you as a pure virgin to him. ³But I am afraid that just as Eve was deceived by the serpent's cunning, your minds may somehow be led astray from your sincere and pure devotion to Christ. ⁴For if someone comes to you and preaches a Jesus other than the Jesus we preached, or if you receive a different spirit from the one you received, or a different gospel from the one you accepted, you put up with it easily enough. ⁵But I do not think I am in the least inferior to those "super-apostles." ⁶I may not be a trained speaker, but I do have knowledge. We have made this perfectly clear to you in every way.

⁷Was it a sin for me to lower myself in order to elevate you by preaching the gospel of God to you free of charge? ⁸I robbed other churches by receiving support from them so as to serve you. ⁹And when I was with you and needed something, I was not a burden to anyone, for the brothers who came from Macedonia supplied what I needed. I have kept myself from being a burden to you in any way, and will continue to do so. ¹⁰As surely as the truth of Christ is in me, nobody in the regions of Achaia will stop this boasting of mine. ¹¹Why? Because I do not love you? God knows I do! ¹²And I will keep on doing what I am doing in order to cut the ground from under those who want an opportunity to be considered equal with us in the things they boast about.

¹³For such men are false apostles, deceitful workmen, masquerading as apostles of Christ. ¹⁴And no wonder, for Satan himself masquerades as an angel of light. ¹⁵It is not surprising, then, if his servants masquerade as servants of righteousness. Their end will be what their actions deserve.

Paul Boasts About His Sufferings

¹⁶I repeat: Let no one take me for a fool. But if you do, then receive me just as you would a fool, so that I may do a little boasting. ¹⁷In this self-confident boasting I am not talking as the Lord would, but as a fool. ¹⁸Since many are boasting in the way the world does, I too will boast. ¹⁹You gladly put up with fools since you are so wise! ²⁰In fact, you even put up with anyone who enslaves you or exploits you or takes advantage of you or pushes himself forward or slaps you in the face. ²¹To my shame I admit that we were too weak for that!

What anyone else dares to boast about—I am speaking as a fool—I also dare to boast about. ²²Are they Hebrews? So am I. Are they Israelites? So am I. Are they Abraham's descendants? So am I. ²³Are they servants of Christ? (I am out of my mind to talk like this.) I am more. I have worked much harder, been in prison more frequently, been flogged more severely, and been exposed to death again and again. ²⁴Five times I received from the Jews the forty lashes minus one. ²⁵Three times I was beaten with rods, once I was stoned, three times I was shipwrecked, I spent a night and a day in the open sea, ²⁶I have been constantly on the move. I have been in danger from

46
2Co 12:20

86
1Th 3:13

rivers, in danger from bandits, in danger from my own countrymen, in danger from Gentiles; in danger in the city, in danger in the country, in danger at sea; and in danger from false brothers. 27I have labored and toiled and have often gone without sleep; I have known hunger and thirst and have often gone without food; I have been cold and naked. 28Besides everything else, I face daily the pressure of my concern for all the churches. 29Who is weak, and I do not feel weak? Who is led into sin, and I do not inwardly burn?

30If I must boast, I will boast of the things that show my weakness. 31The God and Father of the Lord Jesus, who is to be praised forever, knows that I am not lying. 32In Damascus the governor under King Aretas had the city of the Damascenes guarded in order to arrest me. 33But I was lowered in a basket from a window in the wall and slipped through his hands.

Paul's Vision and His Thorn

12 I must go on boasting. Although there is nothing to be gained, I will go on to visions and revelations from the Lord. 2I know a man in Christ who fourteen years ago was caught up to the third heaven. Whether it was in the body or out of the body I do not know—God knows. 3And I know that this man—whether in the body or apart from the body I do not know, but God knows— 4was caught up to paradise. He heard inexpressible things, things that man is not permitted to tell. 5I will boast about a man like that, but I will not boast about myself, except about my weaknesses. 6Even if I should choose to boast, I would not be a fool, because I would be speaking the truth. But I refrain, so no one will think more of me than is warranted by what I do or say.

7To keep me from becoming conceited because of these surpassingly great revelations, there was given me a thorn in my flesh, a messenger of Satan, to torment me. 8Three times I pleaded with the Lord to take it away from me. 9But he said to me, "My grace is sufficient for you, for my power is made perfect in weakness." Therefore I will boast all the more gladly about my weaknesses, so that Christ's power may rest on me. 10That is why, for Christ's sake, I delight in weaknesses, in insults, in hardships, in persecutions, in difficulties. For when I am weak, then I am strong.

91
Php 1:29

Paul's Concern for the Corinthians

11I have made a fool of myself, but you drove me to it. I ought to have been commended by you, for I am not in the least inferior to the "super-apostles," even though I am nothing. 12The things that mark an apostle— signs, wonders and miracles— were done among you with great perseverance. 13How were you inferior to the other churches, except that I was never a burden to you? Forgive me this wrong!

67
2Ti 1:12

14Now I am ready to visit you for the third time, and I will not be a burden to you, because what I want is not your possessions but you. After all, children should not have to save up for their parents, but parents for their children. 15So I will very gladly spend for you everything I have and expend myself as well. If I love you more, will you love me less? 16Be that as it may, I have not been a burden to you. Yet, crafty fellow that I am, I caught you by trickery! [17]Did I exploit you through any of the men I sent you? [18]I urged Titus to go to you and I sent our brother with him. Titus did not exploit you, did he? Did we not act in the same spirit and follow the same course?

[19]Have you been thinking all along that we have been defending ourselves to you? We have been speaking in the sight of God as those in Christ; and everything we do, dear friends, is for your strengthening. [20]For I am afraid that when I come I may not find you as I want you to be, and you may not find me as you want me to be. I fear that there may be quarreling, jealousy, outbursts of anger, factions, slander, gossip, arrogance and disorder. [21]I am afraid that when I come again my God will humble me before you, and I will be grieved over many who have sinned earlier and have not repented of the impurity, sexual sin and debauchery in which they have indulged.

Final Warnings

13 This will be my third visit to you. "Every matter must be established by the testimony of two or three witnesses."[a] [2]I already gave you a warning when I was with you the second time. I now repeat it while absent: On my return I will not spare those who sinned earlier or any of the others, [3]since you are demanding proof that Christ is speaking through me. He is not weak in dealing with you, but is powerful among you.

[4]For to be sure, he was crucified in weakness, yet he lives by God's power. Likewise, we are weak in him, yet by God's power we will live with him to serve you.

[5]Examine yourselves to see whether you are in the faith; test yourselves. Do you not realize that Christ Jesus is in you—unless, of course, you fail the test? [6]And I trust that you will discover that we have not failed the test. [7]Now we pray to God that you will not do anything wrong. Not that people will see that we have stood the test but that you will do what is right even though we may seem to have failed. [8]For we cannot do anything against the truth, but only for the truth. [9]We are glad whenever we are weak but you are strong; and our prayer is for your perfection. [10]This is why I write these things when I am absent, that when I come I may not have to be harsh in my use of authority—the authority the Lord gave me for building you up, not for tearing you down.

Final Greetings

[11]Finally, brothers, good-by. Aim for perfection, listen to my appeal, be of one mind, live in peace. And the God of love and peace will be with you.

[12]Greet one another with a holy kiss. [13]All the saints send their greetings.

[14]May the grace of the Lord Jesus Christ, and the love of God, and the fellowship of the Holy Spirit be with you all.

46
Gal 5:20,21

79
1Th 5:23

---

[a]*1* Deut. 19:15

Galatians

1 Paul, an apostle—sent not from men nor by man, but by Jesus Christ and God the Father, who raised him from the dead— ²and all the brothers with me,

To the churches in Galatia:

³Grace and peace to you from God our Father and the Lord Jesus Christ, ⁴who gave himself for our sins to rescue us from the present evil age, according to the will of our God and Father, ⁵to whom be glory for ever and ever. Amen.

No Other Gospel

⁶I am astonished that you are so quickly deserting the one who called you by the grace of Christ and are turning to a different gospel— ⁷which is really no gospel at all. Evidently some people are throwing you into confusion and are trying to pervert the gospel of Christ. ⁸But even if we or an angel from heaven should preach a gospel other than the one we preached to you, let him be eternally condemned! ⁹As we have already said, so now I say again: If anybody is preaching to you a gospel other than what you accepted, let him be eternally condemned!

¹⁰Am I now trying to win the approval of men, or of God? Or am I trying to please men? If I were still trying to please men, I would not be a servant of Christ.

Paul Called by God

¹¹I want you to know, brothers, that the gospel I preached is not something that man made up. ¹²I did not receive it from any man, nor was I taught it; rather, I received it by revelation from Jesus Christ.

¹³For you have heard of my previous way of life in Judaism, how intensely I persecuted the church of God and tried to destroy it. ¹⁴I was advancing in Judaism beyond many Jews of my own age and was extremely zealous for the traditions of my fathers. ¹⁵But when God, who set me apart from birth[a] and called me by his grace, was pleased ¹⁶to reveal his Son in me so that I might preach him among the Gentiles, I did not consult any man, ¹⁷nor did I go up to Jerusalem to see those who were apostles before I was, but I went immediately into Arabia and later returned to Damascus.

¹⁸Then after three years, I went up to Jerusalem to get acquainted with Peter[b] and stayed with him fifteen days. ¹⁹I saw none of the other apostles—only James, the Lord's brother. ²⁰I assure you before God that what I am writing you is no lie. ²¹Later I went to Syria and Cilicia. ²²I was personally unknown to the churches of Judea that are in Christ. ²³They only heard the report: "The man who formerly persecuted us is now preaching the faith he once tried to destroy." ²⁴And they praised God because of me.

Paul Accepted by the Apostles

2 Fourteen years later I went up again to Jerusalem, this time with Barnabas. I took Titus

---

[a]15 Or *from my mother's womb*   [b]18 Greek *Cephas*

along also. [2]I went in response to a revelation and set before them the gospel that I preach among the Gentiles. But I did this privately to those who seemed to be leaders, for fear that I was running or had run my race in vain. [3]Yet not even Titus, who was with me, was compelled to be circumcised, even though he was a Greek. [4]This matter arose, because some false brothers had infiltrated our ranks to spy on the freedom we have in Christ Jesus and to make us slaves. [5]We did not give in to them for a moment, so that the truth of the gospel might remain with you.

[6]As for those who seemed to be important—whatever they were makes no difference to me; God does not judge by external appearance—those men added nothing to my message. [7]On the contrary, they saw that I had been entrusted with the task of preaching the gospel to the Gentiles,[a] just as Peter had been to the Jews.[b] [8]For God, who was at work in the ministry of Peter as an apostle to the Jews, was also at work in my ministry as an apostle to the Gentiles. [9]James, Peter[c] and John, those reputed to be pillars, gave me and Barnabas the right hand of fellowship when they recognized the grace given to me. They agreed that we should go to the Gentiles, and they to the Jews. [10]All they asked was that we should continue to remember the poor, the very thing I was eager to do.

Paul Opposes Peter

[11]When Peter came to Antioch, I opposed him to his face, because he was clearly in the wrong. [12]Before certain men came from James, he used to eat with the Gentiles. But when they arrived, he began to draw back and separate himself from the Gentiles because he was afraid of those who belonged to the circumcision group. [13]The other Jews joined him in his hypocrisy, so that by their hypocrisy even Barnabas was led astray.

[14]When I saw that they were not acting in line with the truth of the gospel, I said to Peter in front of them all, "You are a Jew, yet you live like a Gentile and not like a Jew. How is it, then, that you force Gentiles to follow Jewish customs?

[15]"We who are Jews by birth and not 'Gentile sinners' [16]know that a man is not justified by observing the law, but by faith in Jesus Christ. So we, too, have put our faith in Christ Jesus that we may be justified by faith in Christ and not by observing the law, because by observing the law no one will be justified.

[17]"If, while we seek to be justified in Christ, it becomes evident that we ourselves are sinners, does that mean that Christ promotes sin? Absolutely not! [18]If I rebuild what I destroyed, I prove that I am a lawbreaker. [19]For through the law I died to the law so that I might live for God. [20]I have been crucified with Christ and I no longer live, but Christ lives in me. The life I live in the body, I live by faith in the Son of God, who loved me and gave himself for me. [21]I do not set aside the grace of God, for if righteousness could be gained through the law, Christ died for nothing!"[d]

87
Eph 1:

---

[a]7 Greek *uncircumcised*   [b]7 Greek *circumcised*; also in verses 8 and 9   [c]9 Greek *Cephas*; also in verses 11 and 14   [d]21 Some interpreters end the quotation after verse 14.

*Faith or Observance
of the Law*

3 You foolish Galatians! Who has bewitched you? Before your very eyes Jesus Christ was clearly portrayed as crucified. [2]I would like to learn just one thing from you: Did you receive the Spirit by observing the law, or by believing what you heard? [3]Are you so foolish? After beginning with the Spirit, are you now trying to attain your goal by human effort? [4]Have you suffered so much for nothing—if it really was for nothing? [5]Does God give you his Spirit and work miracles among you because you observe the law, or because you believe what you heard?

[6]Consider Abraham: "He believed God, and it was credited to him as righteousness."[a] [7]Understand, then, that those who believe are children of Abraham. [8]The Scripture foresaw that God would justify the Gentiles by faith, and announced the gospel in advance to Abraham: "All nations will be blessed through you."[b] [9]So those who have faith are blessed along with Abraham, the man of faith.

[10]All who rely on observing the law are under a curse, for it is written: "Cursed is everyone who does not continue to do everything written in the Book of the Law."[c] [11]Clearly no one is justified before God by the law, because, "The righteous will live by faith."[d] [12]The law is not based on faith; on the contrary, "The man who does these things will live by them."[e] [13]Christ redeemed us from the curse of the law by becoming a curse for us, for it is written: "Cursed is everyone

who is hung on a tree."[f] [14]He redeemed us in order that the blessing given to Abraham might come to the Gentiles through Christ Jesus, so that by faith we might receive the promise of the Spirit.

The Law and the Promise

[15]Brothers, let me take an example from everyday life. Just as no one can set aside or add to a human covenant that has been duly established, so it is in this case. [16]The promises were spoken to Abraham and to his seed. The Scripture does not say "and to seeds," meaning many people, but "and to your seed,"[g] meaning one person, who is Christ. [17]What I mean is this: The law, introduced 430 years later, does not set aside the covenant previously established by God and thus do away with the promise. [18]For if the inheritance depends on the law, then it no longer depends on a promise; but God in his grace gave it to Abraham through a promise.

[19]What, then, was the purpose of the law? It was added because of transgressions until the Seed to whom the promise referred had come. The law was put into effect through angels by a mediator. [20]A mediator, however, does not represent just one party; but God is one.

[21]Is the law, therefore, opposed to the promises of God? Absolutely not! For if a law had been given that could impart life, then righteousness would certainly have come by the law. [22]But the Scripture declares that the whole world is a prisoner of sin, so that what was promised, being given through faith in Jesus Christ,

50
Jas 2:10

72
Gal 4:4,5

---

[a]6 Gen. 15:6   [b]8 Gen. 12:3; 18:18; 22:18   [c]10 Deut. 27:26   [d]11 Hab. 2:4
[e]12 Lev. 18:5   [f]13 Deut. 21:23   [g]16 Gen. 12:7; 13:15; 24:7

might be given to those who believe.

23Before this faith came, we were held prisoners by the law, locked up until faith should be revealed. 24So the law was put in charge to lead us to Christ[a] that we might be justified by faith. 25Now that faith has come, we are no longer under the supervision of the law.

Sons of God

24
Heb 11:6

26You are all sons of God through faith in Christ Jesus, 27for all of you who were baptized into Christ have clothed yourselves with Christ. 28There is neither Jew nor Greek, slave nor free, male nor female, for you are all one in Christ Jesus. 29If you belong to Christ, then you are Abraham's seed, and heirs according to the promise.

4 What I am saying is that as long as the heir is a child, he is no different from a slave, although he owns the whole estate. 2He is subject to guardians and trustees until the time set by his father. 3So also, when we were children, we were in slavery under the basic principles of the world. 4But when the time

72
1Pe 1:18,19

had fully come, God sent his Son, born of a woman, born under law, 5to redeem those under law, that we might receive the full rights of sons. 6Because you are sons, God sent the Spirit of his Son into our hearts, the Spirit who calls out, "Abba,[b] Father." 7So you are no longer a slave, but a son; and since you are a son, God has made you also an heir.

Paul's Concern for the Galatians

8Formerly, when you did not know God, you were slaves to those who by nature are not gods. 9But now that you know God—or rather are known by God—how is it that you are turning back to those weak and miserable principles? Do you wish to be enslaved by them all over again? 10You are observing special days and months and seasons and years! 11I fear for you, that somehow I have wasted my efforts on you.

12I plead with you, brothers, become like me, for I became like you. You have done me no wrong. 13As you know, it was because of an illness that I first preached the gospel to you. 14Even though my illness was a trial to you, you did not treat me with contempt or scorn. Instead, you welcomed me as if I were an angel of God, as if I were Christ Jesus himself. 15What has happened to all your joy? I can testify that, if you could have done so, you would have torn out your eyes and given them to me. 16Have I now become your enemy by telling you the truth?

17Those people are zealous to win you over, but for no good. What they want is to alienate you from us, so that you may be zealous for them. 18It is fine to be zealous, provided the purpose is good, and to be so always and not just when I am with you. 19My dear children, for whom I am again in the pains of childbirth until Christ is formed in you, 20how I wish I could be with you now and change my tone, because I am perplexed about you!

Hagar and Sarah

21Tell me, you who want to be under the law, are you not aware of what the law says? 22For it is

---

a24 Or charge until Christ came   b6 Aramaic for Father

written that Abraham had two sons, one by the slave woman and the other by the free woman. 23His son by the slave woman was born in the ordinary way; but his son by the free woman was born as the result of a promise.

24These things may be taken figuratively, for the women represent two covenants. One covenant is from Mount Sinai and bears children who are to be slaves: This is Hagar. 25Now Hagar stands for Mount Sinai in Arabia and corresponds to the present city of Jerusalem, because she is in slavery with her children. 26But the Jerusalem that is above is free, and she is our mother. 27For it is written:

"Be glad, O barren woman,
    who bears no children;
break forth and cry aloud,
    you who have no labor
        pains;
because more are the children
        of the desolate woman
    than of her who has a
        husband."[a]

28Now you, brothers, like Isaac, are children of promise. 29At that time the son born in the ordinary way persecuted the son born by the power of the Spirit. It is the same now. 30But what does the Scripture say? "Get rid of the slave woman and her son, for the slave woman's son will never share in the inheritance with the free woman's son."[b] 31Therefore, brothers, we are not children of the slave woman, but of the free woman.

Freedom in Christ

30
Pe 2:16,17

5 It is for freedom that Christ has set us free. Stand firm, then, and do not let yourselves be burdened again by a yoke of slavery.

2Mark my words! I, Paul, tell you that if you let yourselves be circumcised, Christ will be of no value to you at all. 3Again I declare to every man who lets himself be circumcised that he is obligated to obey the whole law. 4You who are trying to be justified by law have been alienated from Christ; you have fallen away from grace. 5But by faith we eagerly await through the Spirit the righteousness for which we hope. 6For in Christ Jesus neither circumcision nor uncircumcision has any value. The only thing that counts is faith expressing itself through love.

7You were running a good race. Who cut in on you and kept you from obeying the truth? 8That kind of persuasion does not come from the one who calls you. 9"A little yeast works through the whole batch of dough." 10I am confident in the Lord that you will take no other view. The one who is throwing you into confusion will pay the penalty, whoever he may be. 11Brothers, if I am still preaching circumcision, why am I still being persecuted? In that case the offense of the cross has been abolished. 12As for those agitators, I wish they would go the whole way and emasculate themselves!

13You, my brothers, were called to be free. But do not use your freedom to indulge the sinful nature[c]; rather, serve one another in love. 14The entire law is summed up in a single command: "Love your neighbor as yourself."[d] 15If you keep on biting and devouring each other, watch out or you will be destroyed by each other.

a27 Isaiah 54:1   b30 Gen. 21:10   c13 Or the flesh; also in verses 16, 17, 19 and 24
d14 Lev. 19:18

Life by the Spirit

16So I say, live by the Spirit, and you will not gratify the desires of the sinful nature. 17For the sinful nature desires what is contrary to the Spirit, and the Spirit what is contrary to the sinful nature. They are in conflict with each other, so that you do not do what you want. 18But if you are led by the Spirit, you are not under law.

88
2Ti 3:2-5

19The acts of the sinful nature are obvious: sexual immorality,

46

impurity and debauchery; 20idolatry and witchcraft; hatred, discord, jealousy, fits of rage, selfish ambition, dissensions, factions 21and envy; drunkenness, orgies, and the like. I warn you, as I did before, that those who live like this will not inherit the kingdom of God.

89
Gal 6:1

22But the fruit of the Spirit is love, joy, peace, patience, kindness, goodness, faithfulness, 23gentleness and self-control. Against such things there is no law. 24Those who belong to Christ Jesus have crucified the sinful nature with its passions and desires. 25Since we live by the Spirit, let us keep in step with the Spirit. 26Let us not become conceited, provoking and envying each other.

Doing Good to All

5
Heb 3:12,13

6 Brothers, if someone is caught in a sin, you who are spiritual should restore him gently. But watch yourself, or you also may be tempted. 2Carry each other's burdens, and in this way you will fulfill the law of Christ. 3If anyone thinks he is something when he is nothing, he deceives himself. 4Each one should test his

89
Eph 5:18-21

35
Php 2:4

55
Jas 2:1-4

70
Eph 2:8,9

own actions. Then he can take pride in himself, without comparing himself to somebody else, 5for each one should carry his own load.

82
Eph 5:28

6Anyone who receives instruction in the word must share all good things with his instructor.

7Do not be deceived: God cannot be mocked. A man reaps what he sows. 8The one who sows to please his sinful nature, from that nature*a* will reap destruction; the one who sows to please the Spirit, from the Spirit will reap eternal life. 9Let us not become weary in doing good, for at the proper time we will reap a harvest if we do not give up. 10Therefore, as we have opportunity, let us do good to all people, especially to those who belong to the family of believers.

16
Php 4:8-13

Not Circumcision but a New Creation

11See what large letters I use as I write to you with my own hand! 12Those who want to make a good impression outwardly are trying to compel you to be circumcised. The only reason they do this is to avoid being persecuted for the cross of Christ. 13Not even those who are circumcised obey the law, yet they want you to be circumcised that they may boast about your flesh. 14May I never boast except in the cross of our Lord Jesus Christ, through which*b* the world has been crucified to me, and I to the world. 15Neither circumcision nor uncircumcision means anything; what counts is a new creation. 16Peace and mercy to all who follow this rule, even to the Israel of God.

---

*a*8 Or *his flesh, from the flesh*   *b*14 Or *whom*

17Finally, let no one cause me trouble, for I bear on my body the marks of Jesus.

18The grace of our Lord Jesus Christ be with your spirit, brothers. Amen.

Ephesians

1 Paul, an apostle of Christ Jesus by the will of God,

To the saints in Ephesus,a the faithfulb in Christ Jesus:

2Grace and peace to you from God our Father and the Lord Jesus Christ.

Spiritual Blessings in Christ

3Praise be to the God and Father of our Lord Jesus Christ, who has blessed us in the heavenly realms with every spiritual blessing in Christ. 4For he chose us in him before the creation of the world to be holy and blameless in his sight. In love 5hec predestined us to be adopted as his sons through Jesus Christ, in accordance with his pleasure and will— 6to the praise of his glorious grace, which he has freely given us in the One he loves.

28
1Jn 1:9,10
7In him we have redemption through his blood, the forgiveness of sins, in accordance with the riches of God's grace 8that he lavished on us with all wisdom and understanding. 9And hed made known to us the mystery of his will according to his good pleasure, which he purposed in Christ, 10to be put into effect when the times will have reached their fulfillment—to bring all things in heaven and on earth together under one head, even Christ.

87
Eph 2:19-22
11In him we were also chosen, having been predestined according to the plan of him who works out everything in conformity with the purpose of his will, 12in order that we, who were the first to hope in Christ, might be for the praise of his glory. 13And you also were included in Christ when you heard the word of truth, the gospel of your salvation. Having believed, you were marked in him with a seal, the promised Holy Spirit, 14who is a deposit guaranteeing our inheritance until the redemption of those who are God's possession—to the praise of his glory.

Thanksgiving and Prayer

15For this reason, ever since I heard about your faith in the Lord Jesus and your love for all the saints, 16I have not stopped giving thanks for you, remembering you in my prayers. 17I keep asking that the God of our Lord Jesus Christ, the glorious Father, may give you the Spirite of wisdom and revelation, so that you may know him better. 18I pray also that the eyes of your heart may be enlightened in order that you may know the hope to which he has called you, the riches of his glorious inheritance in the saints, 19and his incomparably great power for us who believe. That power is like the working of his mighty strength, 20which he exerted in Christ when he raised him from the dead and seated him at his right

---

a1 Some early manuscripts do not have *in Ephesus.*   b1 Or *believers who are*
c4,5 Or *sight in love.*   dHe   e8,9 Or *us. With all wisdom and understanding,* 9he
f11 Or *were made heirs*   g17 Or *a spirit*

hand in the heavenly realms, [21]far above all rule and authority, power and dominion, and every title that can be given, not only in the present age but also in the one to come. [22]And God placed all things under his feet and appointed him to be head over everything for the church, [23]which is his body, the fullness of him who fills everything in every way.

Made Alive in Christ

18
Eph 5:3-7

2 As for you, you were dead in your transgressions and sins, [2]in which you used to live when you followed the ways of this world and of the ruler of the kingdom of the air, the spirit who is now at work in those who are disobedient. [3]All of us also lived among them at one time, gratifying the cravings of our sinful nature[a] and following its desires and thoughts. Like the rest, we were by nature objects of wrath. [4]But because of his great love for us, God, who is rich in mercy, [5]made us alive with Christ even when we were dead in transgressions—it is by grace you have been saved. [6]And God raised us up with Christ and seated us with him in the heavenly realms in Christ Jesus, [7]in order that in the coming ages he might show the incomparable riches of his grace, expressed in his kindness to us in Christ Jesus. [8]For it is by grace you have been saved, through faith—and this not from yourselves, it is the gift of God— [9]not by works, so that no one can boast. [10]For we are God's workmanship, created in Christ Jesus to do good works, which God prepared in advance for us to do.

70

One in Christ

[11]Therefore, remember that formerly you who are Gentiles by birth and called "uncircumcised" by those who call themselves "the circumcision" (that done in the body by the hands of men)— [12]remember that at that time you were separate from Christ, excluded from citizenship in Israel and foreigners to the covenants of the promise, without hope and without God in the world. [13]But now in Christ Jesus you who once were far away have been brought near through the blood of Christ.

[14]For he himself is our peace, who has made the two one and has destroyed the barrier, the dividing wall of hostility, [15]by abolishing in his flesh the law with its commandments and regulations. His purpose was to create in himself one new man out of the two, thus making peace, [16]and in this one body to reconcile both of them to God through the cross, by which he put to death their hostility. [17]He came and preached peace to you who were far away and peace to those who were near. [18]For through him we both have access to the Father by one Spirit.

71
Col 1:19,20

[19]Consequently, you are no longer foreigners and aliens, but fellow citizens with God's people and members of God's household, [20]built on the foundation of the apostles and prophets, with Christ Jesus himself as the chief cornerstone. [21]In him the whole building is joined together and rises to become a holy temple in the Lord. [22]And in him you too are being built together to become a dwelling in which God lives by his Spirit.

1
Eph 3:12,13
8
Heb 10:25
87
Php 1:12

---

[a]3 Or *our flesh*

Paul the Preacher to the Gentiles

3 For this reason I, Paul, the prisoner of Christ Jesus for the sake of you Gentiles—

²Surely you have heard about the administration of God's grace that was given to me for you, ³that is, the mystery made known to me by revelation, as I have already written briefly. ⁴In reading this, then, you will be able to understand my insight into the mystery of Christ, ⁵which was not made known to men in other generations as it has now been revealed by the Spirit to God's holy apostles and prophets. ⁶This mystery is that through the gospel the Gentiles are heirs together with Israel, members together of one body, and sharers together in the promise in Christ Jesus.

⁷I became a servant of this gospel by the gift of God's grace given me through the working of his power. ⁸Although I am less than the least of all God's people, this grace was given me: to preach to the Gentiles the unsearchable riches of Christ, ⁹and to make plain to everyone the administration of this mystery, which for ages past was kept hidden in God, who created all things. ¹⁰His intent was that now, through the church, the manifold wisdom of God should be made known to the rulers and authorities in the heavenly realms, ¹¹according to his eternal purpose which he accomplished in Christ Jesus our Lord. ¹²In him and through faith in him we may approach God with freedom and confidence. ¹³I ask you, therefore, not to be discouraged because of my sufferings for you, which are your glory.

1
Jas 2:1-4

A Prayer for the Ephesians

¹⁴For this reason I kneel before the Father, ¹⁵from whom his whole family[a] in heaven and on earth derives its name. ¹⁶I pray that out of his glorious riches he may strengthen you with power through his Spirit in your inner being, ¹⁷so that Christ may dwell in your hearts through faith. And I pray that you, being rooted and established in love, ¹⁸may have power, together with all the saints, to grasp how wide and long and high and deep is the love of Christ, ¹⁹and to know this love that surpasses knowledge—that you may be filled to the measure of all the fullness of God.

²⁰Now to him who is able to do immeasurably more than all we ask or imagine, according to his power that is at work within us, ²¹to him be glory in the church and in Christ Jesus throughout all generations, for ever and ever! Amen.

99
Heb 13:15,16

Unity in the Body of Christ

4 As a prisoner for the Lord, then, I urge you to live a life worthy of the calling you have received. ²Be completely humble and gentle; be patient, bearing with one another in love. ³Make every effort to keep the unity of the Spirit through the bond of peace. ⁴There is one body and one Spirit— just as you were called to one hope when you were called— ⁵one Lord, one faith, one baptism; ⁶one God and Father of all, who is over all and through all and in all.

7
Col 2:6

97
Eph 4:13

57
Eph 5:22-33

⁷But to each one of us grace has been given as Christ apportioned it. ⁸This is why it[b] says:

"When he ascended on high,

---

[a]15 Or *whom all fatherhood*   [b]8 Or *God*

he led captives in his train
and gave gifts to men."[a]

⁹(What does "he ascended"
mean except that he also descended to the lower, earthly regions[b]? ¹⁰He who descended is
the very one who ascended
higher than all the heavens, in
order to fill the whole universe.)
¹¹It was he who gave some to be
apostles, some to be prophets,
some to be evangelists, and some
to be pastors and teachers, ¹²to
prepare God's people for works
of service, so that the body of
Christ may be built up ¹³until we
all reach unity in the faith and in
the knowledge of the Son of God
and become mature, attaining to
the whole measure of the fullness
of Christ.

¹⁴Then we will no longer be infants, tossed back and forth by
the waves, and blown here and
there by every wind of teaching
and by the cunning and craftiness of men in their deceitful
scheming. ¹⁵Instead, speaking
the truth in love, we will in all
things grow up into him who is
the Head, that is, Christ. ¹⁶From
him the whole body, joined and
held together by every support-
ing ligament, grows and builds
itself up in love, as each part does
its work.

Living as Children of Light

¹⁷So I tell you this, and insist on
it in the Lord, that you must no
longer live as the Gentiles do, in
the futility of their thinking.
¹⁸They are darkened in their
understanding and separated
from the life of God because of
the ignorance that is in them due
to the hardening of their hearts.
¹⁹Having lost all sensitivity, they
have given themselves over to

58 Php 1:6

97 Php 2:1,2

56 Eph 4:25

34 Col 1:9-11

sensuality so as to indulge in
every kind of impurity, with a
continual lust for more.

²⁰You, however, did not come
to know Christ that way. ²¹Surely
you heard of him and were
taught in him in accordance with
the truth that is in Jesus. ²²You
were taught, with regard to your
former way of life, to put off your
old self, which is being corrupted
by its deceitful desires; ²³to be
made new in the attitude of your
minds; ²⁴and to put on the new
self, created to be like God in true
righteousness and holiness.

²⁵Therefore each of you must
put off falsehood and speak
truthfully to his neighbor, for we
are all members of one body.
²⁶"In your anger do not sin"[c]: Do
not let the sun go down while
you are still angry, ²⁷and do not
give the devil a foothold. ²⁸He
who has been stealing must steal
no longer, but must work, doing
something useful with his own
hands, that he may have something to share with those in need.

²⁹Do not let any unwholesome
talk come out of your mouths,
but only what is helpful for building others up according to their
needs, that it may benefit those
who listen. ³⁰And do not grieve
the Holy Spirit of God, with
whom you were sealed for the
day of redemption. ³¹Get rid of
all bitterness, rage and anger,
brawling and slander, along with
every form of malice. ³²Be kind
and compassionate to one another, forgiving each other, just
as in Christ God forgave you.

5 Be imitators of God, therefore, as dearly loved children
²and live a life of love, just as
Christ loved us and gave himself
up for us as a fragrant offering
and sacrifice to God.

59 Heb 8:10

56 Eph 5:8-10

3 Eph 4:31

90 Tit 2:9,10

49 1Th 5:15

3 Jas 1:19,20

29 Col 3:13

---

[a] 8 Psalm 68:18   [b] 9 Or *the depths of the earth*   [c] 26 Psalm 4:4

18
2Th 1:7-9
3But among you there must not be even a hint of sexual immorality, or of any kind of impurity, or of greed, because these are improper for God's holy people. 4Nor should there be obscenity, foolish talk or coarse joking, which are out of place, but rather thanksgiving. 5For of this you can be sure: No immoral, impure or greedy person—such a man is an idolater—has any inheritance in the kingdom of Christ and of God.*

85
Eph 5:11
6Let no one deceive you with empty words, for because of such things God's wrath comes on those who are disobedient. 7Therefore do not be partners with them.

9
Tit 3:3-8
8For you were once darkness, but now you are light in the Lord.

56
Php 4:8
Live as children of light 9(for the fruit of the light consists in all goodness, righteousness and truth) 10and find out what pleases the Lord.

85
Rev 9:20,21
11Have nothing to do with the fruitless deeds of darkness, but rather expose them. 12For it is shameful even to mention what the disobedient do in secret. 13But everything exposed by the light becomes visible, 14for it is light that makes everything visible. This is why it is said:

"Wake up, O sleeper,
  rise from the dead,
  and Christ will shine on you."

15Be very careful, then, how you live—not as unwise but as wise, 16making the most of every opportunity, because the days

98
Col 1:9,10
are evil. 17Therefore do not be foolish, but understand what the

21
1Ti 3:16
Lord's will is. 18Do not get drunk on wine, which leads to debauchery. Instead, be filled with the

89
2Pe 1:5-8
Spirit. 19Speak to one another with psalms, hymns and spiritual songs. Sing and make music

94
Col 3:17
in your heart to the Lord, 20always giving thanks to God the Father for everything, in the name of our Lord Jesus Christ.

21Submit to one another out of reverence for Christ.

44
Php 2:5-11

Wives and Husbands

22Wives, submit to your husbands as to the Lord. 23For the husband is the head of the wife as Christ is the head of the church, his body, of which he is the Savior. 24Now as the church submits to Christ, so also wives should submit to their husbands in everything.

25
Col 3:18-21

57
Col 3:18,19

25Husbands, love your wives, just as Christ loved the church and gave himself up for her 26to make her holy, cleansing* her by the washing with water through the word, 27and to present her to himself as a radiant church, without stain or wrinkle or any other blemish, but holy and blameless. 28In this same way, husbands ought to love their wives as their own bodies. He who loves his wife loves himself. 29After all, no one ever hated his own body, but he feeds and cares for it, just as Christ does the church— 30for we are members of his body. 31"For this reason a man will leave his father and mother and be united to his wife, and the two will become one flesh."* 32This is a profound mystery—but I am talking about Christ and the church. 33However, each one of you also must love his wife as he loves himself, and the wife must respect her husband.

82
2Ti 4:7

Children and Parents

6 Children, obey your parents in the Lord, for this is right. 2"Honor your father and mother"—which is the first commandment with a promise— 3"that it may go well with you

17
2Ti 1:7

*5 Or kingdom of the Christ and God   *26 Or having cleansed   *31 Gen. 2:24

and that you may enjoy long life on the earth."[a]

4Fathers, do not exasperate your children; instead, bring them up in the training and instruction of the Lord.

Slaves and Masters

5Slaves, obey your earthly masters with respect and fear, and with sincerity of heart, just as you would obey Christ. 6Obey them not only to win their favor when their eye is on you, but like slaves of Christ, doing the will of God from your heart. 7Serve wholeheartedly, as if you were serving the Lord, not men, 8because you know that the Lord will reward everyone for whatever good he does, whether he is slave or free.

9And masters, treat your slaves in the same way. Do not threaten them, since you know that he who is both their Master and yours is in heaven, and there is no favoritism with him.

The Armor of God

10Finally, be strong in the Lord and in his mighty power. 11Put on the full armor of God so that you can take your stand against the devil's schemes. 12For our struggle is not against flesh and blood, but against the rulers, against the authorities, against the powers of this dark world and against the spiritual forces of evil in the heavenly realms. 13Therefore put on the full armor of God, so that when the day of evil comes, you may be able to stand your ground, and after you have done everything, to stand. 14Stand firm then, with the belt of truth buckled around your waist, with the breastplate of righteousness in place, 15and with your feet fitted with the readiness that comes from the gospel of peace. 16In addition to all this, take up the shield of faith, with which you can extinguish all the flaming arrows of the evil one. 17Take the helmet of salvation and the sword of the Spirit, which is the word of God. 18And pray in the Spirit on all occasions with all kinds of prayers and requests. With this in mind, be alert and always keep on praying for all the saints.

19Pray also for me, that whenever I open my mouth, words may be given me so that I will fearlessly make known the mystery of the gospel, 20for which I am an ambassador in chains. Pray that I may declare it fearlessly, as I should.

Final Greetings

21Tychicus, the dear brother and faithful servant in the Lord, will tell you everything, so that you also may know how I am and what I am doing. 22I am sending him to you for this very purpose, that you may know how we are, and that he may encourage you.

23Peace to the brothers, and love with faith from God the Father and the Lord Jesus Christ. 24Grace to all who love our Lord Jesus Christ with an undying love.

a3 Deut. 5:16

Philippians

from Rome

1 Paul and Timothy, servants of Christ Jesus,

To all the saints in Christ Jesus at Philippi, together with the overseers[a] and deacons:

[2] Grace and peace to you from God our Father and the Lord Jesus Christ.

Thanksgiving and Prayer

[3] I thank my God every time I remember you. [4] In all my prayers for all of you, I always pray with joy [5] because of your partnership in the gospel from the first day until now, [6] being confident of this, that he who began a good work in you will carry it on to completion until the day of Christ Jesus.

58
Col 4:12

81
2Ti 2:13

[7] It is right for me to feel this way about all of you, since I have you in my heart; for whether I am in chains or defending and confirming the gospel, all of you share in God's grace with me. [8] God can testify how I long for all of you with the affection of Christ Jesus.

[9] And this is my prayer: that your love may abound more and more in knowledge and depth of insight, [10] so that you may be able to discern what is best and may be pure and blameless until the day of Christ, [11] filled with the fruit of righteousness that comes through Jesus Christ—to the glory and praise of God.

Paul's Chains Advance the Gospel

87
hp 2:12,13

[12] Now I want you to know, brothers, that what has happened to me has really served to advance the gospel. [13] As a result, it has become clear throughout the whole palace guard[b] and to everyone else that I am in chains for Christ. [14] Because of my chains, most of the brothers in the Lord have been encouraged to speak the word of God more courageously and fearlessly.

[15] It is true that some preach Christ out of envy and rivalry, but others out of goodwill. [16] The latter do so in love, knowing that I am put here for the defense of the gospel. [17] The former preach Christ out of selfish ambition, not sincerely, supposing that they can stir up trouble for me while I am in chains.[c] [18] But what does it matter? The important thing is that in every way, whether from false motives or true, Christ is preached. And because of this I rejoice.

Yes, and I will continue to rejoice, [19] for I know that through your prayers and the help given by the Spirit of Jesus Christ, what has happened to me will turn out for my deliverance.[d] [20] I eagerly expect and hope that I will in no way be ashamed, but will have sufficient courage so that now as always Christ will be exalted in my body, whether by life or by death. [21] For to me, to live is Christ and to die is gain. [22] If I am to go on living in the body, this will mean fruitful labor for me. Yet what shall I choose? I do not know! [23] I am torn between the two: I desire to depart and be with Christ, which is better by far; [24] but it is more necessary for you that I remain in the body.

53
Php 3:8

---

[a] 1 Traditionally *bishops*   [b] 13 Or *whole palace*   [c] 16,17 Some late manuscripts have verses 16 and 17 in reverse order.   [d] 19 Or *salvation*

²⁵Convinced of this, I know that I will remain, and I will continue with all of you for your progress and joy in the faith, ²⁶so that through my being with you again your joy in Christ Jesus will overflow on account of me.

²⁷Whatever happens, conduct yourselves in a manner worthy of the gospel of Christ. Then, whether I come and see you or only hear about you in my absence, I will know that you stand firm in one spirit, contending as one man for the faith of the gospel ²⁸without being frightened in any way by those who oppose you. This is a sign to them that they will be destroyed, but that you will be saved—and that by God. ²⁹For it has been granted to you on behalf of Christ not only to believe on him, but also to suffer for him, ³⁰since you are going through the same struggle you saw I had, and now hear that I still have.

91
2Ti 3:12

Imitating Christ's Humility

97
Col 3:14

2 If you have any encouragement from being united with Christ, if any comfort from his love, if any fellowship with the Spirit, if any tenderness and compassion, ²then make my joy complete by being like-minded, having the same love, being one in spirit and purpose. ³Do nothing out of selfish ambition or vain conceit, but in humility consider others better than yourselves. ⁴Each of you should look not only to your own interests, but also to the interests of others.

19
Php 2:21

35
1Th 2:10-12

⁵Your attitude should be the same as that of Christ Jesus:

44
1Pe 5:5,6

⁶Who, being in very nature[a]
   God,

15
Heb 1:8

did not consider equality
   with God something to
   be grasped,
⁷but made himself nothing,
   taking the very nature[b] of a
   servant,
being made in human
   likeness.
⁸And being found in
   appearance as a man,
he humbled himself
and became obedient to
   death—
   even death on a cross!
⁹Therefore God exalted him to
   the highest place
and gave him the name that
   is above every name,
¹⁰that at the name of Jesus
   every knee should bow,
in heaven and on earth and
   under the earth,
¹¹and every tongue confess that
   Jesus Christ is Lord,
to the glory of God the
   Father.

10
Jas 5:16

Shining as Stars

¹²Therefore, my dear friends, as you have always obeyed—not only in my presence, but now much more in my absence—continue to work out your salvation with fear and trembling, ¹³for it is God who works in you to will and to act according to his good purpose.

87
Col 2:2,3

¹⁴Do everything without complaining or arguing, ¹⁵so that you may become blameless and pure, children of God without fault in a crooked and depraved generation, in which you shine like stars in the universe ¹⁶as you hold out[c] the word of life—in order that I may boast on the day of Christ that I did not run or labor for nothing. ¹⁷But even if I am being poured out like a drink offering on the sacrifice and service com-

ᵃ6 Or *in the form of*   ᵇ7 Or *the form*   ᶜ16 Or *hold on to*

ing from your faith, I am glad and rejoice with all of you. [18]So you too should be glad and rejoice with me.

Timothy and Epaphroditus

[19]I hope in the Lord Jesus to send Timothy to you soon, that I also may be cheered when I receive news about you. [20]I have no one else like him, who takes a genuine interest in your welfare. [21]For everyone looks out for his own interests, not those of Jesus Christ. [22]But you know that Timothy has proved himself, because as a son with his father he has served with me in the work of the gospel. [23]I hope, therefore, to send him as soon as I see how things go with me. [24]And I am confident in the Lord that I myself will come soon.

[25]But I think it is necessary to send back to you Epaphroditus, my brother, fellow worker and fellow soldier, who is also your messenger, whom you sent to take care of my needs. [26]For he longs for all of you and is distressed because you heard he was ill. [27]Indeed he was ill, and almost died. But God had mercy on him, and not on him only but also on me, to spare me sorrow upon sorrow. [28]Therefore I am all the more eager to send him, so that when you see him again you may be glad and I may have less anxiety. [29]Welcome him in the Lord with great joy, and honor men like him, [30]because he almost died for the work of Christ, risking his life to make up for the help you could not give me.

No Confidence in the Flesh

3 Finally, my brothers, rejoice in the Lord! It is no trouble for me to write the same things to you again, and it is a safeguard for you.

[2]Watch out for those dogs, those men who do evil, those mutilators of the flesh. [3]For it is we who are the circumcision, we who worship by the Spirit of God, who glory in Christ Jesus, and who put no confidence in the flesh— [4]though I myself have reasons for such confidence.

If anyone else thinks he has reasons to put confidence in the flesh, I have more: [5]circumcised on the eighth day, of the people of Israel, of the tribe of Benjamin, a Hebrew of Hebrews; in regard to the law, a Pharisee; [6]as for zeal, persecuting the church; as for legalistic righteousness, faultless.

[7]But whatever was to my profit I now consider loss for the sake of Christ. [8]What is more, I consider everything a loss compared to the surpassing greatness of knowing Christ Jesus my Lord, for whose sake I have lost all things. I consider them rubbish, that I may gain Christ [9]and be found in him, not having a righteousness of my own that comes from the law, but that which is through faith in Christ—the righteousness that comes from God and is by faith. [10]I want to know Christ and the power of his resurrection and the fellowship of sharing in his sufferings, becoming like him in his death, [11]and so, somehow, to attain to the resurrection from the dead.

Pressing on Toward the Goal

[12]Not that I have already obtained all this, or have already been made perfect, but I press on to take hold of that for which Christ Jesus took hold of me. [13]Brothers, I do not consider myself yet to have taken hold of it. But one thing I do: Forgetting what is behind and straining toward what is ahead, [14]I press on toward the goal to win the

84
ls 3:13-16

53
1Th 4:13

66
Col 1:28

prize for which God has called me heavenward in Christ Jesus.

¹⁵All of us who are mature should take such a view of things. And if on some point you think differently, that too God will make clear to you. ¹⁶Only let us live up to what we have already attained.

¹⁷Join with others in following my example, brothers, and take note of those who live according to the pattern we gave you. ¹⁸For, as I have often told you before and now say again even with tears, many live as enemies of the cross of Christ. ¹⁹Their destiny is destruction, their god is their stomach, and their glory is in their shame. Their mind is on earthly things. ²⁰But our citizenship is in heaven. And we eagerly await a Savior from there, the Lord Jesus Christ, ²¹who, by the power that enables him to bring everything under his control, will transform our lowly bodies so that they will be like his glorious body.

4 Therefore, my brothers, you whom I love and long for, my joy and crown, that is how you should stand firm in the Lord, dear friends!

Exhortations

²I plead with Euodia and I plead with Syntyche to agree with each other in the Lord. ³Yes, and I ask you, loyal yokefellow,ᵃ help these women who have contended at my side in the cause of the gospel, along with Clement and the rest of my fellow workers, whose names are in the book of life.

⁴Rejoice in the Lord always. I will say it again: Rejoice! ⁵Let your gentleness be evident to all. The Lord is near. ⁶Do not be anxious about anything, but in everything, by prayer and petition, with thanksgiving, present your requests to God. ⁷And the peace of God, which transcends all understanding, will guard your hearts and your minds in Christ Jesus.

⁸Finally, brothers, whatever is true, whatever is noble, whatever is right, whatever is pure, whatever is lovely, whatever is admirable—if anything is excellent or praiseworthy—think about such things. ⁹Whatever you have learned or received or heard from me, or seen in me—put it into practice. And the God of peace will be with you.

Thanks for Their Gifts

¹⁰I rejoice greatly in the Lord that at last you have renewed your concern for me. Indeed, you have been concerned, but you had no opportunity to show it. ¹¹I am not saying this because I am in need, for I have learned to be content whatever the circumstances. ¹²I know what it is to be in need, and I know what it is to have plenty. I have learned the secret of being content in any and every situation, whether well fed or hungry, whether living in plenty or in want. ¹³I can do everything through him who gives me strength.

¹⁴Yet it was good of you to share in my troubles. ¹⁵Moreover, as you Philippians know, in the early days of your acquaintance with the gospel, when I set out from Macedonia, not one church shared with me in the matter of giving and receiving, except you only; ¹⁶for even when I was in Thessalonica, you sent me aid again and again when I was in need. ¹⁷Not that I am looking for a gift, but I am looking for what may be credited to your account.

Cross references:

75 Ps 16:10

4 1Pe 5:7

16 2Th 3:11–

56 Col 3:9,10

65 Col 3:15

13 1Ti 6:6–10

26 1Jn 4:18

ᵃ3 Or loyal Syzygus

¹⁸I have received full payment and even more; I am amply supplied, now that I have received from Epaphroditus the gifts you sent. They are a fragrant offering, an acceptable sacrifice, pleasing to God. ¹⁹And my God will meet all your needs according to his glorious riches in Christ Jesus.

²⁰To our God and Father be glory for ever and ever. Amen.

Final Greetings

²¹Greet all the saints in Christ Jesus. The brothers who are with me send greetings. ²²All the saints send you greetings, especially those who belong to Caesar's household.

²³The grace of the Lord Jesus Christ be with your spirit. Amen.*a*

Colossians

1 Paul, an apostle of Christ Jesus by the will of God, and Timothy our brother,

²To the holy and faithful*b* brothers in Christ at Colosse:

Grace and peace to you from God our Father.*c*

Thanksgiving and Prayer

³We always thank God, the Father of our Lord Jesus Christ, when we pray for you, ⁴because we have heard of your faith in Christ Jesus and of the love you have for all the saints— ⁵the faith and love that spring from the hope that is stored up for you in heaven and that you have already heard about in the word of truth, the gospel ⁶that has come to you. All over the world this gospel is bearing fruit and growing, just as it has been doing among you since the day you heard it and understood God's grace in all its truth. ⁷You learned it from Epaphras, our dear fellow servant, who is a faithful minister of Christ on our*d* behalf, ⁸and who also told us of your love in the Spirit.

⁹For this reason, since the day we heard about you, we have not stopped praying for you and asking God to fill you with the knowledge of his will through all spiritual wisdom and understanding. ¹⁰And we pray this in order that you may live a life worthy of the Lord and may please him in every way: bearing fruit in every good work, growing in the knowledge of God, ¹¹being strengthened with all power according to his glorious might so that you may have great endurance and patience, and joyfully ¹²giving thanks to the Father, who has qualified you*e* to share in the inheritance of the saints in the kingdom of light. ¹³For he has rescued us from the dominion of darkness and brought us into the kingdom of the Son he loves, ¹⁴in whom we have redemption,*f* the forgiveness of sins.

The Supremacy of Christ

¹⁵He is the image of the invisible God, the firstborn over all creation. ¹⁶For by him all things were created: things in heaven and on earth, visible and invisible, whether thrones or powers or

---

*a*23 Some manuscripts do not have *Amen.*   *b*2 Or *believing*   *c*2 Some manuscripts
Father and the Lord Jesus Christ   *d*7 Some manuscripts *your*   *e*12 Some manuscripts
us   *f*14 A few late manuscripts *redemption through his blood*

43
n 2:16,17

34
1Th 5:11

98
1Pe 2:15,16

rulers or authorities; all things were created by him and for him. [17]He is before all things, and in him all things hold together. [18]And he is the head of the body, the church; he is the beginning and the firstborn from among the dead, so that in everything he might have the supremacy. [19]For God was pleased to have all his fullness dwell in him, [20]and through him to reconcile to himself all things, whether things on earth or things in heaven, by making peace through his blood, shed on the cross.

71
1Pe 3:18

[21]Once you were alienated from God and were enemies in your minds because of[a] your evil behavior. [22]But now he has reconciled you by Christ's physical body through death to present you holy in his sight, without blemish and free from accusation— [23]if you continue in your faith, established and firm, not moved from the hope held out in the gospel. This is the gospel that you heard and that has been proclaimed to every creature under heaven, and of which I, Paul, have become a servant.

Paul's Labor for the Church

[24]Now I rejoice in what was suffered for you, and I fill up in my flesh what is still lacking in regard to Christ's afflictions, for the sake of his body, which is the church. [25]I have become its servant by the commission God gave me to present to you the word of God in its fullness— [26]the mystery that has been kept hidden for ages and generations, but is now disclosed to the saints. [27]To them God has chosen to make known among the Gentiles the glorious riches of this mystery, which is Christ in you, the hope of glory.

[a]21 Or *minds, as shown by*

[28]We proclaim him, admonishing and teaching everyone with all wisdom, so that we may present everyone perfect in Christ. [29]To this end I labor, struggling with all his energy, which so powerfully works in me.

66
Ps 34:6

2 I want you to know how much I am struggling for you and for those at Laodicea, and for all who have not met me personally. [2]My purpose is that they may be encouraged in heart and united in love, so that they may have the full riches of complete understanding, in order that they may know the mystery of God, namely, Christ, [3]in whom are hidden all the treasures of wisdom and knowledge. [4]I tell you this so that no one may deceive you by fine-sounding arguments. [5]For though I am absent from you in body, I am present with you in spirit and delight to see how orderly you are and how firm your faith in Christ is.

87
1Ti 2:7

Freedom From Human Regulations Through Life With Christ

[6]So then, just as you received Christ Jesus as Lord, continue to live in him, [7]rooted and built up in him, strengthened in the faith as you were taught, and overflowing with thankfulness.

7
Tit 2:11-3

[8]See to it that no one takes you captive through hollow and deceptive philosophy, which depends on human tradition and the basic principles of this world rather than on Christ.

[9]For in Christ all the fullness of the Deity lives in bodily form, [10]and you have been given fullness in Christ, who is the head over every power and authority. [11]In him you were also circum-

cised, in the putting off of the sinful nature,[a] not with a circumcision done by the hands of men but with the circumcision done by Christ, [12]having been buried with him in baptism and raised with him through your faith in the power of God, who raised him from the dead.

[13]When you were dead in your sins and in the uncircumcision of your sinful nature,[b] God made you[c] alive with Christ. He forgave us all our sins, [14]having canceled the written code, with its regulations, that was against us and that stood opposed to us; he took it away, nailing it to the cross. [15]And having disarmed the powers and authorities, he made a public spectacle of them, triumphing over them by the cross.[d]

[16]Therefore do not let anyone judge you by what you eat or drink, or with regard to a religious festival, a New Moon celebration or a Sabbath day. [17]These are a shadow of the things that were to come; the reality, however, is found in Christ. [18]Do not let anyone who delights in false humility and the worship of angels disqualify you for the prize. Such a person goes into great detail about what he has seen, and his unspiritual mind puffs him up with idle notions. [19]He has lost connection with the Head, from whom the whole body, supported and held together by its ligaments and sinews, grows as God causes it to grow.

[20]Since you died with Christ to the basic principles of this world, why, as though you still belonged to it, do you submit to its rules: [21]"Do not handle! Do not taste! Do not touch!"? [22]These are

all destined to perish with use, because they are based on human commands and teachings. [23]Such regulations indeed have an appearance of wisdom, with their self-imposed worship, their false humility and their harsh treatment of the body, but they lack any value in restraining sensual indulgence.

Rules for Holy Living

3 Since, then, you have been raised with Christ, set your hearts on things above, where Christ is seated at the right hand of God. [2]Set your minds on things above, not on earthly things. [3]For you died, and your life is now hidden with Christ in God. [4]When Christ, who is your[e] life, appears, then you also will appear with him in glory.

[5]Put to death, therefore, whatever belongs to your earthly nature: sexual immorality, impurity, lust, evil desires and greed, which is idolatry. [6]Because of these, the wrath of God is coming.[f] [7]You used to walk in these ways, in the life you once lived. [8]But now you must rid yourselves of all such things as these: anger, rage, malice, slander, and filthy language from your lips. [9]Do not lie to each other, since you have taken off your old self with its practices [10]and have put on the new self, which is being renewed in knowledge in the image of its Creator. [11]Here there is no Greek or Jew, circumcised or uncircumcised, barbarian, Scythian, slave or free, but Christ is all, and is in all.

[12]Therefore, as God's chosen people, holy and dearly loved, clothe yourselves with compassion, kindness, humility, gentle-

51
1Jn 5:12

42

56
Rev 21:8

---

[a]11 Or *the flesh*   [b]13 Or *your flesh*   [c]13 Some manuscripts *us*   [d]15 Or *them in him*
[e]4 Some manuscripts *our*   [f]6 Some early manuscripts *coming on those who are disobedient*

29 ness and patience. 13Bear with each other and forgive whatever grievances you may have against one another. Forgive as the Lord
97 forgave you. 14And over all these virtues put on love, which binds them all together in perfect unity.

65
Heb 12:14,15
15Let the peace of Christ rule in your hearts, since as members of one body you were called to peace. And be thankful. 16Let the word of Christ dwell in you richly as you teach and admonish one another with all wisdom, and as you sing psalms, hymns and spiritual songs with gratitude in
94
1Th 5:18
your hearts to God. 17And whatever you do, whether in word or deed, do it all in the name of the Lord Jesus, giving thanks to God the Father through him.

Rules for Christian Households

25
1Ti 5:8
18Wives, submit to your husbands, as is fitting in the Lord.
57
Heb 13:4
19Husbands, love your wives and do not be harsh with them.
20Children, obey your parents in everything, for this pleases the Lord.
21Fathers, do not embitter your children, or they will become discouraged.
22Slaves, obey your earthly masters in everything; and do it, not only when their eye is on you and to win their favor, but with sincerity of heart and reverence for the Lord. 23Whatever you do,
76
2Ti 4:8
work at it with all your heart, as working for the Lord, not for men, 24since you know that you will receive an inheritance from the Lord as a reward. It is the Lord Christ you are serving.
25Anyone who does wrong will be repaid for his wrong, and there is no favoritism.

4 Masters, provide your slaves with what is right and fair, because you know that you also have a Master in heaven.

Further Instructions

2Devote yourselves to prayer, being watchful and thankful. 3And pray for us, too, that God may open a door for our message, so that we may proclaim the mystery of Christ, for which I am in chains. 4Pray that I may proclaim it clearly, as I should. 5Be wise in the way you act toward outsiders; make the most of every opportunity. 6Let your conversation be always full of grace, seasoned with salt, so that you may know how to answer everyone.

Final Greetings

7Tychicus will tell you all the news about me. He is a dear brother, a faithful minister and fellow servant in the Lord. 8I am sending him to you for the express purpose that you may know about oura circumstances and that he may encourage your hearts. 9He is coming with Onesimus, our faithful and dear brother, who is one of you. They will tell you everything that is happening here.
10My fellow prisoner Aristarchus sends you his greetings, as does Mark, the cousin of Barnabas. (You have received instructions about him; if he comes to you, welcome him.) 11Jesus, who is called Justus, also sends greetings. These are the only Jews among my fellow workers for the kingdom of God, and they have proved a comfort to me.
12Epaphras, who is one of you
58
Heb 2:1

a8 Some manuscripts that he may know about your

and a servant of Christ Jesus, sends greetings. He is always wrestling in prayer for you, that you may stand firm in all the will of God, mature and fully assured. ¹³I vouch for him that he is working hard for you and for those at Laodicea and Hierapolis. ¹⁴Our dear friend Luke, the doctor, and Demas send greetings. ¹⁵Give my greetings to the brothers at Laodicea, and to Nympha and the church in her house.

¹⁶After this letter has been read to you, see that it is also read in the church of the Laodiceans and that you in turn read the letter from Laodicea.

¹⁷Tell Archippus: "See to it that you complete the work you have received in the Lord."

¹⁸I, Paul, write this greeting in my own hand. Remember my chains. Grace be with you.

1 Thessalonians

1 Paul, Silas*ᵃ* and Timothy,

To the church of the Thessalonians in God the Father and the Lord Jesus Christ:

Grace and peace to you. *ᵇ*

Thanksgiving for the Thessalonians' Faith

²We always thank God for all of you, mentioning you in our prayers. ³We continually remember before our God and Father your work produced by faith, your labor prompted by love, and your endurance inspired by hope in our Lord Jesus Christ.

⁴For we know, brothers loved by God, that he has chosen you, ⁵because our gospel came to you not simply with words, but also with power, with the Holy Spirit and with deep conviction. You know how we lived among you for your sake. ⁶You became imitators of us and of the Lord; in spite of severe suffering, you welcomed the message with the joy given by the Holy Spirit. ⁷And so you became a model to all the believers in Macedonia and Achaia. ⁸The Lord's message rang out from you not only in Macedonia and Achaia—your faith in God has become known everywhere. Therefore we do not need to say anything about it, ⁹for they themselves report what kind of reception you gave us. They tell how you turned to God from idols to serve the living and true God, ¹⁰and to wait for his Son from heaven, whom he raised from the dead—Jesus, who rescues us from the coming wrath.

Paul's Ministry in Thessalonica

2 You know, brothers, that our visit to you was not a failure. ²We had previously suffered and been insulted in Philippi, as you know, but with the help of our God we dared to tell you his gospel in spite of strong opposition. ³For the appeal we make does not spring from error or impure motives, nor are we trying to trick you. ⁴On the contrary, we speak as men approved by God to be entrusted with the gospel. We are not trying to please men but God, who tests our hearts. ⁵You know we never used flattery, nor did we put on a mask to cover up greed—God is our witness. ⁶We

14
Ti 3:14,15

ᵃ1 Greek *Silvanus*, a variant of *Silas*　*ᵇ1* Some early manuscripts *you from God our Father and the Lord Jesus Christ*

were not looking for praise from men, not from you or anyone else.

As apostles of Christ we could have been a burden to you, [7]but we were gentle among you, like a mother caring for her little children. [8]We loved you so much that we were delighted to share with you not only the gospel of God but our lives as well, because you had become so dear to us. [9]Surely you remember, brothers, our toil and hardship; we worked night and day in order not to be a burden to anyone while we preached the gospel of God to you.

35
Jas 5:19,20

[10]You are witnesses, and so is God, of how holy, righteous and blameless we were among you who believed. [11]For you know that we dealt with each of you as a father deals with his own children, [12]encouraging, comforting and urging you to live lives worthy of God, who calls you into his kingdom and glory.

45
2Ti 3:16,17

[13]And we also thank God continually because, when you received the word of God, which you heard from us, you accepted it not as the word of men, but as it actually is, the word of God, which is at work in you who believe. [14]For you, brothers, became imitators of God's churches in Judea, which are in Christ Jesus: You suffered from your own countrymen the same things those churches suffered from the Jews, [15]who killed the Lord Jesus and the prophets and also drove us out. They displease God and are hostile to all men [16]in their effort to keep us from speaking to the Gentiles so that they may be saved. In this way they always heap up their sins to

38
Ps 11:5

the limit. The wrath of God has come upon them at last.[a]

Paul's Longing to See the Thessalonians

[17]But, brothers, when we were torn away from you for a short time (in person, not in thought), out of our intense longing we made every effort to see you. [18]For we wanted to come to you— certainly I, Paul, did, again and again—but Satan stopped us. [19]For what is our hope, our joy, or the crown in which we will glory in the presence of our Lord Jesus when he comes? Is it not you? [20]Indeed, you are our glory and joy.

3 So when we could stand it no longer, we thought it best to be left by ourselves in Athens. [2]We sent Timothy, who is our brother and God's fellow worker[b] in spreading the gospel of Christ, to strengthen and encourage you in your faith, [3]so that no one would be unsettled by these trials. You know quite well that we were destined for them. [4]In fact, when we were with you, we kept telling you that we would be persecuted. And it turned out that way, as you well know. [5]For this reason, when I could stand it no longer, I sent to find out about your faith. I was afraid that in some way the tempter might have tempted you and our efforts might have been useless.

93
Heb 10:3

Timothy's Encouraging Report

[6]But Timothy has just now come to us from you and has brought good news about your faith and love. He has told us that you always have pleasant memories of us and that you long to see

---

[a]16 Or them fully   [b]2 Some manuscripts brother and fellow worker; other manuscripts brother and God's servant

us, just as we also long to see you. 7Therefore, brothers, in all our distress and persecution we were encouraged about you because of your faith. 8For now we really live, since you are standing firm in the Lord. 9How can we thank God enough for you in return for all the joy we have in the presence of our God because of you? 10Night and day we pray most earnestly that we may see you again and supply what is lacking in your faith.

11Now may our God and Father himself and our Lord Jesus clear the way for us to come to you. 12May the Lord make your love increase and overflow for each other and for everyone else, just as ours does for you. 13May he strengthen your hearts so that you will be blameless and holy in the presence of our God and Father when our Lord Jesus comes with all his holy ones.

86
2Ti 2:15

Living to Please God

4 Finally, brothers, we instructed you how to live in order to please God, as in fact you are living. Now we ask you and urge you in the Lord Jesus to do this more and more. 2For you know what instructions we gave you by the authority of the Lord Jesus.

3It is God's will that you should be sanctified: that you should avoid sexual immorality; 4that each of you should learn to control his own body*a* in a way that is holy and honorable, 5not in passionate lust like the heathen, who do not know God; 6and that in this matter no one should wrong his brother or take advantage of him. The Lord will punish men for all such sins, as we have already told you and warned you. 7For God did not call us to be

83
Th 5:4-8

impure, but to live a holy life. 8Therefore, he who rejects this instruction does not reject man but God, who gives you his Holy Spirit.

9Now about brotherly love we do not need to write to you, for you yourselves have been taught by God to love each other. 10And in fact, you do love all the brothers throughout Macedonia. Yet we urge you, brothers, to do so more and more.

11Make it your ambition to lead a quiet life, to mind your own business and to work with your hands, just as we told you, 12so that your daily life may win the respect of outsiders and so that you will not be dependent on anybody.

The Coming of the Lord

13Brothers, we do not want you to be ignorant about those who fall asleep, or to grieve like the rest of men, who have no hope. 14We believe that Jesus died and rose again and so we believe that God will bring with Jesus those who have fallen asleep in him. 15According to the Lord's own word, we tell you that we who are still alive, who are left till the coming of the Lord, will certainly not precede those who have fallen asleep. 16For the Lord himself will come down from heaven, with a loud command, with the voice of the archangel and with the trumpet call of God, and the dead in Christ will rise first. 17After that, we who are still alive and are left will be caught up together with them in the clouds to meet the Lord in the air. And so we will be with the Lord forever. 18Therefore encourage each other with these words.

53
Ps 23
80
Tit 2:13

5 Now, brothers, about times and dates we do not need to

---

a4 Or learn to live with his own wife; or learn to acquire a wife

write to you, ²for you know very well that the day of the Lord will come like a thief in the night. ³While people are saying, "Peace and safety," destruction will come on them suddenly, as labor pains on a pregnant woman, and they will not escape.

⁴But you, brothers, are not in darkness so that this day should surprise you like a thief. ⁵You are all sons of the light and sons of the day. We do not belong to the night or to the darkness. ⁶So then, let us not be like others, who are asleep, but let us be alert and self-controlled. ⁷For those who sleep, sleep at night, and those who get drunk, get drunk at night. ⁸But since we belong to the day, let us be self-controlled, putting on faith and love as a breastplate, and the hope of salvation as a helmet. ⁹For God did not appoint us to suffer wrath but to receive salvation through our Lord Jesus Christ. ¹⁰He died for us so that, whether we are awake or asleep, we may live together with him. ¹¹Therefore encourage one another and build each other up, just as in fact you are doing.

Final Instructions

¹²Now we ask you, brothers, to respect those who work hard among you, who are over you in the Lord and who admonish you. ¹³Hold them in the highest regard in love because of their work. Live in peace with each other. ¹⁴And we urge you, brothers, warn those who are idle, encourage the timid, help the weak, be patient with everyone. ¹⁵Make sure that nobody pays back wrong for wrong, but always try to be kind to each other and to everyone else.

¹⁶Be joyful always; ¹⁷pray continually; ¹⁸give thanks in all circumstances, for this is God's will for you in Christ Jesus.

¹⁹Do not put out the Spirit's fire; ²⁰do not treat prophecies with contempt. ²¹Test everything. Hold on to the good. ²²Avoid every kind of evil.

²³May God himself, the God of peace, sanctify you through and through. May your whole spirit, soul and body be kept blameless at the coming of our Lord Jesus Christ. ²⁴The one who calls you is faithful and he will do it.

²⁵Brothers, pray for us. ²⁶Greet all the brothers with a holy kiss. ²⁷I charge you before the Lord to have this letter read to all the brothers.

²⁸The grace of our Lord Jesus Christ be with you.

2 Thessalonians

1 Paul, Silas*a* and Timothy,

To the church of the Thessalonians in God our Father and the Lord Jesus Christ:

²Grace and peace to you from God the Father and the Lord Jesus Christ.

Thanksgiving and Prayer

³We ought always to thank God for you, brothers, and rightly so, because your faith is growing more and more, and the love every one of you has for each other is increasing. ⁴Therefore, among God's churches we boast

---

a1 Greek *Silvanus*, a variant of *Silas*

Margin references:
83 2Ti 1:7
34 2Ti 2:15
64 Heb 10:
49 1Pe 4:8
69 1Ti 2:1
94 Ps 118:1
79 Tit 2:11

about your perseverance and faith in all the persecutions and trials you are enduring.

⁵All this is evidence that God's judgment is right, and as a result you will be counted worthy of the kingdom of God, for which you are suffering. ⁶God is just: He will pay back trouble to those who trouble you ⁷and give relief to you who are troubled, and to us as well. This will happen when the Lord Jesus is revealed from heaven in blazing fire with his powerful angels. ⁸He will punish those who do not know God and do not obey the gospel of our Lord Jesus. ⁹They will be punished with everlasting destruction and shut out from the presence of the Lord and from the majesty of his power ¹⁰on the day he comes to be glorified in his holy people and to be marveled at among all those who have believed. This includes you, because you believed our testimony to you.

¹¹With this in mind, we constantly pray for you, that our God may count you worthy of his calling, and that by his power he may fulfill every good purpose of yours and every act prompted by your faith. ¹²We pray this so that the name of our Lord Jesus may be glorified in you, and you in him, according to the grace of our God and the Lord Jesus Christ.ᵃ

The Man of Lawlessness

2 Concerning the coming of our Lord Jesus Christ and our being gathered to him, we ask you, brothers, ²not to become easily unsettled or alarmed by some prophecy, report or letter supposed to have come from us, saying that the day of the Lord

has already come. ³Don't let anyone deceive you in any way, for ˌthat day will not comeˌ until the rebellion occurs and the man of lawlessnessᵇ is revealed, the man doomed to destruction. ⁴He will oppose and will exalt himself over everything that is called God or is worshiped, so that he sets himself up in God's temple, proclaiming himself to be God.

⁵Don't you remember that when I was with you I used to tell you these things? ⁶And now you know what is holding him back, so that he may be revealed at the proper time. ⁷For the secret power of lawlessness is already at work; but the one who now holds it back will continue to do so till he is taken out of the way. ⁸And then the lawless one will be revealed, whom the Lord Jesus will overthrow with the breath of his mouth and destroy by the splendor of his coming. ⁹The coming of the lawless one will be in accordance with the work of Satan displayed in all kinds of counterfeit miracles, signs and wonders, ¹⁰and in every sort of evil that deceives those who are perishing. They perish because they refused to love the truth and so be saved. ¹¹For this reason God sends them a powerful delusion so that they will believe the lie ¹²and so that all will be condemned who have not believed the truth but have delighted in wickedness.

Stand Firm

¹³But we ought always to thank God for you, brothers loved by the Lord, because from the beginning God chose youᶜ to be saved through the sanctifying work of the Spirit and through belief in the truth. ¹⁴He called you

to this through our gospel, that you might share in the glory of our Lord Jesus Christ. ¹⁵So then, brothers, stand firm and hold to the teachings^a we passed on to you, whether by word of mouth or by letter.

¹⁶May our Lord Jesus Christ himself and God our Father, who loved us and by his grace gave us eternal encouragement and good hope, ¹⁷encourage your hearts and strengthen you in every good deed and word.

43
Heb 6:19

Request for Prayer

3 Finally, brothers, pray for us that the message of the Lord may spread rapidly and be honored, just as it was with you. ²And pray that we may be delivered from wicked and evil men, for not everyone has faith. ³But the Lord is faithful, and he will strengthen and protect you from the evil one. ⁴We have confidence in the Lord that you are doing and will continue to do the things we command. ⁵May the Lord direct your hearts into God's love and Christ's perseverance.

92
Heb 2:18

Warning Against Idleness

⁶In the name of the Lord Jesus Christ, we command you, brothers, to keep away from every brother who is idle and does not live according to the teaching^b you received from us. ⁷For you yourselves know how you ought to follow our example. We were not idle when we were with you, ⁸nor did we eat anyone's food without paying for it. On the contrary, we worked night and day, laboring and toiling so that we would not be a burden to any of you. ⁹We did this, not because we do not have the right to such help, but in order to make ourselves a model for you to follow. ¹⁰For even when we were with you, we gave you this rule: "If a man will not work, he shall not eat."

¹¹We hear that some among you are idle. They are not busy; they are busybodies. ¹²Such people we command and urge in the Lord Jesus Christ to settle down and earn the bread they eat. ¹³And as for you, brothers, never tire of doing what is right.

16
Heb 13:6

¹⁴If anyone does not obey our instruction in this letter, take special note of him. Do not associate with him, in order that he may feel ashamed. ¹⁵Yet do not regard him as an enemy, but warn him as a brother.

Final Greetings

¹⁶Now may the Lord of peace himself give you peace at all times and in every way. The Lord be with all of you.

¹⁷I, Paul, write this greeting in my own hand, which is the distinguishing mark in all my letters. This is how I write.

¹⁸The grace of our Lord Jesus Christ be with you all.

1 Timothy

1 Paul, an apostle of Christ Jesus by the command of God our Savior and of Christ Jesus our hope,

²To Timothy my true son in the faith:

Grace, mercy and peace from

---

^a15 Or *traditions*   ^b6 Or *tradition*

God the Father and Christ Jesus
our Lord.

Warning Against False Teachers of the Law

96
Heb 3:19

³As I urged you when I went
into Macedonia, stay there in
Ephesus so that you may command certain men not to teach
false doctrines any longer ⁴nor to
devote themselves to myths and
endless genealogies. These pro-
mote controversies rather than
God's work—which is by faith.

12
1Ti 1:19

⁵The goal of this command is
love, which comes from a pure
heart and a good conscience and
a sincere faith. ⁶Some have wandered away from these and
turned to meaningless talk.
⁷They want to be teachers of the
law, but they do not know what
they are talking about or what
they so confidently affirm.

⁸We know that the law is good
if one uses it properly. ⁹We also
know that law*a* is made not for
the righteous but for lawbreakers
and rebels, the ungodly and sinful, the unholy and irreligious;
for those who kill their fathers or
mothers, for murderers, ¹⁰for
adulterers and perverts, for slave
traders and liars and perjurers—
and for whatever else is contrary
to the sound doctrine ¹¹that con-
forms to the glorious gospel of
the blessed God, which he entrusted to me.

The Lord's Grace to Paul

¹²I thank Christ Jesus our Lord,
who has given me strength, that
he considered me faithful, ap-
pointing me to his service. ¹³Even
though I was once a blasphemer
and a persecutor and a violent
man, I was shown mercy because
I acted in ignorance and unbelief.
¹⁴The grace of our Lord was

poured out on me abundantly,
along with the faith and love that
are in Christ Jesus.

¹⁵Here is a trustworthy saying
that deserves full acceptance:
Christ Jesus came into the world
to save sinners—of whom I am
the worst. ¹⁶But for that very reason I was shown mercy so that in
me, the worst of sinners, Christ
Jesus might display his unlimited
patience as an example for those
who would believe on him and
receive eternal life. ¹⁷Now to the
King eternal, immortal, invisible,
the only God, be honor and glory
for ever and ever. Amen.

¹⁸Timothy, my son, I give you
this instruction in keeping with
the prophecies once made about
you, so that by following them
you may fight the good fight,
¹⁹holding on to faith and a good
conscience. Some have rejected
these and so have shipwrecked
their faith. ²⁰Among them are
Hymenaeus and Alexander,
whom I have handed over to Satan to be taught not to blaspheme.

12
Heb 10:22-25

Instructions on Worship

2 I urge, then, first of all, that
requests, prayers, interces-
sion and thanksgiving be made
for everyone— ²for kings and all
those in authority, that we may
live peaceful and quiet lives in all
godliness and holiness. ³This is
good, and pleases God our Savior, ⁴who wants all men to be
saved and to come to a knowledge of the truth. ⁵For there is
one God and one mediator between God and men, the man
Christ Jesus, ⁶who gave himself
as a ransom for all men—the testimony given in its proper time.
⁷And for this purpose I was appointed a herald and an apos-

69
Ps 61:1,2

87
1Pe 2:4,5

*a*9 Or that the law

tle—I am telling the truth, I am not lying—and a teacher of the true faith to the Gentiles.

[8]I want men everywhere to lift up holy hands in prayer, without anger or disputing.

[9]I also want women to dress modestly, with decency and propriety, not with braided hair or gold or pearls or expensive clothes, [10]but with good deeds, appropriate for women who profess to worship God.

[11]A woman should learn in quietness and full submission. [12]I do not permit a woman to teach or to have authority over a man; she must be silent. [13]For Adam was formed first, then Eve. [14]And Adam was not the one deceived; it was the woman who was deceived and became a sinner. [15]But women[a] will be saved[b] through childbearing—if they continue in faith, love and holiness with propriety.

Overseers and Deacons

60
1 Ti 4:11-16

3 Here is a trustworthy saying: If anyone sets his heart on being an overseer,[c] he desires a noble task. [2]Now the overseer must be above reproach, the husband of but one wife, temperate, self-controlled, respectable, hospitable, able to teach, [3]not given to drunkenness, not violent but gentle, not quarrelsome, not a lover of money. [4]He must manage his own family well and see that his children obey him with proper respect. [5](If anyone does not know how to manage his own family, how can he take care of God's church?) [6]He must not be a recent convert, or he may become conceited and fall under the same judgment as the devil. [7]He must also have a good reputation with outsiders, so that he

61
1 Ti 6:6-10

will not fall into disgrace and into the devil's trap.

21
1 Pe 4:3

[8]Deacons, likewise, are to be men worthy of respect, sincere, not indulging in much wine, and not pursuing dishonest gain. [9]They must keep hold of the deep truths of the faith with a clear conscience. [10]They must first be tested; and then if there is nothing against them, let them serve as deacons.

[11]In the same way, their wives[d] are to be women worthy of respect, not malicious talkers but temperate and trustworthy in everything.

[12]A deacon must be the husband of but one wife and must manage his children and his household well. [13]Those who have served well gain an excellent standing and great assurance in their faith in Christ Jesus.

[14]Although I hope to come to you soon, I am writing you these instructions so that, [15]if I am delayed, you will know how people ought to conduct themselves in God's household, which is the church of the living God, the pillar and foundation of the truth. [16]Beyond all question, the mystery of godliness is great:

> He[e] appeared in a body,[f]
>   was vindicated by the Spirit,
> was seen by angels,
>   was preached among the
>   nations,
> was believed on in the world,
>   was taken up in glory.

Instructions to Timothy

4 The Spirit clearly says that in later times some will abandon the faith and follow deceiving spirits and things taught by demons. [2]Such teachings come through hypocritical liars, whose

---

[a]15 Greek *she*   [b]15 Or *restored*   [c]1 Traditionally *bishop*; also in verse 2   [d]11 Or *way, deaconesses*   [e]16 Some manuscripts *God*   [f]16 Or *in the flesh*

consciences have been seared as with a hot iron. [3]They forbid people to marry and order them to abstain from certain foods, which God created to be received with thanksgiving by those who believe and who know the truth. [4]For everything God created is good, and nothing is to be rejected if it is received with thanksgiving, [5]because it is consecrated by the word of God and prayer.

[6]If you point these things out to the brothers, you will be a good minister of Christ Jesus, brought up in the truths of the faith and of the good teaching that you have followed. [7]Have nothing to do with godless myths and old wives' tales; rather, train yourself to be godly. [8]For physical training is of some value, but godliness has value for all things, holding promise for both the present life and the life to come.

[9]This is a trustworthy saying that deserves full acceptance [10](and for this we labor and strive), that we have put our hope in the living God, who is the Savior of all men, and especially of those who believe.

[11]Command and teach these things. [12]Don't let anyone look down on you because you are young, but set an example for the believers in speech, in life, in love, in faith and in purity. [13]Until I come, devote yourself to the public reading of Scripture, to preaching and to teaching. [14]Do not neglect your gift, which was given you through a prophetic message when the body of elders laid their hands on you.

[15]Be diligent in these matters; give yourself wholly to them, so that everyone may see your progress. [16]Watch your life and doctrine closely. Persevere in them, because if you do, you will save both yourself and your hearers.

Advice About Widows, Elders and Slaves

[5] Do not rebuke an older man harshly, but exhort him as if he were your father. Treat younger men as brothers, [2]older women as mothers, and younger women as sisters, with absolute purity.

[3]Give proper recognition to those widows who are really in need. [4]But if a widow has children or grandchildren, these should learn first of all to put their religion into practice by caring for their own family and so repaying their parents and grandparents, for this is pleasing to God. [5]The widow who is really in need and left all alone puts her hope in God and continues night and day to pray and to ask God for help. [6]But the widow who lives for pleasure is dead even while she lives. [7]Give the people these instructions, too, so that no one may be open to blame. [8]If anyone does not provide for his relatives, and especially for his immediate family, he has denied the faith and is worse than an unbeliever.

[9]No widow may be put on the list of widows unless she is over sixty, has been faithful to her husband,[a] [10]and is well known for her good deeds, such as bringing up children, showing hospitality, washing the feet of the saints, helping those in trouble and devoting herself to all kinds of good deeds.

[11]As for younger widows, do not put them on such a list. For when their sensual desires overcome their dedication to Christ,

[a]9 Or has had but one husband

they want to marry. ¹²Thus they bring judgment on themselves, because they have broken their first pledge. ¹³Besides, they get into the habit of being idle and going about from house to house. And not only do they become idlers, but also gossips and busybodies, saying things they ought not to. ¹⁴So I counsel younger widows to marry, to have children, to manage their homes and to give the enemy no opportunity for slander. ¹⁵Some have in fact already turned away to follow Satan.

¹⁶If any woman who is a believer has widows in her family, she should help them and not let the church be burdened with them, so that the church can help those widows who are really in need.

¹⁷The elders who direct the affairs of the church well are worthy of double honor, especially those whose work is preaching and teaching. ¹⁸For the Scripture says, "Do not muzzle the ox while it is treading out the grain,"ᵃ and "The worker deserves his wages."ᵇ ¹⁹Do not entertain an accusation against an elder unless it is brought by two or three witnesses. ²⁰Those who sin are to be rebuked publicly, so that the others may take warning.

²¹I charge you, in the sight of God and Christ Jesus and the elect angels, to keep these instructions without partiality, and to do nothing out of favoritism.

²²Do not be hasty in the laying on of hands, and do not share in the sins of others. Keep yourself pure.

²³Stop drinking only water, and use a little wine because of your stomach and your frequent illnesses.

²⁴The sins of some men are obvious, reaching the place of judgment ahead of them; the sins of others trail behind them. ²⁵In the same way, good deeds are obvious, and even those that are not cannot be hidden.

6 All who are under the yoke of slavery should consider their masters worthy of full respect, so that God's name and our teaching may not be slandered. ²Those who have believing masters are not to show less respect for them because they are brothers. Instead, they are to serve them even better, because those who benefit from their service are believers, and dear to them. These are the things you are to teach and urge on them.

Love of Money

³If anyone teaches false doctrines and does not agree to the sound instruction of our Lord Jesus Christ and to godly teaching, ⁴he is conceited and understands nothing. He has an unhealthy interest in controversies and quarrels about words that result in envy, strife, malicious talk, evil suspicions ⁵and constant friction between men of corrupt mind, who have been robbed of the truth and who think that godliness is a means to financial gain.

⁶But godliness with contentment is great gain. ⁷For we brought nothing into the world, and we can take nothing out of it. ⁸But if we have food and clothing, we will be content with that. ⁹People who want to get rich fall into temptation and a trap and into many foolish and harmful desires that plunge men into ruin and destruction. ¹⁰For the love of money is a root of all kinds of evil. Some people, eager for

13 Heb 13:5

33 1Ti 6:18

61 2Ti 3:2-5

ᵃ18 Deut. 25:4   ᵇ18 Luke 10:7

money, have wandered from the faith and pierced themselves with many griefs.

Paul's Charge to Timothy

[11]But you, man of God, flee from all this, and pursue righteousness, godliness, faith, love, endurance and gentleness. [12]Fight the good fight of the faith. Take hold of the eternal life to which you were called when you made your good confession in the presence of many witnesses. [13]In the sight of God, who gives life to everything, and of Christ Jesus, who while testifying before Pontius Pilate made the good confession, I charge you [14]to keep this command without spot or blame until the appearing of our Lord Jesus Christ, [15]which God will bring about in his own time—God, the blessed and only Ruler, the King of kings and Lord of lords, [16]who alone is immortal and who lives in unapproachable

31
1Jn 4:8

light, whom no one has seen or can see. To him be honor and might forever. Amen.

[17]Command those who are rich in this present world not to be arrogant nor to put their hope in wealth, which is so uncertain, but to put their hope in God, who richly provides us with everything for our enjoyment. [18]Command them to do good, to be rich in good deeds, and to be generous and willing to share. [19]In this way they will lay up treasure for themselves as a firm foundation for the coming age, so that they may take hold of the life that is truly life.

[20]Timothy, guard what has been entrusted to your care. Turn away from godless chatter and the opposing ideas of what is falsely called knowledge, [21]which some have professed and in so doing have wandered from the faith.

Grace be with you.

37
1Pe 1:6

33
2Ti 3:2-5

2 Timothy

1 Paul, an apostle of Christ Jesus by the will of God, according to the promise of life that is in Christ Jesus,

[2]To Timothy, my dear son:

Grace, mercy and peace from God the Father and Christ Jesus our Lord.

Encouragement to Be Faithful

[3]I thank God, whom I serve, as my forefathers did, with a clear conscience, as night and day I constantly remember you in my prayers. [4]Recalling your tears, I long to see you, so that I may be filled with joy. [5]I have been reminded of your sincere faith,

which first lived in your grandmother Lois and in your mother Eunice and, I am persuaded, now lives in you also. [6]For this reason I remind you to fan into flame the gift of God, which is in you through the laying on of my hands. [7]For God did not give us a spirit of timidity, but a spirit of power, of love and of self-discipline.

[8]So do not be ashamed to testify about our Lord, or ashamed of me his prisoner. But join with me in suffering for the gospel, by the power of God, [9]who has saved us and called us to a holy life—not because of anything we have done but because of his own pur-

17
Tit 1:8

20
Heb 7:25

83
2Ti 3:2-5

pose and grace. This grace was given us in Christ Jesus before the beginning of time, [10]but it has now been revealed through the appearing of our Savior, Christ Jesus, who has destroyed death and has brought life and immortality to light through the gospel. [11]And of this gospel I was appointed a herald and an apostle and a teacher. [12]That is why I am suffering as I am. Yet I am not ashamed, because I know whom I have believed, and am convinced that he is able to guard what I have entrusted to him for that day.

67
2Ti 2:12,13

[13]What you heard from me, keep as the pattern of sound teaching, with faith and love in Christ Jesus. [14]Guard the good deposit that was entrusted to you—guard it with the help of the Holy Spirit who lives in us.

[15]You know that everyone in the province of Asia has deserted me, including Phygelus and Hermogenes.

[16]May the Lord show mercy to the household of Onesiphorus, because he often refreshed me and was not ashamed of my chains. [17]On the contrary, when he was in Rome, he searched hard for me until he found me. [18]May the Lord grant that he will find mercy from the Lord on that day! You know very well in how many ways he helped me in Ephesus.

2 You then, my son, be strong in the grace that is in Christ Jesus. [2]And the things you have heard me say in the presence of many witnesses entrust to reliable men who will also be qualified to teach others. [3]Endure hardship with us like a good soldier of Christ Jesus. [4]No one serving as a soldier gets involved in civilian affairs—he wants to please his commanding officer.

[5]Similarly, if anyone competes as an athlete, he does not receive the victor's crown unless he competes according to the rules. [6]The hardworking farmer should be the first to receive a share of the crops. [7]Reflect on what I am saying, for the Lord will give you insight into all this.

[8]Remember Jesus Christ, raised from the dead, descended from David. This is my gospel, [9]for which I am suffering even to the point of being chained like a criminal. But God's word is not chained. [10]Therefore I endure everything for the sake of the elect, that they too may obtain the salvation that is in Christ Jesus, with eternal glory.

22
1Pe 1:1,2

[11]Here is a trustworthy saying:

If we died with him,
    we will also live with him;
[12]if we endure,
    we will also reign with him.
If we disown him,
    he will also disown us;
[13]if we are faithless,
    he will remain faithful,
    for he cannot disown
        himself.

67
Heb 4:16

73
1Pe 2:19

81
Heb 6:19

A Workman Approved by God

[14]Keep reminding them of these things. Warn them before God against quarreling about words; it is of no value, and only ruins those who listen. [15]Do your best to present yourself to God as one approved, a workman who does not need to be ashamed and who correctly handles the word of truth. [16]Avoid godless chatter, because those who indulge in it will become more and more ungodly. [17]Their teaching will spread like gangrene. Among them are Hymenaeus and Philetus, [18]who have wandered away from the truth. They say that the resurrection has already taken

34
Heb 6:11,

60
2Ti 4:1-5

86
1Jn 3:19-2

place, and they destroy the faith of some. [19]Nevertheless, God's solid foundation stands firm, sealed with this inscription: "The Lord knows those who are his,"[a] and, "Everyone who confesses the name of the Lord must turn away from wickedness."

[20]In a large house there are articles not only of gold and silver, but also of wood and clay; some are for noble purposes and some for ignoble. [21]If a man cleanses himself from the latter, he will be an instrument for noble purposes, made holy, useful to the Master and prepared to do any good work.

[22]Flee the evil desires of youth, and pursue righteousness, faith, love and peace, along with those who call on the Lord out of a pure heart. [23]Don't have anything to do with foolish and stupid arguments, because you know they produce quarrels. [24]And the Lord's servant must not quarrel; instead, he must be kind to everyone, able to teach, not resentful. [25]Those who oppose him he must gently instruct, in the hope that God will grant them repentance leading them to a knowledge of the truth, [26]and that they will come to their senses and escape from the trap of the devil, who has taken them captive to do his will.

Godlessness in the Last Days

3 But mark this: There will be terrible times in the last days. [2]People will be lovers of themselves, lovers of money, boastful, proud, abusive, disobedient to their parents, ungrateful, unholy, [3]without love, unforgiving, slanderous, without self-control, brutal, not lovers of the good, [4]treacherous, rash, conceited, lovers of pleasure rather than

lovers of God— [5]having a form of godliness but denying its power. Have nothing to do with them.

[6]They are the kind who worm their way into homes and gain control over weak-willed women, who are loaded down with sins and are swayed by all kinds of evil desires, [7]always learning but never able to acknowledge the truth. [8]Just as Jannes and Jambres opposed Moses, so also these men oppose the truth—men of depraved minds, who, as far as the faith is concerned, are rejected. [9]But they will not get very far because, as in the case of those men, their folly will be clear to everyone.

Paul's Charge to Timothy

[10]You, however, know all about my teaching, my way of life, my purpose, faith, patience, love, endurance, [11]persecutions, sufferings—what kinds of things happened to me in Antioch, Iconium and Lystra, the persecutions I endured. Yet the Lord rescued me from all of them. [12]In fact, everyone who wants to live a godly life in Christ Jesus will be persecuted, [13]while evil men and impostors will go from bad to worse, deceiving and being deceived. [14]But as for you, continue in what you have learned and have become convinced of, because you know those from whom you learned it, [15]and how from infancy you have known the holy Scriptures, which are able to make you wise for salvation through faith in Christ Jesus. [16]All Scripture is God-breathed and is useful for teaching, rebuking, correcting and training in righteousness, [17]so that the man of God may be thoroughly equipped for every good work.

74

18
eb 3:18,19
33
61
Heb 13:5
83
Tit 2:1
88
o 10:26,27

91
1Pe 1:6,7

14
Jas 2:9

45
Heb 4:12

---

[a]19 Num. 16:5 (see Septuagint)

60
Tit 1:7-9

4 In the presence of God and of Christ Jesus, who will judge the living and the dead, and in view of his appearing and his kingdom, I give you this charge: [2]Preach the Word; be prepared in season and out of season; correct, rebuke and encourage—with great patience and careful instruction. [3]For the time will come when men will not put up with sound doctrine. Instead, to suit their own desires, they will gather around them a great number of teachers to say what their itching ears want to hear. [4]They will turn their ears away from the truth and turn aside to myths. [5]But you, keep your head in all situations, endure hardship, do the work of an evangelist, discharge all the duties of your ministry.

[6]For I am already being poured out like a drink offering, and the time has come for my departure.

82
1Pe 2:15,16

[7]I have fought the good fight, I have finished the race, I have kept the faith.

76
1Pe 1:7

[8]Now there is in store for me the crown of righteousness, which the Lord, the righteous Judge, will award to me on that day—and not only to me, but also to all who have longed for his appearing.

Personal Remarks

[9]Do your best to come to me quickly, [10]for Demas, because he loved this world, has deserted me and has gone to Thessalonica. Crescens has gone to Galatia, and Titus to Dalmatia. [11]Only Luke is with me. Get Mark and bring him with you, because he is helpful to me in my ministry. [12]I sent Tychicus to Ephesus. [13]When you come, bring the cloak that I left with Carpus at Troas, and my scrolls, especially the parchments.

[14]Alexander the metalworker did me a great deal of harm. The Lord will repay him for what he has done. [15]You too should be on your guard against him, because he strongly opposed our message.

[16]At my first defense, no one came to my support, but everyone deserted me. May it not be held against them. [17]But the Lord stood at my side and gave me strength, so that through me the message might be fully proclaimed and all the Gentiles might hear it. And I was delivered from the lion's mouth. [18]The Lord will rescue me from every evil attack and will bring me safely to his heavenly kingdom. To him be glory for ever and ever. Amen.

Final Greetings

[19]Greet Priscilla[a] and Aquila and the household of Onesiphorus. [20]Erastus stayed in Corinth, and I left Trophimus sick in Miletus. [21]Do your best to get here before winter. Eubulus greets you, and so do Pudens, Linus, Claudia and all the brothers.

[22]The Lord be with your spirit. Grace be with you.

---

[a]19 Greek *Prisca*, a variant of *Priscilla*

Titus

1 Paul, a servant of God and an apostle of Jesus Christ for the faith of God's elect and the knowledge of the truth that leads to godliness— ²a faith and knowledge resting on the hope of eternal life, which God, who does not lie, promised before the beginning of time, ³and at his appointed season he brought his word to light through the preaching entrusted to me by the command of God our Savior,

⁴To Titus, my true son in our common faith:

Grace and peace from God the Father and Christ Jesus our Savior.

Titus' Task on Crete

⁵The reason I left you in Crete was that you might straighten out what was left unfinished and appointᵃ elders in every town, as I directed you. ⁶An elder must be blameless, the husband of but one wife, a man whose children believe and are not open to the charge of being wild and disobedient. ⁷Since an overseerᵇ is entrusted with God's work, he must be blameless—not overbearing, not quick-tempered, not given to drunkenness, not violent, not pursuing dishonest gain. ⁸Rather he must be hospitable, one who loves what is good, who is self-controlled, upright, holy and disciplined. ⁹He must hold firmly to the trustworthy message as it has been taught, so that he can encourage others by sound doctrine and refute those who oppose it.

¹⁰For there are many rebellious people, mere talkers and deceivers, especially those of the circumcision group. ¹¹They must be silenced, because they are ruining whole households by teaching things they ought not to teach—and that for the sake of dishonest gain. ¹²Even one of their own prophets has said, "Cretans are always liars, evil brutes, lazy gluttons." ¹³This testimony is true. Therefore, rebuke them sharply, so that they will be sound in the faith ¹⁴and will pay no attention to Jewish myths or to the commands of those who reject the truth. ¹⁵To the pure, all things are pure, but to those who are corrupted and do not believe, nothing is pure. In fact, both their minds and consciences are corrupted. ¹⁶They claim to know God, but by their actions they deny him. They are detestable, disobedient and unfit for doing anything good.

What Must Be Taught to Various Groups

2 You must teach what is in accord with sound doctrine. ²Teach the older men to be temperate, worthy of respect, self-controlled, and sound in faith, in love and in endurance.

³Likewise, teach the older women to be reverent in the way they live, not to be slanderers or addicted to much wine, but to teach what is good. ⁴Then they can train the younger women to love their husbands and children, ⁵to be self-controlled and pure, to be busy at home, to be kind, and to be subject to their

60

17
b 12:5-11

ᵃ5 Or *ordain*   ᵇ7 Traditionally *bishop*

husbands, so that no one will malign the word of God.

⁸³
1Pe 5:8

⁶Similarly, encourage the young men to be self-controlled. ⁷In everything set them an example by doing what is good. In your teaching show integrity, seriousness ⁸and soundness of speech that cannot be condemned, so that those who oppose you may be ashamed because they have nothing bad to say about us.

90

⁹Teach slaves to be subject to their masters in everything, to try to please them, not to talk back to them, ¹⁰and not to steal from them, but to show that they can be fully trusted, so that in every way they will make the teaching about God our Savior attractive.

7
79
Heb 12:14

¹¹For the grace of God that brings salvation has appeared to all men. ¹²It teaches us to say "No" to ungodliness and worldly passions, and to live self-controlled, upright and godly lives in

80
1Jn 3:1-3

this present age, ¹³while we wait for the blessed hope—the glorious appearing of our great God and Savior, Jesus Christ, ¹⁴who gave himself for us to redeem us from all wickedness and to purify for himself a people that are his very own, eager to do what is good.

¹⁵These, then, are the things you should teach. Encourage and rebuke with all authority. Do not let anyone despise you.

Doing What Is Good

9
1Pe 3:8,9

3 Remind the people to be subject to rulers and authorities, to be obedient, to be ready to do whatever is good, ²to slander no one, to be peaceable and considerate, and to show true humility toward all men.

³At one time we too were foolish, disobedient, deceived and enslaved by all kinds of passions and pleasures. We lived in malice and envy, being hated and hating one another. ⁴But when the kindness and love of God our Savior appeared, ⁵he saved us, not because of righteous things we had done, but because of his mercy. He saved us through the washing of rebirth and renewal by the Holy Spirit, ⁶whom he poured out on us generously through Jesus Christ our Savior, ⁷so that, having been justified by his grace, we might become heirs having the hope of eternal life. ⁸This is a trustworthy saying. And I want you to stress these things, so that those who have trusted in God may be careful to devote themselves to doing what is good. These things are excellent and profitable for everyone.

62
1Pe 1:23

⁹But avoid foolish controversies and genealogies and arguments and quarrels about the law, because these are unprofitable and useless. ¹⁰Warn a divisive person once, and then warn him a second time. After that, have nothing to do with him. ¹¹You may be sure that such a man is warped and sinful; he is self-condemned.

Final Remarks

¹²As soon as I send Artemas or Tychicus to you, do your best to come to me at Nicopolis, because I have decided to winter there. ¹³Do everything you can to help Zenas the lawyer and Apollos on their way and see that they have everything they need. ¹⁴Our people must learn to devote themselves to doing what is good, in order that they may provide for daily necessities and not live unproductive lives.

¹⁵Everyone with me sends you greetings. Greet those who love us in the faith.

Grace be with you all.

Philemon

¹Paul, a prisoner of Christ Jesus, and Timothy our brother,

To Philemon our dear friend and fellow worker, ²to Apphia our sister, to Archippus our fellow soldier and to the church that meets in your home:

³Grace to you and peace from God our Father and the Lord Jesus Christ.

Thanksgiving and Prayer

Heb 10:25

⁴I always thank my God as I remember you in my prayers, ⁵because I hear about your faith in the Lord Jesus and your love for all the saints. ⁶I pray that you may be active in sharing your faith, so that you will have a full understanding of every good thing we have in Christ. ⁷Your love has given me great joy and encouragement, because you, brother, have refreshed the hearts of the saints.

Paul's Plea for Onesimus

⁸Therefore, although in Christ I could be bold and order you to do what you ought to do, ⁹yet I appeal to you on the basis of love. I then, as Paul—an old man and now also a prisoner of Christ Jesus— ¹⁰I appeal to you for my son Onesimus,ᵃ who became my son while I was in chains. ¹¹Formerly he was useless to you, but now he has become useful both to you and to me.

¹²I am sending him—who is my very heart—back to you. ¹³I would have liked to keep him with me so that he could take your place in helping me while I am in chains for the gospel. ¹⁴But I did not want to do anything without your consent, so that any favor you do will be spontaneous and not forced. ¹⁵Perhaps the reason he was separated from you for a little while was that you might have him back for good— ¹⁶no longer as a slave, but better than a slave, as a dear brother. He is very dear to me but even dearer to you, both as a man and as a brother in the Lord.

¹⁷So if you consider me a partner, welcome him as you would welcome me. ¹⁸If he has done you any wrong or owes you anything, charge it to me. ¹⁹I, Paul, am writing this with my own hand. I will pay it back—not to mention that you owe me your very self. ²⁰I do wish, brother, that I may have some benefit from you in the Lord; refresh my heart in Christ. ²¹Confident of your obedience, I write to you, knowing that you will do even more than I ask.

²²And one thing more: Prepare a guest room for me, because I hope to be restored to you in answer to your prayers.

²³Epaphras, my fellow prisoner in Christ Jesus, sends you greetings. ²⁴And so do Mark, Aristarchus, Demas and Luke, my fellow workers.

²⁵The grace of the Lord Jesus Christ be with your spirit.

ᵃ10 Onesimus means useful.

Hebrews

The Son Superior to Angels

1Pe 1:8,9

6 **1** In the past God spoke to our forefathers through the prophets at many times and in various ways, ²but in these last days he has spoken to us by his Son, whom he appointed heir of all things, and through whom he made the universe. ³The Son is the radiance of God's glory and the exact representation of his being, sustaining all things by his powerful word. After he had provided purification for sins, he sat down at the right hand of the Majesty in heaven. ⁴So he became as much superior to the angels as the name he has inherited is superior to theirs.

⁵For to which of the angels did God ever say,

"You are my Son;
 today I have become your
  Father"*a*,*b*?

Or again,

"I will be his Father,
 and he will be my Son"*c*?

⁶And again, when God brings his firstborn into the world, he says,

"Let all God's angels worship
  him."*d*

⁷In speaking of the angels he says,

"He makes his angels winds,
 his servants flames of fire."*e*

15 ⁸But about the Son he says,

"Your throne, O God, will last
  for ever and ever,
 and righteousness will be
  the scepter of your
  kingdom.
⁹You have loved righteousness
  and hated wickedness;
therefore God, your God,
  has set you above your
   companions
by anointing you with the
  oil of joy."*f*

¹⁰He also says,

"In the beginning, O Lord,
  you laid the foundations
   of the earth,
and the heavens are the
  work of your hands.
¹¹They will perish, but you
   remain;
 they will all wear out like a
  garment.
¹²You will roll them up like a
   robe;
 like a garment they will be
  changed.
But you remain the same,
 and your years will never
  end."*g*

¹³To which of the angels did God ever say,

"Sit at my right hand
until I make your enemies
 a footstool for your feet"*h*?

¹⁴Are not all angels ministering spirits sent to serve those who will inherit salvation?

Warning to Pay Attention

2 We must pay more careful attention, therefore, to what we have heard, so that we do not drift away. ²For if the message spoken by angels was binding,

58
Heb 5:14

---

a5 Or *have begotten you*   *b5* Psalm 2:7   *c5* 2 Samuel 7:14; 1 Chron. 17:13
d6 Deut. 32:43 (see Dead Sea Scrolls and Septuagint)   *e7* Psalm 104:4
f9 Psalm 45:6,7   *g12* Psalm 102:25-27   *h13* Psalm 110:1

and every violation and disobedience received its just punishment, ³how shall we escape if we ignore such a great salvation? This salvation, which was first announced by the Lord, was confirmed to us by those who heard him. ⁴God also testified to it by signs, wonders and various miracles, and gifts of the Holy Spirit distributed according to his will.

as 5:13-16

95

Jesus Made Like His Brothers

⁵It is not to angels that he has subjected the world to come, about which we are speaking. ⁶But there is a place where someone has testified:

"What is man that you are
      mindful of him,
   the son of man that you
      care for him?
⁷You made him a little[a] lower
      than the angels;
   you crowned him with glory
      and honor
⁸   and put everything under
      his feet."[b]

In putting everything under him, God left nothing that is not subject to him. Yet at present we do not see everything subject to him. ⁹But we see Jesus, who was made a little lower than the angels, now crowned with glory and honor because he suffered death, so that by the grace of God he might taste death for everyone.

¹⁰In bringing many sons to glory, it was fitting that God, for whom and through whom everything exists, should make the author of their salvation perfect through suffering. ¹¹Both the one who makes men holy and those who are made holy are of the same family. So Jesus is not ashamed to call them brothers. ¹²He says,

"I will declare your name to
      my brothers;
   in the presence of the
      congregation I will sing
      your praises."[c]

¹³And again,

"I will put my trust in him."[d]

And again he says,

"Here am I, and the children
      God has given me."[e]

¹⁴Since the children have flesh and blood, he too shared in their humanity so that by his death he might destroy him who holds the power of death—that is, the devil— ¹⁵and free those who all their lives were held in slavery by their fear of death. ¹⁶For surely it is not angels he helps, but Abraham's descendants. ¹⁷For this reason he had to be made like his brothers in every way, in order that he might become a merciful and faithful high priest in service to God, and that he might make atonement for[f] the sins of the people. ¹⁸Because he himself suffered when he was tempted, he is able to help those who are being tempted.

92
Heb 11:25

Jesus Greater Than Moses

3 Therefore, holy brothers, who share in the heavenly calling, fix your thoughts on Jesus, the apostle and high priest whom we confess. ²He was faithful to the one who appointed him, just as Moses was faithful in all God's house. ³Jesus has been found worthy of greater honor than Moses, just as the builder of a house has greater honor than the house itself. ⁴For every house

---

7 Or *him for a little while; also in verse 9*   *8* Psalm 8:4-6   *12* Psalm 22:22
13 Isaiah 8:17   *13* Isaiah 8:18   *17* Or *and that he might turn aside God's wrath, taking away*

is built by someone, but God is the builder of everything. [5]Moses was faithful as a servant in all God's house, testifying to what would be said in the future. [6]But Christ is faithful as a son over God's house. And we are his house, if we hold on to our courage and the hope of which we boast.

Warning Against Unbelief

[7]So, as the Holy Spirit says:

"Today, if you hear his voice,
[8] do not harden your hearts
  as you did in the rebellion,
    during the time of testing in
     the desert,
[9]where your fathers tested and
    tried me
  and for forty years saw
    what I did.
[10]That is why I was angry with
    that generation,
  and I said, 'Their hearts are
    always going astray,
  and they have not known
    my ways.'
[11]So I declared on oath in my
    anger,
  'They shall never enter my
    rest.' " [a]

[12]See to it, brothers, that none of you has a sinful, unbelieving heart that turns away from the living God. [13]But encourage one another daily, as long as it is called Today, so that none of you may be hardened by sin's deceitfulness. [14]We have come to share in Christ if we hold firmly till the end the confidence we had at first. [15]As has just been said:

"Today, if you hear his voice,
  do not harden your hearts
  as you did in the rebellion." [b]

[16]Who were they who heard and rebelled? Were they not all those Moses led out of Egypt? [17]And with whom was he angry for forty years? Was it not with those who sinned, whose bodies fell in the desert? [18]And to whom did God swear that they would never enter his rest if not to those who disobeyed[c]? [19]So we see that they were not able to enter, because of their unbelief.

A Sabbath-Rest for the People of God

4 Therefore, since the promise of entering his rest still stands, let us be careful that none of you be found to have fallen short of it. [2]For we also have had the gospel preached to us, just as they did; but the message they heard was of no value to them, because those who heard did not combine it with faith.[d] [3]Now we who have believed enter that rest, just as God has said,

"So I declared on oath in my
  anger,
  'They shall never enter my
  rest.' " [e]

And yet his work has been finished since the creation of the world. [4]For somewhere he has spoken about the seventh day in these words: "And on the seventh day God rested from all his work."[f] [5]And again in the passage above he says, "They shall never enter my rest."

[6]It still remains that some will enter that rest, and those who formerly had the gospel preached to them did not go in, because of their disobedience. [7]Therefore God again set a certain day, calling it Today, when a

Side references:
18 Ps 111:10
96 Heb 11:6
5 Heb 10:22

long time later he spoke through David, as was said before:

"Today, if you hear his voice,
do not harden your
hearts."[a]

[8]For if Joshua had given them rest, God would not have spoken later about another day. [9]There remains, then, a Sabbath-rest for the people of God; [10]for anyone who enters God's rest also rests from his own work, just as God did from his. [11]Let us, therefore, make every effort to enter that rest, so that no one will fall by following their example of disobedience.

45
Pe 1:19-21

[12]For the word of God is living and active. Sharper than any double-edged sword, it penetrates even to dividing soul and spirit, joints and marrow; it judges the thoughts and attitudes of the heart. [13]Nothing in all creation is hidden from God's sight Everything is uncovered and laid bare before the eyes of him to whom we must give account.

Jesus the Great High Priest

[14]Therefore, since we have a great high priest who has gone through the heavens,[b] Jesus the Son of God, let us hold firmly to the faith we profess. [15]For we do not have a high priest who is unable to sympathize with our weaknesses, but we have one who has been tempted in every way, just as we are—yet was without sin. [16]Let us then approach the throne of grace with confidence, so that we may receive mercy and find grace to help us in our time of need.

11
Heb 10:35

67
Jas 1:3

5 Every high priest is selected from among men and is appointed to represent them in

matters related to God, to offer gifts and sacrifices for sins. [2]He is able to deal gently with those who are ignorant and are going astray, since he himself is subject to weakness. [3]This is why he has to offer sacrifices for his own sins, as well as for the sins of the people.

[4]No one takes this honor upon himself; he must be called by God, just as Aaron was. [5]So Christ also did not take upon himself the glory of becoming a high priest. But God said to him,

"You are my Son;
today I have become your
Father."[c][d]

[6]And he says in another place,

"You are a priest forever,
in the order of
Melchizedek."[e]

[7]During the days of Jesus' life on earth, he offered up prayers and petitions with loud cries and tears to the one who could save him from death, and he was heard because of his reverent submission. [8]Although he was a son, he learned obedience from what he suffered [9]and, once made perfect, he became the source of eternal salvation for all who obey him [10]and was designated by God to be high priest in the order of Melchizedek.

Warning Against Falling Away

[11]We have much to say about this, but it is hard to explain because you are slow to learn. [12]In fact, though by this time you ought to be teachers, you need someone to teach you the elementary truths of God's word all over again. You need milk, not

[a]7 Psalm 95:7,8   [b]14 Or gone into heaven   [c]5 Or have begotten you
[d]6 Psalm 110:4   [e]5 Psalm 2:7

solid food! ¹³Anyone who lives on milk, being still an infant, is not acquainted with the teaching about righteousness. ¹⁴But solid food is for the mature, who by constant use have trained themselves to distinguish good from evil.

6 Therefore let us leave the elementary teachings about Christ and go on to maturity, not laying again the foundation of repentance from acts that lead to death,ᵃ and of faith in God, ²instruction about baptisms, the laying on of hands, the resurrection of the dead, and eternal judgment. ³And God permitting, we will do so.

⁴It is impossible for those who have once been enlightened, who have tasted the heavenly gift, who have shared in the Holy Spirit, ⁵who have tasted the goodness of the word of God and the powers of the coming age, ⁶if they fall away, to be brought back to repentance, becauseᵇ to their loss they are crucifying the Son of God all over again and subjecting him to public disgrace.

⁷Land that drinks in the rain often falling on it and that produces a crop useful to those for whom it is farmed receives the blessing of God. ⁸But land that produces thorns and thistles is worthless and is in danger of being cursed. In the end it will be burned.

⁹Even though we speak like this, dear friends, we are confident of better things in your case—things that accompany salvation. ¹⁰God is not unjust; he will not forget your work and the love you have shown him as you have helped his people and continue to help them. ¹¹We want each of you to show this same diligence to the very end, in or-

der to make your hope sure. ¹²We do not want you to become lazy, but to imitate those who through faith and patience inherit what has been promised.

The Certainty of God's Promise

¹³When God made his promise to Abraham, since there was no one greater for him to swear by, he swore by himself, ¹⁴saying, "I will surely bless you and give you many descendants."ᶜ ¹⁵And so after waiting patiently, Abraham received what was promised.

¹⁶Men swear by someone greater than themselves, and the oath confirms what is said and puts an end to all argument. ¹⁷Because God wanted to make the unchanging nature of his purpose very clear to the heirs of what was promised, he confirmed it with an oath. ¹⁸God did this so that, by two unchangeable things in which it is impossible for God to lie, we who have fled to take hold of the hope offered to us may be greatly encouraged. ¹⁹We have this hope as an anchor for the soul, firm and secure. It enters the inner sanctuary behind the curtain, ²⁰where Jesus, who went before us, has entered on our behalf. He has become a high priest forever, in the order of Melchizedek.

Melchizedek the Priest

7 This Melchizedek was king of Salem and priest of God Most High. He met Abraham returning from the defeat of the kings and blessed him, ²and Abraham gave him a tenth of everything. First, his name means "king of righteousness"; then also, "king of Salem" means "king of peace." ³Without father or

ᵃ1 Or from useless rituals   ᵇ6 Or repentance while   ᶜ14 Gen. 22:17

mother, without genealogy, without beginning of days or end of life, like the Son of God he remains a priest forever.

⁴Just think how great he was: Even the patriarch Abraham gave him a tenth of the plunder! ⁵Now the law requires the descendants of Levi who become priests to collect a tenth from the people—that is, their brothers—even though their brothers are descended from Abraham. ⁶This man, however, did not trace his descent from Levi, yet he collected a tenth from Abraham and blessed him who had the promises. ⁷And without doubt the lesser person is blessed by the greater. ⁸In the one case, the tenth is collected by men who die; but in the other case, by him who is declared to be living. ⁹One might even say that Levi, who collects the tenth, paid the tenth through Abraham, ¹⁰because when Melchizedek met Abraham, Levi was still in the body of his ancestor.

Jesus Like Melchizedek

¹¹If perfection could have been attained through the Levitical priesthood (for on the basis of it the law was given to the people), why was there still need for another priest to come—one in the order of Melchizedek, not in the order of Aaron? ¹²For when there is a change of the priesthood, there must also be a change of the law. ¹³He of whom these things are said belonged to a different tribe, and no one from that tribe has ever served at the altar. ¹⁴For it is clear that our Lord descended from Judah, and in regard to that tribe Moses said nothing about priests. ¹⁵And what we have said is even more clear if another priest like Melchizedek

appears, ¹⁶one who has become a priest not on the basis of a regulation as to his ancestry but on the basis of the power of an indestructible life. ¹⁷For it is declared:

"You are a priest forever,
  in the order of
    Melchizedek."ᵃ

¹⁸The former regulation is set aside because it was weak and useless ¹⁹(for the law made nothing perfect), and a better hope is introduced, by which we draw near to God.

²⁰And it was not without an oath! Others became priests without any oath, ²¹but he became a priest with an oath when God said to him:

"The Lord has sworn
  and will not change his
    mind:
  'You are a priest forever.' "ᵃ

²²Because of this oath, Jesus has become the guarantee of a better covenant.

²³Now there have been many of those priests, since death prevented them from continuing in office; ²⁴but because Jesus lives forever, he has a permanent priesthood. ²⁵Therefore he is able to save completelyᵇ those who come to God through him, because he always lives to intercede for them.

²⁶Such a high priest meets our need—one who is holy, blameless, pure, set apart from sinners, exalted above the heavens. ²⁷Unlike the other high priests, he does not need to offer sacrifices day after day, first for his own sins, and then for the sins of the people. He sacrificed for their sins once for all when he offered himself. ²⁸For the law appoints as high priests men who are weak; but the oath, which came after

20
Heb 12:2

ᵃ17,21 Psalm 110:4   ᵇ25 Or forever

the law, appointed the Son, who has been made perfect forever.

The High Priest of a New Covenant

8 The point of what we are saying is this: We do have such a high priest, who sat down at the right hand of the throne of the Majesty in heaven, [2]and who serves in the sanctuary, the true tabernacle set up by the Lord, not by man.

[3]Every high priest is appointed to offer both gifts and sacrifices, and so it was necessary for this one also to have something to offer. [4]If he were on earth, he would not be a priest, for there are already men who offer the gifts prescribed by the law. [5]They serve at a sanctuary that is a copy and shadow of what is in heaven. This is why Moses was warned when he was about to build the tabernacle: "See to it that you make everything according to the pattern shown you on the mountain."[a] [6]But the ministry Jesus has received is as superior to theirs as the covenant of which he is mediator is superior to the old one, and it is founded on better promises.

[7]For if there had been nothing wrong with that first covenant, no place would have been sought for another. [8]But God found fault with the people and said[b]:

"The time is coming, declares the Lord,
    when I will make a new covenant
with the house of Israel
    and with the house of Judah.
[9]It will not be like the covenant
    I made with their forefathers
when I took them by the hand

to lead them out of Egypt,
because they did not remain
    faithful to my covenant,
    and I turned away from them,
        declares the Lord.
[10]This is the covenant I will
    make with the house of Israel
    after that time, declares the Lord.
I will put my laws in their minds
    and write them on their hearts.
I will be their God,
    and they will be my people.
[11]No longer will a man teach his neighbor,
    or a man his brother,
        saying, 'Know the Lord,'
because they will all know me,
    from the least of them to the greatest.
[12]For I will forgive their wickedness
    and will remember their sins no more."[c]

[13]By calling this covenant "new," he has made the first one obsolete; and what is obsolete and aging will soon disappear.

Worship in the Earthly Tabernacle

9 Now the first covenant had regulations for worship and also an earthly sanctuary. [2]A tabernacle was set up. In its first room were the lampstand, the table and the consecrated bread; this was called the Holy Place. [3]Behind the second curtain was a room called the Most Holy Place, [4]which had the golden altar of incense and the gold-covered ark of the covenant. This ark contained the gold jar of manna, Aaron's

59
Ps 64:5,6

---

[a]5 Exodus 25:40   [b]8 Some manuscripts may be translated *fault and said to the people.*
[c]12 Jer. 31:31-34

staff that had budded, and the stone tablets of the covenant. [5]Above the ark were the cherubim of the Glory, overshadowing the atonement cover.[d] But we cannot discuss these things in detail now.

[6]When everything had been arranged like this, the priests entered regularly into the outer room to carry on their ministry. [7]But only the high priest entered the inner room, and that only once a year, and never without blood, which he offered for himself and for the sins the people had committed in ignorance. [8]The Holy Spirit was showing by this that the way into the Most Holy Place had not yet been disclosed as long as the first tabernacle was still standing. [9]This is an illustration for the present time, indicating that the gifts and sacrifices being offered were not able to clear the conscience of the worshiper. [10]They are only a matter of food and drink and various ceremonial washings—external regulations applying until the time of the new order.

The Blood of Christ

[11]When Christ came as high priest of the good things that are already here,[b] he went through the greater and more perfect tabernacle that is not man-made, that is to say, not a part of this creation. [12]He did not enter by means of the blood of goats and calves; but he entered the Most Holy Place once for all by his own blood, having obtained eternal redemption. [13]The blood of goats and bulls and the ashes of a heifer sprinkled on those who are ceremonially unclean sanctify them so that they are outwardly

clean. [14]How much more, then, will the blood of Christ, who through the eternal Spirit offered himself unblemished to God, cleanse our consciences from acts that lead to death,[c] so that we may serve the living God!

[15]For this reason Christ is the mediator of a new covenant, that those who are called may receive the promised eternal inheritance—now that he has died as a ransom to set them free from the sins committed under the first covenant.

[16]In the case of a will,[d] it is necessary to prove the death of the one who made it, [17]because a will is in force only when somebody has died; it never takes effect while the one who made it is living. [18]This is why even the first covenant was not put into effect without blood. [19]When Moses had proclaimed every commandment of the law to all the people, he took the blood of calves, together with water, scarlet wool and branches of hyssop, and sprinkled the scroll and all the people. [20]He said, "This is the blood of the covenant, which God has commanded you to keep."[e] [21]In the same way, he sprinkled with the blood both the tabernacle and everything used in its ceremonies. [22]In fact, the law requires that nearly everything be cleansed with blood, and without the shedding of blood there is no forgiveness.

[23]It was necessary, then, for the copies of the heavenly things to be purified with these sacrifices, but the heavenly things themselves with better sacrifices than these. [24]For Christ did not enter a man-made sanctuary that was only a copy of the true one; he

---

[a]5 Traditionally *the mercy seat*   [b]11 Some early manuscripts *are to come*   [c]14 Or *from useless rituals*   [d]16 Same Greek word as *covenant*; also in verse 17
[e]20 Exodus 24:8

entered heaven itself, now to appear for us in God's presence. [25]Nor did he enter heaven to offer himself again and again, the way the high priest enters the Most Holy Place every year with blood that is not his own. [26]Then Christ would have had to suffer many times since the creation of the world. But now he has appeared once for all at the end of the ages to do away with sin by the sacrifice of himself. [27]Just as man is destined to die once, and after that to face judgment, [28]so Christ was sacrificed once to take away the sins of many people; and he will appear a second time, not to bear sin, but to bring salvation to those who are waiting for him.

Christ's Sacrifice Once for All

10 The law is only a shadow of the good things that are coming—not the realities themselves. For this reason it can never, by the same sacrifices repeated endlessly year after year, make perfect those who draw near to worship. [2]If it could, would they not have stopped being offered? For the worshipers would have been cleansed once for all, and would no longer have felt guilty for their sins. [3]But those sacrifices are an annual reminder of sins, [4]because it is impossible for the blood of bulls and goats to take away sins.

[5]Therefore, when Christ came into the world, he said:

"Sacrifice and offering you did
   not desire,
   but a body you prepared for
      me;
[6]with burnt offerings and sin
      offerings
   you were not pleased.

[7]Then I said, 'Here I am—it is
      written about me in the
      scroll—
   I have come to do your will,
      O God.' "[a]

[8]First he said, "Sacrifices and offerings, burnt offerings and sin offerings you did not desire, nor were you pleased with them" (although the law required them to be made). [9]Then he said, "Here I am, I have come to do your will." He sets aside the first to establish the second. [10]And by that will, we have been made holy through the sacrifice of the body of Jesus Christ once for all.

[11]Day after day every priest stands and performs his religious duties; again and again he offers the same sacrifices, which can never take away sins. [12]But when this priest had offered for all time one sacrifice for sins, he sat down at the right hand of God. [13]Since that time he waits for his enemies to be made his footstool, [14]because by one sacrifice he has made perfect forever those who are being made holy.

[15]The Holy Spirit also testifies to us about this. First he says:

[16]"This is the covenant I will
      make with them
   after that time, says the
      Lord.
I will put my laws in their
      hearts,
   and I will write them on
      their minds."[b]

[17]Then he adds:

"Their sins and lawless acts
   I will remember no more."[c]

[18]And where these have been forgiven, there is no longer any sacrifice for sin.

[a]7 Psalm 40:6-8 (see Septuagint)   [b]16 Jer. 31:33   [c]17 Jer. 31:34

A Call to Persevere

[19] Therefore, brothers, since we have confidence to enter the Most Holy Place by the blood of Jesus, [20] by a new and living way opened for us through the curtain, that is, his body, [21] and since we have a great priest over the house of God, [22] let us draw near to God with a sincere heart in full assurance of faith, having our hearts sprinkled to cleanse us from a guilty conscience and having our bodies washed with pure water. [23] Let us hold unswervingly to the hope we profess, for he who promised is faithful. [24] And let us consider how we may spur one another on toward love and good deeds. [25] Let us not give up meeting together, as some are in the habit of doing, but let us encourage one another—and all the more as you see the Day approaching.

[26] If we deliberately keep on sinning after we have received the knowledge of the truth, no sacrifice for sins is left, [27] but only a fearful expectation of judgment and of raging fire that will consume the enemies of God. [28] Anyone who rejected the law of Moses died without mercy on the testimony of two or three witnesses. [29] How much more severely do you think a man deserves to be punished who has trampled the Son of God under foot, who has treated as an unholy thing the blood of the covenant that sanctified him, and who has insulted the Spirit of grace? [30] For we know him who said, "It is mine to avenge; I will repay,"[a] and again, "The Lord will judge his people."[b] [31] It is a dreadful thing to fall into the hands of the living God.

[32] Remember those earlier days after you had received the light, when you stood your ground in a great contest in the face of suffering. [33] Sometimes you were publicly exposed to insult and persecution; at other times you stood side by side with those who were so treated. [34] You sympathized with those in prison and joyfully accepted the confiscation of your property, because you knew that you yourselves had better and lasting possessions.

[35] So do not throw away your confidence; it will be richly rewarded. [36] You need to persevere so that when you have done the will of God, you will receive what he has promised. [37] For in just a very little while,

"He who is coming will come
        and will not delay.
[38]   But my righteous one[c] will
            live by faith.
    And if he shrinks back,
        I will not be pleased with
            him."[d]

[39] But we are not of those who shrink back and are destroyed, but of those who believe and are saved.

By Faith

11

Now faith is being sure of what we hope for and certain of what we do not see. [2] This is what the ancients were commended for.

[3] By faith we understand that the universe was formed at God's command, so that what is seen was not made out of what was visible.

[4] By faith Abel offered God a better sacrifice than Cain did. By faith he was commended as a

---

Cross references (margin):
93 Jas 1:2,3
64 Jas 5:7,8
11 1Jn 2:28
5 1Jn 5:3-5
12 1Pe 3:16
43 Ps 25:5
8 Jas 1:26,27
27 1Jn 1:3
36 Ps 19:13
41 Dev 20:11-15
88 1Jn 1:8-10

---

[a]30 Deut. 32:35;   [b]30 Deut. 32:36; Psalm 135:14   [c]38 One early manuscript *But the righteous*   [d]38 Hab. 2:3,4

righteous man, when God spoke well of his offerings. And by faith he still speaks, even though he is dead.

⁵By faith Enoch was taken from this life, so that he did not experience death; he could not be found, because God had taken him away. For before he was taken, he was commended as one who pleased God. ⁶And without faith it is impossible to please God, because anyone who comes to him must believe that he exists and that he rewards those who earnestly seek him.

⁷By faith Noah, when warned about things not yet seen, in holy fear built an ark to save his family. By his faith he condemned the world and became heir of the righteousness that comes by faith.

⁸By faith Abraham, when called to go to a place he would later receive as his inheritance, obeyed and went, even though he did not know where he was going. ⁹By faith he made his home in the promised land like a stranger in a foreign country; he lived in tents, as did Isaac and Jacob, who were heirs with him of the same promise. ¹⁰For he was looking forward to the city with foundations, whose architect and builder is God.

¹¹By faith Abraham, even though he was past age—and Sarah herself was barren—was enabled to become a father because he*ᵈ* considered him faithful who had made the promise. ¹²And so from this one man, and he as good as dead, came descendants as numerous as the stars in the sky and as countless as the sand on the seashore.

¹³All these people were still living by faith when they died.

24 Ps 37:5
78 1Jn 1:9
96

They did not receive the things promised; they only saw them and welcomed them from a distance. And they admitted that they were aliens and strangers on earth. ¹⁴People who say such things show that they are looking for a country of their own. ¹⁵If they had been thinking of the country they had left, they would have had opportunity to return. ¹⁶Instead, they were longing for a better country—a heavenly one. Therefore God is not ashamed to be called their God, for he has prepared a city for them.

¹⁷By faith Abraham, when God tested him, offered Isaac as a sacrifice. He who had received the promises was about to sacrifice his one and only son, ¹⁸even though God had said to him, "It is through Isaac that your offspringᵇ will be reckoned."ᶜ ¹⁹Abraham reasoned that God could raise the dead, and figuratively speaking, he did receive Isaac back from death.

²⁰By faith Isaac blessed Jacob and Esau in regard to their future.

²¹By faith Jacob, when he was dying, blessed each of Joseph's sons, and worshiped as he leaned on the top of his staff.

²²By faith Joseph, when his end was near, spoke about the exodus of the Israelites from Egypt and gave instructions about his bones.

²³By faith Moses' parents hid him for three months after he was born, because they saw he was no ordinary child, and they were not afraid of the king's edict.

²⁴By faith Moses, when he had grown up, refused to be known as the son of Pharaoh's daughter. ²⁵He chose to be mistreated along

92 Jas 1:13,14

ᵃ11 Or By faith even Sarah, who was past age, was enabled to bear children because she ᵇ18 Greek seed ᶜ18 Gen. 21:12

with the people of God rather than to enjoy the pleasures of sin for a short time. [26]He regarded disgrace for the sake of Christ as of greater value than the treasures of Egypt, because he was looking ahead to his reward. [27]By faith he left Egypt, not fearing the king's anger; he persevered because he saw him who is invisible. [28]By faith he kept the Passover and the sprinkling of blood, so that the destroyer of the firstborn would not touch the firstborn of Israel.

[29]By faith the people passed through the Red Sea[z] as on dry land; but when the Egyptians tried to do so, they were drowned.

[30]By faith the walls of Jericho fell, after the people had marched around them for seven days.

[31]By faith the prostitute Rahab, because she welcomed the spies, was not killed with those who were disobedient.[b]

[32]And what more shall I say? I do not have time to tell about Gideon, Barak, Samson, Jephthah, David, Samuel and the prophets, [33]who through faith conquered kingdoms, administered justice, and gained what was promised; who shut the mouths of lions, [34]quenched the fury of the flames, and escaped the edge of the sword; whose weakness was turned to strength; and who became powerful in battle and routed foreign armies. [35]Women received back their dead, raised to life again. Others were tortured and refused to be released, so that they might gain a better resurrection. [36]Some faced jeers and flogging, while still others were chained and put in prison. [37]They were stoned[c]; they were sawed in two; they were put to death by the sword. They went about in sheepskins and goatskins, destitute, persecuted and mistreated— [38]the world was not worthy of them. They wandered in deserts and mountains, and in caves and holes in the ground.

[39]These were all commended for their faith, yet none of them received what had been promised. [40]God had planned something better for us so that only together with us would they be made perfect.

God Disciplines His Sons

12 Therefore, since we are surrounded by such a great cloud of witnesses, let us throw off everything that hinders and the sin that so easily entangles, and let us run with perseverance the race marked out for us. [2]Let us fix our eyes on Jesus, the author and perfecter of our faith, who for the joy set before him endured the cross, scorning its shame, and sat down at the right hand of the throne of God. [3]Consider him who endured such opposition from sinful men, so that you will not grow weary and lose heart.

[4]In your struggle against sin, you have not yet resisted to the point of shedding your blood. [5]And you have forgotten that word of encouragement that addresses you as sons:

"My son, do not make light of
    the Lord's discipline,
  and do not lose heart when
    he rebukes you,
[6]because the Lord disciplines
    those he loves,
  and he punishes everyone
    he accepts as a son."[d]

20 Jas 1:5,6

17

⁷Endure hardship as discipline; God is treating you as sons. For what son is not disciplined by his father? ⁸If you are not disciplined (and everyone undergoes discipline), then you are illegitimate children and not true sons. ⁹Moreover, we have all had human fathers who disciplined us and we respected them for it. How much more should we submit to the Father of our spirits and live! ¹⁰Our fathers disciplined us for a little while as they thought best; but God disciplines us for our good, that we may share in his holiness. ¹¹No discipline seems pleasant at the time, but painful. Later on, however, it produces a harvest of righteousness and peace for those who have been trained by it.

¹²Therefore, strengthen your feeble arms and weak knees. ¹³"Make level paths for your feet,"ᵃ so that the lame may not be disabled, but rather healed.

Warning Against Refusing God

¹⁴Make every effort to live in peace with all men and to be holy; without holiness no one will see the Lord. ¹⁵See to it that no one misses the grace of God and that no bitter root grows up to cause trouble and defile many. ¹⁶See that no one is sexually immoral, or is godless like Esau, who for a single meal sold his inheritance rights as the oldest son. ¹⁷Afterward, as you know, when he wanted to inherit this blessing, he was rejected. He could bring about no change of mind, though he sought the blessing with tears.

¹⁸You have not come to a mountain that can be touched and that is burning with fire; to darkness, gloom and storm; ¹⁹to a trumpet blast or to such a voice speaking words that those who heard it begged that no further word be spoken to them, ²⁰because they could not bear what was commanded: "If even an animal touches the mountain, it must be stoned."ᵇ ²¹The sight was so terrifying that Moses said, "I am trembling with fear."ᶜ

²²But you have come to Mount Zion, to the heavenly Jerusalem, the city of the living God. You have come to thousands upon thousands of angels in joyful assembly, ²³to the church of the firstborn, whose names are written in heaven. You have come to God, the judge of all men, to the spirits of righteous men made perfect, ²⁴to Jesus the mediator of a new covenant, and to the sprinkled blood that speaks a better word than the blood of Abel.

²⁵See to it that you do not refuse him who speaks. If they did not escape when they refused him who warned them on earth, how much less will we, if we turn away from him who warns us from heaven? ²⁶At that time his voice shook the earth, but now he has promised, "Once more I will shake not only the earth but also the heavens."ᵈ ²⁷The words "once more" indicate the removing of what can be shaken—that is, created things—so that what cannot be shaken may remain.

²⁸Therefore, since we are receiving a kingdom that cannot be shaken, let us be thankful, and so worship God acceptably with reverence and awe, ²⁹for our "God is a consuming fire."ᵉ

Concluding Exhortations

13 Keep on loving each other as brothers. ²Do not forget

65
79
Jas 4:7,8

ᵃ13 Prov. 4:26   ᵇ20 Exodus 19:12,13   ᶜ21 Deut. 9:19   ᵈ26 Haggai 2:6
ᵉ29 Deut. 4:24

to entertain strangers, for by so doing some people have entertained angels without knowing it. ³Remember those in prison as if you were their fellow prisoners, and those who are mistreated as if you yourselves were suffering.

⁴Marriage should be honored by all, and the marriage bed kept pure, for God will judge the adulterer and all the sexually immoral. ⁵Keep your lives free from the love of money and be content with what you have, because God has said,

"Never will I leave you;
    never will I forsake you."ᵃ

⁶So we say with confidence,

"The Lord is my helper; I will
    not be afraid.
What can man do to me?"ᵇ

⁷Remember your leaders, who spoke the word of God to you. Consider the outcome of their way of life and imitate their faith. ⁸Jesus Christ is the same yesterday and today and forever.

⁹Do not be carried away by all kinds of strange teachings. It is good for our hearts to be strengthened by grace, not by ceremonial foods, which are of no value to those who eat them. ¹⁰We have an altar from which those who minister at the tabernacle have no right to eat.

¹¹The high priest carries the blood of animals into the Most Holy Place as a sin offering, but the bodies are burned outside the camp. ¹²And so Jesus also suffered outside the city gate to make the people holy through his own blood. ¹³Let us, then, go

to him outside the camp, bearing the disgrace he bore. ¹⁴For here we do not have an enduring city, but we are looking for the city that is to come.

¹⁵Through Jesus, therefore, let us continually offer to God a sacrifice of praise—the fruit of lips that confess his name. ¹⁶And do not forget to do good and to share with others, for with such sacrifices God is pleased.

¹⁷Obey your leaders and submit to their authority. They keep watch over you as men who must give an account. Obey them so that their work will be a joy, not a burden, for that would be of no advantage to you.

¹⁸Pray for us. We are sure that we have a clear conscience and desire to live honorably in every way. ¹⁹I particularly urge you to pray so that I may be restored to you soon.

²⁰May the God of peace, who through the blood of the eternal covenant brought back from the dead our Lord Jesus, that great Shepherd of the sheep, ²¹equip you with everything good for doing his will, and may he work in us what is pleasing to him, through Jesus Christ, to whom be glory for ever and ever. Amen.

²²Brothers, I urge you to bear with my word of exhortation, for I have written you only a short letter.

²³I want you to know that our brother Timothy has been released. If he arrives soon, I will come with him to see you.

²⁴Greet all your leaders and all God's people. Those from Italy send you their greetings.

²⁵Grace be with you all.

ᵃ5 Deut. 31:6   ᵇ6 Psalm 118:6,7

Margin references

2 Ps 51
57 1Pe 3:1-7
13
52 Ps 27:10
61 Ps 15:5

16 Ps 27:14

68 1Pe 1:3
99 1Pe 1:17

63 Jas 1:22-25

James

1 James, a servant of God and of the Lord Jesus Christ,

To the twelve tribes scattered among the nations:

Greetings.

Trials and Temptations

93 [2]Consider it pure joy, my brothers, whenever you face trials of many kinds, [3]because you know that the testing of your faith develops perseverance. [4]Perseverance must finish its work so that you may be mature and complete, not lacking anything. [5]If any of you lacks wisdom, he should ask God, who gives generously to all without finding fault, and it will be given to him. [6]But when he asks, he must believe and not doubt, because he who doubts is like a wave of the sea, blown and tossed by the wind. [7]That man should not think he will receive anything from the Lord; [8]he is a double-minded man, unstable in all he does.

67
Jas 1:12

58

20
1Jn 1:7

[9]The brother in humble circumstances ought to take pride in his high position. [10]But the one who is rich should take pride in his low position, because he will pass away like a wild flower. [11]For the sun rises with scorching heat and withers the plant; its blossom falls and its beauty is destroyed. In the same way, the rich man will fade even while he goes about his business.

67 [12]Blessed is the man who perseveres under trial, because when he has stood the test, he will receive the crown of life that God has promised to those who love him.

[13]When tempted, no one should say, "God is tempting me." For God cannot be tempted by evil, nor does he tempt anyone; [14]but each one is tempted when, by his own evil desire, he is dragged away and enticed. [15]Then, after desire has conceived, it gives birth to sin; and sin, when it is full-grown, gives birth to death.

92

[16]Don't be deceived, my dear brothers. [17]Every good and perfect gift is from above, coming down from the Father of the heavenly lights, who does not change like shifting shadows. [18]He chose to give us birth through the word of truth, that we might be a kind of firstfruits of all he created.

Listening and Doing

[19]My dear brothers, take note of this: Everyone should be quick to listen, slow to speak and slow to become angry, [20]for man's anger does not bring about the righteous life that God desires. [21]Therefore, get rid of all moral filth and the evil that is so prevalent and humbly accept the word planted in you, which can save you.

3
Jas 3:14

[22]Do not merely listen to the word, and so deceive yourselves. Do what it says. [23]Anyone who listens to the word but does not do what it says is like a man who looks at his face in a mirror [24]and, after looking at himself, goes away and immediately forgets what he looks like. [25]But the man who looks intently into the perfect law that gives freedom, and continues to do this, not forgetting what he has heard, but do-

63
1Pe 1:2

ing it—he will be blessed in what he does.

⁸
_{Rev 2}

²⁶If anyone considers himself religious and yet does not keep a tight rein on his tongue, he deceives himself and his religion is worthless. ²⁷Religion that God our Father accepts as pure and faultless is this: to look after orphans and widows in their distress and to keep oneself from being polluted by the world.

Favoritism Forbidden

¹
⁴⁷
⁵⁵
_{1Pe 1:22}

2 My brothers, as believers in our glorious Lord Jesus Christ, don't show favoritism. ²Suppose a man comes into your meeting wearing a gold ring and fine clothes, and a poor man in shabby clothes also comes in. ³If you show special attention to the man wearing fine clothes and say, "Here's a good seat for you," but say to the poor man, "You stand there" or "Sit on the floor by my feet," ⁴have you not discriminated among yourselves and become judges with evil thoughts?

⁵Listen, my dear brothers: Has not God chosen those who are poor in the eyes of the world to be rich in faith and to inherit the kingdom he promised those who love him? ⁶But you have insulted the poor. Is it not the rich who are exploiting you? Are they not the ones who are dragging you into court? ⁷Are they not the ones who are slandering the noble name of him to whom you belong?

⁸If you really keep the royal law found in Scripture, "Love your neighbor as yourself,"ᵃ you are doing right. ⁹But if you show favoritism, you sin and are convicted by the law as lawbreakers.

¹⁴
_{Jude 15}

⁵⁰
_{Ps 19:7}

¹⁰For whoever keeps the whole law and yet stumbles at just one point is guilty of breaking all of it. ¹¹For he who said, "Do not commit adultery,"ᵇ also said, "Do not murder."ᶜ If you do not commit adultery but do commit murder, you have become a lawbreaker.

¹²Speak and act as those who are going to be judged by the law that gives freedom, ¹³because judgment without mercy will be shown to anyone who has not been merciful. Mercy triumphs over judgment!

Faith and Deeds

¹⁴What good is it, my brothers, if a man claims to have faith but has no deeds? Can such faith save him? ¹⁵Suppose a brother or sister is without clothes and daily food. ¹⁶If one of you says to him, "Go, I wish you well; keep warm and well fed," but does nothing about his physical needs, what good is it? ¹⁷In the same way, faith by itself, if it is not accompanied by action, is dead.

¹⁸But someone will say, "You have faith; I have deeds."

Show me your faith without deeds, and I will show you my faith by what I do. ¹⁹You believe that there is one God. Good! Even the demons believe that—and shudder.

²⁰You foolish man, do you want evidence that faith without deeds is useless?ᵈ ²¹Was not our ancestor Abraham considered righteous for what he did when he offered his son Isaac on the altar? ²²You see that his faith and his actions were working together, and his faith was made complete by what he did. ²³And the scripture was fulfilled that says, "Abraham believed God, and it was credited to him as righteousness,"ᵉ and he was called God's

---

ᵃ8 Lev. 19:18   ᵇ11 Exodus 20:14; Deut. 5:18   ᶜ11 Exodus 20:13; Deut. 5:17
ᵈ20 Some early manuscripts *dead*   ᵉ23 Gen. 15:6

friend. 24You see that a person is justified by what he does and not by faith alone.

25In the same way, was not even Rahab the prostitute considered righteous for what she did when she gave lodging to the spies and sent them off in a different direction? 26As the body without the spirit is dead, so faith without deeds is dead.

Taming the Tongue

3 Not many of you should presume to be teachers, my brothers, because you know that we who teach will be judged more strictly. 2We all stumble in many ways. If anyone is never at fault in what he says, he is a perfect man, able to keep his whole body in check.

3When we put bits into the mouths of horses to make them obey us, we can turn the whole animal. 4Or take ships as an example. Although they are so large and are driven by strong winds, they are steered by a very small rudder wherever the pilot wants to go. 5Likewise the tongue is a small part of the body, but it makes great boasts. Consider what a great forest is set on fire by a small spark. 6The tongue also is a fire, a world of evil among the parts of the body. It corrupts the whole person, sets the whole course of his life on fire, and is itself set on fire by hell.

7All kinds of animals, birds, reptiles and creatures of the sea are being tamed and have been tamed by man, 8but no man can tame the tongue. It is a restless evil, full of deadly poison.

9With the tongue we praise our Lord and Father, and with it we curse men, who have been made in God's likeness. 10Out of the

same mouth come praise and cursing. My brothers, this should not be. 11Can both fresh water and salt*a* water flow from the same spring? 12My brothers, can a fig tree bear olives, or a grapevine bear figs? Neither can a salt spring produce fresh water.

Two Kinds of Wisdom

13Who is wise and understanding among you? Let him show it by his good life, by deeds done in the humility that comes from wisdom. 14But if you harbor bitter envy and selfish ambition in your hearts, do not boast about it or deny the truth. 15Such "wisdom" does not come down from heaven but is earthly, unspiritual, of the devil. 16For where you have envy and selfish ambition, there you find disorder and every evil practice.

17But the wisdom that comes from heaven is first of all pure; then peace-loving, considerate, submissive, full of mercy and good fruit, impartial and sincere. 18Peacemakers who sow in peace raise a harvest of righteousness.

Submit Yourselves to God

4 What causes fights and quarrels among you? Don't they come from your desires that battle within you? 2You want something but don't get it. You kill and covet, but you cannot have what you want. You quarrel and fight. You do not have, because you do not ask God. 3When you ask, you do not receive, because you ask with wrong motives, that you may spend what you get on your pleasures.

4You adulterous people, don't you know that friendship with the world is hatred toward God? Anyone who chooses to be a friend of the world becomes an

84

3
Ps 2:12

---

*a11 Greek *bitter* (see also verse 14)

enemy of God. ⁵Or do you think Scripture says without reason that the spirit he caused to live in us envies intensely?ᵃ ⁶But he gives us more grace. That is why Scripture says:

"God opposes the proud
    but gives grace to the
    humble."ᵇ

79 ⁷Submit yourselves, then, to God. Resist the devil, and he will flee from you. ⁸Come near to God and he will come near to you. Wash your hands, you sinners, and purify your hearts, you double-minded. ⁹Grieve, mourn and wail. Change your laughter to mourning and your joy to gloom. ¹⁰Humble yourselves before the Lord, and he will lift you up.

¹¹Brothers, do not slander one another. Anyone who speaks against his brother or judges him speaks against the law and judges it. When you judge the law, you are not keeping it, but sitting in judgment on it. ¹²There is only one Lawgiver and Judge, the one who is able to save and destroy. But you—who are you to judge your neighbor?

Boasting About Tomorrow

¹³Now listen, you who say, "Today or tomorrow we will go to this or that city, spend a year there, carry on business and make money." ¹⁴Why, you do not even know what will happen tomorrow. What is your life? You are a mist that appears for a little while and then vanishes. ¹⁵Instead, you ought to say, "If it is the Lord's will, we will live and do this or that." ¹⁶As it is, you boast and brag. All such boasting is evil. ¹⁷Anyone, then, who

knows the good he ought to do and doesn't do it, sins.

Warning to Rich Oppressors

5 Now listen, you rich people, weep and wail because of the misery that is coming upon you. ²Your wealth has rotted, and moths have eaten your clothes. ³Your gold and silver are corroded. Their corrosion will testify against you and eat your flesh like fire. You have hoarded wealth in the last days. ⁴Look! The wages you failed to pay the workmen who mowed your fields are crying out against you. The cries of the harvesters have reached the ears of the Lord Almighty. ⁵You have lived on earth in luxury and self-indulgence. You have fattened yourselves in the day of slaughter.ᶜ ⁶You have condemned and murdered innocent men, who were not opposing you.

Patience in Suffering

⁷Be patient, then, brothers, un- 64 til the Lord's coming. See how the farmer waits for the land to yield its valuable crop and how patient he is for the autumn and spring rains. ⁸You too, be patient and stand firm, because the Lord's coming is near. ⁹Don't grumble against each other, brothers, or you will be judged. The Judge is standing at the door!

¹⁰Brothers, as an example of patience in the face of suffering, take the prophets who spoke in the name of the Lord. ¹¹As you know, we consider blessed those who have persevered. You have heard of Job's perseverance and have seen what the Lord finally

---

ᵃ5 Or that God jealously longs for the spirit that he made to live in us; or that the Spirit he caused to live in us longs jealously   ᵇ6 Prov. 3:34   ᶜ5 Or yourselves as in a day of feasting

brought about. The Lord is full of compassion and mercy.

¹²Above all, my brothers, do not swear—not by heaven or by earth or by anything else. Let your "Yes" be yes, and your "No," no, or you will be condemned.

The Prayer of Faith

39 ¹³Is any one of you in trouble? He should pray. Is anyone happy? Let him sing songs of praise. ¹⁴Is any one of you sick? He should call the elders of the church to pray over him and anoint him with oil in the name of the Lord. ¹⁵And the prayer offered in faith will make the sick person well; the Lord will raise him up. If he has sinned, he will be forgiven. ¹⁶Therefore confess your sins to each other and pray for each other so that you may be healed. The prayer of a righteous man is powerful and effective.

10 1Jn 1:9,10

¹⁷Elijah was a man just like us. He prayed earnestly that it would not rain, and it did not rain on the land for three and a half years. ¹⁸Again he prayed, and the heavens gave rain, and the earth produced its crops.

¹⁹My brothers, if one of you should wander from the truth and someone should bring him back, ²⁰remember this: Whoever turns a sinner from the error of his way will save him from death and cover over a multitude of sins.

35

1 Peter

22 2Pe 1:10

1 Peter, an apostle of Jesus Christ,

To God's elect, strangers in the world, scattered throughout Pontus, Galatia, Cappadocia, 63 Asia and Bithynia, ²who have been chosen according to the foreknowledge of God the Father, through the sanctifying work of the Spirit, for obedience to Jesus Christ and sprinkling by his blood:

Grace and peace be yours in abundance.

Praise to God for a Living Hope

68 Ps 16:11

³Praise be to the God and Father of our Lord Jesus Christ! In his great mercy he has given us new birth into a living hope through the resurrection of Jesus Christ from the dead, ⁴and into an inheritance that can never perish, spoil or fade—kept in heaven for you, ⁵who through faith are shielded by God's power until the coming of the salvation that is ready to be revealed in the last time. ⁶In this you greatly rejoice, though now for a little while you may have had to suffer grief in all kinds of trials. ⁷These have come so that your faith—of greater worth than gold, which perishes even though refined by fire— may be proved genuine and may result in praise, glory and honor when Jesus Christ is revealed. ⁸Though you have not seen him, you love him; and even though you do not see him now, you believe in him and are filled with an inexpressible and glorious joy, ⁹for you are receiving the goal of your faith, the salvation of your souls.

37 Ps 16:11
91 1Pe 2:20
76 1Pe 5:4

6 1Pe 1:18,

¹⁰Concerning this salvation, the prophets, who spoke of the grace that was to come to you, searched intently and with the

greatest care, [11]trying to find out the time and circumstances to which the Spirit of Christ in them was pointing when he predicted the sufferings of Christ and the glories that would follow. [12]It was revealed to them that they were not serving themselves but you, when they spoke of the things that have now been told you by those who have preached the gospel to you by the Holy Spirit sent from heaven. Even angels long to look into these things.

Be Holy

[13]Therefore, prepare your minds for action; be self-controlled; set your hope fully on the grace to be given you when Jesus Christ is revealed. [14]As obedient children, do not conform to the evil desires you had when you lived in ignorance. [15]But just as he who called you is holy, so be holy in all you do; [16]for it is written: "Be holy, because I am holy."[a]

[17]Since you call on a Father who judges each man's work impartially, live your lives as strangers here in reverent fear. [18]For you know that it was not with perishable things such as silver or gold that you were redeemed from the empty way of life handed down to you from your forefathers, [19]but with the precious blood of Christ, a lamb without blemish or defect. [20]He was chosen before the creation of the world, but was revealed in these last times for your sake. [21]Through him you believe in God, who raised him from the dead and glorified him, and so your faith and hope are in God.

[22]Now that you have purified yourselves by obeying the truth so that you have sincere love for your brothers, love one another deeply, from the heart.[b] [23]For you have been born again, not of perishable seed, but of imperishable, through the living and enduring word of God. [24]For,

"All men are like grass,
  and all their glory is like the
    flowers of the field;
the grass withers and the
    flowers fall,
[25] but the word of the Lord
    stands forever."[c]

And this is the word that was preached to you.

2 Therefore, rid yourselves of all malice and all deceit, hypocrisy, envy, and slander of every kind. [2]Like newborn babies, crave pure spiritual milk, so that by it you may grow up in your salvation, [3]now that you have tasted that the Lord is good.

The Living Stone and a Chosen People

[4]As you come to him, the living Stone—rejected by men but chosen by God and precious to him— [5]you also, like living stones, are being built into a spiritual house to be a holy priesthood, offering spiritual sacrifices acceptable to God through Jesus Christ. [6]For in Scripture it says:

"See, I lay a stone in Zion,
  a chosen and precious
    cornerstone,
and the one who trusts in him
    will never be put to
    shame."[d]

[7]Now to you who believe, this stone is precious. But to those who do not believe,

"The stone the builders
    rejected
  has become the capstone,[e]"[f]

Margin references

99 Jude 24,25
6 1Jn 2:2
72 Ps 26:11
55 1Jn 4:19-21
62
34 2Pe 1:5
87 1Pe 2:9,10

---

[a]16 Lev. 11:44,45; 19:2; 20:7   [b]22 Some early manuscripts from a pure heart
[c]25 Isaiah 40:6-8   [d]6 Isaiah 28:16   [e]7 Or cornerstone   [f]7 Psalm 118:22

⁸and,

> "A stone that causes men to
> stumble
>   and a rock that makes them
>   fall." [a]

They stumble because they disobey the message—which is also what they were destined for.

87
Ps 139:16
⁹But you are a chosen people, a royal priesthood, a holy nation, a people belonging to God, that you may declare the praises of him who called you out of darkness into his wonderful light. ¹⁰Once you were not a people, but now you are the people of God; once you had not received mercy, but now you have received mercy.

¹¹Dear friends, I urge you, as aliens and strangers in the world, to abstain from sinful desires, which war against your soul. ¹²Live such good lives among the pagans that, though they accuse you of doing wrong, they may see your good deeds and glorify God on the day he visits us.

Submission to Rulers and Masters

¹³Submit yourselves for the Lord's sake to every authority instituted among men: whether to the king, as the supreme authority, ¹⁴or to governors, who are sent by him to punish those who do wrong and to commend those who do right. ¹⁵For it is God's will that by doing good you should silence the ignorant talk of foolish men. ¹⁶Live as free men, but do not use your freedom as a cover-up for evil; live as servants of God. ¹⁷Show proper respect to everyone: Love the brotherhood of believers, fear God, honor the king.

82
98
Ps 19:14
30

¹⁸Slaves, submit yourselves to your masters with all respect, not only to those who are good and considerate, but also to those who are harsh. ¹⁹For it is commendable if a man bears up under the pain of unjust suffering because he is conscious of God. ²⁰But how is it to your credit if you receive a beating for doing wrong and endure it? But if you suffer for doing good and you endure it, this is commendable before God. ²¹To this you were called, because Christ suffered for you, leaving you an example, that you should follow in his steps.

73
Ps 27:10

91
1Pe 4:12-

²²"He committed no sin,
    and no deceit was found in
    his mouth." [b]

²³When they hurled their insults at him, he did not retaliate; when he suffered, he made no threats. Instead, he entrusted himself to him who judges justly. ²⁴He himself bore our sins in his body on the tree, so that we might die to sins and live for righteousness; by his wounds you have been healed. ²⁵For you were like sheep going astray, but now you have returned to the Shepherd and Overseer of your souls.

Wives and Husbands

3 Wives, in the same way be submissive to your husbands so that, if any of them do not believe the word, they may be won over without words by the behavior of their wives, ²when they see the purity and reverence of your lives. ³Your beauty should not come from outward adornment, such as braided hair and the wearing of gold jewelry and fine clothes. ⁴Instead, it should be that of your inner self, the unfading beauty of a gentle and qui-

25
Ps 68:6

57

---

[a]8 Isaiah 8:14   [b]22 Isaiah 53:9

et spirit, which is of great worth in God's sight. [5]For this is the way the holy women of the past who put their hope in God used to make themselves beautiful. They were submissive to their own husbands, [6]like Sarah, who obeyed Abraham and called him her master. You are her daughters if you do what is right and do not give way to fear.

[7]Husbands, in the same way be considerate as you live with your wives, and treat them with respect as the weaker partner and as heirs with you of the gracious gift of life, so that nothing will hinder your prayers.

Suffering for Doing Good

9
19:8-11

[8]Finally, all of you, live in harmony with one another; be sympathetic, love as brothers, be compassionate and humble. [9]Do not repay evil with evil or insult with insult, but with blessing, because to this you were called so that you may inherit a blessing. [10]For,

"Whoever would love life
    and see good days
must keep his tongue from
    evil
    and his lips from deceitful
        speech.
[11]He must turn from evil and
    do good;
he must seek peace and
    pursue it.
[12]For the eyes of the Lord are
    on the righteous
    and his ears are attentive to
        their prayer,
but the face of the Lord is
    against those who do
    evil."[a]

[13]Who is going to harm you if you are eager to do good? [14]But even if you should suffer for

what is right, you are blessed. "Do not fear what they fear[b]; do not be frightened."[c] [15]But in your hearts set apart Christ as Lord. Always be prepared to give an answer to everyone who asks you to give the reason for the hope that you have. But do this with gentleness and respect, [16]keeping a clear conscience, so that those who speak maliciously against your good behavior in Christ may be ashamed of their slander. [17]It is better, if it is God's will, to suffer for doing good than for doing evil. [18]For Christ died for sins once for all, the righteous for the unrighteous, to bring you to God. He was put to death in the body but made alive by the Spirit, [19]through whom[d] also he went and preached to the spirits in prison [20]who disobeyed long ago when God waited patiently in the days of Noah while the ark was being built. In it only a few people, eight in all, were saved through water, [21]and this water symbolizes baptism that now saves you also—not the removal of dirt from the body but the pledge[e] of a good conscience toward God. It saves you by the resurrection of Jesus Christ, [22]who has gone into heaven and is at God's right hand—with angels, authorities and powers in submission to him.

Living for God

4 Therefore, since Christ suffered in his body, arm yourselves also with the same attitude, because he who has suffered in his body is done with sin. [2]As a result, he does not live the rest of his earthly life for evil human desires, but rather for the will of God. [3]For you have spent enough time in the past doing

12
1Pe 3:21

71

12
Ps 19:12

21

---

[a]12 Psalm 34:12-16   [b]14 Or not fear their threats   [c]14 Isaiah 8:12   [d]18,19 Or alive in the spirit, [19]through which   [e]21 Or response

what pagans choose to do—living in debauchery, lust, drunkenness, orgies, carousing and detestable idolatry. ⁴They think it strange that you do not plunge with them into the same flood of dissipation, and they heap abuse on you. ⁵But they will have to give account to him who is ready to judge the living and the dead. ⁶For this is the reason the gospel was preached even to those who are now dead, so that they might be judged according to men in regard to the body, but live according to God in regard to the spirit.

⁷The end of all things is near. Therefore be clear minded and self-controlled so that you can pray. ⁸Above all, love each other deeply, because love covers over a multitude of sins. ⁹Offer hospitality to one another without grumbling. ¹⁰Each one should use whatever gift he has received to serve others, faithfully administering God's grace in its various forms. ¹¹If anyone speaks, he should do it as one speaking the very words of God. If anyone serves, he should do it with the strength God provides, so that in all things God may be praised through Jesus Christ. To him be the glory and the power for ever and ever. Amen.

Suffering for Being a Christian

¹²Dear friends, do not be surprised at the painful trial you are suffering, as though something strange were happening to you. ¹³But rejoice that you participate in the sufferings of Christ, so that you may be overjoyed when his glory is revealed. ¹⁴If you are insulted because of the name of Christ, you are blessed, for the Spirit of glory and of God rests on you. ¹⁵If you suffer, it should not be as a murderer or thief or any other kind of criminal, or even as a meddler. ¹⁶However, if you suffer as a Christian, do not be ashamed, but praise God that you bear that name. ¹⁷For it is time for judgment to begin with the family of God; and if it begins with us, what will the outcome be for those who do not obey the gospel of God? ¹⁸And,

"If it is hard for the righteous
    to be saved,
what will become of the
    ungodly and the
    sinner?"ᵃ

¹⁹So then, those who suffer according to God's will should commit themselves to their faithful Creator and continue to do good.

To Elders and Young Men

5 To the elders among you, I appeal as a fellow elder, a witness of Christ's sufferings and one who also will share in the glory to be revealed: ²Be shepherds of God's flock that is under your care, serving as overseers—not because you must, but because you are willing, as God wants you to be; not greedy for money, but eager to serve; ³not lording it over those entrusted to you, but being examples to the flock. ⁴And when the Chief Shepherd appears, you will receive the crown of glory that will never fade away.

⁵Young men, in the same way be submissive to those who are older. All of you, clothe yourselves with humility toward one another, because,

"God opposes the proud

---

49 Ps 34:8

91

76 Ps 84:11

44 Ps 19:12

ᵃ18 Prov. 11:31

but gives grace to the
humble."[a]

[Ps 43:5] [4]

6Humble yourselves, therefore, under God's mighty hand, that he may lift you up in due time. 7Cast all your anxiety on him because he cares for you.

[83]

8Be self-controlled and alert. Your enemy the devil prowls around like a roaring lion looking for someone to devour. 9Resist him, standing firm in the faith, because you know that your brothers throughout the world are undergoing the same kind of sufferings.

10And the God of all grace, who called you to his eternal glory in Christ, after you have suffered a little while, will himself restore you and make you strong, firm and steadfast. 11To him be the power for ever and ever. Amen.

Final Greetings

12With the help of Silas,[b] whom I regard as a faithful brother, I have written to you briefly, encouraging you and testifying that this is the true grace of God. Stand fast in it.

13She who is in Babylon, chosen together with you, sends you her greetings, and so does my son Mark. 14Greet one another with a kiss of love.

Peace to all of you who are in Christ.

2 Peter

1 Simon Peter, a servant and apostle of Jesus Christ,

To those who through the righteousness of our God and Savior Jesus Christ have received a faith as precious as ours:

2Grace and peace be yours in abundance through the knowledge of God and of Jesus our Lord.

Making One's Calling and Election Sure

3His divine power has given us everything we need for life and godliness through our knowledge of him who called us by his own glory and goodness. 4Through these he has given us his very great and precious promises, so that through them you may participate in the divine nature and escape the corruption in the world caused by evil desires.

5For this very reason, make every effort to add to your faith goodness; and to goodness, knowledge; 6and to knowledge, self-control; and to self-control, perseverance; and to perseverance, godliness; 7and to godliness, brotherly kindness; and to brotherly kindness, love. 8For if you possess these qualities in increasing measure, they will keep you from being ineffective and unproductive in your knowledge of our Lord Jesus Christ. 9But if anyone does not have them, he is nearsighted and blind, and has forgotten that he has been cleansed from his past sins.

[34] [2Pe 3:18]
[89] [1Jn 2:15-17]

10Therefore, my brothers, be all the more eager to make your calling and election sure. For if you do these things, you will never fall, 11and you will receive a rich welcome into the eternal kingdom of our Lord and Savior Jesus Christ.

[22]

---

a5 Prov. 3:34   b12 Greek *Silvanus*, a variant of *Silas*

Prophecy of Scripture

12So I will always remind you of these things, even though you know them and are firmly established in the truth you now have. 13I think it is right to refresh your memory as long as I live in the tent of this body, 14because I know that I will soon put it aside, as our Lord Jesus Christ has made clear to me. 15And I will make every effort to see that after my departure you will always be able to remember these things.

16We did not follow cleverly invented stories when we told you about the power and coming of our Lord Jesus Christ, but we were eyewitnesses of his majesty. 17For he received honor and glory from God the Father when the voice came to him from the Majestic Glory, saying, "This is my Son, whom I love; with him I am well pleased."a 18We ourselves heard this voice that came from heaven when we were with him on the sacred mountain.

45
Ps 19:7,8

19And we have the word of the prophets made more certain, and you will do well to pay attention to it, as to a light shining in a dark place, until the day dawns and the morning star rises in your hearts. 20Above all, you must understand that no prophecy of Scripture came about by the prophet's own interpretation. 21For prophecy never had its origin in the will of man, but men spoke from God as they were carried along by the Holy Spirit.

False Teachers and Their Destruction

2 But there were also false prophets among the people, just as there will be false teachers among you. They will secretly introduce destructive heresies, even denying the sovereign Lord who bought them—bringing swift destruction on themselves. 2Many will follow their shameful ways and will bring the way of truth into disrepute. 3In their greed these teachers will exploit you with stories they have made up. Their condemnation has long been hanging over them, and their destruction has not been sleeping.

4For if God did not spare angels when they sinned, but sent them to hell,b putting them into gloomy dungeonsc to be held for judgment; 5if he did not spare the ancient world when he brought the flood on its ungodly people, but protected Noah, a preacher of righteousness, and seven others; 6if he condemned the cities of Sodom and Gomorrah by burning them to ashes, and made them an example of what is going to happen to the ungodly; 7and if he rescued Lot, a righteous man, who was distressed by the filthy lives of lawless men 8(for that righteous man, living among them day after day, was tormented in his righteous soul by the lawless deeds he saw and heard)— 9if this is so, then the Lord knows how to rescue godly men from trials and to hold the unrighteous for the day of judgment, while continuing their punishment.d 10This is especially true of those who follow the corrupt desire of the sinful naturee and despise authority.

Bold and arrogant, these men are not afraid to slander celestial beings; 11yet even angels, although they are stronger and more powerful, do not bring

a17 Matt. 17:5; Mark 9:7; Luke 9:35   b4 Greek Tartarus   c4 Some manuscripts into chains of darkness   d9 Or unrighteous for punishment until the day of judgment   e10 Or slanderous accusations against such beings in the presence of the Lord. [12]But these men blaspheme in matters they do not understand. They are like brute beasts, creatures of instinct, born only to be caught and destroyed, and like beasts they too will perish.

[13]They will be paid back with harm for the harm they have done. Their idea of pleasure is to carouse in broad daylight. They are blots and blemishes, reveling in their pleasures while they feast with you.[a] [14]With eyes full of adultery, they never stop sinning; they seduce the unstable; they are experts in greed—an accursed brood! [15]They have left the straight way and wandered off to follow the way of Balaam son of Beor, who loved the wages of wickedness. [16]But he was rebuked for his wrongdoing by a donkey—a beast without speech—who spoke with a man's voice and restrained the prophet's madness.

[17]These men are springs without water and mists driven by a storm. Blackest darkness is reserved for them. [18]For they mouth empty, boastful words and, by appealing to the lustful desires of sinful human nature, they entice people who are just escaping from those who live in error. [19]They promise them freedom, while they themselves are slaves of depravity—for a man is a slave to whatever has mastered him. [20]If they have escaped the corruption of the world by knowing our Lord and Savior Jesus Christ and are again entangled in it and overcome, they are worse off at the end than they were at the beginning. [21]It would have been better for them not to have known the way of righteousness, than to have known it and then

to turn their backs on the sacred command that was passed on to them. [22]Of them the proverbs are true: "A dog returns to its vomit,"[b] and, "A sow that is washed goes back to her wallowing in the mud."

The Day of the Lord

3 Dear friends, this is now my second letter to you. I have written both of them as reminders to stimulate you to wholesome thinking. [2]I want you to recall the words spoken in the past by the holy prophets and the command given by our Lord and Savior through your apostles.

[3]First of all, you must understand that in the last days scoffers will come, scoffing and following their own evil desires. [4]They will say, "Where is this 'coming' he promised? Ever since our fathers died, everything goes on as it has since the beginning of creation." [5]But they deliberately forget that long ago by God's word the heavens existed and the earth was formed out of water and by water. [6]By these waters also the world of that time was deluged and destroyed. [7]By the same word the present heavens and earth are reserved for fire, being kept for the day of judgment and destruction of ungodly men.

[8]But do not forget this one thing, dear friends: With the Lord a day is like a thousand years, and a thousand years are like a day. [9]The Lord is not slow in keeping his promise, as some understand slowness. He is patient with you, not wanting anyone to perish, but everyone to come to repentance.

[10]But the day of the Lord will come like a thief. The heavens will disappear with a roar; the

---

[a]13 Some manuscripts *in their love feasts*   [b]22 Prov. 26:11

elements will be destroyed by fire, and the earth and everything in it will be laid bare.*

[11] Since everything will be destroyed in this way, what kind of people ought you to be? You ought to live holy and godly lives [12] as you look forward to the day of God and speed its coming.* That day will bring about the destruction of the heavens by fire, and the elements will melt in the heat. [13] But in keeping with his promise we are looking forward to a new heaven and a new earth, the home of righteousness.

[14] So then, dear friends, since you are looking forward to this, make every effort to be found spotless, blameless and at peace with him. [15] Bear in mind that our Lord's patience means salvation, just as our dear brother Paul also wrote you with the wisdom that God gave him. [16] He writes the same way in all his letters, speaking in them of these matters. His letters contain some things that are hard to understand, which ignorant and unstable people distort, as they do the other Scriptures, to their own destruction.

[17] Therefore, dear friends, since you already know this, be on your guard so that you may not be carried away by the error of lawless men and fall from your secure position. [18] But grow in the grace and knowledge of our Lord and Savior Jesus Christ. To him be glory both now and forever! Amen.

81
1Jn 5:18

34

1 John

The Word of Life

1 That which was from the beginning, which we have heard, which we have seen with our eyes, which we have looked at and our hands have touched—this we proclaim concerning the Word of life. [2] The life appeared; we have seen it and testify to it, and we proclaim to you the eternal life, which was with the Father and has appeared to us. [3] We proclaim to you what we have seen and heard, so that you also may have fellowship with us. And our fellowship is with the Father and with his Son, Jesus Christ. [4] We write this to make our* joy complete.

27
Ps 133

Walking in the Light

[5] This is the message we have heard from him and declare to you: God is light; in him there is no darkness at all. [6] If we claim to have fellowship with him yet walk in the darkness, we lie and do not live by the truth. [7] But if we walk in the light, as he is in the light, we have fellowship with one another, and the blood of Jesus, his Son, purifies us from all* sin.

20
1Jn 3:14

[8] If we claim to be without sin, we deceive ourselves and the truth is not in us. [9] If we confess our sins, he is faithful and just and will forgive us our sins and purify us from all unrighteousness. [10] If we claim we have not sinned, we make him out to be a liar and his word has no place in our lives.

88
1Jn 3:6

78
1Jn 5:13

10
Ps 32:5

28
Ps 86:15

2 My dear children, I write this to you so that you will not sin. But if anybody does sin, we have one who speaks to the Fa-

*10 Some manuscripts *be burned up come*   *12 Or *as you wait eagerly for the day of God to come*   *4 Some manuscripts *your*   *7 Or *every*

ther in our defense—Jesus Christ, the Righteous One. ²He is the atoning sacrifice for our sins, and not only for ours but also for[a] the sins of the whole world.

³We know that we have come to know him if we obey his commands. ⁴The man who says, "I know him," but does not do what he commands is a liar, and the truth is not in him. ⁵But if anyone obeys his word, God's love[b] is truly made complete in him. This is how we know we are in him: ⁶Whoever claims to live in him must walk as Jesus did.

⁷Dear friends, I am not writing you a new command but an old one, which you have had since the beginning. This old command is the message you have heard. ⁸Yet I am writing you a new command; its truth is seen in him and you, because the darkness is passing and the true light is already shining.

⁹Anyone who claims to be in the light but hates his brother is still in the darkness. ¹⁰Whoever loves his brother lives in the light, and there is nothing in him[c] to make him stumble. ¹¹But whoever hates his brother is in the darkness and walks around in the darkness; he does not know where he is going, because the darkness has blinded him.

¹²I write to you, dear children,
  because your sins have been
    forgiven on account of
      his name.
¹³I write to you, fathers,
  because you have known
    him who is from the
      beginning.
I write to you, young men,
  because you have overcome the
    evil one.

I write to you, dear children,
  because you have known
    the Father.
¹⁴I write to you, fathers,
  because you have known
    him who is from the
      beginning.
I write to you, young men,
  because you are strong,
    and the word of God lives
      in you,
  and you have overcome the
    evil one.

Do Not Love the World

¹⁵Do not love the world or anything in the world. If anyone loves the world, the love of the Father is not in him. ¹⁶For everything in the world—the cravings of sinful man, the lust of his eyes and the boasting of what he has and does—comes not from the Father but from the world. ¹⁷The world and its desires pass away, but the man who does the will of God lives forever.

89
Ps 1:1,2

Warning Against Antichrists

¹⁸Dear children, this is the last hour; and as you have heard that the antichrist is coming, even now many antichrists have come. This is how we know it is the last hour. ¹⁹They went out from us, but they did not really belong to us. For if they had belonged to us, they would have remained with us; but their going showed that none of them belonged to us. ²⁰But you have an anointing from the Holy One, and all of you know the truth.[d] ²¹I do not write to you because you do not know the truth, but because you do know it and because no lie comes

---

[a]2 Or *He is the one who turns aside God's wrath, taking away our sins, and not only ours but also*   [b]5 Or *word, love for God*   [c]10 Or *it*   [d]20 Some manuscripts *and you know all things*

from the truth. ²²Who is the liar? It is the man who denies that Jesus is the Christ. Such a man is the antichrist—he denies the Father and the Son. ²³No one who denies the Son has the Father; whoever acknowledges the Son has the Father also.

²⁴See that what you have heard from the beginning remains in you. If it does, you also will remain in the Son and in the Father. ²⁵And this is what he promised us—even eternal life.

²⁶I am writing these things to you about those who are trying to lead you astray. ²⁷As for you, the anointing you received from him remains in you, and you do not need anyone to teach you. But as his anointing teaches you about all things and as that anointing is real, not counterfeit—just as it has taught you, remain in him.

Children of God

11
1Jn 4:17,18

²⁸And now, dear children, continue in him, so that when he appears we may be confident and unashamed before him at his coming.

²⁹If you know that he is righteous, you know that everyone who does what is right has been born of him.

80
Rev 22:12

3 How great is the love the Father has lavished on us, that we should be called children of God! And that is what we are! The reason the world does not know us is that it did not know him. ²Dear friends, now we are children of God, and what we will be has not yet been made known. But we know that when he appears,ᵃ we shall be like him, for we shall see him as he is. ³Everyone who has this hope in him purifies himself, just as he is pure.

⁴Everyone who sins breaks the law; in fact, sin is lawlessness. ⁵But you know that he appeared so that he might take away our sins. And in him is no sin. ⁶No one who lives in him keeps on sinning. No one who continues to sin has either seen him or known him.

88
1Jn 3:9

⁷Dear children, do not let anyone lead you astray. He who does what is right is righteous, just as he is righteous. ⁸He who does what is sinful is of the devil, because the devil has been sinning from the beginning. The reason the Son of God appeared was to destroy the devil's work. ⁹No one who is born of God will continue to sin, because God's seed remains in him; he cannot go on sinning, because he has been born of God. ¹⁰This is how we know who the children of God are and who the children of the devil are: Anyone who does not do what is right is not a child of God; nor is anyone who does not love his brother.

88

Love One Another

¹¹This is the message you heard from the beginning: We should love one another. ¹²Do not be like Cain, who belonged to the evil one and murdered his brother. And why did he murder him? Because his own actions were evil and his brother's were righteous. ¹³Do not be surprised, my brothers, if the world hates you. ¹⁴We know that we have passed from death to life, because we love our brothers. Anyone who does not love remains in death. ¹⁵Anyone who hates his brother is a murderer, and you know that no murderer has eternal life in him.

20

ᵃ2 Or *when it is made known*

¹⁶This is how we know what love is: Jesus Christ laid down his life for us. And we ought to lay down our lives for our brothers. ¹⁷If anyone has material possessions and sees his brother in need but has no pity on him, how can the love of God be in him? ¹⁸Dear children, let us not love with words or tongue but with actions and in truth. ¹⁹This then is how we know that we belong to the truth, and how we set our hearts at rest in his presence ²⁰whenever our hearts condemn us. For God is greater than our hearts, and he knows everything.

²¹Dear friends, if our hearts do not condemn us, we have confidence before God ²²and receive from him anything we ask, because we obey his commands and do what pleases him. ²³And this is his command: to believe in the name of his Son, Jesus Christ, and to love one another as he commanded us. ²⁴Those who obey his commands live in him, and he in them. And this is how we know that he lives in us: We know it by the Spirit he gave us.

Test the Spirits

4 Dear friends, do not believe every spirit, but test the spirits to see whether they are from God, because many false prophets have gone out into the world. ²This is how you can recognize the Spirit of God: Every spirit that acknowledges that Jesus Christ has come in the flesh is from God, ³but every spirit that does not acknowledge Jesus is not from God. This is the spirit of the antichrist, which you have heard is coming and even now is already in the world.

⁴You, dear children, are from God and have overcome them,

because the one who is in you is greater than the one who is in the world. ⁵They are from the world and therefore speak from the viewpoint of the world, and the world listens to them. ⁶We are from God, and whoever knows God listens to us; but whoever is not from God does not listen to us. This is how we recognize the Spirit^a of truth and the spirit of falsehood.

God's Love and Ours

⁷Dear friends, let us love one another, for love comes from God. Everyone who loves has been born of God and knows God. ⁸Whoever does not love does not know God, because God is love. ⁹This is how God showed his love among us: He sent his one and only Son^b into the world that we might live through him. ¹⁰This is love: not that we loved God, but that he loved us and sent his Son as an atoning sacrifice for^c our sins. ¹¹Dear friends, since God so loved us, we also ought to love one another. ¹²No one has ever seen God; but if we love one another, God lives in us and his love is made complete in us.

¹³We know that we live in him and he in us, because he has given us of his Spirit. ¹⁴And we have seen and testify that the Father has sent his Son to be the Savior of the world. ¹⁵If anyone acknowledges that Jesus is the Son of God, God lives in him and he in God. ¹⁶And so we know and rely on the love God has for us.

God is love. Whoever lives in love lives in God, and God in him. ¹⁷In this way, love is made complete among us so that we will have confidence on the day

---

86
Ps 44:15

31
1Jn 4:16

54

31
1Jn 5:20

11
1Jn 5:14

---

^a6 Or *spirit* ^b9 Or *his only begotten Son* ^c10 Or *as the one who would turn aside his wrath, taking away*

of judgment, because in this world we are like him. ¹⁸There is no fear in love. But perfect love drives out fear, because fear has to do with punishment. The one who fears is not made perfect in love.

¹⁹We love because he first loved us. ²⁰If anyone says, "I love God," yet hates his brother, he is a liar. For anyone who does not love his brother, whom he has seen, cannot love God, whom he has not seen. ²¹And he has given us this command: Whoever loves God must also love his brother.

Faith in the Son of God

5 Everyone who believes that Jesus is the Christ is born of God, and everyone who loves the father loves his child as well. ²This is how we know that we love the children of God: by loving God and carrying out his commands. ³This is love for God: to obey his commands. And his commands are not burdensome, ⁴for everyone born of God overcomes the world. This is the victory that has overcome the world, even our faith. ⁵Who is it that overcomes the world? Only he who believes that Jesus is the Son of God.

⁶This is the one who came by water and blood—Jesus Christ. He did not come by water only, but by water and blood. And it is the Spirit who testifies, because the Spirit is the truth. ⁷For there are three that testify: ⁸the^a Spirit, the water and the blood; and the three are in agreement. ⁹We accept man's testimony, but God's testimony is greater because it is the testimony of God, which he has given about his Son. ¹⁰Any-

one who believes in the Son of God has this testimony in his heart. Anyone who does not believe God has made him out to be a liar, because he has not believed the testimony God has given about his Son. ¹¹And this is the testimony: God has given us eternal life, and this life is in his Son. ¹²He who has the Son has life; he who does not have the Son of God does not have life.

Concluding Remarks

¹³I write these things to you who believe in the name of the Son of God so that you may know that you have eternal life. ¹⁴This is the confidence we have in approaching God: that if we ask anything according to his will, he hears us. ¹⁵And if we know that he hears us—whatever we ask—we know that we have what we asked of him.

¹⁶If anyone sees his brother commit a sin that does not lead to death, he should pray and God will give him life. I refer to those whose sin does not lead to death. There is a sin that leads to death. I am not saying that he should pray about that. ¹⁷All wrongdoing is sin, and there is sin that does not lead to death.

¹⁸We know that anyone born of God does not continue to sin; the one who was born of God keeps him safe, and the evil one cannot harm him. ¹⁹We know that we are children of God, and that the whole world is under the control of the evil one. ²⁰We know also that the Son of God has come and has given us understanding, so that we may know him who is true. And we are in him who is true—even in his Son Jesus

Margin references:
26 Ps 34:7
55
5 Ps 51:10-12

51 Ps 39:4,5

78 Rev 3:20
11 Ps 71:5,6

81 Ps 5:11

31 Ps 14:1

---

*a*7,8 Late manuscripts of the Vulgate *testify in heaven: the Father, the Word and the Holy Spirit, and these three are one.* *8And there are three that testify on earth: the* (not found in any Greek manuscript before the sixteenth century)

Christ. He is the true God and eternal life.

²¹Dear children, keep yourselves from idols.

2 John

¹The elder,

To the chosen lady and her children, whom I love in the truth—and not I only, but also all who know the truth— ²because of the truth, which lives in us and will be with us forever:

³Grace, mercy and peace from God the Father and from Jesus Christ, the Father's Son, will be with us in truth and love.

⁴It has given me great joy to find some of your children walking in the truth, just as the Father commanded us. ⁵And now, dear lady, I am not writing you a new command but one we have had from the beginning. I ask that we love one another. ⁶And this is love: that we walk in obedience to his commands. As you have heard from the beginning, his command is that you walk in love.

⁷Many deceivers, who do not acknowledge Jesus Christ as coming in the flesh, have gone out into the world. Any such person is the deceiver and the antichrist. ⁸Watch out that you do not lose what you have worked for, but that you may be rewarded fully. ⁹Anyone who runs ahead and does not continue in the teaching of Christ does not have God; whoever continues in the teaching has both the Father and the Son. ¹⁰If anyone comes to you and does not bring this teaching, do not take him into your house or welcome him. ¹¹Anyone who welcomes him shares in his wicked work.

¹²I have much to write to you, but I do not want to use paper and ink. Instead, I hope to visit you and talk with you face to face, so that our joy may be complete.

¹³The children of your chosen sister send their greetings.

3 John

¹The elder,

To my dear friend Gaius, whom I love in the truth.

²Dear friend, I pray that you may enjoy good health and that all may go well with you, even as your soul is getting along well. ³It gave me great joy to have some brothers come and tell about your faithfulness to the truth and how you continue to walk in the truth. ⁴I have no greater joy than to hear that my children are walking in the truth.

⁵Dear friend, you are faithful in what you are doing for the brothers, even though they are strangers to you. ⁶They have told the church about your love. You will do well to send them on their way in a manner worthy of God. ⁷It was for the sake of the Name that they went out, receiving no help from the pagans. ⁸We ought therefore to show hospitality to such men so that we may work together for the truth.

⁹I wrote to the church, but Diotrephes, who loves to be first, will have nothing to do with us. ¹⁰So if I come, I will call attention to what he is doing, gossiping maliciously about us. Not satisfied with that, he refuses to welcome the brothers. He also stops those who want to do so and puts them out of the church.

¹¹Dear friend, do not imitate what is evil but what is good. Anyone who does what is good is from God. Anyone who does what is evil has not seen God. ¹²Demetrius is well spoken of by everyone—and even by the truth itself. We also speak well of him, and you know that our testimony is true.

¹³I have much to write you, but I do not want to do so with pen and ink. ¹⁴I hope to see you soon, and we will talk face to face.

Peace to you. The friends here send their greetings. Greet the friends there by name.

Jude

¹Jude, a servant of Jesus Christ and a brother of James,

To those who have been called, who are loved by God the Father and kept by[a] Jesus Christ:

²Mercy, peace and love be yours in abundance.

The Sin and Doom of Godless Men

³Dear friends, although I was very eager to write to you about the salvation we share, I felt I had to write and urge you to contend for the faith that was once for all entrusted to the saints. ⁴For certain men whose condemnation was written about[b] long ago have secretly slipped in among you. They are godless men, who change the grace of our God into a license for immorality and deny Jesus Christ our only Sovereign and Lord.

a 1 Or for; or in   b 4 Or men who were marked out for condemnation

[5]Though you already know all this, I want to remind you that the Lord[d] delivered his people out of Egypt, but later destroyed those who did not believe. [6]And the angels who did not keep their positions of authority but abandoned their own home—these he has kept in darkness, bound with everlasting chains for judgment on the great Day. [7]In a similar way, Sodom and Gomorrah and the surrounding towns gave themselves up to sexual immorality and perversion. They serve as an example of those who suffer the punishment of eternal fire.

[8]In the very same way, these dreamers pollute their own bodies, reject authority and slander celestial beings. [9]But even the archangel Michael, when he was disputing with the devil about the body of Moses, did not dare to bring a slanderous accusation against him, but said, "The Lord rebuke you!" [10]Yet these men speak abusively against whatever they do not understand; and what things they do understand by instinct, like unreasoning animals—these are the very things that destroy them.

[11]Woe to them! They have taken the way of Cain; they have rushed for profit into Balaam's error; they have been destroyed in Korah's rebellion. [12]These men are blemishes at your love feasts, eating with you without the slightest qualm—shepherds who feed only themselves. They are clouds without rain, blown along by the wind; autumn trees, without fruit and uprooted—twice dead. [13]They are wild waves of the sea, foaming up their shame; wandering stars, for whom blackest darkness has been reserved forever.

[14]Enoch, the seventh from Adam, prophesied about these men: "See, the Lord is coming with thousands upon thousands of his holy ones [15]to judge every- 14 one, and to convict all the ungodly of all the ungodly acts they have done in the ungodly way, and of all the harsh words ungodly sinners have spoken against him." [16]These men are grumblers and faultfinders; they follow their own evil desires; they boast about themselves and flatter others for their own advantage.

A Call to Persevere

[17]But, dear friends, remember what the apostles of our Lord Jesus Christ foretold. [18]They said to you, "In the last times there will be scoffers who will follow their own ungodly desires." [19]These are the men who divide you, who follow mere natural instincts and do not have the Spirit.

[20]But you, dear friends, build yourselves up in your most holy faith and pray in the Holy Spirit. [21]Keep yourselves in God's love as you wait for the mercy of our Lord Jesus Christ to bring you to eternal life.

[22]Be merciful to those who doubt; [23]snatch others from the fire and save them; to others show mercy, mixed with fear—hating even the clothing stained by corrupted flesh.

Doxology

[24]To him who is able to keep 99 you from falling and to present [Rev 5:9,10] you before his glorious presence without fault and with great joy— [25]to the only God our Savior

---

[d]5 Some early manuscripts Jesus

be glory, majesty, power and authority, through Jesus Christ our Lord, before all ages, now and forevermore! Amen.

Revelation

Prologue

1 The revelation of Jesus Christ, which God gave him to show his servants what must soon take place. He made it known by sending his angel to his servant John, ²who testifies to everything he saw—that is, the word of God and the testimony of Jesus Christ. ³Blessed is the one who reads the words of this prophecy, and blessed are those who hear it and take to heart what is written in it, because the time is near.

Greetings and Doxology

⁴John,

To the seven churches in the province of Asia:

Grace and peace to you from him who is, and who was, and who is to come, and from the seven spirits*a* before his throne, ⁵and from Jesus Christ, who is the faithful witness, the firstborn from the dead, and the ruler of the kings of the earth.

To him who loves us and has freed us from our sins by his blood, ⁶and has made us to be a kingdom and priests to serve his God and Father—to him be glory and power for ever and ever! Amen.

⁷Look, he is coming with the clouds,
    and every eye will see him,
    even those who pierced him;

and all the peoples of the earth will mourn because of him.

So shall it be! Amen.

⁸"I am the Alpha and the Omega," says the Lord God, "who is, and who was, and who is to come, the Almighty."

One Like a Son of Man

⁹I, John, your brother and companion in the suffering and kingdom and patient endurance that are ours in Jesus, was on the island of Patmos because of the word of God and the testimony of Jesus. ¹⁰On the Lord's Day I was in the Spirit, and I heard behind me a loud voice like a trumpet, ¹¹which said: "Write on a scroll what you see and send it to the seven churches: to Ephesus, Smyrna, Pergamum, Thyatira, Sardis, Philadelphia and Laodicea."

¹²I turned around to see the voice that was speaking to me. And when I turned I saw seven golden lampstands, ¹³and among the lampstands was someone "like a son of man,"*b* dressed in a robe reaching down to his feet and with a golden sash around his chest. ¹⁴His head and hair were white like wool, as white as snow, and his eyes were like blazing fire. ¹⁵His feet were like bronze glowing in a furnace, and his voice was like the sound of rushing waters. ¹⁶In his right hand he held seven stars, and out of his mouth came a sharp dou-

*a*4 Or the sevenfold Spirit   *b*13 Daniel 7:13

ble-edged sword. His face was like the sun shining in all its brilliance.

¹⁷When I saw him, I fell at his feet as though dead. Then he placed his right hand on me and said: "Do not be afraid. I am the First and the Last. ¹⁸I am the Living One; I was dead, and behold I am alive for ever and ever! And I hold the keys of death and Hades.

¹⁹"Write, therefore, what you have seen, what is now and what will take place later. ²⁰The mystery of the seven stars that you saw in my right hand and of the seven golden lampstands is this: The seven stars are the angels[a] of the seven churches, and the seven lampstands are the seven churches.

To the Church in Ephesus

2 "To the angel[b] of the church in Ephesus write:

These are the words of him who holds the seven stars in his right hand and walks among the seven golden lampstands: ²I know your deeds, your hard work and your perseverance. I know that you cannot tolerate wicked men, that you have tested those who claim to be apostles but are not, and have found them false. ³You have persevered and have endured hardships for my name, and have not grown weary.

⁴Yet I hold this against you: You have forsaken your first love. ⁵Remember the height from which you have fallen! Repent and do the things you did at first. If you do not repent, I will come to you and remove your lampstand from its place. ⁶But you have this in your favor: You hate the practices of the Nicolaitans, which I also hate.

⁷He who has an ear, let him hear what the Spirit says to the churches. To him who overcomes, I will give the right to eat from the tree of life, which is in the paradise of God.

To the Church in Smyrna

⁸"To the angel of the church in Smyrna write:

These are the words of him who is the First and the Last, who died and came to life again. ⁹I know your afflictions and your poverty—yet you are rich! I know the slander of those who say they are Jews and are not, but are a synagogue of Satan. ¹⁰Do not be afraid of what you are about to suffer. I tell you, the devil will put some of you in prison to test you, and you will suffer persecution for ten days. Be faithful, even to the point of death, and I will give you the crown of life.

¹¹He who has an ear, let him hear what the Spirit says to the churches. He who overcomes will not be hurt at all by the second death.

To the Church in Pergamum

¹²"To the angel of the church in Pergamum write:

These are the words of him who has the sharp, double-edged sword. ¹³I know where you live—where Satan has his throne. Yet you remain true to my name. You did not renounce your faith in me, even in the days of Antipas, my faithful witness, who was put

---

[a]20 Or *messengers*   [b]1 Or *messenger*; also in verses 8, 12 and 18

to death in your city—where Satan lives.

[14]Nevertheless, I have a few things against you: You have people there who hold to the teaching of Balaam, who taught Balak to entice the Israelites to sin by eating food sacrificed to idols and by committing sexual immorality. [15]Likewise you also have those who hold to the teaching of the Nicolaitans. [16]Repent therefore! Otherwise, I will soon come to you and will fight against them with the sword of my mouth.

[17]He who has an ear, let him hear what the Spirit says to the churches. To him who overcomes, I will give some of the hidden manna. I will also give him a white stone with a new name written on it, known only to him who receives it.

To the Church in Thyatira

[18]"To the angel of the church in Thyatira write:

These are the words of the Son of God, whose eyes are like blazing fire and whose feet are like burnished bronze. [19]I know your deeds, your love and faith, your service and perseverance, and that you are now doing more than you did at first.

[20]Nevertheless, I have this against you: You tolerate that woman Jezebel, who calls herself a prophetess. By her teaching she misleads my servants into sexual immorality and the eating of food sacrificed to idols. [21]I have given her time to repent of her immorality, but she is unwilling. [22]So I will cast her on a bed of

suffering, and I will make those who commit adultery with her suffer intensely, unless they repent of her ways. [23]I will strike her children dead. Then all the churches will know that I am he who searches hearts and minds, and I will repay each of you according to your deeds. [24]Now I say to the rest of you in Thyatira, to you who do not hold to her teaching and have not learned Satan's so-called deep secrets (I will not impose any other burden on you): [25]Only hold on to what you have until I come.

[26]To him who overcomes and does my will to the end, I will give authority over the nations—

[27]'He will rule them with an iron scepter;
   he will dash them to pieces like pottery'[a]—

just as I have received authority from my Father. [28]I will also give him the morning star. [29]He who has an ear, let him hear what the Spirit says to the churches.

To the Church in Sardis

3 "To the angel[b] of the church in Sardis write: 8

These are the words of him who holds the seven spirits[c] of God and the seven stars. I know your deeds; you have a reputation of being alive, but you are dead. [2]Wake up! Strengthen what remains and is about to die, for I have not found your deeds complete in the sight of my God. [3]Remember, therefore, what you have received and heard; obey it, and repent. But if you do not wake up, I will come like a thief, and you will not know at what time I will come to you.

⁴Yet you have a few people in Sardis who have not soiled their clothes. They will walk with me, dressed in white, for they are worthy. ⁵He who overcomes will, like them, be dressed in white. I will never blot out his name from the book of life, but will acknowledge his name before my Father and his angels. ⁶He who has an ear, let him hear what the Spirit says to the churches.

To the Church in Philadelphia

⁷"To the angel of the church in Philadelphia write:

These are the words of him who is holy and true, who holds the key of David. What he opens no one can shut, and what he shuts no one can open. ⁸I know your deeds. See, I have placed before you an open door that no one can shut. I know that you have little strength, yet you have kept my word and have not denied my name. ⁹I will make those who are of the synagogue of Satan, who claim to be Jews though they are not, but are liars—I will make them come and fall down at your feet and acknowledge that I have loved you. ¹⁰Since you have kept my command to endure patiently, I will also keep you from the hour of trial that is going to come upon the whole world to test those who live on the earth.

¹¹I am coming soon. Hold on to what you have, so that no one will take your crown. ¹²Him who overcomes I will make a pillar in the temple of my God. Never again will he leave it. I will write on him the name of my God and the name of the city of my God, the new Jerusalem, which is coming down out of heaven from my God; and I will also write on him my new name. ¹³He who has an ear, let him hear what the Spirit says to the churches.

To the Church in Laodicea

¹⁴"To the angel of the church in Laodicea write:

These are the words of the Amen, the faithful and true witness, the ruler of God's creation. ¹⁵I know your deeds, that you are neither cold nor hot. I wish you were either one or the other! ¹⁶So, because you are lukewarm—neither hot nor cold—I am about to spit you out of my mouth. ¹⁷You say, 'I am rich; I have acquired wealth and do not need a thing.' But you do not realize that you are wretched, pitiful, poor, blind and naked. ¹⁸I counsel you to buy from me gold refined in the fire, so you can become rich; and white clothes to wear, so you can cover your shameful nakedness; and salve to put on your eyes, so you can see.

¹⁹Those whom I love I rebuke and discipline. So be earnest, and repent. ²⁰Here I am! I stand at the door and knock. If anyone hears my voice and opens the door, I will come in and eat with him, and he with me.

²¹To him who overcomes, I will give the right to sit with me on my throne, just as I overcame and sat down with my Father on his throne. ²²He

78

who has an ear, let him hear what the Spirit says to the churches."

The Throne in Heaven

4 After this I looked, and there before me was a door standing open in heaven. And the voice I had first heard speaking to me like a trumpet said, "Come up here, and I will show you what must take place after this." ²At once I was in the Spirit, and there before me was a throne in heaven with someone sitting on it. ³And the one who sat there had the appearance of jasper and carnelian. A rainbow, resembling an emerald, encircled the throne. ⁴Surrounding the throne were twenty-four other thrones, and seated on them were twenty-four elders. They were dressed in white and had crowns of gold on their heads. ⁵From the throne came flashes of lightning, rumblings and peals of thunder. Before the throne, seven lamps were blazing. These are the seven spirits*a* of God. ⁶Also before the throne there was what looked like a sea of glass, clear as crystal.

In the center, around the throne, were four living creatures, and they were covered with eyes, in front and in back. ⁷The first living creature was like a lion, the second was like an ox, the third had a face like a man, the fourth was like a flying eagle. ⁸Each of the four living creatures had six wings and was covered with eyes all around, even under his wings. Day and night they never stop saying:

"Holy, holy, holy
is the Lord God Almighty,
who was, and is, and is to
come."

⁹Whenever the living creatures give glory, honor and thanks to him who sits on the throne and who lives for ever and ever, ¹⁰the twenty-four elders fall down before him who sits on the throne, and worship him who lives for ever and ever. They lay their crowns before the throne and say:

¹¹"You are worthy, our Lord
and God,
to receive glory and honor
and power,
for you created all things,
and by your will they were
created
and have their being."

The Scroll and the Lamb

5 Then I saw in the right hand of him who sat on the throne a scroll with writing on both sides and sealed with seven seals. ²And I saw a mighty angel proclaiming in a loud voice, "Who is worthy to break the seals and open the scroll?" ³But no one in heaven or on earth or under the earth could open the scroll or even look inside it. ⁴I wept and wept because no one was found who was worthy to open the scroll or look inside. ⁵Then one of the elders said to me, "Do not weep! See, the Lion of the tribe of Judah, the Root of David, has triumphed. He is able to open the scroll and its seven seals."

⁶Then I saw a Lamb, looking as if it had been slain, standing in the center of the throne, encircled by the four living creatures and the elders. He had seven horns and seven eyes, which are the seven spirits*a* of God sent out into all the earth. ⁷He came and took the scroll from the right hand of him who sat on the throne. ⁸And when he had taken

*a*5,6 Or *the sevenfold Spirit*

it, the four living creatures and the twenty-four elders fell down before the Lamb. Each one had a harp and they were holding golden bowls full of incense, which are the prayers of the

99   saints. ⁹And they sang a new
Ps 19:14   song:

> "You are worthy to take the
>   scroll
>   and to open its seals,
> because you were slain,
>   and with your blood you
>   purchased men for God
> from every tribe and
>   language and people
>   and nation.
> ¹⁰You have made them to be a
>   kingdom and priests to
>   serve our God,
>   and they will reign on the
>   earth."

¹¹Then I looked and heard the voice of many angels, numbering thousands upon thousands, and ten thousand times ten thousand. They encircled the throne and the living creatures and the elders. ¹²In a loud voice they sang:

> "Worthy is the Lamb, who
>   was slain,
> to receive power and wealth
>   and wisdom and
>   strength
> and honor and glory and
>   praise!"

¹³Then I heard every creature in heaven and on earth and under the earth and on the sea, and all that is in them, singing:

> "To him who sits on the
>   throne and to the Lamb
> be praise and honor and glory
>   and power,
>   for ever and ever!"

¹⁴The four living creatures said,

"Amen," and the elders fell down and worshiped.

The Seals

6 I watched as the Lamb opened the first of the seven seals. Then I heard one of the four living creatures say in a voice like thunder, "Come!" ²I looked, and there before me was a white horse! Its rider held a bow, and he was given a crown, and he rode out as a conqueror bent on conquest.

³When the Lamb opened the second seal, I heard the second living creature say, "Come!" ⁴Then another horse came out, a fiery red one. Its rider was given power to take peace from the earth and to make men slay each other. To him was given a large sword.

⁵When the Lamb opened the third seal, I heard the third living creature say, "Come!" I looked, and there before me was a black horse! Its rider was holding a pair of scales in his hand. ⁶Then I heard what sounded like a voice among the four living creatures, saying, "A quart*d* of wheat for a day's wages,*b* and three quarts of barley for a day's wages,*b* and do not damage the oil and the wine!"

⁷When the Lamb opened the fourth seal, I heard the voice of the fourth living creature say, "Come!" ⁸I looked, and there before me was a pale horse! Its rider was named Death, and Hades was following close behind him. They were given power over a fourth of the earth to kill by sword, famine and plague, and by the wild beasts of the earth.

⁹When he opened the fifth seal, I saw under the altar the souls of those who had been slain be-

---

*6 Greek a choinix (probably about a liter)   *b 6 Greek a denarius

cause of the word of God and the testimony they had maintained. [10]They called out in a loud voice, "How long, Sovereign Lord, holy and true, until you judge the inhabitants of the earth and avenge our blood?" [11]Then each of them was given a white robe, and they were told to wait a little longer, until the number of their fellow servants and brothers who were to be killed as they had been was completed.

[12]I watched as he opened the sixth seal. There was a great earthquake. The sun turned black like sackcloth made of goat hair, the whole moon turned blood red, [13]and the stars in the sky fell to earth, as late figs drop from a fig tree when shaken by a strong wind. [14]The sky receded like a scroll, rolling up, and every mountain and island was removed from its place.

[15]Then the kings of the earth, the princes, the generals, the rich, the mighty, and every slave and every free man hid in caves and among the rocks of the mountains. [16]They called to the mountains and the rocks, "Fall on us and hide us from the face of him who sits on the throne and from the wrath of the Lamb! [17]For the great day of their wrath has come, and who can stand?"

144,000 Sealed

7 After this I saw four angels standing at the four corners of the earth, holding back the four winds of the earth to prevent any wind from blowing on the land or on the sea or on any tree. [2]Then I saw another angel coming up from the east, having the seal of the living God. He called out in a loud voice to the four angels who had been given power to harm the land and the sea: [3]"Do not harm the land or the sea or the trees until we put a seal on the foreheads of the servants of our God." [4]Then I heard the number of those who were sealed: 144,000 from all the tribes of Israel.

[5]From the tribe of Judah 12,000 were sealed,
from the tribe of Reuben 12,000,
from the tribe of Gad 12,000,
[6]from the tribe of Asher 12,000,
from the tribe of Naphtali 12,000,
from the tribe of Manasseh 12,000,
[7]from the tribe of Simeon 12,000,
from the tribe of Levi 12,000,
from the tribe of Issachar 12,000,
[8]from the tribe of Zebulun 12,000,
from the tribe of Joseph 12,000,
from the tribe of Benjamin 12,000.

The Great Multitude in White Robes

[9]After this I looked and there before me was a great multitude that no one could count, from every nation, tribe, people and language, standing before the throne and in front of the Lamb. They were wearing white robes and were holding palm branches in their hands. [10]And they cried out in a loud voice:

"Salvation belongs to our God,
who sits on the throne,
and to the Lamb."

[11]All the angels were standing around the throne and around the elders and the four living creatures. They fell down on

their faces before the throne and worshiped God, ¹²saying:

"Amen!
Praise and glory
and wisdom and thanks and
    honor
and power and strength
be to our God for ever and
    ever.
Amen!"

¹³Then one of the elders asked me, "These in white robes—who are they, and where did they come from?"

¹⁴I answered, "Sir, you know."

And he said, "These are they who have come out of the great tribulation; they have washed their robes and made them white in the blood of the Lamb. ¹⁵Therefore,

"they are before the throne of
    God
    and serve him day and
        night in his temple;
and he who sits on the throne
    will spread his tent over
    them.
¹⁶Never again will they hunger;
    never again will they thirst.
The sun will not beat upon
    them,
    nor any scorching heat.
¹⁷For the Lamb at the center of
    the throne will be their
    shepherd;
    he will lead them to springs
        of living water.
And God will wipe away
    every tear from their
    eyes."

The Seventh Seal and the Golden Censer

8 When he opened the seventh seal, there was silence in heaven for about half an hour.

²And I saw the seven angels who stand before God, and to them were given seven trumpets.

³Another angel, who had a golden censer, came and stood at the altar. He was given much incense to offer, with the prayers of all the saints, on the golden altar before the throne. ⁴The smoke of the incense, together with the prayers of the saints, went up before God from the angel's hand. ⁵Then the angel took the censer, filled it with fire from the altar, and hurled it on the earth; and there came peals of thunder, rumblings, flashes of lightning and an earthquake.

The Trumpets

⁶Then the seven angels who had the seven trumpets prepared to sound them.

⁷The first angel sounded his trumpet, and there came hail and fire mixed with blood, and it was hurled down upon the earth. A third of the earth was burned up, a third of the trees were burned up, and all the green grass was burned up.

⁸The second angel sounded his trumpet, and something like a huge mountain, all ablaze, was thrown into the sea. A third of the sea turned into blood, ⁹a third of the living creatures in the sea died, and a third of the ships were destroyed.

¹⁰The third angel sounded his trumpet, and a great star, blazing like a torch, fell from the sky on a third of the rivers and on the springs of water— ¹¹the name of the star is Wormwood.ᵈ A third of the waters turned bitter, and many people died from the waters that had become bitter.

¹²The fourth angel sounded his trumpet, and a third of the sun was struck, a third of the moon, and a third of the stars, so that a

ᵈ11 That is, Bitterness

third of them turned dark. A third of the day was without light, and also a third of the night.

¹³As I watched, I heard an eagle that was flying in midair call out in a loud voice: "Woe! Woe! Woe to the inhabitants of the earth, because of the trumpet blasts about to be sounded by the other three angels!"

9 The fifth angel sounded his trumpet, and I saw a star that had fallen from the sky to the earth. The star was given the key to the shaft of the Abyss. ²When he opened the Abyss, smoke rose from it like the smoke from a gigantic furnace. The sun and sky were darkened by the smoke from the Abyss. ³And out of the smoke locusts came down upon the earth and were given power like that of scorpions of the earth. ⁴They were told not to harm the grass of the earth or any plant or tree, but only those people who did not have the seal of God on their foreheads. ⁵They were not given power to kill them, but only to torture them for five months. And the agony they suffered was like that of the sting of a scorpion when it strikes a man. ⁶During those days men will seek death, but will not find it; they will long to die, but death will elude them.

⁷The locusts looked like horses prepared for battle. On their heads they wore something like crowns of gold, and their faces resembled human faces. ⁸Their hair was like women's hair, and their teeth were like lions' teeth. ⁹They had breastplates like breastplates of iron, and the sound of their wings was like the thundering of many horses and chariots rushing into battle.

¹⁰They had tails and stings like scorpions, and in their tails they had power to torment people for five months. ¹¹They had as king over them the angel of the Abyss, whose name in Hebrew is Abaddon, and in Greek, Apollyon.ᵃ

¹²The first woe is past; two other woes are yet to come.

¹³The sixth angel sounded his trumpet, and I heard a voice coming from the hornsᵇ of the golden altar that is before God. ¹⁴It said to the sixth angel who had the trumpet, "Release the four angels who are bound at the great river Euphrates." ¹⁵And the four angels who had been kept ready for this very hour and day and month and year were released to kill a third of mankind. ¹⁶The number of the mounted troops was two hundred million. I heard their number.

¹⁷The horses and riders I saw in my vision looked like this: Their breastplates were fiery red, dark blue, and yellow as sulfur. The heads of the horses resembled the heads of lions, and out of their mouths came fire, smoke and sulfur. ¹⁸A third of mankind was killed by the three plagues of fire, smoke and sulfur that came out of their mouths. ¹⁹The power of the horses was in their mouths and in their tails; for their tails were like snakes, having heads with which they inflict injury.

²⁰The rest of mankind that were not killed by these plagues still did not repent of the work of their hands; they did not stop worshiping demons, and idols of gold, silver, bronze, stone and wood—idols that cannot see or hear or walk. ²¹Nor did they repent of their murders, their magic arts, their sexual immorality or their thefts.

85
Rev 18:4

ᵃ11 *Abaddon* and *Apollyon* mean *Destroyer*.   ᵇ13 That is, projections

The Angel and the Little Scroll

10 Then I saw another mighty angel coming down from heaven. He was robed in a cloud, with a rainbow above his head; his face was like the sun, and his legs were like fiery pillars. ²He was holding a little scroll, which lay open in his hand. He planted his right foot on the sea and his left foot on the land, ³and he gave a loud shout like the roar of a lion. When he shouted, the voices of the seven thunders spoke. ⁴And when the seven thunders spoke, I was about to write; but I heard a voice from heaven say, "Seal up what the seven thunders have said and do not write it down."

⁵Then the angel I had seen standing on the sea and on the land raised his right hand to heaven. ⁶And he swore by him who lives for ever and ever, who created the heavens and all that is in them, the earth and all that is in it, and the sea and all that is in it, and said, "There will be no more delay! ⁷But in the days when the seventh angel is about to sound his trumpet, the mystery of God will be accomplished, just as he announced to his servants the prophets."

⁸Then the voice that I had heard from heaven spoke to me once more: "Go, take the scroll that lies open in the hand of the angel who is standing on the sea and on the land."

⁹So I went to the angel and asked him to give me the little scroll. He said to me, "Take it and eat it. It will turn your stomach sour, but in your mouth it will be as sweet as honey." ¹⁰I took the little scroll from the angel's hand and ate it. It tasted as sweet as honey in my mouth, but when I had eaten it, my stomach turned sour. ¹¹Then I was told, "You must prophesy again about many peoples, nations, languages and kings."

The Two Witnesses

11 I was given a reed like a measuring rod and was told, "Go and measure the temple of God and the altar, and count the worshipers there. ²But exclude the outer court; do not measure it, because it has been given to the Gentiles. They will trample on the holy city for 42 months. ³And I will give power to my two witnesses, and they will prophesy for 1,260 days, clothed in sackcloth." ⁴These are the two olive trees and the two lampstands that stand before the Lord of the earth. ⁵If anyone tries to harm them, fire comes from their mouths and devours their enemies. This is how anyone who wants to harm them must die. ⁶These men have power to shut up the sky so that it will not rain during the time they are prophesying; and they have power to turn the waters into blood and to strike the earth with every kind of plague as often as they want.

⁷Now when they have finished their testimony, the beast that comes up from the Abyss will attack them, and overpower and kill them. ⁸Their bodies will lie in the street of the great city, which is figuratively called Sodom and Egypt, where also their Lord was crucified. ⁹For three and a half days men from every people, tribe, language and nation will gaze on their bodies and refuse them burial. ¹⁰The inhabitants of the earth will gloat over them and will celebrate by sending each other gifts, because these two

prophets had tormented those who live on the earth.

[11]But after the three and a half days a breath of life from God entered them, and they stood on their feet, and terror struck those who saw them. [12]Then they heard a loud voice from heaven saying to them, "Come up here." And they went up to heaven in a cloud, while their enemies looked on.

[13]At that very hour there was a severe earthquake and a tenth of the city collapsed. Seven thousand people were killed in the earthquake, and the survivors were terrified and gave glory to the God of heaven.

[14]The second woe has passed; the third woe is coming soon.

The Seventh Trumpet

[15]The seventh angel sounded his trumpet, and there were loud voices in heaven, which said:

"The kingdom of the world
has become the kingdom
of our Lord and of his
Christ,
and he will reign for ever
and ever."

[16]And the twenty-four elders, who were seated on their thrones before God, fell on their faces and worshiped God, [17]saying:

"We give thanks to you, Lord
God Almighty,
the One who is and who
was,
because you have taken your
great power
and have begun to reign.
[18]The nations were angry;
and your wrath has come.
The time has come for judging
the dead,
and for rewarding your
servants the prophets

and your saints and those
who reverence your
name,
both small and great—
and for destroying those who
destroy the earth."

[19]Then God's temple in heaven was opened, and within his temple was seen the ark of his covenant. And there came flashes of lightning, rumblings, peals of thunder, an earthquake and a great hailstorm.

The Woman and the Dragon

12 A great and wondrous sign appeared in heaven: a woman clothed with the sun, with the moon under her feet and a crown of twelve stars on her head. [2]She was pregnant and cried out in pain as she was about to give birth. [3]Then another sign appeared in heaven: an enormous red dragon with seven heads and ten horns and seven crowns on his heads. [4]His tail swept a third of the stars out of the sky and flung them to the earth. The dragon stood in front of the woman who was about to give birth, so that he might devour her child the moment it was born. [5]She gave birth to a son, a male child, who will rule all the nations with an iron scepter. And her child was snatched up to God and to his throne. [6]The woman fled into the desert to a place prepared for her by God, where she might be taken care of for 1,260 days.

[7]And there was war in heaven. Michael and his angels fought against the dragon, and the dragon and his angels fought back. [8]But he was not strong enough, and they lost their place in heaven. [9]The great dragon was hurled down—that ancient serpent called the devil, or Satan, who leads the whole world

astray. He was hurled to the earth, and his angels with him.

[10]Then I heard a loud voice in heaven say:

"Now have come the
    salvation and the power
    and the kingdom of our
    God,
and the authority of his
    Christ.
For the accuser of our
    brothers,
    who accuses them before
        our God day and night,
    has been hurled down.
[11]They overcame him
    by the blood of the Lamb
    and by the word of their
        testimony;
they did not love their lives so
    much
    as to shrink from death.
[12]Therefore rejoice, you heavens
    and you who dwell in them!
But woe to the earth and the
    sea,
    because the devil has gone
        down to you!
He is filled with fury,
    because he knows that his
        time is short."

[13]When the dragon saw that he had been hurled to the earth, he pursued the woman who had given birth to the male child. [14]The woman was given the two wings of a great eagle, so that she might fly to the place prepared for her in the desert, where she would be taken care of for a time, times and half a time, out of the serpent's reach. [15]Then from his mouth the serpent spewed water like a river, to overtake the woman and sweep her away with the torrent. [16]But the earth helped the woman by opening its mouth and swallowing the river that the dragon had spewed out

of his mouth. [17]Then the dragon was enraged at the woman and went off to make war against the rest of her offspring—those who obey God's commandments and hold to the testimony of Jesus.

13 [1]And the dragon[a] stood on the shore of the sea.

The Beast out of the Sea

And I saw a beast coming out of the sea. He had ten horns and seven heads, with ten crowns on his horns, and on each head a blasphemous name. [2]The beast I saw resembled a leopard, but had feet like those of a bear and a mouth like that of a lion. The dragon gave the beast his power and his throne and great authority. [3]One of the heads of the beast seemed to have had a fatal wound, but the fatal wound had been healed. The whole world was astonished and followed the beast. [4]Men worshiped the dragon because he had given authority to the beast, and they also worshiped the beast and asked, "Who is like the beast? Who can make war against him?"

[5]The beast was given a mouth to utter proud words and blasphemies and to exercise his authority for forty-two months. [6]He opened his mouth to blaspheme God, and to slander his name and his dwelling place and those who live in heaven. [7]He was given power to make war against the saints and to conquer them. And he was given authority over every tribe, people, language and nation. [8]All inhabitants of the earth will worship the beast—all whose names have not been written in the book of life belonging to the Lamb that was slain from the creation of the world.[b]

---

[a]1 Some late manuscripts And I   [b]8 Or written from the creation of the world in the book of life belonging to the Lamb that was slain

⁹He who has an ear, let him hear.

¹⁰If anyone is to go into
      captivity,
   into captivity he will go.
   If anyone is to be killed*a* with
      the sword,
   with the sword he will be
      killed.

This calls for patient endurance and faithfulness on the part of the saints.

The Beast out of the Earth

¹¹Then I saw another beast, coming out of the earth. He had two horns like a lamb, but he spoke like a dragon. ¹²He exercised all the authority of the first beast on his behalf, and made the earth and its inhabitants worship the first beast, whose fatal wound had been healed. ¹³And he performed great and miraculous signs, even causing fire to come down from heaven to earth in full view of men. ¹⁴Because of the signs he was given power to do on behalf of the first beast, he deceived the inhabitants of the earth. He ordered them to set up an image in honor of the beast who was wounded by the sword and yet lived. ¹⁵He was given power to give breath to the image of the first beast, so that it could speak and cause all who refused to worship the image to be killed. ¹⁶He also forced everyone, small and great, rich and poor, free and slave, to receive a mark on his right hand or on his forehead, ¹⁷so that no one could buy or sell unless he had the mark, which is the name of the beast or the number of his name.

¹⁸This calls for wisdom. If anyone has insight, let him calculate the number of the beast, for it is man's number. His number is 666.

The Lamb and the 144,000

14 Then I looked, and there before me was the Lamb, standing on Mount Zion, and with him 144,000 who had*b* his name and his Father's name written on their foreheads. ²And I heard a sound from heaven like the roar of rushing waters and like a loud peal of thunder. The sound I heard was like that of harpists playing their harps. ³And they sang a new song before the throne and before the four living creatures and the elders. No one could learn the song except the 144,000 who had been redeemed from the earth. ⁴These are those who did not defile themselves with women, for they kept themselves pure. They follow the Lamb wherever he goes. They were purchased from among men and offered as firstfruits to God and the Lamb. ⁵No lie was found in their mouths; they are blameless.

The Three Angels

⁶Then I saw another angel flying in midair, and he had the eternal gospel to proclaim to those who live on the earth—to every nation, tribe, language and people. ⁷He said in a loud voice, "Fear God and give him glory, because the hour of his judgment has come. Worship him who made the heavens, the earth, the sea and the springs of water."

⁸A second angel followed and said, "Fallen! Fallen is Babylon the Great, which made all the nations drink the maddening wine of her adulteries."

⁹A third angel followed them and said in a loud voice: "If any-

---

a10 Some manuscripts *anyone kills*

one worships the beast and his image and receives his mark on the forehead or on the hand, [10]he, too, will drink of the wine of God's fury, which has been poured full strength into the cup of his wrath. He will be tormented with burning sulfur in the presence of the holy angels and of the Lamb. [11]And the smoke of their torment rises for ever and ever. There is no rest day or night for those who worship the beast and his image, or for anyone who receives the mark of his name." [12]This calls for patient endurance on the part of the saints who obey God's commandments and remain faithful to Jesus.

[13]Then I heard a voice from heaven say, "Write: Blessed are the dead who die in the Lord from now on."

"Yes," says the Spirit, "they will rest from their labor, for their deeds will follow them."

The Harvest of the Earth

[14]I looked, and there before me was a white cloud, and seated on the cloud was one "like a son of man"[a] with a crown of gold on his head and a sharp sickle in his hand. [15]Then another angel came out of the temple and called in a loud voice to him who was sitting on the cloud, "Take your sickle and reap, because the time to reap has come, for the harvest of the earth is ripe." [16]So he who was seated on the cloud swung his sickle over the earth, and the earth was harvested.

[17]Another angel came out of the temple in heaven, and he too had a sharp sickle. [18]Still another angel, who had charge of the fire, came from the altar and called in a loud voice to him who had the sharp sickle, "Take your sharp sickle and gather the clusters of grapes from the earth's vine, because its grapes are ripe." [19]The angel swung his sickle on the earth, gathered its grapes and threw them into the great winepress of God's wrath. [20]They were trampled in the winepress outside the city, and blood flowed out of the press, rising as high as the horses' bridles for a distance of 1,600 stadia.[b]

Seven Angels With Seven Plagues

15 I saw in heaven another great and marvelous sign: seven angels with the seven last plagues—last, because with them God's wrath is completed. [2]And I saw what looked like a sea of glass mixed with fire and, standing beside the sea, those who had been victorious over the beast and his image and over the number of his name. They held harps given them by God [3]and sang the song of Moses the servant of God and the song of the Lamb:

"Great and marvelous are
    your deeds,
  Lord God Almighty.
Just and true are your ways,
  King of the ages.
[4]Who will not fear you,
  O Lord,
  and bring glory to your
    name?
For you alone are holy.
All nations will come
  and worship before you,
for your righteous acts have
  been revealed."

[5]After this I looked and in heaven the temple, that is, the tabernacle of the Testimony, was opened. [6]Out of the temple came the seven angels with the seven plagues. They were dressed in

[a]14 Daniel 7:13   [b]20 That is, about 180 miles (about 300 kilometers)

clean, shining linen and wore golden sashes around their chests. ⁷Then one of the four living creatures gave to the seven angels seven golden bowls filled with the wrath of God, who lives for ever and ever. ⁸And the temple was filled with smoke from the glory of God and from his power, and no one could enter the temple until the seven plagues of the seven angels were completed.

The Seven Bowls of God's Wrath

16 Then I heard a loud voice from the temple saying to the seven angels, "Go, pour out the seven bowls of God's wrath on the earth."

²The first angel went and poured out his bowl on the land, and ugly and painful sores broke out on the people who had the mark of the beast and worshiped his image.

³The second angel poured out his bowl on the sea, and it turned into blood like that of a dead man, and every living thing in the sea died.

⁴The third angel poured out his bowl on the rivers and springs of water, and they became blood. ⁵Then I heard the angel in charge of the waters say:

"You are just in these
　　judgments,
　you who are and who were,
　　the Holy One,
because you have so judged;
⁶for they have shed the blood
　　of your saints and
　　prophets,
　and you have given them
　　blood to drink as they
　　deserve."

⁷And I heard the altar respond:

"Yes, Lord God Almighty,
　true and just are your
　　judgments."

⁸The fourth angel poured out his bowl on the sun, and the sun was given power to scorch people with fire. ⁹They were seared by the intense heat and they cursed the name of God, who had control over these plagues, but they refused to repent and glorify him.

¹⁰The fifth angel poured out his bowl on the throne of the beast, and his kingdom was plunged into darkness. Men gnawed their tongues in agony ¹¹and cursed the God of heaven because of their pains and their sores, but they refused to repent of what they had done.

¹²The sixth angel poured out his bowl on the great river Euphrates, and its water was dried up to prepare the way for the kings from the East. ¹³Then I saw three evil*a* spirits that looked like frogs; they came out of the mouth of the dragon, out of the mouth of the beast and out of the mouth of the false prophet. ¹⁴They are spirits of demons performing miraculous signs, and they go out to the kings of the whole world, to gather them for the battle on the great day of God Almighty.

¹⁵"Behold, I come like a thief! Blessed is he who stays awake and keeps his clothes with him, so that he may not go naked and be shamefully exposed."

¹⁶Then they gathered the kings together to the place that in Hebrew is called Armageddon.

¹⁷The seventh angel poured out his bowl into the air, and out of the temple came a loud voice from the throne, saying, "It is done!" ¹⁸Then there came flashes of lightning, rumblings, peals of

---

*a*13 Greek *unclean*

thunder and a severe earthquake. No earthquake like it has ever occurred since man has been on earth, so tremendous was the quake. [19]The great city split into three parts, and the cities of the nations collapsed. God remembered Babylon the Great and gave her the cup filled with the wine of the fury of his wrath. [20]Every island fled away and the mountains could not be found. [21]From the sky huge hailstones of about a hundred pounds each fell upon men. And they cursed God on account of the plague of hail, because the plague was so terrible.

The Woman on the Beast

17 One of the seven angels who had the seven bowls came and said to me, "Come, I will show you the punishment of the great prostitute, who sits on many waters. [2]With her the kings of the earth committed adultery and the inhabitants of the earth were intoxicated with the wine of her adulteries."

[3]Then the angel carried me away in the Spirit into a desert. There I saw a woman sitting on a scarlet beast that was covered with blasphemous names and had seven heads and ten horns. [4]The woman was dressed in purple and scarlet, and was glittering with gold, precious stones and pearls. She held a golden cup in her hand, filled with abominable things and the filth of her adulteries. [5]This title was written on her forehead:

MYSTERY
BABYLON THE GREAT
THE MOTHER OF PROSTITUTES
AND OF THE ABOMINATIONS OF
THE EARTH.

[6]I saw that the woman was drunk with the blood of the saints, the blood of those who bore testimony to Jesus.

When I saw her, I was greatly astonished. [7]Then the angel said to me: "Why are you astonished? I will explain to you the mystery of the woman and of the beast she rides, which has the seven heads and ten horns. [8]The beast, which you saw, once was, now is not, and will come up out of the Abyss and go to his destruction. The inhabitants of the earth whose names have not been written in the book of life from the creation of the world will be astonished when they see the beast, because he once was, now is not, and yet will come.

[9]"This calls for a mind with wisdom. The seven heads are seven hills on which the woman sits. [10]They are also seven kings. Five have fallen, one is, the other has not yet come; but when he does come, he must remain for a little while. [11]The beast who once was, and now is not, is an eighth king. He belongs to the seven and is going to his destruction.

[12]"The ten horns you saw are ten kings who have not yet received a kingdom, but who for one hour will receive authority as kings along with the beast. [13]They have one purpose and will give their power and authority to the beast. [14]They will make war against the Lamb, but the Lamb will overcome them because he is Lord of lords and King of kings—and with him will be his called, chosen and faithful followers."

[15]Then the angel said to me, "The waters you saw, where the prostitute sits, are peoples, multitudes, nations and languages. [16]The beast and the ten horns you saw will hate the prostitute. They will bring her to ruin and leave her naked; they will eat her flesh

and burn her with fire. [17]For God has put it into their hearts to accomplish his purpose by agreeing to give the beast their power to rule, until God's words are fulfilled. [18]The woman you saw is the great city that rules over the kings of the earth."

The Fall of Babylon

18 After this I saw another angel coming down from heaven. He had great authority, and the earth was illuminated by his splendor. [2]With a mighty voice he shouted:

"Fallen! Fallen is Babylon the Great!
 She has become a home for demons
and a haunt for every evil[a] spirit,
 a haunt for every unclean and detestable bird.
[3]For all the nations have drunk the maddening wine of her adulteries.
The kings of the earth committed adultery with her,
 and the merchants of the earth grew rich from her excessive luxuries."

[4]Then I heard another voice from heaven say:

"Come out of her, my people,
 so that you will not share in her sins,
 so that you will not receive any of her plagues;
[5]for her sins are piled up to heaven,
 and God has remembered her crimes.
[6]Give back to her as she has given;
 pay her back double for what she has done.
Mix her a double portion from her own cup.
[7]Give her as much torture and grief
 as the glory and luxury she gave herself.
In her heart she boasts,
 'I sit as queen; I am not a widow,
 and I will never mourn.'
[8]Therefore in one day her plagues will overtake her:
 death, mourning and famine.
She will be consumed by fire,
 for mighty is the Lord God who judges her.

[9]"When the kings of the earth who committed adultery with her and shared her luxury see the smoke of her burning, they will weep and mourn over her. [10]Terrified at her torment, they will stand far off and cry:

"Woe! Woe, O great city,
 O Babylon, city of power!
In one hour your doom has come!'

[11]"The merchants of the earth will weep and mourn over her because no one buys their cargoes any more— [12]cargoes of gold, silver, precious stones and pearls; fine linen, purple, silk and scarlet cloth; every sort of citron wood, and articles of every kind made of ivory, costly wood, bronze, iron and marble; [13]cargoes of cinnamon and spice, of incense, myrrh and frankincense, of wine and olive oil, of fine flour and wheat; cattle and sheep; horses and carriages; and bodies and souls of men.

[14]"They will say, 'The fruit you longed for is gone from you. All your riches and splendor have

---

*a*2 Greek *unclean*

vanished, never to be recovered.' ¹⁵The merchants who sold these things and gained their wealth from her will stand far off, terrified at her torment. They will weep and mourn ¹⁶and they cry out:

" 'Woe! Woe, O great city,
    dressed in fine linen, purple
      and scarlet,
    and glittering with gold,
      precious stones and
      pearls!
¹⁷In one hour such great wealth
    has been brought to
      ruin!'

"Every sea captain, and all who travel by ship, the sailors, and all who earn their living from the sea, will stand far off. ¹⁸When they see the smoke of her burning, they will exclaim, 'Was there ever a city like this great city?' ¹⁹They will throw dust on their heads, and with weeping and mourning cry out:

" 'Woe! Woe, O great city,
    where all who had ships on
      the sea
    became rich through her
      wealth!
In one hour she has been
    brought to ruin!
²⁰Rejoice over her, O heaven!
    Rejoice, saints and apostles
      and prophets!
God has judged her for the
    way she treated you.' "

²¹Then a mighty angel picked up a boulder the size of a large millstone and threw it into the sea, and said:

"With such violence
    the great city of Babylon
      will be thrown down,
    never to be found again.
²²The music of harpists and
    musicians, flute players
      and trumpeters,

will never be heard in you
    again.
No workman of any trade
    will ever be found in you
      again.
The sound of a millstone
    will never be heard in you
      again.
²³The light of a lamp
    will never shine in you
      again.
The voice of bridegroom and
    bride
    will never be heard in you
      again.
Your merchants were the
    world's great men.
By your magic spell all the
    nations were led astray.
²⁴In her was found the blood of
    prophets and of the
      saints,
    and of all who have been
      killed on the earth.' "

Hallelujah!

19 After this I heard what sounded like the roar of a great multitude in heaven shouting:

"Hallelujah!
Salvation and glory and
    power belong to our
      God,
² for true and just are his
      judgments.
He has condemned the great
    prostitute
    who corrupted the earth by
      her adulteries.
He has avenged on her the
    blood of his servants."

³And again they shouted:

"Hallelujah!
The smoke from her goes up
    for ever and ever."

⁴The twenty-four elders and the four living creatures fell down

and worshiped God, who was seated on the throne. And they cried:

"Amen, Hallelujah!"

[5]Then a voice came from the throne, saying:

"Praise our God,
  all you his servants,
you who fear him,
  both small and great!"

[6]Then I heard what sounded like a great multitude, like the roar of rushing waters and like loud peals of thunder, shouting:

"Hallelujah!
  For our Lord God Almighty
    reigns.
[7]Let us rejoice and be glad
  and give him glory!
For the wedding of the Lamb
    has come,
  and his bride has made
    herself ready.
[8]Fine linen, bright and clean,
  was given her to wear."

(Fine linen stands for the righteous acts of the saints.)

[9]Then the angel said to me, "Write: 'Blessed are those who are invited to the wedding supper of the Lamb!'" And he added, "These are the true words of God."

[10]At this I fell at his feet to worship him. But he said to me, "Do not do it! I am a fellow servant with you and with your brothers who hold to the testimony of Jesus. Worship God! For the testimony of Jesus is the spirit of prophecy."

The Rider on the White Horse

[11]I saw heaven standing open and there before me was a white horse, whose rider is called Faithful and True. With justice he judges and makes war. [12]His eyes are like blazing fire, and on his head are many crowns. He has a name written on him that no one knows but he himself. [13]He is dressed in a robe dipped in blood, and his name is the Word of God. [14]The armies of heaven were following him, riding on white horses and dressed in fine linen, white and clean. [15]Out of his mouth comes a sharp sword with which to strike down the nations. "He will rule them with an iron scepter."[a] He treads the winepress of the fury of the wrath of God Almighty. [16]On his robe and on his thigh he has this name written:

KING OF KINGS AND LORD OF
LORDS.

[17]And I saw an angel standing in the sun, who cried in a loud voice to all the birds flying in midair, "Come, gather together for the great supper of God, [18]so that you may eat the flesh of kings, generals, and mighty men, of horses and their riders, and the flesh of all people, free and slave, small and great."

[19]Then I saw the beast and the kings of the earth and their armies gathered together to make war against the rider on the horse and his army. [20]But the beast was captured, and with him the false prophet who had performed the miraculous signs on his behalf. With these signs he had deluded those who had received the mark of the beast and worshiped his image. The two of them were thrown alive into the fiery lake of burning sulfur. [21]The rest of them were killed with the sword that came out of the mouth of the rider on the horse, and all the birds gorged themselves on their flesh.

[a]15 Psalm 2:9

The Thousand Years

20 And I saw an angel coming down out of heaven, having the key to the Abyss and holding in his hand a great chain. ²He seized the dragon, that ancient serpent, who is the devil, or Satan, and bound him for a thousand years. ³He threw him into the Abyss, and locked and sealed it over him, to keep him from deceiving the nations anymore until the thousand years were ended. After that, he must be set free for a short time.

⁴I saw thrones on which were seated those who had been given authority to judge. And I saw the souls of those who had been beheaded because of their testimony for Jesus and because of the word of God. They had not worshiped the beast or his image and had not received his mark on their foreheads or their hands. They came to life and reigned with Christ a thousand years. ⁵(The rest of the dead did not come to life until the thousand years were ended.) This is the first resurrection. ⁶Blessed and holy are those who have part in the first resurrection. The second death has no power over them, but they will be priests of God and of Christ and will reign with him for a thousand years.

Satan's Doom

⁷When the thousand years are over, Satan will be released from his prison ⁸and will go out to deceive the nations in the four corners of the earth—Gog and Magog—to gather them for battle. In number they are like the sand on the seashore. ⁹They marched across the breadth of the earth and surrounded the camp of God's people, the city he loves. But fire came down from heaven and devoured them. ¹⁰And the devil, who deceived them, was thrown into the lake of burning sulfur, where the beast and the false prophet had been thrown. They will be tormented day and night for ever and ever.

The Dead Are Judged

¹¹Then I saw a great white throne and him who was seated on it. Earth and sky fled from his presence, and there was no place for them. ¹²And I saw the dead, great and small, standing before the throne, and books were opened. Another book was opened, which is the book of life. The dead were judged according to what they had done as recorded in the books. ¹³The sea gave up the dead that were in it, and death and Hades gave up the dead that were in them, and each person was judged according to what he had done. ¹⁴Then death and Hades were thrown into the lake of fire. The lake of fire is the second death. ¹⁵If anyone's name was not found written in the book of life, he was thrown into the lake of fire.

The New Jerusalem

21 Then I saw a new heaven and a new earth, for the first heaven and the first earth had passed away, and there was no longer any sea. ²I saw the Holy City, the new Jerusalem, coming down out of heaven from God, prepared as a bride beautifully dressed for her husband. ³And I heard a loud voice from the throne saying, "Now the dwelling of God is with men, and he will live with them. They will be his people, and God himself will be with them and be their God. ⁴He will wipe every tear from their eyes. There will be no more death or mourning or crying or pain, for the old order of things has passed away."

⁵He who was seated on the throne said, "I am making everything new!" Then he said, "Write this down, for these words are trustworthy and true."

⁶He said to me: "It is done. I am the Alpha and the Omega, the Beginning and the End. To him who is thirsty I will give to drink without cost from the spring of the water of life. ⁷He who overcomes will inherit all this, and I will be his God and he will be my son. ⁸But the cowardly, the unbelieving, the vile, the murderers, the sexually immoral, those who practice magic arts, the idolaters and all liars—their place will be in the fiery lake of burning sulfur. This is the second death."

56
Ps 15:1-3

⁹One of the seven angels who had the seven bowls full of the seven last plagues came and said to me, "Come, I will show you the bride, the wife of the Lamb." ¹⁰And he carried me away in the Spirit to a mountain great and high, and showed me the Holy City, Jerusalem, coming down out of heaven from God. ¹¹It shone with the glory of God, and its brilliance was like that of a very precious jewel, like a jasper, clear as crystal. ¹²It had a great, high wall with twelve gates, and with twelve angels at the gates. On the gates were written the names of the twelve tribes of Israel. ¹³There were three gates on the east, three on the north, three on the south and three on the west. ¹⁴The wall of the city had twelve foundations, and on them

were the names of the twelve apostles of the Lamb.

¹⁵The angel who talked with me had a measuring rod of gold to measure the city, its gates and its walls. ¹⁶The city was laid out like a square, as long as it was wide. He measured the city with the rod and found it to be 12,000 stadia*a* in length, and as wide and high as it is long. ¹⁷He measured its wall and it was 144 cubits*b* thick,*c* by man's measurement, which the angel was using. ¹⁸The wall was made of jasper, and the city of pure gold, as pure as glass. ¹⁹The foundations of the city walls were decorated with every kind of precious stone. The first foundation was jasper, the second sapphire, the third chalcedony, the fourth emerald, ²⁰the fifth sardonyx, the sixth carnelian, the seventh chrysolite, the eighth beryl, the ninth topaz, the tenth chrysoprase, the eleventh jacinth, and the twelfth amethyst.*d* ²¹The twelve gates were twelve pearls, each gate made of a single pearl. The great street of the city was of pure gold, like transparent glass.

²²I did not see a temple in the city, because the Lord God Almighty and the Lamb are its temple. ²³The city does not need the sun or the moon to shine on it, for the glory of God gives it light, and the Lamb is its lamp. ²⁴The nations will walk by its light, and the kings of the earth will bring their splendor into it. ²⁵On no day will its gates ever be shut, for there will be no night there. ²⁶The glory and honor of the nations will be brought into it. ²⁷Nothing impure will ever enter it, nor will anyone who does what is shame-

---

a16 That is, about 1,400 miles (about 2,200 kilometers)   *b17* That is, about 200 feet (about 65 meters)   *c17* Or *high*   *d20* The precise identification of some of these precious stones is uncertain.

ful or deceitful, but only those whose names are written in the Lamb's book of life.

The River of Life

22 Then the angel showed me the river of the water of life, as clear as crystal, flowing from the throne of God and of the Lamb 2down the middle of the great street of the city. On each side of the river stood the tree of life, bearing twelve crops of fruit, yielding its fruit every month. And the leaves of the tree are for the healing of the nations. 3No longer will there be any curse. The throne of God and of the Lamb will be in the city, and his servants will serve him. 4They will see his face, and his name will be on their foreheads. 5There will be no more night. They will not need the light of a lamp or the light of the sun, for the Lord God will give them light. And they will reign for ever and ever.

6The angel said to me, "These words are trustworthy and true. The Lord, the God of the spirits of the prophets, sent his angel to show his servants the things that must soon take place."

Jesus Is Coming

7"Behold, I am coming soon! Blessed is he who keeps the words of the prophecy in this book."

8I, John, am the one who heard and saw these things. And when I had heard and seen them, I fell down to worship at the feet of the angel who had been showing them to me. 9But he said to me, "Do not do it! I am a fellow servant with you and with your brothers the prophets and of all who keep the words of this book. Worship God!"

10Then he told me, "Do not seal up the words of the prophecy of this book, because the time is near. 11Let him who does wrong continue to do wrong; let him who is vile continue to be vile; let him who does right continue to do right; and let him who is holy continue to be holy."

12"Behold, I am coming soon! 80 My reward is with me, and I will give to everyone according to what he has done. 13I am the Alpha and the Omega, the First and the Last, the Beginning and the End.

14"Blessed are those who wash their robes, that they may have the right to the tree of life and may go through the gates into the city. 15Outside are the dogs, those who practice magic arts, the sexually immoral, the murderers, the idolaters and everyone who loves and practices falsehood.

16"I, Jesus, have sent my angel to give you*a* this testimony for the churches. I am the Root and the Offspring of David, and the bright Morning Star."

17The Spirit and the bride say, "Come!" And let him who hears say, "Come!" Whoever is thirsty, let him come; and whoever wishes, let him take the free gift of the water of life.

18I warn everyone who hears the words of the prophecy of this book: If anyone adds anything to them, God will add to him the plagues described in this book. 19And if anyone takes words away from this book of proph-

---

*a16 The Greek is plural.

ecy, God will take away from him his share in the tree of life and in the holy city, which are described in this book.

²⁰He who testifies to these things says, "Yes, I am coming soon."

Amen. Come, Lord Jesus.

²¹The grace of the Lord Jesus be with God's people. Amen.

The Book
of
Psalms

Psalms

BOOK I

Psalms 1-41

Psalm 1

89 ¹Blessed is the man
  who does not walk in the
    counsel of the wicked
  or stand in the way of sinners
  or sit in the seat of mockers.
²But his delight is in the law of
    the LORD,
  and on his law he meditates
    day and night.
³He is like a tree planted by
    streams of water,
  which yields its fruit in
    season
  and whose leaf does not
    wither.
  Whatever he does prospers.

⁴Not so the wicked!
  They are like chaff
    that the wind blows away.
⁵Therefore the wicked will not
    stand in the judgment,
  nor sinners in the assembly
    of the righteous.

⁶For the LORD watches over the
    way of the righteous,
  but the way of the wicked
    will perish.

Psalm 2

¹Why do the nations conspire*a*
  and the peoples plot in
    vain?
²The kings of the earth take
    their stand
  and the rulers gather
    together
  against the LORD

and against his Anointed
    One.*b*
³"Let us break their chains,"
    they say,
  "and throw off their
    fetters."

⁴The One enthroned in heaven
    laughs;
  the Lord scoffs at them.
⁵Then he rebukes them in his
    anger
  and terrifies them in his
    wrath, saying,
⁶"I have installed my King*c*
    on Zion, my holy hill."

⁷I will proclaim the decree of
the LORD:

  He said to me, "You are my
    Son*d*;
  today I have become your
    Father.*e*
⁸Ask of me,
  and I will make the nations
    your inheritance,
  the ends of the earth your
    possession.
⁹You will rule them with an
    iron scepter*f*;
  you will dash them to
    pieces like pottery."

¹⁰Therefore, you kings, be wise;
  be warned, you rulers of the
    earth.
¹¹Serve the LORD with fear
  and rejoice with trembling.
¹²Kiss the Son, lest he be angry   3
  and you be destroyed in   Ps 7:11
    your way,
  for his wrath can flare up in a
    moment.
  Blessed are all who take
    refuge in him.

---

*a1 Hebrew; Septuagint rage   b2 Or anointed one   c6 Or king   d7 Or son; also in
verse 12   e7 Or have begotten you   f9 Or will break them with a rod of iron*

Psalm 3

A psalm of David. When he fled
from his son Absalom.

[1]O Lord, how many are my
      foes!
   How many rise up against
      me!
[2]Many are saying of me,
   "God will not deliver him."
                          Selah[a]

[3]But you are a shield around
      me, O Lord;
   you bestow glory on me
      and lift[b] up my head.
[4]To the Lord I cry aloud,
   and he answers me from his
      holy hill.   *Selah*

[5]I lie down and sleep;
   I wake again, because the
      Lord sustains me.
[6]I will not fear the tens of
      thousands
   drawn up against me on
      every side.

[7]Arise, O Lord!
   Deliver me, O my God!
   Strike all my enemies on the
      jaw;
   break the teeth of the
      wicked.

[8]From the Lord comes
      deliverance.
   May your blessing be on
      your people.   *Selah*

Psalm 4

For the director of music. With
stringed instruments.
A psalm of David.

[1]Answer me when I call to
      you,
   O my righteous God.

Give me relief from my
      distress;
   be merciful to me and hear
      my prayer.

[2]How long, O men, will you
   turn my glory into
      shame[c]?
   How long will you love
   delusions and seek false
      gods[d]?   *Selah*
[3]Know that the Lord has set
   apart the godly for
      himself;
   the Lord will hear when I
      call to him.

[4]In your anger do not sin;
   when you are on your beds,
   search your hearts and be
      silent.   *Selah*
[5]Offer right sacrifices
   and trust in the Lord.

[6]Many are asking, "Who can
   show us any good?"
   Let the light of your face
   shine upon us, O Lord.
[7]You have filled my heart with
      greater joy
   than when their grain and
      new wine abound.
[8]I will lie down and sleep in
      peace,
   for you alone, O Lord,
   make me dwell in safety.

Psalm 5

For the director of music. For flutes.
A psalm of David.

[1]Give ear to my words,
   O Lord,
   consider my sighing.
[2]Listen to my cry for help,
   my King and my God,
   for to you I pray.
[3]In the morning, O Lord, you
      hear my voice;

---

[a]2 A word of uncertain meaning, occurring frequently in the Psalms; possibly a
musical term   [b]3 Or Lord, / my Glorious One, who lifts   [c]2 Or you dishonor my
Glorious One   [d]2 Or seek lies

in the morning I lay my
requests before you
and wait in expectation.

⁴You are not a God who takes
pleasure in evil;
with you the wicked cannot
dwell.
⁵The arrogant cannot stand in
your presence;
you hate all who do wrong.
⁶You destroy those who tell
lies;
bloodthirsty and deceitful
men
the LORD abhors.

⁷But I, by your great mercy,
will come into your house;
in reverence will I bow down
toward your holy temple.
⁸Lead me, O LORD, in your
righteousness
because of my enemies—
make straight your way
before me.

⁹Not a word from their mouth
can be trusted;
their heart is filled with
destruction.
Their throat is an open grave;
with their tongue they
speak deceit.
¹⁰Declare them guilty, O God!
Let their intrigues be their
downfall.
Banish them for their many
sins,
for they have rebelled
against you.

¹¹But let all who take refuge in
you be glad;
let them ever sing for joy.
Spread your protection over
them,
that those who love your
name may rejoice in you.
¹²For surely, O LORD, you bless
the righteous;

81
Ps 12:5

you surround them with
your favor as with a
shield.

Psalm 6

For the director of music. With
stringed instruments. According to
sheminith.^a A psalm of David.

¹O LORD, do not rebuke me in
your anger
or discipline me in your
wrath.
²Be merciful to me, LORD, for I
am faint;
O LORD, heal me, for my
bones are in agony.
³My soul is in anguish.
How long, O LORD, how
long?

⁴Turn, O LORD, and deliver
me;
save me because of your
unfailing love.
⁵No one remembers you when
he is dead.
Who praises you from the
grave^b?

⁶I am worn out from groaning;
all night long I flood my
bed with weeping
and drench my couch with
tears.
⁷My eyes grow weak with
sorrow;
they fail because of all my
foes.

⁸Away from me, all you who
do evil,
for the LORD has heard my
weeping.
⁹The LORD has heard my cry
for mercy;
the LORD accepts my prayer.
¹⁰All my enemies will be
ashamed and dismayed;
they will turn back in
sudden disgrace.

^aTitle: Probably a musical term   ^b5 Hebrew *Sheol*

Psalm 7

*A shiggaion[a] of David, which he sang
to the LORD concerning Cush, a
Benjamite.*

1 O LORD my God, I take refuge
    in you;
  save and deliver me from all
    who pursue me,
2 or they will tear me like a lion
  and rip me to pieces with
    no one to rescue me.

3 O LORD my God, if I have
    done this
  and there is guilt on my
    hands—
4 if I have done evil to him who
    is at peace with me
  or without cause have
    robbed my foe—
5 then let my enemy pursue
    and overtake me;
  let him trample my life to
    the ground
  and make me sleep in the
    dust.   *Selah*

6 Arise, O LORD, in your anger;
  rise up against the rage of
    my enemies.
  Awake, my God; decree
    justice.
7 Let the assembled peoples
    gather around you.
  Rule over them from on
    high;
8   let the LORD judge the
    peoples.
  Judge me, O LORD, according
    to my righteousness,
  according to my integrity,
    O Most High.
9 O righteous God,
  who searches minds and
    hearts,
  bring to an end the violence
    of the wicked
  and make the righteous
    secure.

10 My shield[b] is God Most High,
  who saves the upright in
    heart.
11 God is a righteous judge,   3
  a God who expresses his
    wrath every day.
12 If he does not relent,
  he[c] will sharpen his sword;
  he will bend and string his
    bow.
13 He has prepared his deadly
    weapons;
  he makes ready his flaming
    arrows.
14 He who is pregnant with evil
  and conceives trouble gives
    birth to disillusionment.
15 He who digs a hole and
    scoops it out
  falls into the pit he has
    made.
16 The trouble he causes recoils
    on himself;
  his violence comes down on
    his own head.

17 I will give thanks to the LORD
    because of his
    righteousness
  and will sing praise to the
    name of the LORD Most
    High.

Psalm 8

*For the director of music. According
to gittith.[d] A psalm of David.*

1 O LORD, our Lord,
  how majestic is your name
    in all the earth!

You have set your glory
  above the heavens.
2 From the lips of children and
    infants
  you have ordained praise[e]
because of your enemies,
  to silence the foe and the
    avenger.

---

a Title: Probably a literary or musical term   *b* 10 Or *sovereign*   *c* 12 Or *If a man does
not repent, / God*   *d* Title: Probably a musical term   *e* 2 Or *strength*

³When I consider your
        heavens,
    the work of your fingers,
  the moon and the stars,
    which you have set in place,
⁴what is man that you are
        mindful of him,
    the son of man that you
        care for him?
⁵You made him a little lower
        than the heavenly
        beingsᵃ
    and crowned him with glory
        and honor.

⁶You made him ruler over the
        works of your hands;
    you put everything under
        his feet:
⁷all flocks and herds,
    and the beasts of the field,
⁸the birds of the air,
    and the fish of the sea,
    all that swim the paths of
        the seas.

⁹O Lord, our Lord,
    how majestic is your name
        in all the earth!

Psalm 9ᵇ

For the director of music. To the
tune of, "The Death of the Son."
A psalm of David.

¹I will praise you, O Lord,
        with all my heart;
    I will tell of all your
        wonders.
²I will be glad and rejoice in
        you;
    I will sing praise to your
        name, O Most High.

³My enemies turn back;
    they stumble and perish
        before you.
⁴For you have upheld my right
        and my cause;

you have sat on your
        throne, judging
        righteously.
⁵You have rebuked the nations
        and destroyed the
        wicked;
    you have blotted out their
        name for ever and
        ever.
⁶Endless ruin has overtaken
        the enemy,
    you have uprooted their
        cities;
    even the memory of them
        has perished.

⁷The Lord reigns forever;
    he has established his
        throne for judgment.
⁸He will judge the world in
        righteousness;
    he will govern the peoples
        with justice.
⁹The Lord is a refuge for the
        oppressed,
    a stronghold in times of
        trouble.
¹⁰Those who know your name
        will trust in you,
    for you, Lord, have never
        forsaken those who seek
        you.

¹¹Sing praises to the Lord,
        enthroned in Zion;
    proclaim among the nations
        what he has done.
¹²For he who avenges blood
        remembers;
    he does not ignore the cry
        of the afflicted.
¹³O Lord, see how my enemies
        persecute me!
    Have mercy and lift me up
        from the gates of death,
¹⁴that I may declare your
        praises
    in the gates of the Daughter
        of Zion

ᵃ5 Or *than God*   ᵇPsalms 9 and 10 may have been originally a single acrostic poem,
the stanzas of which begin with the successive letters of the Hebrew alphabet. In the
Septuagint they constitute one psalm.

and there rejoice in your
    salvation.
[15]The nations have fallen into
    the pit they have dug;
  their feet are caught in the
    net they have hidden.
[16]The LORD is known by his
    justice;
  the wicked are ensnared by
    the work of their hands.
        Higgaion.[a] *Selah*
[17]The wicked return to the
    grave,[b]
  all the nations that forget
    God.
[18]But the needy will not always
    be forgotten,
  nor the hope of the afflicted
    ever perish.

[19]Arise, O LORD, let not man
    triumph;
  let the nations be judged in
    your presence.
[20]Strike them with terror,
    O LORD;
  let the nations know they
    are but men.   *Selah*

Psalm 10[c]

[1]Why, O LORD, do you stand
    far off?
  Why do you hide yourself
    in times of trouble?

[2]In his arrogance the wicked
    man hunts down the
    weak,
  who are caught in the
    schemes he devises.
[3]He boasts of the cravings of
    his heart;
  he blesses the greedy and
    reviles the LORD.
[4]In his pride the wicked does
    not seek him;
  in all his thoughts there is
    no room for God.

[5]His ways are always
    prosperous;
  he is haughty and your laws
    are far from him;
  he sneers at all his enemies.
[6]He says to himself, "Nothing
    will shake me;
  I'll always be happy and
    never have trouble."
[7]His mouth is full of curses
    and lies and threats;
  trouble and evil are under
    his tongue.
[8]He lies in wait near the
    villages;
  from ambush he murders
    the innocent,
  watching in secret for his
    victims.
[9]He lies in wait like a lion in
    cover;
  he lies in wait to catch the
    helpless;
  he catches the helpless and
    drags them off in his
    net.
[10]His victims are crushed, they
    collapse;
  they fall under his strength.
[11]He says to himself, "God has
    forgotten;
  he covers his face and never
    sees."

[12]Arise, LORD! Lift up your
    hand, O God.
  Do not forget the helpless.
[13]Why does the wicked man
    revile God?
  Why does he say to himself,
    "He won't call me to
    account"?
[14]But you, O God, do see
    trouble and grief;
  you consider it to take it in
    hand.
  The victim commits himself to
    you;

---

[a]16 Or *Meditation;* possibly a musical notation   [b]17 Hebrew *Sheol*   [c]Psalms 9 and
10 may have been originally a single acrostic poem, the stanzas of which begin with
the successive letters of the Hebrew alphabet. In the Septuagint they constitute one
psalm.

you are the helper of the
fatherless.

[15]Break the arm of the wicked
and evil man;
call him to account for his
wickedness
that would not be found
out.

[16]The LORD is King for ever and
ever;
the nations will perish from
his land.

[17]You hear, O LORD, the desire
of the afflicted;
you encourage them, and
you listen to their cry,

[18]defending the fatherless and
the oppressed,
in order that man, who is of
the earth, may terrify no
more.

Psalm 11

For the director of music. Of David.

[1]In the LORD I take refuge.
How then can you say to
me:
"Flee like a bird to your
mountain.

[2]For look, the wicked bend
their bows;
they set their arrows against
the strings
to shoot from the shadows
at the upright in heart.

[3]When the foundations are
being destroyed,
what can the righteous
do[a]?"

[4]The LORD is in his holy
temple;
the LORD is on his heavenly
throne.
He observes the sons of men;
his eyes examine them.

38 [5]The LORD examines the
righteous,

but the wicked[b] and those
who love violence
his soul hates.

[6]On the wicked he will rain
fiery coals and burning
sulfur;
a scorching wind will be
their lot.

[7]For the LORD is righteous,
he loves justice;
upright men will see his
face.

Psalm 12

*For the director of music. According
to sheminith.[c] A psalm of David.*

[1]Help, LORD, for the godly are
no more;
the faithful have vanished
from among men.

[2]Everyone lies to his neighbor;
their flattering lips speak
with deception.

[3]May the LORD cut off all
flattering lips
and every boastful tongue

[4]that says, "We will triumph
with our tongues;
we own our lips[d]—who is
our master?"

[5]"Because of the oppression of   81
the weak   Ps 91:1,2
and the groaning of the
needy,
I will now arise," says the
LORD.
"I will protect them from
those who malign
them."

[6]And the words of the LORD
are flawless,
like silver refined in a
furnace of clay,
purified seven times.

[7]O LORD, you will keep us safe

---

[a]3 Or *what is the Righteous One doing*   [b]5 Or *The LORD, the Righteous One, examines
the wicked,* | [c]Title: Probably a musical term   [d]4 Or *our lips are our plowshares*

and protect us from such
  people forever.
[8]The wicked freely strut about
    when what is vile is
    honored among men.

Psalm 13

For the director of music.
A psalm of David.

[1]How long, O LORD? Will you
    forget me forever?
  How long will you hide
    your face from me?
[2]How long must I wrestle with
    my thoughts
  and every day have sorrow
    in my heart?
  How long will my enemy
    triumph over me?

[3]Look on me and answer,
    O LORD my God.
  Give light to my eyes, or I
    will sleep in death;
[4]my enemy will say, "I have
    overcome him,"
  and my foes will rejoice
    when I fall.

[5]But I trust in your unfailing
    love;
  my heart rejoices in your
    salvation.
[6]I will sing to the LORD,
  for he has been good to me.

Psalm 14

For the director of music. Of David.

31 [1]The fool[a] says in his heart,
    "There is no God."
  They are corrupt, their deeds
    are vile;
    there is no one who does
    good.

[2]The LORD looks down from
    heaven
  on the sons of men
  to see if there are any who
    understand,

any who seek God.
[3]All have turned aside,
  they have together become
    corrupt;
  there is no one who does
    good,
    not even one.

[4]Will evildoers never learn—
  those who devour my
    people as men eat bread
  and who do not call on the
    LORD?
[5]There they are, overwhelmed
    with dread,
  for God is present in the
    company of the
    righteous.
[6]You evildoers frustrate the
    plans of the poor,
  but the LORD is their refuge.

[7]Oh, that salvation for Israel
    would come out of Zion!
  When the LORD restores the
    fortunes of his people,
  let Jacob rejoice and Israel
    be glad!

Psalm 15

A psalm of David.

[1]LORD, who may dwell in your 56
    sanctuary?
  Who may live on your holy
    hill?

[2]He whose walk is blameless
  and who does what is
    righteous,
  who speaks the truth from his
    heart
[3] and has no slander on his
    tongue,
  who does his neighbor no
    wrong
  and casts no slur on his
    fellowman,
[4]who despises a vile man
  but honors those who fear
    the LORD,
  who keeps his oath

---

[a]1 The Hebrew words rendered *fool* in Psalms denote one who is morally deficient.

even when it hurts,
61 ⁵who lends his money without
        usury
   and does not accept a bribe
        against the innocent.

He who does these things
        will never be shaken.

Psalm 16

A miktam[a] *of David.*

¹Keep me safe, O God,
   for in you I take refuge.

²I said to the LORD, "You are
        my Lord;
   apart from you I have no
        good thing."
³As for the saints who are in
        the land,
   they are the glorious ones in
        whom is all my delight.[b]
⁴The sorrows of those will
        increase
   who run after other gods.
   I will not pour out their
        libations of blood
   or take up their names on
        my lips.

⁵LORD, you have assigned me
        my portion and my cup;
   you have made my lot
        secure.
⁶The boundary lines have
        fallen for me in pleasant
        places;
   surely I have a delightful
        inheritance.

⁷I will praise the LORD, who
        counsels me;
   even at night my heart
        instructs me.
⁸I have set the LORD always
        before me.
   Because he is at my right
        hand,
   I will not be shaken.

⁹Therefore my heart is glad
        and my tongue rejoices;
   my body also will rest
        secure,
¹⁰because you will not abandon   75
        me to the grave,[c]
   nor will you let your Holy
        One[d] see decay.
¹¹You have made[e] known to me   37
        the path of life;   Ps 68:4
   you will fill me with joy in   68
        your presence,   Ps 34:1
   with eternal pleasures at
        your right hand.

Psalm 17

A prayer of David.

¹Hear, O LORD, my righteous
        plea;
   listen to my cry.
   Give ear to my prayer—
        it does not rise from
        deceitful lips.
²May my vindication come
        from you;
   may your eyes see what is
        right.

³Though you probe my heart
        and examine me at
        night,
   though you test me, you
        will find nothing;
   I have resolved that my
        mouth will not sin.
⁴As for the deeds of men—
        by the word of your lips
   I have kept myself
        from the ways of the
        violent.
⁵My steps have held to your
        paths;
   my feet have not slipped.

⁶I call on you, O God, for you
        will answer me;
   give ear to me and hear my
        prayer.

---

[a]Title: Probably a literary or musical term
[b]3 Or *As for the pagan priests who are in
the land / and the nobles in whom all delight, I said:*   [c]10 Hebrew *Sheol*   [d]10 Or *your
faithful one*   [e]11 Or *You will make*

⁷Show the wonder of your
   great love,
      you who save by your right
         hand
         those who take refuge in
            you from their foes.
⁸Keep me as the apple of your
   eye;
      hide me in the shadow of
         your wings
⁹from the wicked who assail
   me,
      from my mortal enemies
         who surround me.

¹⁰They close up their callous
   hearts,
      and their mouths speak
         with arrogance.
¹¹They have tracked me down,
   they now surround me,
      with eyes alert, to throw me
         to the ground.
¹²They are like a lion hungry for
   prey,
      like a great lion crouching in
         cover.

¹³Rise up, O LORD, confront
   them, bring them down;
      rescue me from the wicked
         by your sword.
¹⁴O LORD, by your hand save
   me from such men,
      from men of this world
         whose reward is in this
            life.

You still the hunger of those
   you cherish;
      their sons have plenty,
         and they store up wealth for
            their children.
¹⁵And I—in righteousness I will
   see your face;
      when I awake, I will be
         satisfied with seeing
            your likeness.

Psalm 18

For the director of music. Of David
the servant of the LORD. He sang to
the LORD the words of this song
when the LORD delivered him from
the hand of all his enemies and from
the hand of Saul. He said:

¹I love you, O LORD, my
   strength.

²The LORD is my rock, my
   fortress and my
      deliverer;
      my God is my rock, in
         whom I take refuge.
      He is my shield and the
         horn[a] of my salvation,
            my stronghold.
³I call to the LORD, who is
   worthy of praise,
      and I am saved from my
         enemies.

⁴The cords of death entangled
   me;
      the torrents of destruction
         overwhelmed me.
⁵The cords of the grave[b] coiled
   around me;
      the snares of death
         confronted me.
⁶In my distress I called to the
   LORD;
      I cried to my God for help.
   From his temple he heard my
      voice;
      my cry came before him,
         into his ears.

⁷The earth trembled and
   quaked,
      and the foundations of the
         mountains shook;
      they trembled because he
         was angry.
⁸Smoke rose from his nostrils;
   consuming fire came from
      his mouth,

---

a2 Horn here symbolizes strength.   *b5 Hebrew Sheol*

burning coals blazed out
of it.
⁹He parted the heavens and
came down;
dark clouds were under his
feet.
¹⁰He mounted the cherubim
and flew;
he soared on the wings of
the wind.
¹¹He made darkness his
covering, his
canopy around
him—
the dark rain clouds of the
sky.
¹²Out of the brightness of his
presence clouds
advanced,
with hailstones and bolts of
lightning.
¹³The LORD thundered from
heaven;
the voice of the Most High
resounded.ᵃ
¹⁴He shot his arrows and
scattered the
enemies,
great bolts of lightning and
routed them.
¹⁵The valleys of the sea were
exposed
and the foundations of the
earth laid bare
at your rebuke, O LORD,
at the blast of breath from
your nostrils.
¹⁶He reached down from on
high and took hold of
me;
he drew me out of deep
waters.
¹⁷He rescued me from my
powerful enemy,
from my foes, who were too
strong for me.
¹⁸They confronted me in the
day of my disaster,

but the LORD was my
support.
¹⁹He brought me out into a
spacious place;
he rescued me because he
delighted in me.

²⁰The LORD has dealt with me
according to my
righteousness;
according to the cleanness
of my hands he has
rewarded me.
²¹For I have kept the ways of
the LORD;
I have not done evil by
turning from my God.
²²All his laws are before me;
I have not turned away
from his decrees.
²³I have been blameless before
him
and have kept myself from
sin.
²⁴The LORD has rewarded me
according to my
righteousness,
according to the cleanness
of my hands in his sight.

²⁵To the faithful you show
yourself faithful,
to the blameless you show
yourself blameless,
²⁶to the pure you show yourself
pure,
but to the crooked you
show yourself shrewd.
²⁷You save the humble
but bring low those whose
eyes are haughty.
²⁸You, O LORD, keep my lamp
burning;
my God turns my darkness
into light.
²⁹With your help I can advance
against a troopᵇ;
with my God I can scale a
wall.

ᵃ13 Some Hebrew manuscripts and Septuagint (see also 2 Samuel 22:14); most
Hebrew manuscripts *resounded, / amid hailstones and bolts of lightning*   ᵇ29 Or *can run
through a barricade*

30As for God, his way is perfect;
  the word of the LORD is
    flawless.
He is a shield
  for all who take refuge in
    him.
31For who is God besides the
    LORD?
  And who is the Rock except
    our God?
32It is God who arms me with
    strength
  and makes my way perfect.
33He makes my feet like the feet
    of a deer;
  he enables me to stand on
    the heights.
34He trains my hands for battle;
  my arms can bend a bow of
    bronze.
35You give me your shield of
    victory,
  and your right hand
    sustains me;
  you stoop down to make
    me great.
36You broaden the path beneath
    me,
  so that my ankles do not
    turn.
37I pursued my enemies and
    overtook them;
  I did not turn back till they
    were destroyed.
38I crushed them so that they
    could not rise;
  they fell beneath my feet.
39You armed me with strength
    for battle;
  you made my adversaries
    bow at my feet.
40You made my enemies turn
    their backs in flight,
  and I destroyed my foes.
41They cried for help, but there
    was no one to save
    them—
  to the LORD, but he did not
    answer.
42I beat them as fine as dust
    borne on the wind;

I poured them out like mud
    in the streets.

43You have delivered me from
    the attacks of the people;
  you have made me the head
    of nations;
  people I did not know are
    subject to me.
44As soon as they hear me, they
    obey me;
  foreigners cringe before me.
45They all lose heart;
  they come trembling from
    their strongholds.
46The LORD lives! Praise be to
    my Rock!
  Exalted be God my Savior!
47He is the God who avenges
    me,
  who subdues nations under
    me,
48 who saves me from my
    enemies.
You exalted me above my
    foes;
  from violent men you
    rescued me.
49Therefore I will praise you
    among the nations,
    O LORD;
  I will sing praises to your
    name.
50He gives his king great
    victories;
  he shows unfailing kindness
    to his anointed,
  to David and his
    descendants forever.

Psalm 19

*For the director of music.
A psalm of David.*

1The heavens declare the glory
    of God;
  the skies proclaim the work
    of his hands.
2Day after day they pour forth
    speech;

night after night they
    display knowledge.
³There is no speech or
    language
    where their voice is not
    heard.ᵃ
⁴Their voiceᵇ goes out into all
    the earth,
    their words to the ends of
    the world.

In the heavens he has pitched
    a tent for the sun,
⁵ which is like a bridegroom
    coming forth from his
    pavilion,
    like a champion rejoicing to
    run his course.
⁶It rises at one end of the
    heavens
    and makes its circuit to the
    other;
    nothing is hidden from its
    heat.

45
50
⁷The law of the LORD is
    perfect,
    reviving the soul.
The statutes of the LORD are
    trustworthy,
    making wise the simple.

9
Ps 84:11
⁸The precepts of the LORD are
    right,
    giving joy to the heart.
The commands of the LORD
    are radiant,
    giving light to the eyes.
⁹The fear of the LORD is pure,
    enduring forever.
The ordinances of the LORD
    are sure
    and altogether righteous.
¹⁰They are more precious than
    gold,
    than much pure gold;
    they are sweeter than honey,
    than honey from the comb.
¹¹By them is your servant
    warned;
    in keeping them there is
    great reward.

¹²Who can discern his errors?
    Forgive my hidden faults.
¹³Keep your servant also from
    willful sins;
    may they not rule over me.
Then will I be blameless,
    innocent of great
    transgression.

12
44
Ps 25:9

36
Ps 32:5

¹⁴May the words of my mouth
    and the meditation of
    my heart
    be pleasing in your sight,
O LORD, my Rock and my
    Redeemer.

98
Ps 25:14

99

Psalm 20

For the director of music.
A psalm of David.

¹May the LORD answer you
    when you are in
    distress;
    may the name of the God of
    Jacob protect you.
²May he send you help from
    the sanctuary
    and grant you support from
    Zion.
³May he remember all your
    sacrifices
    and accept your burnt
    offerings.   *Selah*
⁴May he give you the desire of
    your heart
    and make all your plans
    succeed.
⁵We will shout for joy when
    you are victorious
    and will lift up our banners
    in the name of our God.
May the LORD grant all your
    requests.

⁶Now I know that the LORD
    saves his anointed;
    he answers him from his
    holy heaven
    with the saving power of
    his right hand.

ᵃ3 Or *They have no speech, there are no words; / no sound is heard from them*
ᵇ4 Septuagint, Jerome and Syriac; Hebrew *line*

7Some trust in chariots and
 some in horses,
 but we trust in the name of
 the LORD our God.
8They are brought to their
 knees and fall,
 but we rise up and stand
 firm.

9O LORD, save the king!
 Answer[a] us when we call!

Psalm 21

For the director of music.
A psalm of David.

1O LORD, the king rejoices in
 your strength.
 How great is his joy in the
 victories you give!
2You have granted him the
 desire of his heart
 and have not withheld the
 request of his lips.   *Selah*
3You welcomed him with rich
 blessings
 and placed a crown of pure
 gold on his head.
4He asked you for life, and you
 gave it to him—
 length of days, for ever and
 ever.
5Through the victories you
 gave, his glory is great;
 you have bestowed on him
 splendor and majesty.
6Surely you have granted him
 eternal blessings
 and made him glad with the
 joy of your presence.
7For the king trusts in the
 LORD;
 through the unfailing love
 of the Most High
 he will not be shaken.

8Your hand will lay hold on all
 your enemies;
 your right hand will seize
 your foes.
9At the time of your appearing

you will make them like a
 fiery furnace.
 In his wrath the LORD will
 swallow them up,
 and his fire will consume
 them.
10You will destroy their
 descendants from the
 earth,
 their posterity from
 mankind.
11Though they plot evil against
 you
 and devise wicked schemes,
 they cannot succeed;
12for you will make them turn
 their backs
 when you aim at them with
 drawn bow.

13Be exalted, O LORD, in your
 strength;
 we will sing and praise your
 might.

Psalm 22

For the director of music. To the
tune of, "The Doe of the Morning."
A psalm of David.

1My God, my God, why have
 you forsaken me?
 Why are you so far from
 saving me,
 so far from the words of my
 groaning?
2O my God, I cry out by day,
 but you do not answer,
 by night, and am not silent.

3Yet you are enthroned as the
 Holy One;
 you are the praise of Israel.[b]
4In you our fathers put their
 trust;
 they trusted and you
 delivered them.
5They cried to you and were
 saved;
 in you they trusted and
 were not disappointed.

---

*a*9 Or save! / O King, answer   *b*3 Or Yet you are holy, / enthroned on the praises of Israel

⁶But I am a worm and not a
man,
scorned by men and
despised by the people.
⁷All who see me mock me;
they hurl insults, shaking
their heads:
⁸"He trusts in the LORD;
let the LORD rescue him.
Let him deliver him,
since he delights in him."
⁹Yet you brought me out of the
womb;
you made me trust in you
even at my mother's breast.
¹⁰From birth I was cast upon
you;
from my mother's womb
you have been my God.
¹¹Do not be far from me,
for trouble is near
and there is no one to help.
¹²Many bulls surround me;
strong bulls of Bashan
encircle me.
¹³Roaring lions tearing their
prey
open their mouths wide
against me.
¹⁴I am poured out like water,
and all my bones are out of
joint.
My heart has turned to wax;
it has melted away within
me.
¹⁵My strength is dried up like a
potsherd,
and my tongue sticks to the
roof of my mouth;
you lay me*a* in the dust of
death.
¹⁶Dogs have surrounded me;
a band of evil men has
encircled me,
they have pierced*b* my
hands and my feet.
¹⁷I can count all my bones;
people stare and gloat over
me.

¹⁸They divide my garments
among them
and cast lots for my
clothing.
¹⁹But you, O LORD, be not far
off;
O my Strength, come
quickly to help me.
²⁰Deliver my life from the
sword,
my precious life from the
power of the dogs.
²¹Rescue me from the mouth of
the lions;
save*c* me from the horns of
the wild oxen.
²²I will declare your name to
my brothers;
in the congregation I will
praise you.
²³You who fear the LORD, praise
him!
All you descendants of
Jacob, honor him!
Revere him, all you
descendants of Israel!
²⁴For he has not despised or
disdained
the suffering of the afflicted
one;
he has not hidden his face
from him
but has listened to his cry
for help.
²⁵From you comes the theme of
my praise in the great
assembly;
before those who fear you*d*
will I fulfill my vows.
²⁶The poor will eat and be
satisfied;
they who seek the LORD will
praise him—
may your hearts live
forever!
²⁷All the ends of the earth
will remember and turn to
the LORD,

---

*a*15 Or / I am laid   *b*16 Some Hebrew manuscripts, Septuagint and Syriac; most
Hebrew manuscripts / like the lion,   *c*21 Or / you have heard   *d*25 Hebrew him

and all the families of the
  nations
    will bow down before
      him,
²⁸for dominion belongs to the
  LORD
    and he rules over the
      nations.

²⁹All the rich of the earth will
  feast and worship;
  all who go down to the dust
    will kneel before him—
  those who cannot keep
    themselves alive.
³⁰Posterity will serve him;
  future generations will be
    told about the Lord.
³¹They will proclaim his
  righteousness
  to a people yet unborn—
    for he has done it.

Psalm 23

A psalm of David.

53
Ps 43:5

¹The LORD is my shepherd, I
  shall not be in want.
² He makes me lie down in
  green pastures,
he leads me beside quiet
  waters,
³ he restores my soul.
He guides me in paths of
  righteousness
  for his name's sake.
⁴Even though I walk
  through the valley of the
    shadow of death,ᵃ
I will fear no evil,
  for you are with me;
your rod and your staff,
  they comfort me.

⁵You prepare a table before
  me
  in the presence of my
    enemies.
You anoint my head with oil;
  my cup overflows.

⁶Surely goodness and love will
  follow me
all the days of my life,
and I will dwell in the house
  of the LORD
forever.

Psalm 24

Of David. A psalm.

¹The earth is the LORD's, and
  everything in it,
  the world, and all who live
    in it;
²for he founded it upon the
  seas
  and established it upon the
    waters.

³Who may ascend the hill of
  the LORD?
  Who may stand in his holy
    place?
⁴He who has clean hands and
  a pure heart,
  who does not lift up his
    soul to an idol
  or swear by what is false.ᵇ
⁵He will receive blessing from
  the LORD
  and vindication from God
    his Savior.
⁶Such is the generation of
  those who seek him,
  who seek your face, O God
    of Jacob.ᶜ
              Selah

⁷Lift up your heads, O you
  gates;
  be lifted up, you ancient
    doors,
  that the King of glory may
    come in.
⁸Who is this King of glory?
  The LORD strong and
    mighty,
  the LORD mighty in battle.
⁹Lift up your heads, O you
  gates;

ᵃ4 Or *through the darkest valley*   ᵇ4 Or *swear falsely*   ᶜ6 Two Hebrew manuscripts
and Syriac (see also Septuagint); most Hebrew manuscripts *face, Jacob*

lift them up, you ancient
  doors,
that the King of glory may
  come in.
¹⁰Who is he, this King of glory?
The LORD Almighty—
  he is the King of glory.

Selah

Psalm 25ᵃ

Of David.

¹To you, O LORD, I lift up my
  soul;
² in you I trust, O my God.
Do not let me be put to
  shame,
  nor let my enemies triumph
    over me.
³No one whose hope is in you
  will ever be put to shame,
but they will be put to shame
  who are treacherous without
    excuse.

⁴Show me your ways, O LORD,
  teach me your paths;

43
Ps 33:20
⁵guide me in your truth and
  teach me,
  for you are God my Savior,
  and my hope is in you all
    day long.
⁶Remember, O LORD, your
  great mercy and love,
  for they are from of old.
⁷Remember not the sins of my
  youth
  and my rebellious ways;
according to your love
  remember me,
  for you are good, O LORD.

⁸Good and upright is the LORD;
  therefore he instructs
    sinners in his ways.
44
Ps 147:6
⁹He guides the humble in what
  is right
  and teaches them his way.

¹⁰All the ways of the LORD are
  loving and faithful
for those who keep the
  demands of his
    covenant.
¹¹For the sake of your name,
  O LORD;
  forgive my iniquity, though
    it is great.
¹²Who, then, is the man that
  fears the LORD?
  He will instruct him in the
    way chosen for him.
¹³He will spend his days in
  prosperity,
  and his descendants will
    inherit the land.
98
Ps 90:12
¹⁴The LORD confides in those
  who fear him;
  he makes his covenant
    known to them.
¹⁵My eyes are ever on the
  LORD,
  for only he will release my
    feet from the snare.

¹⁶Turn to me and be gracious to
  me,
  for I am lonely and afflicted.
¹⁷The troubles of my heart have
  multiplied;
  free me from my anguish.
¹⁸Look upon my affliction and
  my distress
  and take away all my sins.
¹⁹See how my enemies have
  increased
  and how fiercely they hate
    me!
²⁰Guard my life and rescue me;
  let me not be put to shame,
  for I take refuge in you.
²¹May integrity and uprightness
  protect me,
  because my hope is in you.

²²Redeem Israel, O God,
  from all their troubles!

ᵃThis psalm is an acrostic poem, the verses of which begin with the successive letters
of the Hebrew alphabet.

Psalm 26

Of David.

¹Vindicate me, O LORD,
　for I have led a blameless
　　life;
I have trusted in the LORD
　without wavering.
²Test me, O LORD, and try me,
　examine my heart and my
　　mind;
³for your love is ever before
　　me,
　and I walk continually in
　　your truth.
⁴I do not sit with deceitful
　　men,
　nor do I consort with
　　hypocrites;
⁵I abhor the assembly of
　　evildoers
　and refuse to sit with the
　　wicked.
⁶I wash my hands in
　　innocence,
　and go about your altar,
　　O LORD,
⁷proclaiming aloud your praise
　and telling of all your
　　wonderful deeds.
⁸I love the house where you
　　live, O LORD,
　the place where your glory
　　dwells.

⁹Do not take away my soul
　along with sinners,
　my life with bloodthirsty
　　men,
¹⁰in whose hands are wicked
　　schemes,
　whose right hands are full
　　of bribes.
¹¹But I lead a blameless life;
　redeem me and be merciful
　　to me.

¹²My feet stand on level
　　ground;
　in the great assembly I will
　　praise the LORD.

72
Ps 49:15

Psalm 27

Of David.

¹The LORD is my light and my
　　salvation—
　whom shall I fear?
The LORD is the stronghold of
　　my life—
　of whom shall I be afraid?
²When evil men advance
　　against me
　to devour my flesh,ᵃ
when my enemies and my
　　foes attack me,
　they will stumble and fall.
³Though an army besiege me,
　my heart will not fear;
　though war break out against
　　me,
　even then will I be
　　confident.

⁴One thing I ask of the LORD,
　this is what I seek:
　that I may dwell in the house
　　of the LORD
　all the days of my life,
to gaze upon the beauty of
　　the LORD
　and to seek him in his
　　temple.
⁵For in the day of trouble
　he will keep me safe in his
　　dwelling;
he will hide me in the shelter
　　of his tabernacle
　and set me high upon a
　　rock.
⁶Then my head will be exalted
　above the enemies who
　　surround me;
at his tabernacle will I sacrifice
　with shouts of joy;
　I will sing and make music
　　to the LORD.

⁷Hear my voice when I call,
　　O LORD,
　be merciful to me and
　　answer me.

ᵃ2 Or _to slander me_

[8]My heart says of you, "Seek
his[a] face!"
Your face, LORD, I will seek.
[9]Do not hide your face from
me,
do not turn your servant
away in anger;
you have been my helper.
Do not reject me or forsake
me,
O God my Savior.

52 [10]Though my father and mother
Ps 119:92   forsake me,
73   the LORD will receive me.
Ps 37:25
[11]Teach me your way, O LORD;
lead me in a straight path
because of my oppressors.
[12]Do not turn me over to the
desire of my foes,
for false witnesses rise up
against me,
breathing out violence.

[13]I am still confident of this:
I will see the goodness of
the LORD
in the land of the living.

16 [14]Wait for the LORD;
Ps 42:5   be strong and take heart
and wait for the LORD.

Psalm 28

Of David.

[1]To you I call, O LORD my
Rock;
do not turn a deaf ear to
me.
For if you remain silent,
I will be like those who
have gone down to the
pit.
[2]Hear my cry for mercy
as I call to you for help,
as I lift up my hands
toward your Most Holy
Place.

[3]Do not drag me away with
the wicked,
with those who do evil,

who speak cordially with their
neighbors
but harbor malice in their
hearts.
[4]Repay them for their deeds
and for their evil work;
repay them for what their
hands have done
and bring back upon them
what they deserve.
[5]Since they show no regard for
the works of the LORD
and what his hands have
done,
he will tear them down
and never build them up
again.

[6]Praise be to the LORD,
for he has heard my cry for
mercy.
[7]The LORD is my strength and
my shield;
my heart trusts in him, and
I am helped.
My heart leaps for joy
and I will give thanks to
him in song.

[8]The LORD is the strength of
his people,
a fortress of salvation for his
anointed one.
[9]Save your people and bless
your inheritance;
be their shepherd and carry
them forever.

Psalm 29

A psalm of David.

[1]Ascribe to the LORD,
O mighty ones,
ascribe to the LORD glory
and strength.
[2]Ascribe to the LORD the glory
due his name;
worship the LORD in the
splendor of his[b]
holiness.

_____
[a]8 Or To you, O my heart, he has said, "Seek my   [b]2 Or LORD with the splendor of

³The voice of the LORD is over
the waters;
the God of glory thunders,
the LORD thunders over the
mighty waters.
⁴The voice of the LORD is
powerful;
the voice of the LORD is
majestic.
⁵The voice of the LORD breaks
the cedars;
the LORD breaks in pieces
the cedars of Lebanon.
⁶He makes Lebanon skip like a
calf,
Sirion*a* like a young wild
ox.
⁷The voice of the LORD strikes
with flashes of lightning.
⁸The voice of the LORD shakes
the desert;
the LORD shakes the Desert
of Kadesh.*b*
⁹The voice of the LORD twists
the oaks*b*
and strips the forests bare.
And in his temple all cry,
"Glory!"

¹⁰The LORD sits*c* enthroned over
the flood;
the LORD is enthroned as
King forever.
¹¹The LORD gives strength to his
people;
the LORD blesses his people
with peace.

Psalm 30

A psalm. A song. For the dedication
of the temple.*d* Of David.

¹I will exalt you, O LORD,
for you lifted me out of the
depths
and did not let my enemies
gloat over me.

²O LORD my God, I called to
you for help
and you healed me.
³O LORD, you brought me up
from the grave*e*;
you spared me from going
down into the pit.

⁴Sing to the LORD, you saints
of his;
praise his holy name.
⁵For his anger lasts only a
moment,
but his favor lasts a lifetime;
weeping may remain for a
night,
but rejoicing comes in the
morning.

⁶When I felt secure, I said,
"I will never be shaken."
⁷O LORD, when you favored
me,
you made my mountain*f*
stand firm;
but when you hid your face,
I was dismayed.

⁸To you, O LORD, I called;
to the Lord I cried for
mercy:
⁹"What gain is there in my
destruction,*g*
in my going down into the
pit?
Will the dust praise you?
Will it proclaim your
faithfulness?
¹⁰Hear, O LORD, and be
merciful to me;
O LORD, be my help."

¹¹You turned my wailing into
dancing;
you removed my sackcloth
and clothed me with joy,
¹²that my heart may sing to you
and not be silent.
O LORD my God, I will give
you thanks forever.

---

*a6 That is, Mount Hermon   *b9 Or LORD makes the deer give birth   *c10 Or sat
*d Title: Or palace   *e3 Hebrew Sheol   *f7 Or hill country   *g9 Or there if I am silenced

Psalm 31

For the director of music.
A psalm of David.

[1]In you, O Lord, I have taken
refuge;
let me never be put to
shame;
deliver me in your
righteousness.
[2]Turn your ear to me,
come quickly to my rescue;
be my rock of refuge,
a strong fortress to save me.
[3]Since you are my rock and my
fortress,
for the sake of your name
lead and guide me.
[4]Free me from the trap that is
set for me,
for you are my refuge.
[5]Into your hands I commit my
spirit;
redeem me, O Lord, the
God of truth.

[6]I hate those who cling to
worthless idols;
I trust in the Lord.
[7]I will be glad and rejoice in
your love,
for you saw my affliction
and knew the anguish of
my soul.
[8]You have not handed me over
to the enemy
but have set my feet in a
spacious place.

[9]Be merciful to me, O Lord,
for I am in distress;
my eyes grow weak with
sorrow,
my soul and my body with
grief.
[10]My life is consumed by
anguish
and my years by groaning;
my strength fails because of
my affliction,[a]
and my bones grow weak.

[11]Because of all my enemies,
I am the utter contempt of
my neighbors;
I am a dread to my friends—
those who see me on the
street flee from me.
[12]I am forgotten by them as
though I were dead;
I have become like broken
pottery.
[13]For I hear the slander of
many;
there is terror on every side;
they conspire against me
and plot to take my life.

[14]But I trust in you, O Lord;
I say, "You are my God."
[15]My times are in your hands;
deliver me from my enemies
and from those who pursue
me.
[16]Let your face shine on your
servant;
save me in your unfailing
love.
[17]Let me not be put to shame,
O Lord,
for I have cried out to you;
but let the wicked be put to
shame
and lie silent in the grave.[b]
[18]Let their lying lips be
silenced,
for with pride and contempt
they speak arrogantly
against the righteous.

[19]How great is your goodness,
which you have stored up
for those who fear you,
which you bestow in the sight
of men
on those who take refuge in
you.
[20]In the shelter of your presence
you hide them
from the intrigues of men;
in your dwelling you keep
them safe
from accusing tongues.

[a]10 Or guilt   [b]17 Hebrew Sheol

²¹Praise be to the LORD,
    for he showed his
        wonderful love to me
    when I was in a besieged
        city.
²²In my alarm I said,
    "I am cut off from your
        sight!"
  Yet you heard my cry for
      mercy
    when I called to you for
        help.
²³Love the LORD, all his saints!
    The LORD preserves the
        faithful,
    but the proud he pays back
        in full.
²⁴Be strong and take heart,
    all you who hope in the
        LORD.

Psalm 32

Of David. A *maskil.*ᵃ

¹Blessed is he
    whose transgressions are
        forgiven,
    whose sins are covered.
²Blessed is the man
    whose sin the LORD does
        not count against him
    and in whose spirit is no
        deceit.

³When I kept silent,
    my bones wasted away
        through my groaning all day
        long.
⁴For day and night
    your hand was heavy upon
        me;
    my strength was sapped
        as in the heat of summer.
                  Selah

10
Ps 66:16

36
Ps 38:4

⁵Then I acknowledged my sin
    to you
    and did not cover up my
        iniquity.
  I said, "I will confess

    my transgressions to the
        LORD"—
  and you forgave
    the guilt of my sin.   *Selah*

⁶Therefore let everyone who is
    godly pray to you
    while you may be found;
  surely when the mighty
      waters rise,
    they will not reach him.
⁷You are my hiding place;
    you will protect me from
        trouble
    and surround me with
        songs of deliverance.
                  Selah

⁸I will instruct you and teach
    you in the way you
        should go;
    I will counsel you and
        watch over you.
⁹Do not be like the horse or
    the mule,
    which have no
        understanding
  but must be controlled by bit
      and bridle
    or they will not come to
        you.
¹⁰Many are the woes of the
    wicked,
    but the LORD's unfailing
        love
    surrounds the man who
        trusts in him.
¹¹Rejoice in the LORD and be
    glad, you righteous;
    sing, all you who are
        upright in heart!

Psalm 33

¹Sing joyfully to the LORD, you
    righteous;
    it is fitting for the upright to
        praise him.
²Praise the LORD with the harp;

ᵃTitle: Probably a literary or musical term

make music to him on the
ten-stringed lyre.
³Sing to him a new song;
play skillfully, and shout for
joy.

⁴For the word of the LORD is
right and true;
he is faithful in all he does.
⁵The LORD loves righteousness
and justice;
the earth is full of his
unfailing love.

⁶By the word of the LORD were
the heavens made,
their starry host by the
breath of his mouth.
⁷He gathers the waters of the
sea into jars*ᵃ*;
he puts the deep into
storehouses.
⁸Let all the earth fear the LORD;
let all the people of the
world revere him.
⁹For he spoke, and it came to
be;
he commanded, and it stood
firm.
¹⁰The LORD foils the plans of
the nations;
he thwarts the purposes of
the peoples.
¹¹But the plans of the LORD
stand firm forever,
the purposes of his heart
through all generations.

¹²Blessed is the nation whose
God is the LORD,
the people he chose for his
inheritance.
¹³From heaven the LORD looks
down
and sees all mankind;
¹⁴from his dwelling place he
watches
all who live on earth—
¹⁵he who forms the hearts of
all,

who considers everything
they do.
¹⁶No king is saved by the size
of his army;
no warrior escapes by his
great strength.
¹⁷A horse is a vain hope for
deliverance;
despite all its great strength
it cannot save.
¹⁸But the eyes of the LORD are
on those who fear him,
on those whose hope is in
his unfailing love,
¹⁹to deliver them from death
and keep them alive in
famine.

²⁰We wait in hope for the LORD;   43
he is our help and our   Ps 71:5
shield.
²¹In him our hearts rejoice,
for we trust in his holy
name.
²²May your unfailing love rest
upon us, O LORD,
even as we put our hope in
you.

Psalm 34*ᵇ*

Of David. When he pretended to be
insane before Abimelech, who drove
him away, and he left.

¹I will extol the LORD at all   68
times;   Ps 111
his praise will always be on
my lips.
²My soul will boast in the
LORD;
let the afflicted hear and
rejoice.
³Glorify the LORD with me;
let us exalt his name
together.
⁴I sought the LORD, and he
answered me;

---

*ᵃ7 Or *sea as into a heap*   *ᵇThis psalm is an acrostic poem, the verses of which begin
with the successive letters of the Hebrew alphabet.

he delivered me from all my
fears.
⁵Those who look to him are
radiant;
their faces are never covered
with shame.

66
Ps 37:7

⁶This poor man called, and the
LORD heard him;
he saved him out of all his
troubles.

26
Ps 34:17

⁷The angel of the LORD
encamps around those
who fear him,
and he delivers them.

49

⁸Taste and see that the LORD is
good;
blessed is the man who
takes refuge in him.
⁹Fear the LORD, you his saints,
for those who fear him lack
nothing.
¹⁰The lions may grow weak and
hungry,
but those who seek the
LORD lack no good thing.
¹¹Come, my children, listen to
me;
I will teach you the fear of
the LORD.
¹²Whoever of you loves life
and desires to see many
good days,
¹³keep your tongue from evil
and your lips from speaking
lies.
¹⁴Turn from evil and do good;
seek peace and pursue it.
¹⁵The eyes of the LORD are on
the righteous
and his ears are attentive to
their cry;
¹⁶the face of the LORD is against
those who do evil,
to cut off the memory of
them from the earth.

26
Ps 34:19

¹⁷The righteous cry out, and the
LORD hears them;
he delivers them from all
their troubles.

¹⁸The LORD is close to the
brokenhearted
and saves those who are
crushed in spirit.

26
Ps 56:11

¹⁹A righteous man may have
many troubles,
but the LORD delivers him
from them all;
²⁰he protects all his bones,
not one of them will be
broken.
²¹Evil will slay the wicked;
the foes of the righteous
will be condemned.
²²The LORD redeems his
servants;
no one will be condemned
who takes refuge in him.

Psalm 35

Of David.

¹Contend, O LORD, with those
who contend with me;
fight against those who fight
against me.
²Take up shield and buckler;
arise and come to my aid.
³Brandish spear and javelin*ᵃ*
against those who pursue
me.
Say to my soul,
"I am your salvation."

⁴May those who seek my life
be disgraced and put to
shame;
may those who plot my ruin
be turned back in dismay.
⁵May they be like chaff before
the wind,
with the angel of the LORD
driving them away;
⁶may their path be dark and
slippery,
with the angel of the LORD
pursuing them.
⁷Since they hid their net for me
without cause

ᵃ3 Or and block the way

and without cause dug a pit
for me,
[8]may ruin overtake them by
surprise—
may the net they hid
entangle them,
may they fall into the pit, to
their ruin.
[9]Then my soul will rejoice in
the Lord
and delight in his salvation.
[10]My whole being will exclaim,
"Who is like you, O Lord?
You rescue the poor from
those too strong for
them,
the poor and needy from
those who rob them."

[11]Ruthless witnesses come
forward;
they question me on things
I know nothing about.
[12]They repay me evil for good
and leave my soul forlorn.
[13]Yet when they were ill, I put
on sackcloth
and humbled myself with
fasting.
When my prayers returned to
me unanswered,
[14]   I went about mourning
as though for my friend or
brother.
I bowed my head in grief
as though weeping for my
mother.
[15]But when I stumbled, they
gathered in glee;
attackers gathered against
me when I was unaware.
They slandered me without
ceasing.
[16]Like the ungodly they
maliciously mocked[a];
they gnashed their teeth at
me.
[17]O Lord, how long will you
look on?
Rescue my life from their
ravages,

my precious life from these
lions.
[18]I will give you thanks in the
great assembly;
among throngs of people I
will praise you.

[19]Let not those gloat over me
who are my enemies
without cause;
let not those who hate me
without reason
maliciously wink the eye.
[20]They do not speak peaceably,
but devise false accusations
against those who live
quietly in the land.
[21]They gape at me and say,
"Aha! Aha!
With our own eyes we have
seen it."

[22]O Lord, you have seen this;
be not silent.
Do not be far from me,
O Lord.
[23]Awake, and rise to my
defense!
Contend for me, my God
and Lord.
[24]Vindicate me in your
righteousness, O Lord
my God;
do not let them gloat over
me.
[25]Do not let them think, "Aha,
just what we wanted!"
or say, "We have swallowed
him up."

[26]May all who gloat over my
distress
be put to shame and
confusion;
may all who exalt themselves
over me
be clothed with shame and
disgrace.
[27]May those who delight in my
vindication
shout for joy and gladness;

---

[a]16 Septuagint; Hebrew may mean *ungodly circle of mockers.*

may they always say, "The
LORD be exalted,
who delights in the
well-being of his
servant."
²⁸My tongue will speak of your
righteousness
and of your praises all day
long.

Psalm 36

For the director of music. Of David
the servant of the LORD.

¹An oracle is within my heart
concerning the sinfulness of
the wicked:ᵃ
There is no fear of God
before his eyes.
²For in his own eyes he flatters
himself
too much to detect or hate
his sin.
³The words of his mouth are
wicked and deceitful;
he has ceased to be wise
and to do good.
⁴Even on his bed he plots evil;
he commits himself to a
sinful course
and does not reject what is
wrong.

⁵Your love, O LORD, reaches to
the heavens,
your faithfulness to the
skies.
⁶Your righteousness is like the
mighty mountains,
your justice like the great
deep.
O LORD, you preserve both
man and beast.
⁷   How priceless is your
unfailing love!
Both high and low among
men
findᵇ refuge in the shadow
of your wings.

⁸They feast on the abundance
of your house;
you give them drink from
your river of delights.
⁹For with you is the fountain
of life;
in your light we see light.

¹⁰Continue your love to those
who know you,
your righteousness to the
upright in heart.
¹¹May the foot of the proud not
come against me,
nor the hand of the wicked
drive me away.
¹²See how the evildoers lie
fallen—
thrown down, not able to
rise!

Psalm 37ᶜ

Of David.

¹Do not fret because of evil
men
or be envious of those who
do wrong;
²for like the grass they will
soon wither,
like green plants they will
soon die away.

³Trust in the LORD and do
good;
dwell in the land and enjoy
safe pasture.
⁴Delight yourself in the LORD
and he will give you the
desires of your heart.

⁵Commit your way to the   24
LORD;
trust in him and he will do
this:
⁶He will make your
righteousness
shine like the dawn,

ᵃ1 Or heart: / Sin proceeds from the wicked.   ᵇ7 Or love, O God! / Men find; or love! /
Both heavenly beings and men / find   ᶜThis psalm is an acrostic poem, the stanzas of
which begin with the successive letters of the Hebrew alphabet.

the justice of your cause like
the noonday sun.

66   7Be still before the LORD and
Ps 119:96   wait patiently for him;
do not fret when men
succeed in their ways,
when they carry out their
wicked schemes.

8Refrain from anger and turn
from wrath;
do not fret—it leads only to
evil.
9For evil men will be cut off,
but those who hope in the
LORD will inherit the
land.

10A little while, and the wicked
will be no more;
though you look for them,
they will not be found.
11But the meek will inherit the
land
and enjoy great peace.

12The wicked plot against the
righteous
and gnash their teeth at
them;
13but the Lord laughs at the
wicked,
for he knows their day is
coming.

14The wicked draw the sword
and bend the bow
to bring down the poor and
needy,
to slay those whose ways
are upright.
15But their swords will pierce
their own hearts,
and their bows will be
broken.

16Better the little that the
righteous have
than the wealth of many
wicked;
17for the power of the wicked
will be broken,
but the LORD upholds the
righteous.

18The days of the blameless are
known to the LORD,
and their inheritance will
endure forever.
19In times of disaster they will
not wither;
in days of famine they will
enjoy plenty.

20But the wicked will perish:
The LORD's enemies will be
like the beauty of the
fields,
they will vanish—vanish
like smoke.

21The wicked borrow and do
not repay,
but the righteous give
generously;
22those the LORD blesses will
inherit the land,
but those he curses will be
cut off.

23If the LORD delights in a
man's way,
he makes his steps firm;
24though he stumble, he will
not fall,
for the LORD upholds him
with his hand.

25I was young and now I am   73
old,
yet I have never seen the
righteous forsaken
or their children begging
bread.
26They are always generous and
lend freely;
their children will be
blessed.

27Turn from evil and do good;   48
then you will dwell in the   Ps 119:121
land forever.
28For the LORD loves the just
and will not forsake his
faithful ones.

They will be protected
forever,
but the offspring of the
wicked will be cut off;

29the righteous will inherit the
    land
    and dwell in it forever.
30The mouth of the righteous
    man utters wisdom,
    and his tongue speaks what
    is just.
31The law of his God is in his
    heart;
    his feet do not slip.
32The wicked lie in wait for the
    righteous,
    seeking their very lives;
33but the LORD will not leave
    them in their power
    or let them be condemned
    when brought to trial.

34Wait for the LORD
    and keep his way.
    He will exalt you to inherit
    the land;
    when the wicked are cut
    off, you will see it.

35I have seen a wicked and
    ruthless man
    flourishing like a green tree
    in its native soil,
36but he soon passed away and
    was no more;
    though I looked for him, he
    could not be found.

37Consider the blameless,
    observe the upright;
    there is a future^a for the
    man of peace.
38But all sinners will be
    destroyed;
    the future^b of the wicked
    will be cut off.

39The salvation of the righteous
    comes from the LORD;
    he is their stronghold in
    time of trouble.
40The LORD helps them and
    delivers them;
    he delivers them from the
    wicked and saves them,

because they take refuge in
    him.

Psalm 38

A psalm of David. A petition.

1O LORD, do not rebuke me in
    your anger
    or discipline me in your
    wrath.
2For your arrows have pierced
    me,
    and your hand has come
    down upon me.
3Because of your wrath there is
    no health in my body;
    my bones have no
    soundness because of
    my sin.
4My guilt has overwhelmed me   36
    like a burden too heavy to   Ps 69:5
    bear.
5My wounds fester and are
    loathsome
    because of my sinful folly.
6I am bowed down and
    brought very low;
    all day long I go about
    mourning.
7My back is filled with searing
    pain;
    there is no health in my
    body.
8I am feeble and utterly
    crushed;
    I groan in anguish of heart.

9All my longings lie open
    before you, O Lord;
    my sighing is not hidden
    from you.
10My heart pounds, my
    strength fails me;
    even the light has gone
    from my eyes.
11My friends and companions
    avoid me because of my
    wounds;
    my neighbors stay far away.

^a37 Or there will be posterity   ^b38 Or posterity

¹²Those who seek my life set
    their traps,
  those who would harm me
    talk of my ruin;
  all day long they plot
    deception.

¹³I am like a deaf man, who
    cannot hear,
  like a mute, who cannot
    open his mouth;
¹⁴I have become like a man who
    does not hear,
  whose mouth can offer no
    reply.

¹⁵I wait for you, O LORD;
  you will answer, O Lord my
    God.
¹⁶For I said, "Do not let them
    gloat
  or exalt themselves over me
    when my foot slips."

¹⁷For I am about to fall,
  and my pain is ever with
    me.
¹⁸I confess my iniquity;
  I am troubled by my sin.
¹⁹Many are those who are my
    vigorous enemies;
  those who hate me without
    reason are numerous.
²⁰Those who repay my good
    with evil
  slander me when I pursue
    what is good.

²¹O LORD, do not forsake me;
  be not far from me, O my
    God.
²²Come quickly to help me,
  O Lord my Savior.

Psalm 39

For the director of music. For
Jeduthun. A psalm of David.

¹I said, "I will watch my ways
    and keep my tongue from
    sin;
  I will put a muzzle on my
    mouth

as long as the wicked are in
    my presence."
²But when I was silent and
    still,
  not even saying anything
    good,
  my anguish increased.
³My heart grew hot within me,
  and as I meditated, the fire
    burned;
  then I spoke with my
    tongue:

⁴"Show me, O LORD, my life's   51
    end
  and the number of my days;
  let me know how fleeting is
    my life.
⁵You have made my days a
    mere handbreadth;
  the span of my years is as
    nothing before you.
  Each man's life is but a
    breath.   *Selah*
⁶Man is a mere phantom as he
    goes to and fro:
  He bustles about, but only
    in vain;
  he heaps up wealth, not
    knowing who will get it.

⁷"But now, Lord, what do I
    look for?
  My hope is in you.
⁸Save me from all my
    transgressions;
  do not make me the scorn
    of fools.
⁹I was silent; I would not open
    my mouth,
  for you are the one who has
    done this.
¹⁰Remove your scourge from
    me;
  I am overcome by the blow
    of your hand.
¹¹You rebuke and discipline
    men for their sin;
  you consume their wealth
    like a moth—
  each man is but a breath.
                        Selah

12"Hear my prayer, O LORD,
  listen to my cry for help;
  be not deaf to my weeping.
For I dwell with you as an
    alien,
  a stranger, as all my fathers
    were.
13Look away from me, that I
    may rejoice again
  before I depart and am no
    more."

Psalm 40

For the director of music. Of David.
A psalm.

1I waited patiently for the
    LORD;
  he turned to me and heard
    my cry.
2He lifted me out of the slimy
    pit,
  out of the mud and mire;
  he set my feet on a rock
  and gave me a firm place to
    stand.
3He put a new song in my
    mouth,
  a hymn of praise to our
    God.
Many will see and fear
  and put their trust in the
    LORD.

4Blessed is the man
  who makes the LORD his
    trust,
who does not look to the
    proud,
  to those who turn aside to
    false gods.a
5Many, O LORD my God,
  are the wonders you have
    done.
The things you planned for us
  no one can recount to you;

were I to speak and tell of
    them,
  they would be too many to
    declare.
6Sacrifice and offering you did
    not desire,
  but my ears you have
    piercedb,c;
burnt offerings and sin
    offerings
  you did not require.
7Then I said, "Here I am, I
    have come—
  it is written about me in the
    scroll.d
8I desire to do your will, O my
    God;
  your law is within my
    heart."

9I proclaim righteousness in
    the great assembly;
  I do not seal my lips,
  as you know, O LORD.
10I do not hide your
    righteousness in my
    heart;
  I speak of your faithfulness
    and salvation.
I do not conceal your love and
    your truth
  from the great assembly.

11Do not withhold your mercy
    from me, O LORD;
  may your love and your
    truth always protect me.
12For troubles without number
    surround me;
  my sins have overtaken me,
    and I cannot see.
They are more than the hairs
    of my head,
  and my heart fails within
    me.
13Be pleased, O LORD, to save
    me;

---

a4 Or to falsehood b6 Hebrew; Septuagint but a body you have prepared for me (see also
Symmachus and Theodotion) c6 Or opened d7 Or come / with the scroll written for
me

O Lord, come quickly to
help me.
[14]May all who seek to take my
life
be put to shame and
confusion;
may all who desire my ruin
be turned back in disgrace.
[15]May those who say to me,
"Aha! Aha!"
be appalled at their own
shame.
[16]But may all who seek you
rejoice and be glad in you;
may those who love your
salvation always say,
"The Lord be exalted!"

[17]Yet I am poor and needy;
may the Lord think of me.
You are my help and my
deliverer;
O my God, do not delay.

Psalm 41

For the director of music.
A psalm of David.

[1]Blessed is he who has regard
for the weak;
the Lord delivers him in
times of trouble.
[2]The Lord will protect him and
preserve his life;
he will bless him in the land
and not surrender him to
the desire of his foes.
[3]The Lord will sustain him on
his sickbed
and restore him from his
bed of illness.

[4]I said, "O Lord, have mercy
on me;
heal me, for I have sinned
against you."
[5]My enemies say of me in
malice,
"When will he die and his
name perish?"

[6]Whenever one comes to see
me,
he speaks falsely, while his
heart gathers slander;
then he goes out and
spreads it abroad.

[7]All my enemies whisper
together against me;
they imagine the worst for
me, saying,
[8]"A vile disease has beset him;
he will never get up from
the place where he lies."
[9]Even my close friend, whom I
trusted,
he who shared my bread,
has lifted up his heel
against me.

[10]But you, O Lord, have mercy
on me;
raise me up, that I may
repay them.
[11]I know that you are pleased
with me,
for my enemy does not
triumph over me.
[12]In my integrity you uphold
me
and set me in your presence
forever.

[13]Praise be to the Lord, the
God of Israel,
from everlasting to
everlasting.
Amen and Amen.

BOOK II

Psalms 42-72

Psalm 42[a]

For the director of music. A *maskil*[b]
of the Sons of Korah.

[1]As the deer pants for streams
of water,

---

[a]In many Hebrew manuscripts Psalms 42 and 43 constitute one psalm.   [b]Title:
Probably a literary or musical term

so my soul pants for you,
O God.
2My soul thirsts for God, for
the living God.
When can I go and meet
with God?
3My tears have been my food
day and night,
while men say to me all day
long,
"Where is your God?"
4These things I remember
as I pour out my soul:
how I used to go with the
multitude,
leading the procession to
the house of God,
with shouts of joy and
thanksgiving
among the festive throng.

16
Ps 56:4
5Why are you downcast, O my
soul?
Why so disturbed within
me?
Put your hope in God,
for I will yet praise him,
my Savior and 6my God.

My*a* soul is downcast within
me;
therefore I will remember
you
from the land of the Jordan,
the heights of
Hermon—from
Mount Mizar.
7Deep calls to deep
in the roar of your
waterfalls;
all your waves and breakers
have swept over me.

8By day the LORD directs his
love,
at night his song is with
me—
a prayer to the God of my
life.

9I say to God my Rock,

"Why have you forgotten
me?
Why must I go about
mourning,
oppressed by the enemy?"
10My bones suffer mortal agony
as my foes taunt me,
saying to me all day long,
"Where is your God?"

11Why are you downcast, O my
soul?
Why so disturbed within
me?
Put your hope in God,
for I will yet praise him,
my Savior and my God.

Psalm 43*b*

1Vindicate me, O God,
and plead my cause against
an ungodly nation;
rescue me from deceitful
and wicked men.
2You are God my stronghold.
Why have you rejected me?
Why must I go about
mourning,
oppressed by the enemy?
3Send forth your light and
your truth,
let them guide me;
let them bring me to your
holy mountain,
to the place where you
dwell.
4Then will I go to the altar of
God,
to God, my joy and my
delight.
I will praise you with the
harp,
O God, my God.

4
53
5Why are you downcast, O my
soul?
Why so disturbed within
me?
Put your hope in God,

*a5,6 A few Hebrew manuscripts, Septuagint and Syriac; most Hebrew manuscripts
praise him for his saving help. / 6O my God, my   b In many Hebrew manuscripts
Psalms 42 and 43 constitute one psalm.*

for I will yet praise him,
my Savior and my God.

Psalm 44

For the director of music. Of the
Sons of Korah. A maskil.[a]

¹We have heard with our ears,
    O God;
  our fathers have told us
what you did in their days,
    in days long ago.
²With your hand you drove
    out the nations
    and planted our fathers;
you crushed the peoples
    and made our fathers
    flourish.
³It was not by their sword that
    they won the land,
    nor did their arm bring
    them victory;
  it was your right hand, your
    arm,
    and the light of your face,
    for you loved them.

⁴You are my King and my
    God,
  who decrees[b] victories for
    Jacob.
⁵Through you we push back
    our enemies;
  through your name we
    trample our foes.
⁶I do not trust in my bow,
  my sword does not bring
    me victory;
⁷but you give us victory over
    our enemies,
  you put our adversaries to
    shame.
⁸In God we make our boast all
    day long,
  and we will praise your
    name forever.   Selah
⁹But now you have rejected
    and humbled us;
  you no longer go out with
    our armies.

¹⁰You made us retreat before
    the enemy,
  and our adversaries have
    plundered us.
¹¹You gave us up to be
    devoured like
    sheep
  and have scattered us
    among the nations.
¹²You sold your people for a
    pittance,
  gaining nothing from their
    sale.

¹³You have made us a reproach
    to our neighbors,
  the scorn and derision of
    those around us.
¹⁴You have made us a byword
    among the nations;
  the peoples shake their
    heads at us.
¹⁵My disgrace is before me all   86
    day long,
  and my face is covered with
    shame
¹⁶at the taunts of those who
    reproach and revile me,
  because of the enemy, who
    is bent on revenge.

¹⁷All this happened to us,
    though we had not
    forgotten you
  or been false to your
    covenant.
¹⁸Our hearts had not turned
    back;
  our feet had not strayed
    from your path.
¹⁹But you crushed us and made
    us a haunt for jackals
  and covered us over with
    deep darkness.

²⁰If we had forgotten the name
    of our God
  or spread out our hands to
    a foreign god,
²¹would not God have
    discovered it,

ᵃTitle: Probably a literary or musical term
Hebrew King, O God; ᶫ command   ᵇ4 Septuagint, Aquila and Syriac;

since he knows the secrets
of the heart?
²²Yet for your sake we face
death all day long;
we are considered as sheep
to be slaughtered.

²³Awake, O Lord! Why do you
sleep?
Rouse yourself! Do not
reject us forever.
²⁴Why do you hide your face
and forget our misery and
oppression?

²⁵We are brought down to the
dust;
our bodies cling to the
ground.
²⁶Rise up and help us;
redeem us because of your
unfailing love.

Psalm 45

For the director of music. To the
tune of, "Lilies." Of the Sons of
Korah. A *maskil.ᵃ* A wedding song.

¹My heart is stirred by a noble
theme
as I recite my verses for the
king;
my tongue is the pen of a
skillful writer.

²You are the most excellent of
men
and your lips have been
anointed with grace,
since God has blessed you
forever.
³Gird your sword upon your
side, O mighty one;
clothe yourself with
splendor and majesty.
⁴In your majesty ride forth
victoriously
in behalf of truth, humility
and righteousness;
let your right hand display
awesome deeds.

⁵Let your sharp arrows pierce
the hearts of the king's
enemies;
let the nations fall beneath
your feet.
⁶Your throne, O God, will last
for ever and ever;
a scepter of justice will be
the scepter of your
kingdom.
⁷You love righteousness and
hate wickedness;
therefore God, your God,
has set you above your
companions
by anointing you with the
oil of joy.
⁸All your robes are fragrant
with myrrh and aloes
and cassia;
from palaces adorned with
ivory
the music of the strings
makes you glad.
⁹Daughters of kings are among
your honored women;
at your right hand is the
royal bride in gold of
Ophir.

¹⁰Listen, O daughter, consider
and give ear:
Forget your people and your
father's house.
¹¹The king is enthralled by your
beauty;
honor him, for he is your
lord.
¹²The Daughter of Tyre will
come with a gift,ᵇ
men of wealth will seek
your favor.

¹³All glorious is the princess
within her chamber;
her gown is interwoven
with gold.
¹⁴In embroidered garments she
is led to the king;
her virgin companions
follow her

ᵃTitle: Probably a literary or musical term   ᵇ12 Or *A Tyrian robe is among the gifts*

and are brought to you.
¹⁵They are led in with joy and
          gladness;
     they enter the palace of the
          king.

¹⁶Your sons will take the place
          of your fathers;
     you will make them princes
          throughout the land.
¹⁷I will perpetuate your memory
          through all generations;
     therefore the nations will
          praise you for ever and
          ever.

Psalm 46

For the director of music. Of the
Sons of Korah. According to
alamoth.ᵃ A song.

¹God is our refuge and
          strength,
     an ever-present help in
          trouble.
²Therefore we will not fear,
          though the earth give
          way
     and the mountains fall into
          the heart of the sea,
³though its waters roar and
          foam
     and the mountains quake
          with their surging.   *Selah*

⁴There is a river whose streams
          make glad the city of
          God,
     the holy place where the
          Most High dwells.
⁵God is within her, she will
          not fall;
     God will help her at break
          of day.
⁶Nations are in uproar,
          kingdoms fall;
     he lifts his voice, the earth
          melts.

⁷The LORD Almighty is with
          us;

the God of Jacob is our
          fortress.   *Selah*

⁸Come and see the works of
          the LORD,
     the desolations he has
          brought on the earth.
⁹He makes wars cease to the
          ends of the earth;
     he breaks the bow and
          shatters the spear,
     he burns the shieldsᵇ with
          fire.
¹⁰"Be still, and know that I am
          God;
     I will be exalted among the
          nations,
     I will be exalted in the
          earth."
¹¹The LORD Almighty is with
          us;
     the God of Jacob is our
          fortress.   *Selah*

Psalm 47

For the director of music. Of the
Sons of Korah. A psalm.

¹Clap your hands, all you
          nations;
     shout to God with cries of
          joy.
²How awesome is the LORD
          Most High,
     the great King over all the
          earth!
³He subdued nations under us,
     peoples under our feet.
⁴He chose our inheritance for
          us,
     the pride of Jacob, whom he
          loved.   *Selah*

⁵God has ascended amid
          shouts of joy,
     the LORD amid the sounding
          of trumpets.
⁶Sing praises to God, sing
          praises;
     sing praises to our King,
          sing praises.

ᵃTitle: Probably a musical term   ᵇ9 Or *chariots*

⁷For God is the King of all the
earth;
sing to him a psalm[a] of
praise.
⁸God reigns over the nations;
God is seated on his holy
throne.
⁹The nobles of the nations
assemble
as the people of the God of
Abraham,
for the kings[b] of the earth
belong to God;
he is greatly exalted.

Psalm 48

*A song. A psalm of the Sons of
Korah.*

¹Great is the LORD, and most
worthy of praise,
in the city of our God, his
holy mountain.
²It is beautiful in its loftiness,
the joy of the whole earth.
Like the utmost heights of
Zaphon[c] is Mount Zion,
the[d] city of the Great King.
³God is in her citadels;
he has shown himself to be
her fortress.

⁴When the kings joined forces,
when they advanced
together,
⁵they saw her, and were
astounded;
they fled in terror.
⁶Trembling seized them there,
pain like that of a woman in
labor.
⁷You destroyed them like ships
of Tarshish
shattered by an east wind.

⁸As we have heard,
so have we seen
in the city of the LORD
Almighty,
in the city of our God:

God makes her secure
forever.   *Selah*
⁹Within your temple, O God,
we meditate on your
unfailing love.
¹⁰Like your name, O God,
your praise reaches to the
ends of the earth;
your right hand is filled
with righteousness.
¹¹Mount Zion rejoices,
the villages of Judah are
glad
because of your judgments.

¹²Walk about Zion, go around
her,
count her towers,
¹³consider well her ramparts,
view her citadels,
that you may tell of them to
the next generation.
¹⁴For this God is our God for
ever and ever;
he will be our guide even to
the end.

Psalm 49

*For the director of music. Of the
Sons of Korah. A psalm.*

¹Hear this, all you peoples;
listen, all who live in this
world,
²both low and high,
rich and poor alike:
³My mouth will speak words
of wisdom;
the utterance from my heart
will give understanding.
⁴I will turn my ear to a
proverb;
with the harp I will
expound my riddle:

⁵Why should I fear when evil
days come,
when wicked deceivers
surround me—

---

[a]7 Or *a maskil* (probably a literary or musical term) [b]9 Or *shields* [c]2 *Zaphon* can
refer to a sacred mountain or the direction north. [d]2 Or *earth, | Mount Zion, on the
northern side | of the*

⁶those who trust in their
    wealth
  and boast of their great
    riches?
⁷No man can redeem the life of
    another
  or give to God a ransom for
    him—
⁸the ransom for a life is costly,
  no payment is ever
    enough—
⁹that he should live on forever
  and not see decay.

¹⁰For all can see that wise men
    die;
  the foolish and the senseless
    alike perish
  and leave their wealth to
    others.
¹¹Their tombs will remain their
    houses*ᵃ* forever,
  their dwellings for endless
    generations,
  though they had*ᵇ* named
    lands after themselves.

¹²But man, despite his riches,
    does not endure;
  he is*ᶜ* like the beasts that
    perish.

¹³This is the fate of those who
    trust in themselves,
  and of their followers, who
    approve their sayings.
                        Selah
¹⁴Like sheep they are destined
    for the grave,*ᵈ*
  and death will feed on
    them.
  The upright will rule over
    them in the morning;
  their forms will decay in the
    grave,*ᵈ*
  far from their princely
    mansions.
72 ¹⁵But God will redeem my life*ᵉ*
    from the grave;

he will surely take me to
    himself.   *Selah*

¹⁶Do not be overawed when a
    man grows rich,
  when the splendor of his
    house increases;
¹⁷for he will take nothing with
    him when he dies,
  his splendor will not
    descend with him.
¹⁸Though while he lived he
    counted himself
    blessed—
  and men praise you when
    you prosper—
¹⁹he will join the generation of
    his fathers,
  who will never see the light
    of life.

²⁰A man who has riches
    without understanding
  is like the beasts that perish.

Psalm 50

A psalm of Asaph.

¹The Mighty One, God, the
    Lord,
  speaks and summons the
    earth
  from the rising of the sun to
    the place where it sets.
²From Zion, perfect in beauty,
  God shines forth.
³Our God comes and will not
    be silent;
  a fire devours before him,
  and around him a tempest
    rages.
⁴He summons the heavens
    above,
  and the earth, that he may
    judge his people:
⁵"Gather to me my consecrated
    ones,

---

*ᵃ11 Septuagint and Syriac; Hebrew In their thoughts their houses will remain   *ᵇ11 Or
/ for they have   *ᶜ12 Hebrew; Septuagint and Syriac read verse 12 the same as
verse 20.   *ᵈ14 Hebrew Sheol; also in verse 15   *ᵉ15 Or soul

who made a covenant with
  me by sacrifice."
[6]And the heavens proclaim his
    righteousness,
  for God himself is judge.

Selah

[7]"Hear, O my people, and I
    will speak,
  O Israel, and I will testify
    against you:
  I am God, your God.
[8]I do not rebuke you for your
    sacrifices
  or your burnt offerings,
    which are ever before
    me.
[9]I have no need of a bull from
    your stall
  or of goats from your pens,
[10]for every animal of the forest
    is mine,
  and the cattle on a thousand
    hills.
[11]I know every bird in the
    mountains,
  and the creatures of the
    field are mine.
[12]If I were hungry I would not
    tell you,
  for the world is mine, and
    all that is in it.
[13]Do I eat the flesh of bulls
  or drink the blood of goats?
[14]Sacrifice thank offerings to
    God,
  fulfill your vows to the Most
    High,
[15]and call upon me in the day
    of trouble;
  I will deliver you, and you
    will honor me."

[16]But to the wicked, God says:

  "What right have you to recite
    my laws
  or take my covenant on
    your lips?
[17]You hate my instruction
  and cast my words behind
    you.

[18]When you see a thief, you
    join with him;
  you throw in your lot with
    adulterers.
[19]You use your mouth for evil
  and harness your tongue to
    deceit.
[20]You speak continually against
    your brother
  and slander your own
    mother's son.
[21]These things you have done
    and I kept silent;
  you thought I was
    altogether[a] like you.
  But I will rebuke you
  and accuse you to your face.

[22]"Consider this, you who
    forget God,
  or I will tear you to pieces,
    with none to rescue:
[23]He who sacrifices thank
    offerings honors me,
  and he prepares the way
  so that I may show him[b] the
    salvation of God."

Psalm 51

For the director of music. A psalm of
David. When the prophet Nathan
came to him after David had
committed adultery with Bathsheba.

[1]Have mercy on me, O God,   2
    according to your unfailing
    love;
  according to your great
    compassion
  blot out my transgressions.
[2]Wash away all my iniquity
  and cleanse me from my
    sin.

[3]For I know my transgressions,
  and my sin is always before
    me.
[4]Against you, you only, have I
    sinned
  and done what is evil in
    your sight,

[a]21 Or *thought the 'I AM' was*   [b]23 Or *and to him who considers his way / I will show*

so that you are proved right
        when you speak
    and justified when you
        judge.
⁵Surely I was sinful at birth,
    sinful from the time my
        mother conceived me.
⁶Surely you desire truth in the
        inner parts*ᵃ*;
    you teach*ᵇ* me wisdom in
        the inmost place.

⁷Cleanse me with hyssop, and
        I will be clean;
    wash me, and I will be
        whiter than snow.
⁸Let me hear joy and gladness;
    let the bones you have
        crushed rejoice.
⁹Hide your face from my sins
    and blot out all my iniquity.

⁵ ¹⁰Create in me a pure heart,
        O God,
    and renew a steadfast spirit
        within me.
¹¹Do not cast me from your
        presence
    or take your Holy Spirit
        from me.
¹²Restore to me the joy of your
        salvation
    and grant me a willing
        spirit, to sustain me.

¹³Then I will teach transgressors
        your ways,
    and sinners will turn back
        to you.
¹⁴Save me from bloodguilt,
        O God,
    the God who saves me,
    and my tongue will sing of
        your righteousness.
¹⁵O Lord, open my lips,
    and my mouth will declare
        your praise.
¹⁶You do not delight in
        sacrifice, or I would
        bring it;

you do not take pleasure in
        burnt offerings.
¹⁷The sacrifices of God are*ᶜ* a
        broken spirit;
    a broken and contrite heart,
        O God, you will not
        despise.

¹⁸In your good pleasure make
        Zion prosper;
    build up the walls of
        Jerusalem.
¹⁹Then there will be righteous
        sacrifices,
    whole burnt offerings to
        delight you;
    then bulls will be offered on
        your altar.

Psalm 52

For the director of music. A *maskil*ᵈ
of David. When Doeg the Edomite
had gone to Saul and told him:
"David has gone to the house of
Ahimelech."

¹Why do you boast of evil, you
        mighty man?
    Why do you boast all day
        long,
    you who are a disgrace in
        the eyes of God?
²Your tongue plots destruction;
    it is like a sharpened razor,
    you who practice deceit.
³You love evil rather than
        good,
    falsehood rather than
        speaking the truth. *Selah*
⁴You love every harmful word,
    O you deceitful tongue!

⁵Surely God will bring you
        down to everlasting ruin:
    He will snatch you up and
        tear you from your tent;
    he will uproot you from the
        land of the living. *Selah*
⁶The righteous will see and
        fear;

ᵃ6 The meaning of the Hebrew for this phrase is uncertain.   *ᵇ6* Or *you desired . . . ; /
you taught*   *ᶜ17* Or *My sacrifice, O God, is*   ᵈTitle: Probably a literary or musical
term

they will laugh at him,
saying,
7"Here now is the man
who did not make God his
stronghold
but trusted in his great wealth
and grew strong by
destroying others!"

8But I am like an olive tree
flourishing in the house of
God;
I trust in God's unfailing love
for ever and ever.
9I will praise you forever for
what you have done;
in your name I will hope,
for your name is good.
I will praise you in the
presence of your saints.

Psalm 53

*For the director of music. According
to* mahalath.*ᵃ A* maskil*ᵇ of David.*

1The fool says in his heart,
"There is no God."
They are corrupt, and their
ways are vile;
there is no one who does
good.

2God looks down from heaven
on the sons of men
to see if there are any who
understand,
any who seek God.

3Everyone has turned away,
they have together become
corrupt;
there is no one who does
good,
not even one.

4Will the evildoers never
learn—
those who devour my
people as men eat bread
and who do not call on
God?

5There they were,
overwhelmed with
dread,
where there was nothing to
dread.
God scattered the bones of
those who attacked you;
you put them to shame, for
God despised them.

6Oh, that salvation for Israel
would come out of Zion!
When God restores the
fortunes of his people,
let Jacob rejoice and Israel
be glad!

Psalm 54

*For the director of music. With
stringed instruments. A* maskil*ᵇ of
David. When the Ziphites had gone
to Saul and said, "Is not David
hiding among us?"*

1Save me, O God, by your
name;
vindicate me by your might.
2Hear my prayer, O God;
listen to the words of my
mouth.

3Strangers are attacking me;
ruthless men seek my life—
men without regard for
God.   *Selah*

4Surely God is my help;
the Lord is the one who
sustains me.

5Let evil recoil on those who
slander me;
in your faithfulness destroy
them.

6I will sacrifice a freewill
offering to you;
I will praise your name,
O LORD,
for it is good.
7For he has delivered me from
all my troubles,

ᵃTitle: Probably a musical term   ᵇTitle: Probably a literary or musical term

and my eyes have looked in
    triumph on my foes.

Psalm 55

For the director of music. With
stringed instruments. A *maskil*[a] of
David.

[1]Listen to my prayer, O God,
    do not ignore my plea;
2   hear me and answer me.
My thoughts trouble me and I
    am distraught
3   at the voice of the enemy,
    at the stares of the wicked;
for they bring down suffering
    upon me
    and revile me in their anger.

[4]My heart is in anguish within
    me;
    the terrors of death assail
    me.
[5]Fear and trembling have beset
    me;
    horror has overwhelmed
    me.
[6]I said, "Oh, that I had the
    wings of a dove!
    I would fly away and be at
    rest—
[7]I would flee far away
    and stay in the desert; *Selah*
[8]I would hurry to my place of
    shelter,
    far from the tempest and
    storm."

[9]Confuse the wicked, O Lord,
    confound their speech,
    for I see violence and strife
    in the city.
[10]Day and night they prowl
    about on its walls;
    malice and abuse are
    within it.
[11]Destructive forces are at work
    in the city;
    threats and lies never leave
    its streets.

[12]If an enemy were insulting
    me,
    I could endure it;
if a foe were raising himself
    against me,
    I could hide from him.
[13]But it is you, a man like
    myself,
    my companion, my close
    friend,
[14]with whom I once enjoyed
    sweet fellowship
    as we walked with the
    throng at the house of
    God.

[15]Let death take my enemies by
    surprise;
    let them go down alive to
    the grave,[b]
    for evil finds lodging among
    them.

[16]But I call to God,
    and the LORD saves me.
[17]Evening, morning and noon
    I cry out in distress,
    and he hears my voice.
[18]He ransoms me unharmed
    from the battle waged
    against me,
    even though many oppose
    me.
[19]God, who is enthroned
    forever,
    will hear them and afflict
    them—   *Selah*
men who never change their
    ways
    and have no fear of God.

[20]My companion attacks his
    friends;
    he violates his covenant.
[21]His speech is smooth as
    butter,
    yet war is in his heart;
his words are more soothing
    than oil,
    yet they are drawn swords.

---

[a]Title: Probably a literary or musical term   [b]15 Hebrew *Sheol*

²²Cast your cares on the LORD
and he will sustain you;
he will never let the
righteous fall.

²³But you, O God, will bring
down the wicked
into the pit of corruption;
bloodthirsty and deceitful men
will not live out half their
days.

But as for me, I trust in you.

Psalm 56

For the director of music. To the
tune of, "A Dove on Distant Oaks."
Of David. A miktam.ᵃ When the
Philistines had seized him in Gath.

¹Be merciful to me, O God, for
men hotly pursue me;
all day long they press their
attack.

²My slanderers pursue me all
day long;
many are attacking me in
their pride.

³When I am afraid,
I will trust in you.

16 ⁴In God, whose word I praise,
Ps 69:1,2   in God I trust; I will not be
afraid.
What can mortal man do to
me?

⁵All day long they twist my
words;
they are always plotting to
harm me.

⁶They conspire, they lurk,
they watch my steps,
eager to take my life.

⁷On no account let them
escape;
in your anger, O God, bring
down the nations.

⁸Record my lament;
list my tears on your
scrollᵇ—
are they not in your record?

⁹Then my enemies will turn
back
when I call for help.
By this I will know that God
is for me.

¹⁰In God, whose word I praise,
in the LORD, whose word I
praise—

11 ¹¹in God I trust; I will not be
Ps 91:5-8   afraid.
What can man do to me?

¹²I am under vows to you,
O God;
I will present my thank
offerings to you.

¹³For you have delivered meᶜ
from death
and my feet from stumbling,
that I may walk before God
in the light of life.ᵈ

Psalm 57

For the director of music. To the
tune of, "Do Not Destroy." Of
David. A miktam.ᵃ When he had fled
from Saul into the cave.

¹Have mercy on me, O God,
have mercy on me,
for in you my soul takes
refuge.
I will take refuge in the
shadow of your wings
until the disaster has
passed.

²I cry out to God Most High,
to God, who fulfills his
purpose for me.

³He sends from heaven and
saves me,
rebuking those who hotly
pursue me;   Selah
God sends his love and his
faithfulness.

⁴I am in the midst of lions;
I lie among ravenous
beasts—

ᵃTitle: Probably a literary or musical term   ᵇ8 Or / put my tears in your wineskin
ᶜ13 Or my soul   ᵈ13 Or the land of the living

men whose teeth are spears
    and arrows,
  whose tongues are sharp
    swords.

⁵Be exalted, O God, above the
    heavens;
  let your glory be over all the
    earth.

⁶They spread a net for my
    feet—
  I was bowed down in
    distress.
  They dug a pit in my path—
  but they have fallen into it
    themselves.   *Selah*

⁷My heart is steadfast, O God,
  my heart is steadfast;
  I will sing and make music.
⁸Awake, my soul!
  Awake, harp and lyre!
  I will awaken the dawn.

⁹I will praise you, O Lord,
    among the nations;
  I will sing of you among the
    peoples.
¹⁰For great is your love,
    reaching to the
    heavens;
  your faithfulness reaches to
    the skies.

¹¹Be exalted, O God, above the
    heavens;
  let your glory be over all the
    earth.

Psalm 58

For the director of music. To the
tune of "Do Not Destroy." Of
David. A *miktam.* ᵈ

¹Do you rulers indeed speak
    justly?
  Do you judge uprightly
    among men?

²No, in your heart you devise
    injustice,
  and your hands mete out
    violence on the earth.

³Even from birth the wicked go
    astray;
  from the womb they are
    wayward and speak
    lies.

⁴Their venom is like the venom
    of a snake,
  like that of a cobra that has
    stopped its ears,
⁵that will not heed the tune of
    the charmer,
  however skillful the
    enchanter may be.

⁶Break the teeth in their
    mouths, O God;
  tear out, O LORD, the fangs
    of the lions!
⁷Let them vanish like water
    that flows away;
  when they draw the bow,
  let their arrows be
    blunted.
⁸Like a slug melting away as it
    moves along,
  like a stillborn child, may
    they not see the sun.

⁹Before your pots can feel the
    heat of the thorns—
  whether they be green or
    dry—the wicked will be
    swept away.ᵇ

¹⁰The righteous will be glad
    when they are
    avenged,
  when they bathe their feet
    in the blood of the
    wicked.
¹¹Then men will say,
  "Surely the righteous still
    are rewarded;
  surely there is a God who
    judges the earth."

ᵈTitle: Probably a literary or musical term

ᵇ9 The meaning of the Hebrew for this
verse is uncertain.

Psalm 59

For the director of music. To the
tune of "Do Not Destroy." Of
David. A *miktam*.[a] When Saul had
sent men to watch David's house in
order to kill him.

¹Deliver me from my enemies,
    O God;
  protect me from those who
    rise up against me.
²Deliver me from evildoers
  and save me from
    bloodthirsty men.

³See how they lie in wait for
    me!
  Fierce men conspire against
    me
  for no offense or sin of
    mine, O LORD.
⁴I have done no wrong, yet
    they are ready to attack
    me.
  Arise to help me; look on
    my plight!
⁵O LORD God Almighty, the
    God of Israel,
  rouse yourself to punish all
    the nations;
  show no mercy to wicked
    traitors.   *Selah*

⁶They return at evening,
    snarling like dogs,
  and prowl about the city.
⁷See what they spew from
    their mouths—
  they spew out swords from
    their lips,
  and they say, "Who can
    hear us?"
⁸But you, O LORD, laugh at
    them;
  you scoff at all those
    nations.

⁹O my Strength, I watch for
    you;
  you, O God, are my
    fortress, ¹⁰my loving
    God.

God will go before me
  and will let me gloat over
    those who slander me.
¹¹But do not kill them, O Lord
    our shield,[b]
  or my people will forget.
In your might make them
    wander about,
  and bring them down.
¹²For the sins of their mouths,
  for the words of their lips,
    let them be caught in their
    pride.
For the curses and lies they
    utter,
¹³   consume them in wrath,
    consume them till they are
    no more.
Then it will be known to the
    ends of the earth
  that God rules over Jacob.
                        Selah

¹⁴They return at evening,
    snarling like dogs,
  and prowl about the city.
¹⁵They wander about for food
  and howl if not satisfied.
¹⁶But I will sing of your
    strength,
  in the morning I will sing of
    your love;
for you are my fortress,
  my refuge in times of
    trouble.

¹⁷O my Strength, I sing praise
    to you;
  you, O God, are my
    fortress, my loving God.

ᵃTitle: Probably a literary or musical term   ᵇ11 Or *sovereign*

Psalm 60

For the director of music. To ,the tune of, "The Lily of the Covenant." A *miktam*[a] of David. For teaching. When he fought Aram Naharaim[b] and Aram Zobah,[c] and when Joab returned and struck down twelve thousand Edomites in the Valley of Salt.

¹You have rejected us, O God,
    and burst forth upon us;
  you have been angry—now
      restore us!
²You have shaken the land and
      torn it open;
  mend its fractures, for it is
      quaking.
³You have shown your people
      desperate times;
  you have given us wine that
      makes us stagger.

⁴But for those who fear you,
    you have raised a banner
  to be unfurled against the
      bow.   *Selah*

⁵Save us and help us with your
      right hand,
  that those you love may be
      delivered.
⁶God has spoken from his
      sanctuary:
    "In triumph I will parcel out
        Shechem
    and measure off the Valley
        of Succoth.
⁷Gilead is mine, and Manasseh
      is mine;
  Ephraim is my helmet,
  Judah my scepter.
⁸Moab is my washbasin,
    upon Edom I toss my
        sandal;
    over Philistia I shout in
        triumph."

⁹Who will bring me to the
      fortified city?

Who will lead me to Edom?
¹⁰Is it not you, O God, you
    who have rejected us
  and no longer go out with
      our armies?
¹¹Give us aid against the
      enemy,
  for the help of man is
      worthless.
¹²With God we will gain the
      victory,
  and he will trample down
      our enemies.

Psalm 61

For the director of music. With stringed instruments. Of David.

¹Hear my cry, O God;
  listen to my prayer.

²From the ends of the earth I
      call to you,
  I call as my heart grows
      faint;
  lead me to the rock that is
      higher than I.
³For you have been my refuge,
  a strong tower against the
      foe.

⁴I long to dwell in your tent
      forever
  and take refuge in the
      shelter of your wings.
                              Selah
⁵For you have heard my vows,
      O God;
  you have given me the
      heritage of those who
      fear your name.

⁶Increase the days of the king's
      life,
  his years for many
      generations.
⁷May he be enthroned in God's
      presence forever;

---

[a]Title: Probably a literary or musical term   [b]Title: That is, Arameans of Northwest
Mesopotamia   [c]Title: That is, Arameans of central Syria

appoint your love and
  faithfulness to protect
  him.
[8]Then will I ever sing praise to
    your name
  and fulfill my vows day
    after day.

Psalm 62

For the director of music. For
Jeduthun. A psalm of David.

[1]My soul finds rest in God
    alone;
  my salvation comes from
    him.
[2]He alone is my rock and my
    salvation;
  he is my fortress, I will
    never be shaken.

[3]How long will you assault a
    man?
  Would all of you throw him
    down—
  this leaning wall, this
    tottering fence?
[4]They fully intend to topple
    him
  from his lofty place;
  they take delight in lies.
With their mouths they bless,
  but in their hearts they
    curse.   *Selah*

[5]Find rest, O my soul, in God
    alone;
  my hope comes from him.
[6]He alone is my rock and my
    salvation;
  he is my fortress, I will not
    be shaken.
[7]My salvation and my honor
    depend on God[a];
  he is my mighty rock, my
    refuge.
[8]Trust in him at all times,
    O people;
  pour out your hearts to
    him,
  for God is our refuge.   *Selah*

[9]Lowborn men are but a
    breath,
  the highborn are but a lie;
if weighed on a balance, they
    are nothing;
  together they are only a
    breath.
[10]Do not trust in extortion
  or take pride in stolen
    goods;
though your riches increase,
  do not set your heart on
    them.

[11]One thing God has spoken,
  two things have I heard:
that you, O God, are strong,
[12] and that you, O Lord, are
    loving.
Surely you will reward each
    person
  according to what he has
    done.

Psalm 63

A psalm of David. When he was in
the Desert of Judah.

[1]O God, you are my God,
  earnestly I seek you;
my soul thirsts for you,
  my body longs for you,
in a dry and weary land
  where there is no water.

[2]I have seen you in the
    sanctuary
  and beheld your power and
    your glory.
[3]Because your love is better
    than life,
  my lips will glorify you.
[4]I will praise you as long as I
    live,
  and in your name I will lift
    up my hands.
[5]My soul will be satisfied as
    with the richest of foods;
  with singing lips my mouth
    will praise you.

[a]7 Or / *God Most High is my salvation and my honor*

⁶On my bed I remember you;
    I think of you through the
        watches of the night.
⁷Because you are my help,
    I sing in the shadow of your
        wings.
⁸My soul clings to you;
    your right hand upholds
        me.

⁹They who seek my life will be
        destroyed;
    they will go down to the
        depths of the earth.
¹⁰They will be given over to the
        sword
    and become food for jackals.

¹¹But the king will rejoice in
        God;
    all who swear by God's
        name will praise him,
    while the mouths of liars
        will be silenced.

Psalm 64

For the director of music.
A psalm of David.

¹Hear me, O God, as I voice
        my complaint;
    protect my life from the
        threat of the enemy.
²Hide me from the conspiracy
        of the wicked,
    from that noisy crowd of
        evildoers.

³They sharpen their tongues
        like swords
    and aim their words like
        deadly arrows.
⁴They shoot from ambush at
        the innocent man;
    they shoot at him suddenly,
        without fear.

⁵They encourage each other in
        evil plans,
    they talk about hiding their
        snares;

they say, "Who will see
        them*ᵃ*?"
⁶They plot injustice and say,
    "We have devised a perfect
        plan!"
    Surely the mind and heart
        of man are cunning.

⁷But God will shoot them with
        arrows;
    suddenly they will be struck
        down.
⁸He will turn their own
        tongues against them
    and bring them to ruin;
    all who see them will shake
        their heads in scorn.

⁹All mankind will fear;
    they will proclaim the works
        of God
    and ponder what he has
        done.
¹⁰Let the righteous rejoice in the
        LORD
    and take refuge in him;
    let all the upright in heart
        praise him!

Psalm 65

For the director of music.
A psalm of David. A song.

¹Praise awaits*ᵇ* you, O God, in
        Zion;
    to you our vows will be
        fulfilled.
²O you who hear prayer,
    to you all men will come.
³When we were overwhelmed
        by sins,
    you forgave*ᶜ* our
        transgressions.
⁴Blessed are those you choose
    and bring near to live in
        your courts!
We are filled with the good
        things of your house,
    of your holy temple.

---

*ᵃ5 Or us   *ᵇ1 Or befits;* the meaning of the Hebrew for this word is uncertain.
ᶜ3 Or made atonement for

⁵You answer us with awesome
deeds of righteousness,
O God our Savior,
the hope of all the ends of the
earth
and of the farthest seas,
⁶who formed the mountains by
your power,
having armed yourself with
strength,
⁷who stilled the roaring of the
seas,
the roaring of their waves,
and the turmoil of the
nations.
⁸Those living far away fear
your wonders;
where morning dawns and
evening fades
you call forth songs of joy.

⁹You care for the land and
water it;
you enrich it abundantly.
The streams of God are filled
with water
to provide the people with
grain,
for so you have ordained it.ᵃ
¹⁰You drench its furrows
and level its ridges;
you soften it with showers
and bless its crops.
¹¹You crown the year with your
bounty,
and your carts overflow
with abundance.
¹²The grasslands of the desert
overflow;
the hills are clothed with
gladness.
¹³The meadows are covered
with flocks
and the valleys are mantled
with grain;
they shout for joy and sing.

Psalm 66

For the director of music. A song.
A psalm.

¹Shout with joy to God, all the
earth!
² Sing the glory of his name;
make his praise glorious!
³Say to God, "How awesome
are your deeds!
So great is your power
that your enemies cringe
before you.
⁴All the earth bows down to
you;
they sing praise to you,
they sing praise to your
name."   *Selah*

⁵Come and see what God has
done,
how awesome his works in
man's behalf!
⁶He turned the sea into dry
land,
they passed through the
waters on foot—
come, let us rejoice in him.
⁷He rules forever by his power,
his eyes watch the nations—
let not the rebellious rise up
against him.   *Selah*

⁸Praise our God, O peoples,
let the sound of his praise
be heard;
⁹he has preserved our lives
and kept our feet from
slipping.
¹⁰For you, O God, tested us;
you refined us like silver.
¹¹You brought us into prison
and laid burdens on our
backs.
¹²You let men ride over our
heads;

ᵃ9 *Or for that is how you prepare the land*

we went through fire and
water,
but you brought us to a
place of abundance.

¹³I will come to your temple
with burnt offerings
and fulfill my vows to
you—
¹⁴vows my lips promised and
my mouth spoke
when I was in trouble.
¹⁵I will sacrifice fat animals to
you
and an offering of rams;
I will offer bulls and goats.
                              Selah

10 ¹⁶Come and listen, all you who
fear God;
let me tell you what he has
done for me.
¹⁷I cried out to him with my
mouth;
his praise was on my
tongue.
¹⁸If I had cherished sin in my
heart,
the Lord would not have
listened;
¹⁹but God has surely listened
and heard my voice in
prayer.
²⁰Praise be to God,
who has not rejected my
prayer
or withheld his love from
me!

Psalm 67 PRAISE

For the director of music. With
stringed instruments. A psalm.
A song.

¹May God be gracious to us
and bless us
and make his face shine
upon us,   *Selah*
²that your ways may be known
on earth,
your salvation among all
nations.

³May the peoples praise you,
O God;
may all the peoples praise
you.
⁴May the nations be glad and
sing for joy,
for you rule the peoples
justly
and guide the nations of the
earth.   *Selah*
⁵May the peoples praise you,
O God;
may all the peoples praise
you.
⁶Then the land will yield its
harvest,
and God, our God, will
bless us.
⁷God will bless us,
and all the ends of the earth
will fear him.

Psalm 68

For the director of music. Of David.
A psalm. A song.

¹May God arise, may his
enemies be scattered;
may his foes flee before
him.
²As smoke is blown away by
the wind,
may you blow them away;
as wax melts before the fire,
may the wicked perish
before God.
³But may the righteous be glad
and rejoice before God;
may they be happy and
joyful.

⁴Sing to God, sing praise to his   37
name,   Ps 97:1
extol him who rides on the
clouds—
his name is the LORD—
and rejoice before him.
⁵A father to the fatherless, a
defender of widows,
is God in his holy dwelling.

---

⁴ Or / prepare the way for him who rides through the deserts

25 ⁶God sets the lonely in
      families,ᵃ
   he leads forth the prisoners
      with singing;
   but the rebellious live in a
      sun-scorched land.

⁷When you went out before
      your people, O God,
   when you marched through
      the wasteland,   Selah
⁸the earth shook,
   the heavens poured down
      rain,
   before God, the One of Sinai,
   before God, the God of
      Israel.
⁹You gave abundant showers,
      O God;
   you refreshed your weary
      inheritance.
¹⁰Your people settled in it,
   and from your bounty,
      O God, you provided
      for the poor.

¹¹The Lord announced the
      word,
   and great was the company
      of those who proclaimed
      it:
¹²"Kings and armies flee in
      haste;
   in the camps men divide the
      plunder.
¹³Even while you sleep among
      the campfires,ᵇ
   the wings of my dove are
      sheathed with silver,
   its feathers with shining
      gold."
¹⁴When the Almightyᶜ scattered
      the kings in the land,
   it was like snow fallen on
      Zalmon.

¹⁵The mountains of Bashan are
      majestic mountains;
   rugged are the mountains of
      Bashan.

¹⁶Why gaze in envy, O rugged
      mountains,
   at the mountain where God
      chooses to reign,
   where the LORD himself will
      dwell forever?
¹⁷The chariots of God are tens
      of thousands
   and thousands of
      thousands;
   the Lord has come from
      Sinai into his sanctuary.
¹⁸When you ascended on high,
   you led captives in your
      train;
   you received gifts from
      men,
   even fromᵈ the rebellious—
   that you,ᵉ O LORD God,
      might dwell there.

¹⁹Praise be to the Lord, to God
      our Savior,
   who daily bears our
      burdens.   Selah
²⁰Our God is a God who saves;
   from the Sovereign LORD
      comes escape from
      death.

²¹Surely God will crush the
      heads of his enemies,
   the hairy crowns of those
      who go on in their
      sins.
²²The Lord says, "I will bring
      them from Bashan;
   I will bring them from the
      depths of the sea,
²³that you may plunge your feet
      in the blood of your
      foes,
   while the tongues of your
      dogs have their share."

²⁴Your procession has come into
      view, O God,
   the procession of my God
      and King into the
      sanctuary.

─────────────
ᵃ6 Or the desolate in a homeland   ᵇ13 Or saddlebags   ᶜ14 Hebrew Shaddai   ᵈ18 Or
gifts for men, / even   ᵉ18 Or they

²⁵In front are the singers, after
    them the musicians;
  with them are the maidens
    playing tambourines.
²⁶Praise God in the great
    congregation;
  praise the LORD in the
    assembly of Israel.
²⁷There is the little tribe of
    Benjamin, leading
    them,
  there the great throng of
    Judah's princes,
  and there the princes of
    Zebulun and of
    Naphtali.

²⁸Summon your power, O God[a];
  show us your strength,
    O God, as you have
    done before.
²⁹Because of your temple at
    Jerusalem
  kings will bring you gifts.
³⁰Rebuke the beast among the
    reeds,
  the herd of bulls among the
    calves of the nations.
  Humbled, may it bring bars of
    silver.
  Scatter the nations who
    delight in war.
³¹Envoys will come from Egypt;
  Cush[b] will submit herself to
    God.

³²Sing to God, O kingdoms of
    the earth,
  sing praise to the Lord,
              Selah
³³to him who rides the ancient
    skies above,
  who thunders with mighty
    voice.
³⁴Proclaim the power of God,
  whose majesty is over
    Israel,
  whose power is in the skies.
³⁵You are awesome, O God, in
    your sanctuary;

the God of Israel gives
    power and strength to
    his people.

Praise be to God!

Psalm 69

*For the director of music. To the
tune of, "Lilies." Of David.*

¹Save me, O God,   16
  for the waters have come up Ps 88:3-9
    to my neck.
²I sink in the miry depths,
  where there is no foothold.
I have come into the deep
    waters;
  the floods engulf me.
³I am worn out calling for help;
  my throat is parched.
My eyes fail,
  looking for my God.
⁴Those who hate me without
    reason
  outnumber the hairs of my
    head;
many are my enemies without
    cause,
  those who seek to destroy
    me.
I am forced to restore
  what I did not steal.

⁵You know my folly, O God;   36
  my guilt is not hidden from
    you.

⁶May those who hope in you
  not be disgraced because of
    me,
  O Lord, the LORD Almighty;
  may those who seek you
  not be put to shame because
    of me,
  O God of Israel.
⁷For I endure scorn for your
    sake,
  and shame covers my face.
⁸I am a stranger to my
    brothers,

---

[a]28 Many Hebrew manuscripts, Septuagint and Syriac; most Hebrew manuscripts
Your God has summoned power for you   [b]31 That is, the upper Nile region

an alien to my own
    mother's sons;
⁹for zeal for your house
    consumes me,
and the insults of those who
    insult you fall on me.
¹⁰When I weep and fast,
    I must endure scorn;
¹¹when I put on sackcloth,
    people make sport of me.
¹²Those who sit at the gate
    mock me,
and I am the song of the
    drunkards.

¹³But I pray to you, O Lord,
    in the time of your favor;
in your great love, O God,
    answer me with your sure
    salvation.
¹⁴Rescue me from the mire,
    do not let me sink;
deliver me from those who
    hate me,
    from the deep waters.
¹⁵Do not let the floodwaters
    engulf me
or the depths swallow me
    up
or the pit close its mouth
    over me.
¹⁶Answer me, O Lord, out of
    the goodness of your
    love;
in your great mercy turn to
    me.
¹⁷Do not hide your face from
    your servant;
answer me quickly, for I am
    in trouble.
¹⁸Come near and rescue me;
    redeem me because of my
    foes.

¹⁹You know how I am scorned,
    disgraced and shamed;
all my enemies are before
    you.
²⁰Scorn has broken my heart
    and has left me helpless;
I looked for sympathy, but
    there was none,

for comforters, but I found
    none.
²¹They put gall in my food
    and gave me vinegar for my
    thirst.

²²May the table set before them
    become a snare;
may it become retribution
    and^a a trap.
²³May their eyes be darkened so
    they cannot see,
and their backs be bent
    forever.
²⁴Pour out your wrath on them;
    let your fierce anger
    overtake them.
²⁵May their place be deserted;
    let there be no one to dwell
    in their tents.
²⁶For they persecute those you
    wound
and talk about the pain of
    those you hurt.
²⁷Charge them with crime upon
    crime;
do not let them share in
    your salvation.
²⁸May they be blotted out of the
    book of life
and not be listed with the
    righteous.

²⁹I am in pain and distress;
    may your salvation, O God,
    protect me.

³⁰I will praise God's name in
    song
and glorify him with
    thanksgiving.
³¹This will please the Lord
    more than an ox,
more than a bull with its
    horns and hoofs.
³²The poor will see and be
    glad—
you who seek God, may
    your hearts live!
³³The Lord hears the needy
    and does not despise his
    captive people.

---

^a22 Or *snare / and their fellowship become*

³⁴Let heaven and earth praise
    him,
  the seas and all that move
    in them,
³⁵for God will save Zion
  and rebuild the cities of
    Judah.
Then people will settle there
    and possess it;
³⁶ the children of his servants
    will inherit it,
  and those who love his
    name will dwell there.

Psalm 70

For the director of music. Of David.
A petition.

¹Hasten, O God, to save me;
  O LORD, come quickly to
    help me.
²May those who seek my life
  be put to shame and
    confusion;
may all who desire my ruin
  be turned back in disgrace.
³May those who say to me,
    "Aha! Aha!"
  turn back because of their
    shame.
⁴But may all who seek you
  rejoice and be glad in you;
may those who love your
    salvation always say,
    "Let God be exalted!"

⁵Yet I am poor and needy;
  come quickly to me, O God.
You are my help and my
    deliverer;
  O LORD, do not delay.

Psalm 71

¹In you, O LORD, I have taken
    refuge;
  let me never be put to
    shame.
²Rescue me and deliver me in
    your righteousness;
  turn your ear to me and
    save me.

³Be my rock of refuge,
  to which I can always go;
give the command to save me,
  for you are my rock and my
    fortress.
⁴Deliver me, O my God, from
    the hand of the wicked,
  from the grasp of evil and
    cruel men.

⁵For you have been my hope,
    O Sovereign LORD,
  my confidence since my
    youth.
⁶From birth I have relied on
    you;
  you brought me forth from
    my mother's womb.
I will ever praise you.
⁷I have become like a portent
    to many,
  but you are my strong
    refuge.
⁸My mouth is filled with your
    praise,
  declaring your splendor all
    day long.

⁹Do not cast me away when I
    am old;
  do not forsake me when my
    strength is gone.
¹⁰For my enemies speak against
    me;
  those who wait to kill me
    conspire together.
¹¹They say, "God has forsaken
    him;
  pursue him and seize him,
  for no one will rescue him."
¹²Be not far from me, O God;
  come quickly, O my God, to
    help me.
¹³May my accusers perish in
    shame;
  may those who want to
    harm me
  be covered with scorn and
    disgrace.

¹⁴But as for me, I will always
  have hope;

I will praise you more and
more.

[15]My mouth will tell of your
righteousness,
of your salvation all day
long,
though I know not its
measure.

[16]I will come and proclaim your
mighty acts, O Sovereign
LORD;
I will proclaim your
righteousness, yours
alone.

[17]Since my youth, O God, you
have taught me,
and to this day I declare
your marvelous deeds.

[18]Even when I am old and gray,
do not forsake me, O God,
till I declare your power to the
next generation,
your might to all who are to
come.

[19]Your righteousness reaches to
the skies, O God,
you who have done great
things.
Who, O God, is like you?

[20]Though you have made me
see troubles, many and
bitter,
you will restore my life
again;
from the depths of the earth
you will again bring me up.

[21]You will increase my honor
and comfort me once again.

[22]I will praise you with the harp
for your faithfulness, O my
God;
I will sing praise to you with
the lyre,
O Holy One of Israel.

[23]My lips will shout for joy
when I sing praise to you—
I, whom you have
redeemed.

[24]My tongue will tell of your
righteous acts
all day long,
for those who wanted to harm
me
have been put to shame and
confusion.

Psalm 72

Of Solomon.

[1]Endow the king with your
justice, O God,
the royal son with your
righteousness.

[2]He will[a] judge your people in
righteousness,
your afflicted ones with
justice.

[3]The mountains will bring
prosperity to the people,
the hills the fruit of
righteousness.

[4]He will defend the afflicted
among the people
and save the children of the
needy;
he will crush the oppressor.

[5]He will endure[b] as long as the
sun,
as long as the moon,
through all generations.

[6]He will be like rain falling on
a mown field,
like showers watering the
earth.

[7]In his days the righteous will
flourish;
prosperity will abound till
the moon is no more.

[8]He will rule from sea to sea
and from the River[c] to the
ends of the earth.[d]

[9]The desert tribes will bow
before him
and his enemies will lick the
dust.

---

[a]2 Or *May he;* similarly in verses 3-11 and 17   [b]5 Septuagint; Hebrew *You will be
feared*   [c]8 That is, the Euphrates   [d]8 Or *the end of the land*

¹⁰The kings of Tarshish and of
    distant shores
  will bring tribute to him;
the kings of Sheba and Seba
  will present him gifts.
¹¹All kings will bow down to
    him
  and all nations will serve
    him.

¹²For he will deliver the needy
    who cry out,
  the afflicted who have no
    one to help.
¹³He will take pity on the weak
    and the needy
  and save the needy from
    death.
¹⁴He will rescue them from
    oppression and violence,
  for precious is their blood in
    his sight.

¹⁵Long may he live!
  May gold from Sheba be
    given him.
May people ever pray for him
  and bless him all day long.
¹⁶Let grain abound throughout
    the land;
  on the tops of the hills may
    it sway.
Let its fruit flourish like
    Lebanon;
  let it thrive like the grass of
    the field.
¹⁷May his name endure forever;
  may it continue as long as
    the sun.

All nations will be blessed
    through him,
  and they will call him
    blessed.

¹⁸Praise be to the LORD God,
    the God of Israel,
  who alone does marvelous
    deeds.

¹⁹Praise be to his glorious name
    forever;
  may the whole earth be
    filled with his glory.
Amen and Amen.

²⁰This concludes the prayers of
  David son of Jesse.

BOOK III

Psalms 73-89

Psalm 73

A psalm of Asaph.

¹Surely God is good to Israel,
  to those who are pure in
    heart.

²But as for me, my feet had
    almost slipped;
  I had nearly lost my
    foothold.
³For I envied the arrogant
  when I saw the prosperity
    of the wicked.

⁴They have no struggles;
  their bodies are healthy and
    strong.ª
⁵They are free from the
    burdens common to
    man;
  they are not plagued by
    human ills.
⁶Therefore pride is their
    necklace;
  they clothe themselves with
    violence.
⁷From their callous hearts
    comes iniquityᵇ;
  the evil conceits of their
    minds know no limits.
⁸They scoff, and speak with
    malice;
  in their arrogance they
    threaten oppression.

ª4 With a different word division of the Hebrew; Masoretic Text *struggles at their death; / their bodies are healthy*   ᵇ7 Syriac (see also Septuagint); Hebrew *Their eyes bulge with fat*

⁹Their mouths lay claim to
      heaven,
  and their tongues take
      possession of the earth.
¹⁰Therefore their people turn to
      them
  and drink up waters in
      abundance.ᵃ
¹¹They say, "How can God
      know?
  Does the Most High have
      knowledge?"

¹²This is what the wicked are
      like—
  always carefree, they
      increase in wealth.

¹³Surely in vain have I kept my
      heart pure;
  in vain have I washed my
      hands in innocence.
¹⁴All day long I have been
      plagued;
  I have been punished every
      morning.

¹⁵If I had said, "I will speak
      thus,"
  I would have betrayed your
      children.
¹⁶When I tried to understand all
      this,
  it was oppressive to me
¹⁷till I entered the sanctuary of
      God;
  then I understood their final
      destiny.

¹⁸Surely you place them on
      slippery ground;
  you cast them down to ruin.
¹⁹How suddenly are they
      destroyed,
  completely swept away by
      terrors!
²⁰As a dream when one
      awakes,
  so when you arise, O Lord,
  you will despise them as
      fantasies.

²¹When my heart was grieved
      and my spirit embittered,
²²I was senseless and ignorant;
  I was a brute beast before
      you.

²³Yet I am always with you;
  you hold me by my right
      hand.
²⁴You guide me with your
      counsel,
  and afterward you will take
      me into glory.
²⁵Whom have I in heaven but
      you?
  And earth has nothing I
      desire besides you.
²⁶My flesh and my heart may
      fail,
  but God is the strength of
      my heart
  and my portion forever.

²⁷Those who are far from you
      will perish;
  you destroy all who are
      unfaithful to you.
²⁸But as for me, it is good to be
      near God.
  I have made the Sovereign
      Lord my refuge;
  I will tell of all your deeds.

Psalm 74

A maskilᵇ of Asaph.

¹Why have you rejected us
      forever, O God?
  Why does your anger
      smolder against the
      sheep of your pasture?
²Remember the people you
      purchased of old,
  the tribe of your inheritance,
      whom you redeemed—
  Mount Zion, where you
      dwelt.
³Turn your steps toward these
      everlasting ruins,

ᵃ10 The meaning of the Hebrew for this verse is uncertain.   ᵇTitle: Probably a
literary or musical term

all this destruction the
enemy has brought on
the sanctuary.

⁴Your foes roared in the place
where you met with us;
they set up their standards
as signs.

⁵They behaved like men
wielding axes
to cut through a thicket of
trees.

⁶They smashed all the carved
paneling
with their axes and
hatchets.

⁷They burned your sanctuary
to the ground;
they defiled the dwelling
place of your Name.

⁸They said in their hearts, "We
will crush them
completely!"
They burned every place
where God was
worshiped in the land.

⁹We are given no miraculous
signs;
no prophets are left,
and none of us knows how
long this will be.

¹⁰How long will the enemy
mock you, O God?
Will the foe revile your
name forever?

¹¹Why do you hold back your
hand, your right hand?
Take it from the folds of
your garment and
destroy them!

¹²But you, O God, are my king
from of old;
you bring salvation upon
the earth.

¹³It was you who split open the
sea by your power;
you broke the heads of the
monster in the waters.

¹⁴It was you who crushed the
heads of Leviathan

and gave him as food to the
creatures of the desert.

¹⁵It was you who opened up
springs and streams;
you dried up the ever
flowing rivers.

¹⁶The day is yours, and yours
also the night;
you established the sun and
moon.

¹⁷It was you who set all the
boundaries of the earth;
you made both summer and
winter.

¹⁸Remember how the enemy
has mocked you,
O LORD,
how foolish people have
reviled your name.

¹⁹Do not hand over the life of
your dove to wild beasts;
do not forget the lives of
your afflicted people
forever.

²⁰Have regard for your
covenant,
because haunts of violence
fill the dark places of the
land.

²¹Do not let the oppressed
retreat in disgrace;
may the poor and needy
praise your name.

²²Rise up, O God, and defend
your cause;
remember how fools mock
you all day long.

²³Do not ignore the clamor of
your adversaries,
the uproar of your enemies,
which rises continually.

Psalm 75

For the director of music. To the
tune of, "Do Not Destroy." A psalm
of Asaph. A song.

¹We give thanks to you,
O God,

we give thanks, for your
Name is near;
men tell of your wonderful
deeds.

2You say, "I choose the
appointed time;
it is I who judge uprightly.
3When the earth and all its
people quake,
it is I who hold its pillars
firm.   *Selah*
4To the arrogant I say, 'Boast
no more,'
and to the wicked, 'Do not
lift up your horns.
5Do not lift your horns against
heaven;
do not speak with
outstretched neck.' "

6No one from the east or the
west
or from the desert can exalt
a man.
7But it is God who judges:
He brings one down, he
exalts another.
8In the hand of the LORD is a
cup
full of foaming wine mixed
with spices;
he pours it out, and all the
wicked of the earth
drink it down to its very
dregs.

9As for me, I will declare this
forever;
I will sing praise to the God
of Jacob.
10I will cut off the horns of all
the wicked,
but the horns of the
righteous will be lifted
up.

Psalm 76

For the director of music. With
stringed instruments. A psalm of
Asaph. A song.

1In Judah God is known;
his name is great in Israel.
2His tent is in Salem,
his dwelling place in Zion.
3There he broke the flashing
arrows,
the shields and the swords,
the weapons of war.
                                Selah

4You are resplendent with
light,
more majestic than
mountains rich with
game.
5Valiant men lie plundered,
they sleep their last sleep;
not one of the warriors
can lift his hands.
6At your rebuke, O God of
Jacob,
both horse and chariot lie
still.
7You alone are to be feared.
Who can stand before you
when you are angry?
8From heaven you pronounced
judgment,
and the land feared and was
quiet—
9when you, O God, rose up to
judge,
to save all the afflicted of
the land.   *Selah*
10Surely your wrath against
men brings you praise,
and the survivors of your
wrath are restrained.a

11Make vows to the LORD your
God and fulfill them;

---

a10 Or *Surely the wrath of men brings you praise, / and with the remainder of wrath you
arm yourself*

let all the neighboring lands
bring gifts to the One to be
feared.
¹²He breaks the spirit of rulers;
he is feared by the kings of
the earth.

Psalm 77

For the director of music. For
Jeduthun. Of Asaph. A psalm.

¹I cried out to God for help;
I cried out to God to hear
me.
²When I was in distress, I
sought the Lord;
at night I stretched out
untiring hands
and my soul refused to be
comforted.

³I remembered you, O God,
and I groaned;
I mused, and my spirit grew
faint.   *Selah*
⁴You kept my eyes from
closing;
I was too troubled to speak.
⁵I thought about the former
days,
the years of long ago;
⁶I remembered my songs in the
night.
My heart mused and my
spirit inquired:

⁷"Will the Lord reject forever?
Will he never show his
favor again?
⁸Has his unfailing love
vanished forever?
Has his promise failed for
all time?
⁹Has God forgotten to be
merciful?
Has he in anger withheld
his compassion?"   *Selah*

¹⁰Then I thought, "To this I will
appeal:

the years of the right hand
of the Most High.''
¹¹I will remember the deeds of
the LORD;
yes, I will remember your
miracles of long ago.
¹²I will meditate on all your
works
and consider all your
mighty deeds.

¹³Your ways, O God, are holy.
What god is so great as our
God?
¹⁴You are the God who
performs miracles;
you display your power
among the peoples.
¹⁵With your mighty arm you
redeemed your people,
the descendants of Jacob
and Joseph.   *Selah*

¹⁶The waters saw you, O God,
the waters saw you and
writhed;
the very depths were
convulsed.
¹⁷The clouds poured down
water,
the skies resounded with
thunder;
your arrows flashed back
and forth.
¹⁸Your thunder was heard in
the whirlwind,
your lightning lit up the
world;
the earth trembled and
quaked.
¹⁹Your path led through the
sea,
your way through the
mighty waters,
though your footprints were
not seen.
²⁰You led your people like a
flock
by the hand of Moses and
Aaron.

Psalm 78

A maskil[a] of Asaph.

¹O my people, hear my
teaching;
   listen to the words of my
   mouth.
²I will open my mouth in
parables,
   I will utter hidden things,
   things from of old—
³what we have heard and
known,
   what our fathers have told
   us.
⁴We will not hide them from
their children;
   we will tell the next
   generation
the praiseworthy deeds of the
Lord,
   his power, and the wonders
   he has done.
⁵He decreed statutes for Jacob
   and established the law in
   Israel,
which he commanded our
forefathers
   to teach their children,
⁶so the next generation would
know them,
   even the children yet to be
   born,
   and they in turn would tell
   their children.
⁷Then they would put their
trust in God
   and would not forget his
   deeds
   but would keep his
   commands.
⁸They would not be like their
forefathers—
   a stubborn and rebellious
   generation,
whose hearts were not loyal
to God,
   whose spirits were not
   faithful to him.

⁹The men of Ephraim, though
armed with bows,
   turned back on the day of
   battle;
¹⁰they did not keep God's
covenant
   and refused to live by his
   law.
¹¹They forgot what he had
done,
   the wonders he had shown
   them.
¹²He did miracles in the sight of
their fathers
   in the land of Egypt, in the
   region of Zoan.
¹³He divided the sea and led
them through;
   he made the water stand
   firm like a wall.
¹⁴He guided them with the
cloud by day
   and with light from the fire
   all night.
¹⁵He split the rocks in the
desert
   and gave them water as
   abundant as the seas;
¹⁶he brought streams out of a
rocky crag
   and made water flow down
   like rivers.

¹⁷But they continued to sin
against him,
   rebelling in the desert
   against the Most
   High.
¹⁸They willfully put God to the
test
   by demanding the food they
   craved.
¹⁹They spoke against God,
saying,
   "Can God spread a table in
   the desert?
²⁰When he struck the rock,
water gushed out,
   and streams flowed
   abundantly.

ᵃTitle: Probably a literary or musical term

But can he also give us food?
Can he supply meat for his
people?"
²¹When the LORD heard them,
he was very angry;
his fire broke out against
Jacob,
and his wrath rose against
Israel,
²²for they did not believe in
God
or trust in his deliverance.
²³Yet he gave a command to the
skies above
and opened the doors of the
heavens;
²⁴he rained down manna for the
people to eat,
he gave them the grain of
heaven.
²⁵Men ate the bread of angels;
he sent them all the food
they could eat.
²⁶He let loose the east wind
from the heavens
and led forth the south
wind by his power.
²⁷He rained meat down on
them like dust,
flying birds like sand on the
seashore.
²⁸He made them come down
inside their camp,
all around their tents.
²⁹They ate till they had more
than enough,
for he had given them what
they craved.
³⁰But before they turned from
the food they craved,
even while it was still in
their mouths,
³¹God's anger rose against
them;
he put to death the sturdiest
among them,
cutting down the young
men of Israel.

³²In spite of all this, they kept
on sinning;

in spite of his wonders,
they did not believe.
³³So he ended their days in
futility
and their years in terror.
³⁴Whenever God slew them,
they would seek him;
they eagerly turned to him
again.
³⁵They remembered that God
was their Rock,
that God Most High was
their Redeemer.
³⁶But then they would flatter
him with their mouths,
lying to him with their
tongues;
³⁷their hearts were not loyal to
him,
they were not faithful to his
covenant.
³⁸Yet he was merciful;
he forgave their iniquities
and did not destroy them.
Time after time he restrained
his anger
and did not stir up his full
wrath.
³⁹He remembered that they
were but flesh,
a passing breeze that does
not return.
⁴⁰How often they rebelled
against him in the
desert
and grieved him in the
wasteland!
⁴¹Again and again they put God
to the test;
they vexed the Holy One of
Israel.
⁴²They did not remember his
power—
the day he redeemed them
from the oppressor,
⁴³the day he displayed his
miraculous signs in
Egypt,
his wonders in the region of
Zoan.

⁴⁴He turned their rivers to
  blood;
    they could not drink from
    their streams.
⁴⁵He sent swarms of flies that
  devoured them,
    and frogs that devastated
    them.
⁴⁶He gave their crops to the
  grasshopper,
    their produce to the locust.
⁴⁷He destroyed their vines with
  hail
    and their sycamore-figs with
    sleet.
⁴⁸He gave over their cattle to
  the hail,
    their livestock to bolts of
    lightning.
⁴⁹He unleashed against them
  his hot anger,
    his wrath, indignation and
    hostility—
    a band of destroying angels.
⁵⁰He prepared a path for his
  anger;
    he did not spare them from
    death
    but gave them over to the
    plague.
⁵¹He struck down all the
  firstborn of Egypt,
    the firstfruits of manhood in
    the tents of Ham.
⁵²But he brought his people out
  like a flock;
    he led them like sheep
    through the desert.
⁵³He guided them safely, so
  they were unafraid;
    but the sea engulfed their
    enemies.
⁵⁴Thus he brought them to the
  border of his holy land,
    to the hill country his right
    hand had taken.
⁵⁵He drove out nations before
  them
    and allotted their lands to
    them as an inheritance;
    he settled the tribes of Israel
    in their homes.

⁵⁶But they put God to the test
  and rebelled against the
    Most High;
    they did not keep his
    statutes.
⁵⁷Like their fathers they were
  disloyal and faithless,
    as unreliable as a faulty
    bow.
⁵⁸They angered him with their
  high places;
    they aroused his jealousy
    with their idols.
⁵⁹When God heard them, he
  was very angry;
    he rejected Israel
    completely.
⁶⁰He abandoned the tabernacle
  of Shiloh,
    the tent he had set up
    among men.
⁶¹He sent the ark of his might
  into captivity,
    his splendor into the hands
    of the enemy.
⁶²He gave his people over to
  the sword;
    he was very angry with his
    inheritance.
⁶³Fire consumed their young
  men,
    and their maidens had no
    wedding songs;
⁶⁴their priests were put to the
  sword,
    and their widows could not
    weep.
⁶⁵Then the Lord awoke as from
  sleep,
    as a man wakes from the
    stupor of wine.
⁶⁶He beat back his enemies;
    he put them to everlasting
    shame.
⁶⁷Then he rejected the tents of
  Joseph,
    he did not choose the tribe of
    Ephraim;
⁶⁸but he chose the tribe of
  Judah,
    Mount Zion, which he
    loved.

⁶⁹He built his sanctuary like the
    heights,
  like the earth that he
    established forever.
⁷⁰He chose David his servant
    and took him from the
    sheep pens;
⁷¹from tending the sheep he
    brought him
  to be the shepherd of his
    people Jacob,
  of Israel his inheritance.
⁷²And David shepherded them
    with integrity of heart;
  with skillful hands he led
    them.

Psalm 79

A psalm of Asaph.

¹O God, the nations have
    invaded your
    inheritance;
  they have defiled your holy
    temple,
  they have reduced
    Jerusalem to rubble.
²They have given the dead
    bodies of your servants
  as food to the birds of the
    air,
  the flesh of your saints to
    the beasts of the earth.
³They have poured out blood
    like water
  all around Jerusalem,
  and there is no one to bury
    the dead.
⁴We are objects of reproach to
    our neighbors,
  of scorn and derision to
    those around us.

⁵How long, O LORD? Will you
    be angry forever?
  How long will your jealousy
    burn like fire?
⁶Pour out your wrath on the
    nations
  that do not acknowledge
    you,

on the kingdoms
    that do not call on your
    name;
⁷for they have devoured Jacob
    and destroyed his
    homeland.
⁸Do not hold against us the
    sins of the fathers;
  may your mercy come
    quickly to meet us,
  for we are in desperate
    need.

⁹Help us, O God our Savior,
  for the glory of your name;
  deliver us and forgive our sins
    for your name's sake.
¹⁰Why should the nations say,
    "Where is their God?"
  Before our eyes, make known
    among the nations
  that you avenge the
    outpoured blood of your
    servants.
¹¹May the groans of the
    prisoners come before
    you;
  by the strength of your arm
    preserve those condemned
    to die.

¹²Pay back into the laps of our
    neighbors seven times
  the reproach they have
    hurled at you, O Lord.
¹³Then we your people, the
    sheep of your pasture,
  will praise you forever;
  from generation to generation
  we will recount your praise.

Psalm 80

*For the director of music. To the
tune of, "The Lilies of the
Covenant." Of Asaph. A psalm.*

¹Hear us, O Shepherd of
    Israel,
  you who lead Joseph like a
    flock;

you who sit enthroned
    between the cherubim,
    shine forth
2   before Ephraim, Benjamin
    and Manasseh.
Awaken your might;
    come and save us.

3Restore us, O God;
    make your face shine upon
    us,
    that we may be saved.

4O Lord God Almighty,
    how long will your anger
    smolder
    against the prayers of your
    people?
5You have fed them with the
    bread of tears;
    you have made them drink
    tears by the bowlful.
6You have made us a source of
    contention to our
    neighbors,
    and our enemies mock us.

7Restore us, O God Almighty;
    make your face shine upon
    us,
    that we may be saved.

8You brought a vine out of
    Egypt;
    you drove out the nations
    and planted it.
9You cleared the ground for it,
    and it took root and filled
    the land.
10The mountains were covered
    with its shade,
    the mighty cedars with its
    branches.
11It sent out its boughs to the
    Sea,[a]
    its shoots as far as the
    River.[b]

12Why have you broken down
    its walls

so that all who pass by pick
    its grapes?
13Boars from the forest ravage it
    and the creatures of the
    field feed on it.
14Return to us, O God
    Almighty!
    Look down from heaven
    and see!
Watch over this vine,
15   the root your right hand has
    planted,
    the son[c] you have raised up
    for yourself.

16Your vine is cut down, it is
    burned with fire;
    at your rebuke your people
    perish.
17Let your hand rest on the
    man at your right hand,
    the son of man you have
    raised up for yourself.
18Then we will not turn away
    from you;
    revive us, and we will call
    on your name.

19Restore us, O Lord God
    Almighty;
    make your face shine upon
    us,
    that we may be saved.

Psalm 81

For the director of music. According
to *gittith*.[d] Of Asaph.

1Sing for joy to God our
    strength;
    shout aloud to the God of
    Jacob!
2Begin the music, strike the
    tambourine,
    play the melodious harp
    and lyre.

3Sound the ram's horn at the
    New Moon,

---

[a]11 Probably the Mediterranean   [b]11 That is, the Euphrates   [c]15 Or *branch*
[d]Title: Probably a musical term

and when the moon is full,
  on the day of our Feast;
⁴this is a decree for Israel,
  an ordinance of the God of
  Jacob.
⁵He established it as a statute
  for Joseph
  when he went out against
  Egypt,
  where we heard a language
  we did not understand.ᵃ
⁶He says, "I removed the
  burden from their
  shoulders;
  their hands were set free
  from the basket.
⁷In your distress you called
  and I rescued you,
  I answered you out of a
  thundercloud;
  I tested you at the waters of
  Meribah.   Selah

⁸"Hear, O my people, and I
  will warn you—
  if you would but listen to
  me, O Israel!
⁹You shall have no foreign god
  among you;
  you shall not bow down to
  an alien god.
¹⁰I am the LORD your God,
  who brought you up out of
  Egypt.
  Open wide your mouth and
  I will fill it.

¹¹"But my people would not
  listen to me;
  Israel would not submit to
  me.
¹²So I gave them over to their
  stubborn hearts
  to follow their own devices.

¹³"If my people would but
  listen to me,
  if Israel would follow my
  ways,
¹⁴how quickly would I subdue
  their enemies

and turn my hand against
  their foes!
¹⁵Those who hate the LORD
  would cringe before
  him,
  and their punishment would
  last forever.
¹⁶But you would be fed with
  the finest of wheat;
  with honey from the rock I
  would satisfy you."

Psalm 82

A psalm of Asaph.

¹God presides in the great
  assembly;
  he gives judgment among
  the "gods":

²"How long will youᵇ defend
  the unjust
  and show partiality to the
  wicked?   Selah
³Defend the cause of the weak
  and fatherless;
  maintain the rights of the
  poor and oppressed.
⁴Rescue the weak and needy;
  deliver them from the hand
  of the wicked.

⁵"They know nothing, they
  understand nothing.
  They walk about in
  darkness;
  all the foundations of the
  earth are shaken.

⁶"I said, 'You are "gods";
  you are all sons of the Most
  High.'
⁷But you will die like mere
  men;
  you will fall like every other
  ruler."

⁸Rise up, O God, judge the
  earth,
  for all the nations are your
  inheritance.

ᵃ5 Or / and we heard a voice we had not known   ᵇ2 The Hebrew is plural.

Psalm 83

A song. A psalm of Asaph.

¹O God, do not keep silent;
  be not quiet, O God, be not
  still.
²See how your enemies are
  astir,
  how your foes rear their
  heads.
³With cunning they conspire
  against your people;
  they plot against those you
  cherish.
⁴"Come," they say, "let us
  destroy them as a
  nation,
  that the name of Israel be
  remembered no more."

⁵With one mind they plot
  together;
  they form an alliance against
  you—
⁶the tents of Edom and the
  Ishmaelites,
  of Moab and the Hagrites,
⁷Gebal,[a] Ammon and Amalek,
  Philistia, with the people of
  Tyre.
⁸Even Assyria has joined them
  to lend strength to the
  descendants of Lot. *Selah*

⁹Do to them as you did to
  Midian,
  as you did to Sisera and
  Jabin at the river Kishon,
¹⁰who perished at Endor
  and became like refuse on
  the ground.
¹¹Make their nobles like Oreb
  and Zeeb,
  all their princes like Zebah
  and Zalmunna,
¹²who said, "Let us take
  possession
  of the pasturelands of God."

¹³Make them like tumbleweed,
  O my God,
  like chaff before the wind.

¹⁴As fire consumes the forest
  or a flame sets the
  mountains ablaze,
¹⁵so pursue them with your
  tempest
  and terrify them with your
  storm.
¹⁶Cover their faces with shame
  so that men will seek your
  name, O LORD.

¹⁷May they ever be ashamed
  and dismayed;
  may they perish in disgrace.
¹⁸Let them know that you,
  whose name is the
  LORD—
  that you alone are the Most
  High over all the earth.

Psalm 84

*For the director of music. According
to gittith.[b] Of the Sons of Korah.
A psalm.*

¹How lovely is your dwelling
  place,
  O LORD Almighty!
²My soul yearns, even faints,
  for the courts of the LORD;
  my heart and my flesh cry out
  for the living God.

³Even the sparrow has found a
  home,
  and the swallow a nest for
  herself,
  where she may have her
  young—
  a place near your altar,
  O LORD Almighty, my King
  and my God.
⁴Blessed are those who dwell
  in your house;
  they are ever praising you.
    Selah

⁵Blessed are those whose
  strength is in you,
  who have set their hearts on
  pilgrimage.

---

*a7 That is, Byblos   bTitle: Probably a musical term

⁶As they pass through the
        Valley of Baca,
    they make it a place of
        springs;
    the autumn rains also cover
        it with pools.ᵃ
⁷They go from strength to
        strength,
    till each appears before God
        in Zion.

⁸Hear my prayer, O Lᴏʀᴅ God
        Almighty;
    listen to me, O God of
        Jacob.   Selah
⁹Look upon our shield,ᵇ
        O God;
    look with favor on your
        anointed one.

¹⁰Better is one day in your
        courts
    than a thousand elsewhere;
    I would rather be a
        doorkeeper in the
        house of my God
    than dwell in the tents of
        the wicked.
ⁱ¹For the Lᴏʀᴅ God is a sun
        and shield;
    the Lᴏʀᴅ bestows favor and
        honor;
    no good thing does he
        withhold
    from those whose walk is
        blameless.

¹²O Lᴏʀᴅ Almighty,
    blessed is the man who
        trusts in you.

Psalm 85

For the director of music. Of the
Sons of Korah. A psalm.

¹You showed favor to your
        land, O Lᴏʀᴅ;
    you restored the fortunes of
        Jacob.

²You forgave the iniquity of
        your people
    and covered all their sins.
                            Selah
³You set aside all your wrath
    and turned from your fierce
        anger.

⁴Restore us again, O God our
        Savior,
    and put away your
        displeasure
        toward us.
⁵Will you be angry with us
        forever?
    Will you prolong your anger
        through all generations?
⁶Will you not revive us again,
    that your people may rejoice
        in you?
⁷Show us your unfailing love,
        O Lᴏʀᴅ,
    and grant us your salvation.

⁸I will listen to what God the
        Lᴏʀᴅ will say;
    he promises peace to his
        people, his saints—
    but let them not return to
        folly.
⁹Surely his salvation is near
        those who fear him,
    that his glory may dwell in
        our land.

¹⁰Love and faithfulness meet
        together;
    righteousness and peace
        kiss each other.
¹¹Faithfulness springs forth
        from the earth,
    and righteousness looks
        down from heaven.
¹²The Lᴏʀᴅ will indeed give
        what is good,
    and our land will yield its
        harvest.
¹³Righteousness goes before
        him
    and prepares the way for
        his steps.

ᵃ6 Or blessings   ᵇ9 Or sovereign

Psalm 86

A prayer of David.

¹Hear, O LORD, and answer
  me,
  for I am poor and needy.
²Guard my life, for I am
  devoted to you.
  You are my God; save your
  servant
  who trusts in you.
³Have mercy on me, O Lord,
  for I call to you all day long.
⁴Bring joy to your servant,
  for to you, O Lord,
  I lift up my soul.

⁵You are forgiving and good,
  O Lord,
  abounding in love to all
  who call to you.
⁶Hear my prayer, O LORD;
  listen to my cry for mercy.
⁷In the day of my trouble I will
  call to you,
  for you will answer me.

⁸Among the gods there is none
  like you, O Lord;
  no deeds can compare with
  yours.
⁹All the nations you have
  made
  will come and worship
  before you, O Lord;
  they will bring glory to your
  name.
¹⁰For you are great and do
  marvelous deeds;
  you alone are God.

¹¹Teach me your way, O LORD,
  and I will walk in your
  truth;
  give me an undivided heart,
  that I may fear your name.
¹²I will praise you, O Lord my
  God, with all my heart;
  I will glorify your name
  forever.

¹³For great is your love toward
  me;
  you have delivered me from
  the depths of the grave.ᵃ

¹⁴The arrogant are attacking me,
  O God;
  a band of ruthless men
  seeks my life—
  men without regard for you.
¹⁵But you, O Lord, are a
  compassionate and
  gracious God,
  slow to anger, abounding in
  love and faithfulness.
¹⁶Turn to me and have mercy
  on me;
  grant your strength to your
  servant
  and save the son of your
  maidservant.ᵇ
¹⁷Give me a sign of your
  goodness,
  that my enemies may see it
  and be put to shame,
  for you, O LORD, have
  helped me and
  comforted me.

Psalm 87

Of the Sons of Korah. A psalm.
A song.

¹He has set his foundation on
  the holy mountain;
² the LORD loves the gates of
  Zion
  more than all the dwellings
  of Jacob.
³Glorious things are said of
  you,
  O city of God: *Selah*
⁴"I will record Rahabᶜ and
  Babylon
  among those who
  acknowledge me—
  Philistia too, and Tyre, along
  with Cushᵈ—

ᵃ13 Hebrew *Sheol*   ᵇ16 Or *save your faithful son*   ᶜ4 A poetic name for Egypt
ᵈ4 That is, the upper Nile region

and will say, 'This*a* one was
    born in Zion.' "
[5]Indeed, of Zion it will be said,
    "This one and that one
        were born in her,
    and the Most High himself
        will establish her."
[6]The LORD will write in the
        register of the peoples:
    "This one was born in
        Zion."   *Selah*
[7]As they make music they will
        sing,
    "All my fountains are in
        you."

Psalm 88

A song. A psalm of the Sons of
Korah. For the director of music.
According to *mahalath leannoth.*[b] A
maskil[c] of Heman the Ezrahite.

[1]O LORD, the God who saves
        me,
    day and night I cry out
        before you.
[2]May my prayer come before
        you;
    turn your ear to my cry.

16 [3]For my soul is full of trouble
    and my life draws near the
        grave.[d]
[4]I am counted among those
        who go down to the pit;
    I am like a man without
        strength.
[5]I am set apart with the dead,
    like the slain who lie in the
        grave,
    whom you remember no
        more,
    who are cut off from your
        care.
[6]You have put me in the
        lowest pit,
    in the darkest depths.
[7]Your wrath lies heavily upon
        me;

you have overwhelmed
    me with all your waves.
                                Selah
[8]You have taken from me my
        closest friends
    and have made me
        repulsive to them.
    I am confined and cannot
        escape;
[9]   my eyes are dim with grief.

I call to you, O LORD, every
        day;
    I spread out my hands to
        you.
[10]Do you show your wonders to
        the dead?
    Do those who are dead rise
        up and praise you? *Selah*
[11]Is your love declared in the
        grave,
    your faithfulness in
        Destruction[e]?
[12]Are your wonders known in
        the place of darkness,
    or your righteous deeds in
        the land of oblivion?

[13]But I cry to you for help,
        O LORD;
    in the morning my prayer
        comes before you.
[14]Why, O LORD, do you reject
        me
    and hide your face from
        me?
[15]From my youth I have been
        afflicted and close to
        death;
    I have suffered your terrors
        and am in despair.
[16]Your wrath has swept over
        me;
    your terrors have destroyed
        me.
[17]All day long they surround
        me like a flood;
    they have completely
        engulfed me.

*a*4 Or "O Rahab and Babylon, / Philistia, Tyre and Cush, / I will record concerning those
who acknowledge me: / This   *b*Title: Possibly a tune, "The Suffering of Affliction"
*c*Title: Probably a literary or musical term   *d*3 Hebrew *Sheol*   *e*11 Hebrew *Abaddon*

¹⁸You have taken my
    companions and loved
    ones from me;
  the darkness is my closest
    friend.

Psalm 89

A maskil^a of Ethan the Ezrahite.

¹I will sing of the LORD's great
    love forever;
  with my mouth I will make
    your faithfulness known
    through all generations.
²I will declare that your love
    stands firm forever,
  that you established your
    faithfulness in heaven
    itself.

³You said, "I have made a
    covenant with my
    chosen one,
  I have sworn to David my
    servant,
⁴'I will establish your line
    forever
  and make your throne firm
    through all
    generations.'"   *Selah*

⁵The heavens praise your
    wonders, O LORD,
  your faithfulness too, in the
    assembly of the holy
    ones.
⁶For who in the skies above
    can compare with the
    LORD?
  Who is like the LORD among
    the heavenly beings?
⁷In the council of the holy ones
    God is greatly feared;
  he is more awesome than all
    who surround him.
⁸O LORD God Almighty, who
    is like you?
  You are mighty, O LORD,
    and your faithfulness
    surrounds you.

⁹You rule over the surging sea;
  when its waves mount up,
    you still them.
¹⁰You crushed Rahab like one of
    the slain;
  with your strong arm you
    scattered your enemies.
¹¹The heavens are yours, and
    yours also the earth;
  you founded the world and
    all that is in it.
¹²You created the north and the
    south;
  Tabor and Hermon sing for
    joy at your name.
¹³Your arm is endued with
    power;
  your hand is strong, your
    right hand exalted.

¹⁴Righteousness and justice are
    the foundation of your
    throne;
  love and faithfulness go
    before you.
¹⁵Blessed are those who have
    learned to acclaim you,
  who walk in the light of
    your presence,
    O LORD.
¹⁶They rejoice in your name all
    day long;
  they exult in your
    righteousness.
¹⁷For you are their glory and
    strength,
  and by your favor you exalt
    our horn.^b
¹⁸Indeed, our shield^c belongs to
    the LORD,
  our king to the Holy One of
    Israel.

¹⁹Once you spoke in a vision,
  to your faithful people you
    said:
  "I have bestowed strength on
    a warrior;
  I have exalted a young man
    from among the people.

^aTitle: Probably a literary or musical term   ^b17 *Horn* here symbolizes strong one.
^c18 Or *sovereign*

20I have found David my
  servant;
    with my sacred oil I have
      anointed him.
21My hand will sustain him;
    surely my arm will
      strengthen him.
22No enemy will subject him to
      tribute;
    no wicked man will oppress
      him.
23I will crush his foes before
      him
    and strike down his
      adversaries.
24My faithful love will be with
      him,
    and through my name his
      horna will be exalted.
25I will set his hand over the
      sea,
    his right hand over the
      rivers.
26He will call out to me, 'You
      are my Father,
    my God, the Rock my
      Savior.'
27I will also appoint him my
      firstborn,
    the most exalted of the
      kings of the earth.
28I will maintain my love to him
      forever,
    and my covenant with him
      will never fail.
29I will establish his line
      forever,
    his throne as long as the
      heavens endure.

30"If his sons forsake my law
    and do not follow my
      statutes,
31if they violate my decrees
    and fail to keep my
      commands,
32I will punish their sin with the
      rod,
    their iniquity with flogging;
33but I will not take my love
    from him,

nor will I ever betray my
      faithfulness.
34I will not violate my covenant
    or alter what my lips have
      uttered.
35Once for all, I have sworn by
      my holiness—
    and I will not lie to David—
36that his line will continue
      forever
    and his throne endure
      before me like the
        sun;
37it will be established forever
      like the moon,
    the faithful witness in the
      sky."   Selah

38But you have rejected, you
      have spurned,
    you have been very angry
      with your anointed one.
39You have renounced the
      covenant with your
        servant
    and have defiled his crown
      in the dust.
40You have broken through all
      his walls
    and reduced his strongholds
      to ruins.
41All who pass by have
      plundered him;
    he has become the scorn of
      his neighbors.
42You have exalted the right
      hand of his foes;
    you have made all his
      enemies rejoice.
43You have turned back the
      edge of his sword
    and have not supported him
      in battle.
44You have put an end to his
      splendor
    and cast his throne to the
      ground.
45You have cut short the days
      of his youth;
    you have covered him with
      a mantle of shame. Selah

a24 Horn here symbolizes strength.

⁴⁶How long, O LORD? Will you
    hide yourself forever?
  How long will your wrath
    burn like fire?
⁴⁷Remember how fleeting is my
    life.
  For what futility you have
    created all men!
⁴⁸What man can live and not
    see death,
  or save himself from the
    power of the graveᵃ?
                              Selah
⁴⁹O Lord, where is your former
    great love,
  which in your faithfulness
    you swore to David?
⁵⁰Remember, Lord, how your
    servant hasᵇ been
    mocked,
  how I bear in my heart the
    taunts of all the nations,
⁵¹the taunts with which your
    enemies have mocked,
    O LORD,
  with which they have
    mocked every step of
    your anointed one.

⁵²Praise be to the LORD forever!
  Amen and Amen.

BOOK IV

Psalms 90-106

Psalm 90

A prayer of Moses the man of God.

¹Lord, you have been our
    dwelling place
  throughout all generations.
²Before the mountains were
    born
  or you brought forth the
    earth and the world,
  from everlasting to
    everlasting you are God.

³You turn men back to dust,
  saying, "Return to dust,
    O sons of men."
⁴For a thousand years in your
    sight
  are like a day that has just
    gone by,
  or like a watch in the night.
⁵You sweep men away in the
    sleep of death;
  they are like the new grass
    of the morning—
⁶though in the morning it
    springs up new,
  by evening it is dry and
    withered.

⁷We are consumed by your
    anger
  and terrified by your
    indignation.
⁸You have set our iniquities
    before you,
  our secret sins in the light
    of your presence.
⁹All our days pass away under
    your wrath;
  we finish our years with a
    moan.
¹⁰The length of our days is
    seventy years—
  or eighty, if we have the
    strength;
  yet their spanᶜ is but trouble
    and sorrow,
  for they quickly pass, and
    we fly away.

¹¹Who knows the power of
    your anger?
  For your wrath is as great as
    the fear that is due you.
¹²Teach us to number our days   98
    aright,
  that we may gain a heart of
    wisdom.
¹³Relent, O LORD! How long
    will it be?
  Have compassion on your
    servants.

ᵃ48 Hebrew *Sheol*   ᵇ50 Or *your servants have*   ᶜ10 Or *yet the best of them*

¹⁴Satisfy us in the morning with
　　your unfailing love,
　　that we may sing for joy
　　and be glad all
　　our days.
¹⁵Make us glad for as many
　　days as you have
　　afflicted us,
　　for as many years as we
　　have seen trouble.
¹⁶May your deeds be shown to
　　your servants,
　　your splendor to their
　　children.

¹⁷May the favor*a* of the Lord
　　our God rest upon us;
　　establish the work of our
　　hands for us—
　　yes, establish the work of
　　our hands.

Psalm 91

81 ¹He who dwells in the shelter
　　of the Most High
　　will rest in the shadow of
　　the Almighty.*b*
²I will say*c* of the LORD, "He is
　　my refuge and my
　　fortress,
　　my God, in whom I trust."

³Surely he will save you from
　　the fowler's snare
　　and from the deadly
　　pestilence.
⁴He will cover you with his
　　feathers,
　　and under his wings you
　　will find refuge;
　　his faithfulness will be your
　　shield and rampart.

26 ⁵You will not fear the terror of
　　night,
　　nor the arrow that flies by
　　day,
⁶nor the pestilence that stalks
　　in the darkness,

nor the plague that destroys
　　at midday.
⁷A thousand may fall at your
　　side,
　　ten thousand at your right
　　hand,
　　but it will not come near
　　you.
⁸You will only observe with
　　your eyes
　　and see the punishment of
　　the wicked.

⁹If you make the Most High
　　your dwelling—
　　even the LORD, who is my
　　refuge—
¹⁰then no harm will befall you,
　　no disaster will come near
　　your tent.
¹¹For he will command his
　　angels concerning you
　　to guard you in all your
　　ways;
¹²they will lift you up in their
　　hands,
　　so that you will not strike
　　your foot against a
　　stone.
¹³You will tread upon the lion
　　and the cobra;
　　you will trample the great
　　lion and the serpent.

¹⁴"Because he loves me," says
　　the LORD, "I will rescue
　　him;
　　I will protect him, for he
　　acknowledges my name.
¹⁵He will call upon me, and I
　　will answer him;
　　I will be with him in
　　trouble,
　　I will deliver him and honor
　　him.
¹⁶With long life will I satisfy
　　him
　　and show him my
　　salvation."

*a*17 Or *beauty*　　*b*1 Hebrew *Shaddai*　　*c*2 Or *He says*

Psalm 92

A psalm. A song. For the Sabbath
day.

[1]It is good to praise the LORD
    and make music to your
        name, O Most High,
[2]to proclaim your love in the
        morning
    and your faithfulness at
        night,
[3]to the music of the
        ten-stringed lyre
    and the melody of the harp.

[4]For you make me glad by
        your deeds, O LORD;
    I sing for joy at the works of
        your hands.
[5]How great are your works,
        O LORD,
    how profound your
        thoughts!
[6]The senseless man does not
        know,
    fools do not understand,
[7]that though the wicked spring
        up like grass
    and all evildoers flourish,
they will be forever destroyed.

[8]But you, O LORD, are exalted
        forever.

[9]For surely your enemies,
        O LORD,
    surely your enemies will
        perish;
    all evildoers will be
        scattered.
[10]You have exalted my horn[a]
        like that of a wild ox;
    fine oils have been poured
        upon me.
[11]My eyes have seen the defeat
        of my adversaries;
    my ears have heard the rout
        of my wicked foes.

[12]The righteous will flourish like
        a palm tree,
    they will grow like a cedar
        of Lebanon;

[a]10 Horn here symbolizes strength.

[13]planted in the house of the
        LORD,
    they will flourish in the
        courts of our God.
[14]They will still bear fruit in old
        age,
    they will stay fresh and
        green,
[15]proclaiming, "The LORD is
        upright;
    he is my Rock, and there is
        no wickedness in him."

Psalm 93

[1]The LORD reigns, he is robed
        in majesty;
    the LORD is robed in
        majesty
    and is armed with strength.
The world is firmly
        established;
    it cannot be moved.
[2]Your throne was established
        long ago;
    you are from all eternity.

[3]The seas have lifted up,
        O LORD,
    the seas have lifted up their
        voice;
    the seas have lifted up their
        pounding waves.
[4]Mightier than the thunder of
        the great waters,
    mightier than the breakers
        of the sea—
    the LORD on high is mighty.

[5]Your statutes stand firm;
    holiness adorns your house
    for endless days, O LORD.

Psalm 94

[1]O LORD, the God who
        avenges,
    O God who avenges, shine
        forth.

²Rise up, O Judge of the earth;
    pay back to the proud what
        they deserve.
³How long will the wicked,
        O LORD,
    how long will the wicked be
        jubilant?
⁴They pour out arrogant
        words;
    all the evildoers are full of
        boasting.
⁵They crush your people,
        O LORD;
    they oppress your
        inheritance.
⁶They slay the widow and the
        alien;
    they murder the fatherless.
⁷They say, "The LORD does not
        see;
    the God of Jacob pays no
        heed."

⁸Take heed, you senseless ones
        among the people;
    you fools, when will you
        become wise?
⁹Does he who implanted the
        ear not hear?
    Does he who formed the
        eye not see?
¹⁰Does he who disciplines
        nations not punish?
    Does he who teaches man
        lack knowledge?
¹¹The LORD knows the thoughts
        of man;
    he knows that they are
        futile.

¹²Blessed is the man you
        discipline, O LORD,
    the man you teach from
        your law;
¹³you grant him relief from days
        of trouble,
    till a pit is dug for the
        wicked.
¹⁴For the LORD will not reject
        his people;
    he will never forsake his
        inheritance.

¹⁵Judgment will again be
        founded on
        righteousness,
    and all the upright in heart
        will follow it.

¹⁶Who will rise up for me
        against the wicked?
    Who will take a stand for
        me against evildoers?
¹⁷Unless the LORD had given
        me help,
    I would soon have dwelt in
        the silence of death.
¹⁸When I said, "My foot is
        slipping,"
    your love, O LORD,
        supported me.
¹⁹When anxiety was great
        within me,
    your consolation brought
        joy to my soul.

²⁰Can a corrupt throne be allied
        with you—
    one that brings on misery
        by its decrees?
²¹They band together against
        the righteous
    and condemn the innocent
        to death.
²²But the LORD has become my
        fortress,
    and my God the rock in
        whom I take refuge.
²³He will repay them for their
        sins
    and destroy them for their
        wickedness;
    the LORD our God will
        destroy them.

Psalm 95

¹Come, let us sing for joy to
        the LORD;
    let us shout aloud to the
        Rock of our salvation.
²Let us come before him with
        thanksgiving
    and extol him with music
        and song.

³For the LORD is the great God,
   the great King above all
      gods.
⁴In his hand are the depths of
      the earth,
   and the mountain peaks
      belong to him.
⁵The sea is his, for he made it,
   and his hands formed the
      dry land.

⁶Come, let us bow down in
      worship,
   let us kneel before the LORD
      our Maker;
⁷for he is our God
   and we are the people of his
      pasture,
   the flock under his care.

Today, if you hear his voice,
⁸   do not harden your hearts
         as you did at Meribah,ᵃ
   as you did that day at
      Massahᵇ in the desert,
⁹where your fathers tested and
      tried me,
   though they had seen what
      I did.
¹⁰For forty years I was angry
      with that generation;
   I said, "They are a people
      whose hearts go astray,
   and they have not known
      my ways."
¹¹So I declared on oath in my
      anger,
   "They shall never enter my
      rest."

Psalm 96

¹Sing to the LORD a new song;
   sing to the LORD, all the
      earth.
²Sing to the LORD, praise his
      name;

   proclaim his salvation day
      after day.
³Declare his glory among the
      nations,
   his marvelous deeds among
      all peoples.

⁴For great is the LORD and
      most worthy of praise;
   he is to be feared above all
      gods.
⁵For all the gods of the nations
      are idols,
   but the LORD made the
      heavens.
⁶Splendor and majesty are
      before him;
   strength and glory are in his
      sanctuary.

⁷Ascribe to the LORD,
   O families of nations,
   ascribe to the LORD glory
      and strength.
⁸Ascribe to the LORD the glory
      due his name;
   bring an offering and come
      into his courts.
⁹Worship the LORD in the
      splendor of hisᶜ holiness;
   tremble before him, all the
      earth.

¹⁰Say among the nations, "The
      LORD reigns."
   The world is firmly
      established, it cannot be
      moved;
   he will judge the peoples
      with equity.
¹¹Let the heavens rejoice, let the
      earth be glad;
   let the sea resound, and all
      that is in it;
¹²   let the fields be jubilant,
         and everything in them.
   Then all the trees of the forest
      will sing for joy;

ᵃ8 Meribah means quarreling.   ᵇ8 Massah means testing.   ᶜ9 Or LORD with the splendor of

¹³ they will sing before the
        LORD, for he comes,
he comes to judge the earth.
He will judge the world in
        righteousness
    and the peoples in his truth.

Psalm 97

37 ¹The LORD reigns, let the earth
        be glad;
    let the distant shores rejoice.

²Clouds and thick darkness
        surround him;
    righteousness and justice
        are the foundation of his
        throne.
³Fire goes before him
    and consumes his foes on
        every side.
⁴His lightning lights up the
        world;
    the earth sees and trembles.
⁵The mountains melt like wax
        before the LORD,
    before the Lord of all the
        earth.
⁶The heavens proclaim his
        righteousness,
    and all the peoples see his
        glory.

⁷All who worship images are
        put to shame,
    those who boast in idols—
    worship him, all you gods!

⁸Zion hears and rejoices
    and the villages of Judah are
        glad
    because of your judgments,
        O LORD.
⁹For you, O LORD, are the
        Most High over all the
        earth;
    you are exalted far above all
        gods.

¹⁰Let those who love the LORD
        hate evil,
    for he guards the lives of
        his faithful ones

and delivers them from the
        hand of the wicked.
¹¹Light is shed upon the
        righteous
    and joy on the upright in
        heart.
¹²Rejoice in the LORD, you who
        are righteous,
    and praise his holy name.

Psalm 98

A psalm.

¹Sing to the LORD a new song,
    for he has done marvelous
        things;
    his right hand and his holy
        arm
    have worked salvation for
        him.
²The LORD has made his
        salvation known
    and revealed his
        righteousness to the
        nations.
³He has remembered his love
    and his faithfulness to the
        house of Israel;
all the ends of the earth have
        seen
    the salvation of our God.

⁴Shout for joy to the LORD, all
        the earth,
    burst into jubilant song with
        music;
⁵make music to the LORD with
        the harp,
    with the harp and the
        sound of singing,
⁶with trumpets and the blast of
        the ram's horn—
    shout for joy before the
        LORD, the King.

⁷Let the sea resound, and
        everything in it,
    the world, and all who live
        in it.
⁸Let the rivers clap their
        hands,

let the mountains sing
    together for joy;
⁹let them sing before the LORD,
    for he comes to judge the
    earth.
He will judge the world in
    righteousness
    and the peoples with equity.

Psalm 99

¹The LORD reigns,
    let the nations tremble;
he sits enthroned between the
    cherubim,
    let the earth shake.
²Great is the LORD in Zion;
    he is exalted over all the
    nations.
³Let them praise your great
    and awesome name—
    he is holy.

⁴The King is mighty, he loves
    justice—
    you have established equity;
in Jacob you have done
    what is just and right.
⁵Exalt the LORD our God
    and worship at his footstool;
    he is holy.

⁶Moses and Aaron were among
    his priests,
    Samuel was among those
    who called on his name;
they called on the LORD
    and he answered them.
⁷He spoke to them from the
    pillar of cloud;
    they kept his statutes and
    the decrees he gave
    them.

⁸O LORD our God,
    you answered them;
you were to Israel[a] a forgiving
    God,
    though you punished their
    misdeeds.[b]
⁹Exalt the LORD our God

and worship at his holy
    mountain,
    for the LORD our God is
    holy.

Psalm 100

A psalm. For giving thanks.

¹Shout for joy to the LORD, all
    the earth.
² Worship the LORD with
    gladness;
    come before him with joyful
    songs.
³Know that the LORD is God.
    It is he who made us, and
    we are his[c];
    we are his people, the
    sheep of his pasture.

⁴Enter his gates with
    thanksgiving
    and his courts with praise;
    give thanks to him and
    praise his name.
⁵For the LORD is good and his
    love endures forever;
    his faithfulness continues
    through all generations.

Psalm 101

Of David. A psalm.

¹I will sing of your love and
    justice;
    to you, O LORD, I will sing
    praise.
²I will be careful to lead a
    blameless life—
    when will you come to me?

I will walk in my house
    with blameless heart.
³I will set before my eyes
    no vile thing.

The deeds of faithless men I
    hate;
    they will not cling to me.

ᵃ8 Hebrew *them*   ᵇ8 Or *I an avenger of the wrongs done to them*   ᶜ3 Or *and not we
ourselves*

⁴Men of perverse heart shall be
    far from me;
  I will have nothing to do
    with evil.

⁵Whoever slanders his
    neighbor in secret,
  him I will put to silence;
whoever has haughty eyes
    and a proud heart,
  him I will not endure.

⁶My eyes will be on the faithful
    in the land,
  that they may dwell with
    me;
he whose walk is blameless
  will minister to me.

⁷No one who practices deceit
    will dwell in my house;
no one who speaks falsely
  will stand in my presence.

⁸Every morning I will put to
    silence
  all the wicked in the land;
I will cut off every evildoer
  from the city of the LORD.

Psalm 102

A prayer of an afflicted man. When
he is faint and pours out his lament
before the LORD.

¹Hear my prayer, O LORD;
  let my cry for help come to
    you.
²Do not hide your face from
    me
  when I am in distress.
Turn your ear to me;
  when I call, answer me
    quickly.

³For my days vanish like
    smoke;
  my bones burn like glowing
    embers.
⁴My heart is blighted and
    withered like grass;
  I forget to eat my food.
⁵Because of my loud groaning

I am reduced to skin and
    bones.
⁶I am like a desert owl,
  like an owl among the
    ruins.
⁷I lie awake; I have become
  like a bird alone on a roof.
⁸All day long my enemies
    taunt me;
  those who rail against me
    use my name as a curse.
⁹For I eat ashes as my food
  and mingle my drink with
    tears
¹⁰because of your great wrath,
  for you have taken me up
    and thrown me aside.
¹¹My days are like the evening
    shadow;
  I wither away like grass.

¹²But you, O LORD, sit
    enthroned forever;
  your renown endures
    through all
    generations.
¹³You will arise and have
    compassion on Zion,
  for it is time to show favor
    to her;
  the appointed time has
    come.
¹⁴For her stones are dear to
    your servants;
  her very dust moves them
    to pity.
¹⁵The nations will fear the name
    of the LORD,
  all the kings of the earth
    will revere your glory.
¹⁶For the LORD will rebuild Zion
  and appear in his glory.
¹⁷He will respond to the prayer
    of the destitute;
  he will not despise their
    plea.

¹⁸Let this be written for a future
    generation,
  that a people not yet created
    may praise the LORD:

¹⁹"The LORD looked down from
his sanctuary on high,
from heaven he viewed the
earth,
²⁰to hear the groans of the
prisoners
and release those
condemned to death."
²¹So the name of the LORD will
be declared in Zion
and his praise in Jerusalem
²²when the peoples and the
kingdoms
assemble to worship the
LORD.

²³In the course of my life*a* he
broke my strength;
he cut short my days.
²⁴So I said:
"Do not take me away,
O my God, in the midst
of my days;
your years go on through all
generations.
²⁵In the beginning you laid the
foundations of the earth,
and the heavens are the
work of your hands.
²⁶They will perish, but you
remain;
they will all wear out like a
garment.
Like clothing you will change
them
and they will be discarded.
²⁷But you remain the same,
and your years will never
end.
²⁸The children of your servants
will live in your
presence;
their descendants will be
established before you."

Psalm 103

Of David.

¹Praise the LORD, O my soul;
all my inmost being, praise
his holy name.

²Praise the LORD, O my soul,
and forget not all his
benefits—
³who forgives all your sins 28
and heals all your diseases,
⁴who redeems your life from
the pit
and crowns you with love
and compassion,
⁵who satisfies your desires
with good things
so that your youth is
renewed like the eagle's.

⁶The LORD works righteousness
and justice for all the
oppressed.

⁷He made known his ways to
Moses,
his deeds to the people of
Israel:
⁸The LORD is compassionate
and gracious,
slow to anger, abounding in
love.
⁹He will not always accuse,
nor will he harbor his anger
forever;
¹⁰he does not treat us as our
sins deserve
or repay us according to our
iniquities.
¹¹For as high as the heavens are
above the earth,
so great is his love for those
who fear him;
¹²as far as the east is from the
west,
so far has he removed our
transgressions from us.
¹³As a father has compassion on
his children,
so the LORD has compassion
on those who fear him;
¹⁴for he knows how we are
formed,
he remembers that we are
dust.
¹⁵As for man, his days are like
grass,

a23 Or By his power

he flourishes like a flower of
  the field;
[16]the wind blows over it and it
  is gone,
  and its place remembers it
  no more.
[17]But from everlasting to
  everlasting
  the LORD's love is with
  those who fear him,
  and his righteousness with
  their children's
  children—
[18]with those who keep his
  covenant
  and remember to obey his
  precepts.

[19]The LORD has established his
  throne in heaven,
  and his kingdom rules over
  all.

[20]Praise the LORD, you his
  angels,
  you mighty ones who do
  his bidding,
  who obey his word.
[21]Praise the LORD, all his
  heavenly hosts,
  you his servants who do his
  will.
[22]Praise the LORD, all his works
  everywhere in his
  dominion.

  Praise the LORD, O my soul.

Psalm 104

[1]Praise the LORD, O my soul.

  O LORD my God, you are very
  great;
  you are clothed with
  splendor and majesty.
[2]He wraps himself in light as
  with a garment;
  he stretches out the heavens
  like a tent
[3] and lays the beams of his
  upper chambers on their
  waters.

He makes the clouds his
  chariot
  and rides on the wings of
  the wind.
[4]He makes winds his
  messengers,[a]
  flames of fire his servants.

[5]He set the earth on its
  foundations;
  it can never be moved.
[6]You covered it with the deep
  as with a garment;
  the waters stood above the
  mountains.
[7]But at your rebuke the waters
  fled,
  at the sound of your
  thunder they took to
  flight;
[8]they flowed over the
  mountains,
  they went down into the
  valleys,
  to the place you assigned
  for them.
[9]You set a boundary they
  cannot cross;
  never again will they cover
  the earth.

[10]He makes springs pour water
  into the ravines;
  it flows between the
  mountains.
[11]They give water to all the
  beasts of the field;
  the wild donkeys quench
  their thirst.
[12]The birds of the air nest by
  the waters;
  they sing among the
  branches.
[13]He waters the mountains from
  his upper chambers;
  the earth is satisfied by the
  fruit of his work.
[14]He makes grass grow for the
  cattle,
  and plants for man to
  cultivate—

[a]4 Or *angels*

bringing forth food from the
earth:
¹⁵wine that gladdens the heart
of man,
oil to make his face shine,
and bread that sustains his
heart.
¹⁶The trees of the LORD are well
watered,
the cedars of Lebanon that
he planted.
¹⁷There the birds make their
nests;
the stork has its home in
the pine trees.
¹⁸The high mountains belong to
the wild goats;
the crags are a refuge for
the coneys.[a]

¹⁹The moon marks off the
seasons,
and the sun knows when to
go down.
²⁰You bring darkness, it
becomes night,
and all the beasts of the
forest prowl.
²¹The lions roar for their prey
and seek their food from
God.
²²The sun rises, and they steal
away;
they return and lie down in
their dens.
²³Then man goes out to his
work,
to his labor until evening.

²⁴How many are your works,
O LORD!
In wisdom you made them
all;
the earth is full of your
creatures.
²⁵There is the sea, vast and
spacious,
teeming with creatures
beyond number—
living things both large and
small.

²⁶There the ships go to and fro,
and the leviathan, which
you formed to frolic
there.

²⁷These all look to you
to give them their food at
the proper time.
²⁸When you give it to them,
they gather it up;
when you open your hand,
they are satisfied with good
things.
²⁹When you hide your face,
they are terrified;
when you take away their
breath,
they die and return to the
dust.
³⁰When you send your Spirit,
they are created,
and you renew the face of
the earth.

³¹May the glory of the LORD
endure forever;
may the LORD rejoice in his
works—
³²he who looks at the earth,
and it trembles,
who touches the mountains,
and they smoke.

³³I will sing to the LORD all my
life;
I will sing praise to my God
as long as I live.
³⁴May my meditation be
pleasing to him,
as I rejoice in the LORD.
³⁵But may sinners vanish from
the earth
and the wicked be no more.

Praise the LORD, O my soul.

Praise the LORD.[b]

Psalm 105

¹Give thanks to the LORD, call
on his name;

---

[a]18 That is, the hyrax or rock badger   [b]35 Hebrew *Hallelu Yah*; in the Septuagint
this line stands at the beginning of Psalm 105.

make known among the
nations what he has
done.
²Sing to him, sing praise to
him;
tell of all his wonderful acts.
³Glory in his holy name;
let the hearts of those who
seek the LORD rejoice.
⁴Look to the LORD and his
strength;
seek his face always.

⁵Remember the wonders he
has done,
his miracles, and the
judgments he
pronounced,
⁶O descendants of Abraham
his servant,
O sons of Jacob, his chosen
ones.
⁷He is the LORD our God;
his judgments are in all the
earth.

⁸He remembers his covenant
forever,
the word he commanded,
for a thousand
generations,
⁹the covenant he made with
Abraham,
the oath he swore to Isaac.
¹⁰He confirmed it to Jacob as a
decree,
to Israel as an everlasting
covenant:
¹¹"To you I will give the land of
Canaan
as the portion you will
inherit."

¹²When they were but few in
number,
few indeed, and strangers
in it,
¹³they wandered from nation to
nation,
from one kingdom to
another.
¹⁴He allowed no one to oppress
them;

for their sake he rebuked
kings:
¹⁵"Do not touch my anointed
ones;
do my prophets no harm."

¹⁶He called down famine on the
land
and destroyed all their
supplies of food;
¹⁷and he sent a man before
them—
Joseph, sold as a slave.
¹⁸They bruised his feet with
shackles,
his neck was put in irons,
¹⁹till what he foretold came to
pass,
till the word of the LORD
proved him true.
²⁰The king sent and released
him,
the ruler of peoples set him
free.
²¹He made him master of his
household,
ruler over all he possessed,
²²to instruct his princes as he
pleased
and teach his elders
wisdom.

²³Then Israel entered Egypt;
Jacob lived as an alien in the
land of Ham.
²⁴The LORD made his people
very fruitful;
he made them too
numerous for
their foes,
²⁵whose hearts he turned to
hate his people,
to conspire against his
servants.
²⁶He sent Moses his servant,
and Aaron, whom he had
chosen.
²⁷They performed his
miraculous signs among
them,
his wonders in the land of
Ham.

²⁸He sent darkness and made
the land dark—
for had they not rebelled
against his words?
²⁹He turned their waters into
blood,
causing their fish to die.
³⁰Their land teemed with frogs,
which went up into the
bedrooms of their rulers.
³¹He spoke, and there came
swarms of flies,
and gnats throughout their
country.
³²He turned their rain into hail,
with lightning throughout
their land;
³³he struck down their vines
and fig trees
and shattered the trees of
their country.
³⁴He spoke, and the locusts
came,
grasshoppers without
number;
³⁵they ate up every green thing
in their land,
ate up the produce of their
soil.
³⁶Then he struck down all the
firstborn in their land,
the firstfruits of all their
manhood.
³⁷He brought out Israel, laden
with silver and gold,
and from among their tribes
no one faltered.
³⁸Egypt was glad when they
left,
because dread of Israel had
fallen on them.
³⁹He spread out a cloud as a
covering,
and a fire to give light at
night.
⁴⁰They asked, and he brought
them quail
and satisfied them with the
bread of heaven.

⁴¹He opened the rock, and
water gushed out;
like a river it flowed in the
desert.

⁴²For he remembered his holy
promise
given to his servant
Abraham.
⁴³He brought out his people
with rejoicing,
his chosen ones with shouts
of joy;
⁴⁴he gave them the lands of the
nations,
and they fell heir to what
others had toiled for—
⁴⁵that they might keep his
precepts
and observe his laws.

Praise the LORD. [a]

Psalm 106

¹Praise the LORD. [b]

Give thanks to the LORD, for
he is good;
his love endures forever.
²Who can proclaim the mighty
acts of the LORD
or fully declare his praise?
³Blessed are they who maintain
justice,
who constantly do what is
right.
⁴Remember me, O LORD, when
you show favor to your
people,
come to my aid when you
save them,
⁵that I may enjoy the
prosperity of your
chosen ones,
that I may share in the joy
of your nation
and join your inheritance in
giving praise.

---

[a]45 Hebrew *Hallelu Yah*   [b]1 Hebrew *Hallelu Yah*; also in verse 48

⁶We have sinned, even as our
     fathers did;
  we have done wrong and
     acted wickedly.
⁷When our fathers were in
     Egypt,
  they gave no thought to
     your miracles;
  they did not remember your
     many kindnesses,
  and they rebelled by the
     sea, the Red Sea.ᵃ
⁸Yet he saved them for his
     name's sake,
  to make his mighty power
     known.
⁹He rebuked the Red Sea, and
     it dried up;
  he led them through the
     depths as through a
     desert.
¹⁰He saved them from the hand
     of the foe;
  from the hand of the enemy
     he redeemed them.
¹¹The waters covered their
     adversaries;
  not one of them survived.
¹²Then they believed his
     promises
  and sang his praise.

¹³But they soon forgot what he
     had done
  and did not wait for his
     counsel.
¹⁴In the desert they gave in to
     their craving;
  in the wasteland they put
     God to the test.
¹⁵So he gave them what they
     asked for,
  but sent a wasting disease
     upon them.

¹⁶In the camp they grew
     envious of Moses
  and of Aaron, who was
     consecrated to the LORD.
¹⁷The earth opened up and
     swallowed Dathan;

it buried the company of
     Abiram.
¹⁸Fire blazed among their
     followers;
  a flame consumed the
     wicked.

¹⁹At Horeb they made a calf
  and worshiped an idol cast
     from metal.
²⁰They exchanged their Glory
  for an image of a bull,
     which eats grass.
²¹They forgot the God who
     saved them,
  who had done great things
     in Egypt,
²²miracles in the land of Ham
  and awesome deeds by the
     Red Sea.
²³So he said he would destroy
     them—
  had not Moses, his chosen
     one,
  stood in the breach before him
  to keep his wrath from
     destroying them.

²⁴Then they despised the
     pleasant land;
  they did not believe his
     promise.
²⁵They grumbled in their tents
  and did not obey the LORD.
²⁶So he swore to them with
     uplifted hand
  that he would make them
     fall in the desert,
²⁷make their descendants fall
     among the nations
  and scatter them throughout
     the lands.

²⁸They yoked themselves to the
     Baal of Peor
  and ate sacrifices offered to
     lifeless gods;
²⁹they provoked the LORD to
     anger by their wicked
     deeds,
  and a plague broke out
     among them.

ᵃ7 Hebrew *Yam Suph*; that is, Sea of Reeds; also in verses 9 and 22

³⁰But Phinehas stood up and
intervened,
and the plague was
checked.
³¹This was credited to him as
righteousness
for endless generations to
come.

³²By the waters of Meribah they
angered the LORD,
and trouble came to Moses
because of them;
³³for they rebelled against the
Spirit of God,
and rash words came from
Moses' lips.ᵈ

³⁴They did not destroy the
peoples
as the LORD had
commanded them,
³⁵but they mingled with the
nations
and adopted their customs.
³⁶They worshiped their idols,
which became a snare to
them.
³⁷They sacrificed their sons
and their daughters to
demons.
³⁸They shed innocent blood,
the blood of their sons and
daughters,
whom they sacrificed to the
idols of Canaan,
and the land was desecrated
by their blood.
³⁹They defiled themselves by
what they did;
by their deeds they
prostituted
themselves.

⁴⁰Therefore the LORD was angry
with his people
and abhorred his
inheritance.
⁴¹He handed them over to the
nations,

and their foes ruled over
them.
⁴²Their enemies oppressed them
and subjected them to their
power.
⁴³Many times he delivered
them,
but they were bent on
rebellion
and they wasted away in
their sin.

⁴⁴But he took note of their
distress
when he heard their cry;
⁴⁵for their sake he remembered
his covenant
and out of his great love he
relented.
⁴⁶He caused them to be pitied
by all who held them
captive.

⁴⁷Save us, O LORD our God,
and gather us from the
nations,
that we may give thanks to
your holy name
and glory in your praise.

⁴⁸Praise be to the LORD, the
God of Israel,
from everlasting to
everlasting.
Let all the people say,
"Amen!"

Praise the LORD.

BOOK V

Psalms 107-150

Psalm 107

¹Give thanks to the LORD, for
he is good;
his love endures forever.
²Let the redeemed of the LORD
say this—
those he redeemed from the
hand of the foe,

ᵈ33 Or *against his spirit, / and rash words came from his lips*

³those he gathered from the
    lands,
  from east and west, from
    north and south.ᵃ

⁴Some wandered in desert
    wastelands,
  finding no way to a city
    where they could settle.
⁵They were hungry and
    thirsty,
  and their lives ebbed away.
⁶Then they cried out to the
    Lᴏʀᴅ in their trouble,
  and he delivered them from
    their distress.
⁷He led them by a straight way
  to a city where they could
    settle.
⁸Let them give thanks to the
    Lᴏʀᴅ for his unfailing
    love
  and his wonderful deeds for
    men,
⁹for he satisfies the thirsty
  and fills the hungry with
    good things.

¹⁰Some sat in darkness and the
    deepest gloom,
  prisoners suffering in iron
    chains,
¹¹for they had rebelled against
    the words of God
  and despised the counsel of
    the Most High.
¹²So he subjected them to bitter
    labor;
  they stumbled, and there
    was no one to help.
¹³Then they cried to the Lᴏʀᴅ
    in their trouble,
  and he saved them from
    their distress.
¹⁴He brought them out of
    darkness and the
    deepest gloom
  and broke away their
    chains.
¹⁵Let them give thanks to the
    Lᴏʀᴅ for his unfailing
    love

and his wonderful deeds for
    men,
¹⁶for he breaks down gates of
    bronze
  and cuts through bars of
    iron.

¹⁷Some became fools through
    their rebellious ways
  and suffered affliction
    because of their
    iniquities.
¹⁸They loathed all food
  and drew near the gates of
    death.
¹⁹Then they cried to the Lᴏʀᴅ
    in their trouble,
  and he saved them from
    their distress.
²⁰He sent forth his word and
    healed them;
  he rescued them from the
    grave.
²¹Let them give thanks to the
    Lᴏʀᴅ for his unfailing
    love
  and his wonderful deeds for
    men.
²²Let them sacrifice thank
    offerings
  and tell of his works with
    songs of joy.

²³Others went out on the sea in
    ships;
  they were merchants on the
    mighty waters.
²⁴They saw the works of the
    Lᴏʀᴅ,
  his wonderful deeds in the
    deep.
²⁵For he spoke and stirred up a
    tempest
  that lifted high the waves.
²⁶They mounted up to the
    heavens and went down
    to the depths;
  in their peril their courage
    melted away.
²⁷They reeled and staggered like
    drunken men;
  they were at their wits' end.

ᵃ3 Hebrew *north and the sea*

²⁸Then they cried out to the
LORD in their trouble,
and he brought them out of
their distress.
²⁹He stilled the storm to a
whisper;
the waves of the sea were
hushed.
³⁰They were glad when it grew
calm,
and he guided them to their
desired haven.
³¹Let them give thanks to the
LORD for his unfailing
love
and his wonderful deeds for
men.
³²Let them exalt him in the
assembly of the people
and praise him in the
council of the elders.

³³He turned rivers into a desert,
flowing springs into thirsty
ground,
³⁴and fruitful land into a salt
waste,
because of the wickedness
of those who lived there.
³⁵He turned the desert into
pools of water
and the parched ground
into flowing springs;
³⁶there he brought the hungry
to live,
and they founded a city
where they could settle.
³⁷They sowed fields and
planted vineyards
that yielded a fruitful
harvest;
³⁸he blessed them, and their
numbers greatly
increased,
and he did not let their
herds diminish.

³⁹Then their numbers
decreased, and they
were humbled
by oppression, calamity and
sorrow;
⁴⁰he who pours contempt on
nobles
made them wander in a
trackless waste.
⁴¹But he lifted the needy out of
their affliction
and increased their families
like flocks.
⁴²The upright see and rejoice,
but all the wicked shut their
mouths.

⁴³Whoever is wise, let him heed
these things
and consider the great love
of the LORD.

Psalm 108

A song. A psalm of David.

¹My heart is steadfast, O God;
I will sing and make music
with all my soul.
²Awake, harp and lyre!
I will awaken the dawn.
³I will praise you, O LORD,
among the nations;
I will sing of you among the
peoples.
⁴For great is your love, higher
than the heavens;
your faithfulness reaches to
the skies.
⁵Be exalted, O God, above the
heavens,
and let your glory be over
all the earth.

⁶Save us and help us with your
right hand,
that those you love may be
delivered.
⁷God has spoken from his
sanctuary:
"In triumph I will parcel out
Shechem
and measure off the Valley
of Succoth.
⁸Gilead is mine, Manasseh is
mine;
Ephraim is my helmet,

Judah my scepter.
⁹Moab is my washbasin,
  upon Edom I toss my
    sandal;
  over Philistia I shout in
    triumph."

¹⁰Who will bring me to the
    fortified city?
  Who will lead me to Edom?
¹¹Is it not you, O God, you
    who have rejected us
  and no longer go out with
    our armies?
¹²Give us aid against the
    enemy,
  for the help of man is
    worthless.
¹³With God we will gain the
    victory,
  and he will trample down
    our enemies.

Psalm 109

For the director of music. Of David.
A psalm.

¹O God, whom I praise,
  do not remain silent,
²for wicked and deceitful men
    have opened their mouths
    against me;
  they have spoken against
    me with lying tongues.
³With words of hatred they
    surround me;
  they attack me without
    cause.
⁴In return for my friendship
    they accuse me,
  but I am a man of prayer.
⁵They repay me evil for good,
  and hatred for my
    friendship.

⁶Appoint*a* an evil man*b* to
    oppose him;
  let an accuser*c* stand at his
    right hand.

⁷When he is tried, let him be
    found guilty,
  and may his prayers
    condemn him.
⁸May his days be few;
  may another take his place
    of leadership.
⁹May his children be fatherless
  and his wife a widow.
¹⁰May his children be
    wandering
    beggars;
  may they be driven*d* from
    their ruined homes.
¹¹May a creditor seize all he
    has;
  may strangers plunder the
    fruits of his labor.
¹²May no one extend kindness
    to him
  or take pity on his fatherless
    children.
¹³May his descendants be cut
    off,
  their names blotted out from
    the next generation.
¹⁴May the iniquity of his fathers
    be remembered before
    the LORD;
  may the sin of his mother
    never be blotted out.
¹⁵May their sins always remain
    before the LORD,
  that he may cut off the
    memory of them from
    the earth.

¹⁶For he never thought of doing
    a kindness,
  but hounded to death the
    poor
  and the needy and the
    brokenhearted.
¹⁷He loved to pronounce a
    curse—
  may it*e* come on him;
  he found no pleasure in
    blessing—
  may it be*f* far from him.

a6 Or They say: "Appoint (with quotation marks at the end of verse 19)   *b6 Or the
Evil One   *c6 Or let Satan   *d10 Septuagint; Hebrew sought   *e17 Or curse, / and it
has   *f17 Or blessing, / and it is*

¹⁸He wore cursing as his
    garment;
  it entered into his body like
    water,
  into his bones like oil.
¹⁹May it be like a cloak
    wrapped about him,
  like a belt tied forever
    around him.
²⁰May this be the LORD's
    payment to my accusers,
  to those who speak evil of
    me.

²¹But you, O Sovereign LORD,
    deal well with me for your
    name's sake;
  out of the goodness of your
    love, deliver me.
²²For I am poor and needy,
  and my heart is wounded
    within me.
²³I fade away like an evening
    shadow;
  I am shaken off like a
    locust.
²⁴My knees give way from
    fasting;
  my body is thin and gaunt.
²⁵I am an object of scorn to my
    accusers;
  when they see me, they
    shake their heads.

²⁶Help me, O LORD my God;
  save me in accordance with
    your love.
²⁷Let them know that it is your
    hand,
  that you, O LORD, have
    done it.
²⁸They may curse, but you will
    bless;
  when they attack they will
    be put to shame,
  but your servant will rejoice.
²⁹My accusers will be clothed
    with disgrace
  and wrapped in shame as in
    a cloak.

³⁰With my mouth I will greatly
    extol the LORD;
  in the great throng I will
    praise him.
³¹For he stands at the right
    hand of the needy
    one,
  to save his life from those
    who condemn him.

Psalm 110

Of David. A psalm.

¹The LORD says to my Lord:
  "Sit at my right hand
  until I make your enemies
    a footstool for your feet."

²The LORD will extend your
    mighty scepter from
    Zion;
  you will rule in the midst of
    your enemies.
³Your troops will be willing
  on your day of battle.
Arrayed in holy majesty,
  from the womb of the dawn
  you will receive the dew of
    your youth.^a

⁴The LORD has sworn
  and will not change his
    mind:
  "You are a priest forever,
  in the order of
    Melchizedek."

⁵The Lord is at your right
    hand;
  he will crush kings on the
    day of his wrath.
⁶He will judge the nations,
    heaping up the dead
  and crushing the rulers of
    the whole earth.
⁷He will drink from a brook
    beside the way^b;
  therefore he will lift up his
    head.

^a3 Or / your young men will come to you like the dew   ^b7 Or / The One who grants
succession will set him in authority

Psalm 111 [a]

68 [1]Praise the LORD. [b]

I will extol the LORD with all
   my heart
  in the council of the upright
   and in the assembly.

[2]Great are the works of the
   LORD;
  they are pondered by all
   who delight in them.
[3]Glorious and majestic are his
   deeds,
  and his righteousness
   endures forever.
[4]He has caused his wonders to
   be remembered;
  the LORD is gracious and
   compassionate.
[5]He provides food for those
   who fear him;
  he remembers his covenant
   forever.
[6]He has shown his people the
   power of his works,
  giving them the lands of
   other nations.
[7]The works of his hands are
   faithful and just;
  all his precepts are
   trustworthy.
[8]They are steadfast for ever
   and ever,
  done in faithfulness and
   uprightness.
[9]He provided redemption for
   his people;
  he ordained his covenant
   forever—
  holy and awesome is his
   name.

[10]The fear of the LORD is the
   beginning of wisdom;
  all who follow his precepts
   have good
   understanding.

To him belongs eternal
  praise.

Psalm 112 [a]

[1]Praise the LORD. [b]

Blessed is the man who fears
   the LORD,
  who finds great delight in
   his commands.

[2]His children will be mighty in
   the land;
  the generation of the
   upright will be blessed.
[3]Wealth and riches are in his
   house,
  and his righteousness
   endures forever.
[4]Even in darkness light dawns
   for the upright,
  for the gracious and
   compassionate and
   righteous man. [c]
[5]Good will come to him who is
   generous and lends
   freely,
  who conducts his affairs
   with justice.
[6]Surely he will never be
   shaken;
  a righteous man will be
   remembered forever.
[7]He will have no fear of bad
   news;
  his heart is steadfast,
   trusting in the LORD.
[8]His heart is secure, he will
   have no fear;
  in the end he will look in
   triumph on his foes.
[9]He has scattered abroad his
   gifts to the poor,
  his righteousness endures
   forever;
  his horn [d] will be lifted high
   in honor.

---

[a]This psalm is an acrostic poem, the lines of which begin with the successive letters
of the Hebrew alphabet.   [b]1 Hebrew *Hallelu Yah*   [c]4 Or *I for the LORD, is gracious
and compassionate and righteous*   [d]9 *Horn* here symbolizes dignity.

¹⁰The wicked man will see and
be vexed,
he will gnash his teeth and
waste away;
the longings of the wicked
will come to nothing.

Psalm 113

¹Praise the LORD.ᵃ

Praise, O servants of the
LORD,
praise the name of the
LORD.
²Let the name of the LORD be
praised,
both now and forevermore.
³From the rising of the sun to
the place where it sets,
the name of the LORD is to
be praised.

⁴The LORD is exalted over all
the nations,
his glory above the heavens.
⁵Who is like the LORD our
God,
the One who sits enthroned
on high,
⁶who stoops down to look
on the heavens and the
earth?

⁷He raises the poor from the
dust
and lifts the needy from the
ash heap;
⁸he seats them with princes,
with the princes of their
people.
⁹He settles the barren woman
in her home
as a happy mother of
children.

Praise the LORD.

Psalm 114

¹When Israel came out of
Egypt,

the house of Jacob from a
people of foreign
tongue,
²Judah became God's
sanctuary,
Israel his dominion.

³The sea looked and fled,
the Jordan turned back;
⁴the mountains skipped like
rams,
the hills like lambs.

⁵Why was it, O sea, that you
fled,
O Jordan, that you turned
back,
⁶you mountains, that you
skipped like rams,
you hills, like lambs?

⁷Tremble, O earth, at the
presence of the Lord,
at the presence of the God
of Jacob,
⁸who turned the rock into a
pool,
the hard rock into springs of
water.

Psalm 115

¹Not to us, O LORD, not to us
but to your name be the
glory,
because of your love and
faithfulness.

²Why do the nations say,
"Where is their God?"
³Our God is in heaven;
he does whatever pleases
him.
⁴But their idols are silver and
gold,
made by the hands of men.
⁵They have mouths, but cannot
speak,
eyes, but they cannot see;
⁶they have ears, but cannot
hear,

ᵃ*1* Hebrew *Hallelu Yah;* also in verse 9

noses, but they cannot
smell;
[7]they have hands, but cannot
feel,
feet, but they cannot walk;
nor can they utter a sound
with their throats.
[8]Those who make them will be
like them,
and so will all who trust in
them.

[9]O house of Israel, trust in the
LORD—
he is their help and shield.
[10]O house of Aaron, trust in the
LORD—
he is their help and shield.
[11]You who fear him, trust in the
LORD—
he is their help and shield.

[12]The LORD remembers us and
will bless us:
He will bless the house of
Israel,
he will bless the house of
Aaron,
[13]he will bless those who fear
the LORD—
small and great alike.

[14]May the LORD make you
increase,
both you and your children.
[15]May you be blessed by the
LORD,
the Maker of heaven and
earth.

[16]The highest heavens belong to
the LORD,
but the earth he has given
to man.
[17]It is not the dead who praise
the LORD,
those who go down to
silence;
[18]it is we who extol the LORD,
both now and forevermore.

Praise the LORD.[a]

Psalm 116

[1]I love the LORD, for he heard
my voice;
he heard my cry for mercy.
[2]Because he turned his ear to
me,
I will call on him as long as
I live.

[3]The cords of death entangled
me,
the anguish of the grave[b]
came upon me;
I was overcome by trouble
and sorrow.
[4]Then I called on the name of
the LORD:
"O LORD, save me!"

[5]The LORD is gracious and
righteous;
our God is full of
compassion.
[6]The LORD protects the
simplehearted;
when I was in great need,
he saved me.

[7]Be at rest once more, O my
soul,
for the LORD has been good
to you.

[8]For you, O LORD, have
delivered my soul from
death,
my eyes from tears,
my feet from stumbling,
[9]that I may walk before the
LORD
in the land of the living.
[10]I believed; therefore[c] I said,
"I am greatly afflicted."
[11]And in my dismay I said,
"All men are liars."

[12]How can I repay the LORD
for all his goodness to me?
[13]I will lift up the cup of
salvation

---

[a]18 Hebrew *Hallelu Yah*　[b]3 Hebrew *Sheol*　[c]10 Or *believed even when*

and call on the name of the
LORD.
¹⁴I will fulfill my vows to the
LORD
in the presence of all his
people.

¹⁵Precious in the sight of the
LORD
is the death of his saints.
¹⁶O LORD, truly I am your
servant;
I am your servant, the son
of your maidservant[a];
you have freed me from my
chains.

¹⁷I will sacrifice a thank offering
to you
and call on the name of the
LORD.
¹⁸I will fulfill my vows to the
LORD
in the presence of all his
people,
¹⁹in the courts of the house of
the LORD—
in your midst, O Jerusalem.

Praise the LORD.[b]

Psalm 117

¹Praise the LORD, all you
nations;
extol him, all you peoples.
²For great is his love toward
us,
and the faithfulness of the
LORD endures forever.

Praise the LORD.[b]

Psalm 118

94
Ps 119:62

¹Give thanks to the LORD, for
he is good;
his love endures forever.

²Let Israel say:
"His love endures forever."

³Let the house of Aaron say:
"His love endures forever."
⁴Let those who fear the LORD
say:
"His love endures forever."

⁵In my anguish I cried to the
LORD,
and he answered by setting
me free.
⁶The LORD is with me; I will
not be afraid.
What can man do to me?
⁷The LORD is with me; he is
my helper.
I will look in triumph on my
enemies.

⁸It is better to take refuge in
the LORD
than to trust in man.
⁹It is better to take refuge in
the LORD
than to trust in princes.
¹⁰All the nations surrounded
me,
but in the name of the LORD
I cut them off.
¹¹They surrounded me on every
side,
but in the name of the LORD
I cut them off.
¹²They swarmed around me like
bees,
but they died out as quickly
as burning thorns;
in the name of the LORD I
cut them off.
¹³I was pushed back and about
to fall,
but the LORD helped me.
¹⁴The LORD is my strength and
my song;
he has become my
salvation.

¹⁵Shouts of joy and victory
resound in the tents of the
righteous:
"The LORD's right hand has
done mighty things!

---

[a]16 Or servant, your faithful son   [b]19,2 Hebrew Hallelu Yah

16 The LORD's right hand is
    lifted high;
      the LORD's right hand has
      done mighty things!''

17I will not die but live,
    and will proclaim what the
    LORD has done.
18The LORD has chastened me
    severely,
      but he has not given me
      over to death.

19Open for me the gates of
    righteousness;
      I will enter and give thanks
      to the LORD.
20This is the gate of the LORD
    through which the righteous
    may enter.
21I will give you thanks, for you
    answered me;
      you have become my
      salvation.

22The stone the builders
    rejected
      has become the capstone;
23the LORD has done this,
    and it is marvelous in our
    eyes.
24This is the day the LORD has
    made;
      let us rejoice and be glad
      in it.

25O LORD, save us;
    O LORD, grant us success.
26Blessed is he who comes in
    the name of the LORD.
      From the house of the LORD
      we bless you.ᵃ
27The LORD is God,
    and he has made his light
    shine upon us.
      With boughs in hand, join in
      the festal procession
      upᵇ to the horns of the altar.

28You are my God, and I will
    give you thanks;

you are my God, and I will
    exalt you.
29Give thanks to the LORD, for
    he is good;
      his love endures forever.

Psalm 119ᶜ

א Aleph

1Blessed are they whose ways
    are blameless,
      who walk according to the
      law of the LORD.
2Blessed are they who keep his
    statutes
      and seek him with all their
      heart.
3They do nothing wrong;
    they walk in his ways.
4You have laid down precepts
    that are to be fully obeyed.
5Oh, that my ways were
    steadfast
      in obeying your decrees!
6Then I would not be put to
    shame
      when I consider all your
      commands.
7I will praise you with an
    upright heart
      as I learn your righteous
      laws.
8I will obey your decrees;
    do not utterly forsake me.

77
Ps 119:75

ב Beth

9How can a young man keep
    his way pure?
      By living according to your
      word.
10I seek you with all my heart;
    do not let me stray from
    your commands.
11I have hidden your word in
    my heart

ᵃ26 The Hebrew is plural. ᵇ27 Or *Bind the festal sacrifice with ropes / and take it*
ᶜThis psalm is an acrostic poem; the verses of each stanza begin with the same letter
of the Hebrew alphabet.

that I might not sin against
  you.
¹²Praise be to you, O LORD;
  teach me your decrees.
¹³With my lips I recount
  all the laws that come from
    your mouth.
¹⁴I rejoice in following your
    statutes
  as one rejoices in great
    riches.
¹⁵I meditate on your precepts
  and consider your ways.
¹⁶I delight in your decrees;
  I will not neglect your
    word.

ג   Gimel

¹⁷Do good to your servant, and
    I will live;
  I will obey your word.
¹⁸Open my eyes that I may see
  wonderful things in your
    law.
¹⁹I am a stranger on earth;
  do not hide your commands
    from me.
²⁰My soul is consumed with
    longing
  for your laws at all times.
²¹You rebuke the arrogant, who
    are cursed
  and who stray from your
    commands.
²²Remove from me scorn and
    contempt,
  for I keep your statutes.
²³Though rulers sit together and
    slander me,
  your servant will meditate
    on your decrees.
²⁴Your statutes are my delight;
  they are my counselors.

ד   Daleth

²⁵I am laid low in the dust;
  preserve my life according
    to your word.

²⁶I recounted my ways and you
    answered me;
  teach me your decrees.
²⁷Let me understand the
    teaching of your
    precepts;
  then I will meditate on your
    wonders.
²⁸My soul is weary with sorrow;
  strengthen me according to
    your word.
²⁹Keep me from deceitful ways;
  be gracious to me through
    your law.
³⁰I have chosen the way of
    truth;
  I have set my heart on your
    laws.
³¹I hold fast to your statutes,
    O LORD;
  do not let me be put to
    shame.
³²I run in the path of your
    commands,
  for you have set my heart
    free.

ה   He

³³Teach me, O LORD, to follow
    your decrees;
  then I will keep them to the
    end.
³⁴Give me understanding, and I
    will keep your law
  and obey it with all my
    heart.
³⁵Direct me in the path of your
    commands,
  for there I find delight.
³⁶Turn my heart toward your
    statutes
  and not toward selfish gain.
³⁷Turn my eyes away from
    worthless things;
  preserve my life according
    to your word.[a]
³⁸Fulfill your promise to your
    servant,

---

[a] 37 Two manuscripts of the Masoretic Text and Dead Sea Scrolls; most manuscripts of
the Masoretic Text *life in your way*

so that you may be feared.
³⁹Take away the disgrace I
    dread,
    for your laws are good.
⁴⁰How I long for your precepts!
    Preserve my life in your
    righteousness.

ו Waw

⁴¹May your unfailing love come
    to me, O LORD,
    your salvation according to
    your promise;
⁴²then I will answer the one
    who taunts me,
    for I trust in your word.
⁴³Do not snatch the word of
    truth from my mouth,
    for I have put my hope in
    your laws.
⁴⁴I will always obey your law,
    for ever and ever.
⁴⁵I will walk about in freedom,
    for I have sought out your
    precepts.
⁴⁶I will speak of your statutes
    before kings
    and will not be put to
    shame,
⁴⁷for I delight in your
    commands
    because I love them.
⁴⁸I lift up my hands to[a] your
    commands, which I love,
    and I meditate on your
    decrees.

ז Zayin

⁴⁹Remember your word to your
    servant,
    for you have given me
    hope.
⁵⁰My comfort in my suffering is
    this:
    Your promise preserves my
    life.
⁵¹The arrogant mock me
    without restraint,
    but I do not turn from your
    law.

⁵²I remember your ancient laws,
    O LORD,
    and I find comfort in them.
⁵³Indignation grips me because
    of the wicked,
    who have forsaken your
    law.
⁵⁴Your decrees are the theme of
    my song
    wherever I lodge.
⁵⁵In the night I remember your
    name, O LORD,
    and I will keep your law.
⁵⁶This has been my practice:
    I obey your precepts.

ח Heth

⁵⁷You are my portion, O LORD;
    I have promised to obey
    your words.
⁵⁸I have sought your face with
    all my heart;
    be gracious to me according
    to your promise.
⁵⁹I have considered my ways
    and have turned my steps
    to your statutes.
⁶⁰I will hasten and not delay
    to obey your commands.
⁶¹Though the wicked bind me
    with ropes,
    I will not forget your law.
⁶²At midnight I rise to give you
    thanks   94
    for your righteous laws.   Ps 138:1,2
⁶³I am a friend to all who fear
    you,
    to all who follow your
    precepts.
⁶⁴The earth is filled with your
    love, O LORD;
    teach me your decrees.

ט Teth

⁶⁵Do good to your servant
    according to your word,
    O LORD.
⁶⁶Teach me knowledge and
    good judgment,

^a48 Or for

for I believe in your
commands.
⁶⁷Before I was afflicted I went
astray,
but now I obey your word.
⁶⁸You are good, and what you
do is good;
teach me your decrees.
⁶⁹Though the arrogant have
smeared me with lies,
I keep your precepts with
all my heart.
⁷⁰Their hearts are callous and
unfeeling,
but I delight in your law.
⁷¹It was good for me to be
afflicted
so that I might learn your
decrees.
⁷²The law from your mouth is
more precious to me
than thousands of pieces of
silver and gold.

י Yodh

⁷³Your hands made me and
formed me;
give me understanding to
learn your commands.
⁷⁴May those who fear you
rejoice when they see
me,
for I have put my hope in
your word.
77 ⁷⁵I know, O Lᴏʀᴅ, that your
laws are righteous,
and in faithfulness you have
afflicted me.
⁷⁶May your unfailing love be
my comfort,
according to your promise
to your servant.
⁷⁷Let your compassion come to
me that I may live,
for your law is my delight.
⁷⁸May the arrogant be put to
shame for wronging me
without cause;
but I will meditate on your
precepts.

⁷⁹May those who fear you turn
to me,
those who understand your
statutes.
⁸⁰May my heart be blameless
toward your decrees,
that I may not be put to
shame.

כ Kaph

⁸¹My soul faints with longing
for your salvation,
but I have put my hope in
your word.
⁸²My eyes fail, looking for your
promise;
I say, "When will you
comfort me?"
⁸³Though I am like a wineskin
in the smoke,
I do not forget your decrees.
⁸⁴How long must your servant
wait?
When will you punish my
persecutors?
⁸⁵The arrogant dig pitfalls for
me,
contrary to your law.
⁸⁶All your commands are
trustworthy;
help me, for men persecute
me without cause.
⁸⁷They almost wiped me from
the earth,
but I have not forsaken your
precepts.
⁸⁸Preserve my life according to
your love,
and I will obey the statutes
of your mouth.

ל Lamedh

⁸⁹Your word, O Lᴏʀᴅ, is
eternal;
it stands firm in the
heavens.
⁹⁰Your faithfulness continues
through all generations;

you established the earth,
and it endures.
91Your laws endure to this day,
for all things serve you.
52 92If your law had not been my
delight,
I would have perished in
my affliction.
93I will never forget your
precepts,
for by them you have
preserved my life.
94Save me, for I am yours;
I have sought out your
precepts.
95The wicked are waiting to
destroy me,
but I will ponder your
statutes.
66 96To all perfection I see a limit;
but your commands are
boundless.

מ Mem

97Oh, how I love your law!
I meditate on it all day long.
98Your commands make me
wiser than my enemies,
for they are ever with me.
99I have more insight than all
my teachers,
for I meditate on your
statutes.
100I have more understanding
than the elders,
for I obey your precepts.
101I have kept my feet from
every evil path
so that I might obey your
word.
102I have not departed from
your laws,
for you yourself have taught
me.
103How sweet are your words to
my taste,
sweeter than honey to my
mouth!
104I gain understanding from
your precepts;

therefore I hate every wrong
path.

נ Nun

105Your word is a lamp to my
feet
and a light for my path.
106I have taken an oath and
confirmed it,
that I will follow your
righteous laws.
107I have suffered much;
preserve my life, O LORD,
according to your word.
108Accept, O LORD, the willing
praise of my mouth,
and teach me your laws.
109Though I constantly take my
life in my hands,
I will not forget your law.
110The wicked have set a snare
for me,
but I have not strayed from
your precepts.
111Your statutes are my heritage
forever;
they are the joy of my
heart.
112My heart is set on keeping
your decrees
to the very end.

ס Samekh

113I hate double-minded men,
but I love your law.
114You are my refuge and my
shield;
I have put my hope in your
word.
115Away from me, you
evildoers,
that I may keep the
commands of my God!
116Sustain me according to your
promise, and I will live;
do not let my hopes be
dashed.
117Uphold me, and I will be
delivered;

I will always have regard for
   your decrees.
118You reject all who stray from
   your decrees,
for their deceitfulness is in
   vain.
119All the wicked of the earth
   you discard like dross;
therefore I love your
   statutes.
120My flesh trembles in fear of
   you;
I stand in awe of your laws.

‎ע‎ Ayin

48 121I have done what is righteous
   and just;
do not leave me to my
   oppressors.
122Ensure your servant's
   well-being;
let not the arrogant oppress
   me.
123My eyes fail, looking for your
   salvation,
looking for your righteous
   promise.
124Deal with your servant
   according to your love
and teach me your decrees.
125I am your servant; give me
   discernment
that I may understand your
   statutes.
126It is time for you to act,
   O LORD;
your law is being broken.
127Because I love your
   commands
more than gold, more than
   pure gold,
128and because I consider all
   your precepts right,
I hate every wrong path.

‎פ‎ Pe

129Your statutes are wonderful;
   therefore I obey them.
130The unfolding of your words
   gives light;

it gives understanding to
   the simple.
131I open my mouth and pant,
   longing for your commands.
132Turn to me and have mercy
   on me,
as you always do to those
   who love your name.
133Direct my footsteps according
   to your word;
let no sin rule over me.
134Redeem me from the
   oppression of men,
that I may obey your
   precepts.
135Make your face shine upon
   your servant
and teach me your decrees.
136Streams of tears flow from
   my eyes,
for your law is not obeyed.

‎צ‎ Tsadhe

137Righteous are you, O LORD,
   and your laws are right.
138The statutes you have laid
   down are righteous;
they are fully trustworthy.
139My zeal wears me out,
   for my enemies ignore your
   words.
140Your promises have been
   thoroughly tested,
and your servant loves
   them.
141Though I am lowly and
   despised,
I do not forget your
   precepts.
142Your righteousness is
   everlasting
and your law is true.
143Trouble and distress have
   come upon me,
but your commands are my
   delight.
144Your statutes are forever
   right;
give me understanding that
   I may live.

ק Qoph

¹⁴⁵I call with all my heart;
    answer me, O LORD,
    and I will obey your
      decrees.
¹⁴⁶I call out to you; save me
    and I will keep your
      statutes.
¹⁴⁷I rise before dawn and cry for
      help;
    I have put my hope in your
      word.
¹⁴⁸My eyes stay open through
      the watches of the night,
    that I may meditate on your
      promises.
¹⁴⁹Hear my voice in accordance
      with your love;
    preserve my life, O LORD,
      according to your laws.
¹⁵⁰Those who devise wicked
      schemes are near,
    but they are far from your
      law.
¹⁵¹Yet you are near, O LORD,
    and all your commands are
      true.
¹⁵²Long ago I learned from your
      statutes
    that you established them to
      last forever.

ר Resh

¹⁵³Look upon my suffering and
      deliver me,
    for I have not forgotten
      your law.
¹⁵⁴Defend my cause and redeem
      me;
    preserve my life according
      to your promise.
¹⁵⁵Salvation is far from the
      wicked,
    for they do not seek out
      your decrees.
¹⁵⁶Your compassion is great,
      O LORD;
    preserve my life according
      to your laws.
¹⁵⁷Many are the foes who
      persecute me,

but I have not turned from
      your statutes.
¹⁵⁸I look on the faithless with
      loathing,
    for they do not obey your
      word.
¹⁵⁹See how I love your precepts;
    preserve my life, O LORD,
      according to your love.
¹⁶⁰All your words are true;
    all your righteous laws are
      eternal.

ש Sin and Shin

¹⁶¹Rulers persecute me without
      cause,
    but my heart trembles at
      your word.
¹⁶²I rejoice in your promise
    like one who finds great
      spoil.
¹⁶³I hate and abhor falsehood
    but I love your law.
¹⁶⁴Seven times a day I praise
      you
    for your righteous laws.
¹⁶⁵Great peace have they who
      love your law,
    and nothing can make them
      stumble.
¹⁶⁶I wait for your salvation,
      O LORD,
    and I follow your
      commands.
¹⁶⁷I obey your statutes,
    for I love them greatly.
¹⁶⁸I obey your precepts and
      your statutes,
    for all my ways are known
      to you.

ת Taw

¹⁶⁹May my cry come before you,
      O LORD;
    give me understanding
      according to your word.
¹⁷⁰May my supplication come
      before you;
    deliver me according to your
      promise.

171May my lips overflow with
    praise,
  for you teach me your
    decrees.
172May my tongue sing of your
    word,
  for all your commands are
    righteous.
173May your hand be ready to
    help me,
  for I have chosen your
    precepts.
174I long for your salvation,
    O LORD,
  and your law is my delight.
175Let me live that I may praise
    you,
  and may your laws sustain
    me.
176I have strayed like a lost
    sheep.
  Seek your servant,
  for I have not forgotten
    your commands.

Psalm 120

A song of ascents.

1I call on the LORD in my
    distress,
  and he answers me.
2Save me, O LORD, from lying
    lips
  and from deceitful tongues.

3What will he do to you,
  and what more besides,
    O deceitful tongue?
4He will punish you with a
    warrior's sharp arrows,
  with burning coals of the
    broom tree.

5Woe to me that I dwell in
    Meshech,
  that I live among the tents
    of Kedar!
6Too long have I lived
  among those who hate
    peace.
7I am a man of peace;
  but when I speak, they are
    for war.

Psalm 121

A song of ascents.

1I lift up my eyes to the hills—
  where does my help come
    from?
2My help comes from the
    LORD,
  the Maker of heaven and
    earth.

3He will not let your foot slip—
  he who watches over you
    will not slumber;
4indeed, he who watches over
    Israel
  will neither slumber nor
    sleep.

5The LORD watches over you—
  the LORD is your shade at
    your right hand;
6the sun will not harm you by
    day,
  nor the moon by night.

7The LORD will keep you from
    all harm—
  he will watch over your life;
8the LORD will watch over your
    coming and going
  both now and forevermore.

Psalm 122

A song of ascents. Of David.

1I rejoiced with those who said
    to me,
  "Let us go to the house of
    the LORD."
2Our feet are standing
  in your gates, O Jerusalem.

3Jerusalem is built like a city
  that is closely compacted
    together.
4That is where the tribes go
    up,
  the tribes of the LORD,
  to praise the name of the
    LORD
  according to the statute
    given to Israel.

⁵There the thrones for
  judgment stand,
  the thrones of the house of
    David.

⁶Pray for the peace of
  Jerusalem:
  "May those who love you
    be secure.
⁷May there be peace within
  your walls
  and security within your
    citadels."
⁸For the sake of my brothers
  and friends,
  I will say, "Peace be within
    you."
⁹For the sake of the house of
  the Lord our God,
  I will seek your prosperity.

Psalm 123

A song of ascents.

¹I lift up my eyes to you,
  to you whose throne is in
    heaven.
²As the eyes of slaves look to
    the hand of their master,
  as the eyes of a maid look
    to the hand of her
    mistress,
so our eyes look to the Lord
    our God,
  till he shows us his mercy.

³Have mercy on us, O Lord,
  have mercy on us,
  for we have endured much
    contempt.
⁴We have endured much
    ridicule from the proud,
  much contempt from the
    arrogant.

Psalm 124

A song of ascents. Of David.

¹If the Lord had not been on
    our side—
  let Israel say—

²if the Lord had not been on
    our side
  when men attacked us,
³when their anger flared
    against us,
  they would have swallowed
    us alive;
⁴the flood would have
    engulfed us,
  the torrent would have
    swept over us,
⁵the raging waters
  would have swept us away.

⁶Praise be to the Lord,
  who has not let us be torn
    by their teeth.
⁷We have escaped like a bird
  out of the fowler's snare;
the snare has been broken,
  and we have escaped.
⁸Our help is in the name of the
    Lord,
  the Maker of heaven and
    earth.

Psalm 125

A song of ascents.

¹Those who trust in the Lord
    are like Mount Zion,
  which cannot be shaken but
    endures forever.
²As the mountains surround
    Jerusalem,
  so the Lord surrounds his
    people
  both now and forevermore.

³The scepter of the wicked will
    not remain
  over the land allotted to the
    righteous,
for then the righteous might
    use
  their hands to do evil.

⁴Do good, O Lord, to those
    who are good,
  to those who are upright in
    heart.

5But those who turn to crooked
ways
  the LORD will banish with
    the evildoers.

Peace be upon Israel.

Psalm 126

A song of ascents.

1When the LORD brought back
    the captives to*a* Zion,
  we were like men who
    dreamed.*b*
2Our mouths were filled with
    laughter,
  our tongues with songs of
    joy.
Then it was said among the
    nations,
  "The LORD has done great
    things for them."
3The LORD has done great
    things for us,
  and we are filled with joy.

4Restore our fortunes,*c*
    O LORD,
  like streams in the Negev.
5Those who sow in tears
  will reap with songs of
    joy.
6He who goes out weeping,
    carrying seed to sow,
will return with songs of joy,
  carrying sheaves with him.

Psalm 127

A song of ascents. Of Solomon.

1Unless the LORD builds the
    house,
  its builders labor in vain.
Unless the LORD watches over
    the city,
  the watchmen stand guard
    in vain.
2In vain you rise early
  and stay up late,

toiling for food to eat—
  for he grants sleep to*d* those
    he loves.

3Sons are a heritage from the
    LORD,
  children a reward from
    him.
4Like arrows in the hands of a
    warrior
  are sons born in one's
    youth.
5Blessed is the man
  whose quiver is full of
    them.
They will not be put to shame
  when they contend with
    their enemies in the
    gate.

Psalm 128

A song of ascents.

1Blessed are all who fear the
    LORD,
  who walk in his ways.
2You will eat the fruit of your
    labor;
  blessings and prosperity will
    be yours.
3Your wife will be like a
    fruitful vine
  within your house;
your sons will be like olive
    shoots
  around your table.
4Thus is the man blessed
  who fears the LORD.

5May the LORD bless you from
    Zion
  all the days of your life;
may you see the prosperity of
    Jerusalem,
6 and may you live to see
    your children's
    children.

Peace be upon Israel.

---

*a*1 Or LORD *restored the fortunes of*   *b*1 Or *men restored to health*   *c*4 Or *Bring back our captives*   *d*2 Or *eat— / for while they sleep he provides for*

Psalm 129

A song of ascents.

¹They have greatly oppressed
       me from my youth—
   let Israel say—
²they have greatly oppressed
       me from my youth,
   but they have not gained
       the victory over me.
³Plowmen have plowed my
       back
   and made their furrows
       long.
⁴But the Lord is righteous;
   he has cut me free from the
       cords of the wicked.

⁵May all who hate Zion
   be turned back in shame.
⁶May they be like grass on the
       roof,
   which withers before it can
       grow;
⁷with it the reaper cannot fill
       his hands,
   nor the one who gathers fill
       his arms.
⁸May those who pass by not
       say,
   "The blessing of the Lord
       be upon you;
   we bless you in the name of
       the Lord."

Psalm 130

A song of ascents.

¹Out of the depths I cry to
       you, O Lord;
²   O Lord, hear my voice.
   Let your ears be attentive
       to my cry for mercy.

³If you, O Lord, kept a record
       of sins,
   O Lord, who could stand?
⁴But with you there is
       forgiveness;
   therefore you are feared.

⁵I wait for the Lord, my soul
       waits,

   and in his word I put my
       hope.
⁶My soul waits for the Lord
   more than watchmen wait
       for the morning,
   more than watchmen wait
       for the morning.

⁷O Israel, put your hope in the
       Lord,
   for with the Lord is
       unfailing love
   and with him is full
       redemption.
⁸He himself will redeem Israel
   from all their sins.

Psalm 131

A song of ascents. Of David.

¹My heart is not proud,
       O Lord,
   my eyes are not haughty;
   I do not concern myself with
       great matters
   or things too wonderful for
       me.
²But I have stilled and quieted
       my soul;
   like a weaned child with its
       mother,
   like a weaned child is my
       soul within me.

³O Israel, put your hope in the
       Lord
   both now and forevermore.

Psalm 132

A song of ascents.

¹O Lord, remember David
   and all the hardships he
       endured.

²He swore an oath to the Lord
   and made a vow to the
       Mighty One of Jacob:
³"I will not enter my house
   or go to my bed—
⁴I will allow no sleep to my
       eyes,
   no slumber to my eyelids,

5till I find a place for the LORD,
  a dwelling for the Mighty
    One of Jacob.''

6We heard it in Ephrathah,
  we came upon it in the
    fields of Jaar*ᵇ
7''Let us go to his dwelling
  place;
  let us worship at his
    footstool—
8arise, O LORD, and come to
  your resting place,
  you and the ark of your
    might.
9May your priests be clothed
  with righteousness;
  may your saints sing for
    joy.''

10For the sake of David your
  servant,
  do not reject your anointed
    one.
11The LORD swore an oath to
  David,
  a sure oath that he will not
    revoke:
  "One of your own
    descendants
  I will place on your
    throne—
12if your sons keep my
  covenant
  and the statutes I teach
    them,
  then their sons will sit
  on your throne for ever and
    ever.''

13For the LORD has chosen
  Zion,
  he has desired it for his
    dwelling:
14"This is my resting place for
  ever and ever;
  here I will sit enthroned, for
    I have desired it—
15I will bless her with abundant
  provisions;

her poor will I satisfy with
  food.
16I will clothe her priests with
  salvation,
  and her saints will ever sing
    for joy.

17"Here I will make a hornᶜ
  grow for David
  and set up a lamp for my
    anointed one.
18I will clothe his enemies with
  shame,
  but the crown on his head
    will be resplendent.''

Psalm 133

A song of ascents. Of David.

1How good and pleasant it is   27
  when brothers live together
    in unity!
2It is like precious oil poured
  on the head,
  running down on the beard,
  running down on Aaron's
    beard,
  down upon the collar of his
    robes.
3It is as if the dew of Hermon
  were falling on Mount Zion.
For there the LORD bestows
  his blessing,
  even life forevermore.

Psalm 134

A song of ascents.

1Praise the LORD, all you
  servants of the LORD
  who minister by night in
    the house of the LORD.
2Lift up your hands in the
  sanctuary
  and praise the LORD.

3May the LORD, the Maker of
  heaven and earth,
  bless you from Zion.

---

*ᵃ6 That is, Kiriath Jearim   ᵇ6 Or heard of it in Ephrathah, / we found it in the fields of
Jaar. (And no quotes around verses 7-9)   ᶜ17 Horn here symbolizes strong one, that
is, king.*

Psalm 135

¹Praise the LORD.ᵃ

Praise the name of the LORD;
  praise him, you servants of
    the LORD,
²you who minister in the
    house of the LORD,
  in the courts of the house of
    our God.

³Praise the LORD, for the LORD
    is good;
  sing praise to his name, for
    that is pleasant.
⁴For the LORD has chosen Jacob
    to be his own,
  Israel to be his treasured
    possession.

⁵I know that the LORD is great,
  that our Lord is greater than
    all gods.
⁶The LORD does whatever
    pleases him,
  in the heavens and on the
    earth,
  in the seas and all their
    depths.
⁷He makes clouds rise from the
    ends of the earth;
  he sends lightning with the
    rain
  and brings out the wind
    from his storehouses.

⁸He struck down the firstborn
    of Egypt,
  the firstborn of men and
    animals.
⁹He sent his signs and
    wonders into your
    midst, O Egypt,
  against Pharaoh and all his
    servants.
¹⁰He struck down many nations
  and killed mighty kings—
¹¹Sihon king of the Amorites,
  Og king of Bashan
  and all the kings of
    Canaan—

¹²and he gave their land as an
    inheritance,
  an inheritance to his people
    Israel.

¹³Your name, O LORD, endures
    forever,
  your renown, O LORD,
  through all generations.
¹⁴For the LORD will vindicate his
    people
  and have compassion on his
    servants.

¹⁵The idols of the nations are
    silver and gold,
  made by the hands of men.
¹⁶They have mouths, but cannot
    speak,
  eyes, but they cannot see;
¹⁷they have ears, but cannot
    hear,
  nor is there breath in their
    mouths.
¹⁸Those who make them will be
    like them,
  and so will all who trust in
    them.

¹⁹O house of Israel, praise the
    LORD;
  O house of Aaron, praise
    the LORD;
²⁰O house of Levi, praise the
    LORD;
  you who fear him, praise
    the LORD.
²¹Praise be to the LORD from
    Zion,
  to him who dwells in
    Jerusalem.

Praise the LORD.

Psalm 136

¹Give thanks to the LORD, for
    he is good.
    His love endures forever.
²Give thanks to the God of
    gods.
    His love endures forever.

ᵃ1 Hebrew *Hallelu Yah;* also in verses 3 and 21

3Give thanks to the Lord of
     lords:
          His love endures forever.

4to him who alone does great
     wonders,
          His love endures forever.
5who by his understanding
     made the heavens,
          His love endures forever.
6who spread out the earth
     upon the waters,
          His love endures forever.
7who made the great lights—
          His love endures forever.
8the sun to govern the day,
          His love endures forever.
9the moon and stars to govern
     the night;
          His love endures forever.

10to him who struck down the
     firstborn of Egypt
          His love endures forever.
11and brought Israel out from
     among them
          His love endures forever.
12with a mighty hand and
     outstretched arm;
          His love endures forever.
13to him who divided the Red
     Sea*a* asunder
          His love endures forever.
14and brought Israel through
     the midst of it,
          His love endures forever.
15but swept Pharaoh and his
     army into the Red Sea;
          His love endures forever.
16to him who led his people
     through the desert,
          His love endures forever.
17who struck down great kings,
          His love endures forever.
18and killed mighty kings—
          His love endures forever.
19Sihon king of the Amorites
          His love endures forever.
20and Og king of Bashan—
          His love endures forever.

21and gave their land as an
     inheritance,
          His love endures forever.
22an inheritance to his servant
     Israel;
          His love endures forever.
23to the One who remembered
     us in our low estate
          His love endures forever.
24and freed us from our
     enemies,
          His love endures forever.
25and who gives food to every
     creature.
          His love endures forever.
26Give thanks to the God of
     heaven.
          His love endures forever.

Psalm 137

1By the rivers of Babylon we
     sat and wept
     when we remembered Zion.
2There on the poplars
     we hung our harps,
3for there our captors asked us
     for songs,
     our tormentors demanded
       songs of joy;
     they said, "Sing us one of
       the songs of Zion!"

4How can we sing the songs of
     the LORD
     while in a foreign land?
5If I forget you, O Jerusalem,
     may my right hand forget
       its skill.
6May my tongue cling to the
     roof of my mouth
     if I do not remember you,
     if I do not consider Jerusalem
       my highest joy.

7Remember, O LORD, what the
     Edomites did
     on the day Jerusalem fell.
"Tear it down," they cried,
     "tear it down to its
       foundations!"

a13 Hebrew *Yam Suph;* that is, Sea of Reeds; also in verse 15

⁸O Daughter of Babylon,
    doomed to destruction,
  happy is he who repays you
    for what you have done to
      us—
⁹he who seizes your infants
    and dashes them against the
      rocks.

Psalm 138

Of David.

¹I will praise you, O LORD,
    with all my heart;
  before the "gods" I will sing
    your praise.
²I will bow down toward your
    holy temple
  and will praise your name
    for your love and your
      faithfulness,
  for you have exalted above all
      things
    your name and your word.
³When I called, you answered
    me;
  you made me bold and
    stouthearted.

⁴May all the kings of the earth
    praise you, O LORD,
  when they hear the words
    of your mouth.
⁵May they sing of the ways of
    the LORD,
  for the glory of the LORD is
    great.

⁶Though the LORD is on high,
    he looks upon the lowly,
  but the proud he knows
    from afar.
⁷Though I walk in the midst of
    trouble,
    you preserve my life;
  you stretch out your hand
    against the anger of my
      foes,
  with your right hand you
    save me.

⁸The LORD will fulfill his
    purpose for me;
  your love, O LORD, endures
    forever—
  do not abandon the works
    of your hands.

Psalm 139

For the director of music. Of David.
A psalm.

¹O LORD, you have searched
    me
  and you know me.
²You know when I sit and
    when I rise;
  you perceive my thoughts
    from afar.
³You discern my going out and
    my lying down;
  you are familiar with all my
    ways.
⁴Before a word is on my
    tongue
  you know it completely,
    O LORD.

⁵You hem me in—behind and
    before;
  you have laid your hand
    upon me.
⁶Such knowledge is too
    wonderful for me,
  too lofty for me to attain.

⁷Where can I go from your
    Spirit?
  Where can I flee from your
    presence?
⁸If I go up to the heavens, you
    are there;
  if I make my bed in the
    depths,ᵃ you are there.
⁹If I rise on the wings of the
    dawn,
  if I settle on the far side of
    the sea,
¹⁰even there your hand will
    guide me,

ᵃ8 Hebrew *Sheol*

your right hand will hold
    me fast.

11If I say, "Surely the darkness
        will hide me
    and the light become night
        around me,"
12even the darkness will not be
        dark to you;
    the night will shine like the
        day,
    for darkness is as light to
        you.

13For you created my inmost
        being;
    you knit me together in my
        mother's womb.
14I praise you because I am
        fearfully and wonderfully
        made;
    your works are wonderful,
    I know that full well.
15My frame was not hidden
        from you
    when I was made in the
        secret place.
    When I was woven together
        in the depths of the
        earth,
87 16   your eyes saw my
        unformed body.
    All the days ordained for me
        were written in your book
        before one of them came
        to be.

17How precious to*a* me are your
        thoughts, O God!
    How vast is the sum of
        them!
18Were I to count them,
    they would outnumber the
        grains of sand.
    When I awake,
    I am still with you.

19If only you would slay the
        wicked, O God!
    Away from me, you
        bloodthirsty men!
20They speak of you with evil
        intent;

*a*17 Or *concerning*

your adversaries misuse
    your name.
21Do I not hate those who hate
        you, O LORD,
    and abhor those who rise
        up against you?
22I have nothing but hatred for
        them;
    I count them my enemies.

23Search me, O God, and know
        my heart;
    test me and know my
        anxious thoughts.
24See if there is any offensive
        way in me,
    and lead me in the way
        everlasting.

Psalm 140

For the director of music.
A psalm of David.

1Rescue me, O LORD, from evil
        men;
    protect me from men of
        violence,
2who devise evil plans in their
        hearts
    and stir up war every day.
3They make their tongues as
        sharp as a serpent's;
    the poison of vipers is on
        their lips.   *Selah*

4Keep me, O LORD, from the
        hands of the wicked;
    protect me from men of
        violence
    who plan to trip my feet.
5Proud men have hidden a
        snare for me;
    they have spread out the
        cords of their net
    and have set traps for me
        along my path.   *Selah*

6O LORD, I say to you, "You
        are my God."
    Hear, O LORD, my cry for
        mercy.

[7]O Sovereign LORD, my strong
        deliverer,
    who shields my head in the
        day of battle—
[8]do not grant the wicked their
        desires, O LORD;
    do not let their plans
        succeed,
    or they will become proud.
                              Selah

[9]Let the heads of those who
        surround me
    be covered with the trouble
        their lips have caused.
[10]Let burning coals fall upon
        them;
    may they be thrown into
        the fire,
    into miry pits, never to rise.
[11]Let slanderers not be
        established in the land;
    may disaster hunt down
        men of violence.

[12]I know that the LORD secures
        justice for the poor
    and upholds the cause of
        the needy.
[13]Surely the righteous will
        praise your name
    and the upright will live
        before you.

Psalm 141

A psalm of David.

[1]O LORD, I call to you; come
        quickly to me.
    Hear my voice when I call
        to you.
[2]May my prayer be set before
        you like incense;
    may the lifting up of my
        hands be like the
        evening sacrifice.

[3]Set a guard over my mouth,
        O LORD;
    keep watch over the door of
        my lips.

[4]Let not my heart be drawn to
        what is evil,
    to take part in wicked deeds
with men who are evildoers;
    let me not eat of their
        delicacies.

[5]Let a righteous man[a] strike
        me—it is a kindness;
    let him rebuke me—it is oil
        on my head.
    My head will not refuse it.

Yet my prayer is ever against
        the deeds of evildoers;
[6] their rulers will be thrown
        down from the cliffs,
    and the wicked will learn
        that my words were well
        spoken.
[7]They will say, "As one plows
        and breaks up the earth,
    so our bones have been
        scattered at the mouth of
        the grave.[b]"

[8]But my eyes are fixed on you,
        O Sovereign LORD;
    in you I take refuge—do not
        give me over to death.
[9]Keep me from the snares they
        have laid for me,
    from the traps set by
        evildoers.
[10]Let the wicked fall into their
        own nets,
    while I pass by in safety.

Psalm 142

A *maskil*[c] of David. When he was in
        the cave. A prayer.

[1]I cry aloud to the LORD;
    I lift up my voice to the
        LORD for mercy.
[2]I pour out my complaint
        before him;
    before him I tell my trouble.

[3]When my spirit grows faint
        within me,

---

[a]5 Or *Let the Righteous One*   [b]7 Hebrew *Sheol*   [c]Title: Probably a literary or musical
term

it is you who know my
way.
In the path where I walk
men have hidden a snare
for me.
⁴Look to my right and see;
no one is concerned for me.
I have no refuge;
no one cares for my life.

⁵I cry to you, O LORD;
I say, "You are my refuge,
my portion in the land of
the living."
⁶Listen to my cry,
for I am in desperate need;
rescue me from those who
pursue me,
for they are too strong for
me.
⁷Set me free from my prison,
that I may praise your
name.

Then the righteous will gather
about me
because of your goodness to
me.

Psalm 143

A psalm of David.

¹O LORD, hear my prayer,
listen to my cry for mercy;
in your faithfulness and
righteousness
come to my relief.
²Do not bring your servant into
judgment,
for no one living is
righteous before
you.

³The enemy pursues me,
he crushes me to the
ground;
he makes me dwell in
darkness
like those long dead.
⁴So my spirit grows faint
within me;
my heart within me is
dismayed.

⁵I remember the days of long
ago;
I meditate on all your works
and consider what your
hands have done.
⁶I spread out my hands to you;
my soul thirsts for you like
a parched land.   Selah

⁷Answer me quickly, O LORD;
my spirit fails.
Do not hide your face from
me
or I will be like those who
go down to the pit.
⁸Let the morning bring me
word of your unfailing
love,
for I have put my trust in
you.
Show me the way I should
go,
for to you I lift up my soul.
⁹Rescue me from my enemies,
O LORD,
for I hide myself in you.
¹⁰Teach me to do your will,
for you are my God;
may your good Spirit
lead me on level ground.

¹¹For your name's sake,
O LORD, preserve my
life;
in your righteousness, bring
me out of trouble.
¹²In your unfailing love, silence
my enemies;
destroy all my foes,
for I am your servant.

Psalm 144

Of David.

¹Praise be to the LORD my
Rock,
who trains my hands for
war,
my fingers for battle.
²He is my loving God and my
fortress,

my stronghold and my
    deliverer,
my shield, in whom I take
    refuge,
who subdues peoples[a]
    under me.

³O Lord, what is man that you
    care for him,
the son of man that you
    think of him?
⁴Man is like a breath;
    his days are like a fleeting
    shadow.

⁵Part your heavens, O Lord,
    and come down;
touch the mountains, so
    that they smoke.
⁶Send forth lightning and
    scatter the enemies;
shoot your arrows and rout
    them.
⁷Reach down your hand from
    on high;
deliver me and rescue me
    from the mighty waters,
    from the hands of foreigners
⁸whose mouths are full of lies,
    whose right hands are
    deceitful.

⁹I will sing a new song to you,
    O God;
on the ten-stringed lyre I
    will make music to you,
¹⁰to the One who gives victory
    to kings,
who delivers his servant
    David from the deadly
    sword.

¹¹Deliver me and rescue me
    from the hands of foreigners
whose mouths are full of lies,
    whose right hands are
    deceitful.

¹²Then our sons in their youth
will be like well-nurtured
    plants,
and our daughters will be like
    pillars
carved to adorn a palace.
¹³Our barns will be filled
    with every kind of
    provision.
Our sheep will increase by
    thousands,
    by tens of thousands in our
    fields;
¹⁴   our oxen will draw heavy
    loads.[b]
There will be no breaching of
    walls,
    no going into captivity,
    no cry of distress in our
    streets.

¹⁵Blessed are the people of
    whom this is true;
blessed are the people
    whose God is the Lord.

Psalm 145[c]

A psalm of praise. Of David.

¹I will exalt you, my God the
    King;
I will praise your name for
    ever and ever.
²Every day I will praise you
    and extol your name for
    ever and ever.
³Great is the Lord and most
    worthy of praise;
his greatness no one can
    fathom.
⁴One generation will commend
    your works to another;
they will tell of your mighty
    acts.
⁵They will speak of the
    glorious splendor of your
    majesty,

---

[a]2 Many manuscripts of the Masoretic Text, Dead Sea Scrolls, Aquila, Jerome and Syriac; most manuscripts of the Masoretic Text *subdues my people*   [b]14 *Or our chieftains will be firmly established*   [c]This psalm is an acrostic poem, the verses of which (including verse 13b) begin with the successive letters of the Hebrew alphabet.

and I will meditate on your
wonderful works.[a]
[6]They will tell of the power of
your awesome works,
and I will proclaim your
great deeds.
[7]They will celebrate your
abundant goodness
and joyfully sing of your
righteousness.

[8]The LORD is gracious and
compassionate,
slow to anger and rich in
love.
[9]The LORD is good to all;
he has compassion on all he
has made.
[10]All you have made will praise
you, O LORD;
your saints will extol you.
[11]They will tell of the glory of
your kingdom
and speak of your might,
[12]so that all men may know of
your mighty acts
and the glorious splendor of
your kingdom.
[13]Your kingdom is an
everlasting kingdom,
and your dominion endures
through all generations.

The LORD is faithful to all his
promises
and loving toward all he has
made.[b]
[14]The LORD upholds all those
who fall
and lifts up all who are
bowed down.
[15]The eyes of all look to you,
and you give them their
food at the proper time.
[16]You open your hand
and satisfy the desires of
every living thing.

[17]The LORD is righteous in all
his ways
and loving toward all he has
made.
[18]The LORD is near to all who
call on him,
to all who call on him in
truth.
[19]He fulfills the desires of those
who fear him;
he hears their cry and saves
them.
[20]The LORD watches over all
who love him,
but all the wicked he will
destroy.

[21]My mouth will speak in praise
of the LORD.
Let every creature praise his
holy name
for ever and ever.

Psalm 146

[1]Praise the LORD.[c]

Praise the LORD, O my soul.
[2] I will praise the LORD all my
life;
I will sing praise to my God
as long as I live.

[3]Do not put your trust in
princes,
in mortal men, who cannot
save.
[4]When their spirit departs,
they return to the
ground;
on that very day their plans
come to nothing.

[5]Blessed is he whose help is
the God of Jacob,
whose hope is in the LORD
his God,

---

[a]5 Dead Sea Scrolls and Syriac (see also Septuagint); Masoretic Text *On the glorious
splendor of your majesty / and on your wonderful works I will meditate*   [b]13 One
manuscript of the Masoretic Text, Dead Sea Scrolls and Syriac (see also Septuagint);
most manuscripts of the Masoretic Text do not have the last two lines of verse 13.
[c]1 Hebrew *Hallelu Yah*; also in verse 10

[6]the Maker of heaven and
   earth,
   the sea, and everything in
       them—
   the LORD, who remains
       faithful forever.
[7]He upholds the cause of the
   oppressed
   and gives food to the
       hungry.
The LORD sets prisoners free,
[8] the LORD gives sight to the
       blind,
   the LORD lifts up those who
       are bowed down,
   the LORD loves the
       righteous.
[9]The LORD watches over the
   alien
   and sustains the fatherless
       and the widow,
   but he frustrates the ways
       of the wicked.

[10]The LORD reigns forever,
   your God, O Zion, for all
       generations.

Praise the LORD.

Psalm 147

[1]Praise the LORD.[a]

How good it is to sing praises
   to our God,
   how pleasant and fitting to
       praise him!

[2]The LORD builds up
   Jerusalem;
   he gathers the exiles of
       Israel.
[3]He heals the brokenhearted
   and binds up their wounds.
[4]He determines the number of
   the stars
   and calls them each by
       name.
[5]Great is our Lord and mighty
   in power;

his understanding has no
   limit.
[6]The LORD sustains the humble   44
   but casts the wicked to the
       ground.

[7]Sing to the LORD with
   thanksgiving;
   make music to our God on
       the harp.
[8]He covers the sky with
   clouds;
   he supplies the earth with
       rain
   and makes grass grow on
       the hills.
[9]He provides food for the cattle
   and for the young ravens
       when they call.

[10]His pleasure is not in the
   strength of the horse,
   nor his delight in the legs of
       a man;
[11]the LORD delights in those
   who fear him,
   who put their hope in his
       unfailing love.

[12]Extol the LORD, O Jerusalem;
   praise your God, O Zion,
[13]for he strengthens the bars of
   your gates
   and blesses your people
       within you.
[14]He grants peace to your
   borders
   and satisfies you with the
       finest of wheat.

[15]He sends his command to the
   earth;
   his word runs swiftly.
[16]He spreads the snow like
   wool
   and scatters the frost like
       ashes.
[17]He hurls down his hail like
   pebbles.
   Who can withstand his icy
       blast?

[a]1 Hebrew *Hallelu Yah*; also in verse 20

¹⁸He sends his word and melts
them;
    he stirs up his breezes, and
        the waters flow.

¹⁹He has revealed his word to
Jacob,
    his laws and decrees to
        Israel.
²⁰He has done this for no other
nation;
    they do not know his laws.

Praise the LORD.

Psalm 148

¹Praise the LORD.ᵃ

Praise the LORD from the
heavens,
    praise him in the heights
        above.
²Praise him, all his angels,
    praise him, all his heavenly
        hosts.
³Praise him, sun and moon,
    praise him, all you shining
        stars.
⁴Praise him, you highest
heavens
    and you waters above the
        skies.
⁵Let them praise the name of
the LORD,
    for he commanded and they
        were created.
⁶He set them in place for ever
and ever;
    he gave a decree that will
        never pass away.

⁷Praise the LORD from the
earth,
    you great sea creatures and
        all ocean depths,
⁸lightning and hail, snow and
clouds,
    stormy winds that do his
        bidding,
⁹you mountains and all hills,
    fruit trees and all cedars,

¹⁰wild animals and all cattle,
    small creatures and flying
        birds,
¹¹kings of the earth and all
nations,
    you princes and all rulers
        on earth,
¹²young men and maidens,
    old men and children.

¹³Let them praise the name of
the LORD,
    for his name alone is
        exalted;
    his splendor is above the
        earth and the heavens.
¹⁴He has raised up for his
people a horn,ᵇ
    the praise of all his saints,
    of Israel, the people close to
        his heart.

Praise the LORD.

Psalm 149

¹Praise the LORD.ᶜ

Sing to the LORD a new song,
    his praise in the assembly of
        the saints.

²Let Israel rejoice in their
Maker;
    let the people of Zion be
        glad in their King.
³Let them praise his name with
dancing
    and make music to him
        with tambourine and
        harp.
⁴For the LORD takes delight in
his people;
    he crowns the humble with
        salvation.
⁵Let the saints rejoice in this
honor
    and sing for joy on their
        beds.

⁶May the praise of God be in
their mouths

ᵃ1 Hebrew *Hallelu Yah*; also in verse 14
is, king.   ᶜ1 Hebrew *Hallelu Yah*; also in verse 9   ᵇ14 *Horn* here symbolizes strong one, that

and a double-edged sword
in their hands,
⁷to inflict vengeance on the
nations
and punishment on the
peoples,
⁸to bind their kings with
fetters,
their nobles with shackles of
iron,
⁹to carry out the sentence
written against them.
This is the glory of all his
saints.

Praise the LORD.

Psalm 150

¹Praise the LORD.ᵃ

Praise God in his sanctuary;

praise him in his mighty
heavens.
²Praise him for his acts of
power;
praise him for his
surpassing greatness.
³Praise him with the sounding
of the trumpet,
praise him with the harp
and lyre,
⁴praise him with tambourine
and dancing,
praise him with the strings
and flute,
⁵praise him with the clash of
cymbals,
praise him with resounding
cymbals.

⁶Let everything that has breath
praise the LORD.

Praise the LORD.

ᵃ1 Hebrew *Hallelu Yah*; also in verse 6

Index of Topics

No.	Topic	References/Summary of Biblical Teaching
	abused	*See* love, rejection, security.
1	**acceptance**	*Jn 3:16; 5:41-44; 6:37; 14:23; Ac 10:34,35; Ro 15:7; Eph 2:19-22; 3:12,13; Jas 2:1-4.* In Christ, God accepts people from every nation; God also expects us to be accepting of all persons and not show favoritism or prejudice.
	accomplishment	*See* ministry, rewards, significance.
	accountability	*See* guilt, ministry, salvation (plan of), shame.
2	**adultery**	*Mt 5:27,28,31,32; 15:19; 19:9; Jn 8:2-11; 1Co 6:9-11; Heb 13:4; Ps 51.* Sex outside of marriage is forbidden; it is a selfish sin that destroys the marriage bond—a rejection of God and one's spouse.
	afraid	*See* fear.
	aggression	*See* anger, hate.
	age	*See* anxiety, wisdom.
	alcohol	*See* drunkenness.
3	**anger**	*Mt 5:22; Mk 3:5; Lk 15:28; Ro 8:7; Eph 4:26,31; Jas 1:19,20; 3:14; Ps 2:12; 7:11.* Anger is emotional energy that may be directed to accomplish good (indignation); however, uncontrolled rage, passive hostility toward others, and resentment are all condemned as sin.
4	**anxiety**	*Mt 6:25-34; 11:28-30; Lk 12:22-26; Php 4:6,7; 1Pe 5:7; Ps 43:5.* God promises to care for all our needs; lack of faith, or failure to trust him, is a root cause of anxiety.
	apprehensive	*See* anxiety, fear, security.
	approval	*See* acceptance, testing.
	authority	*See* inspiration, will of God.
	ashamed	*See* guilt, repentance, shame.
	assurance	*See* confidence, doubt, salvation (plan of), security.
	atonement	*See* Christ, forgiveness (God's), redemption, salvation (plan of).
5	**backsliding**	*Jn 21:15-17; Gal 6:1; Heb 3:12,13; 10:22; 1Jn 5:3-5; Ps 51:10-12.* When someone through carelessness falls back into sin,

No.	Topic	References/Summary of Biblical Teaching
	condemned	*See* acceptance, forgiveness (God's), guilt, judging, love, security.
9	conduct	*Mt 22:37,38; Eph 5:8-14; Tit 3:3-8; 1Pe 3:8,9; Ps 19:8-11; 84:11.* The conduct of Christians is distinctive; principles and standards of conduct are given throughout the Bible.
10	confession	*Mt 10:32,33; Ac 19:18; Php 2:11; Jas 5:16; 1Jn 1:9,10; Ps 32:5; 66:16.* We are encouraged to confess our sins, faults, and imperfections to God and each other so that we may be forgiven and accepted. We also confess Christ as our Savior and Lord.
11	confidence	*Heb 4:16; 10:35; 1Jn 2:28; 4:17,18; 5:14; Ps 71:5,6.* Faith in Christ makes it possible for us to face all situations in life with confidence.
	conflict	*See* anger, forgiveness (of others), humility.
	confused	*See* anxiety, guidance, will of God.
12	conscience	*Ro 2:15; 1Co 8:10-12; 1Ti 1:5,19; Heb 10:22-25; 1Pe 3:16,21; Ps 19:12.* When our consciences are properly educated in the law of God as expressed in the Bible, they help us judge what is right or wrong in our lives.
	consistency	*See* growth, security, significance.
	conspicuous	*See* acceptance, security.
13	contentment	*2Co 1:3,4; Php 4:12; 1Ti 6:6-10; Heb 13:5,6.* Godliness and contentment are the positive virtues that contrast with sin and greed.
	conversion	*See* conduct, new birth, salvation (plan of).
14	conviction	*Jn 16:7-11; 1Th 1:5; 2Ti 3:14,15; Jas 2:9; Jude 15.* The Holy Spirit convicts sinners because they refuse to believe in Christ, the only remedy for sin; without Christ, judgment for sin is inevitable.
	counseling	*See* guidance, love (for others).
	courage	*See* confidence, perseverance, security.
	critical	*See* forgiveness (of others), judging, patience.
	crushed	*See* love, rejection, security, significance.
	death	*See* loss, love (of God), security.
	deceit	*See* conduct, lying.

No.	Topic	References/Summary of Biblical Teaching
	decisions	*See* evangelism, salvation (plan of), will of God.
	dedication	*See* growth, sanctification, spirituality.
15	**deity**	Mt 16:16; Jn 1:1,2,14; 10:30,33; 20:28; Php 2:6; Heb 1:8. Jesus Christ is not merely *like* God, he *is* God.
	defeated	*See* depression, loss, love (of God).
	defensive	*See* confidence, security, significance.
	denial	*See* disobedience, lying, rejection.
16	**depression**	Lk 18:1-8; Jn 16:33; 2Co 4:1,2, 16,17; Gal 6:9,10; Php 4:8-13; 2Th 3:11-13; Heb 13:6; Ps 27:14; 42:5; 56:4; 69:1,2; 88:3-9. Depression is a chronic feeling of hopeless despair. The Bible shows that there is hope, love, meaning, and security in Christ; we are encouraged not to "give up," but rather to be involved in helping others.
	dependence	*See* confidence, faith, hope, security.
	despair	*See* depression, loss.
	desperate	*See* anxiety, fear, security.
	despised	*See* love, security.
	development	*See* conduct, growth, spirituality.
	direction	*See* conduct, guidance.
	disappointed	*See* depression, loss.
	discipling	*See* growth, guidance.
17	**discipline**	1Co 11:32; Eph 6:1-4; 2Ti 1:7; Tit 1:8; Heb 12:5-11. Just as parents discipline their children if they love them, God disciplines and trains all his children; we should not resent it.
	discouraged	*See* depression, love (of God), security.
	disgusted	*See* anger, patience, perseverance.
	disillusioned	*See* Christianity, evangelism, salvation (plan of).
18	**disobedience**	Ro 10:21; Eph 2:1,2; 5:3-7; 2Th 1:7-9; 2Ti 3:2-5; Heb 3:18,19; Ps 111:10. All people are born in sin; we *naturally* rebel against doing God's will, and disobedience is characteristic of the life of unbelievers.
	distressed	*See* anxiety, loss, love (of God), security.
	disturbed	*See* anger, anxiety, security.
19	**divorce**	Mt 5:31,32; 19:4-6; Mk 10:11,12; Lk 16:18; 1Co 7:10,11,27; Php 2:3. Marriage is sacred and intended to be permanent; divorce is permitted where adultery has already broken the union.

No.	Topic	References/Summary of Biblical Teaching
20	**doubt**	*Ro 4:3,18-21; 8:16; 2Ti 1:7; Heb 7:25; 12:2; Jas 1:5,6; 1Jn 1:7; 3:14.* Doubt is a lack of faith; it is not the same as rejection or disobedience. Doubters need encouragement, not rebuke.
21	**drunkenness**	*Ro 14:21; 1Co 6:9-11; 10:31,32; Eph 5:18; 1Ti 3:8; 1Pe 4:3.* Drunkenness results from a lack of self-control; it is condemned as sin, but we can conquer it by yielding control to the Holy Spirit.
	edification	*See* conduct, growth, sanctification, spirituality.
22	**election**	*Mt 24:31; Mk 13:20; Ro 8:28-30; 9:11; 11:7; 2Ti 2:10; 1Pe 1:1,2; 2Pe 1:10.* Through his grace and mercy, and not our merit, God chose us as his people in Christ.
	embarrassed	*See* confidence, self-acceptance, significance.
	emotions	*See* anger, anxiety, depression.
	empathy	*See* guidance, love (for others), ministry.
	empty	*See* loss, security, significance.
	encouragement	*See* guidance, ministry.
	endurance	*See* depression, patience, spirituality.
	envy	*See* conduct, greed, hate, jealousy.
23	**evangelism**	*Mt 3:7-10; 7:24-27; 28:19,20; Lu 4:18; 19:10; Jn 6:29; Ac 1:8; 5:42; Ro 1:16; 1Co 1:18; 2Co 5:17-21; Ps 126:6. See also salvation (plan of).* One of the reasons for the existence of the church is evangelism; we are to make known the gospel, answer objections, and call all unbelievers to repentance and faith in Christ.
	evil	*See* conduct, sin, spirituality.
	excuses	*See* evangelism.
	exhausted	*See* depression, guidance, perseverance.
	failure	*See* depression, faith, fear.
24	**faith**	*Mt 8:9-11; Mk 11:24; Jn 20:31; Ac 16:31; Ro 10:17; Gal 3:26; Heb 11:6; Ps 37:5.* To be saved from our sins, we need to trust in Jesus Christ as Lord and Savior. This belief is not merely intellectual assent, but is a complete commitment to Christ.
	fathers	*See* family.

No.	Topic	References/Summary of Biblical Teaching
		1Ti 6:15,16; 1Jn 4:8,16; 5:20; Ps 14:1. The true God is the creator and sustainer of all things; he is not at all like idols of wood and stone.
	godless	*See* sin, spirituality, will of God.
	goodness	*See* Christianity, humility, kindness, obedience, will of God.
32	gospel	*Lk 9:6; Ac 2:22-24; 8:40; 10:34-43; Ro 1:16; 2:12-16.* The "good news" is that Jesus Christ came, fulfilling the promises of the Old Testament prophets. He lived a righteous life, died in our place to save us from our sins, and then rose from the dead.
	gossip	*See* hate, love (for others), lying, sin.
	grace	*See* acceptance, Christianity.
33	greed	*Mt 6:19-21,24; 23:25; Mk 7:22; 1Ti 6:6-10,18; 2Ti 3:2-5.* Greed is the opposite of faith and contentment with what God has given; it is a root of all kinds of evil.
	grief	*See* loss, love (of God), security.
34	growth	*1Co 3:1; Eph 4:16; Col 1:9-11; 1Th 5:11; 2Ti 2:15; Heb 6:11,12; 1Pe 2:1-3; 2Pe 1:5; 3:18.* Christians are regenerated by the grace of God; after the new birth, they grow to spiritual maturity in Christ with the help of the whole family of God.
35	guidance	*Jn 16:7,13; 2Co 1:3,4; Gal 6:2; Php 2:4; 1Th 2:10-12; Jas 5:19,20.* We are not only our brother's keeper, but his counselor as well; all Christians are responsible to help and encourage each other daily in the Christian life.
36	guilt	*Jn 15:22-25; Ro 2:5-11; 3:19,20; 8:1; Heb 10:26,27; Ps 19:13; 32:5; 38:4; 69:5.* Guilt is not so much the feeling as the fact of having broken God's law; no one is without guilt, but we are no longer under a sentence of condemnation if we accept Christ.
37	happiness	*Mt 6:19-21; Lk 12:15; Ac 20:35; 1Ti 6:17; 1Pe 1:6; Ps 16:11; 68:4; 97:1.* True happiness is the joy of salvation that sustains us even in suffering. Happiness is impossible without faith.
38	hate	*Mt 5:21,22; Jn 15:23; Ro 8:7; 12:18,19; 1Th 2:14-16; Ps 11:5.* Hatred is a basic

No.	Topic	References/Summary of Biblical Teaching
		characteristic of the old nature; the natural man is hostile to God and abusive and disobedient to others.
	hated	See love (of God), rejection, security.
39	healing	Mt 8:14-17; Ac 3:16; 10:38; 1Co 12:9; Heb 2:4; Jas 5:13-16. Jesus and the apostles performed miracles of healing to confirm the coming of the kingdom of God.
	heart	See conduct, spirituality.
	heartbroken	See depression, hope, loss, rejection.
40	heaven	Mt 8:11; Lk 16:22-26; Ro 2:5-11; 1Co 2:9,10; Rev 21:1-4. Heaven is the promised, eternal home of the people of God, where there is no more grief, pain, or death.
41	hell	Mk 9:47,48; Lk 16:22-26; Ro 2:5-11; Heb 10:26-31; Rev 20:11-15. Hell is the eternal place of punishment prepared for the devil and those who refuse to accept salvation in Christ.
	help	See growth, guidance.
	helpless	See depression, hope, rejection.
	holiness	See conduct, maturity, sanctification.
	Holy Spirit	See God, spirituality.
	homesick	See acceptance, love (of God), security.
42	homosexuality	Ro 6:12-14; 1Co 6:9-11; Col 3:5. Those who engage in homosexual activity have no part in the kingdom of God; however, God loves sinners and will freely forgive all who come to him through Christ.
43	hope	Ro 4:17-23; 5:5; Php 4:19; 2Th 2:16,17; Heb 6:19; 10:22-25; Ps 25:5; 33:20; 71:5,14. God is the God of all hope and can do anything; if God is for us, we can have hope against impossible odds.
	hostility	See anger, forgiveness (of others).
	humiliated	See love (of God), pride, rejection.
44	humility	Lk 18:9-14; Eph 5:21; Php 2:5-11; 1Pe 5:5,6; Ps 19:12-14; 25:9; 147:6. Humility is a total commitment to God and his will as opposed to our own will; a humble life involves doing things God's way.
	hurt	See anger, rejection, security, significance.
	husbands	See family, marriage.
	hypocrisy	See Christianity, evangelism.

No.	Topic	References/Summary of Biblical Teaching
	identity	*See* security, significance.
	ignored	*See* love (of God), significance.
	immorality	*See* adultery, lying, sin.
	impatient	*See* love (for others), patience.
	important	*See* significance.
	inadequate	*See* acceptance, confidence, patience.
	incompetent	*See* acceptance, maturity, perfectionism.
	indecisive	*See* ministry, will of God.
	indifferent	*See* love (for others).
	indignation	*See* anger, conduct, forgiveness.
	inferior	*See* depression, patience.
	inhibited	*See* confidence, maturity.
	insecure	*See* security.
	insignificant	*See* significance.
45	**inspiration**	Lk 24:45; 1Th 2:13; 2Ti 3:16,17; Heb 4:12; 2Pe 1:19-21; Ps 19:7,8. The Bible is God's Word; as such it must be obeyed without question in all matters of faith and conduct, in whatever statements it makes explicitly or implicitly.
	intercession	*See* prayer.
	intimidated	*See* ministry, security, significance.
	irrational	*See* anger, depression, fear, will of God.
	irritated	*See* anger, conduct.
46	**jealousy**	Ro 13:13; 1Co 3:3; 2Co 11:2; 12:20; Gal 5:20,21. Jealousy is a selfish and suspicious anger against another person; it is almost always sinful and shows a lack of faith.
	joy	*See* happiness.
47	**judging**	Mt 7:1-5; 23:23,24; Ro 2:1-4; Jas 2:1-4. Unjust judging is condemned as sinful hypocrisy; it is not based on fact but on assumptions.
48	**justification**	Lk 18:9-14; Jn 5:30; Ro 3:26; 5:1,11; Ps 37:27,28; 119:121. Justification means that God declares us righteous and acceptable on the basis of Christ's death on the cross.
49	**kindness**	Eph 4:29-32; 1Th 5:15; 1Pe 4:8-10; Ps 34:8. Just as God is good and kind toward us in forgiving our sins, he expects us to be good, kind, and forgiving of others.
50	**law**	Jn 1:17; Ro 3:19,20; 4:13; Gal 3:10,11; Jas 2:10; Ps 19:7. We are all condemned by God because we have not obeyed his

No.	Topic	References/Summary of Biblical Teaching
		law. But Christ has fulfilled the law and experienced the punishment we deserved so that we can be accepted as righteous by God.
51	life	Mt 7:13,14; Jn 3:36; Ro 8:9-11; Col 3:1-4; 1Jn 5:12; Ps 39:4,5. Eternal life is freedom from the condemnation and punishment of God; it is total acceptance by God and is gained through faith in Christ.
	light	See conduct.
52	loneliness	Mt 11:28-30; 18:20; 28:20; Heb 13:5; Ps 27:10; 119:92. Contentment and happiness are God's will for the Christian; God has promised that he will never leave us alone.
53	loss	Mt 5:4; Jn 11:25,26; 14:1-6; 16:22; Ro 14:8; 1Co 15:54-58; 2Co 4:8,9; 5:1; Php 1:21-23; 3:8; 1Th 4:13; Ps 23; 43:5. In loss or grief, God himself is our Shepherd; he promises to care for us, give us security and rest, and restore us.
	lost	See evangelism, salvation (plan of).
54	love (God's)	Mt 23:37-39; Jn 3:16; 15:13; Ro 5:8; 8:35-39; 10:21; 1Jn 4:13-16. God loves us with an everlasting love; he gave his only Son to die for our salvation.
55	love (for others)	Lk 6:27-36; Jn 13:35; 1Co 13; Gal 6:2; Jas 2:1-4; 1Pe 1:22; 1Jn 4:19-21. We are responsible to love God and others as well as ourselves; this love is possible because God first loved us.
	low	See depression, perseverance, security.
	lust	See adultery.
56	lying	Jn 8:44; Eph 4:15,25; 5:8-10; Php 4:8; Col 3:9,10; Rev 21:8; Ps 15:1-3. God requires truth; it is essential to the character of God and his children.
	mad	See anger.
	maligned	See hate, security.
	manipulated	See freedom, humility, love (for others).
57	marriage	1Co 7:1-7; Eph 4:2; 5:22-33; Col 3:18,19; Heb 13:4; 1Pe 3:1-7. Marriage is approved by God as sacred; sex outside of marriage is immoral and condemned by God.
58	maturity	Eph 4:13,14; Php 1:6; Col 4:12; Heb 2:1;

No.	Topic	References/Summary of Biblical Teaching
		5:14; 6:1,2; Jas 1:4. Normal Christian life moves from its beginning in the new birth toward maturity in the same manner that children develop into mature adults.
	meaning	*See* significance.
59	mind	*Ro 8:5; 12:1,2; 2Co 4:4; 5:16,17; Eph 4:23; Heb 8:10; Ps 64:5,6.* Our minds or beliefs (world view) are transformed when we have faith in Christ; we are responsible to live not by wrong assumptions but by the assumptions of faith.
60	ministry	*Lk 10:27; 1Co 3:5-9; 4:1-5; 12:4-11; 2Co 5:17-21; 1Ti 3:1-13; 4:11-16; 2Ti 2:15; 4:1-5; Tit 1:7-9.* God gives various spiritual gifts to us by his Spirit; with them comes the responsibility for the ministry of reconciliation.
	miserable	*See* depression, happiness, security.
	mission	*See* evangelism, ministry.
	mistreated	*See* anxiety, depression, fear, loneliness.
	misunderstood	*See* depression, loneliness, security.
	mocked	*See* anxiety, loneliness, security.
61	money	*Mt 6:19-21,24; Mk 12:41-44; Lk 3:14; Ac 8:20; 2Co 9:6,7,11; 1Ti 3:3; 6:6-10; 2Ti 3:2-5; Heb 13:5; Ps 15:5.* The desire for money is a root of all kinds of evil; God promises to meet all our needs if we seek his kingdom first.
	moody	*See* depression, security.
	morbid	*See* depression, happiness, security.
	motivation	*See* growth, ministry, significance.
	naughty	*See* disobedience, sin.
	negative	*See* forgiveness (of others), hate.
	neglected	*See* anxiety, depression, loneliness.
	neighbor	*See* love (for others), ministry.
	nervous	*See* anxiety, fear.
62	new birth	*Jn 1:12,13; 3:3-7; Ro 5:16,17; Tit 3:5; 1Pe 1:23-25.* Unless a person is born again or "saved," he cannot go to heaven; spiritual rebirth is absolutely necessary.
63	obedience	*Jn 14:15,23; Ac 3:22,23; 5:29,32; Heb 13:17; Jas 1:22-25; 1Pe 1:2.* A chief characteristic of believers in Christ is obedience; all God's children have within them the desire to do God's will.
	obsessive	*See* anxiety, ministry.

No.	Topic	References/Summary of Biblical Teaching
	oppressed	*See* anxiety, depression, loneliness, security.
	outraged	*See* anger, conduct.
	overworked	*See* contentment, depression, perseverance, self-control.
	pain	*See* anxiety, perseverance.
	panicky	*See* faith, fear, patience.
	parents	*See* family.
64	patience	Ro 12:12; 15:4; 1Co 13:4; 1Th 5:14; Heb 10:34; Jas 5:7,8. We should be willing to put up with the faults of others because we love them; we must also endure the difficult circumstances of life with patience.
65	peace	Mt 11:28-30; 14:27; Ro 5:1,2; Php 4:8,9; Col 3:15; Heb 12:14,15. Through Christ we have peace with God; this also makes it possible for us to live without hostility toward others.
66	perfectionism	Lk 18:9-14; Ro 3:23; 4:2-5; 1Co 8:12; 13:10; Php 3:12; Col 1:28; Ps 34:6; 37:7; 119:96. God's justice causes him to require perfection as a goal but his grace accepts us as we are; no human is perfect, and to insist on perfection in ourselves or others causes deep psychological problems.
	perplexed	*See* confidence, salvation (plan of), will of God.
	persecution	*See* anxiety, depression, love (of God), security, suffering.
67	perseverance	1Co 13:7; 2Co 12:12; 2Ti 1:12; 2:12,13; Heb 4:16; Jas 1:3,12. Perseverance means continuing in the work of God even though the going gets tough; we are asked to endure to the end through faith.
	personality	*See* acceptance, growth, mind, self-control.
	pleasing	*See* acceptance, kindness, obedience, will of God.
68	praise	Ro 8:31,32; Heb 13:15,16; 1Pe 1:3; Ps 16:11; 34:1; 111. Praise is a part of worship; we find our deepest fulfillment in bringing praise and thanksgiving to God.
69	prayer	Mt 6:9-13; 7:7,8; 18:19; Lk 18:1; Jn 14:13,14; 1Th 5:17; 1Ti 2:1; Ps 61:1,2. Prayer involves adoration of God, confession, thanksgiving, and supplication

No.	Topic	References/Summary of Biblical Teaching
		for the needs of ourselves and others.
	prejudice	*See* acceptance, judging, love (for others).
	pressured	*See* anxiety.
70	**pride**	Mt 9:12,13; 1Co 1:26-29; Gal 6:3; Eph 2:8,9. Pride is thinking you are something when you are nothing; while arrogance is condemned, we should take "pride" in the accomplishments of others as well as our own.
	procrastination	*See* salvation (plan of).
	projection	*See* guilt, maturity.
	protection	*See* security.
	provoked	*See* anger.
	punishment	*See* acceptance, family, guilt.
	purpose	*See* significance, will of God.
	puzzled	*See* significance, will of God.
	rage	*See* anger.
	rationalization	*See* guilt, maturity.
	rebelliousness	*See* disobedience, humility, love (of God).
71	**reconciliation**	Mt 5:23,24; 1Co 7:11; 2Co 5:17-21; Eph 2:16; Col 1:19,20; 1Pe 3:18. Reconciliation is reestablishing proper relationships. We are reconciled to God through Christ's death. We ought to maintain a proper relation with God as well as with other people.
72	**redemption**	Ro 3:22-26; Gal 3:13,14; 4:4,5; 1Pe 1:18,19; Ps 26:11; 49:15. To redeem is to buy back with money or something valuable; we were bought with a high price, the death of Christ on the cross, so that we might become God's people.
	regeneration	*See* new birth.
	regret	*See* forgiveness (God's), repentance.
73	**rejection**	Mt 10:28-31; 23:37-39; Jn 5:40; Ro 10:21; 1Co 4:11-13; 2Ti 2:12; 1Pe 2:19; Ps 27:10; 37:25. The feeling of rejection is the painful opposite of feeling loved; God accepts us in Christ without any other conditions. We ought to accept others in the same way.
	remarriage	*See* divorce, family, marriage.
	renewal	*See* conduct, mind, new birth, sanctification.
74	**repentance**	Mt 3:2; Lk 13:3; Ac 2:38; 17:30,31; 20:21; Ro 2:1-4; 2Co 7:9,10; 2Ti 2:25. To repent means to change one's mind, to turn from

No.	Topic	References/Summary of Biblical Teaching
		sin and turn to God; God calls everyone to repent, and he freely accepts all who come to him through Christ.
	resentment	See anger.
	resolutions	See conduct.
	respect	See family, love (for others), marriage, obedience.
	responsibility	See family, guilt, repentance, rewards.
	restless	See anxiety, fear, salvation (plan of).
75	resurrection	Mk 16:6; Lk 24:36-46; Jn 11:25,26; 1Co 15:20-23,42-44,50-52; Php 3:20,21; Ps 16:10. The resurrection of Christ from the dead is an authenticated fact that gives solid basis for the expectation that we shall rise from the dead at his coming.
	revenge	See forgiveness (of others).
76	rewards	Mt 6:2-4; Ro 12:17; 1Co 3:11-15; Col 3:23,24; 2Ti 4:8; 1Pe 1:7; 5:4; Ps 84:11. God rewards us for ministry of all kinds and for good works; his rewards may be in this life or in the next, but they are certain.
	ridicule	See kindness, rejection, security, significance.
77	righteousness	Mt 6:33; 9:13; Lk 14:14; Ac 3:14; Ro 3:21-26; 4:13; 1Co 1:30; Ps 119:7,75. Jesus Christ is our righteousness; when we accept him as Savior, God counts our faith in him as righteousness and perfection.
	rivalry	See anger, hate, jealousy, unity.
	sad	See anger, depression.
78	salvation (plan of)	Lk 18:9-14; Jn 1:12; 3:16-18; 5:24; 20:31; Ac 10:43; Ro 3:23; 6:21-23; 8:1; 10:9,10,13; 2Co 6:2; Heb 11:6; 1Jn 1:9; 5:13; Rev 3:20. Anyone who acknowledges his need of salvation, confesses his guilt, accepts Jesus Christ as his Lord, and believes that God raised him from the dead will be saved. We are justified by the death of Christ on the cross and saved from God's wrath through him.
79	sanctification	Jn 17:17-19; Ac 26:17,18; Ro 12:1,2; 2Co 13:9; 1Th 5:23,24; Tit 2:11-14; Heb 12:14; Jas 4:7,8. As God's people, we are set apart from the world by the Holy Spirit;

No.	Topic	References/Summary of Biblical Teaching
		the indwelling Spirit enables us to live godly lives of self-control.
	satisfaction	*See* contentment, happiness.
	saved	*See* salvation (plan of).
	scared	*See* fear.
	Scripture	*See* inspiration.
80	**second coming**	*Mt 24:27; Ac 1:11; 1Th 4:13-18; Tit 2:13; 1Jn 3:1-3; Rev 22:12.* The incarnation, or advent, was the coming of Christ into the world; after his resurrection, he was taken up into heaven with the promise that he would come again.
81	**security**	*Jn 5:24; 10:28; 14:18; Ro 8:28,37-39; 2Co 9:8; Php 1:6; 2Ti 2:13; Heb 6:19; 2Pe 3:17; 1Jn 5:18; Ps 5:11; 12:5; 91:1,2.* Security is a basic human need; those who are in Christ are protected in God's will—nothing at all can separate us from the love of God in Christ.
82	**self-acceptance**	*Mt 6:26; Ro 14:16-18,22; 1Co 4:3; Gal 6:4,5; Eph 5:28; 2Ti 4:7; 1Pe 2:15,16.* We need to accept ourselves as worthwhile. God accepts us in Christ and calls us to accept others without prejudice.
83	**self-control**	*1Th 4:4; 5:4-8; 2Ti 1:7; 3:2-5; Tit 2:1,6; 1Pe 5:8.* Self-control is one of the fruits of the Spirit; when the self is dedicated to the will of God, it is controlled by the Spirit of God who lives in us.
	self-hate	*See* conduct, humility, love, security, self-acceptance, significance.
	self-identity	*See* conduct, growth, maturity, mind.
84	**selfishness**	*Mt 16:24; Lk 9:23-25; 1Co 10:24; 2Co 5:14,15; Php 2:3,21; Jas 3:13-16.* Selfishness is at the center of sin; to be saved we must deny self and follow Christ.
	self-pity	*See* depression.
	self-respect	*See* growth, maturity, significance.
	self-will	*See* disobedience.
	sensitive	*See* anger, forgiveness (of others), pride, security.
	sensual	*See* adultery, conduct.
85	**separation**	*Ro 10:20,21; 1Co 3:16,17; 2Co 6:14-18; Eph 5:6,7,11; Rev 9:20,21; 18:4.* Christians are not to be patterned after the sinful world system and its values. We

No.	Topic	References/Summary of Biblical Teaching
		should be separated from these and to God. We are God's special people and this is to be reflected in our lives.
	service	*See* guidance, happiness, ministry.
	sex	*See* adultery, conduct, marriage.
86	shame	*Lk 17:3; Ro 10:11; 1Co 4:14; 6:5; 2Co 11:21; 1Th 3:13; 2Ti 2:15; 1Jn 3:19-22; Ps 44:15.* Shame, the painful feeling arising from knowing we have done something wrong, is replaced by joyous confidence when we confess our sins and follow God's will.
	shy	*See* confidence, self-acceptance.
	sickness	*See* love (of God), prayer, suffering.
87	significance	*Ro 8:29-32; 1Co 12:4-11; 2Co 5:5; Gal 2:20; Eph 1:11,12; 2:19-22; Php 1:12; 2:12,13; Col 2:2,3; 1Ti 2:7; 1Pe 2:4,5,9,10; Ps 139:16.* An understanding of individual significance and importance in life—a reason for being—is a basic human need; for the Christian, life has meaning, purpose, and goals, no matter what else happens.
88	sin	*Mt 7:24-27; Jn 8:34; Ro 3:10; Gal 5:19-21; 2Ti 3:2-5; Heb 10:26,27; 1Jn 1:8-10; 3:6,9.* Sin is any thought, word, or deed that is contrary to the will of God; all have sinned, but God forgives and accepts us in Christ.
	slander	*See* hate, love (for others), lying, sin.
	sorry	*See* acceptance, loss, repentance.
89	spirituality	*Gal 5:22,23; 6:1; Eph 5:18-21; 2Pe 1:5-8; 1Jn 2:15-17; Ps 1:1,2.* We ought to be dedicated to God; the more dedicated we are, the more we do God's will instead of our own.
90	stealing	*Mk 10:19; Ro 2:21; 13:9; Eph 4:28; Tit 2:9,10.* Stealing is sin; whatever we may have done before accepting Christ is past, and the new life must be lived according to new standards.
	stifled	*See* acceptance, love (of God), patience, significance.
	stress	*See* anxiety, significance.
	stupid	*See* confidence.
	submission	*See* family, humility, marriage.

No.	Topic	References/Summary of Biblical Teaching
91	**suffering**	*Jn 15:20,21; Ac 5:41; 9:16; Ro 5:3,4; 8:16-18; 2Co 12:9,10; Php 1:29; 2Ti 3:12; 1Pe 1:6,7; 2:20; 4:12-19.* God sometimes permits suffering in our lives; if he does, he also gives grace and patience so that we may endure and glorify him in it.
	suicide	*See depression, hope, love (of God), salvation (plan of), testing.*
	sympathy	*See kindness, love (for others), ministry.*
	teaching	*See evangelism, ministry.*
	temper	*See anger.*
92	**temptation**	*Mt 5:10,11,22; Ac 14:22; 2Th 3:3; Heb 2:18; 11:25; Jas 1:13,14.* Temptation to evil is the work of Satan; Christ himself was tempted in the same way and is able to help us overcome temptation.
	tense	*See anxiety, fear, peace.*
93	**testing**	*Ro 14:12; 1Co 10:13; 1Th 3:3,4; Heb 10:32-34; Jas 1:2,3.* Testing is for our good even though it is difficult; God will give us strength, and quality of character will increase with each test.
94	**thankfulness**	*Ac 27:35; 1Co 15:10; 2Co 2:14; Eph 5:20; Col 3:17; 1Th 5:18; Ps 3:17; 119:62; 138:1,2.* We should cultivate a thankful attitude always; humility and submission to God's will are elements of a positive underlying strength that helps us cope with stress.
	threatened	*See anxiety, fear, peace.*
	timid	*See confidence, doubt.*
	tired	*See depression.*
95	**tongues**	*Ac 2:4; 10:46; 19:6; 1Co 12:10,28,30; 13:1; 14:1-3,22,39,40; Heb 2:4.* The miracle of speaking in tongues confirmed that the coming of Christ and the phenomenon of the Christian church were fulfillments of God's promises in the Old Testament.
	transformation	*See conduct, mind, new birth.*
	trapped	*See anxiety, freedom, happiness, security, significance, testing.*
	trials	*See temptations, testing.*
	troubled	*See anxiety, depression, fear, guilt.*
	trust	*See Christianity, faith, hope.*
	ugly	*See love (of God), security, self-acceptance, significance.*

No.	Topic	References/Summary of Biblical Teaching
	unappreciated	*See* ministry, patience, security, significance.
96	**unbelief**	*Mk 9:24; Lk 12:46; Jn 3:18; 8:24; 2Th 2:11,12; 1Ti 1:3; Heb 3:19; 11:6.* Unbelief is, in effect, a rejection of God and his loving offer of salvation in Christ; unbelief results in condemnation.
	uneasy	*See* anxiety, confidence, fear, security.
	uncertain	*See* doubt, security, will of God.
	understanding	*See* patience.
	unfaithfulness	*See* adultery, conduct, marriage.
	unhappy	*See* happiness, ministry, peace, salvation (plan of).
97	**unity**	*Jn 17:23; Ro 15:5,6; 1Co 1:10; Eph 4:1-6,13; Php 2:1,2; Col 3:14.* The common beliefs, standards, and hopes of all Christians bind us together in a unity that we are encouraged to preserve.
	unqualified	*See* confidence, ministry, significance.
	unsatisfied	*See* confidence, contentment, ministry, significance.
	unsettled	*See* anxiety, doubt, fear.
	unsure	*See* anxiety, doubt, fear, security.
	unworthy	*See* self-acceptance.
	upset	*See* anxiety.
	used	*See* confidence, security, self-acceptance.
	useless	*See* confidence, self-acceptance.
	vengeance	*See* forgiveness (of others).
	vulnerable	*See* love of God, security.
	weak	*See* confidence, self-control, testing.
	weary	*See* depression, perseverance.
	willful	*See* disobedience, selfishness.
98	**will of God**	*Mt 6:10; 7:21; Jn 4:34; 7:17; Ac 20:27; Eph 5:17; Col 1:9,10; 1Pe 2:15,16; Ps 19:14; 25:14; 90:12.* Christians have an intuitive desire to do the things that please God; his will may be discovered directly from the explicit or implicit teaching of the Bible along with the guidance of the Holy Spirit.
	wisdom	*See* growth, mind, will of God.
	witness	*See* evangelism, ministry.
	wives	*See* family, marriage.
	Word	*See* inspiration.
	works	*See* evangelism, ministry, salvation (plan of).

No.	Topic	References/Summary of Biblical Teaching
99	**worship**	*Jn 4:23; Eph 3:20,21; Heb 13:15,16; 1Pe 1:17; Jude 24,25; Rev 5:9,10; Ps 19:14.* We are created to worship God; ultimate satisfaction is possible only when we offer to God the sacrifices of praise and thanksgiving through Jesus Christ.
	worthless	*See* confidence, self-acceptance.
	worldliness	*See* conduct, growth, sin, spirituality.
	worry	*See* anxiety, fear.
	wrath	*See* anger.
	wronged	*See* forgiveness (of others), security, testing.

PRAISE — WORSHIP

LINDA   WALDO WERNING
JOSH   MATT WELDE
SARAH   Jerry Sander
THELMA   Pastor Williamson
MOTHER   Bob Campbell
SLUGGER

MIKE
RICHARD
Church

Community

Daryl Hoffmaster

Bill Smith

Kevin Perotta

Betty Moore

Ray Bridgham

Brad Long

Todd Wetzel

Armand Welly

Vernon Stoop

JIM KUSHNER
      HIGBEE

PAUL JOHNSTON

TIM BAYLY
DON BLOESCH
DARREL ANDERSON
JIM HEIDINGER

Clauses
personal rights relinquished